Ius Comparatum - Global Studies in Comparative Law

Volume 13

More information about this series at http://www.springer.com/series/11943

Académie Internationale de Droit Comparé
International Academy of Comparative Law

Olga Cvejić Jančić
Editor

The Rights of the Child in a Changing World

25 Years after The UN Convention on the Rights of the Child

Springer

Editor
Olga Cvejić Jančić
University Educons – Sremska Kamenica
Faculty of European Legal and Political Studies – Novi Sad
University professor
Novi Sad, Serbia

ISSN 2214-6881 ISSN 2214-689X (electronic)
Ius Comparatum - Global Studies in Comparative Law
ISBN 978-3-319-23188-4 ISBN 978-3-319-23189-1 (eBook)
DOI 10.1007/978-3-319-23189-1

Library of Congress Control Number: 2015956385

Springer Cham Heidelberg New York Dordrecht London

Printed on acid-free paper

Springer International Publishing AG Switzerland is part of Springer Science+Business Media (www.springer.com)

Preface

For a long time in human history, the legal status of the child was not the focus of attention by the state, government, international organisations and even family itself. The child was not treated as an independent holder of rights but rather as a more or less subordinate object of rights of the parents or guardians. More attention began to be paid to children and their position just after the First World War, when, thanks to the efforts and commitments of two sisters, Eglantyne Jebb and Dorothy Buxton, the first Declaration of the Rights of the Child (1924) was adopted. This document highlights a very important maxim *that mankind owes to the child the best that it has to give*, which plausibly had far-reaching consequences for a further improvement of the status of children in the world. After this first Declaration of the Rights of the Child, the second one was adopted in 1959, and only in 1989 was the first legally binding international document regarding children rights adopted as the UN Convention on the Rights of the Child.

Since then, a quarter of a century has been passed, and the 19th Congress of the International Academy of Comparative Law, which took place in Vienna from 20–27 July 2014, was a good opportunity to compare the experiences and results in the implementation of the Convention in different parts of the world. Based on the questionnaire, which is appended at the end of this book, authors from 21 countries from all continents, except Africa, submitted national reports about the status of the rights of the child in their countries. This book compiles these national reports, which come from Australia, Canada, Croatia, Denmark, France, Germany, Greece, India, Iran, Japan, Portugal, Romania, Scotland, Serbia, Solomon Islands, Spain, the Netherlands, the UK, the USA, Uzbekistan and Venezuela. They were also the bases for the general report that represents a synthetic overview of the topic.

On this occasion I would like to thank all national rapporteurs for their research and commitment to the preparation of their reports, without which this comprehensive and profound analysis and overview of the implementation of the Convention on the Rights of the Child in such diverse parts of the world would not be possible. My gratitude also goes to Penny Booth, professor of Law (England), to whom I am deeply indebted for her invaluable assistance in the linguistic revision of my general report.

Novi Sad, Serbia
January 2015

Olga Cvejić Jančić

Contents

About the Authors

Olga Cvejić Jančić taught Family Law, European Family Law, and Inheritance Law at the Faculty of Law, University of Novi Sad (1980–2010), and since then at the Faculty of European Legal and Political Studies, Novi Sad, Educons University, Sremska Kamenica. She is currently a member of the Commission for the Drafting of the Serbian Civil Code, of the Ethical Board of the Clinical Centre of the Province of Vojvodina, and of the Editorial Board of the Kopaonik School of Natural Law.

From 2004 to 2006, she served as a dean of the Faculty of Law, University of Novi Sad, where she also served as a vice dean, director of the Institute of Legal Sciences, president of the Faculty's Senate, secretary of the law journal titled *Zbornik radova Pravnog fakulteta u Novom Sadu* [Bulletin of the Novi Sad Law Faculty] and the head of the Civil Law Department.

Prof. Cvejić Jančić is an associate member of the International Academy of Comparative Law, a councillor of the European Law Institute, a member of the International Society of Family Law, a member of the Executive Board of Directors of the International Academy for the Study of the Jurisprudence of the Family and the president of the Executive Board of the Serbian Association for Comparative Law.

She also sits on the editorial boards of the following journals: *Zeitschrift für das gesamte Familienrecht (FamRZ)*, *Law and Justice Review* and *Human Rights Review* (both published by the Justice Academy of Turkey), *Strani Pravni Život* [Foreign Legal Life] (published by the Institute of Comparative Law, Belgrade) and *Pravo i Politika* [Law and Politics] (published by the Faculty of European Legal and Political Studies, Novi Sad).

In 2010 she was a visiting scholar-in-residence at Washington and Lee University, Lexington, VA, USA. She has published a number of books and textbooks and more than 140 journal articles, book chapters and other papers.

Novi Sad, Serbia

Rita Shackel is an associate professor of Law at Sydney Law School and holds the Chair of The University of Sydney Human Research Ethics Committee. Her research interests revolve around evaluation and reform of legal and social justice processes, with a specific focus on sexual and gender-based violence, the needs of victims and survivors and children's interaction with the law.

Sydney Law School, Law School Building, The University of Sydney, Camperdown, NSW, Australia

Michelle Giroux Université d'Ottawa, Ottawa, ON, Canada

Carmen Lavallée Université de Sherbrooke, Sherbrooke, QC, Canada

Nenad Hlača graduated from the Faculty of Law, University of Rijeka, in 1980. Before he joined the University in 1982, he was a clerk at the Municipal Court in Rijeka. In 1984 he received the master's degree in civil law studies from the Faculty of Law, University of Belgrade. In 1990 he received the title of Doctor of Laws from the Faculty of Law, University of Zagreb, by defending doctorate dissertation on 'Family Law Aspects of the Transgender'. In 1991, Nenad Hlača was nominated an assistant professor, and in 1998 he became the professor of Family Law at the Faculty of Law, University of Rijeka. He was twice elected as a vice dean: from 1990 to 1994 and from 1999 to 2001. From 1991 to 1994, as well as from 2009 to 2011, he acted as the editor in chief of the Collected Papers of the Law Faculty of the University of Rijeka. He is also a member of the international advisory board of the review *FamRZ* (*Zeitschrift für das gesamte Familienrecht mit Betreuungsrecht, Erbrecht, Verfahrensrecht, Öffentlichem Recht*).

Since 1999 to 2015, Professor Nenad Hlača was a vice president of the Croatian Section of the *Commission Internationale de l'Etat Civil* in Strasbourg.

While a member of the working group, formed by the Ministry of Work and Social Welfare of the Republic of Croatia, he worked on the draft proposal on the Family Act (1994–1998). Professor Hlača actively participated in many international and national seminars and conferences and published a number of scientific papers and articles.

Sandra Winkler is a senior research assistant at the Chair of Family Law of the Faculty of Law, University of Rijeka (Croatia). Before she joined the University in 2006, she worked in a law office. In 2009 she received her PhD degree in Law from the Faculty of Law, University of Verona (Italy). She was awarded a research grant at the *Max-Planck-Institut für ausländisches und internationales Privatrecht* in Hamburg (Germany) on two occasions. Her research interests include Family Law and European Family Law. She is a member of the European Law Institute (ELI) and of the Croatian Comparative Law Association (HUPP).

She actively participated in international and national seminars and conferences and published scientific papers and articles in the field of Family Law and European Family Law.

Faculty of Law, University of Rijeka, Rijeka, Croatia

Christina Jeppesen de Boer is a researcher and lecturer at Utrecht University (research group Family and Law) and is further affiliated with UCERF (Utrecht Centre for European Research into Family Law) and the research school IUS Commune. Her main interest is Comparative Family Law and Human Rights Law.

Molengraaff Instituut, Utrecht, The Netherlands

Annette Kronborg is an associate professor at Copenhagen University, Denmark, and is affiliated to the Centre of Legal Culture. She teaches family law courses and has published broadly within family law. Currently, her main interest is Nordic Family Law in a comparative perspective.

Copenhagen University, Copenhagen K, Denmark

Adeline Gouttenoire Professor at the Faculty of Law and Political Science of Bordeaux, Director of the Institute of Minors and CERFAP, President of the Departmental Observatory of the Gironde.

Bordeaux, France

Stefanie Schmahl is a professor of Law and holds the Chair of German and Foreign Public Law, Public International Law and European Union Law at the Julius-Maximilians-University of Würzburg (Germany). She was nominated as a member of the group of specialists on child-friendly justice of the Council of Europe in 2008. The objective of the group was to produce comprehensive European Guidelines on child-friendly justice which were approved by the Committee of Ministers in November 2010. In 2011, Stefanie Schmahl acted as a counsel on behalf of the Federal Government of Germany at a proceeding before the European Court of Human Rights. From 2011 until 2013, she was a member of the Independent Committee concerning the law of member of Parliament at the German Bundestag. Since 2012, she is an alternate member of the Management Board of the European Union Agency for Fundamental Rights, and in 2015, she was elected as a member of the Advisory Board to the International Nuremberg Principles Academy.

Stefanie Schmahl is the author and editor of books and scholarly articles on public international law, European Union and German public law. Inter alia, she has written a Commentary to the Convention on the Rights of the Child (*Kinderrechtskonvention mit Zusatzprotokollen, Handkommentar, Baden-Baden 2013*).

Juristische Fakultät, Julius-Maximilians-Universität Würzburg, Würzburg, Germany

Eleni Micha holds a doctorate degree in law from the University of Athens and a diploma from the International Committee of the Red Cross. Parts of her studies were carried out at Leiden University in the Netherlands. Dr. Micha specialises in Public International Law, and her particular fields of interest are International and

Regional Protection of Human Rights, International Humanitarian Law and Law of War, International Criminal Law and Domestic Application of International Law.

She currently holds a teaching post at the Department of International Studies at the School of Law of the University of Athens. She is attorney at law at the Athens Bar Association dealing mostly with cases regarding protection of human rights. She is a member of the Board of Directors of the NGO 'Human Rights Defense Centre' and an external evaluator of the law journal *International Community Law Review*, published by Brill/Nijhoff.

Dr. Micha participated in various conferences and has published a number of articles in Greece and abroad. Her recent work deals with execution issues of the judgments of the European Court of Human Rights, domestic application of treaties treating human trafficking and justiciability of social rights. She also contributed to the Commentary of the European Convention on Human Rights compiled and edited under the supervision of the Greek judge in the European Court of Human Rights, Professor Linos-Alexander Sicilianos.

School of Law, University of Athens, Athens, Greece

Vishnupriya Yadlapalli did her Master of Arts (MA) with specialisation in Industrial Economics and Master of Laws (LLM) with specialisation in Labour Laws. She did her doctoral degree (PhD) entitled *Child Labour: A Socio-legal Study with Reference to Slate Mines of Markapur in Andhra Pradesh, India*, where concentration of child labour is severe. She also did a Postgraduate Diploma in Industrial Relations and Personnel Management. She has been teaching Labour Law, Family Law, Law of Contracts, Women and Law, Human Rights and Law and Social Change to LLB, LLM and PhD students since June 1989. National and international PhD scholars are doing research under her guidance.

She was a chairperson of Board of Studies in Law from June 2012 to July 2014. *Presently, she is head of the Department of Law, Osmania University.* She is a member of the Governing Body and Selection Committee of different law colleges. She is a member of the Board of Examiners of various universities and public service commissions. She delivered invited lectures in various universities and institutions. She was the regional coordinator of Law Common Entrance Test – 2013, 2014 and 2015 – in the states of Telangana and Andhra Pradesh.

She has published 35 articles in standard legal journals. She participated in 50 national and international seminars/conferences and workshops. She has participated and presented papers in the *16th IVR World Congress on 'Law, Justice and State' which was held at Reykjavik, Iceland, and Women's Worlds Congress at Hyderabad Central University in August 2014.* She has submitted Indian report in the *IACL World Congress organised by the International Academy of Comparative Law (IACL) at Vienna in July 2014.*

She is a member of the Academic Council of Maharashtra National Law University, Mumbai. She is an editorial board member of legal journals such as *Indian Socio-legal Journal, Jaipur,* and *Justicia, Hyderabad.* She is a life member of the Indian Law Institute, New Delhi; Indian Institute of Comparative Law, Jaipur;

and Central Social Welfare Board, New Delhi. She is associated with many NGOs working for human rights.

Her areas of interest are Human Rights, Gender Justice, Child and Law and Law and Social Change.

Department of Law, Osmania University, Hyderabad, Telangana State, 500 007, India

Habiballah Ahmadi Baloutaki is an advocate in Iran Legal System and has received LLB, LLM and PhD degrees in the field of International Human Rights Law, from University College of Law, Osmania University, Hyderabad – 500007 – India.

Education:

LLB/Bachelor of Laws, College of Law, Azad University, Ahwaz, Iran, 1996–2000

LLM/Master of Laws in International Human Rights Law, College of Law, University of Shahid Beheshti, Tehran, Iran, 2003–2006

Thesis topic: 'Freedom of Press in Iran Legal System by View of International Human Rights Law', PhD/Research Scholar at Osmania University, Hyderabad, India. 'Protection of Human Rights in the Developing Countries, a study of Brazil, Kenya and India'

Occupation: attorney at law and legal advisor, in Iran Legal System and PhD in the field of Human Rights, at University College of Law, Osmania University, Hyderabad – 500007 – India

Activities: Participated in many national seminars, international conferences, world congress and workshop and published several articles in prestigious international journals

University College of Law, Osmania University, Hyderabad, Telangana State, 500 007, India

Advocate Law Office, Tehran, Iran

Yoshiaki Ohmura was born in Tokyo in 1963 and graduated from the Faculty of Law, Tokyo University. Ohmura has a legal master's degree (University of Tokyo). Ohmura's field is Private International Law (especially in Family Law matters) and field of interest is Interpersonal Family Law.

Prof. Yoshiaki Ohmura is dean of the Faculty of Law, Chuo-gakuin University, Abiko City, Chiba Prefecture, Japan

Manuela Baptista Lopes The author is secretary general of the Constitutional Court of Portugal and a legal advisor on its permanent staff. She previously served with Ministry of Justice bodies responsible for the jurisdictional protection of minors (civil matters and underage offenders). She spent several years linked to both the international convention protection of children within the framework of the Council of Europe and the Hague Conference on Private International Law and similar questions in the bilateral domain (France and Luxembourg).

Tribunal Constitucional, Lisboa, Portugal

Daniela-Anca Deteşeanu is a lecturer at the Faculty of Law, University of Bucharest, with her major teaching and research interests being in Human Rights Law and International Law. She obtained both her undergraduate degree and the PhD at the University of Bucharest Law School. Currently, Mrs. Deteseanu teaches Human Rights Law, Public International Law, International Humanitarian Law and International Criminal Law at the University of Bucharest Law School. Since February 2015, Mrs. Deteseanu has been appointed as vice dean of the University of Bucharest Law School. She is also a member of the Bucharest Bar Association.

Faculty of Law, University of Bucharest, Bd, Bucharest, Romania

Frankie Mccarthy is a senior lecturer in Private Law at the University of Glasgow. She is the author of *Succession* (2012) and *Family Law* (with Griffiths and Fotheringham, 2013), and her work has been published in *European Human Rights Law Review* and *Child and Family Law Quarterly*, amongst others.

School of Law, University of Glasgow, Glasgow, Scotland

Nevena Vučković Šahović is a professor at the Faculty of Law, Union University, in Belgrade, Serbia, teaching International Public Law with International Organisations and Family Law with Rights of the Child. She is the coordinator of the Master on the Rights of the Child. Nevena Vučković Šahović is the founder and director of Child Rights Centre – Belgrade – which was the first and the only organisation in Serbia exclusively devoted to the promotion and implementation of the Convention on the Rights of the Child. She served on the Committee on the Rights of the Child (2003–2009). She is active in many countries in Europe, Asia and the USA, teaching human rights and rights of the child.

Nevena Vučković Šahović is the author of numerous articles, books and researches. Some include *Implementation of the General Measures of the CRC and the Role of Civil Society* (WP, UNICEF Innocenti Research Centre, Florence, 2010, p. 61), 'Measures to Implement the Convention on the Rights of the Child and Good Governance: The Case of Serbia' (in: Ganguly Thukral, Enakshi, *Every Right for Every Child*, Routledge Taylor and Francis Group, p. 65–89, 2011), *ENOC Study Report on National Human Rights Institutions and Child/Juvenile Delinquency* (ENOC, Council of Europe, Strasbourg, 2012, p. 61) and *The Rights of the Child in International Law* (with Jaap Doek and Jean Zermatten) (Stampfli Publishers, November 2012, p. 420).

Beograd, Serbia

Ivana Savić is an executive director of the Centre for Human Rights and Development Studies (CHRDS), an organisation focused on advancing global, regional and national policies in the areas of human rights, especially of the rights of the child and youth rights, and sustainable development. From 2009 until 2014, she had been one of the Organising Partners for the United Nations Major Group for

Children and Youth (MGCY) with a mandate to coordinate and facilitate young people's participation in the international sustainability negotiations, namely, Rio + 20 and the post-2015 process. Ivana is a member of the UNDP Civil Society Advisory Committee and CIVICUS Youth Advisory Group. Additionally, she has been involved in different child and youth initiatives worldwide and has been internationally recognised as expert in the field of the Rights of the Child, Youth Rights, Human Rights and Environment, Sustainable Development and Young People's Participation. She is a published author in the area of her expertise. Ivana holds an LLM degree in the Rights of the Child and is a doctoral candidate in the Rights of the Child at the Union University, Faculty of Law, in Belgrade, Serbia.

Beograd, Serbia

Jennifer Corrin is a director of the Centre for Public, International and Comparative Law and professor in the TC Beirne School of Law at The University of Queensland. She is the recipient of an Australian Research Council Future Fellowships (project number FT120100642), researching law reform and development in plural legal regimes. Jennifer is a partner investigator in two international research collaborations on legal pluralism funded by the Social Sciences and Humanities Research Council and L'Agence Universitaire de la Francophonie. She is also part of an interdisciplinary team working on environmental issues in Solomon Islands, funded by the MacArthur Foundation. Jennifer has published in the areas of South Pacific Law, Customary Law, Human Rights, Court Systems, Evidence, Civil Procedure, Family Law, Land Law, Constitutional Law and Contract. Jennifer's most recent publications include a third edition of *Introduction to South Pacific Law* and articles on legal pluralism and questions of proof, family law in the South Pacific, and complexities of legal pluralism. Before joining The University of Queensland, Jennifer spent 6 years at the University of the South Pacific, having joined the Faculty after 9 years in her own legal firm in Solomon Islands. Jennifer is a member of the Editorial Board of *The Journal of Legal Pluralism*, the International Editorial Board of the *Journal of South Pacific Law*, and the Editorial Board of the *Comparative Law Journal of the Pacific*.

TC Beirne School of Law, The University of Queensland, Brisbane, QLD, Australia

Gabriel Garcia Cantero born in the Basque Country (San Sebastián 1927), after had exercised judicial functions (1951–1967), he was Professor of Civil Law at the Universities of Santiago de Compostela, San Sebastián and Zaragoza, where he continued to teach Comparative Law and European Law. He is a titular member of the AIDC and the Association of European Lawyers Pavia and President of the Spanish Association of Comparative Law. At the Teheran International Congress (1974) and Brisbane (2002), he was General Rapporteur for Law themes of filiation and family.

Facultad de Derecho, Zaragoza, Espagne

Ton Liefaard holds the UNICEF Chair in Children's Rights at Leiden University, Leiden Law School. He teaches and publishes on children's rights, child law and juvenile justice from an international and comparative perspective and has published widely on the meaning of the UN Convention on the Rights of the Child and related international and regional instruments for the position of children at the national level. He is the programme director of the Master's Programme (LLM) *Advanced Studies in International Children's Rights*, which starts in September 2015. He also coordinates in the Leiden Summer School on International Children's Rights.

Ton Liefaard regularly works as a consultant for international organisations, including agencies of the United Nations, the Council of Europe and the European Union, on issues related to children's rights, juvenile justice, child-friendly justice, child protection, alternative care and violence against children. He is furthermore a deputy juvenile judge at the District Court of Amsterdam and a member of the State Commission advising the Dutch Government on changing parental relationships and the position of children.

His key publications include *Deprivation of Liberty of Children in Light of International Human Rights Law and Standards* (Intersentia 2008), 'Juveniles in Transition from Juvenile Justice to Adult Criminal Justice' (in: R. Loeber et al. (eds.), *Persisters and Desisters in Crime from Adolescence into Adulthood: Explanation, Prevention and Punishment*, Ashgate 2012), 'Child Soldiers: Towards A Rights-Based Imagery' (in: C. Brants, A. Hol and D. Siegel (eds.), *Transitional Justice: Images and Memories*, Ashgate 2013), *Litigating the Rights of the Child* (Springer 2014, edited with J.E. Doek) and 'Juvenile justice from a children's rights perspective' (in: W. Vandenhole et al. (eds.), *Routledge International Handbook of Children's Rights Studies*, Routledge 2015).

Department of Child Law, Leiden Law School, Leiden, The Netherlands

Machteld Vonk is an assistant professor and research fellow of Child and Family Law at the Child Law Department of Leiden University Law School. Her research interests concern the position of children in their families and include research into multi-parent families, same-sex families, families through surrogacy, the legal position of transgender children, the child's right to know his/her origins in the context of these new families and child participation in family matters. Machteld Vonk holds a PhD in Comparative Family Law from Utrecht University (2007), a Master in Law from the University of Amsterdam (2002) and a Master in English from VU University Amsterdam (1991). Machteld Vonk publishes in international and national journals and books. In the summer of fall of 2014, she was a visiting scholar at the University of British Columbia in Vancouver and the University of Victoria in British Columbia, amongst others to do research on the new BC Family Law Act.

Department of Child Law, Leiden Law School, Leiden, The Netherlands

Jenny Driscoll is lecturer in Child Studies and programme director of the MA in Child Studies/International Child Studies at King's College London, where she moved after over a decade of practice at the Independent Family Law Bar in London, specialising in child protection. Her research interests are at the intersection of children's rights and child protection, particularly in relation to children in the care of the state. She is currently an academic advisor to the NGO 'shadow' submission to the UN Committee on the Rights of the Child in response to the UK government's 5th periodic report on implementation of the UN Convention on the Rights of the Child.

Department of Education and Professional Studies, King's College London, London, UK

Nora V. Demleitner Dean Demleitner received her JD from Yale Law School, her BA from Bates College, and an LLM with distinction in International and Comparative Law from Georgetown University Law Center. After law school Dean Demleitner clerked for the Supreme Court Justice Samuel A. Alito, Jr., then a member of the US Court of Appeals for the Third Circuit.

Dean Demleitner teaches and has written widely in the areas of Criminal, Comparative, Human Rights, with a focus on women and children, and Immigration Law and Legal Education. At conferences around the country and abroad, she regularly speaks on sentencing matters, often in a comparative context, and issues pertaining to the state of legal education.

A native of Germany, Dean Demleitner has served as a visiting professor at the University of Michigan Law School, the University of Freiburg in Germany, St. Thomas University School of Law in Miami, and the Sant'Anna Institute of Advanced Research in Pisa, Italy. She has also been a visiting researcher at the Max Planck Institute for Foreign and International Criminal Law in Germany, funded by a German Academic Exchange Service grant. Before joining Washington and Lee University, she was the dean at the Maurice A. Deane School of Law at Hofstra University in New York and a faculty member at St. Mary's University School of Law in San Antonio, Texas.

Dean Demleitner is an editor of the *Federal Sentencing Reporter* and serves on the Board of Editors of Nijhoff Publishers' Studies in Intercultural Human Rights. She is the lead author of *Sentencing Law and Policy*, a major casebook on sentencing law, published by Wolters Kluwer. Her articles have appeared in the Stanford, Michigan, and Minnesota law reviews, amongst others.

Dean Demleitner is an elected member of the American Law Institute, the European Law Institute, and the International Society of Comparative Law and a Fellow of the American Bar Foundation. In 2014 *Virginia Lawyers Weekly* named her one of 'Virginia's Leaders in the Law'.

Washington and Lee University School of Law, Charlottesville, Virginia, USA

Iroda Djuraeva graduated from Tashkent State University of Law (TSUL) where she obtained her master's degree (2003). She holds a PhD in Law from TSUL (2007). She conducted her doctoral studies on *Personal and Property Rights of Spouses in Private International Law* under the supervision of Academic Professor Rakhmankulov H.R.

Recently, she has participated as a researcher in the framework of the project 'Comparative Legal Research on Eurasian Law' at Max Planck Institute for Comparative and International Private Law in Hamburg, Germany (2011–2012). As a result her manuscript on *Personal Non-property Rights of Minors in Uzbekistan* has been published in Germany (2014).

Dr. Iroda Djuraeva currently works as an attorney at law firm 'Mukhiddinova and Partners'. Her main lines of research are International Family Law, Children's Rights and Civil Law.

Tashkent city, Uzbekistan

Alberto Blanco-Uribe Lawyer (1983) and specialist in administrative law (1987) at the Central University of Venezuela (UCV). DESS (Diploma of higher specialized studies) of Environmental Law (1988) and DEA (Diplôme d'études appliquées) of public law (1989) at the Robert Schuman University, Strasbourg, France. Constitutional Justice Specialist (2006) and Human Rights Specialist (2008) at the University of Castilla-La Mancha, Toledo, Spain. Professor of Constitutional Law (undergraduate) and Human Rights (third cycle) at the Central University of Venezuela (UCV). Several specialized legal publications. Advisor, consultant and litigator in partnership with Lawyers Klemprer, Rivas, Perez & Associates.

Caracas, Venezuela

Rights of the Child in a Changing World

The UN Convention on the Rights of the Child: 25 Years After

Olga Cvejić Jančić

The author is indebted to Penny Booth, Law Professor, for her invaluable assistance in the linguistic revision of this paper.

IV A. Droit international public/Public international law.

O.C. Jančić, Ph.D. (✉)
Faculty of European Legal and Political Studies – Novi Sad, Educons University - Sremska Kamenica, Serbia
e-mail: olgacvejic@gmail.com

O. Cvejić Jančić (ed.), *The Rights of the Child in a Changing World*,
Ius Comparatum - Global Studies in Comparative Law 13,
DOI 10.1007/978-3-319-23189-1_1

1 Introduction

Starting from a theoretical and legislative point of view, the importance of the United Nation Convention on the Rights of the Child[1,2] (New York, 20 November 1989) is very salient, having in mind the number of countries that have signed and ratified this Convention. Namely, 195 countries[3] have so far signed and ratified the Convention, while the USA and Somalia have started this process but still have not finished. This Convention, which is among those with the highest number of ratifications, is the result of long-term and persistent international efforts in order to improve the social, economic, health and legal position, and well-being of children around the world.

[1] The general report is based upon the contribution of the 21 national reports from almost all continents (except from Africa) and covers the implementation of children's rights in States Parties of the Convention on the Rights of the Child, which submitted papers for the congress. Although at the time of the congress more than 21 countries, through their national committee, have announced their participation in the Congress, the only 21 mentioned countries submitted their reports. The authors of national reports come from Australia (RITA SHACKEL), Canada (MICHELLE GIROUX, CARMEN LAVALLÉE), Croatia (NENAD HLAČA, SANDRA WINKLER), Denmark (CHRISTINA G. JEPPESEN DE BOER, ANNETTE KRONBORG), France (ADELINE GOUTTENOIRE), Germany (STEFANIE SCHMAHL), Greece (ELENI MICHA), India (VISHNUPRIYA YADLAPALLI), Iran (HABIB ALLAH AHMADI), Japan (YOSHIAKI OHMURA), Portugal (MANUELA BAPTISTA LOPES), Romania (DANIELA-ANCA DETEŞEANU), Scotland (FRANKIE McCARTHY), Serbia (NEVENA VUČKOVIĆ ŠAHOVIĆ, IVANA SAVIĆ), Solomon Islands (JENNIFER CORRIN), Spain (GABRIEL GARCÍA CANTERO), The Netherlands (TON LIEFAARD, MACHTELD VONK), UK (JENNY DRISCOLL), USA (NORA V. DEMLEITNER), Uzbekistan (IRODA DJURAEVA) and Venezuela (ALBERTO BLANCO-URIBE). National reports have been written on the basis of the questionnaire drawn up by the general reporter, with the possibility of each author to add all that is considered to be important for the realisation of children's rights in his/her country. The questionnaire has not encompassed all rights of the child guaranteed by the Convention, but only several of them, which author of the questionnaire deemed as essential and in some way of general value for children. Some important issues in respect of children's right are not included in the reports, such as protection of the child in armed conflicts; protection of the child against prostitution, pornography and prohibition of the sale of children; and protection of the right of the child through the possibility to bring a complaint before the UN Committee on the Rights of the Child, which are part of separate Optional protocols to the Convention (Optional Protocol to the CRC on the involvement of children in armed conflict; the Optional Protocol to the CRC on the sale of children, child prostitution and child pornography; and the Optional Protocol to the CRC on a communications procedure), as well as some others, because it deserves much more spaces and may be a particular topic for some of the Congresses that follow.

[2] Thereafter UN CRC, CRC or simply Convention.

[3] The last two are the State of Palestine which accessed to the Convention on 2 April 2014, available at the website https://treaties.un.org/Pages/ViewDetails.aspx?src=TREATY&mtdsg_no=IV-11&chapter=4&lang=en (access to the site on 1 July 2014) and South Sudan which accessed to the Convention on 23 January 2015, available at the website https://treaties.un.org/Pages/ViewDetails.aspx?src=IND&mtdsg_no=IV-11&chapter=4&lang=en (access to the site in May 2015).

These efforts date back to 1924, when the League of Nations adopted the Declaration of the Rights of the Child, commonly known as the Geneva Declaration.[4] However, many politicians, scholars and other persons and organisations concerned with the rights and welfare of children deemed it insufficient and advocated the adoption of a separate internationally binding document on this matter. This did not happen until 1989, when the UN Convention on the Rights of the Child was adopted, even though in the meantime (in November 1959) the UN General Assembly adopted the second Declaration of the Rights of the Child. Although the governments of a large number of countries have realised that some measures and steps should be taken in order to improve the position of children and to this end have signed and ratified the Convention, it does not automatically mean that the position of children worldwide will indeed be significantly and evenly improved.

Therefore, what are the practical effects of this international instrument in the everyday life of children, are there any outcomes in terms of improvement of their status around the world and the conditions under which they live in the 25 years, since the Convention came into force[5]? The great significance of the Convention is evident firstly from the simple fact that the governments of the numerous countries recognised that 'in all countries in the world, there are children living in exceptionally difficult conditions, and that such children need special consideration'[6] and therefore were ready to undertake necessary measures for improvement of the rights of the child in their countries. The first measure was signature and ratification of this Convention. This was the preliminary step to further measures in the implementation of the provisions of the Convention. However, is that enough for any child to live a better, safer and healthier life? The implementation and realisation of the objectives of the Convention is a process that requires time, resources, efforts, and first and foremost, the willingness to achieve them. Signature and ratification will never be sufficient. Albeit this process is far from being completed, 25 years of the life of the Convention is enough to make some comparative review of its implementation and some evaluations of the achieved results.

It is important to state that after its adoption by the General Assembly of the United Nations (1989), there was and remains significant resistance to the Convention. The most common objections and reasons for non-approval have been directed to the limitation of parental rights and responsibilities owing to the allegation that the child as a legal entity has too many rights and freedom, which weakened

[4] The Draft Declaration was created thanks to the efforts of Ms. Eglantyne Jebb and her sister Dorothy Buxton, who, confronted with the horrors of World War I established in London the Save the Children Fund. Later, in 1923, the International Union of Save the Children prepared a Draft Declaration on the Rights of the Child, which then, in February 1924, Eglantyne Jebb submitted to the League of Nations for approval. Declaration on the Rights of the Child was adopted on 26 September of the same year. See more at http://www.humanium.org/en/childrens-rights-history/references-on-child-rights/geneva-declaration/.

[5] The UNCRC was adopted by resolution 44/25 of the General Assembly of the United Nation of 20. November 1989, entered into force of 2 September 1990, available at http://www.ohchr.org/en/professionalinterest/pages/crc.aspx. Accessed 8 January 2014.

[6] Preamble of the CRC, recital 10.

the position and authority of parents. However, these objections are not justified, since the purpose of the Convention is, in the first place, to provide that '[S]tates Parties undertake to ensure the child such protection and care as is necessary for his or her well-being, taking into account the rights and duties of his or her parents, legal guardians, or other individuals legally responsible for him or her, and, to this end, (States Parties)[7] shall take all appropriate legislative and administrative measures'.[8] Many other provisions of the Convention are also directed at the States Parties, to which are imposed considerable commitments to undertake all necessary measures to support the realisation of the guaranteed rights of the child in order to '[e]nsure to the maximum extent possible the survival and development of the child'.[9] The right to life, survival and development (Art. 6 CRC) is, at the same time, one of the four principles on which the rights of the child are based. The other three are prohibition of discrimination or right to nondiscrimination (Art. 2 CRC),[10] the right to participation (Art. 12 and 13 CRC), and the right to have the best interests of the child respected (Art. 3/1 CRC).

In order that implementation of the Convention would not be left to the goodwill of the States Parties and, in particular, that the Convention would not eventually become a 'dead letter', the Convention established a special body vested with a task to monitor the implementation of it.[11] This body is the Committee on the Rights of the Child (thereafter Committee or ComRC), which consists of ten experts nominated by member states.[12]

Member States are obliged, under the provisions of the Convention, to submit to the Committee a report on the measures they have adopted in order to implement the Convention and on the progress made in that regard. Reports should be submitted every 5 years.[13] A national report should include information on the measures undertaken by the State Party in order to implement the Convention, as well as possible difficulties that affect the fulfilment of the obligations under the Convention (Article 44 paragraph 2 of the CRC).

---

[7] *Added by the author.*

[8] Article 3, paragraph 2 of the CRC.

[9] Article 6, paragraph 2 of the CRC.

[10] The CRC does not use the term of 'right to nondiscrimination', but this phrase is used in General Comment No. 4 (2003) of the Committee on the Rights of the Child, adopted on the 33rd session of the Committee, which took place from 19 May to 6 June 2003, no I/6.

[11] In Article 43 of the CRC, it is expressed very clearly: 'For the purpose of examining the progress made by States Parties in achieving the realisation of the obligations undertaken in the present Convention, there shall be established a Committee on the Rights of the Child, which shall carry out the functions hereinafter provided'.

[12] Each state party may nominate one person for the Committee, but the final election will be performed by secret ballot from a list of persons nominated by States Parties (Art. 43 paragraph 3 of the CRC). The mandate of the members of the Committee shall be for 4 years and they may be reelected if they would be renominated (Art. 43 par. 6).

[13] After the CRC entered into force, Member States were under obligation to submit their first reports within 2 years and thereafter every 5 years (Article 44 paragraph 1, points a. and b.).

2 The Definition of the Child under the National Laws of the States Parties

The CRC defines the child as '[e]very human being below the age of eighteen years unless under the law applicable to the child, majority is attained earlier (Article 1)'. As for the definition of the child in the national laws of the States Parties which submitted national reports, the prevailing situation is that there is no explicit, clear and proper definition of the child as in the CRC (except for several countries, such as the Republic of Uzbekistan, UK and Romania) but rather indirect definition through the determination of the age of majority and the acquisition of full legal capacity, which indirectly leads to conclusion that from that moment the person is no longer a 'child'.

In the Republic of Uzbekistan, the Law on Guarantees of the Rights of the Child (2008) sets the legal definition of the child as a person below 18 years; in Romania, the Law no. 272/2004 regarding the protection of the child defines 'child' as being any person who is below the age of 18 and does not have full civil capacity; in the UK, the Children Act 1989 Section 105 defines the child as 'a person under the age of eighteen', while the Family Law Reform Act 1969 s1(1) states that 'a person shall attain full age on attaining the age of eighteen' (England and Wales).[14]

Apart from these few countries, for most of the others, mainly in the absence of an explicit definition of the child, the notion of the child may be deduced from the notion of majority. According to the submitted national reports, the child acquires the age of majority in most cases at the age of 18. This is the case with Australia; the Canadian province of Quebec (Article 153 of the Civil Code of Québec); Croatia (Article 120, paragraph 1 of the Croatian Family Act); France, in which it is regulated by the French Code Civil (Art. 388 Code civil français); Germany where it is also regulated by the Civil Code (Section 2 of the Bürgerliches Gesetzbuch); India (The Indian Majority Act); Portugal (Article 122 of the Portuguese Civil Code); Scotland (Age of Majority Act 1969); Serbia (Article 37 of the Constitution and Article 11 of the Family Act); Spain (Article 12 of the Constitution); and the Netherlands (Article 1:233 of the Dutch Civil Code); and in Northern Ireland (under the Children Order 1995 s2(2) and the Age of Majority Act 1969 s1(1)), the similar provisions are in effect.

In few countries, the age of majority is lower than 18 (Iran) or higher (some province and territories of Canada, Japan, Solomon Islands) than 18 years. For instance, in Iran, the Civil Code (Article 1210, note 1) provides for the age of majority for boys is 15 lunar years and for girls 9 lunar years.[15] The issue of majority in Iran is raised in connection with the age of maturity for marriage and has particular importance since Article 1041 of Iranian Civil Code sets out that '[M]arriage before the age of majority is prohibited'. Given that such a low age for marriage endangers or may endanger development of children, especially girls, the human rights

[14] See national reports, Uzbekistan, Romania and UK.

[15] A lunar year is a slightly shorter than a solar year.

defenders advocated for a change of this provision in order to raise the threshold for marriageable age. Their efforts were rewarded, so the threshold for girls was raised to 13 and for the boys to 15 years. Even this modest success is compromised by the power of the child's guardian (i.e. his or her father or paternal grandfather, who are, ex lege, the guardians of the child) to consent to marriage of the girl or boy before reaching these ages, if it is, according to their perception, in the child's best interest.[16]

In several Canadian provinces, such as British Columbia, New Brunswick, Newfoundland, Nova Scotia and the three territories, majority is attained at the age of 19 years,[17] while under the Japanese Civil Code (Article 4), the age of majority is 20, but the notion of the 'child' and 'minor' differs.[18] The specific statutes regulate different age threshold for some rights or obligations of the child.

In the Solomon Islands, the age of majority is not regulated by statute, although the Child's Rights Bill had been drafted in 1993, but still not enacted. Hence, the age of majority is governed by the common law (which is in force in the Solomon Islands) under which the age of majority is 21, while the Child's Rights Bill (drafted in 1993, but still not enacted) provides for 18 years as the age of majority.[19] In the USA, there is no general rule that regulates the age of majority because the competence to regulate this issue is divided between the federal and states governments. Although most people deem 18 years as the age of majority, in select areas the specific age at which the child is legally considered an adult varies depending on the context.[20] In Venezuela under Organic Law for the Protection of Boys, Girls and Adolescents (2007), a distinction is made between the child and adolescent. The child is a person under the age of 12, while an adolescent is person older than 12 but younger than 18 (Article 2 of the Organic Law).[21]

In addition to this universal notion of majority (where applicable) as the boundary of childhood, after which starts the period of adulthood and the child acquires a full legal capacity, there is the so-called qualified capacity of the child for the enjoyment of specific rights and protection or for the responsibility, if the child committed a tort or crime, in which cases the age limit for this 'qualified capacity' is less than 18. This 'qualified capacity of the child' is governed by different statutes in different areas of law and differs from country to country, as regards the terms, the ages and the like. In some national reports, it is emphasised that terminology for a minor child is not uniform and that some statutes use the term 'the child' for an underage child until the child reaches some specified years, and then after that period use the term of younger minor, older minor, and then juvenile, adolescent and other similar words, according to the specific years provided for in respective national legislations.

---

[16] National report, Iran.

[17] National report, Canada, 3.

[18] National report, Japan, 1

[19] National report, the Solomon Islands, Personhood and Age of Majority.

[20] National report, USA, I.

[21] National report, Venezuela, II/2.

3 Legal Instruments Devoted to the Rights of the Child

Member States regulate the rights of the child through constitutional guarantee (basic rules and principles), family law legislation and provisions on children's rights, which can be found in the other statutes that govern special areas of law ('sectoral laws'), and, finally, through special statutes on the rights of children. However, although the implementation of the CRC through enactment of a special statute dedicated only to the rights of the child is very desirable,[22] it is very interesting that there are not many countries that had acted in this way. Enactment of special statutes on the rights of the child in each State Party would be very welcome by the ComRC with regard to need to ensure global and equal application of the CRC for all children on whole territory of the States Parties, as expressed by the ComRC in the comments addressed to some countries.[23]

Such a special statute is enacted in Spain (the Organic Law on the Legal Protection of Minors from 15 January 1996), in Romania (the Law no. 272/2004 regarding the protection of the child), in Venezuela (the Organic Law on the Protection of Boys, Girls and Adolescents, 2007, as well as the law on special procedures in the field of family protection of boys, girls and adolescents, 2010), and in Uzbekistan (the Law on Guarantees of the Rights of the Child no 139, from 7 January 2008).[24]

There are also two drafts of similar legal acts, which were prepared but still not enacted (in Serbia, Draft of the Act on the Rights of the Child 2011, and in Wales, the Rights of Children and Young Persons Measure 2011), while in Scotland, the Children and Young People Act is enacted in 2014, but will come into force in the next 2–3 years.[25]

4 Best Interests of the Child

Best interests of the child is one of the four core principles of the CRC.[26] Although this is not a new principle, the CRC, we would say, for the first time, puts a strong emphasis on its importance and need to its universal, holistic and comprehensive

[22] 'The Committee welcomes the development of consolidated children's rights statutes, which can highlight and emphasise the Convention's principles. But the Committee emphasises that it is crucial in addition that all relevant 'sectoral' laws (on education, health, justice and so on) reflect consistently the principles and standards of the Convention'; see general comment of the Committee on the Rights of the Child, no. 5 (2003) (General measures of implementation of the Convention on the rights of the child, paragraph 22). General comments adopted on the 34th session of the Committee, which took place 19 September 2003.

[23] See, for instance, national report Australia, III; national report Canada, Preliminary Remarks; national report the Solomon Islands, Conventions and Protocols; national report UK, Introduction.

[24] See national reports of respective countries.

[25] See national reports of respective countries.

[26] See more about the topic in Jacqueline Rubellin–Devichi, 'The Best Interests Principle in French Law and Practice', *International Journal of Law and Family 8/1994*, Philip Alston, 'The Best

application when child's issues are at stake. The CRC explicitly mentions the best interests of the child in eight articles: 3/1, 9/1 and 9/3, 18/1, 20/1, 21/1, 37/c, 40/2 (b), iii and 40/4.

In Article 3/1, it is provided that the best interests of the child shall be a primary consideration in *all actions concerning children*, no matter 'whether undertaken by public or private social welfare institutions, courts of law, administrative authorities or legislative bodies'. Family surroundings are not mentioned. A content of this principle is clearly elaborated neither by the Convention nor by any other similar international document. This is very often raised as a problem and objections are raised regarding the application of this principle and the Convention itself. However, such a task and efforts to define a full and precise content of the best interest principle would be very problematic to achieve and, in addition, unfruitful. Why is it so? First of all, because this principle is very complex and should be very broadly applied on a case-by-case basis. This means that the best interests of the child should be taken into account in all situations where the child's rights are decided upon, no matter which field of (sectoral) law is at stake, and in each situation, all concrete circumstances of the case should be considered and assessed. All these situations and circumstances cannot be predicted in advance. Secondly, as it is stressed by the Committee, 'The best interests of the child is a dynamic concept that encompasses various issues which are continuously evolving'.[27] This dynamism and evolving concept of the best interest principle is often neglected.

Despite all the difficulties in defining the content of the best interest of the child, the Committee adopted 'General Comment No. 14 (2013) on the right of the child to have his or her best interests taken as a primary consideration' in which it points out, inter alia, the following parts: 'Legal analysis and links with the general principles of the Convention (IV)' and 'Implementation: assessing and determining the child's best interests (V)'. This Comment should serve as a useful guide for States Parties, i.e. its authorities, while applying the Convention and could be helpful in providing a better understanding of the new position of children as the holders of the rights proclaimed and guaranteed by the Convention and as 'a framework for assess-

---

Interests Principle: Towards a Reconciliation of Culture and Human Rights', *International Journal of Law and Family 8/1994*, J. Eekelaar, 'The Interests of the Child and Child's Wishes: The Role of Dynamic Self-Determinism', *International Journal of Law and the Family* 8/1994, U. Basset, The Changing Standard of the 'Best interest of the Child' and its Impact on the Exercise on Parenting and on Children, *International Journal of the Jurisprudence of the Family, Volume 2/2011*, R. Farrugia, Challenges in Balancing Parental Rights and the Child's Best Interests: A Preliminary Analyses of the Malta Divorce Referendum, *International Journal of the Jurisprudence of the Family, Volume 2/2011*, U. Novakovic, Najbolji interes deteta - Zajednicko vršenje roditeljskog prava (The Best Interests of the Child – Joint Exercise of Parental Rights) *Pravni život (Legal life) no.10/2011*, V. Vlaškalić, Problem odredjivanja najboljeg interesa deteta ('The Best Interests of the Child' – Problem of Definition), *Anali Pravnog fakulteta u Beogradu (Annals of the Law Faculty in Belgrade), LX, 1/2012.*

[27] General Comment No. 14 (2013) on the right of the child to have his or her best interests taken as a primary consideration (art. 3, para. 1), Adopted by the Committee at its 60-s session (14 January–1 February 2013), paragraph 11.

ing and determining the child's best interests' without of intention to prescribe what is best for the child in any given situation at any point in time.[28]

The expression 'primary consideration' according to the Comment of the Committee means 'that the child's best interests may not be considered on the same level as all other considerations', i.e. have high priority due to the special situation of the children, such as dependency, maturity, legal status, and, often, voicelessness.[29]

In addition to the right of the child to have his or her interests taken as a primary consideration in all actions, whether undertaken by public or private social welfare institutions, courts of law, administrative authorities or legislative bodies, the best interests of the child must also be taken into account in case of separation of the child from his or her parents. Namely, Art. 9 CRC provides that 'the child shall not be separated from his or her parents against their will, except when competent authorities subject to judicial review determine, in accordance with applicable law and procedures, that such separation is necessary for the best interests of the child'.[30] Having in mind Art. 3 CRC, the best interests of the child shall also be a primary consideration here.

Something similar is regulated in Art. 20/1 which mentions the best interest of the child when the child is temporarily or permanently deprived of his or her family environment, or when *in his or her best interests* cannot be allowed to remain in that environment, the child shall be entitled to special protection and assistance provided by the State. Thereupon, the best interests of the child is to be taken into account under Article 40/2 (b), iii, if the child is alleged as or accused of having infringed the penal law, in which occasion he or she should have at least a guarantee that the matter will be 'determined without delay by a competent, independent, and impartial authority or judicial body in a fair hearing according to law, in the presence of legal or other appropriate assistance and, *unless it is considered not to be in the best interest of the child* (emphasised by the author), in particular, taking into account his or her age or situation, his or her parents or legal guardians'. In the same Article, paragraph 4 mentions *thewell-beingof the child* in the context of a variety of dispositions, which shall be available to the competent authority in order to ensure that children are dealt with in a manner appropriate to their well-being and proportionate both to their circumstances and the offence.

Only Article 18/1 regulates that the best interest of the child has to be taken into account in family law relations, well, not only when someone out of the family decides on children rights but also when the child's parents or guardians do so, since they have the primary responsibility for the upbringing and development of the child, and therefore *the child's best interests* should be their basic concern. Thus, this Article regulates the common responsibilities of both parents (or of the child's legal guardians) for the upbringing and development of the child, in which case the best interests of the child will be their basic concern.

[28] Ibidem.

[29] See General Comment No. 14, paragraph 37 and 39.

[30] Emphasised by the author.

However, in the field of adoption, CRC uses stronger criterion when regulating this issue, using the wording that the best interests of the child shall be the paramount consideration (Art. 20/1).

In the Model Family Code,[31] as well as in the Principles of European Family Law Regarding Parental Responsibilities,[32] the best interest principle is considered also in the ambit of parents–children relations. The Model Family Code proclaims that in all matters concerning these relations, paramount regard must be given to the best interests of the child (Article 3.1). Schwenzer underlines that the child's best interests are neither merely one of many considerations nor a primary consideration but *the* primary consideration.[33] As the author explains, this does not mean that interests of the child's parent should not to be taken into account but that, in cases of conflicting interests, the child's interests always should take priority. In the Principles of European Family Law Regarding Parental Responsibilities, the emphasis is also put on the request that the best interests of the child in all matters *concerning parental responsibilities* (emphasised by the author) should be the primary consideration. Thus, the best interests of the child should always be 'the decisive criterion'.[34] In neither of the two mentioned is the content of this principle discussed in detail. It is explained that the principle is a changing notion and as such depends on many factors, for instance, the prevailing values of the concerned society as regards children, and then the individual situation of each child regarding the age, maturity, personality, needs, abilities, etc.[35]

The best interests principle is represented in all respective States Parties, but as might be expected, not with the same understanding and content. There are great differences between the national legislations regarding protection of children and their well-being, although all of them have ratified the CRC and thus undertook international commitments to recognise the rights of the child, based on the four core principles, and to provide protection of the child and his or her legal position as a holder of these rights.

The way of promotion of the best interest principle varies. From the submitted National reports can be seen that this principle is constitutionally promoted and guaranteed as a general principle only in the Constitution of Venezuela (1999), while in other countries, it is promoted and guaranteed indirectly. The Constitution of Venezuela proclaims (in Art. 78) that '[T]he State, families and society shall guarantee full protection of children and adolescents as an absolute priority, taking into account their best interests in actions and decisions concerning them…'.[36] In

[31] I. Schwenzer, in collaboration with M Dimsey, Model Family Code from a Global Perspective, Intersentia, 2006, p. 92, Article 3.1.

[32] K. Boele-Woelki, F. Ferrand, C. G. Beilfuss, M. Jänterä-Jareborg, N. Lowe, D. Martiny, W. Pintens, Principles of European Family Law Regarding Parental Responsibilities, Intersentia, 2007, p. 34 Principle 3.3.

[33] I. Schwenzer, op.cit.

[34] K. Boele-Woelki and other, op. cit. p. 38.

[35] Ibidem.

[36] National report, Venezuela.

addition, the Venezuelan Constitution guarantees every person the enjoyment and exercise of human rights, respect of which is mandatory for public authorities, if they (i.e. human rights) *contained in treaties signed and ratified by the Republic* (emphasised by the author) or any laws developing the same (Art. 19). Thereupon, the Constitution explicitly enshrines the precedence of international treaties concerning human rights over the national laws (Art. 23).[37]

In the Serbian Constitution (2006), the best interests of the child is also constitutionally promoted, not as a general principle but related to the deprivation of parental rights, which can occur only if it is in the best interest of the child (Article 65 of Serbian Constitution).[38] However, in several countries, this principle has become constitutionally guaranteed, implicitly, through the constitutional provisions governing primacy of ratified international treaties over national law, which therefore apply directly or through decisions of the national Supreme Court, which approves direct application of the CRC, or just through the judicial practice of the courts of lower jurisdiction, which protect the best interests principle enshrined in the different areas of national legislation.

In France, the Supreme Court admits direct application of Article 3 of the CRC, which, as already mentioned, concerns the best interests of the child and very severely supervises decisions of the lower courts in that regard.[39] In the Solomon Islands, where the welfare principle may be in collision with the patriarchal values and customary laws, the courts strive to promote the welfare principle through case law.[40] In other countries, the best interest of the child is mostly enshrined in the Family Code, Civil Code and similar statutes which regulate some specific field of legal relations (labour law, for instance, and other legal provisions which regulate protection of children and juveniles at risk, Roma children, disabled children, and so on). That is the case in Canada,[41] Japan, Greece, Portugal, Romania, Serbia (in addition to the constitutional provision), Scotland, the Netherlands, UK, USA, Uzbekistan and Venezuela.[42]

---

[37] Article 23 of the Venezuelan Constitution reads: 'The treaties, pacts and conventions relating human rights which have been executed and ratified by Venezuela have a constitutional rank, *and prevail over internal legislation*, insofar *as they contain provisions concerning the enjoyment and exercise of such rights* that are more favourable than those established by this Constitution and the laws of the Republic, and shall *be immediately and directly applied* by the courts and other organs of the Public Power', available at http://venezuela-us.org/live/wp-content/uploads/2009/08/constitucioningles.pdf. Accessed 24 May 2014.

[38] Although the Serbian Constitution (2006) in Art. 64 contains a special provision dedicated to the rights of the child, it has been omitted to proclaim the best interest of the child as a general constitutional principle.

[39] National report, France.

[40] National report, the Solomon Islands.

[41] Canadian report refers mostly to the legislation of Quebec.

[42] National reports of respective countries.

5 The Right of the Child to Know About His/Her Origin

5.1 Child Born In and Out of Wedlock

This right of the child is generally not so pronounced in the case of children born in wedlock, since such children from birth know who their mother and father is,[43] except in cases where the legal and biological parenthood do not coincide. However, the right of the child to know about his/her origin is very salient for children born out of wedlock, adopted children and children conceived by biomedical assistance.

Although Art. 7 of the CRC provides for that the child shall have, as far as possible, the right to know and be cared for by his or her parents, there still are the States Parties which forbid or restrict the possibility of contestation of paternity of the child born in wedlock, and thus restrict the right of the child to discover its origin. For instance, under the legislation of Solomon Islands, contestation of legal paternity of the mother's husband is not provided for.[44] The Civil Code of Japan (Art. 772) restricts the right to rebut marital paternity of the child born in wedlock only to mother's husband, who is presumptive, i.e. legal father of the child, and only if the child is born after 200 days after the celebration of marriage or within 300 days after the marriage has come to an end.[45] That means that the Civil Code of Japan requires that the child should be conceived in marriage (not only born in marriage) in order to be considered as marital one. Apart from this, the presumption of paternity of mother's husband does not apply. The child and his/her mother do not have the right to rebut marital paternity of the mother's husband under any circumstances, which is a remnant of the patriarchal concept of family. This does violate the right of the child to know his/her origin. Similar provision is provided by the Family Code of the Republic of Uzbekistan, under which (Art. 63) the right to rebut the paternity of the mother's husband lies only with the mother herself and her husband, while the child has no such a right.[46] The right to rebut the legal paternity of the mother's husband is not recognised for the child under the Greek Civil Code, Indian legislation and Iranian Civil Code.[47]

It seems that the right of the child born out of wedlock to have established his/her maternity or paternity in most States Parties is no longer an issue, since the legal status of the child born out of wedlock is equalised with the child born in wedlock, as it is the case in Australia, Canada, Croatia, Denmark, France, Germany, Portugal, Serbia and Uzbekistan or at least the establishment of the paternity is allowed

[43] As for marital fatherhood and motherhood, among States Parties, it is a very widely accepted legal presumption that the mother is the woman who gave birth to the child and as such is recorded in the birth register, while the father of the child born in a marriage or within 300 days of the termination of marriage is the mother's (former) husband.

[44] National report, the Solomon Islands, The right to information about parents.

[45] National report, Japan, point 4.

[46] National report, Uzbekistan, II point A.

[47] National reports, Greece, India and Iran.

(Japan, Romania, Spain, the Netherlands, UK, USA, Venezuela).[48] However, there still are the countries where the child born out of wedlock has no equal legal position as the child born in wedlock. In India the child born out of wedlock has no right to the establishment of paternity of his/her biological father but only maternity.[49] In some countries, such as Iran, the child born out of wedlock is discriminated as regards the child born in wedlock and cannot be entrusted to his/her 'natural' parents. The 'illegitimate' child has neither the right to maintenance from his/her 'natural' parents nor an inheritance right towards them. They are also deprived of civil, legal and human rights because their parents engaged in an 'illegal' relationship.[50,51] Such legislative solutions and such status of the child directly contravene the provisions of the UN Convention on the Rights of the Child, which prohibit discrimination of any kind, including discrimination based on birth, and are neither in the spirit of the Convention nor acceptable in the modern era.

5.2 Adopted Child

As for the right of an adopted child to know about his/her origin, there are several situations worth mentioning. Namely, in the most States Parties, the data about adoption are confidential, but under certain prerequisites, they can be revealed. The prerequisites may refer to a certain age of the child, consent of adoptive or birth parents, or both, may refer to identifying or non-identifying data and the like.

In Australia this issue is not a federal but a state responsibility, so even in the same country, there are provisions which regulate this matter differently. Most Australian jurisdictions recognise the right of the child under the age of 18 years to have access to the birth registry, usually with the consent of adoptive parents or, in some jurisdictions, with the consent of both, adoptive as well as birth parents. When the child turns 18 years of age, all Australian jurisdictions permit adopted children to access certain identifying and non-identifying information about their origin.[52] In Canada, the child under the age of 14 years can get information about his/her origin if both, adoptive and biological, parents consent.[53] The general rule under Croatian legislation is that a legally mature child has the right to know about his/her origin and, while minor, only if the social welfare centre ascertains that it is in the interest

[48] National reports respective countries. In some national reports (Greece, Solomon Islands), there are no data on the right to establish paternity of the child born out of wedlock.

[49] National report, India.

[50] Mahshid Satad Tabaei, 'Comparative Study of the Illegitimate Children's Rights under English and Iran Laws,' Journal of Basic and Applied Scientific Research, Tehran, 2012, cited in national report Iran.

[51] See national reports from Greece and the Solomon Islands.

[52] National report, Australia.

[53] National report, Canada.

of the adoptee.[54] In England, Wales and Northern Ireland, an adoptee has the right to ascertain the identity of birth parents when he/she reaches adulthood, i.e. with 18 years of age,[55] as well as in Romania and Spain. In Romania, a minor adoptee has no right to get identifying information about his/her biological parents, except on medical grounds,[56] while in Spain minors can have access to data about their origin only if represented by their adoptive parents.[57] In some countries, such as France, the adoptee has the right to know about his/her origin, except if the mother of the child gave birth anonymously (l'accouchement sous X) and objects to the revelation of data about the origin. There are also countries that do not have specific provisions about this right of the child, as Denmark, for instance, but the adoptee can have access to the adoption files at the age of majority. In India the High Court of Karnataka in 2013 found that under the Indian Constitution, the right to know about one's origin is a fundamental right which enables a person to ascertain and preserve their identity, but there are no specific provisions on this right of the child. However, there are the commentators who deem that the legal mechanism should be built up in order to provide this fundamental right of the child and to secure child's protection.[58] Japan and the Netherlands recognise the right of the adoptee to know about his/her origin.[59]

Portugal does not regulate the right of the adoptee to have access to adoption files and thus pays more attention to the protection of fundamental right of adopters and biological parents.[60] In Scotland, the child who has reached 16 years of age, and in Serbia 15 years of age, has the right to inspect the birth register and to know who his/her biological parents are, but before realising this right, the registrar will direct him/her on counselling.[61] Under the legislation of the Solomon Islands, the adoptee can have access to the data about his/her origin only with a court order.[62] In most states of the USA, adoption is 'closed' which means that the adoptee does not have the right to find out who his/her biological parents are.[63] In Uzbekistan adoption is also 'closed' and disclosure of the secrecy of adoption entails criminal responsibility. However, disclosure of data about an adoptee's biological parents is possible if the adopters consent with it, as well as the adopted child if he or she at the time of adoption had reached the age of 10 years or more (Article 155/1 the Family Code of

[54] National report, Croatia.

[55] National report, UK, subtitle 'Specific issues in relation to Family Law, 1: The right of the child to know about his/her origin (Article 7)'.

[56] National report, Romania.

[57] National report, Spain, point B.

[58] National report, India.

[59] National report, Japan, point 5 and National Report the Netherlands, subtitle 'Biological parents, legal parents and knowledge of origins (art.7 CRC)'.

[60] National report, Portugal, subtitle 'Adoption'.

[61] National report, Scotland, subtitle 'Adopted children' and Art. 326 paragraph 3 of the Family Act of Serbia (2005).

[62] National report, Solomon Islands, subtitle 'The Right to Information about Parents'.

[63] National report, USA, subtitle B. 'The Right to Identity'.

the RU).[64] In Venezuela the adoptee does not have the right to know who his/her biological parents are, but can have information about their medical data if it is in his/her best interests.[65]

To summarise, there are some great differences regarding the legal status of the adoptee. There are legislations which recognise the right of an adoptee to disclosure of data about his/her biological origin, under certain conditions. These conditions include the requirement that the adopted child has become of age or that he/she reaches some ages before majority, or the consent of interested person (adoptive or biological parents, or both), or a court order and the like. There are also countries, such as most US states, in which the child has no right to know about origin.

5.3 Child Conceived by Biomedical Assistance

For children conceived by biomedical assistance, as well as for adopted children, very often it is vitally important to know the data about the donor, i.e. his/her biological parent, and, having in mind the CRC, no child should be discriminated on the ground of its origin, which is not so infrequently the case. Enabling the child to learn all information (including identification) about the donor does not mean the establishment of any parental relationship between the child and donor nor the establishment of any rights and obligations between them, but only satisfying a natural human need, especially psychological, to find out from whom they originate. However, we can, quite often, meet resistance to the recognition of such rights to children conceived through biomedical assistance and a quite low level of understanding for such needs of these children, despite the aspirations of the Convention that this right of the child should be guaranteed in all States Parties. The first obstacle to the realisation of this right is lack of legal provisions that establish this right in some countries, and the second is that even if such a right is recognised, there is no legal obligation of the legal parents to inform the child about conception by assisted reproductive technology (thereafter ART), so the child is very often not aware of this circumstance. Since it is in human nature that secrets cannot be hidden for long time, it is advisable that legal parents from early childhood familiarise the child with the truth on his/her origin. Confidence in the legal parents can vanish very fast and give way to distrust, mutual misunderstandings, conflicts and even violence, if they hide the truth and the child in the adult age discovers that the people who cared about him/her are not his/her biological parents. What is the actual situation in terms of the right of the child conceived by biomedical assistance or of assisted reproductive technology (thereafter ART) to know about its origin? The prevailing situation in the countries which submitted national reports is that either the issue is not legally regulated in the country concerned or the child is not vested

[64] National report, Uzbekistan, subtitle B. 'The interests of the child and interests of adoptive parents.'

[65] National report, Venezuela.

with the right to know the full identity of the donor but only his non-identifying data. Only a couple of them recognise this right of the child upon reaching majority or certain ages before majority. However, newer judicial practice manifests a trend that the child should be vested with the right to know his/her origin.

In the Solomon Islands, Iran, Japan and Uzbekistan, there are no specific provisions related to this issue.[66] The same situation is in Denmark, with the difference that the child's right to know information about donor depends on the legal parents' agreement with the sperm bank.[67] In France the child conceived of ART has no right to any information about the donor, and the release of information about the donor is subject to criminal responsibility.[68] In Germany the right of the child to access donor information is balanced with the right of the donor to remain anonymous. However, recently the German Higher Regional Court of Hamm (2013) ruled that the right of the child to know about his/her biological father is superior to the interests of the father to stay anonymous.[69] Although this decision has not yet established a widespread support in case law, it is very important as an indicator of good practice that may affect future trends in this area.

In Australia there is no single solution in all federal states. In South Australia, the child has the right to access the donor's non-identifying information when he/she reaches the age of 16 while identifying information only with donor consent. In Victoria the child born of ART has the right to know identifying data about the donor when reaching the age of 18 and before that age only with the consent of their legal parent. In New South Wales, it is only provided for that the child conceived of ART may have access to the donor's identifying information upon reaching the age of 18, while in Western Australia, this right is given to the child when reaching 16 years of age. For the other Australian jurisdictions, which do not have any legislation about the matter, the National Health and Medical Research Council (NHMRC) ART Guidelines provide direction.[70] It is very important to emphasise that the NHMRC ART Guidelines provide that the child conceived of ART has the right to know identifying data about the donor (genetic parent), as well as that donor cannot be a person who does not consent that his/her identifying data be released to the child conceived with his/her gametes. It seems that such a solution is the most correct, not only regarding the child conceived of ART but also regarding the donors, which should know, before proceeding to ART, that the child will have the right to information about him/her, and based on that information, a potential donor will consider their view on that decision before deciding whether to be a donor. In Canada the child has no right to access information about the donor.

In Croatia the child has the right to identifying information about the donor when they become 18 years of age, and, by that time, the parents should inform the child about the fact that he/she has been conceived using ART. In the UK, the child con-

---

[66] National reports of the respective countries.

[67] National report, Denmark.

[68] National report, France.

[69] National report, Germany, II/point 3.

[70] National report, Australia.

ceived with biomedical assistance has the right to access identifying information about its origin upon becoming 18 years of age, but only if the donor registered on 1st April 2005 or after that date. If the donor registered prior to this date, the child may obtain only non-identifying information about his/her biological parent, pertinent mainly for medical reasons. However, the problem is whether the child will be aware of the circumstances regarding its birth, since there is no legal obligation of the legal parents to inform the child about that issue.[71]

In Greece the records about the identity of the donor are confidential, but the child is deemed as being vested with a legal interest and thus has access of the respective files and information about the identity of their genetic (biological) father.[72] In Portugal the data about medically assisted procreation are confidential, and the child has no right to disclosure of the identifying information about its origin, unless the donor waives such confidentiality. This does not apply to non-identifying information which is significant and important for medical reasons.[73] Similar provisions are provided for in Romania and Serbia. The general rule in Romania is strict confidentiality of donor information, but the court may allow disclosure of such information, in a confidential manner, to the physicians or competent authorities, if health reasons related to the child or his/her descendants so requires. The child is not vested with such right.[74] In Serbia the child conceived by biomedical assistance is entitled to disclosure of medical data from the administration for biomedicine, when they turn 18 years of age and exceptionally when they turn 16 years of age, if they acquired full legal capacity before their legal majority.[75] This provision of the Infertility Treatment Act of Serbia is neither in accordance with the general rule of the Family Act nor with the Constitution of Serbia. Namely, the Family Act sets out that the child, independent of his/her age, has the right to know who his/her parents are (Art. 59/1 FA) as well as that the child who reached the age of 15 and who is mentally capable has the right to inspect the register of births and other documentation related to his/her origin (Art. 59/3 FA).[76] The Constitution of Serbia provides for that '[E]very child shall have the right to personal name, entry in the registry of births, the right to learn about its ancestry, and the right to preserve his own identity (Art. 64/2 of the Constitution)'.[77]

[71] National reports, UK and Scotland.

[72] National report, Greece, II (a).

[73] National report, Portugal.

[74] National report, Romania.

[75] Art. 64 of the Act on Infertility Treatment by Bio-medical Assistance (2009), published in the Official Herald of the Republic Serbia no 72/2009.

[76] The Family Act of Serbia is published in the Official Herald of the RS no.18/2005. However, the FA does not contain detailed rules about the right of the child conceived by biomedical assistance to access birth register and documentation files about their origin, but provides for such rules only in respect of an adopted child.

[77] The Constitution of the Republic of Serbia is published in the Official Herald of the RS no 98/2006, Internet presentation in English on.http://www.srbija.gov.rs/cinjenice_o_srbiji/ustav.php?change_lang=en

In India, as was mentioned above, the right of the child to know about his/her genetic parent is not universally legally recognised, but originates from a recently adopted court decision of the Karnataka High Court (2013) which recognises the right to know one's biological origin as a fundamental right based on the Indian Constitution.[78]

In Spain, the child who is conceived by sperm donation has the right to access non-identifying information about the donor, while identifying data can only be provided to the child when there are extraordinary circumstances that endanger his/her life or health or if there is a criminal proceeding, but disclosure of the donor's identity cannot be used to determine parentage of the child.[79] In the Netherlands, under the legislation from 2004, the child conceived by sperm or eggs donation, when he/she reaches 12 years of age, has the right to know non-identifying information about the donor, and when he/she reaches 16 years of age may apply to have identifying information revealed to him/her. However, as in many other countries, there are no provisions that impose an obligation on legal parents to notify the child about the truth regarding its origins. It is left to the free will of the legal parents to decide on concealment or revelation of these secrets of a child's birth.[80] In the USA, most states do not recognise the right of the child to access information about the donor. However, 'at least 18 states have passed laws that allow such children to gain access upon a showing of cause'.[81] It is also worth mentioning that the California Court of Appeals (2000) decided that the interest in preserving the anonymity of a donor is 'limited and outweighed by the state's interest in preserving the child's right to discover their identity',[82] although there are few countries in the USA which support that view. In Venezuela, the child has the right to know non-identifying data about the donor, mostly related to medical files, and only if it is in his/her best interest.[83]

6 The Right of the Child to Express His/Her Views

This right of the child perhaps best expresses the new position of the child as a holder of rights guaranteed by the Convention,[84] because it puts the child in an active position to participate in all proceedings affecting him/her and thus influencing his/her life. If the child is mentally competent and capable to form his/her view,

---

[78] National report, India.

[79] National report, Spain.

[80] National report, the Netherlands.

[81] National report, USA.

[82] See Johnson v. Superior Ct., 95 Cal. Rptr. 2d 864, 864 (Ct. App. 2000), cited in national report USA.

[83] National report, Venezuela.

[84] In addition to the Article 12 of the CRC, the right of the child to express his/her view is regulated by the European Convention on the Exercise of Children's Rights (Strasbourg 1996). Until 9 December 2014, the total number of ratification/accessions is 18, while 10 countries signed but

irrespective of age, he/she should have the opportunity to express it.[85] It is part of the child's right to participation.[86] As it is stressed in the general comment issued by the Committee on the rights of the child, 'States parties should encourage the child to form a free view and should provide an environment that enables the child to exercise her or his right to be heard'.[87] However, this right does not imply any obligation of the child to express his or her opinion; it is on a voluntary basis on the part of the child. The child can choose whether or not he/she wants to exercise the right to be heard, and there should not be any pressure on the child to express his/her view,[88] especially in sensitive matters and situations which can re-victimise and hurt the child. The child should only be given the opportunity to participate in proceedings which affect him/her and thus contribute to making a decision that will be in his/her best interest.

The Convention on the Rights of the Child does not expressly provide for the application of the right of the child to express his/her view in the frame of his/her family, although many very important decisions affecting the child are taken within the family. This does not mean that the child should not be heard within his/her family. The Committee on the rights of the child welcomes this way of bringing up a child and encourages the family surroundings in which the child can freely express his/her view and in which his/her views will be taken seriously. The Committee emphasises the importance of such a model of family education asserting that '[S]uch an approach to parenting serves to promote individual development, enhance family relations and support children's socialisation and plays a preventive role against all forms of violence in the home and family'.[89]

The right of the child to freely express its view in all proceedings affecting him/her is very differently implemented in the national legislations of the States Parties, as regards the recognition of this right as well as the age from which the child can exercise its right. According to the submitted national reports, this right is provided for each child irrespective of age in Australia, Canada (mainly in Quebec), Croatia, England, Wales and Northern Ireland, while in Germany, Spain, Venezuela and Uzbekistan, a minor has also the right to be heard within the family. In Danish, Scottish and Greek legislation, this right of the child refers to proceedings relating to parental responsibility. In France, the child who is capable of reasoning has the

still not ratified this Convention. Hence, more than a half of the member states of the Council of Europe ratified or is on the way to ratify the Convention.

[85] Article 12 of the Convention reads: '1. States Parties shall assure to the child who is capable of forming his or her own views the right to express those views freely in all matters affecting the child, the views of the child being given due weight in accordance with the age and maturity of the child. 2. For this purpose the child shall in particular be provided the opportunity to be heard in any judicial and administrative proceedings affecting the child, either directly, or through a representative or an appropriate body, in a manner consistent with the procedural rules of national law'.

[86] See more in N. Vučković Šahović, J. E. Doek, J. Zermatten, 'The Rights of the Child in International Law', Stämpfli Publishers, Bern, 2012, pp. 106–117.

[87] See General Comment No. 12 (2009), The right of the child to be heard, part III, paragraph 11.

[88] Ibidem, paragraph 22.

[89] Ibidem, paragraph 90.

right to request to be heard in all proceedings concerning him or her, except in certain cases, such as the proceedings regarding educational assistance or emancipation of the minor, in which (proceedings) the judge for children have ex officio to hear the minor child capable of understanding, no matter whether the child requests it. In Romania, Serbia and Uzbekistan, a child over 10 years has the right to be heard. The child who is under the age of 10 years has this right only if they are able to understand the matter and to form and express his/her view. The Dutch Code of Civil Procedure sets out that every child of 12 years or older has the right to express his/her views in family court proceedings, while the Dutch Civil Code, regarding the exercise of parental responsibility, does not acknowledge the right of the child to be heard. The Supreme Court emphasises the significance of the right of the child to be heard even when they are younger than 12 years. In Iran the child generally has the right to express his/her opinion in family law matters, with a note that he/she has such a right 'if necessary', but there is no explanation about who determines when it is necessary and when it is not. In India the National Plan of Action for Children (2005) promotes participation of children and respect for their views within the family, community, schools and institutions, as well as in judicial and administrative proceedings, in accordance with their age and maturity. However, in practice, participation of the child in the decision-making process that affects his/her interest is still a great challenge since, traditionally, the child is not consulted on family matters or wider. Japanese and Portuguese legislation do not have provisions recognising that a child has the right to be heard in judicial proceedings or family law matters. Similarly, in the Solomon Islands and the USA, with an exception covering a general constitutional provision about the right of each person to freedom of expression or freedom of speech.

7 The Rights of the Child in the Field of Adoption

Adoption is a legal way of creating a family, mostly for children without parents or without adequate parental care, although the child who has one (or both) parent also may be adopted, if the parents consent to the adoption. The consent of the child is usually required if he/she reaches some specified age, as, for instance, 10 years (in Canada, Romania, Serbia, Uzbekistan), 12 years (in Croatia, Denmark, Greece, Portugal, Scotland, Spain, the Netherlands,[90] Venezuela and in several Australian countries – New South Wales, Northern Territory, South Australia, Western Australia), 14 years (Germany) or 15 years (Japan). In the USA, the age of the child who has the capacity to consent to adoption varies from 10 to 14 years, depending on the applicable State law. In some countries, such as Iran, adoption is not recognised, while in others, consent of the child is not a requirement (the Solomon Islands, England). In India, the child's consent should be taken into account before

[90] Also, if the child under the age of 12 years objects to adoption and it is considered that he/she is able to reasonably assess his own interests in the matter, the adoption order will not be granted.

the adoption is completed if the child can understand and express consent, irrespective of age.

According to the CRC, intercountry adoption should be considered as a last resort for resolving the family situation of the child who does not have adequate parental care, if he/she cannot be placed in a foster or an adoptive family or cannot in any suitable manner be cared for in his/her country of origin (Art. 21/1-b). The idea of this provision is to make all efforts in order to find family environment for the child in his/her country and thus avoid the necessity that the child leaves his/her country of origin. Hence, a competent authority has to try to find a suitable solution for the child within his/her country, and if despite all efforts a resolution is not found (no one had applied for adoption of concerned child, no one wants to receive concerned child in foster care and so on), the child will be available for intercountry adoption. Respect for the required procedures will reduce the chances of international child trafficking. This problem arises in underdeveloped countries, which are designated as the countries from which the childless spouses or cohabiting partners from developed countries can easily, and not always in an appropriate or legal manner, find children for adoption. Australia, Canada, France, Germany, Iran, the Netherlands, UK and USA are not among the countries which are faced with problem of adoption of their citizen children by foreign adopters and thus rarely have to deal with the problem of removal of children from his/her country of origin. In other countries, adopters may be, as a general rule, only domestic citizens, but there are exceptions under which the foreigners may also adopt. In some States Parties, in addition to the requirement that the best interests of the child should be taken into account (Venezuela, Spain), it is required, as a prerequisite for intercountry adoption, that it is not possible to find adopters among domestic citizens, within some specified time limit (in Serbia – if more than 1 year has passed from the day of entry of the data on the future adoptee in the Unified Personal Register of Adoptions); thereafter, in Spain, for instance, if the country of origin of the child is not in a state of war or is not affected by natural disaster or if the child – a foreigner – resides in Spain due to a holiday programme, study or medical treatment, he/she cannot be adopted before these circumstances are complete and a minor has commenced an adoption programme.[91] In some countries, the approval of a competent Minister (for welfare matters in Croatia or for family matters in Serbia) is required for intercountries adoption, while in some others, such as Uzbekistan, only those foreign nationals whose countries have their diplomatic missions in Uzbekistan can be adopters.[92] However, among countries that have ratified the Hague Convention on Protection of Children and Co-Operation in Respect of Intercountry Adoption, problems regarding trafficking and sale of children should be avoided, and intercountry adoption should become much easier, as well as much safer. Except for Iran, Japan, the Solomon Islands and Uzbekistan, all other countries, which submitted national reports, had ratified the said Hague Convention.[93]

---

[91] National reports of the respective countries.

[92] National reports of the respective countries.

[93] Hague Convention on Protection of Children and Co-operation in Respect of Inter-country Adoption entered into force in Romania (1 May 1995), Spain (1 November 1995), Canada (1 April

8 The Right of the Child to Freedom of Thought, Conscience and Religion

The CRC prescribed that States Parties shall respect the right of the child to freedom of thought, conscience and religion and that freedom to manifest one's religion or beliefs may be subject only to such limitations as are prescribed by law and are necessary to protect public safety, order, health or morals, or the fundamental rights and freedoms of others (Art. 14/1,3). Hence, some States Parties have introduced religious education in school curriculum as an obligatory or optional subject, in order to make religious education closer to believers among the pupils; some states have forbidden religious education in public schools. As long as this kind of teaching is not compulsory for all children and is equally provided for all believers of different religions and denominations, without of discrimination, it can be said that religious teaching, as part of school curriculum, is not against the CRC. In our opinion, it would be more useful for young people to gain knowledge (through, e.g. subjects like 'religious culture' or similar) about the world's great religions, their meaning and significance for the relevant historical period as well as for the present time than to have religious instruction or to have *only* religious instruction. This knowledge will not only contribute to the general culture of the child but also can help to improve mutual understanding between children of different religions, nations and cultures and contribute to mutual respect and tolerance.

Religious education in school is provided as an optional subject for recognised religions (in Spain), for traditional churches and religious communities (in Serbia) or for some particular religions (in Venezuela). In Australia religious education in government schools is legally recognised as an optional subject. Volunteers from religious organisations can teach interested pupils weekly classes, generally up to 1h, and school are obliged to permit them such education.[94] In Croatia religious education is an optional subject in public schools, but school curriculum offers, also as an optional subject, religious culture, which encompasses comparative knowledge about the world's great religions.[95] Similarly, religious education is available in schools as an optional subject in India, and knowledge of the world's great religions is taught in schools as a part of education.[96]

In some States Parties, religious education is compulsory starting from elementary school. In Denmark religious education is a compulsory school subject and is primarily related to Evangelist-Lutheran Christian teaching. In upper classes of primarily school, the teaching about other religions is included, but in neither of them

1997), Venezuela (1 May 1997), Denmark (1 November 1997), the Netherlands and France (1 October 1998), Australia (1 December 1998), Germany (1 March 2002), UK (1 June 2003), India (1 October 2003), Portugal (1 July 2004), USA (1 April 2008), Greece (1 January 2010), Croatia and Serbia (1 April 2014).

[94] National report, Australia.

[95] National report, Croatia.

[96] National report, India.

is religious instruction included. The child may be excused from religious classes if the parents confirm that the child will learn about religion elsewhere.[97] In Iran, Islamic religious education is compulsory for all Iranians in schools and universities, except for Zoroastrian, Jewish and Christian religious, which are not obliged to follow an Islamic religious education. They are free to practice and be educated in their own religion, while the followers of other religions, which do not belong to the official religion listed in the Constitution, do not have the right to practice their religion and to educate children.[98] In Romania, religious education is compulsory from the elementary school until high school and may be organised for all religions and cults recognised by the state, irrespective of the number of pupils. However, a legal representative of minor children (parents or guardians) or pupils who have reached their majority (in their own behalf) may request exemption from attending religious classes.[99]

In Germany religious education is part of the regular curriculum in state schools, excluding of non-denominational schools, but is not a compulsory subject for everyone regardless of religion of the child. Bases of religious education are principles and rites of the given religion. The child from the age of 12 cannot be forced to follow the religious education of any faith he/she does not belong to.[100] In Scotland, both religious observance and non-confessional religious instruction must be available in all state-funded schools, to pupils of all denominations, unless a contrary decision has been passed by the Education Authority and approved by electors in that local authority area.[101] In the Solomon Islands, the State-run schools provide free education for years 1–9, but a large number of primary and secondary schools are operated by the five main Christian denominations to which are affiliated about 90 % of the population. In schools run by one of the Christian denominations, religious education is obligatory. Although, under the Constitution of Solomon Islands, everyone, including children, has freedom of thought, conscience and religion, in practice, in some areas of the country, the only secondary school is provided by a particular church, which means that the child is, by force of circumstances, compelled to attend that school and receive instruction in the school's faith.[102] In England and Wales, maintained schools (excluding special schools) are obliged to provide religious education for all pupils. Religious teaching is based on the Christian religious traditions, but the other religions represented in Great Britain should also be taken into account. In Northern Ireland, religious education is compulsory in all publicly funded schools for children up to the age of 16. This includes also a daily act of collective worship. Parents have the right to withdraw their child from religious teaching and worship.[103]

---

[97] National report, Denmark.

[98] National report, Iran.

[99] National report, Romania.

[100] National report, Germany.

[101] National report, Scotland.

[102] National report, the Solomon Islands.

[103] National report, UK.

In Portugal, the churches, religious communities and organisations representing worshippers who reside in national territory and who are registered as religious legal persons are free to organise religious education at public primary and secondary schools.[104]

In the USA, religious education is introduced in schools as an optional or compulsory subject, but should not include religious instructions. It should be education about religion, which should neither advance nor inhibit any specific religion.[105]

In several countries, religious education is forbidden, and it is not allowed to be included it in the curriculum, either in public or private schools (Uzbekistan) or only in public schools (Japan).[106]

9 Physical Punishment of the Child

This is one of the very pronounced issues regarding rights of the child. The number of States Parties that resist the banning of physical punishment of children in the family as well as in the institutions that care for children is still not small.[107] The traditional concept of child rearing, which understands that parents are free to decide how to bring up their children, including the right to physical punishment by the parent, is still deeply rooted in some societies. There is no doubt that the raising and upbringing of children is not an easy task, particularly regarding some children who are not receptive to any measure of discipline. However, physical punishment hardly can be regarded as an answer to these difficulties. It should be regarded as being appropriate that some other nonviolent and non-harmful means of disciplining and rearing of children should be used and that such measures can be more fruitful and beneficial, both for children and parents or any other who cares about the children. The Committee on the rights of the child stands firmly on the view that physical (corporal) punishment of children 'is incompatible with the Convention'.[108]

Among States Parties in which corporal punishment of children is not deemed unlawful, either within the family, at school or in institutions that care for children, if it does not exceed 'reasonable chastisement' are Australia, Canada, Iran and most states of the USA.[109]

[104] National report, Portugal.

[105] National report, USA.

[106] National reports, Uzbekistan and Japan.

[107] In General Comment No. 8 (2006) on [T]he right of the child to protection from corporal punishment and other cruel or degrading form of punishments, adopted at the 40-s session of the Committee on the Rights of the Child, Geneva 2006 (published 2 March 2007), paragraph 5 is stated: "Since it began examining States parties' reports the Committee has recommended prohibition of all corporal punishment, in the family and other settings, *to more than 130 States* in all continents" (emphasis added by author).

[108] Ibidem, paragraph 7.

[109] National reports respective countries.

In Croatia physical punishment of children in schools or other institutions for children, as well as within the family, is explicitly forbidden (Croatia).[110] In Serbia, physical punishment of children in schools or other institutions for children is also forbidden, while within the family is not explicitly set out as 'physical punishment' but only as 'humiliating actions and punishments which insult the child's human dignity' (Article 69 paragraph 2 of the Family Act of Serbia).[111] Having in mind that there still are parents who think that corporal chastisement of children is not humiliating and does not insult the child's human dignity,[112] the Draft of the Civil Code of Serbia explicitly sets out that physical punishment of the child within the family shall be forbidden.[113]

In several countries, violence against the child is forbidden, mostly by a criminal code, but physical punishment is not precisely defined. For instance, in Portugal, prohibition of physical punishment of children within a family environment is regulated as a part of the criminal law protection against domestic violence, which leaves some room for measurement whether some violent conduct towards the child may be treated as violence justifying criminal responsibility.[114] In Romania, the general rule about prohibition of physical punishment of children is provided for by the special statute governing the legal status of the child, but criminal law protection refers only to protection against domestic violence, and therefore, it is debatable whether that includes only more serious acts or also includes a less serious act of violence, i.e. whether any physical punishment of the child entails criminal responsibility.[115] The Spanish Penal Code also punishes all acts directed against the physical or mental integrity of minors, committed both within and outside the family. Acts of physical punishment are not explicitly mentioned.[116] It seems that the French society is not very sensitive to physical punishment of children by their parents. Namely, although hitting the child or inflicting even minor injuries to the child under the age of 15 years is forbidden by the Criminal Code, the courts are reluctant to apply such provision in practice, in an informal recognition of a customary 'right of parents to correction', except when the violence may be treated as 'excessive'. However, this customary right of correction, which de facto recognised

[110] Article 94 paragraph 2 of the Family Act of Croatia (2014), National Gazette of the Republic of Croatia, No 75/2014.

[111] The Family Act of Serbia is published in the Official Herald of the Republic of Serbia, No 18/2005.

[112] See more in O. Cvejic Jancic, 'Privacy and Autonomy in Serbian Family Law' International Journal of the Jurisprudence of the Family (IJJF), Volume 4.

[113] Article 87 of the Draft of the Civil Code of Serbia reads 'Parents shall not physically punish the child and are under obligation to protect the child against such conduct of others'. The Draft CC is published (in Serbian) in 'Prednacrt Gradjanskog Zakonika Republike Srbije', Treća knjiga, Porodični odnosi (the Draft of the Civil Code of the Republic of Serbia, Volume 3, Family relationships), Generalni sekretarijat Vlade (General Secretariat of the Government), Belgrade, 2011, p. 37.

[114] National report, Portugal.

[115] National report, Romania.

[116] National report, Spain

by parents, is no longer allowed for teachers or any other person who is in charge of children.[117]

The States Parties in which physical punishment of children is harmonised with the Convention, i.e. which explicitly prohibit it at schools, in home, social welfare institution as well as in any other institutions for children, subject to criminal responsibility, include Denmark, Germany, the Netherlands, Venezuela.[118]

Scottish law forbids physical punishment of children in schools and childcare institutions. Also, holders of parental responsibilities and rights are not permitted to apply physical punishment to children. Physical punishment of children will be treated as a criminal assault, but a defence based on 'justifiable assault' may be presented in court. The court is authorised to determine whether the assault was justified, which would not be in accordance with the CRC, and the Committee recommends that 'all forms of corporal punishment within the family be prohibited as a matter of priority'.[119] Similarly, in the Solomon Islands physical punishment of children under the age of 15 is a criminal offence, but there is not much enthusiasm by the police or courts to prosecute such cases, since a parent, teacher or other person, having the lawful control of the child or young person, has the right to punish them reasonably. This has led to the situation that corporal punishment is still widely practiced in the family, schools and other institutions. The Committee therefore also asserted that all forms of physical and mental violence, including corporal punishment, against children should clearly be treated as unlawful.[120]

In Japan there is a great difference between the right of parents, guardians, foster parents and welfare institutions, on the one hand, which have authority to reprimand their child and ward (including physical punishment), and schools, on the other hand, in which physical punishment is strictly forbidden.[121]

10 Deprivation of Parental Responsibility

Parentage is for the most people a very important part of their life, and they properly and with great satisfaction fulfil their parental duties. Unfortunately, due to manifold reasons, often due to many unhappy living circumstances, there are parents who are not able to create an adequate family environment necessary for the safe survival, upbringing, development and education of their children, and not infrequently are themselves in need of support and assistance. If the child is threatened in his/her family, the state should not remain neutral and leave the child unprotected within his/her family, as was frequently the case in the past, when parents had rather wide powers over their children. The CRC is therefore an important international

---

117 National report, France.

118 National reports of the respective countries.

119 National report, Scotland.

120 National report, the Solomon Islands.

121 National report, Japan.

and national instrument for the protection and security of children, both within and outside their family.

Many States Parties regulate the removal or restriction of parental responsibility of those parents who abuse or roughly neglect their parental duties towards their children, in order to protect such children and prevent any further harmful influence of parent/parents. Such provisions are provided in Canada, Croatia, France, Germany, Greece, Japan, Portugal, Romania, Spain, Serbia, the Netherlands, UK, USA, Uzbekistan and Venezuela.[122]

The authorities competent for deprivation of parental responsibility and removal of the child from the parents are the Family Court, in the countries where it is established (Germany, Iran, Japan), the civil court of general jurisdiction (Australia, Canada, Croatia, Denmark, France, Portugal, Serbia, the Netherlands, UK, Uzbekistan, Venezuela) or the criminal court (Romania).[123] In some states, the competent authority for the removal of parental responsibility may be the civil or the criminal court (the Solomon Islands), or even an administrative body, in addition to the civil or the criminal court, depending on the grounds for the removal of parental responsibility (Spain).[124] In some of them, the courts and state administrative agencies, such as child protective services, may deprive a parent of parental responsibility (USA).[125]

Some authors (India, Iran) report problems of so-called street children which live in very unfavourable situations, homeless and abandoned by their families and forced to take care and to earn a living for themselves, and as such they are very exposed to exploitation in the sex industry, at work in dangerous and unsanitary conditions for which they receive extremely low wages, with no possibility of education and improvement in their life. Very often they must also work to earn money to maintain their families.[126] The problems of such children are indeed the great challenges for the countries concerned, but, despite difficulties, all States Parties of the UN Convention on the Rights of the Child are bound to improve the legal status of children and to ensure children's life, survival and development, because Article 6 of the CRC sets out that '1. States Parties recognise that every child has the inherent right to life. 2. States Parties shall ensure to the maximum extent possible the survival and development of the child'. It seems that implementation of this, as well as other provisions of the Convention, is not understood by all States Parties as a strong international commitment of each country which ratified the Convention to guarantee the protection of all children and their rights, among which, first and foremost, the right to life, survival and development (Art. 6). The process of the implementation of the Convention is a long-lasting process, and, it seems, in some countries, not among the priority tasks.

[122] National reports of the respective countries.

[123] National reports of the respective countries.

[124] National reports, the Solomon Islands and Spain.

[125] National report, USA.

[126] National reports, India and Iran.

11 Medical Consent of the Child

This is a problematic issue especially in the case of the right of the child to independently decide about abortion or to refuse (any) medical consent, particularly if the view of the parents and the child does not coincide, or if refusal of medical intervention may seriously endanger the health or life of the child, or when decisive impact on such a refusal had the religious convictions of the child's parents (followers of the Jehovah's Witnesses, for instance) or similar.

In several countries, the minor child does not have the right to give or refuse medical consent, and the parents or other legal representatives (guardian) will decide instead of him/her. This is so in Croatia, France, India, Iran, the Solomon Islands and Venezuela. [127]

In federal countries, such as Australia, the issue is not resolved uniformly across the country. In some parts of Australia (New South Wales), the age for consent to medical and dental treatment is 14 years, while in South Australia, it is 16 years. Nothing is said about refusal of medical treatment,[128] especially if the child of a certain age refuses medical treatment despite the fact that the proposed treatment is the only medically known way to save the child's life or to prevent severe damage to a child's health. Should the child also have the right to refuse medical treatment in such a situation, especially if his/her decision is affected by pressure of, for example, his/her parents, who, because of religious reasons, do not accept this intervention?

In Canada, under the Quebec Civil Code, the age limit to independent consent to medical treatment is also 14 years. For the children who have not reached 14 years of age, medical consent is given by their parents, but the child may legally refuse medical intervention if such an intervention is not required by his/her state of health, even if they are younger than 14 years of age. The same goes for the child older than 14 years, but it appears that this is not acceptable in cases where the medical treatment is required by a medical condition of the child concerned.[129] The child over 14 years has also the right to give or refuse medical consent in Uzbekistan. Instead of the child under the age of 14, medical consent is given to the parents or legal representatives and in their absence a medical consilium.[130]

Some countries recognise that the child has an independent right to decide about medical consent upon reaching 15 years (Denmark, Serbia) or 16 years of age (Portugal, Spain, the Netherlands, England and Wales).[131] In Spain the child who is capable of reasoning and who understands the medical treatment may give or refuse medical consent without any parental consent, but if the child is not capable of such an assessment, the parents or legal representative can consent, taking into account the child's view, if he/she is older than 12 years of age. Once the child reaches 16

---

[127] National reports of the respective countries.

[128] National report, Australia.

[129] National report, Canada.

[130] National report, Uzbekistan.

[131] National reports of the respective countries.

years of age, he/she is deemed as capable enough to decide independently about medical intervention.[132] In the Netherlands, if the child is younger than 16 years but older than 12, he/she should give medical consent together with the holder of parental responsibilities, except in two situations. Namely, if refusing medical treatment would lead to substantial harm to the child's health, the consent of parents or other holders of parental responsibilities is not necessary if the child gives his/her consent. The second situation occurs if the consent of parents or other holders of parental responsibilities cannot be obtained, but the child has been informed about consequences of the treatment and agrees to it.[133] In England and Wales, the child who is younger than 16 years of age can also consent to some medical treatments if he/she is assessed as competent to give consent.[134]

There are also countries where a child's capacity to give medical consent does not depend on a certain age but the maturity of the child and the type of intervention to be undertaken. Such an approach is accepted in Germany, where the child may independently decide about some medical treatment, and alternatively consent of the parents or another holder of parental responsibility is required. Regarding specific medical treatment which does not affect the child's health if postponed, the child has the right to veto.[135] Similarly, in Scotland, the right of the child to give medical consent does not depend on the age of the child but on his/her degree of maturity and capability to understand, according to the opinion of the practitioner treating the child, the nature and possible consequences of that treatment. As for the right of the child to refuse medical treatment, there is no clear provision about that, but current National Health Service guidance to medical professionals in Scotland recommends that refusal of treatment by a competent person under 16 must be respected. Some Scottish scholars share the same opinion.[136]

In the USA, the issue is highly debated regarding the right of a minor child to abortion. The Supreme Court suggested that the child's right to decide independently about abortion, without parental consent, should be considered depending on the child's maturity and ability to make a decision and upon consultation with a doctor. If the child is not mature enough for such a decision, the Court will approve or refuse abortion.[137]

In Romania, the child acquires the ability to give consent for medical treatment, medical methods of prevention or diagnosis when reaching the age of 18 years, except in cases of emergency, if parents or other holder of parental responsibilities cannot be contacted, and the child is capable of reasoning irrespective of their age. The second exception applies to diagnosis and treatment of reproductive and sexual problems, in which case the child reaching 16 years and over this age has the right to decide independently. A minor cannot give consent to the transplantation of

[132] National report, Spain.

[133] National report, the Netherlands.

[134] National report, UK.

[135] National report, Germany.

[136] National report, Scotland.

[137] National report, USA.

organs, tissues and human body cells, in which cases the medical consent, instead of a minor child, should be given by the child's parents or legal representatives. The same goes for the sampling of organs, tissues and cells. However, many exceptions are provided for specific situations.[138] In Japan the child has the right to give or refuse medical consent independently, but the statutory provisions do not set out the age limit, and views are not unanimous in this regard.[139]

12 The Right of the Child to Change His/Her Personal Name

The personal name of each person is an inseparable part of his/her identity. However, the child may be interested to preserve or change his/her personal name (first name and surname) especially in the case of adoption, contestation or establishment of maternity or paternity, removal of parental right of his/her parents as well as due to other reasons (discontent with his/her personal name, wish to use more modern name, change of a pejorative or ridiculous name and the like). Does the child have the right to change personal name independently or it is reserved only to an adult person? It is resolved differently in the States Parties as is the case with other issues. In India, Iran, Portugal, Spain and Venezuela, the child has no right to change his/her name independently before reaching majority (18 years), or even when he/she reaches some years after majority (25 years, for instance, in the Solomon Islands).[140]

Some countries do not recognise the right of the child to change the name independently, but only at the request of parents or other holder of parental responsibilities (guardian), while the child who has reached a specific age has the right to consent to this change. Such a situation is in Australia and Denmark, where it is required that the child who turns 12 years or is older should consent to the change of name.[141] In Croatia a minor adoptee may change personal name at the request of both parents and adoptive parents, but there is inconsistency in two statutes which regulate this matter. Under the Croatian Personal Name Act, the consent for the change of personal name of the child is required if the child is older than 10 years, while the Family Act prescribes that a consent of the child of 12 years or older is obligatory for the change of the name in case of adoption.[142] In France, the consent of the child who is 13 years or older is needed, while the child has no right to request the change of his/her first name or surname until the age of majority.[143] In England and Wales, the consent of the child who is 16 years or older is required.[144]

In Germany, a change of personal name is strictly regulated and is allowed if the applicant demonstrates a significant reason for this. A minor adopted child may

138 National report, Romania.

139 National report, Japan.

140 National reports of the respective countries.

141 National reports, Australia and Denmark.

142 National report, Croatia.

143 National report, France.

144 National report, UK.

change their first name in case of adoption, upon request of the adoptive parents if the adoptee consents to the change, and the family court, which decides about the change, finds that this is in the best interests of the child. The Federal Constitutional Court ruled that only a transsexual child, even before majority, has the right to change his/her first name, in which case the consent of his/her legal representative is required.[145] In Canada, a child aged 14 years or older may present a request for a change of name before the court in a case of change of affiliation, neglect or the removal of parental authority, subject to the condition that he/she notifies the holder of parental responsibilities. Before this age, the minor child cannot request a change of name independently.[146] In Romania, the parents may request the change of the name of their child, but the child who turns 14 years or older needs to sign the application together with their parents.[147]

In some countries, the child acquires an independent right to change a name after reaching a certain age. This is provided for in Serbia,[148] where a child who is 15 years old or older has a right to change a name, while a child who reached the age of 10 years shall give consent for the change of his/her name. In Scotland and Uzbekistan, the child can change his/her name independently at the age of 16.[149] In cases of change of name in Uzbekistan, the consent of the child who turns 10 years or older is obligatory. In the USA, the child has the right to apply for a change of his/her name irrespective of specific age.[150]

13 The Rights of the Child in Employment

In some countries, exploitation of child labour is quite widespread due to the fact that state control over the employment of children and their working conditions is very loose. Although States Parties to the CRC undertook the obligation to guarantee and protect the rights of the child, there are cases where this obligation is not realised and many children are left on their own, without state and parental protection. There are also countries where the age for employment is very low or is not at all regulated, so children start working in early childhood, without the possibility to go to school or to have time for playing, learning or even taking a rest. Therefore, the Committee on the Rights of the Child issued general comment on State obligations regarding the impact of the business sector on children's rights[151] which

---

145 National report, Germany.

146 National report, Canada.

147 National report, Romania.

148 Article 346/1, 2 Family Act of Serbia.

149 National reports, Scotland and Uzbekistan.

150 National report, USA.

151 General Comment No. 16 (2013) on the State obligations regarding the impact of the business sector on children's rights was adopted by the Committee at its 62nd session held on 14 January–1 February 2013.

stressed, among other important matters, that '[S]tates must take all necessary, appropriate and reasonable measures to prevent business enterprises from causing or contributing to abuses of children's rights'.[152] Since significant numbers of children are engaged in the informal economy,[153] the Comment recommends that 'States should put in place measures to ensure that business activities take place within appropriate legal and institutional frameworks in all circumstances regardless of size or sector of the economy so that children's rights can be clearly recognized and protected'.[154] Has this obligation of States Parties been implemented and how was this implemented?

In most States Parties, protection of children in the field of employment is mainly provided for in similar ways, first of all through the prescription of the age limit under which is forbidden to employ a young person (unless in exceptional cases which are regulated by legislation), but the differences in terms of minimum age for employment of children are significant. Namely, the age limit varies from 13 years (England and Wales), 14 years (Canada,[155] USA, Venezuela), 15 years (Australia,[156] Croatia, Denmark, Germany, Greece, Iran, Japan, Romania, Serbia) to 16 years (France, Portugal, Scotland, Spain, the Netherlands, Uzbekistan).

In a few countries, general rules for employment of children are not provided for, but it depends on the type of work in which children of certain age can be employed. Such is the case in the Solomon Islands. However, in many countries, children may be employed part time even if they are younger than the general age limit for the employment of children, or they may be employed in some special jobs, such as entertainment, engagement in films, theatre, modelling, on light work, in family business, in agriculture and the like (Australia, France, Greece, Scotland, the Netherlands, USA, Uzbekistan). In Denmark, the permission from the police is needed. It is very likely that in other countries, too, children younger than a certain 'regular' age for employment may temporarily or occasionally be employed in some light works, although not specifically mentioned in the national report.

However, there are states, such as India, in which children labour is very widespread since there does not exist a complete ban on the employment of children nor

---

[152] General Comment No. 16 (2013), IV. B. 2./28.

[153] See General Comment No. 16 (2013), V. B./35: 'Also, a concentrated number of children are often found in hidden areas of informal work, such as small family enterprises, agricultural and hospitality sectors. Such work frequently involves precarious employment status, low, irregular or no remuneration, health risks, a lack of social security, limited freedom of association and inadequate protection from discrimination and violence or exploitation'.

[154] General Comment No. 16 (2013), V. B/36.

[155] In Canada provisions about children labour differ from one province and territory to other, but, in general, the child must attend school until 16 years old. This rule does not prevent the child from working part time, national report Canada.

[156] In Australia, although the employment of children is governed by different federal, state and territory laws, the education of children is generally protected by prohibiting children from working 'when employment would prevent them from attending school within the mandatory school age'. The minimum school-leaving age usually is 15 years or over, but children below that age (from 10 or 11 years) may also be part-time employed outside of school hours, national report Australia.

a minimum age for the admission of children into employment is prescribed. Children are forced to find a job due to economic coercion, for a very low salary and to the detriment of their proper education, development and childhood. Even children aged 7 or 8 years are employed, which is very favourable for their employer who may earn considerable amounts of money using children workers, without having to provide adequate reimbursement to them.[157] It seems that the state is powerless (or not interested) to solve the problem in an appropriate way, but the exploitation of children workers represents a rough violation of the Convention on the Rights of the Child, and, inter alia, such bad examples, as well as many others, are a powerful motive for the international forces to fight for the adoption of such international instruments which should contribute to the improvement of the position of children all over the world. However, it seems that that process moves very slowly in some parts of the world.

Authorisation or consent of parents or other legal representative for the employment of a minor child is needed in Japan, Croatia, Denmark, Germany,[158] Romania, Serbia and Spain.[159] In some countries, this is needed only if the child is younger than some specified age. For instance, in Canada the consent of parents (or legal representative) is needed if the child is younger than 14 years; in the most Australian states and territories, as well as in Uzbekistan, it is 15 years; in Portugal, the Netherlands, the USA 16 years, while in the UK parental consent to child's employment is governed by local byelaws.[160]

In the Solomon Islands, children are generally free to choose their own work, but it is common that the child will act in accordance with the wishes of his/her parents when choosing a job.[161] In Scotland, parental consent for child's employment is not usually required.[162] The same judicial approach and practice can be found in France.[163] Iranian legislation has no provision about the issue of whether the consent of parents is needed.[164]

Many States Parties to the Convention also prescribe the prohibition of the night work for children as well as the jobs in which children may not be employed because it may be to the detriment of children's education, health, morals or if it exceeds the child's physical or mental ability or similar. This kind of child protection is provided for in Australia, Canada, Croatia, Denmark, France, Germany, Greece, India, Iran, Japan, Portugal, Romania, Scotland, Serbia, England and Wales and Uzbekistan.[165] In Croatia and Romania, night work is not expressly prohibited, but it can be, possibly, subsumed under the category of work which is detrimental to the safety,

---

[157] National report, India.

[158] In Denmark and German, the child older than 15 years may only change a job independently.

[159] National reports of the respective countries.

[160] National reports of the respective countries.

[161] National report, the Solomon Island.

[162] National report, Scotland.

[163] National report, France.

[164] National report, Iran.

[165] National reports of the respective countries.

health, morals or development of the child. Night work of children in Serbia is allowed only in some exceptional cases, such as work in the area of culture, sports, art and advertising or in case of force majeure, under special conditions (that such work lasts for a definite period of time, that it has to be urgently completed and that the employer has no other older employees available).[166]

In the Solomon Islands, night work (from 6 pm to 6 am) is forbidden for children under the age of 18 except that performed by a male person over the age of 16, with the permission (in writing) of the Commissioner of Labour.[167] In the Netherlands and the USA, prohibition of night work for children is not mentioned, but children are not allowed to work with dangerous substances (in the Netherlands) or jobs which are particularly hazardous or detrimental to their health or well-being (USA).[168] In a few national reports, such as Iran and Greece, the problems of 'street children' are stressed as particularly salient. In Iran, for instance, 'street children' are usually not orphans but children whose parents are drug addicts, refugees or unemployed and therefore force their children to work on the street or otherwise to support the family. These children can very easily become prey for sexual and other forms of exploitation. They live under very bad working, health and other conditions, and their life, health and development are completely threatened, so it is hardly possible to even speak about protection of their rights in Iran.[169] Greece has a problem with Roma children, children which belong to minorities and refuges as well as with children who are victims of trafficking and sexual abuse. The Greek state undertook legislative and other measures for the combat against these problems, but there are still many difficulties and obstacles in the implementation of the prescribed protection of these especially vulnerable children affected by very unfavourable circumstances.[170]

14 Obligation of the Child Towards Parents

In some countries, a reciprocal legal obligation of maintenance between parents and children is provided, meaning that, as parents were obliged to support their children while they were incapable of working or if they attended school, children are obliged to maintain their parents when they remain without of means for satisfying living needs and when they become incapable of earning it by work. In addition to the obligation of children to maintain their parents, in Canada, Croatia,[171] Romania,

[166] National report, Serbia.

[167] National report, the Solomon Islands.

[168] National reports, the Netherlands and USA.

[169] National report, Iran.

[170] National report, Greece.

[171] Articles 89 of the Family Act of Croatia (2014) provide also that a 'child is obliged to respect their parents and assist them in carrying out jobs in the family in accordance with their age and maturity and be considerate of the family members'.

France, the Solomon Islands and Spain, they are also obliged to respect them.[172] Legislation of Uzbekistan provides for that children are obliged to maintain the parents.[173] In Germany mutual support and help is a legal obligation between parents and children, while in Indian legislation, children are obliged to respect their parents.[174] Iranian legislation regulates the obligation of children to obey and respect their parents.[175] In Japan children have legal obligation to acknowledge the parental rights of parents, as well as an obligation of mutual support, while in Portugal and Venezuela, there exists an obligation on the part of children to obey and respect their parents and to mutually support each other.[176] The Serbian Family Act provides for the obligation of children to help their parents in accordance with their age and maturity, as well as obligation of mutual maintenance.[177]

In Australia, Denmark and Scotland, any legal obligation of children towards parents is not provided for, while in the national reports of Greece, the Netherlands, UK and USA, such obligations are not mentioned.[178]

However, the Committee on the Rights of the Child, on the occasion of the Belgian report, in which was mentioned the provision of Belgian Civil Code regarding the obligation of children to respect their parents, objected that such a provision is one-sided and that should include mutual respect for all members of the family. Therefore, the Committee recommended an amendment of the Belgian Civil Code in order to include, in addition, the obligation of parents to respect their children, which the Belgian CC accepted and subsequently adjusted Article 371 of the Belgian CC.[179] This statement reflects the spirit of the Convention and the need to accept a new attitude towards children within the family, as well as outside the family.

15 Summary

In the last 25 years since the Convention on the Rights of the Child was adopted, many States Parties to the Convention made great efforts to pass legislation regulating the rights of the child, committed to improving the legal status of the child. We considered the reports of 21 countries from four continents which submitted their

---

[172] National reports of the respective countries.

[173] National report, Uzbekistan.

[174] National reports, Germany and India.

[175] National report, Iran.

[176] National reports, the respective countries.

[177] National report, Serbia.

[178] National reports of the respective countries.

[179] See Belgium IRCO, Add.38, para 5, cited in N. Vučković Šahović, Prava deteta i porodično zakonodavstvo (Rights of the Child and Family Legislation), published in Novo porodično zakonodavstvo, Zbornik radova sa savetovanja (New Family Legislation, Proceedings of the Conference) Kragujevac, 2006, Gen. editor Zoran Ponjavić, p. 257.

national report at the Congress of the International Academy of Comparative Law. From these reports, it is evident that despite the efforts made in that regard, and despite the fact that many countries have achieved remarkable results, there are still countries in which the status of children remains very difficult, their everyday life threatened and the rights of the child enshrined by the Convention understood very differently from their basic conception. Hence, large differences in terms of understanding and interpretation of children's rights are affected by many factors, including economic development of a given country, the influence of religion, local customs, educational level of parents, the overall educational level of the nation and so on. The most pronounced problem of implementation of the rights of the child is poverty. Is it at all possible to speak about the rights of the child who does not have enough to eat, appropriate clothing to wear, a place to live, who lacks drinking water and water for hygienic purposes, who cannot attend school and whose basic living needs cannot be satisfied? As is stated in the preamble of Declaration on the rights of the child (1924) 'mankind owes to children the best it has', but despite all international efforts, the reality is completely different. In some countries, due to economic constraint, very young children are forced to work for very low wages in order to earn for the family, while in some other countries, there are 'street children' who live and work on the street because their parents are not able to take care of them or even themselves (due to drug addiction, their status as refugees or unemployment).

Fortunately, most States Parties have taken their international obligations very seriously and undertook many legislative and other measures for improvement of status of children and to recognise them as the holders of particular rights in accordance with their age and maturity. Equally, many of them have also properly implemented the provision of the Convention. However, this process is not finished since there always remains some room for further improvement of children's lives, development, well-being and their rights in general. Thereby, one should never forget that, in addition to the financial resources, which may significantly influence and improve children's status, the human resources, commitment and willingness to accept new legal position of the child is also very prominent and important.

The UN Convention on the Rights of the Child: Tracing Australia's Implementation of the Provisions Relating to Family Relations

Rita Shackel

1 Introduction

The United Nations Convention on the Rights of the Child (UNCRC – the Convention) was adopted and opened for signature, ratification and accession by General Assembly Resolution 44/25 of 20 November 1989 and entered into force on 2 September 1990, in accordance with Article 49. The UNCRC is the first legally binding international instrument to incorporate the full range of human rights – civil, cultural, economic, political and social rights.[1] The Convention is premised on the view that 'childhood is entitled to special care and assistance' and 'the child, by reason of his/[her] physical and mental immaturity, needs special safeguards and care, including appropriate legal protection, before as well as after birth'.[2] Currently 194 states are parties to the Convention with 140 signatories,[3] it is the most widely (and rapidly) ratified treaty in history,[4] and only three member states have not ratified it – the United States, Somalia and South Sudan.

Australia signed and ratified the Convention in 1990. Australia's only reservation to the Convention is with respect to Article 37. Although accepting the general principles of Article 37, in relation 'to the second sentence of paragraph (c), the obligation to separate children from adults in prison is accepted only to the extent

[1] UNICEF at <http://www.unicef.org/crc>.

[2] Preamble.

[3] See https://treaties.un.org/Pages/ViewDetails.aspx?mtdsg_no=IV-11&chapter=4&lang=en.

[4] UN News Centre, 'UN issues call on Member States to ratify convention on rights of the child' at http://www.un.org/apps/news/story.asp?NewsID=45894&Cr=children&Cr1=rights#.UlgxaLyKyuQ, 43.

R. Shackel (✉)
Sydney Law School, The University of Sydney,
Law School Building F10, Eastern Avenue, Camperdown, NSW 2006, Australia
e-mail: rita.shackel@sydney.edu.au

O. Cvejić Jančić (ed.), *The Rights of the Child in a Changing World*,
Ius Comparatum - Global Studies in Comparative Law 13,
DOI 10.1007/978-3-319-23189-1_2

that such imprisonment is considered by the responsible authorities to be feasible and consistent with the obligation that children be able to maintain contact with their families, having regard to the geography and demography of Australia'.[5] Australia's ratification therefore is reserved to the extent that it is unable to comply with the obligation imposed by article 37(c). The Committee on the Rights of the Child (CRC) has repeatedly urged Australia to reconsider this reservation[6] on the basis that it 'is unnecessary since there appears to be no contradiction between the logic behind it and the provisions of article 37(c) of the Convention'.[7] Namely, that the concerns expressed by Australia in its reservation are well addressed by article 37(c), 'which provides that every child deprived of liberty shall be separated from adults "unless it is considered in the best interests of the child not to do so" and that the child "shall have the right to maintain contact with his or her family"'.[8] The Australian Government has undertaken to explore possible withdrawal of this reservation with its states and territories,[9] but action is still wanting.

The UNCRC consists of 54 provisions in its entirety. This report examines Australia's efforts over the last 23 years in implementation of provisions in the Convention that relate more specifically to family relations and family law matters and the results that have been achieved. Section 2 of the report begins by examining the definition of child under Australian law. Section 3 then lays out the framework for protection of children's rights in Australia. Section 4 examines the application and implementation of the best interests principle, particularly in family-related laws and policies in Australia. Section 5 discusses implementation of the child's right to be heard in family-related matters in Australia. Section 6 of the report examines Australia's implementation of a child's right to know about his or her origins. Here three key areas are examined: registration of birth, presumptions and rebuttal of parentage, and a child's right to access information relating to genetic origins. Section 7 examines the framework in Australia for protection of a child's rights in adoption processes. Section 8 briefly examines a child's right to freedom of religion within the specific context of school education. Section 9 discusses Australia's protection of children against physical punishment. Section 10 examines provisions under Australian family law that regulate parental responsibility. Section 11 discusses a child's right to medical consent. Section 12 examines a child's right to change name. Section 13 examines the rights of children in employment in Australia. Section 14 discusses a child's obligations towards his or her parent. Section 15 of the report concludes.

The Convention recognises the centrality of the family unit in children's well-being '[r]ecognizing that the child, for the full and harmonious development of his

---

[5] Status of Ratification, Reservations and Declarations, Convention on the Rights of the Child (as at 13-1-2013) at http://treaties.un.org/Pages/ViewDetails.aspx?src=TREATY&mtdsg_no=IV-11&chapter=4&lang=en.

[6] CRC/C/AUS/CO/4 (28 August 2012), [10].

[7] CRC/C/AUS/CO/4 (28 August 2012), [9].

[8] Ibid.

[9] CRC/C/AUS/4 (14 June 2011), [6].

or her personality, should grow up in a family environment, in an atmosphere of happiness, love and understanding'.[10] Further the Convention recognises that 'the family, as the fundamental group of society and the natural environment for the growth and well-being of all its members and particularly children, should be afforded the necessary protection and assistance so that it can fully assume its responsibilities within the community'.[11]

2 Definition of 'Child' Under Australian Laws

Core to the Convention and its implementation is its application to the person as a 'child'. Article 1 of the UNCRC defines a child as 'every human being below the age of 18 years unless under the law applicable to the child, majority is attained earlier'.

Under Australian laws a child is generally deemed to be a person under the age of 18 years. At age 18 a person is no longer a minor in Australia and is generally considered an adult thereafter. For example, the eligibility age for voting in Australia is 18 years.[12] The legal age for purchasing alcohol[13] and tobacco[14] in every Australian state and territory is also 18 years. However, the threshold age of a child varies under different legislative provisions and for different purposes ranging variously from under 14 to under 18 years of age. For example, the *Children and Young Persons (Care and Protection) Act 1988* (NSW)[15] defines a child (except in Chapter 13)[16]

---

[10] Preamble.

[11] Preamble.

[12] *Commonwealth Electoral Act 1918* (Cth) s93(1).

[13] *Liquor Act 2007* (NSW) s 117(1), *Liquor Licensing Act 1997* (SA) s110, *Liquor Control Reform Act 1998* (Vic) s119, *Liquor Control Act 1988* (WA) s121, *Liquor Act 1992* (Qld) s155A, *Liquor Act 2010* (ACT) s112, *Liquor Licensing Act 1990* (Tas) s70.

[14] *Public Health (Tobacco) Act 2008* (NSW) s22, *Tobacco Act 1987* (Vic) s12, *Tobacco and Other Smoking Products Act 1998* (Qld) s10, *Tobacco Products Regulation Act 1997* (SA) s38A, *Public Health Act 1997* (Tas) s64, *Tobacco Control Act 2006* (WA) s6, *Tobacco Act 1927* (ACT) s14.

[15] Pursuant to Section 8, the objects of the Act are to provide:

(a) That children and young persons receive such care and protection as is necessary for their safety, welfare and well-being, having regard to the capacity of their parents or other persons responsible for them
(b) That all institutions, services and facilities responsible for the care and protection of children and young persons provide an environment for them that is free of violence and exploitation and provide services that foster their health, developmental needs, spirituality, self-respect and dignity
(c) That appropriate assistance is rendered to parents and other persons responsible for children and young persons in the performance of their child-rearing responsibilities in order to promote a safe and nurturing environment

[16] Chapter 13 of the Act deals with Children's Employment, and s221 defines a child variously as under the age of 15 or 16 for different purposes.

'as a person under the age of 16 years'.[17] The legal age of consent to sexual activity varies between 16 and 17 years across different Australian jurisdictions,[18] and a child aged less than 14 years is deemed to lack criminal responsibility in all Australian jurisdictions.[19] In most Australian states a child turning 18 years of age is tried as an adult and in an adult court. In Queensland though, for the purposes of the *Juvenile Justice Act 1992*, which is concerned with children who have or are alleged to have committed an offence, a child is a person who has not turned 17 years of age.[20] Accordingly, in Queensland a 17-year-old is treated as an adult in the criminal justice system. It is difficult to justify this different treatment of juveniles in Queensland, compared to other Australian states, particularly as it runs contrary to international standards.[21]

Some Australian legislation defines the age of a child only for specific purposes. For example, under the *Family Law Act* 1975 (Cth), a child is defined as a person under 18 years of age only for the purpose of parenting orders[22]; otherwise, the definition of a child within the Act more generally is not provided.

As a signatory to the UNCR, it may be inferred that in the absence of explicit definition of a child, the default age is 18 years as defined in the Convention.

As the examples provided above suggest, there is scope for greater harmonisation of status as a child across jurisdictions in Australia and in different domains of children's lives, as is the case also for some other States Parties. Variable thresholds in defining childhood arguably permit flexibility in relation to how children may be protected in society and their lives regulated and enable greater recognition of children's diverse needs, particularly, as children mature and develop through adolescence into adulthood. However, ambiguity about status as a child and differing definitions of a 'child' may also lead to policies and laws that treat children inconsistently and which may potentially engender contradictory notions of childhood and the needs of children within a society. The concept of 'youth' as a transition between childhood and adulthood is equally unstable. For example, youth supervision orders and youth attendance orders in Victoria cannot extend beyond the offender's twenty-first birthday, suggesting that this is the upper limit of the Act's understanding of youth,[23] whereas the Australian Institute of Health and Welfare,

---

[17] Section 3 Definitions.

[18] *Crimes Act 1900* (ACT) s55 (16 years), *Crimes Act 1900* (NSW) s66C (16 years), *Act 1983* (NT) s127 (16 years), *Criminal Code Act 1899* (s208 and s215) (the age of consent for anal sex is 18 years and for all other sexual acts is 16 years), *Criminal Law Consolidation Act 1935* (SA) s49 (17 years), *Criminal Code Act 1924* (Tas) (s124) (17 years), *Crimes Act 1958* (Vic) s45 (16 years), *Criminal Code Act Compilation Act 1913* (WA) s321 (16 years).

[19] This is a rebuttable presumption for children aged 10 to under 14 in all jurisdictions: *Crimes Act 1914* (Cth) s4N *2002* (ACT) s26, *Criminal Code* (NT) s38(2), *Criminal Code Act 1899* (Qld) s29(2), *Criminal Code Act 1924* (Tas) s18(2), *Criminal Code Act Compilation Act 1913* (WA) s29 and Common law *doli incapax* (NSW, Victoria and SA).

[20] Schedule 4.

[21] CRC/C/AUS/CO/4 (28 August 2012), [82–83].

[22] Section 3 Definitions. See also Subdivision E of Division 6 of Part VII.

[23] *Children, Youth and Families Act 2005* (VIC) s387; s397.

which studies the provision of health and well-being services to youth, defines this demographic as those aged between 12 and 24 years old. Similarly, the Youth Health Service in South Australia provides free health services to individuals between 12 and 25 years old.[24]

Arguably, generally then in Australia, as is also seen in many jurisdictions around the world, the special status accorded to young people is expanding at least into the third decade of life. The United Nations defines 'youth' as persons falling between the ages of 15 and 24 years.[25] The Australian Government's National Youth Week targets young people aged 12–25 years old,[26] and in order to be eligible for Youth Allowance in Australia, you must be between the ages of 16 and 24 years old.[27]

3 Framework for Protection of the Rights of the Child in Australia

There is no single instrument in Australia that is specifically devoted to the rights of the child. A federal system of government in Australia means that many of the rights covered by the UNCRC fall within the purview of state and territory responsibility. The CRC has expressed concern 'that there continues to be no comprehensive child rights Act at the national level [in Australia] giving full and direct effect to the Convention'.[28] In practice, children living in some parts of Australia may not always be treated equally or have their rights duly recognised relative to other children living in different parts of Australia, where law and policies may be more progressive.

Victoria[29] and the Australian Capital Territory (ACT)[30] are the only two jurisdictions in Australia that have enacted specific human rights legislation applicable to all citizens. In both these jurisdictions the legislation explicitly refers to the child as a rights bearer. Section 17(2) of the Victorian Charter recognises that '[e]very child has the right, without discrimination, to such protection as is in his or her best interests and is needed by him or her by reason of being a child'. The child's right to be protected is not framed in the ACT legislation by the best interests principle, as in the Victorian Charter, but more generally, Section 11(2) of the Act simply states that

[24] Government of South Australia, 'Youth Health Service', *Women's and Children's Health Network*, available at http://cyh.com/SubContent.aspx?p=223.

[25] United Nations, 'Definition of Youth', *United Nations Youth Fact Sheet* available at http://www.un.org/esa/socdev/documents/youth/fact-sheets/youth-definition.pdf.

[26] Australian, State, Territory and Local Government Initiative, 'National Youth Week' available at http://youthweek.com.

[27] Department of Human Services, 'Youth Allowance Eligibility' available at http://www.humanservices.gov.au/customer/services/centrelink/youth-allowance.

[28] CRC/C/AUS/CO/4 (28 August 2012), [11].

[29] *The* Victorian Charter *of Human Rights and Responsibilities Act 2006.*

[30] *The Human Rights Act 2004.*

'[e]very child has the right to the protection needed by the child because of being a child, without distinction or discrimination of any kind'.[31] Sections 23 and 20 of the Victorian and ACT legislation, respectively, specifically protect the rights of the child in the criminal process. Protection in this context is important, and the criminal justice system must demonstrate a heightened sensitivity to the vulnerability of children that come into contact with it. Kelly Richards' study on the rate at which juvenile offenders in Australia are remanded suggests that there has been a substantial increase in the proportion of juvenile detainees being remanded, which is concerning for efforts towards ensuring that detainment is a last resort for juveniles.[32] In 2014, the Queensland Government removed the sentencing principle for juvenile offenders that detention should be used as a last resort and also removed limitations on publishing identifying information about youth offenders.[33]

More generally, children's rights are also protected in Australia by a range of specific legislative provisions, for example, child protection, consumer, education and family law legislation. Furthermore, Australian children are generally protected in most aspects of public life against discrimination on the grounds of race, sex, disability and age, by anti-discrimination legislation at the federal and state level.[34] For example, a disabled child can rely upon Section 22 of the *Disability Discrimination Act 1992* (Cth) to ensure that they are provided equal access to educational institutions.[35]

Despite the existence of a range of legislative provisions that seek to promote recognition and protection of the rights of the child in Australia, albeit at times in a somewhat limited way, the absence of a comprehensive child rights Act at a national level in Australia continues to raise concerns of 'fragmentation and inconsistencies in the implementation of child rights…with children in similar situations being subject to variations in the fulfilment of their rights depending on the state or territory in which they reside'.[36] Unfortunately, although enactment of the UNCRC through special statute is highly desirable, many nation parties like Australia have not taken this course of action.

---

[31] Section 11 in providing examples of distinction or discrimination refers to 'race, colour, sex, sexual orientation, language, religion, political or other opinion, national or social origin, property, birth, disability or other status'.

[32] Kelly Richards, 'Trends in Juvenile Detention in Australia' (2011) *Australian Institute of Criminology: Trends and Issues in Crime and Criminal Justice* No. 416, 5.

[33] *Youth Justice and Other Legislation Amendment Act 2014* (Qld).

[34] At a federal level, see *Australian Human Rights Commission Act 1986*, *Age Discrimination Act 2004*, *Racial Discrimination Act 1975* and *Sex Discrimination Act 1984*. State and territory anti-discrimination laws: *Australian Capital Territory Discrimination Act 1991* (ACT), *New South Wales Anti-Discrimination Act 1977* (NSW), *Northern Territory Anti-Discrimination Act 1996* (NT), *Queensland Anti-Discrimination Act 1991* (QLD), *South Australia Equal Opportunity Act 1984* (SA), *Tasmania Anti-Discrimination Act 1998* (TAS), *Victoria Equal Opportunity Act 1995* (VIC) and *Western Australia Equal Opportunity Act 1984* (WA).

[35] See also, for example, *Age Discrimination Act 2004* (Cth) s 14–15.

[36] CRC/C/AUS/CO/4 (28 August 2012), [11].

Aboriginal children have been identified as one group of Australian children that continue to experience persistent, systemic and structural discrimination[37] and violation of many of their rights. For example, Aboriginal children are overrepresented in the juvenile justice system – the likelihood of detention is at a rate 24 times higher than their non-Aboriginal counterparts.[38] Aboriginal children are also more likely to have contact with the child protection system; out-of-home placements for Aboriginal children are at a rate almost ten times greater than that for non-Aboriginal children.[39]

A comprehensive and coordinated approach to children's rights in Australia would benefit all children in Australia but especially disadvantaged children who often do not have an adequate participatory voice and who more often experience rights' violations including Aboriginal children, children with disabilities[40] and children from non-English speaking backgrounds or ethnic minorities.[41]

It is hoped that with Australia's appointment of its first National Children's Commissioner in 2013,[42] a more unified and national voice in advocating for the rights of all Australian children will be provided over time. However, as cautioned by the CRC, appropriate measures should accompany this appointment to ensure that the National Children's Commissioner is provided with adequate resources for the office to effectively function and fulfil its mandate.[43] Since the Commissioner's appointment in March 2013, significant community consultation with a focus on engagement with children has been undertaken. The Commissioner's *Children's Rights Report* laid out a number of issues that continue to require government action and will be monitored by the Commissioner on an ongoing basis.[44]

Australia in meeting its obligations under the UNCRC should strive for greater coordination in policies, law reform and resource allocation across all jurisdictions, so as to ensure that the rights of all Australian children are recognised and protected equally.

---

[37] Child Rights Taskforce. 'Listen to Children'. *Child Rights NGO Report Australia* (May 2011) available at http://www2.ohchr.org/english/bodies/crc/crcs60.htm, 4. See also, generally, Harris, M. and Gartland, G. 'Children of the Intervention: Aboriginal Children Living in the Northern Territory'. *A Submission to the UN Committee on the Rights of the Child* (June 2011) available at http://www2.ohchr.org/english/bodies/crc/crcs60.htm; National Aboriginal and Torres Strait Islander Legal Services. Shadow Report to the Committee on the Rights of the Child Regarding the Review of Australia (July 2011) available at http://www2.ohchr.org/english/bodies/crc/crcs60.htm.

[38] Ibid.

[39] Ibid.

[40] See, for example, generally, International Disability Alliance, *IDA Recommendations for* Concluding Observations, CRC 60th Session available at http://www2.ohchr.org/english/bodies/crc/crcs60.htm.

[41] Child Rights Taskforce. 'Listen to Children'. *Child Rights NGO Report Australia* (May 2011) available at http://www2.ohchr.org/english/bodies/crc/crcs60.htm, 4–6.

[42] See at http://www.humanrights.gov.au/our-work/childrens-rights/about-childrens-rights.

[43] CRC/C/AUS/CO/4 (28 August 2012), [17–18].

[44] National Children's Commissioner, *Children's Rights Report 2013* (November 2013) Australia Human Rights Commission 36.

4 Implementation of the Best Interests Principle

Article 3(1) of the Convention provides that '[i]n all actions concerning children, whether undertaken by public or private social welfare institutions, courts of law, administrative authorities or legislative bodies, the best interests of the child shall be a primary consideration'.

The best interests of the child (BIC) is the key guiding principle in most legislation in Australia at both federal and state levels that relates to children. For example, child protection legislation in every Australian jurisdiction identifies the paramount importance of the BIC,[45] and each jurisdiction provides guidelines on how such decisions should be reached.[46] However, legislative protection alone seems to have been insufficient in fulfilling this right.[47]

In the context of family law more specifically, the *Family Law Act 1975* (Cth) (the FLA) requires that the BIC is a core consideration in decisions affecting children. Section 60B of the FLA states that the objects of Part VII (Children) are to ensure that the best interests of children are met by:

(a) Ensuring that children have the benefit of both of their parents having meaningful involvement in their lives, to the maximum extent consistent with the best interests of the child
(b) Protecting children from physical or psychological harm from being subjected to, or exposed to, abuse, neglect or family violence
(c) Ensuring that children receive adequate and proper parenting to help them achieve their full potential
(d) Ensuring that parents fulfil their duties and meet their responsibilities, concerning the care, welfare and development of their children

Section 60CA of the FLA requires that the court in deciding whether to make a particular parenting order in relation to a child must have regard to the BIC as the paramount consideration. Section 60CC of the FLA requires the court, in determining what is in the child's best interests, to consider certain primary considerations (subsection (2)) and additional considerations (subsection (3)). The primary considerations are:

(a) The benefit to the child of having a meaningful relationship with both of the child's parents

[45] *Children and Young People Act 2008* (ACT), *Children and Young Persons* (Care *and Protection) Act 1998* (NSW), *Care and Protection Children Act 2007* (NT), *Child Protection Act 1999* (Qld), *Children's Protection Act 1993* (SA), *Children, Young Persons and their Families Act 1997* (Tas), *Children, Youth and Families Act 2005* (Vic), *Children and Community Services Act 2004* (WA).

[46] Holzer, P. and Lamont, A. (2009). 'Australian Child Protection Legislation'. Resource Sheet No. 14 (AIFS) available at: http://www.aifs.gov.au/nch/pubs/sheets/rs14/rs14.html.

[47] Child Rights Taskforce. 'Listen to Children'. *Child Rights NGO Report Australia* (May 2011) available at http://www2.ohchr.org/english/bodies/crc/crcs60.htm, 6.

(b) The need to protect the child from physical or psychological harm from being subjected to, or exposed to, abuse, neglect or family violence

Greater weight is to be accorded to the considerations set out in paragraph (2)(b).[48]

Numerous additional considerations must also be taken into account by the court,[49] amongst these are any views expressed by the child,[50] the nature of the relationship between the child and parents and others,[51] the capacity of the child's parents and of any other person to provide for the needs of the child including emotional and intellectual needs,[52] the extent to which each parent has fulfilled or failed to fulfil parental obligations to maintain the child,[53] the likely effect on the child of any change in circumstances[54] and the attitude to the child and to the responsibilities of parenthood, demonstrated by each of the child's parents.[55]

Courts in Australia including the High Court of Australia have also considered the BIC principle in numerous contexts through common law principles and doctrine, for example, *Cattanach v Melchior* [2003] HCA 38 (16 July 2003) (wrongful birth case) and *Secretary, Department of Health and Community Services v JWB and SMB* (Marion's case) (1992) 175 CLR 218 (concerning sterilisation).[56] In *Cattanach v Melchior* (2003) the High Court considered whether the unintended birth of a child as a result of medical negligence in the performance of or advice pertaining to a sterilisation procedure should give rise to actionable damages on the part of the parents of that child. The High Court assumed that the fact of the child's birth could not be considered a legal wrong for this purpose; however, the costs of raising and maintaining that child could be recovered.[57] The court considered various factors as relevant to whether the child would be impacted adversely by the allowance of this type of claim. Concern was raised as to whether a child would feel devalued in knowing that their parents had sued for the damage associated with and caused by their birth.[58] This was weighed against the child's interest in the alleviation of their parent's financial hardship.[59]

In the context of considering whether medical procedures are in the best interests of a child, the law will place a value on protecting the child's bodily

[48] Paragraph (2A).

[49] Paragraph (3).

[50] Paragraph (3)(a).

[51] Paragraph (3)(b).

[52] Paragraph (3)(f).

[53] Paragraph (ca).

[54] Paragraph (d).

[55] Paragraph (i).

[56] Cited in CRC/C/AUS/4 (4 June 2011), [70].

[57] Cattanach v Melchior (2003) 215 CLR 1, 31-2, 39, 57, 107.

[58] Ibid. 56, 92, 93, 124, 127-8, 139.

[59] Ibid. 75, 144.

integrity and dignity.[60] The medical procedure at issue in Marion's case was the sterilisation of a disabled child. The majority considered that this procedure would only be in the best interests of the child if it furthered the child's welfare and if alternative, less invasive procedures had already failed or were likely to be unsuccessful.[61] The child's welfare in this context was construed as meaning more than simply convenience.[62] When authorising medical procedures as being in the best interests of the child, the court must be cautious because of the irreversibility of the procedure and the 'significant risk of a wrong decision being made'.[63] The court said that ordinarily the best interests of the child would coincide with the wishes of the parents.[64] In this case the 'best interest' test was criticised by Justice Brennan as being void of predictable and consistent content.[65]

A key concern raised by the CRC with respect to Australia's approach to the BIC is that the principle is not 'appropriately integrated and consistently applied in all legislative, administrative and judicial proceedings and in policies, programmes and projects relevant to and with an impact on children'.[66] This is similarly a concern for many States Parties. A particular concern raised for Australia is application of the best interests principle to child asylum seekers, refugee and immigration detention situations.[67] Accordingly the CRC has encouraged Australia to develop procedures and criteria to provide guidance for determining the best interests of the child in every area and to disseminate them to public and private social welfare institutions, courts of law, administrative authorities and legislative bodies. The legal reasoning of all judicial and administrative judgments and decisions should also be based on this principle, specifying the criteria used in the individual assessment of the best interests of the child.[68]

As this discussion highlights, implementation of the best interests principle represents another area where greater harmonisation of approach and application should be pursued in Australia in order to more effectively protect children's interests and their well-being.

---

[60] *Secretary, Department of Health and Community Services v J.W.B and S.M.B* (1992) 175 CLR 218, 232, 253, 265-9, 309-10.

[61] Ibid. 259.

[62] Ibid. 260.

[63] Ibid. 250.

[64] Ibid. 260.

[65] Ibid. 270-1.

[66] CRC/C/AUS/CO/4 (28 August 2012), [31].

[67] CRC/C/AUS/CO/4 (28 August 2012), [31]. See also Child Rights Taskforce. 'Listen to Children'. *Child Rights NGO Report Australia* (May 2011) available at http://www2.ohchr.org/english/bodies/crc/crcs60.htm, 6.

[68] CRC/C/AUS/CO/4 (28 August 2012), [32].

5 Implementation of the Right to Express the Views Freely in All Matters Affecting the Child

Article 12 of the UNCRC recognises that children who are capable of forming their own views have a right to express those views freely in all matters affecting them and accordingly should be 'provided the opportunity to be heard in any judicial and administrative proceedings'. Moreover, Article 13 recognises a child's right 'to freedom of expression'.

A child's right to be heard in proceedings that affect the child is reflected in numerous legislative provisions in Australia both at federal and state levels and in varied contexts. For example, child protection legislation in every jurisdiction in Australia makes provision for a child's view or wishes to be expressed either directly or indirectly in such proceedings.[69] A key cornerstone in most of these provisions is recognition and support of the individual child's needs, level of maturity and his or her abilities. Accordingly, most provisions require the court or other person to provide the child with sufficient information to permit the child to express his or her views or wishes and to meaningfully participate in the decision-making process.

A key consideration in affording a child the opportunity to express his or her view in judicial or administrative proceedings is balancing such opportunity against the potential for distress to the child. In the context of family law proceedings, paragraph 60CC(3)(a) of the *Family Law Act* requires the court to consider any views expressed by a child in deciding whether to make a particular parenting order in relation to the child. Section 60CD of the Act deals with how the court informs itself of views expressed by a child, such means including by way of report to the court,[70] by appointment of an independent children's lawyer[71] or by any other means the court deems appropriate.[72] The Act makes clear however that the child's right to participate is voluntary and that '[n]othing in [the Act] permits the court or any person to require the child to express his or her views in relation to any matter'.[73] There is no age requirement specified in the Act with respect to a child's participation in proceedings; rather, the child's maturity and level of understanding is a factor that the court is to consider in determining the weight that it should give to the child's views.[74] The Act thus encourages consultation between the court and the child in making decisions in such proceedings. It is widely recognised that Australian family law processes 'have made considerable efforts to allow children's voices to

---

[69] *Children, Youth & Families Act 2005* (Vic) s11; *Children and Young People Act 2008* (ACT) s352; *Child Protection Act 1999* (Qld) s5E; *Children and Young Persons (Care and Protection) Act* 1998 (NSW) s10; *Care and Protection Children Act 2007* (NT) s11; *Children's Protection Act 1993* (SA) s4; *Children, Young Persons and their Families Act 1997* (Tas) s56; *Children and Community Services Act 2004* (WA) s10.

[70] Section 60CD(2)(a) pursuant to subsection 62G(2).

[71] Section 60CD(2)(b).

[72] Section 60CD(2)(c).

[73] Section 60CE.

[74] Paragraph 60CC(3)(a).

be heard both in the court process and in cases that are resolved without court intervention'.[75] However, concerns remain in Australia regarding 'inadequate fora for taking into account the views of children who are below the age of 15 and/or of Aboriginal or Torres Strait Islander descent'[76] specifically within the context of family law and welfare matters as well as more generally.

6 The Right of the Child to Know About His/Her Origin

Article 7 of the UNCRC recognises the right of the child to have from birth a name and 'to acquire a nationality and, as far as possible, the right to know and be cared for by his or her parents'.

6.1 *Registration of Birth*

All Australian states and territories require a child to be registered at birth. Entering a person's name as a parent of a child in a register of births or equivalent gives rise to a presumption of parentage.[77]

Evidence suggests that many indigenous Australians however are not registered at birth, and even if they are, they often experience difficulty in accessing their birth certificate.[78] Procedural barriers to registration including difficulties arising from poor literacy levels have been identified as a common problem.[79] It is quite clear that more can be done to streamline birth registration processes in Australia and remove barriers such as fees associated with obtaining copies of a birth certificate, particularly, for disadvantaged Australians such as indigenous Australians. A lack of access to one's birth certificate may start a 'vicious cycle' that prevents access to numerous other key facilities including education and health services and which precludes a person from obtaining a driver's licence and passport.[80]

[75] Child Rights Taskforce. 'Listen to Children'. *Child Rights NGO Report Australia* (May 2011) available at http://www2.ohchr.org/english/bodies/crc/crcs60.htm, 8

[76] CRC/C/AUS/CO/4 (28 August 2012), [33].

[77] Family Law Act (Cth) s69R.

[78] See, generally, Castan Centre for Human Rights Law, Monash University. *Shadow Report to the UN Committee on the Rights of the Child Regarding Australia's Compliance with Article 7 of the Convention of the Rights of the Child* (22 June 2011) available at http://www2.ohchr.org/english/bodies/crc/crcs60.htm.

[79] Ibid.

[80] Ibid.

6.2 Presumptions and Rebuttals of Parentage

Under the *Family Law Act 1975* (Cth), a child born to a woman whilst she is married is generally presumed to be a child of the woman and her husband.[81] The FLA also presumes parentage arising from a woman's cohabitation.[82] Under the FLA such presumptions are rebuttable pursuant to Section 69U. This section does not explicitly state who has standing to make such rebuttal; however, by virtue of Section 69C(2), it seems that proceedings relating to parentage may be initiated by the child, either or both of the child's parents, a grandparent of the child or any other person concerned with the care, welfare or development of the child. No distinction is drawn here under the FLA, as between children born in and outside of marriage. The position under state and territory legislation is similar to that under the FLA.[83]

In the case of a child conceived through medical assistance, the child's mother and her husband are generally presumed to be the parents of the child (assuming the husband consented to the procedure).[84] The woman and man need not be married but must be living together in a bona fide domestic relationship. This presumption is generally rebuttable by the child, parent or anyone who has a proper interest in such a determination.[85]

Thus under Australian law, a child, whether born in or out of a marriage or through assisted technology, may generally rebut parentage of either his or her mother or father as registered at birth or as otherwise presumed at law.

---

[81] Family Law Act (Cth) s69P.

[82] Family Law Act 1975 (Cth) s69Q. Additionally parentage may be presumed by a court's finding of such (s69S) or execution of an instrument acknowledging paternity (s69T).

[83] See *Status of Children Act* (NT), *Status of Children Act 1996* (NSW), *Status of Children Act 1974* (Vic), *Parentage Act 2004* (ACT), *Status of Children Act 1978* (Qld), *Family Relationships Act 1975* (SA), *Status of Children Act 1974* (Tas) and Family Court *Act 1997* (WA). Some jurisdictions also have specific provisions that deal with presumptions of parentage in the context of intestacy.

[84] *Status of Children Act 1978* (Qld) ss14-17, *Status of Children Act 1974* (Tas) Part III, *Status of Children Act 1974* (Vic) Parts II, *Family Law Relationships Act 1975* (SA) Part 2A, *Status of Children Act 1996* (NSW) s14, *Status of Children Act* (NT) Part IIIA, Family Law Act 1975 (Cth) s60H.

[85] *Status of Children Act 1978* (Qld) s 10, *Status of Children Act 1974* (Tas) s10, *Status of Children Act 1974* (Vic) s10, *Family Law Relationships Act 1975* (SA) s9, *Status of Children Act 1996* (NSW) Division 3.

6.3 Right to Access Information Relating to Genetic Origins

6.3.1 Children Conceived Through Biomedical Assistance

The position in Australia in relation to a child's right to access genetic or donor information where the child is born of assisted reproductive technology (ART)[86] varies between jurisdictions. Only four states in Australia (Victoria, NSW, WA and SA) have legislation that specifically regulates ART and the rights of persons conceived using such technology to know their genetic origins.[87] In South Australia, donor offspring have a right to access non-identifying information about donors once they reach the age of 16.[88] Identifying information is only accessible by the conceived person with donor consent. In Victoria children born of donor gametes have a right to access identifying information, but generally, only after they reach the age of 18 or before, with the consent of their parent/guardian.[89] Similarly, in NSW a child conceived of ART may access donor-identifying information upon turning 18 years of age.[90] No provision is made in the NSW legislation for disclosure of any information to a nonadult donor offspring. Western Australia is the only Australian jurisdiction that recognises a child's right (at age 16) to identifying donor information.[91] The child here however is required to have undertaken approved counselling.[92] NSW, Victoria, SA and WA all require certain information to be recorded prior to use of the donor gametes so as to protect and enable the future accessibility of such data.

In Australian jurisdictions where there is no legislation in place that regulates ART and the right of access to information about donor gametes, the National Health and Medical Research Council (NHMRC) ART guidelines provide direction.[93] The NHMRC guidelines recognise the right of a person born of ART to have access to information regarding their genetic parents[94] and prohibit the use of

---

[86]Assisted reproductive technology is the application of laboratory or clinical technology to gametes (human egg or sperm) and/or embryos for the purposes of reproduction: NHMRC at http://www.nhmrc.gov.au/health-ethics/australian-health-ethics-committee-ahec/assisted-reproductive-technology-art/assisted.

[87]*Assisted Reproductive Treatment Act 2008* (Vic), Assisted Reproductive Technology *Act 2007* (NSW) (the NSW legislation is currently under review), *Assisted Reproductive Treatment Act 1988* (SA), *Western Australian Human Reproductive Technology Act 1991(WA)*.

[88]*Reproductive Technology (Code of Ethical Clinical Practice) Regulations 1995* (SA) cl 31(2).

[89]*Assisted Reproductive Treatment Act 2008* (Vic) s59.

[90]Assisted Reproductive Technology *Act 2007* (NSW) s37.

[91]*Western Australian Human Reproductive Technology Act 1991*(WA) s49(2d).

[92]*Western Australian Human Reproductive Technology Act 1991*(WA) s49(2d).

[93]NHMRC, 'Ethical Guidelines on the use of assisted reproductive technology in clinical practice and research' (2007) (ART Guidelines) available at: http://www.nhmrc.gov.au/_files_nhmrc/publications/attachments/e78.pdf.

[94]NHMRC, 'Ethical Guidelines on the use of assisted reproductive technology in clinical practice and research' (2007) (ART Guidelines), paragraph 6.1.

donated gametes in reproductive technologies, unless the donor has consented to the release of identifying information about himself or herself to the persons conceived using his or her gametes.[95]

Importantly although the NHMRC guidelines and the legislation in Victoria, NSW, WA and SA recognise the right of a person conceived of ART to know their genetic parents, there is no requirement that a parent disclose to a person so born that they were conceived by ART. This lack of a duty of disclosure essentially renders 'any access to identifying information [a]s inconsequential if parents do not inform their children that they are donor conceived and entitled to [such information]'.[96]

What is thus clearly lacking in Australia is a mechanism that recognises a child's right to know that they have been conceived through biomedical assistance (or at least a rigorous and standardised process such as counselling that encourages and facilitates such disclosure as appropriate) and thereafter to be able to access identifying and non-identifying information as a matter of right when the child has 'acquired sufficient maturity to appreciate the significance of the request'.[97]

6.3.2 Adopted Children

All Australian jurisdictions have provisions that permit adopted children on turning 18 (16 in NT) to access certain identifying and non-identifying information, where available, about their birth parent.[98] The position however varies between jurisdictions. Most Australian jurisdictions also have provisions for children under 18 years of age to access birth information, but generally the consent of adoptive parents is required,[99] and in some states consent from both adoptive and birth parents may also be necessary depending on the circumstances and information that are sought to be obtained.[100] In Western Australia, however, an adoptee under 18 years of age may apply for access to adoption information in their own right.[101]

---

[95] NHMRC, 'Ethical Guidelines on the use of assisted reproductive technology in clinical practice and research' (2007) (ART Guidelines) paragraph 6.1.

[96] Schneller, E.A. 'The rights of donor inseminated children to know their genetic origins in Australia'. (2005) 19 *Australian Journal of Family Law* 222 (accessed via LexisNexis).

[97] NHMRC, 'Ethical Guidelines on the use of assisted reproductive technology in clinical practice and research' (2007) (ART Guidelines), paragraph 6.11.

[98] Adoption *Act 1988* (Tas) Section 82, *Adoption of Children Act* (NT) Section 64, *Adoption Act 1988* (SA) Section 27, *Adoption Act 1984* (Vic) Section 93, *Adoption Act 2009* (Qld) Part 11, *Adoption Act 2000* (NSW) Section 133C, *Adoption Act 1993* (ACT) Part 5.

[99] Adoption *Act 1988* (Tas) Section 81, *Adoption of Children Act* (ACT) Section 64 (children under 16), *Adoption Act 2000* (NSW) s 133C, *Adoption Act 2009* (Qld) Section 256, *Adoption Act 1984* (Vic) Section 94, *Adoption Act 1993* (ACT) Section 68.

[100] Adoption *Act 1988* (SA) Section 27A.

[101] Adoptions *Act 1994* (WA) Part 4.

There is a clear need for harmonisation of provisions in Australia relating to a child's access to information about adoption, based on the child's best interests and recognition that withholding such information from an adopted child may adversely impact on the child's psychological and emotional well-being.[102]

7 Rights of a Child in Adoption

Adoption in Australia including intercountry adoptions is a state, not federal, responsibility, so legislation varies across different jurisdictions.[103] The best interests of the child or young person is a paramount consideration in adoption decisions in all Australian jurisdictions.[104] The NSW *Adoption Act 2000* as in most other states and territories takes a broad approach to the BIC requiring that in making a decision about the adoption of a child, the decision-maker must (as far as is practicable or appropriate) have regard to the BIC 'both in childhood and later life'.[105] Every state and territory in Australia recognises the importance of 'consulting with the child or young person throughout the adoption process and, wherever possible, taking the child's or young person's views into account'[106] with regard to the child's age or ability to understand.

Australian states and territories however are split on whether a child must consent to the adoption. In NSW, NT, SA and WA, a court must not make an order for adoption of a child aged 12–18 years capable of giving consent unless the child consents.[107] However, in these jurisdictions the court may of itself dispense

---

[102] Richard Chisholm, 'Information Rights and Donor Conception: Lessons from Adoption?' (2012) 19 *Journal of Law and Medicine* 722 and Brooke Skinner-Drawz et al., 'The Role of Adoption Communicative Openness in Information Seeking Among Adoptees From Adolescence to Emerging Adulthood' (2011) 11 *Journal of Family Communication* 181.

[103] Adoption *Act 2000* (NSW), *Adoption Act 1993* (ACT), *Adoption Act 2009* (Qld), *Adoption Act* 1988 (Tas), *Adoption of Children Act* (NT), *Adoption Act* 1988 (SA), *Adoption Act 1994* (WA), *Adoption Act 1984* (Vic).

[104] Adoption *Act 2000* (NSW) s8(1)(a), *Adoption Act 1993* (ACT) s4(a) and 5, *Adoption Act 2009* (Qld) s6(1), *Adoption of Children Act* (NT) s8, *Adoption Act 1988* (Tas) s8, *Adoption Act* 1988 (SA) s7, *Adoption Act 1994* (WA) s3, *Adoption Act 1984* (Vic) s9.

[105] Adoption *Act 2000* (NSW) s8(1)(a), *Adoption Act 2009* (Qld) s6(1) and 9.

[106] Adoption *Act 1993* (ACT) s4(e) and 35B. See also *Adoption Act 2000* (NSW) ss8 and 9, *Adoption of Children Act* (NT) Section 10(1), *Adoption Act 2009* (Qld) Section 44 and 179, *Adoption Act 1984* (Vic) Section 14, *Adoption Act 1988* (Tas) Section 23, *Adoption Act* 1988 (SA) Section 8A and *Adoption Act 1994* (WA) Section 134.

[107] Adoption *Act 2000* (NSW) Section 55(1), *Adoption of Children Act* (NT) Section 10(2), *Adoption Act* 1988 (SA) Section 16 and *Adoption Act 1994* (WA) Section 17. Consent of the child is not required in the ACT: *Adoption Act 1993* (ACT) Section 28 nor does the Qld, Tas and Vic legislation make mention of the need for the child's consent.

with this requirement.[108] For example, in NSW the *Adoption Act 2000* pursuant to Section 55 requires that:

1. The court must not make an adoption order in relation to a child who is 12 or more but less than 18 years of age and who is capable of giving consent unless:
   (a) The child has been counselled as required by Section 63.
   (b) The counsellor has certified that the child understands the effect of signing the instrument of consent (as required by Section 61).
   (c) The child consents to his or her adoption by the prospective adoptive parent or parents, or the court dispenses with the requirement for consent.
2. The court may make an adoption order in relation to such a child who is incapable of giving consent if the court is satisfied that the circumstances are exceptional and that it would be in the best interests of the child to make the order.

The eligibility requirements for overseas adoptions are different in each Australian state and territory[109] and may include criteria concerning partner relationship status, age, citizenship and health. Actual adoption procedures vary depending on the country and category under which the adoption takes place. Generally procedures for adoption involve prospective parents being allocated a child from the overseas country through their state or territory adoption authority; if accepted, they may lodge an adoption visa application for the child; the child is required to undergo medical checks; the adoption is finalised in the overseas country; a visa granting permanent residence to the child is granted and appears in the child's foreign passport.[110]

Although adoption is a state responsibility, the Australian Government, through the Attorney-General's Department, has the responsibility for managing existing adoption programmes and negotiating new programmes with other countries.[111]

There is clearly a need for greater harmonisation across Australia in relation to legislative provisions relating to adoption, particularly, in relation to a child's consent in such matters.[112] Also consistent national eligibility requirements and procedures for overseas adoptions that provide uniformity throughout Australia would assist in removing any impetus for 'forum shopping'.

---

[108] Adoption *Act 2000* (NSW) Section 55(1)(c) and (2), *Adoption of Children Act* (NT) Section 10(2), *Adoption Act* 1988 (SA) Section 18 and *Adoption Act 1994* (WA) Section 24.

[109] Adoption *Act 1993* (ACT) Part 4A; *Adoption of Children Act* (NT) Section 10(2)(b); *Adoption Act 1988* (Tas) Part II, Division 5; *Adoption Act 1994* (WA) Part 3, Division II; *Adoption Act 2000* (NSW) Chapter 5, Part 2; *Adoption Act 2009* (Qld) Part 9. Division 3; *Adoption Act 1984* (Vic) Part IVA; *Adoption Act 1988* (SA) Division 3.

[110] See generally http://www.immi.gov.au/media/fact-sheets/36adopting.htm.

[111] See generally http://www.immi.gov.au/media/fact-sheets/36adopting.htm.

[112] CRC/C/AUS/CO/4 (28 August 2012), [53–54].

8 The Right of the Child to Freedom of Thought, Conscience and Religion

Article 14 of the UNCRC recognises 'the right of the child to freedom of thought, conscience and religion' subject 'only to such limitations as are prescribed by law and are necessary to protect public safety, order, health or morals, or the fundamental rights and freedoms of others'.

There is legal provision for religious education in government schools in all states and territories in Australia.[113] Such religious instruction is not obligatory but optional for students. However, under the current scheme, schools are obliged to permit volunteers from religious organisations to teach weekly classes, generally up to 1 h, to students choosing this instruction (generally through parental/guardian decision-making).[114] Legislation in Australia provides for two types of religious education: general religious education and denominational religious education. The latter form of religious education has dominated religious instruction in Australian state schools. Calls have been made in Australia to revisit the appropriateness of such provisions in secular schools, but the issue is yet to be well argued.

9 Protection of Child Against Physical Punishment

Article 19 of the UNCRC requires that 'appropriate legislative, administrative, social and educational measures' be undertaken 'to protect the child from all forms of physical or mental violence, injury or abuse, neglect or negligent treatment, maltreatment or exploitation, including sexual abuse, while in the care of parent(s), legal guardian(s) or any other person who has the care of the child'.

The position with respect to corporal punishment and discipline of children in Australia varies between jurisdictions. In the context of schooling, the Australian Government has stated it does not endorse corporal punishment as an approach to developing values and respect in students and has legislated that the National Safe Schools Framework now be implemented in every Australian school.[115] This Framework consists 'of a set of nationally agreed principles for a safe and supportive school environment. It includes appropriate responses which schools can adopt to address issues of bullying, violence, harassment, and child abuse and neglect'.[116] Some Australian states have explicitly banned the use of corporal

---

[113] Rossiter, G. 'Religious education in government schools in Australia' available at: http://203.10.46.30/ren/reflag/iarfchap.html.

[114] See, for example, *Education (General Provisions) Act 2006* (Qld) Section 76(1), (5) and (6).

[115] CRC/C/AUS/4 at 18.

[116] Ibid.

punishment in schools,[117] but in other states, it remains unclear whether this ban also extends to nongovernment schools.[118] This is a problem in terms of universal protection of children against corporal punishment as over one million Australian school students attend nongovernment schools, which is just over half the number of students at government schools.[119]

In relation to physical punishment by parents, it remains lawful in all Australian jurisdictions for parents to use reasonable corporal punishment to discipline their children.[120] In some jurisdictions the lawfulness of physical punishment of a child by a parent is provided for by legislation,[121] whilst in others it is permitted by the common law.[122]

The position in Australia therefore with respect to the physical punishment of children in schools, institutional settings and within the home is that physical punishment remains lawful in certain circumstances on the basis of 'reasonable chastisement'. As recommended by the CRC, Australia should '[t]ake all appropriate measures to explicitly prohibit corporal punishment in homes, in public and private schools, detention centres and alternative care settings in all states and territories'.[123]

10 Deprivation of Parental Responsibility

Under Part VII (Children) of the *Family Law Act 1975* (Cth), parental responsibility is understood to mean 'all the duties, powers, responsibilities and authority which, by law, parents have in relation to children'.[124] Each of the parents of a child under

---

[117] Education Act 1990 (NSW) s35 and s47(h), *Education Amendment Act 1999* (Tas) s82A, *Education and Training Reform Act 2006* (Vic) s2.6.60 and s4.3.1(6)(a) and *School Education Regulations 2000* (WA) (only applies to government schools).

[118] For example, in the ACT the purpose of the *Education (Amendment) Act 2004* was to ban punishment in 'all schools'. Although the Act does not explicitly state that it relates to both government and nongovernment schools, the interpretation is that it applies to both school systems: Holzer, P. and Lamont, A. (2010). 'Corporal Punishment: Key Issues'. *NCPC Resource Sheet* (AIFS) available at http://www.aifs.gov.au/nch/pubs/sheets/rs19/rs19.html. See also *Education General Provisions Regulation Act 2006* (Qld) and *Education (Amendment) Act 1991* (SA).

[119] Australian Bureau of Statistics, 'Schools Australia 2013' ABS 4221.0, available at http://www.abs.gov.au/ausstats/abs@.nsf/Lookup/4221.0main+features42013.

[120] Holzer, P. and Lamont, A. (2010). 'Corporal Punishment: Key Issues'. *NCPC Resource Sheet* (AIFS) available at: http://www.aifs.gov.au/nch/pubs/sheets/rs19/rs19.html.

[121] See, e.g. *Crimes Act 1900 (NSW)* s61AA, Criminal Code *Act* (NT) s 27, *Criminal Code Act 1899* (Qld) s280, *Criminal Code Act 1924* (Tas) s50 and *Criminal Code Act 1913* (WA) s 257.

[122] For example, the ACT, SA and Vic.

[123] CRC/C/AUS/CO/4 at 10. See also Bernadette Saunders and Chris Goddard, 'Some Australian Children's Perceptions of Physical Punishment in Childhood' (2008) 22 *Children & Society* 405 and Seunghee Han, 'Corporal Punishment and Student Outcomes in Rural Schools' (2014) 13 *Educational Research for Police and Practice* 221.

[124] Section 61B.

18 years of age has parental responsibility for the child.[125] However, parenting orders may (either expressly or by necessary intendment) diminish or take away all or some aspects of parental responsibility of a parent for their child.[126] The scope of parental responsibility conferred for a child on a person will be determined by the extent to which a parenting order 'confers on the person duties, powers, responsibilities or authority in relation to the child'.[127] The court in making a parenting order 'must apply a presumption that it is in the best interests of the child for the child's parents to have equal shared parental responsibility for the child'.[128] However, consistent with the requirements of Article 19(1) of the UNCRC, the presumption does not apply if there are reasonable grounds to believe that a parent of the child (or a person who lives with a parent of the child) has engaged in abuse of the child or another child in the parent's family or perpetrated family violence.[129] Moreover, the presumption of equal shared parental responsibility may be rebutted by evidence that 'satisfies the court that it would not be in the best interests of the child for the child's parents to have equal shared parental responsibility for the child'.[130] As against other countries the law in Australia with respect to deprivation of parental responsibility seems well developed in protection of children's right to life, survival and development.

11 A Child's Right to Medical Consent

A child's right to give or refuse medical consent in Australia is variously governed by a mix of common law and legislation in the different jurisdictions. Generally speaking, parents and children in Australia hold concurrent rights to refuse or consent to a child's medical treatment, consistent with recognition of a child's increasing competency in decision-making as the child moves towards adulthood.[131] A court may override the decision of a competent child and/or their parent in relation to giving or refusing medical consent by application of the best interests principle.

In NSW the *Minors (Property and Contracts) Act 1970* provides that a child aged 14 years or over may consent to his/her medical or dental treatment. Pursuant to Section 49 of the Act, the consent of the minor will be effective in terms of defending an action for assault or battery relating to the treatment. This Act however does not provide guidance on situations of conflict in consent to medical treatment

---

[125] Section 61C.

[126] Section 61D.

[127] Section 61D(1).

[128] Section 61DA(1).

[129] Section 61DA(2).

[130] Section 61DA(4).

[131] High Court of Australia in *Secretary, Department of Health and Community Services v JWB and SMB* (Marion's case) (1992) 175 CLR 218 approving *Gillick v West Norfolk and Wisbech Area Health Authority* [1986] AC 112.

between a child and his or her parents. In South Australia the *Consent toMedical Treatment and Palliative Care Act 1995* provides that a child aged 16 years of age or over can consent to medical and dental treatment 'as validly and effectively as an adult'. Section 12 of the Act permits a medical practitioner to administer medical treatment in circumstances where the child consents and the medical practitioner is of the opinion 'that the child is capable of understanding the nature, consequences and risks of the treatment and that the treatment is in the best interest of the child's health and well-being'[132] and 'that opinion is supported by the written opinion of at least one other medical practitioner who personally examines the child before the treatment is commenced'.[133]

The child's right to independent consent in medical treatment and interventions whilst well developed in Australia against international standards could be harmonised more nationally.

12 A Child's Right to Change Name

In Australia the law applicable to a child's right to formally change name (i.e. from that recorded on their birth certificate) is state and territory based.[134] Generally a child who is aged under 18 will, unless they have previously been married, require the consent of at least one parent to change their name, and usually consent from both parents is required, exceptions typically include where only one parent is recorded on the birth certificate, the other parent has died or a court orders such change of name. In the case of a child aged 12 years or older (or in the case of South Australia, a child old enough to understand the implications of a change in name), most Australian jurisdictions require the child to consent to a change in name. In most Australian jurisdictions application for change of name of a minor must be lodged by a parent or legal guardian with the appropriate registry of Births, Deaths and Marriages or equivalent government office.[135]

---

[132] Section 12(b)(i).

[133] Section 12(b)(ii).

[134] Births, Deaths and Marriages Registration Act 1997 (ACT); Births, Deaths and Marriages Registration Act 1995 (NSW); Births, Deaths and Marriages Registration Act 2003 (Qld); Births, Deaths and Marriages Registration Act (NT); Births, Deaths and Marriages Registration Act 1996 (SA); Births, Deaths and Marriages Registration Act 1999 (Tas); Births, Deaths and Marriages Registration Act 1996 (Vic); Births, Deaths and Marriages Registration Act 1998 (WA).

[135] See generally http://www.bdm.vic.gov.au/home/change+of+name/change+your+childs+name/, http://www.bdm.nsw.gov.au/bdm_con.html, http://www.qld.gov.au/law/births-deaths-marriages-and-divorces/changing-your-name/changing-your-childs-name/, http://www.justice.tas.gov.au/bdm/changeofname/howtoregister, http://www.cbs.sa.gov.au/assets/files/change_name_child.pdf, http://www.nt.gov.au/justice/bdm/births_deaths_marriages/other/reg_name.shtml, http://www.ors.act.gov.au/community/births_deaths_and_marriages#I%20want%20to%20change%20my%20child%27s%20name and http://www.bdm.dotag.wa.gov.au/H/how_to_register_a_child_s_change_of_name.aspx?uid=4090-9458-2925-3474.

13 Rights and Protection of Children in Employment

In protecting the child against economic exploitation and other types of hazards and harm, Article 32 para (a) of the UNCRC requires States Parties to provide for a minimum age for children's admission to employment.

In Australia the employment of children is governed by a number of different federal, state and territory laws.[136] Most states and territories in Australia have legislation that regulates the minimum conditions of employment for children including the type of work children can undertake and the hours that children may work. For example, in Victoria children can be employed for a maximum of three hours per day during school term and up to six hours a day, and 30 hours a week, during school holidays. Moreover children can only be employed between 6.00 am and 9.00 pm and must receive a 30-minute break every three hours.[137] Moreover, children are only permitted to engage in 'light work' which is not likely to be harmful to a child's health, safety or moral and material welfare.[138] The ACT regulations provide examples of light work which includes going on errands, casual work in and around a private home, work related to sporting activities, clerical work, work as a cashier, gardening, taking care of children in a private home and providing entertainment, e.g. singing, dancing, musical instrument playing, performing on radio, television or film, modelling and a photographic subject.[139] Most states and territories in Australia have comparable laws of child employment.

Generally in Australia, children are prohibited from working when employment would prevent them from attending school within the mandatory school age. In the NT and ACT, the minimum school leaving age is 15 years, and in NSW, Victoria, Queensland, SA, Western Australia and Tasmania, students must stay at school until they have completed Year 10 and have attained at least 15 years of age and thereafter must be in some type of education, vocational training or employment until aged 17. However, children and young people in Australia are generally permitted to be employed part-time outside of school hours with various forms of regulation from 10 to 11 years of age upwards. For example, in Victoria the minimum age for employment generally is 13 years; however, children aged at least 11 can deliver newspapers and other types of advertising material or make deliveries for a registered pharmacist.[140] Moreover there is no minimum age in Victoria for employment of a child in a family business or in the entertainment industry. In most Australian

---

[136] Industrial relations (Child Employment) Act 2006 (NSW), Children and Young Persons (Care and protection) Act 1998 (NSW), Child Employment Act 2003 (Vic), Child Employment Act 2006 (Qld), Children and Community Services Act 2004 (WA), Children and Young People Act (ACT).

[137] See generally http://www.workplaceinfo.com.au/resources/employment-topics-a-z/child-employment-laws.

[138] Ibid.

[139] Children and Young People Regulation 2009 (ACT): cited at http://www.workplaceinfo.com.au/resources/employment-topics-a-z/child-employment-laws.

[140] See generally http://www.workplaceinfo.com.au/resources/employment-topics-a-z/child-employment-laws.

jurisdictions children aged under 15 years must obtain parental consent for employment. Australian law as regards children's employment is generally assessed against international standards, well developed in protecting children from unsafe and unfair working conditions, including wages, minimum age at which children are first allowed to work, types of employment that children can engage in and in balancing children's rights in decisions about employment with the need for parental consent.

14 Obligation of Child Towards Parents

With a number of countries introducing laws and policies that seek to regulate the duties and responsibilities of a child (generally as an adult) towards his or her parents, this issue is of increasing relevance globally.[141] In Australia the relevance of this issue is made even clearer when considered against the changed backdrop of contemporary family and community life.[142] Australia today like many countries has a rapidly ageing population[143]; family breakdown is increasing with one in three marriages ending in divorce and the rate of marriages having markedly fallen in recent decades.[144] Moreover, evidence suggests that elderly Australians are increasingly the victims of abuse and neglect including within their own home.[145] The structure and lifestyle of families in Australia have changed, as have familial relationships. Nevertheless, the fundamental importance of family in community well-being continues to be widely recognised:

> The interconnection of families with their communities is a fundamental building block of strong and resilient societies.
>
> .
> .
> .
>
> Resilience requires support from within and beyond families, tailored to the needs of individual, family and community circumstances.[146]

[141] See generally F Russo, 'Caring for Aging Parents: Should there be a Law? *Time* (Health & Family), 22 July 2013 available at http://healthland.time.com/2013/07/22/caring-for-aging-parents-should-there-be-a-law/.

[142] Hayes, A., Qu, L., Weston, R. and Baxter, J. (2011) 'Families in Australia 2011: Sticking together in good and tough times' (AIFS, Report for National Families Week, March 2011) available at ww.aifs.gov.au/institute/pubs/factssheets/2011/fw2011/fw2011a.html..

[143] Ibid.

[144] Ibid.

[145] Kurrie, S. and Naughtin, G (2008). 'An Overview of Elder Abuse and Neglect in Australia'. 20 *Journal of Elder Abuse & Neglect* 108 and James, M. (1994) 'Abuse and Neglect of Older People'. 37 *Family Matters* 94.

[146] Australian Institute of Family Studies, 'Families in Australia 2011: Sticking Together in Good and Tough Times', *Report of National Families Week* 2011, available at http://www.aifs.gov.au/institute/pubs/factssheets/2011/fw2011/fw2011d.html.

Currently there is no specific legal obligation owed by a child towards his/her parents under any Australian law at either a national or state level. A child however must interact with his/her parents in a way consistent with the laws of Australia and in accordance with basic human rights.

15 Summary

Since ratification of the UNCRC, Australia has made steady progress in implementation of many of its provisions against international efforts and standards. However, as outlined in this report, there are several areas in Australia's implementation of the Convention that need to be further strengthened. Australia is one of the most developed countries in the world, and its implementation of the UNCRC should reflect this status and its economic well-being, which arguably currently is not consistently the case on its current record of achievement towards implementation of the Convention and in recognition of the child's bundle of rights.[147] This report has focused specifically on provisions in the Convention that relate to family law and family relations, and in this domain it is clear that Australia needs to examine how its implementation of the UNCRC can be harmonised to a greater extent across different jurisdictions and domains of children's lives to ensure equal and consistent protection of the rights of all Australian children irrespective of place of domicile, origin of birth, family situation or ethnic or racial background.

Australia's combined fifth and sixth periodic reports are due to be submitted to the CRC by 15 January 2018. It is hoped that some of the weaknesses in Australia's implementation of the Convention highlighted in this report and in the concluding observations of the CRC in response to Australia's fourth periodic report[148] might be addressed by the Australian Government, at least in part prior to its next report being due or at the very least identification of the core areas that require more attention with a plan of action put forward for addressing these areas in the future, in its report to the CRC.

[147] Australian Research Alliance for Children and Youth, Report Card: The Wellbeing of Young Australians (2013) available at: http://www.aracy.org.au/documents/item/126.

[148] CRC/C/AUS/C0/4.

Les droits de l'enfant : Rapport du Canada

Michelle Giroux and Carmen Lavallée

1 Remarques préliminaires

Le Canada est une fédération dont la constitution prévoit le partage des compétences législatives entre le Parlement fédéral et les législatures des 10 provinces et 3 territoires.[1] Selon la Constitution, le gouvernement central a le pouvoir de conclure des traités internationaux, mais leur mise en œuvre doit respecter le partage des compétences. Ce dernier peut aussi intervenir en matière de droit criminel, de mariage (conditions de fond) et de divorce, de citoyenneté, pour ne nommer que celles-ci. Il est également responsable des peuples autochtones vivant dans les réserves. Toutefois, les matières de nature locale, principalement le droit privé, de même que quelques domaines de compétence spécifiquement attribuées, telles que la célébration du mariage, relèvent des provinces ou territoires. Ainsi, plusieurs des sujets abordés dans la Convention relèvent des législatures provinciales et territoriales et non du Parlement fédéral.

Au fil de l'histoire de l'application de la Convention au Canada, il lui a souvent été reproché de ne pas avoir de législation nationale, de cadre juridique global sur l'ensemble de son territoire, permettant de mettre en œuvre de façon uniforme la

[1] *Loi constitutionnelle de 1867* (R.-U.), 30 & 31 Vict., c. 3.

M. Giroux (✉)
Faculté de droit, Section de droit civil, Université d'Ottawa,
57 Louis Pasteur, Ottawa, ON K1N 6N5, Canada
e-mail: Michelle.Giroux@uottawa.ca

C. Lavallée
Faculté de droit, Université de Sherbrooke,
2500 boul. Université, Sherbrooke, QC J1K 2R1, Canada
e-mail: Carmen.Lavallee@usherbrooke.ca

O. Cvejić Jančić (ed.), *The Rights of the Child in a Changing World*,
Ius Comparatum - Global Studies in Comparative Law 13,
DOI 10.1007/978-3-319-23189-1_3

Convention des Nations Unies relative aux droits de l'enfant [la Convention].[2] S'il est vrai que la mise en œuvre d'un texte international pose des défis particuliers dans un État fédéral, le degré de difficulté rencontré dans la mise en œuvre de la Convention ne doit pas servir d'excuse à l'immobilisme. Il faut plutôt chercher plus activement encore le dialogue, la collaboration, la coopération et le partage des ressources entre les différents ordres de gouvernement afin de maximiser la mise en œuvre de cet instrument fondamental de protection des droits de l'enfant.[3]

Le présent rapport met l'accent sur le droit civil de la province du Québec, lorsque les questions abordées relèvent des juridictions provinciales ou territoriales. Il a été impossible, faute de temps et d'espace, de préciser le droit applicable dans le reste du Canada, quoique les réponses juridiques aux problèmes posés soient parfois similaires, d'un océan à l'autre. Toutefois, pour les domaines relevant de la compétence fédérale, le rapport présente le droit applicable partout au Canada. Il en est ainsi, notamment, des questions relatives à la ratification de la Convention et de la question du châtiment corporel des enfants qui relève du *Code criminel* canadien.

2 Ratification par le Canada de la Convention internationale relative aux droits de l'enfant

Le Canada a signé la Convention le 28 mai 1990 et l'a ratifiée le 13 décembre 1991. Elle entrait en vigueur un mois plus tard, le 12 janvier 1992.[4] Pour sa part, le Québec s'est déclaré lié par la Convention, en adoptant un décret à cet effet.[5] Toutefois, dans le système juridique canadien, le droit international n'est pas d'application directe. En vertu de l'approche dualiste, selon laquelle l'ordre interne et l'ordre interna-

---

[2] Voir notamment Comité des droits de l'enfant, *Observations finales sur les troisième et quatrième rapports périodiques du Canada, soumis en un seul document, adoptées par le Comité à sa soixante et unième session (17 septembre – 5 octobre 2012)*, CRC/C/CAN/CO/3–4, 6 décembre 2012, plus précisément aux pp. 2 et s. Nous saluons plus particulièrement la recommandation faite au paragraphe 13 de ce document à l'effet que « le Comité recommande vivement à l'État partie d'adopter une stratégie nationale qui fournisse un cadre global de mise en œuvre aux niveaux des autorités fédérales, provinciales et territoriales, énonçant dûment les priorités, les objectifs et les responsabilités respectives pour la mise en œuvre globale de la Convention, et qui permettra aux provinces et aux territoires d'adopter en conséquence leurs propres plans et stratégies spécifiques [...] ».

[3] Quelques recommandations pertinentes en ce sens se trouvent dans le rapport de la *Coalition canadienne sur les droits des enfants* [CCDE] mais d'autres, au contraire, démontrent la difficulté à comprendre la réalité constitutionnelle au Canada. Voir CCDE, *Des principes à la réalisation. Mise en œuvre de la Convention relative aux droits de l'enfant des Nations Unies*, 2011, 94 pp.

[4] *Convention internationale relative aux droits de l'enfant*, R.T. Can. 1992, n° 3.

[5] *Décret concernant la Convention internationale relative aux droits de l'enfant*, D.1676-91 (1992) 32 G.O. II 51 (09-12-91). Seule la province de l'Alberta a refusé pendant un certain temps de se déclarer liée par la Convention. Voir à ce sujet Ford, Catherine, *Against the Grain: An Irreverent View of Alberta* (Toronto: Random House Digital Inc., 2009,) at 230.

tional évoluent différemment, une loi de mise en vigueur de la Convention est nécessaire pour intégrer la Convention dans l'ordre juridique canadien. Or, une telle loi n'a jamais été adoptée, ce qui signifie que la Convention n'a pas d'application directe au Canada.

En revanche, la Cour suprême du Canada s'est penchée sur la question de l'influence potentielle de la Convention sur le droit canadien dans l'affaire *Baker*.[6] Après avoir rappelé que les conventions internationales ne font pas partie du droit canadien à moins d'être rendues applicables par une loi, la Cour affirme que la Convention n'a aucune application directe au Canada. Cependant, la majorité de la Cour est d'avis que les valeurs exprimées par le droit international des droits de la personne peuvent être prises en compte dans l'approche contextuelle de l'interprétation des lois.[7] Les tribunaux ont, à plusieurs reprises, eu recours à la Convention pour interpréter le droit québécois ou canadien, tentant ainsi de donner tous les effets juridiques possibles à la Convention dans le respect des systèmes juridiques et parlementaires.[8]

3 Statut du fœtus et début de la personnalité juridique (art.1 de la CIDE)

L'article 1 du *Code civil du Québec* stipule que tout être humain a la personnalité juridique. Le Code fournit quelques indices quant à la protection à accorder à l'enfant conçu, mais non encore né,[9] sans toutefois spécifier le moment d'acquisition de la personnalité juridique. La jurisprudence a donc été amenée à trancher le débat sur le début de la vie. D'une part, la Cour suprême du Canada a affirmé qu'une certaine protection est accordée à l'enfant alors qu'il est dans le ventre de sa mère, à la condition qu'il naisse vivant et viable et que la protection en question soit

---

[6] *Baker c. Canada (Ministère de la Citoyenneté et de l'Immigration)*, [1999] 2 R.C.S. 817. Voir aussi Anne-Marie TRAHAN, « Les droits de l'enfant, la Convention des Nations-Unies et l'arrêt *Baker* : une trilogie porteuse d'espoir », dans Benoît MOORE (dir.), *Mélanges Jean Pineau*, Montréal, Les Éditions Thémis, 2013, à la p. 151. Pour la place de l'enfant dans la jurisprudence, voir : Mona Paré, « La mise en œuvre de la *Convention relative aux droits de l'enfant* : une question de principes », dans Le Tribunal des droits de la personne et le Barreau du Québec, *Race, femme, enfant, handicap : les conventions internationales et le droit interne à la lumière des enjeux pratiques du droit à l'égalité*, Cowansville, Yvon Blais, 2010, 391–394.

[7] Pour certains auteurs, il est possible de défendre l'application implicite de la Convention. Voir notamment Brian R HOWE, « Implementing Children's Rights in a Federal State: The Case of Canada's Child Protection System », (2001) 9 *Int'l J Child Rts* 361, aux pp. 364–365, ainsi que Michelle GIROUX et Mariana DE LORENZI, « « Putting the child first »: A necessary step in the recognition of the right to identity », (2011) 27 *C.J.F.L.* 53, à la p. 69.

[8] Carmen LAVALLÉE, « Respect des droits de l'enfant », dans *Jurisclasseur* coll. « Droit civil », *Droit des personnes et de la famille*, Montréal, 2e éd., Les éditions LexisNexis, 2012, Fasc. 3, à la p.10.

[9] Voir par exemple l'art. 192 C.c.Q.

conforme à son intérêt.[10] Dans l'arrêt *Daigle* c. *Tremblay,*[11] le plus haut tribunal du pays ajoute également que l'acquisition de la personnalité juridique est soumise à une condition suspensive, et non résolutoire, de naissance vivante et viable.[12]

L'enfant né vivant et viable acquiert donc la personnalité juridique et par la même occasion, les droits de la personnalité.[13] Néanmoins, avant de pouvoir exercer pleinement ses droits, autrement que dans les cas spécifiquement prévus par la loi,[14] l'enfant mineur doit atteindre l'âge de la majorité, qui est fixée à 18 ans.[15] Durant la minorité, l'enfant est sous l'autorité de ses père et mère,[16] qui sont également ses tuteurs légaux.[17] Exceptionnellement, un tuteur datif peut être nommé à l'enfant.[18] Il faut noter que l'acquisition de la capacité du mineur s'acquiert progressivement et le Code civil précise les actes que le mineur peut faire seul.[19]

4 Reconnaissance des droits de l'enfant malgré l'absence d'instrument particulier de mise en œuvre de la Convention

Au Canada et au Québec, il n'y a pas d'instrument particulier de mise en œuvre de la Convention, dont l'influence est directe au moment de l'interprétation du droit canadien et québécois. L'enfant est tout de même titulaire des droits fondamentaux de la personne. Il bénéficie à ce titre de la protection générale, comme les adultes, et d'une protection spécifique en tant qu'enfant.

---

[10] Voir *Montreal Tramways c. Leveillé*, [1933] R.C.S. 456, où l'on retrouve l'application en droit québécois de la maxime romaine *Infans conceptus pro nato habetur quoties de commodis ejus agitur*, selon laquelle une fiction juridique permettait de considérer l'enfant simplement conçu comme étant déjà né lorsque cela était dans son intérêt.

[11] *Daigle v. Tremblay*, [1989] 2 RCS 530.

[12] Voir également, Édith Deleury et Dominique Goubau, *Le droit des personnes physiques*, para. 222, n. 1, 5 et s., ainsi que Robert P. Kouri et Suzanne Philips-Nootens, *L'intégrité de la personne et le consentement aux soins,* 2e éd., Cowansville (Québec), Éditions Yvon Blais, 2005, à la p. 93 et s.

[13] Tel que, par exemple, le droit à la vie. Voir l'art. 3 C.c.Q.

[14] Art. 155 et s. C.c.Q.

[15] Art. 153 C.c.Q. L'âge de la majorité varie d'une province ou territoires à l'autre. L'Alberta, le Manitoba, l'Ontario, l'Île du Prince-Édouard et la Saskatchewan fixent aussi la majorité à 18 ans. En Colombie-Britannique, au Nouveau-Brunswick, à Terre-Neuve, en Nouvelle-Écosse ainsi que dans les trois territoires, la majorité est atteinte à l'âge de 19 ans.

[16] Art. 597 et s. C.c.Q.

[17] Art. 192 Cc.Q.

[18] Art. 200 et s. C.c.Q.

[19] Pour les pouvoirs accordés au mineur de quatorze ans et plus, voir *infra*.

L'enfant est protégé par la *Charte canadienne des droits et libertés* [Charte canadienne].[20] En tant que sujet de droit, l'enfant bénéficie d'une protection contre toute action gouvernementale qui porte atteinte à la Charte canadienne. Cette dernière est supra législative, ce qui signifie qu'elle a préséance sur les lois. Elle protège les enfants contre la discrimination par le biais du droit à l'égalité (art. 15). Les autres droits importants reconnus à l'enfant sont le droit à la vie, à la liberté et à la sécurité de sa personne (art. 7), le droit d'être protégé contre les fouilles, les perquisitions ou les saisies abusives (art. 8), le droit de ne pas être détenu de façon arbitraire (art. 9), le droit d'être représenté par un avocat et d'être informé de ses droits (art. 10b). L'enfant bénéficie également des libertés fondamentales, telles que la liberté de conscience et de religion, la liberté de pensée, de croyance, d'opinion, d'expression, la liberté de réunion pacifique et la liberté d'association (art. 2). Si les droits reconnus à l'enfant se heurtent aux prérogatives de l'autorité parentale, le conflit qui en résulte doit alors être réglé en vertu de l'article premier, qui permet d'imposer des limites raisonnables dans le cadre d'une société libre et démocratique (art. 1). Les tribunaux doivent alors départager l'importance des droits individuels au regard des autres considérations sociales en présence.[21] La Charte canadienne a été invoquée en matière pénale dans un premier temps, pour s'étendre ensuite à la protection de la jeunesse, à l'adoption et aux relations familiales.[22] Elle a eu une influence particulièrement importante dans les provinces et les territoires qui ne protègent pas adéquatement les droits procéduraux des différents membres de la famille.[23]

L'enfant québécois est aussi protégé par la *Charte des droits et libertés de la personne*[24] [Charte québécoise]. Cette dernière protège l'enfant autant dans ses rapports avec l'État québécois, que dans ses rapports privés. Elle a donc un champ d'application plus vaste que la Charte canadienne. Toutefois, la Charte québécoise ne s'applique qu'au droit québécois, et non pas au droit fédéral.

Les principaux droits reconnus à l'enfant par la Charte québécoise sont le droit à la vie, à la sûreté, à l'intégrité physique et à la liberté (art. 1). L'enfant est aussi protégé contre la discrimination fondée sur l'âge, « sauf dans la mesure prévue par la loi » (art. 10). Cette expression n'empêche pas les tribunaux de réviser la conformité des dispositions législatives québécoises avec la Charte. En effet, la loi peut parfois entrainer des conséquences non prévues sur des personnes d'un âge donné. Dans les situations où ces conséquences sont voulues par le législateur, elles ne

---

[20] *Charte canadienne des droits et libertés*, Partie 1 de la *Loi constitutionnelle de 1982*, constituant l'annexe B de la Loi de 1982 sur le Canada (R.U.), 1982, c. 11.

[21] Lavallée, *supra* note 8, à la p. 3.

[22] Nicholas Bala, et D. Cruickshank, « Children and the Charter of Rights », dans *Children's Rights in the Practice of Family Law*, B. Landau (dir.), Toronto, Carswell, 1986, à la p. 28.

[23] Robert Leckey et Nicholas Bala, « Les trente premières années de la Charte canadienne en droit de la famille » (2012) 42 *R.D.U.S.* 409–457.

[24] *Charte des droits et libertés de la personne*, L.R.Q. c. C-12.

doivent pas avoir comme résultat de reproduire des stéréotypes ou de justifier une forme de discrimination.[25]

Plus précisément, l'article 39 de la Charte québécoise prévoit que « Tout enfant a droit à la protection, à la sécurité et à l'attention que ses parents ou les personnes qui en tiennent lieu peuvent lui donner ».

Le Code civil confère également des droits de la personnalité qui sont applicables aux enfants. Il s'agit du droit à la vie, à l'inviolabilité et à l'intégrité de sa personne, du droit au respect de son nom, de sa réputation et de sa vie privée (art. 3, 10 et 35). Un chapitre particulier du Code civil porte sur les droits de l'enfant (Art. 32 à 34). L'article 32 du Code civil reprend mot à mot le libellé de l'article 39 de la Charte québécoise. L'importance de la notion d'intérêt de l'enfant est affirmée (art. 33) et le droit de l'enfant d'être entendu dans les litiges où son intérêt est en jeu l'est aussi (art. 34).

De plus, la *Loi sur la protection de la jeunesse*[26] protège les enfants dont la sécurité ou le développement est, ou risque d'être, compromis par l'un des motifs expressément prévus dans la loi (abandon, négligence, abus physiques et sexuels, mauvais traitements et troubles de comportement[27]). La loi limite donc le droit des parents d'exercer, comme ils l'entendent leur autorité parentale, qui n'est donc pas considérée au Québec comme étant un droit absolu. La loi québécoise sur la protection de la jeunesse prévoit des dispositions particulières pour les enfants autochtones dans le but de mieux respecter leurs coutumes et leurs traditions.[28] Toutefois, le chevauchement de certaines compétences législatives entre le fédéral, principalement chargé de la mise en œuvre de la protection des enfants autochtones, et les provinces, soulève des questions sur l'adéquation des différentes approches et sur l'iniquité dont les enfants autochtones seraient victimes. En effet, les enfants autochtones, mais aussi les enfants afro-canadiens sont surreprésentés dans les instances visant à assurer les mesures de protection de la jeunesse.[29]

---

[25] *Commission des droits de la personne et des droits de la jeunesse* c. *Québec (Procureur général)*, J.E. 2005–535 (T.D.P.).

[26] *Loi sur la protection de la jeunesse,* L.R.Q., c. P-34.1.

[27] *Ibid.*, à l'art. 38.

[28] *Ibid.,* aux arts. 2.4 et 37.5.

[29] Comité des droits de l'enfant, *supra* note 2, aux pp. 10 et s., ainsi qu'à la p. 17. Voir également à ce sujet Alexandre Breton, Sarah Dufour et Chantal Lavergne, « Les enfants autochtones en protection de la jeunesse au Québec : leur réalité comparée à celle des autres enfants » (2012) 45 : 2 *Crime et jeux de hasard* 157, ainsi que l'étude de Nico Trocmé, Della Knoke et Cindy Blackstock, « Pathways to the Overrepresentation of Aboriginal Children in Canada's Child Welfare System » (2004) 78 : 4 *Social Service Review* 577.

5 Encadrement du principe de l'intérêt de l'enfant (art. 3 de la CIDE)

Le principe fondamental de l'intérêt de l'enfant est reconnu législativement au Québec depuis fort longtemps[30] et s'applique à de nombreuses situations. En plus d'être un principe général, on le retrouve également de manière plus spécifique dans les questions de droit d'accès, de garde, d'adoption, de soins médicaux et dans les cas de protection de la jeunesse. En effet, la législation indique que les décisions prises à l'égard des enfants doivent être prises dans leur intérêt, qu'il s'agisse d'ailleurs de décisions administratives, judiciaires ou de décisions privées prises par exemple par les parents, les éducateurs ou les tuteurs.[31] Au Québec, la notion de l'intérêt de l'enfant se retrouve ainsi à la fois dans le Code civil,[32] dans la *Loi sur la protection de la jeunesse*[33] et dans la Charte québécoise.[34] Dans l'ordre juridique fédéral, on retrouve la notion d'intérêt de l'enfant dans la *Loi sur le divorce.*[35]

Au Québec, la législation ne définit pas précisément la notion d'intérêt de l'enfant, mais elle donne des pistes qui doivent guider les décideurs. Selon l'article 33 du Code civil l'intérêt de l'enfant doit être déterminé en considérant, notamment, ses besoins moraux, intellectuels, affectifs et physiques, son âge, sa santé, son caractère et son milieu familial. Cette liste n'est pas limitative et, selon la situation de l'enfant, certains facteurs seront prioritaires par rapport aux autres.[36]

La Cour suprême du Canada a confirmé à plusieurs reprises la nécessité de tenir compte de l'intérêt de l'enfant au regard des autres éléments à considérer dans l'analyse.[37] En 1987, la Cour suprême affirmait d'ailleurs explicitement

[30] Déjà, l'ancien article 30 du *Code civil du Bas-Canada* précisait que l'intérêt de l'enfant et le respect de ses droits devaient être les motifs déterminants des décisions prises à son sujet.

[31] Deleury et Goubau, *supra* note 12, aux pp. 407 et s. Voir également, par exemple, *Droit de la famille – 2041* [1994] R.D.F. 797, EYB 1994–73449 (C.Q.), *Droit de la famille – 2104* [1995] R.J.Q. 1132, EYB 1995–72342 (C.Q.), ainsi que les commentaires du ministre de la Justice dans les *Débats de l'Assemblée nationale*, 6e session, 31e législature, B-793 et B-798, à l'effet que la disposition sur l'intérêt de l'enfant s'applique à « toute personne qui a des décisions à prendre » au sujet d'un enfant.

[32] Pour la règle générale de protection des enfants, voir notamment les art. 33 et 34 C.c.Q. De manière plus spécifique, voir également les art. 496 et 513 C.c.Q. (séparation de corps), 543, 545, 647, 568, 573 et 574 C.c.Q. (adoption), et 604, 606 et 607 C.c.Q. (exercice et déchéance de l'autorité parentale).

[33] Art. 3 de la *Loi sur la protection de la jeunesse*, *supra* note 26.

[34] Art. 57 et 73 de la Charte québécoise, *supra* note 24.

[35] Art. 16(8) de la *Loi concernant le divorce et les mesures accessoires*, L.R.C. 1985, c. 3, 2e suppl.

[36] Pour plus de détails sur l'importance des critères et les différents niveaux d'interprétation de la notion d'intérêt de l'enfant, voir : Lavallée, *supra* note 8, à la p. 12.

[37] *Beson c. Director of Child Welfare (Nfld.)* [1982] 2 R.C.S. 716 ; *Racine c. Woods* [1983] 2 R.C.S. 173; *King c. Low* [1985] 1 R.C.S. 87; *C. (G.) c. V.-F. (T.)* [1987] 2 R.C.S. 244; *N.-B. (Ministre de la Santé) c. C. (G.C.)* [1988] 1 R.C.S. 1073; *Gordon c. Goertz,* [1996] R.D.F. 209, EYB 1996–30431 (C.S.C.); *W. (V.) c. S. (D.)*, [1996] 2 R.C.S. 108, EYB 1996–67897; *Baker c. Canada (Ministère de la Citoyenneté et de l'Immigration)*, [1999] 2 R.C.S. 817, REJB 1999–13279 et, plus récemment, l'arrêt *Office des services à l'enfant et à la famille de Winnipeg c. K.L.W.*, [2000] 2 R.C.S. 519, REJB 2000–20378.

que « l'intérêt de l'enfant est devenu en droit civil québécois la pierre angulaire des décisions prises à son endroit ».[38] En 1993, dans les arrêts *Young c. Young*[39] et *P.(D.) c. C.(S.)*,[40] elle confirmait que la notion de l'intérêt de l'enfant était conforme aux principes reconnus dans la Charte canadienne. Toutefois, la Cour suprême refuse d'aller plus loin et de reconnaître la notion d'intérêt de l'enfant comme étant un principe de justice fondamentale, en raison de son contenu variable et que d'autres facteurs doivent parfois être considérés.[41] Plus tard, la Cour est venue préciser que dans le contexte d'une autorisation de traitement pour un mineur, la notion d'intérêt de l'enfant doit recevoir une interprétation qui ne soit ni arbitraire, ni discriminatoire en raison d'une distinction fondée sur l'âge, ni contraire au droit à la liberté de religion de l'enfant.[42]

6 Liens biologiques, filiation de l'enfant et connaissance de ses origines (art. 7 et 8 de la CIDE)

6.1 Règles concernant la filiation par le sang

Au Québec, tous les enfants dont la filiation est établie ont les mêmes droits et les mêmes obligations, sans égard aux circonstances de leur naissance.[43] La filiation maternelle ou paternelle s'établit généralement par l'acte de naissance ou à défaut, par la possession constante d'état.[44] La présomption de paternité constitue un autre moyen extrajudiciaire de prouver la filiation lorsque l'enfant nait pendant le mariage ou l'union civile.[45] À défaut de tout autre moyen de preuve, la filiation peut être établie par reconnaissance volontaire.[46] Par contre, bien que seuls le père ou la mère aient le pouvoir de déclarer la filiation d'un enfant à leur égard, lorsque la conception ou la naissance survient pendant le mariage ou l'union civile, l'un des conjoints peut déclarer la filiation de l'enfant à l'égard de l'autre parent.[47]

---

[38] Propos du juge Beetz dans l'arrêt *C. (G.) c. V.-F. (T.)*, [1987] 2 R.C.S. 244, aux para. 169–170.

[39] *Young c. Young*, [1993] 4 R.C.S. 3.

[40] *P. (D.) c. C. (S.)*, [1993] 4 R.C.S. 141.

[41] *Canadian Foundation for Children, Youth and the Law* c. *Canada (Procureur général)*, [2004] 1 R.C.S. 76.

[42] *A.C.* c. *Manitoba (Directeur des services à l'enfant et à la famille)*, [2009] 2 R.C.S. 181.

[43] Art 522 C.c.Q.

[44] Art. 523 et 524 C.c.Q.

[45] Art. 525 C.c.Q.

[46] Art. 526 à 529 C.c.Q.

[47] D'ailleurs, aucune autre personne n'est en mesure de déclarer la filiation à l'égard d'un parent sans son autorisation. Voir l'art. 114 C.c.Q.

Toute personne intéressée,[48] incluant l'enfant, le père ou la mère, peut contester par tout moyen[49] la filiation d'un enfant lorsque la possession constante d'état[50] n'est pas conforme à l'acte de naissance.[51] Il en est de même en matière de réclamation d'état, sous réserve de l'admissibilité de la preuve testimoniale.[52] Le délai pour prendre une action en contestation ou en réclamation d'état est de 30 ans, sous réserve de quelques délais plus courts prévus par la loi, notamment dans le cas des actions en désaveu et en contestation de paternité, visant à repousser l'application de la présomption de paternité.[53] Dans ce cas, le père présumé ou la mère bénéficie d'une année pour intenter une action, soit à partir de la naissance, soit à partir de la connaissance de la naissance lorsque le père ignorait la naissance de l'enfant.[54]

6.2 Règles concernant la filiation adoptive (art. 21 de la CIDE)

En principe, les dossiers d'adoption sont confidentiels.[55] Cependant, l'adopté majeur ou mineur de 14 ans et plus peut obtenir des renseignements sur ses origines, à la condition que ses parents biologiques y ont consenti.[56] Il en va de même pour les parents biologiques, si leur enfant adopté, maintenant majeur, y a consenti.[57] Quant à l'adopté mineur de moins de 14 ans, il peut également retrouver ses parents d'origine lorsque ses parents adoptifs et biologiques y ont consenti.[58]

Le tribunal peut également autoriser de façon anonyme la divulgation de renseignements contenus dans les dossiers d'adoption dans les cas où cela permet de se conformer à la loi ou pour permettre à l'adopté de bénéficier de « privilèges statut-

---

[48] La personne qui prétend que la filiation n'aurait pas dû être établie à son égard est également une personne intéressée.

[49] La preuve peut se faire par test d'ADN, conformément à l'art. 535.1 C.c.Q.

[50] La jurisprudence a reconnu qu'une possession d'état de la naissance jusqu'à l'âge de 16 à 24 mois était suffisamment longue pour en établir la constance. À ce sujet, voir notamment *Droit de la famille 737*, [1990] R.J.Q. 85 (C.A.) et *Droit de la famille 1059*, [1990] R.D.F. 385 (C.A.).

[51] Art. 530, 531 et 535 C.c.Q. Pour plus de détails, voir notamment Jean Pineau et Marie Pratte, *La famille*, Montréal, Éditions Thémis, 2007, aux pp. 632 et s.

[52] Art. 530 et 532, 533, 534 et 535.1 (test d'ADN). Généralement, les personnes intéressées à prendre action sont l'enfant et le père dont la paternité n'est pas reconnue à l'acte de naissance.

[53] Art. 536 et 531(2) C.c.Q.

[54] Art. 531(2) C.c.Q.

[55] Voir les art. 582 et 149 C.c.Q., ainsi que les art. 823.1 et 823.2 du *Code de procédure civile*. Ce principe remonte à l'adoption de la *Loi de l'adoption*, L.Q. 1969, c. 64. Auparavant, la confidentialité des dossiers d'adoption découlait d'une coutume locale. Voir à ce sujet le document Association des centres jeunesse du Québec, *Guide de pratique professionnelle en matière d'antécédents sociobiologiques et de retrouvailles*, Montréal, 2003, à la p. 4 et Alain Roy, *Droit de l'adoption*, 2e éd., Wilson & Lafleur, 2010, à la p. 129.

[56] Art. 583 C.c.Q.

[57] *Ibid.*

[58] *Ibid.* Pour plus de détails, voir Roy, *supra* note 55, aux pp. 129 et s.

aires ou confidentiels dont la mise en œuvre exige la divulgation d'éléments autrement confidentiels ».[59] L'anonymat des parties impliquées doit cependant être respecté et le tribunal doit au préalable soupeser différents éléments importants, tels que « l'objectif, le sérieux et la nécessité de la demande, la portée de celle-ci eu égard à l'ordre public, la pertinence des renseignements recherchés, la possibilité que la consultation puisse malgré tout s'effectuer dans le respect de la confidentialité et, bien entendu, l'intérêt de l'enfant ».[60]

Une autre exception à la règle de la confidentialité permet à la personne adoptée (mineure ou majeure), ou à ses proches parents, d'obtenir des renseignements, avec l'autorisation du tribunal et de façon confidentielle, lorsqu'un préjudice grave risque d'être causé à leur santé.[61]

Depuis plusieurs années déjà, une proposition de réforme majeure du droit de l'adoption est en cours. À la suite du dépôt du rapport du groupe de travail sur le régime québécois de l'adoption,[62] deux projets de loi ont été déposés.[63] L'un et l'autre proposent un renversement du principe du secret de l'adoption. Une fois majeur, l'adopté aurait accès aux renseignements relatifs à ses parents d'origine sauf si ces derniers ont émis un veto interdisant la levée de la confidentialité de leur identité ou un veto interdisant le contact. Le principe serait alors renversé et la divulgation de l'identité des parties deviendrait sans doute la norme. En effet, la réforme proposée limite les situations et le délai pendant lequel l'inscription de ces vetos est possible. Quoi qu'il en soit, la réforme proposée va sans conteste vers une plus grande ouverture en matière d'adoption.[64] La réforme s'inscrit, par ailleurs, dans la perspective du Comité des Nations Unies qui a déjà critiqué le manque d'ouverture de la loi actuelle sur la question de l'accès aux origines.[65]

---

[59] Roy, *supra* note 55, aux pp. 130–131.

[60] Roy, *supra* note 55, à la p. 131.

[61] Art. 584 C.c.Q.

[62] Groupe de travail interministériel sur le régime québécois de l'adoption, sous la présidence de Carmen Lavallée, *Pour une adoption québécoise à la mesure de chaque enfant*, ministère de la Justice et ministère de la Santé et des Services sociaux, mars 2007, 135 pp.

[63] Voir les deux projets de loi récents suivants : *Projet de loi n°81 : Loi modifiant le Code civil et d'autres dispositions législatives en matière d'adoption et d'autorité parentale*, Assemblée nationale du Québec, 2e session, 39e législature, 2012 ; *Projet de loi n°47 : Loi modifiant le Code civil et d'autres dispositions législatives en matière d'adoption, d'autorité parentale et de divulgation de renseignements*, Assemblée nationale du Québec, 1e session, 40e législature, 2013.

[64] Carmen Lavallée et Michelle Giroux, « Le droit de l'enfant québécois à la connaissance de ses origines évalué à l'aune de la Convention internationale relative aux droits de l'enfant », (2013) 72 *R. du B.* 147.

[65] Comité des droits de l'enfant, *Observations finales 2e et 3e rapport,* 34e session, CRC/C/15/Add.215, 27 octobre 2003, aux para. 30 et 31.

6.3 Règles concernant la procréation médicalement assistée

Lorsqu'un enfant est conçu par procréation médicalement assistée avec don de gamètes, la confidentialité est également la règle.[66] Cette question a déjà fait l'objet de critiques.[67] En cas de risque de préjudice grave à l'enfant ainsi conçu ou à ses descendants, l'article 542 du Code civil permet cependant la transmission confidentielle de renseignements, aux autorités médicales concernées, sur autorisation du tribunal.

Le législateur fédéral a tenté de règlementer cet enjeu dans le cadre d'une loi encadrant la procréation médicalement assistée, en invoquant son pouvoir en matière de droit criminel.[68] La Cour suprême est cependant venue invalider plusieurs articles de cette loi, en raison de leur caractère *ultra vires*.[69] Il est donc maintenant clair que les provinces ont la compétence en cette matière. L'affaire *Pratten* en Colombie-Britannique constitue une tentative de faire reconnaître par les tribunaux le droit aux origines des enfants conçus par procréation assistée avec don de gamètes.[70] Bien que le tribunal de première instance ait conclu à la discrimination entre les enfants adoptés et les enfants conçus par procréation assistée avec don anonyme, car les premiers bénéficiaient d'un accès à leurs origines et pas les seconds, la Cour d'appel a renversé cette décision en précisant que les enfants adoptés bénéficiaient d'un programme de discrimination positive sous l'article 15 (2) de la Charte canadienne. Par la suite, la Cour suprême du Canada a rejeté une requête pour permission d'en appeler d'une décision de la Cour d'appel de la Colombie-Britannique,[71] confirmant ainsi la nécessité d'une action législative provinciale dans ce dossier.[72]

---

[66] Art. 542 C.c.Q. Pour une discussion critique de cette règle, voir Lavallée et Giroux, *supra* note 64.

[67] Voir notamment Canada, Senate, Standing Senate Committee on Human Rights, *Children: The Silenced Citizens. Effective Implementation Of Canada's International Obligations With Respect To The Rights Of Children*, Ottawa: Sénat, 2007. Voir aussi les recommandations de la CCDE, *supra* note 3, à la p. 49. On y retrouve une prise de position en faveur de la reconnaissance du droit aux origines pour les enfants adoptés et conçus par procréation médicalement assistée. On y suggère cependant une solution pan canadienne qui n'est pas nécessairement respectueuse de la constitution canadienne, qui prévoit que la question relève des provinces, tel que déjà mentionné.

[68] *Loi sur la procréation assistée*, L.C. 2004, ch. 2.

[69] *Renvoi relatif à la Loi sur la procréation assistée*, 2010 CSC 61, [2010] 3 RCS 457.

[70] *Pratten c. British Columbia (Attorney General)*, 2012 BCCA 480, CSC no 35191.

[71] *Ibid.*

[72] *Ibid.* Pour plus de détails à ce sujet, voir Lavallée et Giroux, *supra* note 64, ainsi que Michelle Giroux et Cheryl Milne, « The right to know one's origins, the *SCC Reference* and *Pratten v. AGBC* : a call for provincial legislative action », [à paraître].

7 L'opinion de l'enfant (art.12 et 13 de la CIDE)

Il n'y a pas si longtemps au Québec, l'enfant était davantage considéré comme un objet de droits plutôt que comme un sujet de droit à part entière. Il était alors presque complètement soumis à l'autorité des adultes. C'est seulement dans les années 1960 que la législation québécoise commence graduellement à reconnaître les enfants, à l'image des adultes, comme étant titulaires à part entière des droits et des libertés fondamentales.[73]

La reconnaissance de l'enfant en tant que sujet de droit s'est accompagnée du droit d'être entendu dans les litiges où son intérêt est en jeu. Une ancienne disposition législative, soit l'article 31 du *Code Civil du Bas-Canada*, prévoyait la possibilité pour le tribunal saisi d'une demande mettant en jeu l'intérêt d'un enfant, de lui donner l'occasion de se faire entendre. La loi actuelle limite le pouvoir discrétionnaire du tribunal. En vertu de l'article 34 du Code civil, lorsqu'un tribunal est saisi d'une demande mettant en jeu l'intérêt d'un enfant, ce dernier a le droit d'être entendu[74] pourvu que son âge et sa capacité de discernement le permettent.[75] Si l'enfant dispose d'une capacité de discernement suffisante, le tribunal a l'obligation de lui donner l'occasion de se faire entendre. La discrétion judiciaire porte maintenant sur la capacité de discernement de l'enfant et non plus sur l'opportunité de l'entendre ou non. Le législateur n'a pas cru bon de fixer un âge précis, mais l'âge constitue tout de même un critère parmi d'autres pour évaluer le discernement de l'enfant. Pour ces raisons, le Code civil est tout à fait conforme à l'article 12 de la Convention en ce qui concerne le droit de l'enfant d'être entendu.[76]

Conformément aux règles de la procédure civile, un enfant appelé à témoigner dans une instance judiciaire a également le droit d'être accompagné par une personne pouvant l'assister ou le rassurer.[77] Le juge peut également l'interroger sans la présence des parties après les en avoir informées. Cette manière de procéder peut s'avérer particulièrement pertinente dans les causes en matières familiales portant sur la garde ou l'attribution des droits d'accès de l'enfant à l'un de ses parents. Toutefois, les procureurs des parties sont normalement présents.

Le tribunal peut également choisir, à sa discrétion, d'entendre l'enfant au lieu où il réside ou à celui où il est gardé ou dans tout autre lieu qui lui paraît approprié.[78]

---

[73] Deleury et Goubau, *supra* note 12, à la p. 534.

[74] Une position confirmée en 2002 par la Cour d'appel du Québec dans la décision *F.(M.) c. L.(J.)*, [2002] CanLII 36783 (QC CA).

[75] Art. 34 C.c.Q. Voir également Michel Tétrault, *Droit de la famille*, 3e éd., Cowansville, Éditions Yvon Blais, 2005, à la p. 1246.

[76] Voir Carmen Lavallée, « La parole de l'enfant devant les instances civiles; une manifestation de son droit de participation selon la Convention internationale relative aux droits de l'enfant », dans *La parole et le droit, Rencontres juridiques Montpellier-Sherbrooke*, Sherbrooke, Éditions R.D.U.S., 2009, à la p.135.

[77] Art. 394.3 *Code de procédure civile.*

[78] Art. 394.4 *Code de procédure civile.*

Au-delà du droit d'être entendu, l'enfant dispose de plusieurs autres droits qui garantissent son droit de participation au sens de l'article 12 de la Convention. En effet, l'enfant a le droit à la représentation par un avocat, un droit garanti par les Chartes et par les différentes législations applicables aux enfants tant en matière de protection de la jeunesse qu'en matière pénale. Au plan civil, l'article 394.1 du *Code de procédure civile* prévoit que dans une instance où l'intérêt d'un mineur est en jeu, le tribunal, doit, même d'office, ajourner la demande jusqu'à ce qu'un procureur soit nommé à l'enfant. De plus, la nomination d'un avocat pour représenter l'enfant n'est pas liée à son statut de partie, ce qui laisse un vaste pouvoir au tribunal de nommer un procureur chaque fois que la chose est nécessaire pour assurer le respect des droits de l'enfant.[79]

Finalement, l'exercice des droits civils de l'enfant relève de la tutelle légale exercée par les parents.[80] Ainsi, les actions en justice de l'enfant sont, en principe, portées au nom de son tuteur. Si l'intérêt de l'enfant est opposé à celui de son tuteur, le tribunal doit lui nommer un tuteur *ad hoc*.[81] En revanche, le Code civil prévoit que l'enfant peut exercer lui-même certains droits sans être représenté par son tuteur. En effet, s'il est préalablement autorisé par le tribunal, l'enfant peut exercer seul les actions relatives à son état, à l'exercice de l'autorité parentale ou à un acte à l'égard duquel il peut agir seul.[82] Dans ce contexte, l'enfant pourra lui-même mandater un avocat pour le représenter.

8 Adoption de l'enfant (art. 21 de la CIDE)

8.1 Consentement à son adoption

Le Code civil permet à l'enfant âgé de 10 ans et plus de prendre part de façon progressive au processus d'adoption. Ainsi, bien que le consentement à l'adoption ne soit pas spécifiquement requis pour les enfants de moins de 10 ans, le tribunal est tout de même tenu de veiller à leur intérêt et doit leur permettre d'être entendus si leur âge et discernement le permettent.[83]

Les enfants âgés de 10 ans ou plus doivent participer au processus d'adoption. Leur consentement doit être libre et éclairé, et il doit être maintenu tout au long de

[79] Lavallée, *supra* note 8, à la p. 20.

[80] Art. 192 C.c.Q.

[81] Art. 394.2 *Code de procédure civile*.

[82] Art. 159 C.c.Q. Par exemple, en matière de changement de nom, voir l'art. 66 C.c.Q.

[83] Roy, *supra* note 55, à la p. 105. Pour une analyse détaillée de la place de l'enfant dans le processus d'adoption en France et au Québec, voir Carmen Lavallée, *L'enfant, ses familles, et les institutions de l'adoption; regards sur le droit français et québécois*, Montréal, Wilson et Lafleur, 2005, aux pp. 299 et s.

la procédure d'adoption.[84] Ce consentement doit également être donné par écrit et devant témoins.[85]

L'enfant âgé entre 10 et 14 ans et qui s'oppose à son adoption n'y fera cependant pas nécessairement obstacle. Par contre, le tribunal devra considérer ce refus sérieusement afin de déterminer si l'adoption est dans son meilleur intérêt ou non.[86]

Le refus d'un enfant de 14 ans et plus à son adoption fait pour sa part complètement obstacle à la démarche. Il détient à cet égard un véritable droit de *veto*.[87]

8.2 Conditions de l'adoption internationale

En ce qui concerne l'adoption internationale, il existe deux cadres juridiques applicables selon que l'enfant est originaire d'un pays signataire de la *Convention de La Haye sur la protection des enfants et la coopération en matière d'adoption internationale* [Convention de La Haye] ou non.[88]

En effet, le Canada est signataire de la Convention de La Haye depuis le 12 avril 1994, l'a ratifiée le 19 décembre 1996 et elle est entrée en vigueur au Canada le 1er avril 1997.[89] En vertu de la Constitution canadienne, l'adoption est un champ de compétence provinciale. Chaque province ou territoire doit donc intégrer les principes de la Convention dans le droit provincial ou territorial. Au Québec, la Convention est applicable en vertu de la *Loi sur la mise en œuvre de la Convention sur la protection des enfants et la coopération en matière d'adoption internationale et modifiant diverses dispositions législatives en matière d'adoption*.[90] En 2012, environ 75 % des enfants adoptés au Québec proviennent d'un pays signataire de la Convention de La Haye.[91] Il s'agit donc de la manière la plus fréquente de procéder à l'adoption

---

[84] À moins d'être absolument dans l'impossibilité de le donner, par exemple en raison de l'état de santé mentale. Voir Roy, *supra* note 55, à la p. 104.

[85] Art. 548 C.c.Q. Voir également Roy, *supra* note 55, à la p. 106, *A.V. (Dans la situation de)*, [2001] R.J.Q. 809 (C.Q.) et *Adoption – 08304*, [2009] R.D.F. 219 (C.Q.).

[86] Dans un tel cas, le tribunal a un pouvoir discrétionnaire. Il peut refuser l'adoption, différer son jugement ou décider de prononcer tout de même l'adoption. Voir l'art. 549(2) C.c.Q.

[87] Art. 550 C.c.Q. Voir également ROY, supra note 55, à la p. 106.

[88] Conférence de La Haye de droit international privé, *33. Convention du 29 mai 1993 sur la protection des enfants et la coopération en matière d'adoption internationale*. Pour l'historique complet de cette convention, voir *Conférence de La Haye de droit international privé*, actes et documents de la 71e session (1993), tome II, *Adoption – coopération*. Ces documents sont disponibles en ligne : www.hcch.net.

[89] *Recueil des traités du Canada*, 1997, no 1, 1997/12.

[90] *Loi sur la mise en œuvre de la Convention sur la protection des enfants et la coopération en matière d'adoption internationale et modifiant diverses dispositions législatives en matière d'adoption*, L.Q. 2004, c. 3. Pour plus d'information voir, Carmen Lavallée, « La Convention sur la protection des enfants et la coopération en matière d'adoption internationale et sa mise en œuvre en droit québécois », (2005) 35 *R.D.U.S.* 356–374.

[91] Selon les statistiques du Secrétariat à l'adoption internationale du Québec, voir, en ligne : http://adoption.gouv.qc.ca/accueil.phtml.

d'un enfant étranger. Si le droit du pays d'origine délègue le pouvoir de prononcer l'adoption au pays de l'adoptant, ce dernier devra présenter une requête en ordonnance de placement préalable au jugement d'adoption.[92] Avant de prononcer l'ordonnance de placement, le tribunal doit s'assurer que toutes les conditions prescrites par la loi ont été respectées, autant celles de la loi québécoise que celles de la loi du pays d'origine de l'enfant.[93] À la fin de la durée du placement, le tribunal prononcera l'adoption plénière de l'enfant, sur la preuve qui lui sera faite de l'intégration de l'enfant à sa famille adoptive.[94]

Si l'adoption a été prononcée dans le pays d'origine de l'enfant avant son départ, il y aura reconnaissance de plein droit de l'adoption sur présentation par les adoptants du certificat de conformité délivré par les autorités étrangères.[95] Après avoir procédé aux vérifications d'usage, le Secrétariat à l'adoption internationale, qui constitue l'autorité centrale au sens de la Convention de La Haye, atteste de la conformité de l'adoption avec la Convention de La Haye. Cette adoption est alors reconnue de plein droit comme si elle avait été prononcée au Québec.[96]

Si le pays d'accueil de l'enfant n'est pas signataire de la Convention de La Haye, il faut voir à qui revient la responsabilité de prononcer l'adoption. Si l'adoption de l'enfant est prononcée avant son départ pour l'étranger, les adoptants devront déposer une requête en reconnaissance d'une adoption étrangère. Le tribunal doit alors s'assurer que les règles concernant les consentements et l'admissibilité de l'enfant à l'adoption ont été respectées.[97]

Si l'adoption doit être prononcée au Québec, elle devra être précédée d'une requête en ordonnance de placement.[98] Le tribunal prononcera l'adoption au terme du placement, sur la preuve que l'enfant s'est intégré à sa famille adoptive.[99]

9 Le droit de l'enfant à la liberté de pensée, de conscience et de religion (art. 14 de la CIDE)

Il n'existe pas de protection spécifique du droit de l'enfant sur cette question. Les libertés de pensée, de conscience et de religion de l'enfant sont protégées, comme celle de toute autre personne par les chartes canadienne et québécoise.[100] La religion

---

[92] Art. 565 C.c.Q.

[93] Pour plus de détails concernant les difficultés d'arrimage du droit des pays d'origine et d'accueil des enfants en matière d'adoption internationale, voir LAVALLÉE, *supra* note 90, aux pp. 158 et s.

[94] Art. 573 C.c.Q.

[95] Art. 565 C.c.Q.

[96] Cette vérification porte sur le respect des conditions de la loi étrangère, selon l'article 3092 C.c.Q. Pour plus d'informations, voir ROY, *supra* note 55, aux pp. 177 et s.

[97] Art. 574 C.c.Q.

[98] Art. 565 C.c.Q.

[99] Art. 573 C.c.Q.

[100] Charte canadienne, *supra* note 20, à l'art. 2, Charte québécoise, *supra* note 24, à l'art. 3.

de l'enfant peut aussi être prise en considération dans la détermination de son intérêt. En cas de litige entre les parents portant sur la garde, les tribunaux insistent sur les effets sur l'enfant de la pratique d'une religion dans l'évaluation de son meilleur intérêt, sans pour autant s'immiscer dans le conflit de valeurs en jeu entre les parents.[101]

L'école n'est plus responsable de l'éducation religieuse des enfants; les parents doivent s'en charger. Dans un contexte où plusieurs confessions religieuses coexistent dans la société, l'État s'implique afin de favoriser le dialogue et une meilleure compréhension de la diversité religieuse. Il guide l'enfant en lui procurant des connaissances générales de base. Au Québec, par exemple, le cours d'*Éthique et culture religieuse* a été développé par le ministère de l'Éducation, du Loisir et du Sport. Il est obligatoire depuis 2008 dans toutes les écoles publiques ou subventionnées du Québec, tant au niveau primaire que secondaire. Le cours se fonde sur divers éléments relatifs à la morale, à l'éthique, ainsi qu'à la compréhension de la diversité religieuse du Canada et d'ailleurs dans le monde. Le ministère estime que ce cours peut contribuer à des relations sociales plus harmonieuses et au respect des différences. Le cours vise ainsi à favoriser chez les jeunes une réflexion sur les questions éthiques et religieuses.[102] Des parents ont voulu remettre en question, mais sans succès, l'enseignement obligatoire de ce cours en alléguant qu'il portait atteinte à la liberté de conscience et de religion prévues à l'article 2a de la *Charte canadienne* et à l'article 3 de la *Charte québécoise*.[103]

10 Encadrement du châtiment corporel à l'égard des enfants (art. 19 de la CIDE)

La loi ne prohibe pas expressément le châtiment corporel à l'égard des enfants. Toutefois, si la correction infligée est telle qu'elle peut être assimilée à des mauvais traitements ou à des abus physiques, ce comportement doit faire l'objet d'un signalement en vertu de la *Loi sur la protection de la jeunesse*.[104] De plus, l'usage de la force à l'endroit d'un enfant peut donner lieu à des accusations de voies de fait[105] et entrainer une accusation criminelle, comme c'est le cas lorsque la victime n'est pas un enfant. Toutefois, dans le cas des enfants, l'article 43 du *Code criminel*, applicable partout au Canada, prévoit que la personne accusée peut alors invoquer

[101] *Young* c. *Young*, *supra* note 39.

[102] Voir le « Programme de formation de l'école québécoise », ministère de l'Éducation, du Loisir et du Sport, gouvernement du Québec, en ligne : http://www1.mels.gouv.qc.ca/sections/programmeFormation/. Pour une analyse plus détaillée à ce sujet, voir André Duhamel et Mireille Estivalèzes, « Vivre ensemble et dialogue : du programme québécois d'éthique et culture religieuse à la délibération démocratique », (2013) 48 : 1 *McGill Journal of Education* 79.

[103] Voir notamment *S.L.* c. *Commission scolaire des Chênes*, 2012 CSC 7, [2012] 1 R.C.S. 235.

[104] Art. 38 de la *Loi sur la protection de la jeunesse*, *supra* note 26.

[105] Art. 265(1) du *Code criminel*, L.R.C. (1985), ch. C-46.

la défense de l'article 43. Cet article se lit ainsi : « Tout instituteur, père et mère est fondé à employer la force pour corriger un enfant [...] pourvu que la force ne dépasse pas la mesure raisonnable dans les circonstances ». Cet article est apparu dans le *Code criminel* en 1892 et n'a pratiquement pas été modifié depuis, sauf pour en retirer l'application aux patrons à l'égard des apprentis. En 2004, une coalition d'organismes canadiens voués à la protection des droits de l'enfant a tenté de faire déclarer inconstitutionnel cet article sur le fondement qu'il constituait une atteinte aux droits à l'égalité et à la dignité des enfants.[106]

Or, la Cour suprême du Canada a confirmé la constitutionnalité de cette disposition.[107] En effet, 6 des 9 juges ont considéré que l'article 43 ne contrevient pas à la Charte canadienne des droits et libertés. Pour la majorité, l'expression « la mesure raisonnable » n'est pas suffisamment imprécise pour constituer une atteinte à la sécurité des enfants en contravention des principes de justice fondamentale. Selon les juges majoritaires, l'usage de la force doit poursuivre un but éducatif et le type et le degré de force doivent être limités. Selon eux, l'enfant doit être en mesure de comprendre la correction et d'en tirer profit, ce qui implique qu'elle ne peut être utilisée à l'encontre d'un enfant de moins de 2 ans ou d'un enfant présentant une déficience particulière. Elle ne doit pas non plus être utilisée contre les adolescents, car elle risque de déclencher des comportements agressifs ou antisociaux. Enfin, elle ne doit pas être appliquée avec des objets, tels que des bâtons, des règles ou des ceintures et ne doit pas viser la tête de l'enfant.

Le fait que les juges majoritaires soient obligés de faire toutes ces nuances démontre bien, selon nous, le caractère imprécis de l'article 43. Une position partagée par la juge Arbour qui aurait invalidé cet article justement à cause de ce motif.[108] L'étude de la jurisprudence canadienne démontre d'ailleurs une absence de consensus judiciaire sur la portée de cette expression. Pour sa part, la juge Deschamps aurait invalidé, elle aussi, la disposition parce que selon elle : « en justifiant ce qui autrement équivaudrait à des voies de fait criminelles, l'art. 43 encourage l'opinion selon laquelle les enfants ne méritent pas la même protection, ni le même respect de leur intégrité que les adultes, opinion qui est fondée sur l'idée désuète que les enfants sont des personnes de statut inférieur ».[109] Le juge Binnie, lui aussi dissident, affirme que cet article porte atteinte au droit à l'égalité et à la dignité des enfants, mais l'atteinte lui apparaît justifiée dans le cadre d'une société libre et démocratique, à l'égard des parents seulement et non des instituteurs. Cette

---

[106] Voir notamment Durrant, J.E., Ensom, R., and Coalition on Physical Punishment of Children and Youth (2004). *Joint Statement on Physical Punishment of Children and Youth*, Ottawa, Coalition on Physical Punishment of Children and Youth, également disponible en français sous le titre : *Déclaration conjointe sur les punitions corporelles données aux enfants et aux adolescents.*

[107] *Canadian Foundation for Children, Youth and the Law* c. *Canada (Procureur général)*, *supra* note 41. Pour une analyse plus approfondie de cette décision, voir Katie Sykes, « Bambi Meets Godzilla: Children's and Parents' Rights in Canadian Foundation for Children, Youth and the Law v. Canada », (2005–2006) 51 *McGill L.J.* 131.

[108] *Canadian Foundation for Children, Youth and the Law* c. *Canada (Procureur général)*, *Ibid.* aux para. 132 et s.

[109] *Ibid.* au para. 232.

justification repose sur la nécessité de limiter l'ingérence du droit criminel dans la vie familiale. Pour lui, il est beaucoup moins impérieux de garder les écoles que les parents à l'abri des sanctions pénales.[110]

À la suite de ce jugement et du refus du législateur canadien d'abroger l'article 43 du *Code criminel*, le Canada fait face à des critiques de la part du Comité des droits de l'enfant de l'ONU sur cette question. Dans ses observations à la suite du dépôt des troisième et quatrième rapports périodiques du Canada,[111] le comité fait état d'une profonde préoccupation quant au fait que les châtiments corporels continuent d'être tolérés par la loi. Le Comité invite clairement le Canada à abroger l'article 43 afin d'interdire expressément toute forme de violence, même légère, contre les enfants. De plus, le Comité invite le Canada à développer la sensibilisation des parents, des professionnels et du public en général, aux autres formes de discipline destinées aux enfants afin de promouvoir le respect des droits de l'enfant.

11 Règles concernant la déchéance de l'autorité parentale et le retrait de certains attributs (art. 18 de la CIDE)

La loi prévoit la possibilité de retirer totalement l'autorité parentale à l'égard de la ou des personnes qui l'exercent (souvent le père, la mère ou les deux), lorsqu'il existe des motifs graves et si l'intérêt de l'enfant le justifie.[112] Dans tous les cas, cette décision revient au tribunal. Des exemples de motifs graves sont l'abandon fautif de l'enfant,[113] mais également le cas où le parent a commis un crime affectant l'enfant, celui où le parent a été négligent et n'a pas respecté ses obligations parentales ou a abusé de son autorité, sexuellement ou autrement.[114]

Si les circonstances ne justifient pas une mesure aussi sévère que la déchéance, le tribunal peut opter pour le retrait d'un attribut de l'autorité parentale (notamment, de la garde ou de l'éducation) ou pour le retrait de l'exercice de cet attribut (par exemple, de l'exercice de la garde).[115]

---

[110] *Ibid.*, aux para. 71 et s.

[111] *Ibid.*, aux para. 212 et s. et Comité des droits de l'enfant, *supra* note 2, à la p. 10.

[112] Conformément aux art. 606 et 607 C.c.Q. Voir aussi *T.V.-F.* c. *C.*, [1987] 2 R.C.S. 244.

[113] À ce sujet, voir notamment l'étude de Marie-Noëlle Pourbaix, « L'abandon des enfants : du Québec à la France en passant par l'Ontario », (1996) 29 *R.G.D.* 133, aux pp. 156 et s. ainsi que Pineau et Pratte, *supra* note 51, aux pp. 869–871.

[114] Pour plus de détails sur les conditions de fond pouvant mener à la déchéance de l'autorité parentale, voir Mireille D. Castelli et Dominique Goubau, *Le droit de la famille au Québec*, 5e éd., Les presses de l'Université Laval, 2005, à la p. 359, ainsi que Pineau et Pratte, *supra* note 51, aux pp. 868 et s.

[115] Art. 606(2) C.c.Q. Dans ce cas, il est alors question de « retrait » de certains attributs de l'autorité parentale. Voir par exemple *Droit de la famille – 2212*, [1995] J.E., 95–1454 (C.A.). Pour une discussion plus approfondie, voir Castelli et Goubau, *supra* note 114, aux pp. 358 et s. ainsi que Pineau et Pratte, *supra* note 51, aux pp. 866 et s.

La déchéance de l'autorité parentale entraine la perte totale de la jouissance et de l'exercice de leur autorité parentale, à l'égard de tous les enfants mineurs nés au moment du jugement,[116] sous réserve pour le tribunal d'en décider autrement.[117] Cependant, elle ne rompt pas le lien de filiation entre l'enfant et le parent déchu. La déchéance entraine également une dispense de l'obligation alimentaire pour l'enfant envers le parent déchu, et ce, bien que le parent déchu conserve pleinement son obligation alimentaire envers l'enfant.[118] Si l'intérêt de l'enfant le commande, la déchéance de l'autorité parentale peut entrainer accessoirement un changement de nom de l'enfant.[119] De plus, la déchéance peut ouvrir la porte à l'admissibilité de l'enfant à l'adoption,[120] ou encore à la perte du droit pour le parent d'hériter de l'enfant, pour cause d'indignité.[121]

La déchéance et le retrait de l'autorité parentale ne sont pas irréversibles, à moins qu'il y ait eu rupture du lien de filiation.[122] Dans certains cas, il est donc possible que le parent retrouve ultérieurement ses droits, s'il fait la preuve de « circonstances nouvelles ».[123]

Dans tous les cas, l'objectif de ces mesures est d'assurer la protection de l'enfant. Toute personne intéressée peut en faire la demande au tribunal. Ce dernier désignera la personne qui exercera l'autorité parentale, ou son attribut, après la déchéance. Si les deux parents dont déchus ou si la filiation n'est établie qu'à l'égard du parent déchu, le tribunal peut nommer un tuteur à l'enfant,[124] Dans ces circonstances, l'enfant pourrait également faire l'objet d'un placement en famille d'accueil ou être adopté.

12 Droits de l'enfant et consentement aux soins médicaux (art. 24 de la CIDE)

Le *Code civil du Québec* accorde une grande place à l'autonomie de la personne, y compris aux mineurs. Le Code opère une distinction entre l'enfant âgé de moins de 14 ans et celui de 14 ans et plus.[125] Le premier n'est pas considéré comme étant apte

---

[116] Pour une discussion sur la non-applicabilité aux enfants à naître et les difficultés pratiques que cela peut entraîner, voir Jean Pineau, *La famille : droit applicable au lendemain de la « loi 89 »*, Montréal, Presses de l'Université de Montréal, 1983, à la p. 289.

[117] Art. 608 C.c.Q.

[118] Art. 609 C.c.Q.

[119] Art 65 C.c.Q.

[120] Art. 559(3) C.c.Q.

[121] Art. 609 et 620(2) C.c.Q.

[122] Voir les art. 609 et 610 C.c.Q., ainsi que l'art 826.1 du *Code de procédure civile*.

[123] Art. 610 C.c.Q. Voir également Castelli et Goubau, *supra* note 114, à la p. 363.

[124] Pour une discussion plus détaillée sur la déchéance de l'autorité parentale et ses effets, voir Tétrault, *supra* note 75, aux pp. 1399 et s., Castelli et Goubau, *supra* note 114, aux pp. 361 et s., ainsi que Pineau et Pratte, *supra* note 51, aux pp. 866 et s.

[125] Pour une discussion détaillée sur le consentement aux soins et le droit à l'intégrité physique des mineurs, voir Deleury et Goubau, *supra* note 12, aux pp. 111 et s. et Michelle Giroux, *Medical*

à donner son consentement aux soins; ses parents consentent pour lui. Ils prennent la décision selon l'intérêt de l'enfant, en soupesant les risques et les bénéfices du traitement proposé. Les volontés de cet enfant pourront être considérées, dans la mesure du possible.[126] Des mesures de protection additionnelles s'appliquent lorsqu'il s'agit de soins non requis par l'état de santé de l'enfant. L'autorisation du tribunal sera au surplus nécessaire « si les soins présentent un risque sérieux pour la santé ou s'ils peuvent causer des effets graves et permanents ».[127] L'enfant de moins de 14 ans peut cependant refuser lui-même des soins qui ne sont pas requis par son état de santé.[128]

Le mineur âgé de 14 ans et plus peut généralement consentir seul aux soins.[129] Tout comme pour le mineur de 14 ans et moins, il est impossible de lui imposer des soins qui ne sont pas requis par son état de santé.[130]

13 Droits de l'enfant et changement de nom

À partir de l'âge de 14 ans, un enfant peut présenter lui-même une demande de changement de nom par voie judiciaire dans les cas précis de changement dans la filiation, d'abandon ou de déchéance de l'autorité parentale, sous réserve d'aviser son titulaire de l'autorité parentale ou, le cas échéant, son tuteur.[131] Avant cet âge, le mineur ne peut faire seul une demande de changement de nom par voie administrative. C'est au tuteur de la faire, au nom du mineur, et à condition d'avoir « un motif sérieux ».[132]

Law Québec, dans Kluwer Law *International, International Encyclopaedia of Laws series, Medical Law – Suppl. 58 (June 2009)*, Kluwer Law International BV, The Netherlands, 2009, aux para. 300 à 313.

[126] Art. 12 C.c.Q. Cet article est modifié par l'article 66 de la *Loi concernant les soins de fin de vie,* L.Q. 2014, c. 2, dont l'entrée en vigueur est prévue le 10 décembre 2015. Dorénavant, les volontés devront être « respectées » dans la mesure du possible. Dans les provinces de common law, l'âge auquel un mineur peut consentir aux soins varie. Par exemple, la loi manitobaine établit la limite à 16 ans. Dans les autres provinces et territoires du Canada, la règle du *mineur mature* vient apporter des nuances à ces règles lorsque le mineur a atteint un degré de maturité considéré comme étant suffisant pour pouvoir consentir seul à ses soins, et ce même s'il n'a pas encore atteint l'âge fixé par la loi. Voir *A.C.* c. *Manitoba (Directeur des services à l'enfant et à la famille),* [2009] 2 R.C.S. 181.

[127] Art. 18 C.c.Q.

[128] Art. 23 C.c.Q.

[129] Art. 14(2) C.c.Q.

[130] Art. 23(2) C.c.Q. et, pour plus de détails, Deleury et Goubau, *supra* note 12, à la p. 133.

[131] Art. 65 et 66 C.c.Q.

[132] Art. 58 et 60 C.c.Q.

14 Droits de l'enfant et conditions pour accéder au marché du travail (art. 32 de la CIDE)

En cette matière, les règles varient grandement d'une province et d'un territoire à l'autre et ne respectent pas toujours l'article 32 de la Convention.[133] En vertu de la *Loi sur l'instruction publique,*[134] l'enfant doit fréquenter l'école jusqu'à 16 ans. Toutefois, la loi n'interdit pas à l'enfant de travailler à temps partiel. En revanche, la *Loi sur les normes minimales de travail*[135] prévoit un encadrement du travail des enfants.

De manière générale, un employeur ne peut pas demander à un enfant d'exercer un travail qui excède ses capacités, compromet son éducation ou affecte négativement sa santé ou son développement physique ou psychologique. La loi interdit à un employeur de faire travailler un enfant tenu de fréquenter l'école durant les heures régulières de classe. Sauf exception, un employeur ne peut pas non plus faire travailler un enfant de nuit, c'est-à-dire entre 23 h 00 et 6 h 00. De plus, avant de faire travailler un enfant âgé de moins de 14 ans, tout employeur doit au préalable obtenir l'accord du titulaire de l'autorité parentale, ou du tuteur, le cas échéant.

L'enfant peut donc travailler, mais sous certaines conditions. Le Code civil respecte le principe de l'acquisition progressive de la capacité de l'enfant, car l'article 156 prévoit que « le mineur de 14 ans et plus est considéré comme une personne majeure pour tous les actes relatifs à son emploi, ou à l'exercice de son art ou de sa profession ». Ainsi, à partir de 14 ans, l'enfant est considéré comme étant apte à prendre ses propres décisions relativement à son emploi ou sa profession. Le mineur de 14 ans et plus se voit ainsi accorder une pleine capacité dans le cadre de son travail. Il peut donc, avec l'autorisation du tribunal, intenter seul une action en justice relative à l'exercice de ce travail.[136]

De manière générale, le mineur gère également le produit de son travail qu'il peut utiliser pour combler ses besoins ordinaires et usuels.[137] Il peut, si son âge et son discernement le permettent, contracter seul dans le but de satisfaire ce type de besoins.[138] Toutefois, si les revenus du mineur sont considérables, ou si les circonstances le requièrent, le tribunal peut limiter les sommes qu'il est autorisé à gérer.[139]

---

[133] Voir le rapport de la CCDE, *supra* note 3, aux pp. 34 et s. Voir également les observations du Comité des droits de l'enfant, *supra* note 2, aux para. 79 et 80.

[134] *Loi sur l'instruction publique*, L.R.Q., c. I-13.3, art. 14.

[135] *Loi sur les normes du travail*, L.R.Q., c. N-1.1, art. 84.2 à 84.7.

[136] Art. 159 C.c.Q.

[137] Art. 220 C.c.Q.

[138] Art. 157 C.c.Q.

[139] Art. 220 C.c.Q.

15 Obligations de l'enfant à l'égard de ses parents

Au Québec, les enfants ont deux principales obligations envers leurs parents. Premièrement, le Code civil impose en tout temps à l'enfant l'obligation de respecter ses parents. Cette disposition a un poids surtout moral puisqu'aucune sanction précise n'est prévue en cas de non-respect.[140]

Deuxièmement, les enfants dont la filiation est établie sont tenus à une obligation alimentaire envers leurs parents. L'obligation alimentaire au Québec existe en effet entre les ascendants et les descendants. Il s'agit d'une obligation d'ordre public, réciproque, mais limité au premier degré. Il n'existe donc pas d'obligation alimentaire entre l'enfant et ses grands-parents, du moins depuis son abolition en 1996.[141]

16 Conclusion

En conclusion, sans avoir explicitement mis en œuvre la *Convention*, le Canada fait bonne figure et respecte généralement les principes qui y sont énoncés. Certains enjeux demeurent cependant moins bien pris en compte par le Canada. Comme les remarques préliminaires le précisaient, les difficultés que soulève la mise en œuvre de la *Convention* dans un État fédéral ne doivent pas justifier un dialogue défaillant ou un manque de collaboration et de coopération, de même qu'un meilleur partage des ressources entre les différents ordres de gouvernement. Il faut poursuivre la mise en œuvre de cet instrument fondamental de protection des droits de l'enfant, plus particulièrement dans certains secteurs. Bien que le rapport ne comportait pas de question spécifique sur les droits et la situation des enfants autochtones (art. 30 de la CIDE), voilà un secteur qui, à titre d'exemple, mérite assurément plus d'attention de la part du gouvernement canadien.

[140] Art. 597 C.c.Q. Voir également l'article de Nicholas Kasirer, « Honour Bound », (2001–2002) 46 *R.D. McGill* 239.

[141] Art. 585 C.c.Q.

The Rights of the Child: Croatian National Report

Nenad Hlača and Sandra Winkler

1 Introduction

The Republic of Croatia became a party to the UN Convention on the Right of the Child on the basis of the succession notification (the Convention was ratified by the former Socialist Federal Republic of Yugoslavia).[1]

The Republic of Croatia became a party to the Convention on 8 October 1991.

Given that the Republic of Croatia succeeded to most of the international treaties the former Yugoslavia State was a party to, one must bear in mind the Constitutional Decision on Sovereignty and Independence of the Republic of Croatia of 1991, which says that the international conventions, to which the Socialist Federal Republic of Yugoslavia was a party, remain in force in the Republic of Croatia, providing it is not contrary to the Constitution and the legal order of the Republic of Croatia.

In addition, Article 141 of the Constitution of the Republic of Croatia provides that once the international treaty has been concluded and ratified in accordance with the Constitution, published and in force, it is a part of the domestic legal order and has a primacy over the domestic law.[2]

---

[1] Konvencija o pravima djeteta, Narodne novine – Međunarodni ugovori, br. 12/93, 20/97 (*Convention on the Rights of the Child, Official Gazette of the Republic of Croatia – International Treaties, No. 12/93, 20/97*).

[2] Ustav RH, Narodne novine, br. 56/90, 135/97, 8/98 (pročišćeni tekst), 113/00, 124/00 (pročišćeni tekst), 28/01, 41/01 (pročišćeni tekst), 55/01 (ispravak), 76/10 i 85/10 (pročišćeni tekst) (Constitution *of Croatia, Official Gazette of the Republic of Croatia, No 56/90, 135/97, 8/98 (consolidated version), 113/00, 124/00 (consolidated text), 28/01, 41/01 (consolidated text), 55/01 (correction), 76/10 and 85/10 (consolidated version).*

N. Hlača (✉) • S. Winkler
Family Law Department, Faculty of Law, University of Rijeka,
Hahlić 6, HR-51000 Rijeka, Croatia
e-mail: neno@pravri.hr; swinkler@pravri.hr

O. Cvejić Jančić (ed.), *The Rights of the Child in a Changing World*,
Ius Comparatum - Global Studies in Comparative Law 13,
DOI 10.1007/978-3-319-23189-1_4

2 Definition of the Child Under Croatian Law

There is no such provision in the domestic law that expressly provides the age below which a human being is deemed to be a child (as it is regulated under Article 1 of the Convention).

However, Article 120 of the Family Act which deals with the legal capacity issue prescribing that one shall acquire a legal capacity either by way of becoming 18 (legal age) or by entering into marriage (as a minor at the age of 16, at least).[3] The latter assumes that a minor has become a parent and the court decision has been rendered in this respect (in a non-litigation procedure).

3 Framework for Protection of the Rights of the Child

There are several provisions (Article 63, Article 64 and Article 65) in the Constitution of the Republic of Croatia dealing with the rights of the child.

Article 63 expressly provides that the State shall protect motherhood, children and youths.

Pursuant to Article 64, paragraph 2, "parents shall be responsible for ensuring the right of their children to the full and harmonious development of their personalities".

Finally, Article 65 stands as a bottom line, imposing the duty to protect children and incapable persons to the whole community and ensuring the protection of children and other "weak" persons in respect of the employment. To be precise, Article 65 paragraph 2 says: "children shall not be employed before reaching the age specified by law, nor shall they be forced or allowed to do any work that is harmful to their health or morality". Article 65 paragraph 3 says: "young people, mothers and disabled persons shall be entitled to special protection at work".

International conventions, according to Article 141 of the Constitution of the Republic of Croatia, form part of the Croatian legal system. Hence, the UN Convention on the Rights of the Child is part of the Croatian legal system too and, what is more, has a primacy over domestic law.

Although both the Constitution and the international conventions are very important, they represent guiding principles only. This means that the main rules are to be created by the laws. In this respect, the rights of the child in the Croatian legal system are predominantly regulated under the Family Act (although not exclusively). In first place it is the section on "Rights and Responsibilities of the Child" (Articles 87 to 90) and the one on "Parental Care" (Articles 91 to 107). The section that starts

[3] Obiteljski zakon, Narodne novine, br. 116/03, 17/04, 136/04, 107/07, 57/11, 61/11, 25/13 (Family Act, *Official Gazette of the Republic of Croatia, No. 116/03, 17/04, 136/04, 107/07, 57/11, 61/11, 25/13*).

with Article 108, on the other hand, prescribes the measures for the protection of the rights and welfare of the child.

Although the Croatian Family Act regulates the majority of the rights of the child, it is worth to mention some other sources as well, such as the Act on the Protection from Domestic Violence,[4] the Personal Name Act,[5] the Medically Assisted Procreation Act,[6] the Act on the Ombudsman for Children,[7] the Act on the Protection of Patients' Rights[8] and the Labour Act.[9]

4 Best Interests Principle

A general provision about BIC is to be found in Article 2 of the Croatian Family Act, which deals with principles the regulation on family relationships is based on. When it comes to the rights of the child, it is worth noting the phrase the legislator is using, i.e. "the protection of wellbeing and rights of the child (…)".

There is no specific definition of the "best interest of the child". However, the doctrine suggests some criteria to be used for the identification of the child's interest, i.e. the child's needs, the parent's will and the ordinary behaviour. Furthermore, the Croatian doctrine observes that the identification of the interest of the child is a very hard and delicate issue. For these reasons, the Croatian legislator decided to use the term "wellbeing" instead of "interest of the child". "Wellbeing" is considered more comprehensive and appropriate expression than interest of the child, because it reflects the "whole, optimal status of the child."[10]

In addition to Article 2 of the Family Act, which can be considered as a general rule, there are many other provisions dealing with the wellbeing of the child in more details.

Article 87 paragraph 3 and paragraph 4 of the Family Act, for example, provide that the child shall have the right to live with his/her parents in accordance with his/her wellbeing. Article 87 paragraph 4 gives the child the right to choose the education and the occupation in accordance with his/her abilities and wellbeing.

---

[4] Zakon o zaštiti od nasilja u obitelji, Narodne novine, br. 137/09, 14/10, 60/10 (*Act on the protection of* domestic violence, *Official Gazette of the Republic of Croatia, No. 137/09, 14/10, 60/10*).

[5] Zakon o osobnom imenu, Narodne novine, br. 118/12 (Personal name *Act, Official Gazette of the Republic of Croatia, No. 118/12*).

[6] Zakon o medicinski pomognutoj oplodnji, Narodne novine, br. 86/12 (*Medically assisted procreation Act, Official Gazette of the Republic of Croatia, No. 86/12*).

[7] Zakon o Pravobranitelju za djecu, Narodne novine, br. 96/03 (*Children's Ombudsperson's Act, Official Gazette of the Republic of Croatia, No. 96/03*).

[8] Zakon o zaštiti prava pacijenata, Narodne novine, br. 169/04, 37/08 (*Act on the Protection of Patients' Rights, Official Gazette, No. 169/04, 37/08*).

[9] Zakon o radu, Narodne novine, br. 149/09, 61/11, 82/12, 73/13 (*Labour Act, Official Gazette RC, No. 149/09, 61/11, 82/12, 73/13*).

[10] Quoting Hrabar, D., in Alinčić et al., Obiteljsko pravo, Narodne novine, 2007, p. 237.

Article 91 paragraph 1 of the Family Act regulates the child's wellbeing in the context of the parental responsibilities, duties and rights (parental care), while in Article 97 it is provided that parents have the right to live with their children, unless it is contrary to the child's wellbeing.

Also, the Croatian Family Act provides an exhaustive list of the rights of the child which is a comprehensive for the authority in charge of the enforcement as well. For instance, pursuant to Article 101 of the Family Act, when the parents cannot reach an agreement regarding some aspect of the exercise of the parental care or regarding the realization of the child's right, it is on the court to make the decision instead of them, having in mind the child's wellbeing.

Article 107 of the Family Act regulates the right of parents, grandparents and others who do not live with the child to visit the child.

In addition, Articles 108–122 of the Family Act prescribe the measures for the protection of the rights and wellbeing of the child.

Finally, Article 125 of the Family Act regulates the preconditions for the adoption. According to its second paragraph, in the adoption procedure, the adopter's character is evaluated in relation to the child's wellbeing.

5 The Right of the Child to Know About His/Her Origin

5.1 Child Born In and Out of Wedlock

In the Croatian legal system, the legal status of a child born out of wedlock is considerably equal to the status of a child born in wedlock. A difference exists in terms of paternity. On the other hand, when it comes to maternity, Article 53 of the Family Act states that "a child's mother is the woman who gave birth to the child".

While the right to know about the origin of the child born out of wedlock is not provided in the legislation explicitly, in some cases, such as adopted child or child conceived with biomedical assistance, the Croatian legislator expressly determines such right as a result of the implementation of the Article 7 of the Convention.

It can be concluded that a child born out of wedlock benefits from this right at the moment his/her right to establish its origin is already consumed.

If maternity or paternity cannot be determined in accordance with the rules which provide legal presumptions of maternity (of a child born in or out of wedlock) or paternity (of a child born in wedlock), it shall be determined by acknowledgement or by a court's decision (Article 55 of the Family Act).

When it comes to the acknowledgement of maternity and paternity, the first paragraph of Article 56 of the Family Act provides that the maternity and paternity may be acknowledged before a Registrar, a welfare authority or a court. The authority in charge shall, without delay, deliver a copy of the acknowledgement to the Registrar in charge of the registration of births.

In accordance with the second paragraph of Article 56 of the Family Act, there is a possibility of the acknowledgement of the maternity or paternity by way of will as well.

As provided under Article 59 of the Family Act (in case of the acknowledgment of maternity) and under Article 62 of the Family Act (in case of the acknowledgement of paternity), if the child has turned 14 and he/she is able to understand the meaning of the acknowledgement, his/her consent to this effect is required.

Moreover, for the acknowledgement of the paternity to be registered, the consent from the child's mother is also required (Article 61 of the Family Act).

It is important to highlight the rule contained in Article 65 of the Family Act, which basically implemented the Convention and says that in case there is no information about the child's father when the child is being registered in the register of births, the Registrar shall inform the mother about the child's right to know who his/her father is and about the procedures that may be taken in order to fulfil that right (i.e. acknowledgement of paternity or establishing paternity by way of a court decision).

The child has the right to file a complaint on the establishment of maternity or paternity until the age of 25 (Article 71, paragraph 1 of the Family Act).

Pursuant to Article 72 of the Family Act, a woman that considers herself to be the mother of the child may file a complaint on the establishment of the maternity or paternity, until the child is 18.

Equally, a complaint on the establishment of the maternity or paternity may be submitted by the man who considers himself to be the father of the child. This can be done within 1 year starting from the day of the reception of the notification that the consent from the mother of the child and/or from the child older than 14 has not been obtained. In any case, his complaint may be submitted at the child's 18th, the latest.

Further, Article 73 of the Family Act gives the social welfare a legal standing for the establishment of the maternity or paternity, providing the child is younger than 18.

Finally, in case the person claimed to be the mother or the father of the child is not alive, a complaint on the establishment of the maternity or paternity shall be submitted against that person's heir. In this case, the complaint has to be filed within 1 year from the death of the person claimed to be the mother or the father of the child or within 6 months from the decision on inheritance (providing it is final and binding).

According to Article 75, paragraph 1 of the Family Act, the child is entitled to rebut the maternity and paternity of the person registered as his/her parent, until the age of 25.

In addition, Article 79 of the Family Act prescribes that the right to contest the paternity is the right of the mother's husband as well. In particular, the mother's husband may contest the paternity of the child born in marriage or within 300 days from the cessation of the marriage, if he considers he is not the father. The complaint may be submitted within a period of 6 months from the day he has found out about the fact that casts doubt upon the paternity registered, but not later than the child's 7th year of age.

Of course, the same right pertains to the mother of the child, i.e. she may contest the paternity within a period of 6 months from the child's birth.

5.2 Adopted Child

Croatian family legislation does not recognize an open adoption. Nevertheless, the Croatian Family Act pays attention to the child's rights, especially those envisaged in Article 7 of the UN Convention. To be precise, the Croatian family law gives the child a right to know about the circumstances in which he/she was adopted as well as a right to know about his/her origin. In this respect one must bear in mind the rules contained in Articles 124 and 142 of the Family Act.

Article 124 of the Family Act gives right to a child to be informed about the fact that he/she was adopted in the sense that it expressly prescribes (in its first paragraph) that in the adoptionprocedure the Social Welfare Centre shall inform the adoptive parents about this right. In its second paragraph, Article 124 highlights that a child has to be informed about the adoption up to the age of 7 or immediately upon the adoption, in case the adopted child is older than 7.

As to the child's right to know about his/her origin, the provisions contained in the Article 142 of the Family Act are to be considered.

The adoption shall take the effect once the administrative procedure before the Social Welfare Centre is terminated. Given that the adoption is confidential, Article 142 paragraph 2 of the Family Act prescribes that the adoption is an official secret.

Nonetheless, Article 142 paragraph 3 of the Family Act says that an adult adopted child, an adoptive parent and a parent who has given consent for the adoption of a child shall be allowed to inspect the files on adoption and the register of births of an adopted child. Even a minor adopted child shall be allowed to inspect the case files and the register of births, if that would be in his/her interest.

5.3 Child Conceived by Biomedical Assistance

A child conceived by biomedical assistance has the right to know who his/her biological parents are. Article 15 of the Medically Assisted Procreation Act envisaged the child's right (if he/she is fully of age) to have an access to all the documents in his/her file related to his/her "biological origin", including the identity of the donor. What is more, the parents are obliged to inform the child about the fact that he/she was conceived with biomedical assistance up to his/her age of 18.

As to the rules on the origin, Article 16 of the Medically Assisted Procreation Act refers to the Family Act's rules (the Croatian Family Act contains some special provisions on maternity and paternity related to a child conceived with medical assistance).

6 The Right of the Child to Express His/Her Views Freely in All Matters Affecting Him/Her

Article 89 paragraph 5 of the Family Act prescribes that, in situations where the child's right or interest is decided upon, the child has the right to learn, in an appropriate way, the important circumstances of the case, to be advised and express its opinion in this respect and to be informed about possible consequences of his/her opinion. The opinion is to be taken into consideration based on the child's age and maturity.

7 The Rights of the Child in the Field of Adoption

According to Article 134 of the Family Act, if the child is at the age of at least 12 and is capable of understanding the significance of the adoption, its consent to the adoption is required. The same is required in case of a change of his/her personal name and ethnicity (Article 145 of the Family Act).

As a general rule, the adoptive parent must be a Croatian citizen (Article 127 of the Family Act). Therefore, a foreigner may be an adoptive parent under exceptional circumstances, providing that this is of a particular benefit of the child. If the adoptive parent is a foreigner, the adoption can take place only with the prior approval of the Minister competent for the welfare matters. Still, general conditions for the adoption, prescribed in Articles 125–134 of the Family Act, are to be met in cases of the intercountry adoption. Even if the international adoption according to the Family Act (Article 135) is taking place, the adoption procedure is to be carried out ex officio by the welfare centre where the child has his/her habitual residence or domicile. Before initiating an adoption procedure, a person who wishes to adopt the child must seek from the welfare centre an opinion concerning his or her suitability to be an adoptive parent.

The Hague Convention on Protection of Children and Co-operation in Respect of Intercountry Adoption, 1993, entered into force in 1995 and has been ratified by 90 countries, including all EU member states. Law on Ratification of the Convention on Protection of Children and Co-operation in Respect of Intercountry Adoption was adopted in the Croatian Parliament in 2013 and was published in the Official Gazette, International Treaties, No. 5 of 2013.[11] The central government body for the implementation of the Convention on Protection of Children and Cooperation of States Regarding Interstate Adoption in the Republic of Croatia shall be established within the Ministry of Social Policy and Youth.

---

[11] Konvencija o zaštiti djece i suradnji u vezi s međudržavnim posvojenjem, Narodne novine, Međunarodni ugovori, br. 5/13 (*Convention on protection of Children and Co-operation in respect of Intercountry* Adoption, *Official gazette of the Republic of Croatia, International Treaties, No. 5/13*).

8 The Right of the Child to Freedom of Thought, Conscience and Religion

As a general rule, Article 93 of the Family Act provides that the upbringing of a child must be in accordance with his age and maturity and with the right of the child to freedom of conscience and religious and other beliefs. Parents have the duty and right to bring up a child as a free, humane, patriotic, moral, sensitive and responsible person, respecting the principles of equality between men and women, so as to be prepared for a harmonious family and social life with a positive attitude towards the nature. Religious education is an optional subject in the public schools. There is also an optional subject for the children whose parents do not want religious education, which deals with comparative knowledge of the world's great religions, or the so-called religious culture.

9 Physical Punishment of the Child

Physical punishment of the child is forbidden in the school and other institutions that take care of the children (social welfare institutions and similar ones). Physical punishment of the child is also forbidden within the family (this relates to the parents, guardians, foster family and any other person holding that parental responsibilities).

Parents and other members of the family may not subject the child to degrading procedures and mental or physical violence or abuse (Article 88 of the Family Act). According to the Family Act, a parent, grandparent, sister or brother or half-sister and half-brother who do not live with the child may be forbidden to approach the child in certain places or at a certain distance or to harass the child on the basis of the court's order issued in a non-litigation procedure. The procedure can be initiated by a welfare centre, a parent or a child.

10 Deprivation of Parental Responsibilities

Pursuant to the Family Act, in a non-litigation procedure, the court will deprive a parent who abuses or grossly violates parental responsibility, duties and rights of the right to parental care (Article 114). A parent is deemed to abuse or grossly violate parental responsibility, duties and rights if he or she:

1. Exerts physical or mental violence on the child, including exposing it to violence among the adult members of the family.
2. Takes sexual advantage of the child.
3. Exploits the child by forcing it to work too hard or to do work that is not appropriate to its age.

4. Allows the child to consume alcohol, drugs or other narcotic substances.
5. Encourages the child to socially unacceptable behaviour.
6. Has abandoned the child.
7. Does not care for a child with which he or she does not live for more than 3 months.
8. In a period of 1 year, does not create the conditions for life together with the child with which he or she does not live without having any particularly good reason for this.
9. Does not care for the basic necessities of life of a child with which he or she lives or does not adhere to the measure that has been previously imposed by a competent body for the sake of the protection of the rights and wellbeing of the child and in the cases that in some other way grossly abuses the rights of the child. The proceeding for deprivation of the right to exercise parental care must be instituted by a welfare centre as soon as it learns of the prescribed circumstances.

A parent who abuses or grossly violates parental responsibility, duties and rights shall be deprived of the right to parental care in a non-litigation procedure. Such a procedure may be initiated by the welfare centre, other parent, the child or ex officio.

In case the procedure on the deprivation of the right to exercise the parental care is instigated in respect of both parents or one of them only, the welfare centre will appoint the child a guardian ad litem, or the so-called special guardian. In such case, the provisions that deal with the guardianship for special cases shall apply accordingly.

Parents are bound to maintain their minor child, even those parents whose right to exercise the parental care has been restricted or forfeited or who do not in fact exercise the parental care (Article 212 of the Family Act). Parents are also obliged to maintain an adult child who is not capable of work due to his/her sickness, mental or physical disability.

11 Medical Consent of the Child

Parents are bound to care for the life and health of a child and to enable it to use measures for improving, preserving and restoring health, in accordance with the regulations from the domain of health care and the requirements of medical science (Article 92 of the Family Act). A parent is also bound to protect a child from the degrading procedures and corporal punishment of other persons.

The Act on the Protection of Patients' Rights in the Republic of Croatia protects the rights of minor patient under provision (Article 17) on the protection of the patient who is unable to give consent. For a patient who is a minor, consent for undertaking medical treatment should be given by legal representative, usually parents or guardian, and such a consent is obligatory. If that would be in the interest of a patient, the person who gave the consent may at any time withdraw it (e.g. for a particular diagnostic or therapeutic procedure). If due to an emergency situation the consent of the legal representative or guardian cannot be obtained, minor patient will undergo a diagnostic or therapeutic procedure only in cases where the failure to take proceedings directly threatens his or her life or when the serious damage to his or her health is certain.

12 The Right of the Child to Change His/Her Personal Name

According to the Croatian Personal Name Act (Article 7), a personal name of a minor child shall be changed upon the request of his/her parents or adoptive parents. Even guardians may request a personal name of a minor child to be changed, providing that they have obtained the approval of the competent Social Welfare Centre. In case minor is older than 10 years, his or her consent in this respect is obligatory.

In case the child is adopted, his/her personal name is determined by the adoptive. If the adopted child is older than 12, his/her consent is mandatory in respect of changing his/her personal name and ethnicity (Article 145 of the Family Act).

The adopted child usually acquires the common surname of the adoptive parents. If the adoptive parents do not have a surname in common, surname of the adopted child will be determined in accordance with a separate law.

According to the Croatian Family Act, an adopted child may keep the name and surname he/she had before the adoption or have it in addition to the surname of the adoptive parent, providing the welfare centre agrees this is in the interest of the child.

13 The Rights of the Child in Employment

Pursuant to Croatian Labour Act (Article 17), there is a general rule that a person under 15 shall not be employed. The same applies to person under 18, providing he/she is taking compulsory primary education.

The labour inspector shall prohibit the work of a minor under 15 or a minor between 15 and 18, if they are taking compulsory primary education.

There is a legal exception to the general rule (Article 18). Namely, if a minor of 15 or more is authorized, by his or her legal representative, to conclude a specific employment contract, except for a minor taking compulsory primary education, such a minor shall have a legal capacity to conclude and rescind the contract at stake and to carry out all the legal actions related to the fulfilment of the rights and obligations arising out of the contract or in relation to the contract.

A dispute that may arise between legal representatives, or one or more legal representatives, and the minor, over an issue of granting an authorization to conclude the employment contract, is to be resolved by the competent social welfare authority, taking into account the minor's best interests.

The legal representative may withdraw or limit the authorization or even terminate the employment agreement on behalf of the minor. The minor's guardian may also give the authorization related to the employment on behalf of the minor. The minor's guardian may give an authorization, providing there is an approval given by for the competent social welfare authority.

The authorization related to the employment of the minor shall be given in writing. It is to be pointed out that, according to the Croatian Labour Act, a minor shall not be employed for a job which threatens his or her safety, health, morals or development. The list of such jobs shall be provided by the competent Ministry.

The employer shall not recruit a minor, without a prior examination of his or her health capacities. The competent Ministry shall make a list of the jobs where the examination of a minor is mandatory, as well as those activities for which a prior approval of the labour inspector is obligatory.

Upon a request of a minor, his or her parents or guardian, works council, trade union or labour inspector, the employer shall offer a minor employee to conclude an employment contract for the performance of other appropriate job and, if there is no such a job, he or she may terminate the minor's employment in the manner and under the conditions prescribed by the Labour Act.

There are special provisions related to this issue (Labour Act, Article 20). For instance, if the labour inspector suspects that the job performed by a minor threatens his or her safety, health, morals or development, he or she may at any time demand from the employer that such employee who is a minor be examined by an authorized physician who should assess, in his or her expert report and opinion, whether the job performed by the minor threatens his or her safety, health, morals or development.

In that case the labour inspector shall fix a time limit within which the employer shall have to obtain an expert report and opinion on whether or not the job performed by the minor threatens his or her health or development.

The costs of the medical examination and expert report and opinion are to be covered by the employer. On the basis of an expert report and opinion given by an authorized physician, the labour inspector may prohibit a minor from performing a specific job.

The initiative for conducting the proceedings of medical examination may be given to the labour inspector by the minor, his or her parent or guardian, the work council or trade union. In case of negative results, the employer shall offer the minor employee to conclude an employment contract for the performance of other appropriate job and, if there is no such job, he or she may terminate the minor's employment in the manner and under the conditions prescribed by the Labour Act.

Special conditions for concluding employment contracts also protect the interests of the minors on the labour market. If a law, other regulation, collective agreement or employment rules prescribe special conditions for the commencement of employment, an employment contract may only be concluded by an employee who meets these conditions (Article 21). The Minister shall, with prior consent of the minister responsible for health, list the jobs which an employee may perform only upon prior and regular examinations of his or her health capacities to perform these jobs carried out in accordance with a special regulation. That ordinance shall prescribe the manner for the examination of health capacities, the intervals at which such examination must be repeated, the contents and procedure for issuing a certificate on health capacities and other issues important for examination of health capacities to perform the jobs.

New provisions related to the protection of the interests of the minors and their property rights are introduced in the Act on the Changes of Family Act in 2007 (Article 36).[12]

Where an agreement or contract is concluded between a minor and natural or legal persons that shall dispose over child's future ownership rights regarding the child's sports, art or similar activities, approval needs to be obtained from the Social Welfare Centre. The Social Welfare Centre shall have a duty to pay special attention to the protection of child's ownership rights and interests, considering the best interest of the child. Duties and obligations set out in the contract shall last until the child has reached the age of majority.

Parents can, with the approval of the competent welfare centre, alienate or burden the property of a minor child for the sake of his/her maintenance, treatment, upbringing, education or training or for the sake of covering some other important needs of the child. The approval of the welfare centre is also important for undertaking of the appropriate procedural actions before a court or government bodies relating to the child's property. Where procedural activities are executed before the court or other state bodies in matters relating to disposal over a property owned by a minor child, approval needs to be obtained from the Social Welfare Centre.

According to the Croatian Family Act (Article 259), a minor child may acquire property through a work, inheritance, gift or some other legal foundation. A minor's property is managed by his/her parents, except for the property that the minor has obtained after his/her 15th birthday.

14 Obligation of the Child Towards His/Her Parents

According to the Croatian Family Act, an adult child is bound to maintain a parent that is not capable of work and does not have enough resources for living or cannot realize resources from his or her assets. A child can be freed from the duty to maintain a parent who for unjustified reasons did not maintain him during the time it was their legal obligation (Article 211 of the Family Act).

---

[12] Zakon o izmjenama i dopunama obiteljskog zakona, Narodne novine, br. 107/07 (*Act on the Changes of* Family Act, *Official Gazette of the Republic of Croatia, No. 107/07*).

15 Summary

The Republic of Croatia is an independent and sovereign state since 1991. The Marriage and Family Relations Act of 1978, amended in 1989, was the source of family law until the 1998 when the Family Act of 1998 entered into force. Legislative activities continued resulting the adoption of a new Family Act in 2003 and later amendments of 2004, 2007, 2011 and 2013. The Ministry of Social Policy and Youth launched in August 2013 public debate on the draft of the (new) Family Act. On the 1st of July 2013, Croatia joined the EU. This report is a summary overview of the positive legislation dealing with the rights of the children and it is guided by the proposed questionnaire. Due to the continuous modifications in the legislation, there is a lack of a proper "feedback" from jurisprudence and theory, as a proof of how the new legal standards are really implemented in the practice. The rights of the child are primarily determined by the international legal standards, especially the UN Convention on the Rights of the Child of 1989. It is evident progress especially through the active role of the Ombudsperson for Children in the Republic of Croatia, in the public life and in the detailed reports, which are annually presented in the Croatian Parliament.

16 Legal Sources

Ustav RH, Narodne novine, br. 56/90, 135/97, 8/98 (pročišćeni tekst), 113/00, 124/00 (pročišćeni tekst), 28/01, 41/01 (pročišćeni tekst), 55/01 (ispravak), 76/10 i 85/10 (pročišćeni tekst) (*Constitution of Croatia, Official Gazette of the Republic of Croatia, No. 56/90, 135/97, 8/98 (consolidated text), 113/00, 124/00 (consolidated text), 28/01, 41/01 (consolidated text), 55/01 (correction), 76/10 and 85/10 (consolidated text)*)

Konvencija o pravima djeteta, Narodne novine – Međunarodni ugovori, br. 12/93, 20/97 (*Convention on the Right of the child, Official Gazette of the Republic of Croatia – International Treaties, No. 12/93, 20/97*)

Konvencija o zaštiti djece i suradnji u vezi s međudržavnim posvojenjem, Narodne novine, Međunarodni ugovori, br. 5/13 (*Convention on protection of Children and Co-operation in respect of Intercountry Adoption, Official gazette of the Republic of Croatia, International Treaties, No. 5/13*)

Obiteljski zakon, Narodne novine, br. 116/03, 17/04, 136/04, 107/07, 57/11, 61/11, 25/13 (*Family Act, Official Gazette of the Republic of Croatia, No. 116/03, 17/04, 136/04, 107/07, 57/11, 61/11, 25/13*)

Zakon o Pravobranitelju za djecu, Narodne novine, br. 96/03 (*Children's Ombudsperson's Act, Official Gazette of the Republic of Croatia, No. 96/03*)

Zakon o zaštiti od nasilja u obitelji, Narodne novine, br. 137/09, 14/10, 60/10 (*Act on the protection of domestic violence, Official Gazette of the Republic of Croatia, No. 137/09, 14/10, 60/10*)

Zakon o medicinski pomognutoj oplodnji, Narodne novine, br. 86/12 (*Medically assisted procreation Act, Official Gazette of the Republic of Croatia, No. 86/12*)
Zakon o osobnom imenu, Narodne novine, br. 118/12 (*Personal name Act, Official Gazette of the Republic of Croatia, No. 118/12*)
Zakon o radu, Narodne novine, br. 149/09, 61/11, 82/12, 73/13 (*Labour Act, Official Gazette of the Republic of Croatia, No. 149/09, 61/11, 82/12, 73/13*)
Zakon o zaštiti prava pacijenata, Narodne novine, br. 169/04, 37/08 (*Act on the Protection of Patients' Rights, Official Gazette of the Republic of Croatia, No. 169/04, 37/08*)

Bibliography

Alinčić et al. 2007. Obiteljsko pravo, Narodne novine, Zagreb.
Hrabar, D. 1994. Dijete – Pravni subjekt u obitelji, Zagreb.
Hrabar, Dubravka. 2012. Podrijetlo djeteta začetog uz medicinski pomognutu oplodnju, Reprodukcijska endokrinologija i neplodnost – Medicinski pomognuta oplodnja IVF/Šimunić, Velimir i sur. (ur.). Zagreb: Školska knjiga, pp. 671–676.
Hrabar, D. 2008. Posvojenje na razmeđi interesa posvojitelja i posvojenika, Zbornik Pravnog fakulteta u Zagrebu, vol. 58, br. 5, pp. 1107–1139.
Jakovac-Lozić, D. 2000. Posvojenje, Split.
Šarčević et al. 2011. *Family law in Croatia*. Wolters Kluwer, Alphen aan den Rijn, The Netherlands.

The Rights of the Child: Danish National Report

Christina G. Jeppesen de Boer and Annette Kronborg

1 Ratification of the Convention on the Rights of the Child

Denmark has ratified the UN Convention on the Rights of the Child (CRC) on July 5, 1991.[1] The Danish Constitution does not directly address the question of which status international law has in national law. Traditionally, the Danish position in relation to international law has been described as dualistic. The dualistic theory considers international law and the national law of states as wholly separate legal entities. However, the Danish position may more accurately be described as that of practical monism since that certain interpretative principles mean that the courts interpret national law in accordance with international law. This is, however, not an adequate description in relation to the CRC which almost only is addressed by the Danish legislature and not by the courts or administrative authorities.[2]

[1] BEK No. 6 of 16.01.1992

[2] See C.G. Jeppesen de Boer, *Joint Parental Authority*, Antwerpen-Oxford-Portland; Intersentia 2008, pp. 107–114

C.G. Jeppesen de Boer (✉)
Utrecht University, Utrecht, The Netherlands
e-mail: c.g.jeppesen@uu.nl

A. Kronborg
Copenhagen University, Copenhagen, Denmark
e-mail: Annette.kronborg@jur.ku.dk

O. Cvejić Jančić (ed.), *The Rights of the Child in a Changing World*,
Ius Comparatum - Global Studies in Comparative Law 13,
DOI 10.1007/978-3-319-23189-1_5

2 Definition of the Child

This question will be dealt with in relation to abortion. Denmark is a Christian Lutheran country and has a liberal legislation in respect of the unconditional right to abortion since 1972. Article 6 of the CRC concerning children's inherent right to life and the state parties' obligation to ensure the survival and development of the child is not interpreted as a prohibition of abortion in Denmark. Denmark did not clarify this point in connection with the ratification as France had already done. According to health law, a woman has a right to abortion during the first 12 weeks of pregnancy. After the 12th week, abortion may be permitted depending upon social and health criteria stated in the legislation. If the fetus is viable, the pregnancy may only be terminated if the fetus has serious disabilities.[3] A termination of pregnancy is considered as an abortion if the fetus is considered to be less than 22 weeks old.[4] Hereafter it is defined as a stillborn child. Parents are allowed to bury a fetus less than 22 weeks old. In 2011, 17 abortions were granted after the 22nd week because of the fetus' disabilities.[5] In conclusion, the fetus' status as a child depends upon the qualification of the matter as concerning abortion or the child's funeral.

3 Framework for the Protection of the Rights of the Child

In Danish law, there is no special legal instrument devoted to the rights of the child. The CRC was not being prioritized when it was considered generally in 2001 which conventions to incorporate into Danish law. It was considered that the legal substance of the CRC was too unclear at the moment.[6] Danish legislation is thus not systematized in a way that collects children's rights in a specific statute regulation. These rights are spread out in different legislation systematized in different manners. The Danish Ombudsman's Children's Division visits institutions for children and also processes complaints from both children and adults about conditions for children.

4 Implementation of the Best Interests Principle

Apart from the EU Charter, the best interest of the child principle is not implemented on a constitutional or general level. In family law, it is implemented in the Act on Parental Responsibility among the introductory provisions. The provision

[3] Act on Health, Chapter 25, BBK No. 13.07.2010

[4] Act on Health, Article 189

[5] Sundhedsstyrelsen statistik 2011

[6] Commission report, No. 1407, Copenhagen 2001, *Inkorporering af menneskerettighedskonventioner i dansk ret*

was redrafted with reference to the CRC Article 3, but the principle itself was already part of Danish law. Section 4 stipulates that: "Decisions made pursuant to the Act will be based on the child's best interests." It should be noted that parents have a high degree of autonomy in deciding matters of parental authority, residence, and contact. Therefore, decisions made according to the Act concern disputes but do not provide for an overall review of parental agreements.[7] In public law concerning the municipalities' duties toward children's welfare (regulating social work), the principle is formulated differently. The consolidation Act on social services provides a more ambitious and detailed principle directed toward *changing* the child's situation.[8]

5 The Right of the Child to Know About His/Her Origin

The establishment of parenthood is covered by a single act called the Children Act.[9] This Act was recently changed to provide a sex neutral parentage law providing the possibility for the mother's female partner to become the legal parent in a simple registration procedure.[10] The Children Act makes no legal distinction between children born in or out of marriage. Differences follow almost only from the fact that marriage is a legal institution which practically makes it easier to establish parentage than if the mother is unmarried. Nevertheless, this lack of distinction has raised the question whether or not an unmarried father has the right to establish his paternity. The father's right to initiate a case is not unlimited. The limitations are set up in Children Act Section 6. As a main rule, the father may initiate the case within 6 months after the birth of the child. If another man has recognized paternity and made an agreement with the mother about joint parental authority, the biological father does not have the right to challenge this agreement unless he was married to the mother or was living with the mother within the period of time 10 months prior to the birth of the child.

A special feature of Danish parentage law is that the state will initiate paternity proceedings if a registration of a second parent does not take place in the central personal register (CPR). The role of the state in the registration of a second parent (primarily the father) dates back to 1938 where children born outside of marriage were granted inheritance rights after the father and had the right to obtain his last name. If such a procedure is initiated, the mother is penally obliged under Section 8 of the Children Act to inform the authorities about any knowledge of the possible father.

[7] Act on Parental Responsibility, No. 652 of 20.11.2012

[8] Act on Social Service, No. 810 of 19.07.2012, Section 19

[9] Children Act, No. 1047 of 08.11.2012

[10] Act No. 652 of 12.06.2013 providing changes to the Children Act

The mother of the child is the woman who gives birth to the child. This was included in the Children Act in the section relating to medically assisted reproduction in 2001. Until then it followed from the principle *mater semper certa est*. It is not possible to give birth anonymously, and it is not possible to challenge maternity, for example, in situations where the mother is not the biological mother (egg donation).

5.1 Challenging Paternity

Within 6 months after the birth of the child, the established paternity may be challenged. Within this time limit, there is no presumption in favor of the existing registration. The father, the mother, and the child's guardian may challenge the registration.

Next to the time limit of 6 months, there exists a time limit of 3 years after the birth of the child. The paternity may be challenged if the existing paternity has been registered by mistake (a mistake as to the person in question/an error in writing), and this may be done by the mother, the registered father, the child's guardian, or the man who was not registered because of the mistake. If the mother or the registered father was aware of the mistake and despite this treated the child as the child of the registered father, the paternity may not be challenged by them. A former husband or cohabitant who has not been informed about the child's birth may challenge the paternity as soon as he is informed and within 3 years after the birth. Furthermore, the paternity may be challenged within 3 years in the case of new information or when there is a presumption that someone else is the father of the child and it is possible to establish his paternity. The relevant criteria are the age of the child, whether or not the child has been treated as the child of the registered father despite existing knowledge disfavoring his paternity, and the information has been known by the party without a challenge being made within a reasonable period of time. In exceptional cases, the paternity may be challenged after 3 years.

Furthermore, the registered father, the mother, and the child who agree to challenge the established paternity are allowed to do so if it is likely that the biological paternity of another man can be established. There is no time limit. Two cases illustrate this situation. In 2002, the Danish Supreme Court decided that two now adult children could have the paternity of the deceased biological father established. They had in fact been living with the biological father since they were 6–7 years old. The children were born in marriage and their legal father consented to the establishment of the paternity of the biological father. The mother was deceased at this point. The biological father's daughter protested. The body of the deceased father was exhumed for the purpose of DNA testing in order to establish paternity.[11] In 2004, the Danish Appeal Court East decided that paternity of the biological father could be established

[11] Supreme Court, 04.09.2002, *Ugeskrift for Retsvæsen*, 2002.2619 H

in a case where the mother before she died had told her daughter, who is now 40 years old, that the mother's husband who was the daughter's legal father was not her biological father. Further, the mother had told the daughter who the biological father was. The biological father had protested against the establishment of his paternity.[12]

5.2 *Adoption*

The Danish legislation does not contain any provision about the child's right to know who his/her biological parents are. The child is a party in the adoption case, and at the age of majority the child may have access to the adoption file and information herein about its origin. Denmark is a member of the Hague Convention on intercountry adoption. According to Article 16.2, the receiving country shall take care not to reveal the identity of the mother and the father if, in the state of origin, these identities may not be disclosed. If the country of origin does disclose information about the biological parents, the grown-up child will have access to the file according to administrative law.[13]

5.3 *Biomedical Assistance*

The Danish legislation does not contain any provision about the child's right to know the egg or sperm donor. The Danish Act on artificial insemination and the Children Act are based on the parent's choice whether or not they want the donor to be anonymous or not. Whether or not the child have a right to know who his biological parents are or more general information about the donor depends on the legal parents agreement with the sperm bank.

6 The Right of the Child to Express His Views

Whether or not the child is allowed to express himself or herself within his family is considered to be outside the legal sphere. The child's involvement in administrative and judicial proceedings is regulated within the different legal fields and their separate piecemeal legislation. The child's procedural position differs depending on the legal field. In the following, mainly family law is described as legislated in the

[12] Eastern Appeal Court (Østre Landsret), 21.06.2004, Section 9, No. B-1308-04

[13] Commission report, No. 1323 *om Haager-konventionen af 29. maj 1993 om beskyttelse af børn og om samarbejde med hensyn til internationale adoptioner sammenholdt med dansk adoptionslovgivning*, p. 53

Act on Parental Responsibility covering the legal issues – parental authority, residence, and contact. The child's right to procedural involvement has not been interpreted as an individual party right but as relating to a more general child perspective in the case. The child's perspective is supposed to work as a guarantee for the best interests of the child. The perspective goes hand in hand with the increase of parents' individual rights to family life with the child and the increased equality between the parents. Nevertheless, the legislative focus on the child's perspective has not been legally clarified. The Act on Parental Responsibility contains an introductory provision in Section 5 referring to the UN Convention on the Rights of the Child in the preliminary draft and reads as follows:

> In all matters relating to the child, the child's own views must be taken into consideration, depending on the child's age and maturity.

Further, Chapter 6 "Case Processing" contains a provision entitled "The Child's Perspective" in Section 34 and reads as follows:

> (1) The child's views must be taken into consideration during a case about parental authority, the child's place of residence or contact by giving the child the opportunity to make its views and opinions known. Information about the child's perspective can be gained through personal interviews, statements from child welfare consultants or other ways that shed light on the child's point of view.
>
> (2) The obligation to directly take the child's views into consideration in the case does not apply if this is deemed too damaging to him or her or considered unnecessary given the circumstances of the case.

In 94 % of the cases the child's perspective is illustrated through the information of the parents.[14] A child who has reached the age of ten can ask the regional state administration to call the parents to a meeting, but neither the child nor the regional state administration can formally initiate a case that results in a decision; see Section 35. Furthermore, if the parents reach an agreement, the authorities do not have a duty to involve the child. The administrative guidelines provide for the main rule concerning child involvement, but this may factually only refer to the cases where agreement is not reached and a decision is made. It has to be kept in mind that the regional state administration cannot, on beforehand, know whether the case will be settled or not. The regulation is therefore not clear.

The legislation does not grant the child an independent right to information, advice, or counsel in order to form his/her view. The involvement of the child is therefore primarily arranged through the parent with whom the child resides.

In welfare law the child has more rights, and an important difference to family law is that the parents cannot deny the child his/her rights. In this field, children may seek the municipality counseling without the consent of the custodial parent on an anonymous and open basis; see Service Act, Section 11. Before a decision on the child's welfare is made, the child must as a main rule be consulted as stated in the Service Act, Section 48 (2). Furthermore, the child has a right to an advisor as stated in Section 48a.

[14] Evaluation of the Act on Parental Responsibility, *Familiestyrelsens evaluering af forældreansvarsloven*, 2011, p. 62

7 Consent to Adoption

The child's right to give his or her consent to adoption is stated in the Danish Adoption Act, Section 6 reading as follows[15]:

> (1) Where the person to be adopted has reached the age of 12, the decree shall be granted only after obtaining the consent of the person to be adopted, except where obtaining consent is considered to be detrimental to the best interests of the child.
>
> (2) The consent of the child should be given in person before a representative of the Regional State Administration or before another authority or institution approved pursuant to subsection (1) of section 8. Before the child gives his or her consent, the child has to attend an interview about the adoption, and the child shall be informed about the legal and other effects of the adoption.
>
> (3) Where the child is under 12, information shall be obtained about the attitude of the child to the adoption, to the extent relevant with regard to the age and maturity of the child and the circumstances of the case. In making the decision the attitude of the child in this respect should be considered to the greatest possible extent.

8 Conditions for Intercountry Adoption

Legally, intercountry adoptions are divided into stepchild adoption, family adoptions, and international (foreign) adoption.

A general condition is set up in the Adoption Act, Section 2, stating as follows:

> Adoption may only be granted if, after an investigation into the matter, it can be assumed to be to the benefit of the person whose adoption is sought, and that person either wishes to be fostered by the adopter or has been fostered by that person, or there is another special reason for the adoption.

Only married couples may adopt together; see Section 5(2). Furthermore, as a main rule, the adopter has to have reached the age of 25; see Section 4.

In addition, there are different conditions in relation to the different forms of adoption:

8.1 Stepchild Adoption

Only a spouse may adopt the child or adoptive child of the other spouse (Section 5a). This applies to same-sex marriage and registered partnership (Section 8a).

[15] Act on Adoption, No. 392 of 22.04.2013

8.2 Family Adoption

As a main rule, an adopter has to be approved as an adopter. Exceptions to this rule are stepchild adoption and cases in which the adopter is closely related to, or has other special ties to, the adoptive child or its parents (Section 4a).

8.3 International Adoption

In the case of international adoption, the adopter needs to be approved as an adopter. An important distinction is whether or not the parent with parental authority gives her consent to adoption. If the adoption is without consent, the adoption will be subject to the investigation of the municipality into the child's circumstances. To coordinate the welfare work of the municipality and the adoption authority, the Adoption Act sets as a condition that the adoption has to be made before the child reaches the age of 1 year. Otherwise, an adoption cannot be granted before the child is at least 3 years old (Section 9).

9 Freedom of Thought, Conscience, and Religion

Religious education is available in schools as an obligatory element. The education is primarily about evangelist-Lutheran Christianity, but it also includes other religions in the upper level of primary school. The subject is knowledge based and it does not include religious instruction.

The holders of parental authority may apply for dispensation if they let the child be taught religion elsewhere. It is not legally controlled if the parents fulfill this condition, but the application procedure is combined with a meeting between the school and the parents, and the parents are informed about the subject; see further the Danish Public School Act, Section 6.[16]

10 Physical Punishment

The Act on Parental Responsibility defines the rights and duties of the holder of parental authority in Section 2. From this section, it follows that children must be treated with respect for their person and not be exposed to corporal punishment or other humiliating treatment. The provision is from 1997 and has since then been the understanding that the civil provision and the criminal act applies the same standard.[17]

[16]The Public School Act, No. 998 from 16/8/2010

[17]Criminal Act, No. 1007 of 24.10.2012, Article 244

This understanding involves that any physical punishment of the child including offenses taking place in school and social welfare institutions is covered by the criminal act. Offenses may lead to a fine or imprisonment up to 3 years depending on how serious it is.

11 Deprivation of Parental Responsibilities

In a dispute between two holders of parental authority, the court may as an exception deprive one of the holders his authority and allocate sole parental authority to the other holder; see Act on Parental Responsibility, Section 11. Any protective measure or alternative care is made without the deprivation of parental authority also in cases where the holder(s) does not give consent. In the case of adoption with or without consent, the parent with parental authority will be deprived his parental authority as well as legal parentage. After adoption, the only legal relation to the child is – as a strict exception – contact if it is considered in the best interests of the child; see Act on Parental Responsibility 21a.

12 Medical Consent

The holder of parental authority has the right to give medical consent until the child is 15 years old, according to Section 2 of the Act on Parental Responsibility. Young people between 15 and 18 years of age have the right to give medical consent themselves, but the holder(s) of parental authority has the right to receive all medical information. The aim is to reach an agreement between the young person and the holder(s), but the young person has the final word; see Act on Health, Section 17.

Young people below the age of 15 years have a right to be involved in the decision process unless it harms them; see Act on Health, Section 20.

13 Change of Name

The child does not have the right to change his name. The competent person(s) is the holder(s) of parental authority. If the child has reached the age of 12, his consent is needed according to the Act on Names.[18] An exception can be permitted administratively. Children below the age of 12 have the right to state their opinion, and it shall as far as reasonable be taken into consideration before a decision is made; see Act on Names, Section 22.

[18] Act on Names, No. 392 of 01.05.2012

14 Child Employment

The Danish Working Environment Act is a framework Act, which lays down the general objectives and requirements in relation to the working environment. The Act aims at preventing accidents and diseases at the workplace and at protecting children and young persons on the labor market through special rules.

Young person's employment is regulated in a separate part named "Young persons under the age of 18." This part incorporates an EU directive (No. 94/33 of 22.06.1994). The main rule is that "young persons who are under the age of 15, or who are subject to compulsory education shall not perform work." The compulsory education lasts 9 years and begins in the year the child reaches the age of 6; see Public School Act, Section 34. Explicit exceptions are made concerning children who have reached the age of 13 and the exceptions are listed in a ministerial regulation. Specific types of jobs are listed.[19] If the employment is part of an education, there is a more liberal approach in the exceptions with an age limit of 14 years used to distinguish children from young persons. Children below 13 years of age may only get a working permission from the police related to a specific activity listed in the regulation such as participating in films, theater, or commercials.

The young person is not allowed to gain employment without the consent of the holder(s) of parental authority. An exception is the dated but valid provision in the Act on Parental Responsibility, Section 43, which allows the young person above 15 years to change employment unless specifically forbidden. It addresses the youngsters' need in the former traditional agriculture society, where it would be too troublesome for the young person being far from home, if he could not change his employment without the parents' consent.

Children's working hours are regulated in the Working Environment Act, Sections 61–62a, and are a combination of legislative regulation and a delegation to the Minister of Employment to lay down special regulation.[20] The main provision is in Section 61:

> **61.-(1)** The working hours for young persons under the age of 18 shall not exceed the normal working hours for adults employed in the same sector, and working hours shall not exceed eight hours per 24-hour period and 40 hours per week. (2) Daily working hours for young persons under the age of 15 years, or young persons subject to compulsory education, must not exceed two hours on school days, and seven hours on other days than school days. However, young persons who have reached 15 years, but who are subject to compulsory education, may work eight hours on days which are not school days. The total working hours per week may not exceed 12 hours in weeks with school days, and 35 hours in weeks other than school weeks. However, young persons who have reached 15 years, but who are still subject to compulsory education may work 40 hours in weeks other than school weeks. Children who are under 15 years, but who are no longer subject to compulsory education may not work for more than seven hours per day and 35 hours per week. (3) If daily working hours exceed 4½ hours, young persons under 18 years shall have a rest period of at least 30 minutes. Such rest period shall be at an appropriate time, and, if possible, continuous. (4)

[19] BEK No. 239 of 06.04.2005

[20] Act on Working Environment, No. 1072 of 07.09.2010

Young persons under the age of 18 shall not work between the hours of 8.00pm and 6.00am.
(5) The Minister for Employment may lay down special regulations concerning:

1. the organisation of working hours, including calculations in cases where young persons work as part of an education course, or where young persons work for more than one employer,
2. the extent to which subsection (1) above may be derogated from for young persons who have reached the age of 15 years and who are no longer subject to compulsory education,
3. that young persons who are subject to compulsory education shall have a period in the school holidays which is entirely free of work, and
4. that the provisions of subsection (4) above may be derogated from for trades or sectors in situations where circumstances make it necessary or desirable for young persons who have reached the age of 15 years, and who are no longer subject to compulsory education. However, the young person must under no circumstances work between the hours of 12.00 midnight and 4.00 a.m.

As explained above, it is listed what type of employment children between 13 and 15 years of age are permitted to have. Concerning young persons above 15 years, the listing is not about the type of jobs but rather about technical tools, paint, and other chemicals they are permitted to work with and a list of specific employment that may involve a risk, disease, or accident for young people which may not be performed by persons below 18 years of age.

15 A Child's Obligations Toward His Parents

In Danish law, children have no legal obligations toward their parents.

Les droits de l'enfant en droit français

Adeline Gouttenoire

1 Introduction

La ratification de la Convention internationale des droits de l'enfant par la France (CIDE) C'est la loi du 2 juillet 1990 qui a autorisé en France la ratification de la CIDE. Le traité est entré en vigueur dans notre pays le 6 septembre 1990.

La définition française de l'enfant Selon l'article 388 du Code civil français, « le mineur est l'individu de l'un ou de l'autre sexe qui n'a point encore l'âge de de dix-huit ans accomplis ».

L'intégration des droits de l'enfant dans la législation française Aucun instrument législatif interne n'est, en France, spécialement consacré aux droits de l'enfant. En revanche plusieurs textes contiennent des dispositions spécifiques aux enfants. On peut notamment citer l'article 388-1 du Code civil qui consacre le droit de l'enfant d'être entendu dans les procédures judiciaires le concernant. Ce texte, dans sa dernière version est issu de la loi n°2007-293 réformant la protection de l'enfance.

L'intérêt supérieur de l'enfant La notion d'intérêt de l'enfant est depuis longtemps, avant la ratification de la CIDE, contenu dans la plupart des articles du Code civil relatifs à la famille, notamment dans le domaine de l'autorité parentale ; toutefois la notion précise d'intérêt supérieur de l'enfant n'a pas fait l'objet en France d'une intégration formelle dans les textes, qu'ils soient législatifs ou constitutionnels. Même lorsque la loi du 5 mars 2007 a modifié l'article 375-7 du Code civil, elle a simplement ajouté que « Le juge peut décider des modalités de l'accueil de l'enfant en considération de l'intérêt de celui-ci ».

A. Gouttenoire (✉)
Faculté de droit et de science politique de Bordeaux, Directrice du CERFAP et de l'Institut des mineurs, 15 rue cendrillon, 33600 Pessac, France
e-mail: adeline.gouttenoire@wanadoo.fr

O. Cvejić Jančić (ed.), *The Rights of the Child in a Changing World*,
Ius Comparatum - Global Studies in Comparative Law 13,
DOI 10.1007/978-3-319-23189-1_6

L'intégration en droit français du critère de l'intérêt supérieur de l'enfant est essentiellement due à la jurisprudence tant de la Cour de cassation, qui a admis l'applicabilité directe de l'article 3 § 1 de la CIDE dans un arrêt du 18 mai 2005, que du Conseil d'Etat qui a affirmé la même solution dans un arrêt Cinar du 22 septembre 1997. Entre 2005 et 2009, la Cour de cassation a exercé une surveillance particulièrement sévère sur la motivation des décisions des juges du fond, procédant à une cassation de leur décision lorsqu'ils ne se fondaient pas formellement sur l'intérêt supérieur de l'enfant. Depuis 2009, elle procède plutôt à un contrôle substantiel de cette motivation, considérant que celle-ci est correcte dès lors qu'elle contient en substance, une appréciation au regard de l'intérêt supérieur de l'enfant, même si ce critère n'est pas formellement évoqué dans la décision.

Dans un certain nombre d'hypothèses, le législateur pose une règle présumée conforme à l'intérêt de l'enfant tout en laissant au juge la possibilité de renverser cette présomption si l'intérêt concret de l'enfant l'exige. Ainsi, l'article 373-2 du Code civil pose le principe d'un exercice en commun de l'autorité parentale par les parents séparés et l'article 373-2-1 dispose que « *si l'intérêt de l'enfant le commande le juge peut confier l'exercice de l'autorité parentale à l'un des deux parents* ». Dans le même sens, l'article 373-3 alinéa 1 du même code pose le principe selon lequel le parent survivant se voit attribuer l'autorité parentale en cas de décès de l'autre parent, et l'article 373-3 alinéa 2 permet au juge, à titre exceptionnel, si l'intérêt de l'enfant l'exige, de confier l'enfant à un tiers dans de telles circonstances. Le législateur a utilisé la même méthode à propos des relations de l'enfant avec d'autres personnes que ses parents. L'article 371-4 du Code civil pose ainsi le principe selon lequel l'enfant a le droit d'entretenir des relations personnelles avec ses ascendants et précise que seul l'intérêt de l'enfant peut faire obstacle à l'exercice de ce droit. De la même façon, l'article 371-5 du Code civil, prévoit que l'enfant ne doit pas être séparé de ses frères et sœurs sauf si son intérêt commande une autre solution. L'arrêt du 19 novembre 2009 fournit une illustration de cette dernière règle. La Cour de cassation a approuvé la Cour d'appel d'avoir écarté le principe de la résidence commune des frères et sœurs, au motif que l'intérêt des deux frères aînés était de rester avec leur père, tandis que leur mère partait vivre outre mer avec leur petite sœur.

2 Le droit de l'enfant de connaitre ses origines (art. 7 CIDE)

2.1 Filiation

Depuis l'ordonnance du 4 juillet 2005, ratifiée par la loi du 16 janvier 2009, l'enfant peut voir sa filiation établie à l'égard de son père et de sa mère, quelle que soit la situation du couple parental, que l'enfant soit né en ou hors mariage. La seule différence qui persiste encore réside dans l'existence d'une présomption de paternité au profit du mari de la mère (article 312 du Code civil).

En vertu de l'article 313 du Code civil, la présomption de paternité est écartée lorsque l'acte de naissance de l'enfant ne désigne pas le mari en qualité de père. Elle est encore écartée, en cas de demande en divorce ou en séparation de corps, lorsque l'enfant est né plus de trois cents jours après la séparation de ses parents. Dans cette hypothèse c'est la mère qui prendra l'initiative d'écarter la présomption. La filiation paternelle (en ou hors mariage) peut en outre être contestée par l'enfant, l'un de ses père et mère ou celui qui se prétend le parent véritable, sauf si l'enfant bénéficie d'une possession d'état de plus de cinq ans. Dans cette hypothèse l'action en contestation de la filiation est fermée à tous, sauf au ministère public.

2.2 Adoption

Lorsqu'il a fait l'objet d'une adoption plénière, l'enfant, s'il en a connaissance, peut demander aux services d'État civil, la communication intégrale de son acte de naissance sur lequel figurent les références du jugement d'adoption. L'acte de naissance intégral porte en effet mention de l'adoption puisqu'il est la transcription d'un jugement d'adoption plénière. Il peut réclamer la copie du jugement d'adoption qui lui révélera l'identité de ses parents de naissance lorsque ceux-ci étaient connus au moment de son adoption. Il peut également demander au juge en vertu de l'article 29 du Code de procédure civile, l'accès au dossier de procédure qui comporte la copie de la requête aux fins d'adoption laquelle indique le consentement à l'adoption. Par ailleurs, en vertu de l'article L. 225-13 du Code de l'action sociale et des familles, « *les organismes autorisées et habilitées pour l'adoption communiquent les dossiers individuels qu'ils détiennent aux intéressés qui leur en font la demande dans les conditions prévues par la loi du 17 juillet 1978* ».

L'adoption internationale est soumise en France aux mêmes conditions que l'adoption nationale (adoption par un couple marié depuis plus de deux ans – de sexe différent ou de même sexe depuis l'entrée en vigueur de la loi n°2013-404 du 17 mai 2013 – dont les membres sont âgés de plus de vingt-huit ans ainsi qu'aux personnes seules ayant atteint cet âge ; différence d'âge d'au moins quinze ans entre l'adopté et l'adoptant). Les articles L. 225-2 et L. 225-17 du Code de l'action sociale et des familles exigent des personnes désirant adopter un enfant pupille de l'État ou confié à un organisme agréée pour l'adoption, ainsi que des personnes souhaitant adopter un enfant étranger, qu'ils obtiennent un agrément délivré par le Président du Conseil général.

2.3 Accouchement anonyme

La question de la connaissance des origines en France pose pour l'essentiel celle du droit de l'enfant né dans le cadre d'un accouchement anonyme. En effet, le droit de la mère de demander que le secret de son admission et de son identité soit préservé lors de son accouchement est consacré par l'article 326 du Code civil. La femme qui accouche est ainsi en droit de ne pas fournir de pièce d'identité et est assurée par la loi qu'il ne sera procédé à aucune enquête. Elle peut bénéficier, ainsi que son enfant, d'une prise en charge médicale – les frais d'hébergement et d'accouchement sont pris en charge par le service de l'Aide sociale à l'enfance du département – tout en dissimulant sa maternité, l'enfant étant dès sa naissance remis à l'Aide sociale à l'enfance et adoptable à l'issue du délai de rétractation du consentement à l'adoption, qui est de deux mois. Même si la femme qui accouche donne son identité aux services médicaux ou sociaux elle est en droit d'exiger que ceux-ci ne communique jamais cette information à l'enfant. L'enfant qui plus tard cherchera à connaitre ses origines se heurtera à un secret légal. Toutefois, la femme qui le met au monde peut, à divers moments, et selon des modalités variables, renoncer à son droit au secret. L'article L. 22-6 du Code de l'action sociale et des familles dispose en effet que « *toute femme qui demande lors de son accouchement, la préservation du secret de son admission et de son identité par un établissement de santé est informée des conséquences juridiques de cette demande et de l'importance pour toute personne de connaître ses origines* ». L'objectif de cette dernière information est d'inciter la mère à laisser des informations pour l'enfant qu'elle abandonne. Le même texte prévoit qu'elle est invitée à laisser des « *renseignements sur sa santé, et celle du père, les origines de l'enfant et les circonstances de la naissance, ainsi que, sous pli fermé, son identité* ». Par ailleurs « *les prénoms de l'enfant et le cas échéant, mention du fait qu'ils ont été donnés par la mère ainsi que le sexe de l'enfant, la date, le lieu et l'heure de sa naissance sont mentionnés à l'extérieur de ce pli* », afin de pouvoir faire le lien entre l'enfant et les renseignements laissés par sa mère biologique. Lorsqu'elle laisse son identité au moment de la naissance, la mère peut accepter que son identité soit communiquée à l'enfant s'il en fait ultérieurement la demande. Dans le cas contraire, elle est informée du fait qu'elle pourra ultérieurement être contactée par le Conseil National de l'Accès aux Origines Personnelles (CNAOP) si l'enfant en fait la demande ; la mère ne pouvant pas, de son côté, demander au CNAOP de contacter l'enfant. Elle se réserve alors la possibilité d'accepter ou non de satisfaire le désir de l'enfant de la connaître. La communication de l'identité de la mère aura lieu si l'enfant en fait la demande alors que la mère est décédée sans avoir été contactée par le CNAOP. La mère peut également se contenter de laisser des renseignements non identifiants. Elle peut cependant, à tout moment, renoncer au secret et communiquer son identité sous pli fermé ou compléter les renseignements qu'elle a donnés au moment de la naissance, permettant alors au CNAOP de la contacter en cas de demande de l'enfant. Elle peut également directement autoriser le CNAOP à répondre favorablement à la demande de l'enfant de connaître ses origines, sans qu'il n'ait besoin, cette fois, de la contacter pour lui demander son accord.

2.4 *Assistance médicale à la procréation*

Les articles 16-8 du Code civil et L. 1211-5 du Code de la santé publique qui posent un principe général d'anonymat du don d'éléments ou de produits du corps humain est applicable au don de gamètes. L'article L. 1244-7 du Code de la santé publique rappelle son application au don d'ovocytes et l'article 2141-6 du même code rappelle à propos du don d'embryon, que « le couple accueillant l'embryon et celui y ayant renoncé ne peuvent connaître leurs identités respectives. » Même un médecin ne peut avoir accès qu'à des « informations médicales non identifiantes en cas de nécessité thérapeutique concernant un enfant conçu par une assistance médicale à la procréation avec tiers donneur ». En cas de procréation médicalement assistée, la transmission du nom du donneur est un délit pénalement sanctionné. La formulation des textes permet même de considérer que le tiers donneur ne peut renoncer à son droit au secret. Les demandes de personnes ayant été conçues par procréation médicalement assistée tendant à se voir communiquer des documents relatifs aux origines de leur conception sont donc rejetées par les Centres d'étude et de conservation des œufs et du sperme humains).

Le législateur a apporté deux dérogations à l'interdiction de communiquer toute information sur le donneur et sur le receveur. D'une part, l'article L. 1244-6 du code de la santé publique prévoit que « *Les organismes et établissements autorisés dans les conditions prévues à l'article L. 2142-1 fournissent aux autorités sanitaires les informations utiles relatives aux donneurs. Un médecin peut accéder auxinformations médicales non identifiantesen cas de nécessité thérapeutique concernant un enfant conçu à partir de gamètes issus de don.* » La loi du 7 juillet 2011 prévoit en outre dans l'article L1131-1-2 du Code de la santé publique qu'en cas de diagnostic d'une anomalie génétique grave susceptible de mesure de prévention, y compris de conseil génétique ou de soins chez le donneur de gamètes, ce dernier peut autoriser le médecin prescripteur à saisir le centre d'assistance médicale à la procréation afin qu'il procède à l'information des enfants issus du don.

3 Le droit de l'enfant d'exprimer son point de vue librement dans toutes les situations qui le concerne

3.1 *Procédures judiciaires*

Selon l'article 388-1 du Code civil français, « *Dans toute procédure le concernant, lemineurcapable de discernement peut, sans préjudice des dispositions prévoyant son intervention ou son consentement, être entendu par le juge ou, lorsque son intérêt le commande, par la personne désignée par le juge à cet effet. Cette audition est de droit lorsque le mineur en fait la demande. Lorsque le mineur refuse d'être entendu, le juge apprécie le bien-fondé de ce refus.* » Ce texte consacre un véritable droit de l'enfant d'être entendu dans toutes les procédures le concernant lorsque celui-ci sollicite cette audition.

Les textes spécifiques sont également relatifs à l'audition de l'enfant peuvent être classés en trois catégories selon l'apport qu'ils constituent au regard du texte général. Certains constituent un simple rappel du texte général (373-2-11 du Code civil en matière d'autorité parentale) tandis que d'autres imposent au juge de prendre l'initiative d'entendre l'enfant. Certaines dispositions subordonnent en outre la décision au consentement de l'enfant ou lui confèrent un droit de veto.

Dans la deuxième catégorie, l'article 1182, alinéa 2, du Code de procédure civile enjoint au juge des enfants d'entendre le mineur capable de discernement dans le cadre de la procédure d'assistance éducative. L'article 4431-2 du Code civil, impose de même au juge d'entendre le mineur avant de prononcer son émancipation. L'article 1234 du Code de procédure civile permet au mineur âgé de seize ans révolus de solliciter la réunion du conseil de famille auprès du juge des tutelles qui ne pourra pas s'y opposer. Lorsque le mineur, doté de discernement, est âgé de moins de seize ans, le juge de tutelles peut refuser de convoquer le conseil de famille à la demande du mineur par une décision spécialement motivée. Par ailleurs, l'article 1236 du Code de procédure civile impose au juge des tutelles d'entendre le mineur doué de discernement préalablement à la réunion du conseil de famille, dans les conditions prévues à l'article 388-1 du Code civil. Enfin, l'article 1234-7 du Code de procédure civile donne au mineur la possibilité d'assister à la réunion du conseil de famille, à titre consultatif, sauf si le juge des tutelles l'estime contraire à son intérêt. Lorsque le mineur n'a pas à donner son consentement dans le cadre de l'adoption, l'article L.223-4 du Code l'action sociale et des familles dispose que, de manière générale, le service de l'aide sociale examine avec le mineur toute décision le concernant et recueille son avis. Plus précisément, une fois le projet d'adoption établi par le tuteur avant que le Conseil de famille se prononce sur lui, le mineur capable de discernement est entendu par le tuteur ou son représentant et par le Conseil de famille ou l'un de ses membres désignés par lui à cet effet (CASF art. L225-4 al. 2).

3.2 Information du mineur sur son droit d'être entendu

Cette question est traitée en droit français dans le cadre de l'audition de l'enfant dans les procédures judiciaires qui le concernent.

Pour que le mineur puisse effectivement exercer son droit d'être entendu dans les procédures le concernant, il doit être informé de ce droit, et de l'existence de la procédure dans le cadre de laquelle il est susceptible de demander à être entendu. L'article 338-1 du Code de procédure civile dispose que le mineur capable de discernement est informé par les titulaires de l'exercice de l'autorité parentale, le tuteur ou le cas échéant, par la personne ou le service à qui il a été confié, de son droit d'être entendu et à être assisté d'un avocat dans toutes les procédures le concernant. L'acte introductif d'instance, requête ou assignation, doit être accompagné d'un avis rappelant les dispositions de ce texte et l'obligation qui incombe aux parents d'informer leur enfant de son droit d'être entendu.

3.3 *Traitements médicaux*

En matière médicale comme dans les autres matières, le principe est que la décision médicale est prise par les parents du mineur. Toutefois un certain nombre de dispositions spécifiques permettent au mineur d'être un sujet actif dans le domaine médical.

Le Code de la santé publique consacre tout d'abord le droit du mineur d'être informé de sa situation médicale même si ce sont ces parents qui prennent la décision médicale et qui sont selon ce texte les premiers bénéficiaires de l'information. L'article L1111-2, alinéa 5, du Code de la santé publique dispose en effet que « *les droits des mineurs ou des majeurs sous tutelle mentionnés au présent article [droit à l'information] sont exercés, selon les cas, par les titulaires de l'autorité parentaleou par le tuteur. Ceux-ci reçoivent l'information prévue par le présent article, sous réserve des dispositions de l'article* L. *1111-5. Les intéressés ont le droit de recevoir eux-mêmes une information et de participer à la prise de décision les concernant, d'une manière adaptée soit à leur degré de maturité s'agissant des mineurs, soit à leurs facultés de discernement s'agissant des majeurs sous tutelle.* »

Certains textes particuliers prévoient une information spéciale du mineur. Il en va ainsi des articles R. 1241-16 et R. 1241-18 du Code de la santé publique, qui prévoit l'information du mineur en cas de prélèvement de moelle osseuse et précise que le comité d'expert chargé d'autoriser le prélèvement doit s'assurer que l'enfant a été informé du prélèvement envisagé et de ses conséquences. En revanche, contrairement à la législation de nombreux pays européens, le droit français ne reconnaît pas au mineur le droit de consulter lui-même son dossier médical.

Ensuite, l'article 1111-2, alinéa 5, du Code de la santé publique consacre le droit du mineur « *de recevoir [lui-même] une information et de participer à la prise de décision [le] concernant d'une manière adaptée à sa maturité* ». L'article L. 1111-4 du Code de la santé publique se montre plus précis en affirmant que le consentement du mineur doit être systématiquement recherché s'il est apte à exprimer sa volonté et à participer à la décision. Les termes du texte imposent incontestablement au médecin de solliciter l'adhésion de l'enfant à l'acte médical. Il ne semble pas en revanche, qu'il le contraigne à obtenir son consentement, la recherche du consentement ne pouvant être assimilée à l'exigence du consentement. Les textes reconnaissent un droit d'expression à l'enfant sans imposer que soit prise une décision conforme au souhait exprimé.

Ainsi la France ne distingue pas en matière médicale en fonction de l'âge du mineur, et ne lui confère qu'une « autonomie participative ». Dans la mesure où il s'agit seulement de rechercher le consentement du mineur, son refus n'est, en théorie, pas un obstacle à la réalisation de l'acte médical, dès lors que ses représentants légaux ont donné leur consentement. On peut cependant difficilement admettre qu'un acte médical soit pratiqué sur un mineur discernant qui le refuse, la contrainte physique qu'il entraînerait étant contraire à la déontologie médicale ; il est donc vraisemblable que le médecin n'effectuerait pas l'acte. Dans l'hypothèse où l'acte envisagé ferait courir au mineur un danger physique ou psychologique, le mineur pourrait saisir le juge des enfants sur le fondement de l'article 375 du Code civil ; celui-ci serait susceptible d'interdire l'acte médical s'il estime qu'il lui fait courir un danger proportionnellement plus important que l'intérêt thérapeutique attendu.

Au delà de la recherche du consentement du mineur, certains textes accordent au mineur un droit de veto lui permettant de s'opposer à l'acte médical proposé par ses parents et les médecins. Ainsi, l'article 1241-3 du Code de la santé publique relatif au prélèvement de moelle osseuse dispose que « *Le refus du mineur fait obstacle au prélèvement* » et l'article L1122-2 du Code de la santé publique relatif à la recherche bio-médicale affirme qu'il ne peut pas être passé outre au refus d'un mineur de participer à une recherche biomédicale.

La mineure se voit enfin reconnaître une capacité autonome en matière de contraception et d'interruption volontaire de grossesse. La prescription et la délivrance de contraceptifs oraux ne sont pas soumis à l'autorité parentale et la mineure peut agir seule en ce domaine (art. L. 5134-1 du Code de la santé publique). Pour ce qui est de l'interruption volontaire de grossesse, si elle est en principe soumise à l'autorisation d'un des parents, le mineur peut demander à ce qu'elle soit pratiquée sans cette autorisation et sans que ses parents n'en soit informés (art. L. 2212-7 du Code de la santé publique). Dans cette hypothèse la loi exige qu'elle soit simplement accompagnée d'une personne majeure.

Surtout, le mineur peut solliciter seul des actes médicaux dans le cadre de l'exercice de son droit au secret consacré par l'article L. 1111-5 du Code de la santé publique selon lequel : « *par dérogation à l'article 371-1 du Code civil, le médecin peut se dispenser d'obtenir le consentement du ou des titulaires de l'autorité parentalesur les décisions à prendre lorsque le traitement ou l'intervention s'impose pour sauvegarder la santé d'une personne mineure, dans les cas où celle-ci s'oppose expressément à la consultation du ou des titulaires de l'autorité parentale afin de garder le secret sur son état de santé* ».

4 Le droit de l'enfant à la liberté de penser, conscience et religion

L'éducation religieuse est un des aspects de l'éducation en général, et en tant que tel, elle relève de l'autorité parentale. Il appartient donc aux parents de choisir la religion de leur enfant, de veiller au suivi de son enseignement et de ses pratiques. Attribut de l'autorité parentale, l'éducation religieuse de l'enfant fait l'objet du pouvoir de décision parentale. Lorsque les deux parents exercent en commun l'autorité parentale, qu'ils soient mariés ou non, unis ou désunis, le père et la mère décident ensemble de l'éducation religieuse du mineur. Lorsque les parents ne sont pas d'accord sur l'éducation religieuse à donner à leur enfant, le juge aux affaires familiales peut imposer le maintien du *statu quo* ou ordonner le retour au *statu quo ante*. Le juge peut interdire à un parent seul de changer la religion d'un enfant. Le choix d'un établissement scolaire est aussi fréquemment source de conflit entre les parents de religions différentes. Il a été jugé qu'une mère ne peut, de sa propre initiative, retirer un enfant d'un établissement religieux choisi antérieurement par les deux parents, pour le mettre dans un établissement laïque. Dans le système scolaire qui relève de l'éducation nationale aucun enseignement portant sur la religion n'est dispensé. Les décisions prises par les père et mère en matière de religion s'imposent aux tiers.

Lorsque les choix des parents en matière religieuse mettent l'enfant en danger, le juge de l'assistance éducative peut prendre les mesures nécessaires à la protection de l'enfant· Les droits des parents en matière d'éducation religieuse de leur enfant trouvent une limitation dans la loi du 15 mars 2004 « *encadrant, en application du principe de laïcité, le port de signes ou de tenues manifestant une appartenance religieuse dans les écoles, collèges et lycées publics* » qui a inséré dans le Code de l'éducation un article L. 141-5-1 selon lequel est interdit le « *port de signes ou de tenues par lesquels les élèves manifestent ostensiblement une appartenance religieuse* ». Les parents ne peuvent plus permettre, ni imposer à leur fille le port du voile islamique à l'école.

En théorie, le mineur ne dispose donc d'aucune autonomie en matière religieuse. La Cour de cassation s'est prononcée dans le sens d'un maintien de la religion de l'enfant dans le domaine de l'autorité parentale en considérant que la volonté d'une mineure de quinze ans de se convertir à la religion des témoins de Jéhovah, ne saurait être effective qu'après sa majorité, déniant ainsi au mineur toute prémajorité religieuse.

5 Les châtiments corporels

Les coups et blessures même légers que des parents administreraient à leur enfant sont susceptibles d'être pénalement incriminés au titre des violences sur mineur de quinze ans alors même qu'elles n'entraînent aucune incapacité de travail notamment sur le fondement de l'article 222-13 du Code pénal qui constitue un texte général non spécifique aux châtiments corporels sur les mineurs, le droit français ne contenant pas ce type de texte. Les poursuites sont particulièrement rares et les juridictions pénales avaient tendance à écarter l'application de l'article 222-13 du Code pénal au nom d'un « droit de correction » coutumier, sauf lorsque les violences étaient considérées comme excessives. Il semble cependant que cette jurisprudence soit désormais plus rare, certaines juridictions du fond ayant condamné des parents pour des châtiments corporels peu graves. La France a fait récemment l'objet d'une condamnation du Comité européen des droits sociaux pour l'absence de législation spéciale prohibant les châtiments corporels.

Dans le cadre scolaire, c'est également le texte général qui s'applique. Toutefois le droit de correction coutumier qui était, de fait, reconnu aux parents, n'est plus du tout admis pour les enseignants ou toute autre personne en charge d'enfants.

6 Le nom et le prénom de l'enfant

Le prénom de l'enfant est choisi par ses parents, sous réserve qu'il ne soit pas contraire à son intérêt. Dans cette dernière hypothèse le procureur de la République peut saisir le juge aux affaires familiales pour qu'il impose aux parents de modifier le prénom de leur enfant. Les parents peuvent également choisir le nom de leur enfant dans certaines limites : ils ont le choix entre le nom de chacun d'eux ou leurs deux noms accolés.

En principe le nom de l'enfant ne peut ensuite être modifié sauf dans le cas exceptionnel où sa filiation à l'égard d'un second parent est établie tardivement. Une procédure administrative de changement de nom est également ouverte lorsque l'enfant a un intérêt légitime à changer de nom, notamment lorsqu'il est ridicule ou qu'il est celui d'une personne qui a commis des actes graves. Dans ce cas, la procédure est intentée par les parents de l'enfant, seul l'enfant de plus de treize ans doit donner son consentement à son changement de nom.

Pour le prénom, le changement est possible en cas d'intérêt légitime dans le cadre d'une procédure judiciaire devant le juge aux affaires familiales. Là encore, la procédure est intentée par les parents de l'enfant, la seule participation de celui-ci consistant à donner son consentement au changement de prénom s'il est âgé de treize ans.

7 Mineur et travail

L'article L. 4153-1 du Code du travail pose le principe de l'interdiction du travail des mineurs de moins de seize ans, soumis à l'obligation scolaire, cette prohibition étant assortie d'une sanction pénale. En outre, la prohibition du travail des enfants de moins de seize ans souffre d'un certain nombre d'exceptions permettant de favoriser l'insertion professionnelle future du mineur. Elle n'interdit pas les travaux légers qui ne portent pas atteinte à l'obligation scolaire, notamment parce qu'ils sont effectués en dehors du temps scolaire, et ne nuisent pas à l'éducation de l'enfant dès lors qu'il est âgé de quatorze ans (Art. L. 4153-1 C. trav.). Par ailleurs, elle n'empêche pas l'emploi d'enfants de moins de seize ans dans les entreprises de spectacles ou de mannequinat ou dans les entreprises familiales (Art. L. 4153-5 C. trav.). L'apprentissage permet également au mineur d'acquérir une formation professionnelle pratique.

Les enfants artistes de moins de seize ans font l'objet une réglementation minutieuse et protectrice sanctionnée pénalement reposant d'une part sur une autorisation administrative et d'autre part sur un encadrement précis des conditions de travail.

Le régime du contrat de travail souscrit par un mineur, défini par la jurisprudence en l'absence de dispositions légales particulières, exclut le système de représentation, en raison de l'engagement personnel qu'il implique de la part du mineur.

Compte tenu de leur plus grande fragilité, notamment physique, les jeunes travailleurs font l'objet d'une protection spécifique. Un certain nombre d'emplois sont interdits aux mineurs même âgés de plus de seize ans. L'article L.3163-2 du Code du travail interdit par ailleurs le travail de nuit pour les jeunes travailleurs âgés de moins de dix-huit ans sauf dérogation exceptionnelle de l'inspecteur du travail pour les établissements commerciaux et ceux du spectacle qui ne peut permettre l'emploi des jeunes travailleurs entre minuit et 4 heures. La partie réglementaire du Code du travail contient en outre des dispositions interdisant certains travaux aux jeunes travailleurs en raison de leur pénibilité ou de leur caractère dangereux. La durée du travail des mineurs ne peut excéder trente-cinq heures par semaine ni sept heures par jour et il est interdit de les faire travailler les jours fériés, sauf dérogation exceptionnelle de l'inspecteur du travail. Les périodes de repos journalier, hebdomadaire et annuel sont également augmentées par rapport à celles accordées aux majeurs. Les inspecteurs du travail peuvent à tout moment demander qu'il soit procédé à un examen des mineurs de plus de seize ans travaillant dans l'entreprise afin de vérifier la compatibilité des tâches qui leur sont confiées avec leurs aptitudes physiques. Pour compenser les obligations particulières que l'embauche de jeunes travailleurs implique pour l'employeur, le salaire que ce dernier est tenu de leur verser est moins important que celui qu'il doit verser aux travailleurs majeurs.

8 Obligation du mineur envers ses parents

8.1 Respect

Selon l'article 371 du Code civil « *L'enfant, à tout âge, doit honneur et respect à ses père et mère* ». La jurisprudence a déduit de l'article 371 un devoir de piété filiale qui impose notamment à l'enfant de supporter les frais d'obsèques de ses parents même s'il renonce à leur succession.

8.2 Aliments

L'article 205 du Code civil dispose que « les enfants doivent des aliments à leur père et mère ou autres ascendants qui sont dans le besoin ». L'article 207, alinéa 2, prévoit la disparition du caractère réciproque de l'obligation alimentaire lorsque celui qui réclame des aliments « aura manqué gravement à ses obligations envers le débiteur ». L'article L. 228-1 alinéa 2 du Code de l'action sociale et des familles établit un régime particulier pour les obligations alimentaires auxquelles sont tenues les pupilles de l'État à l'égard de leurs parents déficients. Le principe est que le pupille de l'État qui a été élevé par le service de l'Aide sociale à l'enfance jusqu'à la fin de la scolarité obligatoire n'est pas redevable de l'obligation alimentaire auprès de ses ascendants, sauf appréciation contraire du juge fondée sur les circonstances, à moins que les frais d'entretien occasionnés par le pupille remis ultérieurement à ses parents n'aient été remboursés au département. De même, selon l'article L.

132-6 du même code, sont dispensés de toute obligation alimentaire à l'égard de leurs ascendants, les enfants qui ont fait l'objet d'un retrait judiciaire de leur milieu familial durant une période de trente-six mois cumulés au cours des douze premières années de leur vie.

9 La limitation ou la privation des droits parentaux

En droit français, la limitation des droits parentaux fait l'objet de de graduation.

9.1 Assistance éducative

Lorsque l'enfant est en danger ou en risque de l'être du fait du comportement de ses parents (maltraitances, négligences ou carences involontaires) le juge des enfants est compétent pour prendre des mesures éducatives sur le fondement de l'article 375 du Code civil. Ces mesures peuvent aller d'une aide à domicile à un placement de l'enfant. Elles sont en principe provisoires et doivent cesser si les parents sont jugés à nouveau aptes à prendre en charge leur enfant.

9.2 Délégation de l'exercice de l'autorité parentale

L'article 377, alinéa 2, du Code civil permet au tiers qui a recueilli un enfant de se faire déléguer l'exercice de l'autorité parentale lorsque les parents sont dans l'impossibilité de l'exercer ou s'ils se sont manifestement désintéressés de l'enfant. La délégation a pour effet de transférer à son bénéficiaire l'exercice de tout ou partie de l'autorité parentale. Les parents peuvent conserver des relations personnelles avec l'enfant. La délégation ne met pas fin à l'obligation d'entretien des parents, et le délégataire peut obtenir d'eux une contribution financière à la prise en charge de l'enfant. Selon l'article 377-2 du Code civil « *La délégation pourra, dans tous les cas, prendre fin ou être transférée par un nouveau jugement, s'il est justifié de circonstances nouvelles.* »

9.3 Retrait de l'autorité parentale

Selon l'article 378, alinéa 1er, du Code civil, « *Peuvent se voir retirer totalement l'autorité parentalepar une disposition expresse du jugement pénal, les père et mère qui sont condamnés, soit comme auteurs, coauteurs ou complices d'un crime ou délit commis sur la personne de leur enfant, soit comme coauteurs ou complices d'un crime ou délit commis par leur enfant, soit comme auteurs, coauteurs ou complices d'un crime sur la personne de l'autre parent* ». Le code pénal prévoit également que le juge pénal peut retirer l'autorité parentale à un parent qui a excercé des violences sur son conjoint.

Le retrait de l'autorité parentale est prononcé à la suite de graves fautes commises par les parents, qu'il s'agisse d'actes ou de manquements dont l'enfant est la victime directe (mauvais traitements, défaut de soins…), ou de comportements qui constituent indirectement une menace pour l'enfant (crime ou acte de délinquance, par ex.).

En dehors de toute condamnation pénale, peuvent se voir retirer totalement l'autorité parentale les parents qui ont gravement manqué à leur fonction. L'article 378-1 du Code civil envisage deux hypothèses : celle des parents dont le comportement est dangereux pour l'enfant et celle du désintérêt des parents après la mise en œuvre d'une mesure d'assistance éducative. Le juge civil compétent est le tribunal de grande instance.

Le retrait de l'autorité parentale entraîne la perte, par le parent déchu, des attributs de l'autorité parentale ou de certains d'entre eux et l'organisation d'un nouveau système de protection de l'enfant. Les modalités de ce système diffèrent selon qu'il reste ou non un parent en état d'exercer l'autorité parentale. Lorsque les deux parents se voient retirer l'autorité parentale ou que l'autre parent a perdu l'exercice de l'autorité parentale sur le fondement de l'article 373 du Code civil, l'article 380 donne au juge le choix entre deux types de protection : soit désigner un tiers auquel l'enfant sera provisoirement confié, à charge pour lui de requérir l'organisation de la tutelle, soit confier l'enfant au service départemental de l'Aide sociale à l'enfance.

The Rights of the Child in Germany: The UN Convention on the Rights of the Child and Its Implementation in National Law

Stefanie Schmahl

1 A Short Survey of the CRC's History of Application in Germany

The history of the application of the UN Convention on the Rights of the Child (CRC) in Germany is more than 20 years long. Coming into force with respect of Germany on 5 April 1992,[1] the Federal Republic of Germany was among the first states adhering to the Convention which entered into force on 2 September 1990 after the 20th instrument of ratification had been deposited in New York.[2] However, the narrative of the international regime of children's rights in Germany was, for a long time, intricate rather than simple. The Federal Government ratified the CRC on 26 January 1990, but the instrument of ratification was deposited on 6 March 1992 only together with five declarations of interpretation which, in substance, had rather the effect of reservations.[3] One of the most famous reservations was the so-called

This report, which has been finalized in October 2013 and updated in January 2014, has first been published in Martin Schmidt-Kessel (ed.), German National Reports on the 19th International Congress of Comparative Law, Tübingen 2014, pp. 581–609, © Mohr Siebeck Tübingen.

[1] See *Bundesgesetzblatt* (Federal Law Gazette) *BGBl.* 1992 II, p. 121, and *BGBl.* 1992 II, p. 990 (proclamation).

[2] The text of the Convention was adopted by General Assembly Resolution 44/25, of 20 November 1989 (UN Doc. A/RES/44/25), and opened to signature to all states. Today, the CRC counts 193 state parties.

[3] See *BGBl.* 1992 II, p. 990. Specific declarations were made with respect to Article 18.1, Article 40.2 lit. b, and Article 38.2 CRC, and more general declarations were made with regard to foreign children and to the scope of (direct) applicability of the CRC in the German legal order.

S. Schmahl (✉)
Chair of German and Foreign Public Law, Public International Law and European Law, Julius Maximilians University of Würzburg, Domerschulstr. 16, Würzburg D-97070, Germany
e-mail: schmahl@jura.uni-wuerzburg.de

O. Cvejić Jančić (ed.), *The Rights of the Child in a Changing World*,
Ius Comparatum - Global Studies in Comparative Law 13,
DOI 10.1007/978-3-319-23189-1_7

foreigner clause according to which the Convention's personal scope was restricted to German nationals only. Children being nationals of third countries were, from the outset, excluded from the ambit of the conventional guarantees.[4] This fact provoked an intense dispute in German legal literature on the scope and lawfulness of reservations to human rights instruments,[5] which only found its end when, on 15 July 2010, the Federal Government withdrew all its reservations to the CRC with effect from 1 November 2010.[6]

By contrast, the Optional Protocols to the CRC were all ratified by Germany without any declaration or reservation. The first Optional Protocol on the involvement of children in armed conflict was signed by Germany on 6 September 2000 and entered into force on 13 January 2005.[7] The second Optional Protocol on the sale of children, child prostitution, and child pornography, however, only came into force with respect of Germany on 15 August 2009, 9 years after it had been signed by the Federal Government on 6 September 2000.[8] This delay was mainly due to the fact that the content of the Protocol was criticized as being too vague because it did (and does) not establish new and effective standards compared to the prohibitions already enshrined in Articles 32–36 CRC.[9] On the other hand, Germany was one of the main supporters of the third Optional Protocol on a communications procedure which was opened for signature in Geneva on 28 February 2012.[10] It is thus not astonishing that the ratification procedure in Germany only took some months and was accomplished on 8 November 2012. The instrument of ratification was deposited on 28 February 2013, exactly 1 year after the Protocol had been opened for signing. The third Optional Protocol will come into force on 14 April 2014, 3 months after the tenth ratification has been deposited by Costa Rica on 14 January 2014.

Since the Federal Government withdrew all of its previous reservations in 2010, the CRC and its protocols are now fully applicable in Germany. Within the German

---

[4] Schmahl, *Kinderrechtskonvention mit Zusatzprotokollen, Handkommentar*, 2013, Einleitung, MN 23.

[5] *Cf.*, e.g., Ullmann, Verfassungs- und völkerrechtliche Widersprüche bei der Ratifikation der UNO-Kinderrechtskonvention, *Zeitschrift für das gesamte Familienrecht* 1991, 889 et seq.; Zimmermann, Neuere Entwicklungen zum Verhältnis zwischen dem UN-Abkommen über die Rechte des Kindes und nationalem Familienrecht, *Praxis des Internationalen Privat- und Verfahrensrechts* 1996, 167, at 173; Cremer, *Die UN-Kinderrechtskonvention: Geltung und Anwendbarkeit in Deutschland nach der Rücknahme der Vorbehalte*, 2011, at 15. The CRC Committee equally criticized the extent of the German declarations, see CRC Committee, Concluding Observations: Germany, UN Doc. CRC/C/15/Add.43, para. 13; and UN Doc. CRC/C/15/Add.226, para. 8.

[6] Lorz/Sauer, Kinderrechte ohne Vorbehalt, *MenschenRechtsMagazin* 2011, 5 et seq.

[7] See *BGBl.* 2004 II, p. 1355, and *BGBl.* 2006 II, p. 1015 (proclamation).

[8] See *BGBl.* 2008 II, p. 1222, and *BGBl.* 2011 II, p. 1288 (proclamation).

[9] More detailed Tomuschat, Mehr Schutz für die Schutzlosen: Die beiden Fakultativprotokolle zu dem Übereinkommen über die Rechte des Kindes, *Vereinte Nationen* 2002, 89, at 91.

[10] *Cf.* Löhr, Die Individualbeschwerde zur Kinderrechtskonvention, *MenschenRechtsMagazin* 2011, 115 et seq.; Lee, Communications procedure under the Convention on the Rights of the Child: 3rd Optional Protocol, *International Journal of Children's Rights* 18 (2010), 567 et seq.

legal system, human rights conventions and their protocols, to the extent that they have come into force for the Federal Republic of Germany, enjoy the status of a federal statute (see Article 59.2 of the Basic Law [*Grundgesetz*]). This classification means that German courts must observe and apply the Convention and its protocols within the limits of methodically justifiable interpretation like other federal statute law.[11] Furthermore, the guarantees of the human rights instruments influence the interpretation of the fundamental rights and constitutional principles of the German Basic Law.[12] The guarantees of the CRC and its protocols, by reason of their status in the hierarchy of norms, are not a direct constitutional standard of review in the German legal system. However, the text of the Convention and the (nonbinding) views given by the Committee on the Rights of the Child (CRC Committee) serve, on the level of constitutional law, as guides to interpretation in determining the content and scope of fundamental rights and constitutional principles of the Basic Law, provided that this does not lead to a restriction or reduction of protection of the individual's fundamental rights under the Basic Law.[13] Against this background, the influence of the CRC on the German legal order, including the fundamental rights system, becomes more and more noticeable in the recent jurisprudence of the Federal Constitutional Court (*Bundesverfassungsgericht*), the Federal Court of Justice (*Bundesgerichtshof*), and the Federal Administrative Court (*Bundesverwalt ungsgericht*).[14]

2 The Personal Scope of the CRC in Germany: Article 1 CRC and Age Limits

As regards the personal scope of the CRC, the German legal order finds itself largely in line with Article 1 CRC according to which a child means every human being below the age of 18 years. Although the Basic Law does not provide for a definition of children, Section 2 of the Civil Code (*Bürgerliches Gesetzbuch*) explicitly sets the age of majority at 18. At that time, parental custody and legal representation of the child by his/her parents or any other legal representative come to an end.[15]

[11] See Decisions of the Federal Constitutional Court (*Entscheidungen des Bundesverfassungsgerichts) BVerfGE* 74, 358 (370); 111, 307 (317, 319 et seq.).

[12] *BVerfGE* 74, 358 (370); 111, 307 (329); 128, 282 (306).

[13] *Cf. mutatis mutandis BVerfGE* 111, 307 (329); 128, 326 (371 et seq.). Particularly with regard to the CRC see recently *BVerfG*, decision of 5 July 2013, 2 BvR 708/12, para. 21.

[14] See, e.g., *BVerfG*, decision of 5 July 2013, 2 BvR 708/12, paras. 22–24 as well as Federal Court of Justice (*Bundesgerichtshof*), decision of 29 May 2013, XII ZB 530/11, paras. 20–22; Federal Administrative Court (*Bundesverwaltungsgericht*), judgment of 29 November 2012, 10 C 4/12, paras. 9–10; and judgment of 21 February 2013, 5 C 9/12, paras. 22–23.

[15] Bamberger in Bamberger/Roth (eds.), *Beck'scher Online Kommentar zum Bürgerlichen Gesetzbuch*, 2013, § 2 MN 2.

The individual gains full contractual capability and further receives the right to vote on federal level according to Article 38.2 of the Basic Law.

In principle, the German legal order does not make use of the so-called flexibility clause[16] as provided for in Article 1 CRC in fine. Majority or full legal capacity is in Germany not attained earlier than at the age of 18. This does not hinder, though, that some federal statutes use more specified and detailed classifications of minors, distinguishing, e.g., between children, juveniles, and/or adolescents. Pursuant to Section 1.1 of the Youth Protection Act (*Jugendschutzgesetz*), for instance, a child is a human being below the age of 14, whereas persons in between 14 and 18 years are defined as adolescents/juveniles. The protection granted by the Youth Protection Act to children is remarkably higher than to juveniles. The same is true with regard to other statutes which differentiate between younger and older children/juveniles such as Section 7.1 of Book VIII of the Social Code (*Sozialgesetzbuch Nr. VIII*), the Youth Court Act (*Jugendgerichtsgesetz*), and the Religious Child Education Act (*Gesetz über die religiöse Kindererziehung*). However, the distinction between children and juveniles/adolescents is always closely related to the respective field of law and has no general significance or purpose.

A delicate question arises with regard to German aliens and asylum laws. According to Section 80.1 of the Residence Act (*Aufenthaltsgesetz*) and according to Section 12.1 of the Administrative Asylum Procedures Act (*Asylverfahrensgesetz*), underage foreigner or refugees are capable of acting from the age of 16 years. These provisions are not unproblematic in view of Article 1 CRC and read in conjunction with Article 2 CRC, which prohibits discrimination on the grounds of national origin and other status. At least insofar as asylum-seeking (unaccompanied) minors are at stake, the early capability of acting in asylum procedures does not favor the minor but is detrimental to him/her.[17] This is all the more valid as the threshold of 18 years is regularly kept in other administrative procedures which do not cover refugees.[18] Furthermore, the asylum-seeking minor, as a rule, is not familiar with the German legal system and the German language.[19] However, the German courts, until now, deem it to be sufficient that the unaccompanied minor, while having the

[16] Critical assessments to this clause can be found by Dorsch, *Die Konvention der Vereinten Nationen über die Rechte des Kindes*, 1994, at 304; Van Bueren, *The International Law on the Rights of the Child*, 1995, at 37 et seq.; and Detrick, *A Commentary on the United Nations Convention on the Rights of the Child*, 1999, at 60.

[17] Heinhold in Kauffmann/Riedelsheimer (eds.), *Kindeswohl oder Ausgrenzung? Flüchtlingskinder in Deutschland nach der Rücknahme der Vorbehalte*, 2010, at 65; Krieger, Die UN Kinderrechtskonvention und die Handlungsfähigkeit unbegleiteter Minderjähriger im deutschen Asyl- und Ausländerrecht, *Recht der Jugend und des Bildungswesens* 2012, 206, at 210 et seq.; Schmahl (note 4), Art. 1 MN 12, and Art. 22 MN 20. Similarly District Court (*Amtsgericht*) of Gießen, decision of 16 July 2010, 244 F 1159/09 VM, paras. 10 et seq.

[18] One exception to this rule is Section 36.1 of Book I the Social Code (*Sozialgesetzbuch Nr. I*), according to which, minors at the age of 15 years are capable of claiming social benefits. However, this provision applies irrespective of the juvenile's nationality or origin.

[19] Löhr, Gesetzliche Konsequenzen aus der Rücknahme des Vorbehalts zur Kinderrechtskonvention, *Zeitschrift für Ausländerrecht und Ausländerpolitik* 2010, 378, at 379; Schmahl (note 4), Art. 2 MN 37.

capability of acting at the age of 16, has the possibility to be represented by a specialized counsel.[20]

A different solution is again given by the German criminal laws. Children and juveniles who commit crimes present a problem to any system of criminal justice, because they are less mature than adults and because criminal sanctions generally have to be a measure of last resort. One consequent difficulty lies in deciding whether children are suitable and responsible for their actions under criminal law, and if so, what the minimum age of criminal responsibility should be. Rule 4 of the UN Standard Minimum Rules for the Administration of Juvenile Justice ("The Beijing Rules")[21] does not specify a minimum age of criminal responsibility. However, the very warning of this rule that the age should not be fixed too low indicates that criminal responsibility and maturity are related concepts. In a similar manner, Article 40.3(a) CRC obliges the state parties to seek to promote the establishment of a minimum age below which children shall be presumed not to have the capacity to infringe penal law. The CRC Committee has recently, in 2007, concluded that a minimum age of criminal responsibility below the age of 12 years is considered not to be internationally acceptable.[22] The German legal order is in accordance with these requirements. The general standard of (limited) criminal responsibility in Germany begins at the age of 14 (see Section 19 of the Criminal Code [*Strafgesetzbuch*]), and full criminal responsibility is only provided for at the age of 18. Furthermore, a person between the age of 18 and 21 years is considered as a "young adult" to whose benefit criminal law relating to young defenders may, in individual cases, still be applicable (see Section 1.2 of the Youth Court Act).

3 Implementation of CRC Standards into the German Legal Order

3.1 Variety of Provisions Regarding Children's Rights

In its Concluding Observations on the State Reports of Germany, the CRC Committee repeatedly expresses concern that children's rights are not specifically mentioned in the German Constitution.[23] In fact, the German legal order does not

[20] See Higher Administrative Court (*Oberverwaltungsgericht*) Nordrhein-Westfalen, decision of 22 May 2012, 5 A 609/11.A, paras. 14–23; as well as Higher Regional Court (*Oberlandesgericht*) of Karlsruhe, decision of 2 December 2010, 2 UF 172/10, paras. 18–27, and decision of 5 March 2012, 18 UF 274/11, paras. 42–46. Similar but not yet decided: Federal Administrative Court (*Bundesverwaltungsgericht*), judgment of 29 November 2012, 10 C 4/12, para. 10.

[21] General Assembly Resolution 44/33, of 29 November 1985, UN Doc. A/RES/40/33, para. 4.

[22] CRC Committee, General Comment No. 10 (2007), UN-Doc. CRC/C/GC/10, paras. 16–18 and 32–35.

[23] See CRC Committee, Concluding Observations: Germany, UN Doc. CRC/C/15/Add.226, paras. 9 et seq.; UN Doc. CRC/C/15/Add.43, para. 14 et seq.; UN Doc. CRC/C/DEU/CO/3-4, paras. 9–10. Further see CRC Committee, General Comment No. 5 (2003), UN Doc. CRC/GC/2003/5, para. 21.

know a special legal regime which is exclusively and comprehensively devoted to the rights of the child. Neither the Basic Law nor the federal law statutes do comprise law books which are, in a consequent manner, only and extensively dedicated to children's rights.[24] The rights of the child are rather encompassed by a variety of provisions depending on the context and the field of law in question. This approach, although being different to the views of the CRC Committee, is to be held as adequate as it corresponds to the German culture and dogmatic tradition and does not lower the guarantees for children in substance.[25] The German legal order grants fundamental rights to "everyone" and does not exclude persons under the age of 18. Provisions addressed exclusively to children are therefore only necessary in those legal areas where children are in need of special protection or where children have to be particularly enabled to active participation.

A specific constitutional children's right is, however, granted by Article 6 of the Basic Law which protects marriage, family, and children. In particular, Article 6.2 of the Basic Law aims at protecting children by defining the grounds and limits of parental custody. For a long time, Article 6.2 of the Basic Law was understood as being primarily a fundamental right of the parents.[26] This interpretation has only been given up in 2008, when the Federal Constitutional Court ruled that it is the child who is the true holder of the right to be cared for in his/her best interests by the parents.[27] Although the decision of the Constitutional Court met some critique in legal literature,[28] there is widespread consensus that the right to care and education is established in favor of the child.[29] The child is not a legal object but an individual to whom parents owe care and education.[30] Also Article 24.1 of the EU Charter of Fundamental Rights grants children the right to such care and protection as is necessary for their well-being. In addition to these provisions entitling children to parental care, minors do enjoy the same fundamental rights of the Basic Law as adults. A

[24] Schmahl (note 4), Einleitung, MN 22.

[25] This aspect, is, however, not undisputed; see, e.g., Cremer, *Aufnahme von Kinderrechten ins Grundgesetz als Maßnahme zur Umsetzung der UN-Kinderrechtskonvention?*, 2011, at 4; Lütkes/Sedlmayr, Auswirkungen einer Grundrechtsänderung auf den Schutz, die Teilhabe und die Förderung von Kindern und Jugendlichen, *Familie Partnerschaft Recht* 2012, 187 et seq.; Hohmann-Dennhart, Kinderrechte ins Grundgesetz – warum?, *Familie Partnerschaft Recht* 2012, 185 et seq.; and – more reluctantly – Schuler-Harms, Kinder in den Mittelpunkt – und ins Grundgesetz, *Kritische Justiz* 2009, Beiheft 1, 133, at 146 et seq.

[26] See, in particular, *BVerfGE* 28, 104 (112) and formerly also Schmitt-Kammler in Sachs (ed.), *Grundgesetz*, 4th ed. 2007, Art. 6 MN 54.

[27] *BVerfGE* 121, 69 (92 et seq.); consenting: von Coelln in Sachs (ed.), *Grundgesetz*, 6th ed. 2011, Art. 6 MN 54, 68.

[28] See, for instance, Jestaedt in *Bonner Kommentar zum Grundgesetz*, 2011, Art. 6 MN 29 et seq.

[29] See *BVerfGE 61*, 358 (371); 121, 69 (92 et seq.); further Brosius-Gersdorf in Dreier (ed.), *Grundgesetz, Band I*, 3rd ed. 2013, Art. 6 MN 152, with further references.

[30] *BVerfGE* 103, 89 (107); 121, 69 (92). See also Jarass in Jarass/Pieroth, *Grundgesetz*, 12th ed. 2012, Art. 6 MN 48; Hohmann-Dennhart (note 25), at 186.

specific age is not required to hold these rights.[31] Whether children can actually exercise these rights depends on their individual intellectual capabilities,[32] and they have, of course, the right to be represented in court by their legal representative or a guardian ad litem.

On the level of federal statute law, there are more legal instruments that aim at protecting children from dangers than provisions which establish subjective rights of the child. The Youth Protection Act, for instance, primarily seeks to protect children from any form of risk which is able to derange or disturb their development.[33] According to the detailed and sophisticated regulations of this Act, e.g., access to guesthouses, for children below the age of 16, it is only permitted when they are accompanied by a person responsible for them.[34] Alcoholic beverages may neither be sold to children younger than 16 years, nor are children of this age-group allowed to consume those products in public.[35] Movies have to be labeled with age restrictions.[36] Also the youth welfare statutes which regulate public benefits toward children through supports given to their parents for education or child day care do only address children in an indirect manner.[37] Merely some more recent provisions consider children as true bearer of rights. In German family law, for instance, Section 1631.2 of the Civil Code now expressly grants children a viable right to an upbringing free of any violence.

3.2 *Implementation of Substantial Standards of the CRC in German Legislation*

The substantial standards of the CRC and its protocols are today widely implemented or reflected in German legislation. This is particularly true for the rules set out in Articles 2, 3, 6, and 12 CRC which the CRC Committee identifies as general and guiding principles of the Convention,[38] but also for other more particular standards enshrined in the Convention and its protocols. It is not the aim of this report – which is limited in pages – to discuss all possible implications of the CRC standards

[31] See, e.g., *BVerfGE* 47, 46 (74); 75, 201 (215), and Sachs, in Sachs (ed.), *Grundgesetz*, 6th ed. 2011, Vor Art. 1 MN 75–76.

[32] Peschel-Gutzeit, Zur Geschichte der Kinderrechte, *Familie Partnerschaft Recht* 2008, 471, at 472.

[33] Liesching, in Erbs/Kohlhaas (eds.), *Strafrechtliche Nebengesetze, Band I*, 2013, Vorbemerkung, MN 2.

[34] Section 4.1 of the Youth Protection Act.

[35] See Section 9 of the Youth Protection Act. The rules for tobacco products are more strict as they encompass all children until the age of 18; see Section 10 of the Youth Protection Act.

[36] Section 14 of the Youth Protection Act.

[37] See, e.g., Section 8.1 of Book VIII of the Social Code (*Sozialgesetzbuch VIII*).

[38] See CRC Committee, General Comment No 5 (2003), UN Doc. CRC/GC/2003/5, para. 12.

on the German legal order. Therefore, only selected issues that are of fundamental importance or which meet particular interest in present times, mostly with respect to family law relations, will be reflected in the following.[39]

3.2.1 Article 3 CRC: The Best Interest of the Child

A general norm comparable to the guiding principle enshrined in Article 3 CRC, which states that the best interests of the child shall be a primary consideration, cannot be found neither in German constitutional nor federal statutes law. However, the best interests of the child are of central importance when interpreting Article 6.2 of the Basic Law. There is no doubt that the constitutional guarantee of the parental rights enshrined in Article 6.2(1) of the Basic Law is primarily aimed at the well-being of the child.[40] The parents' natural right to care for and to educate their child without any state interference does not gear toward a parental domination of the child but, on the contrary, to serve the child's best interests in an altruistic way.[41] The care and upbringing of children is not only a natural right of parents but at the same time a duty primarily incumbent upon them. When conflicts arise between parents' interests and the interests of the child, the latter, depending on their nature and seriousness, shall be given primacy, and they may even override the interests of other parties involved in the conflict.[42] Furthermore, the state has the duty to supervise the parents in the performance of their parental rights (see Article 6.2(2) of the Basic Law). The state is even obliged to take over the duty to care for the child if the parents are strongly incapable or unwilling of doing so.[43] This state duty to watch over the parents in the performance of the care and upbringing of the child is, of course, bound to high prerequisites, inter alia, by giving strict primacy to the well-being of the child.[44]

---

[39] No particular reference will be made to the prohibition of discrimination (Article 2 CRC), including the duty to take affirmative actions, for instance, regarding disabled children (see Article 23 CRC). The ambit of both provisions is too large to be discussed in this report. For further details *cf.* Schmahl (note 4), Art. 2 MN 1–31, and Art. 23 MN 1–13.

[40] See *BVerfGE* 56, 363 (376); 59, 360 (376); 60, 79 (88); 103, 89 (107); 121, 69 (93).

[41] *BVerfGE* 59, 360 (376); 72, 155 (172); 108, 52 (78); 121, 69 (94); Brosius-Gersdorf (note 29), Art. 6 MN 142; Peschel-Gutzeit (note 32), at 473; Schmahl (note 4) Art. 3 MN 18, and Art. 5 MN 11.

[42] See *BVerfGE* 60, 79 (88); 72, 122 (137); 99, 145 (156). Also, according to the ECtHR's case law, the interests of the child may override those of the parents, see, e.g., ECtHR, *Elsholz v. Germany*, judgment of 13 July 2000, no. 25735/94, § 50; *T.P. and K.M. v. the United Kingdom*, judgment of 10 May 2001, no. 28945/95, § 71; *Sahin v. Germany*, judgment of 8 July 2003, no. 30943/96, § 65; *Pini and Other v. Romania*, judgment of 22 June 2004, no. 78028/01, § 155.

[43] Brosius-Gersdorf (note 29), Art. 6 MN 175.

[44] *BVerfGE* 24, 119 (144); 60, 79 (88). Further see von Coelln (note 27), Art. 6 MN 76 et seq.; Brosius-Gersdorf (note 29), Art. 6 MN 176; Uhle in Epping/Hillgruber (eds.), *Beck'scher Online Kommentar zum Grundgesetz*, 2013, Art. 6 MN 59.

The general principle of the best interests of the child is also appropriately integrated and concretized in various family law provisions. Namely, Section 1697a of the Civil Code establishes the duty of family courts to give the highest respect possible to the best interests of the child when deciding on child custody. This provision constitutes a general principle[45] and serves as a catch-all clause in cases where more specified rules which include the obligation to consider the well-being of the child, such as the provisions on foster family and on shared custody of separated parents,[46] do not apply in a given situation.[47] In a similar manner, also Article 24.2 of the EU Charter of Fundamental Rights states that in all actions relating to children, whether taken by public authorities or private institutions, the child's best interests must be a primary consideration.

3.2.2 Article 12 CRC: The Right of the Child to Express His/Her Views Freely in All Matters Affecting Him/Her

The general principle laid down in Article 12 CRC, according to which the child has the right to express his/her views freely in all matters affecting him/her, highlights the role of the child as active participant in the promotion, protection, and monitoring of his/her rights.[48] The opinions of the child have therefore to be given due weight in all matters affecting the child according to the child's age and maturity. In the view of the CRC Committee, Article 12 CRC imposes a clear legal obligation on state parties to recognize this right and ensure its implementation by adopting or revising laws.[49]

The German legal order to a great extent conforms to these parameters.[50] Everyone, including children, holds the right of freedom of expression laid down in Art. 5.1 of the Basic Law.[51] Furthermore, Section 1626.2 of the Civil Code expressly states that parents, when performing parental custody, are obliged to consider the growing abilities of their child. The older and more mature the child grows, the more parents have to take into account the child's views seriously and to seek an understanding with the child.[52] This does not imply a right to co-decision; parents or

[45] Veit in Bamberger/Roth (eds.), *Beck'scher Online Kommentar zum Bürgerlichen Gesetzbuch*, 2013, § 1697a MN 1.

[46] See Section 1632.4 of the Civil Code on foster families and Section 1671.2 of the Civil Code on the shared custody of separated parents.

[47] Götz in Palandt (ed.), 72nd ed. 2013, § 1697a MN 2.

[48] See CRC Committee, General Comment No. 5 (2003), UN Doc. CRC/C/GC/2003/, para. 12.

[49] CRC Committee, General Comment No. 12 (2009), UN Doc. CRC/C/GC/12, 2009, para. 15. It is interesting to note that Article 24.1 of the EU Charter of Fundamental Rights, which also grants children the right to express their view freely, was strongly inspired by Article 12 CRC.

[50] Similarly Baer, Verabschiedung des UN-Übereinkommens über die Rechte des Kindes im November 1989 in New York, *Familie und Recht* 1990, 192, at 193.

[51] Schulze-Fielitz in Dreier (ed.), *Grundgesetz, Band 1*, 3rd ed. 2013, Art. 5 MN 115.

[52] Schmahl (note 4), Art. 5 MN 11.

legal representatives are not obliged to adhere to the opinions expressed by the child or to partially or even fully comply with the child's ideas. But the provision admonishes parents to a moderate style of education by respecting the child as an individual and as a bearer of rights.[53]

The right to give due weight to the child's view in accordance to his/her age and maturity finds its procedural counterparts in the laws governing family law proceedings. Children over the age of 14 have the right to lodge a complaint by themselves in all questions affecting them; they do not need consent of their legal representatives.[54] With regard to younger children, parents might be entitled to complain on behalf of their children in cases where a conflict arises over a minor's interests opposing the parents and the national authorities having custody over the child. Yet, in cases where the holders of parental responsibilities are precluded from representing the child as a result of a conflict of interests with the latter, the child has the right to apply for a special counsel (legal guardian) in proceedings before a court or an administrative authority.[55] A legal guardian is to be appointed, for instance, in proceedings where the deprivation of parental custody is to be expected or where the right to contact, access, and care is concerned.[56] The purpose of the guardian lies in detecting the child's interests and bringing them before court. Thereby, the guardian has not only to consider the subjective will of the child but also his/her objective well-being.[57] In addition, the guardian is obliged to inform the child about the subject of the proceedings, the course of actions to be taken, and the likely outcome of the process. He/she has the duty to continuously inform the child about the progress of the proceedings; it is not sufficient to inform the child just once in the beginning.[58]

During the proceedings, the family courts, in principle, have to hear the child personally. When the child is over the age of 14, the hearing is mandatory.[59] Children below this age have to be heard personally in cases where the wishes of the child are

---

[53] Veit (note 45), § 1626 MN 32; Götz (note 47), § 1626 MN 22--23. More restrictively von Coelln (note 27), Art. 6 MN 69 et seq.

[54] See Section 60 of the Act on Proceedings in Family Cases and in Matters of Non-Contentious Litigation (*Gesetz über das Verfahren in Familiensachen und in den Angelegenheiten der freiwilligen Gerichtsbarkeit)*.

[55] See CRC Committee, General Comment No. 2 (2002), UN Doc. CRC/GC/2002/2, para. 19. Similarly ECtHR, *Scozzari and Giunta v. Italy*, judgment of 13 July 2000, nos. 39221/98 and 41963/98, § 138; *Moser v. Austria*, judgment of 21 September 2006, no. 12643/02, § 60.

[56] See Section 158 of the Act on Proceedings in Family Cases and in Matters of Non-Contentious Litigation.

[57] Schumann in Rauscher et al. (eds.), *Münchener Kommentar zur Zivilprozessordnung*, 4th ed. 2012, § 158 FamFG MN 27; Salgo, Mitwirkung am Zustandekommen einer einvernehmlichen Regelung: Aufgaben und Pflichten des Verfahrensbeistands, *Familie Partnerschaft Recht* 2010, 456, at 458.

[58] Schumann (note 57), § 158 FamFG MN 30.

[59] See Section 159.1 of the Act on Proceedings in Family Cases and in Matters of Non-Contentious Litigation; further *cf.* Schlünder in Hahne/Munzig (eds.), *Beck'scher Online Kommentar zum FamFG*, 2013, § 159 MN 2.

of special importance for the delivering of the decision. In practice, children over the age of 2 years are regularly heard in all cases affecting them, having due regard to their age, maturity, and the circumstances of the case.[60] This practice is in line with Article 9.2 CRC which states that all interested parties in family proceedings shall be given an opportunity to participate in the proceedings and make their views known.[61] It also conforms to the CRC Committee's General Comment No. 12 which discourages states from introducing or maintaining standardized age limits because age should not be a barrier to participate fully in judicial proceedings.[62] Similarly, the ECtHR found, in a finish custody case, a 12-year-old girl sufficiently mature for her views to be taken into account,[63] and the Court ruled, in further custody cases, that the hearing of younger children can be appropriate, depending on the circumstances of the case and the age and maturity of the child concerned.[64] Even if the will and the wishes of a child cannot always be decisive in family matters, it is nevertheless important to know the child's opinion in order to ascertain the child's true wishes.[65]

In administrative proceedings, the participation of children is also widely provided for in various law statutes. For instance, children are to be engaged in all questions of public youth welfare services, and they shall be involved in the planning and arranging of offers of youth work.[66] Furthermore, children are to be informed in an appropriate way about their rights in administrative proceedings as well as in judicial proceedings before the courts. This rule, enshrined, e.g., in Sections 8.1(2) and 17.2 of Book VIII of the Social Code as well as in Section 159.4 of the Act on Proceedings in Family Cases and in Matters of Non-Contentious Litigation*(Gesetz über das Verfahren in Familiensachen und in den Angelegenheiten der freiwilligen Gerichtsbarkeit)*, seeks to make sure that children are informed about their procedural rights in times of conflicts with their parents or legal representatives, particularly in cases where the latter might not accord all necessary information to the child.[67]

---

[60] See Section 159.2 of the Act on Proceedings in Family Cases and in Matters of Non-Contentious Litigation, as well as Schumann (note 57), § 159 FamFG MN 4. *Cf.* also *BVerfG, Zeitschrift für das gesamte Familienrecht* 2007, 1078.

[61] Schmahl (note 4), Art. 9 MN 22.

[62] CRC Committee, General Comment No. 12 (2009), UN Doc. CRC/C/GC/12, 2009, paras. 20–21. See also the UN Guidelines on Justice in Matters involving child victims and witnesses of crime, ECOSOC Resolution 2005/20, of 22 July 2005, para. 18.

[63] ECtHR, *Hokkanen v. Finland*, judgment of 23 September 1994, no. 19823/92, § 61.

[64] ECtHR, *Elsholz v. Germany*, judgment of 13 July 2000, no. 25735/94, § 50; *Sahin v. Germany*, judgment of 8 July 2003, no. 30943/96, § 73.

[65] Schmahl, Existing International and European standards: meeting the needs of children in Council of Europe (ed.), *Compilation of texts related to child-friendly justice*, 2009, 20, at 30.

[66] See Sections 8, 9, and 11 of Book VIII of the Social Code. For more details *cf.* Periodic Report of Germany, 20 October 2010, UN Doc. CRC/C/DEU/3-4, para. 90; Schmahl (note 4), Art. 12 MN 32.

[67] Tillmanns in Säcker/Rixecker (eds.) *Münchener Kommentar zum Bürgerlichen Gesetzbuch, Band 8*, 6th ed. 2012, § 8 SGB VIII MN 5.

If a juvenile between the age of 14 and 18 or a person considered as being a "young adult" (until the age of 21 years) is accused of having committed a crime, the Youth Court Act sets up additional procedural rules in order to protect the child and to give due weight to his/her views in court. According to Section 38 of the Youth Court Act, a guardian ad litem (*Jugendgerichtshilfe*) is to be consulted during all stages of the process against the juvenile. The main task of the guardian is the introduction of educational, social, and care-related aspects to the fore.[68] But also during the enforcement of a sentence, the guardian ad litem has to keep close contact with the juvenile and takes care of his/her social rehabilitation.[69]

The possible role of children and juveniles in criminal proceedings is, of course, not limited to their place as defendants or potential perpetrators. They also serve as witnesses, especially in criminal proceedings concerning sexual offenses of which they have been victims. Such proceedings are often conceived as an ordeal by the victim, in particular when the latter is unwillingly confronted with the defendant. These features are even more prominent in cases involving a minor. Therefore, in criminal proceedings where a child is to be heard as witness, Section 58a.1 of the Code of Criminal Procedure (*Strafprozessordnung*) gives the judge the possibility to question the child in a separate room and to video record the hearing.[70] This option was introduced into the criminal proceedings in 1998 mainly in order to protect minors who have been victim witnesses of sexual crimes, because hearings in court regularly do additional harm to the victim.[71] Like all witnesses, the child shall be instructed before being questioned. Furthermore, the adjudicating court must take into account that some of the information given by a child, particularly a young child, is vague, uncertain, and lacking detail. The court must also have due regard to the possibly leading nature of some questions put to the child during the police interviews.[72] Therefore, children witnesses may avail themselves of the assistance of a legal counsel, and courts regularly call for forensic psychology experts who have special training in and knowledge of the matter.[73]

---

[68] Eisenberg, *Jugendgerichtsgesetz*, 16th ed. 2013, § 38 MN 20.

[69] See Section 38.2 of the Youth Courts Act and Eisenberg (note 68), § 38 MN 19.

[70] Further see *BGBl.* 2013 I, p. 935, at 936, with a new Section 58b having been introduced into the Code of Criminal Procedure in order to facilitate the hearing of witnesses by means of broadcasting.

[71] Senge in Hannich (ed.), *Karlsruher Kommentar zur Strafprozessordnung*, 7th ed. 2013, § 58a MN 6. *Cf.* also ECtHR, *S.N. v. Sweden*, judgment of 2 February 2002, no. 34209/96, § 44 et seq.; *B. v. Finland*, judgment of 24 April 2007, no. 17122/02, § 42.

[72] See ECtHR, *S.N. v. Sweden*, judgment of 2 July 2002, no. 34209/96, § 53. Similarly with regard to family proceedings: Heilmann, Die Gesetzeslage zum Sorge- und Umgangsrecht, *Neue Juristische Wochenschrift* 2012, 16, at 17.

[73] The Federal Ministry of Justice, since a couple of years, does further provide a child-friendly brochure on its web site named "Ich habe Rechte" ("I have rights") which particularly addresses children's rights in criminal proceedings.

3.2.3 Articles 7 CRC: The Right of the Child to Know about His/Her Origin

With the modernization of societies and the increasing biomedical progress, the right of the child to know about his/her origin as guaranteed by Article 7 CRC raises more and more legal problems, which were not known at the time when the Basic Law was drafted in 1948/1949 and even not common when the CRC entered into force in 1990. Therefore, most of the provisions in Germany regulating the right of the child to know about his/her origin are the result of recent developments in legislation.

In 2008, a new provision – Section 1598a – was introduced into the Civil Code[74] after the Federal Constitutional Court had adopted a ruling according to which the legislative had to bring into existence a lawsuit that enables the child to clarify his/her origin irrespective of the question of legal paternity.[75] This so-called origin clarification claim (*Verfahren zur Klärung der Abstammung*) is the result of transforming the personal rights of the child into a specific procedural right. All children – not only children born out of wedlock but also children born in wedlock – have the right to demand their mother and father to consent to biomedical measures in order to clarify their true biological origin.[76] Furthermore, Section 1598a of the Civil Code does not only contain the right to clarify the fatherhood of a child but also the right to question whether the legal mother is in fact the genetic mother.[77] If one of the parents or both do not consent, the competent family court has to substitute the lacking consent if the child so demands (Section 1598a.2 of the Civil Code). On the other hand, also both parents are entitled to demand clarification about the origin of the child. Yet, the family court will stay the proceedings in those cases where the clarification of the origin of the child gravely endangers the well-being of the minor child (see Section 1598a.3 of the Civil Code). The potential biological father who is not the legal father has no right to demand clarification.[78]

If a child is born in wedlock, it is regularly assumed that he/she is the child of the marital father (see Section 1592 of the Civil Code). This rule, although only referring to legal presumptions, has recently been declared compatible with the European Convention on Human Rights by the ECtHR in the case *Ahrens v. Germany* (2012) with the view to the possibility given by law to determine the natural paternity.[79] In fact, according to the newly (in 2008) introduced Section 1600 of the Civil Code,

[74] *BGBl.* 2008 I, p. 441. See further Hahn in Bamberger/Roth (eds), *Beck'scher Online Kommentar zum Bürgerlichen Gesetzbuch*, 2013, § 1598a MN 1.

[75] *BVerfGE* 117, 202 (229 et seq.). See also *BVerfGE* 108, 82 (105).

[76] See also the Periodic Report of Germany, 20 October 2010 (note 66), para. 108.

[77] Wellenhofer in Säcker/Rixecker (eds.), *Münchener Kommentar zum Bürgerlichen Gesetzbuch*, Band 7, 6th ed. 2012, § 1598a MN 22.

[78] Rauscher in v. Staudinger, Bürgerliches Gesetzbuch, *Buch 4: Familienrecht*, 2012, § 1598a MN 9.

[79] ECtHR, *Ahrens v. Germany*, judgment of 22 March 2012, no. 45071/09, § 70 et seq. See also ECtHR, *Kautzor v. Germany*, judgment of 22 March 2012, no. 23338/09, § 69 et seq.

the child, the mother, the legal father, the man who affirms to have lain with the mother during the time of conception, and the authority responsible for the acknowledgment of paternity have the right to appeal paternity (*Vaterschaftsanfechtungsverfahren*). The time limit for appeal is 2 years after having gained knowledge of the circumstances that could indicate the nonexistence of biological fatherhood. The nonexistence of fatherhood will be determined by the family courts. If the legal father is proven not to be the biological father, the presumption given by Section 1592 of the Civil Code is without effect (see Section 1599.1 of the Civil Code). Legal paternity will then have to be determined through a "paternity determination lawsuit" (*Vaterschaftsfeststellungsverfahren*) before the family courts (Section 1600d of the Civil Code). The aforementioned "origin clarification lawsuit" according to Section 1598a of the Civil Code gives a further possibility to clarify fatherhood without having to appeal legal paternity.[80]

Particular problems exist in cases where a child has been legally adopted and is raised in wedlock. Already in January 1989, the Federal Constitutional Court held that is was against the personal right if an adopted person over the age of 18 had no right to know who his/her biological parents were. There is a fundamental right at least for adults to know their proper origin.[81] Today, the federal law statutes go even further. According to Section 9b.2 of the Adoption Agency Act (*Adoptionsvermittlungsgesetz*), adopted children, from the age of 16 years onward, have to be granted access to the papers documenting their adoption and origin. They have the right to information about their biological parents, including their profession, origin, and current family status, as well as about the existence of biological siblings. Access to further information that is not directly related to the personal history of the adopted child is only granted if the child demonstrates a legitimate interest. This restriction is made in order to protect the interests of third persons involved in the adoption procedure.[82] The documents on the adoption procedure have to be kept by the competent authorities for a time period of 60 years starting from the date of birth of the adopted child (see Section 9b.1 of the Adoption Agency Act).

Finally, the most precarious situation occurs when children are conceived with biomedical assistance, particularly via sperm donations. Although it is not disputed that these children do enjoy the same fundamental rights like other individuals, their rights have to be balanced against the rights of the anonymous sperm donator. This balance recently, on 6 February 2013, was made by the Higher Regional Court (*Oberlandesgericht*) of Hamm to the effect that a child conceived via sperm donation has the right to know about his/her biological father. The Court assessed the

---

[80] Brudermüller in Palandt (ed.), Bürgerliches Gesetzbuch, 72nd ed. 2013, § 1598a MN 1. Both claims, of course, do not confer the right to the biological father to have contact with his child. This question is regulated by the newly introduced Section 1686a of the Civil Code (for more details see note 104).

[81] *BVerfGE* 79, 256 (268).

[82] See Reinhardt, *Adoptionsvermittlungsgesetz*, 2012, § 9b MN 8 et seq.

right of the child to know his biological origin as being superior to the interests of the father to stay anonymous. Whereas knowing one's origin is of central importance for the development of the personality, the interests of the donator to stay anonymous are less in need of protection.[83] This argument given by the Court can be agreed with. However, it is to be stressed that the Higher Regional Court's decision has not yet established a consolidated line of case law, and there is, until now, no special legislation regulating the topic in Germany.

By contrast, surrogate motherhood and egg donation are explicitly forbidden in Germany in order to avoid the occurrence of a "divided motherhood."[84] The woman who gives birth to a child is always seen as the legal mother (see Section 1591 of the Civil Code). From a legal perspective, genetic and legal motherhood are thus assumed to be identical. Consequently, there is – besides the general claim pursuant to Section 1598a of the Civil Code – no need for a specific right for a child conceived with biomedical assistance to identify his/her genetic mother. However, as egg donation and surrogate motherhood are allowed in other countries, it is not astonishing that, on 5 September 2012, the Administrative Court (*Verwaltungsgericht*) of Berlin had to decide on an "egg cell tourism" case. A German married couple traveled to the Ukraine and found a surrogate mother to deliver their cognate baby. After the birth which had taken place in the Ukraine, the German couple applied for a German passport for the baby. The request was dismissed by the German authorities arguing that the Ukrainian woman, who gave birth to the child, was the child's legal mother, and her Ukrainian husband was the legal father. The child was therefore considered a Ukrainian national. The Administrative Court of Berlin confirmed this view. It stressed that under German law, "divided motherhood" was to be avoided and only the woman having given birth could be regarded as the legal mother of the child. The genetic mother, i.e., the woman from whom the egg cell derives, can only become a legal mother through adoption.[85] The child concerned, however, has the right, according to Section 1598a of the Civil Code, to demand his/her genetic mother to consent to biomedical measures in order to clarify his/her origin.[86] This "origin clarification claim" does, of course, not help in determining the nationality status.

[83] Higher Regional Court (*Oberlandesgericht*) of Hamm, judgment of 6 February 2013, I-14 U 7/12, *Zeitschrift für das gesamte Familienrecht* 2013, 637 (639 et seq.). Critical Fink/Grün, Der Auskunftsanspruch über die Abstammung des durch heterologe Insemination gezeugten Kindes gegen den Arzt, *Neue Juristische Wochenschrift* 2013, 1913–1916.

[84] See, with more details, Günther in Günther/Taupitz/Kaiser (eds.), *Embryonenschutzgesetz*, 2008, § 1 II, MN. 4.

[85] Administrative Court (*Verwaltungsgericht*) of Berlin, judgment of 5 September 2012, VG 23 L 283.12, *Zeitschrift für das gesamte Familienrecht* 2013, 738–740. See also the concurrent view of the Higher Regional Court (*Oberlandesgericht*) of Stuttgart, judgment of 7 February 2012, 8 W 46/12, *Zeitschrift für das gesamte Familienrecht* 2012, 1740 et seq., in a similar case concerning egg donation.

[86] Brudermüller (note 80), § 1598a MN 6.

3.2.4 Articles 7, 8 CRC: The Right of the Child to Change His/Her Personal Name

According to Articles 7.1 and 8.1 CRC, children shall have the right from birth to a name, and state parties shall respect the child's right to preserve his/her identity, including the name. There is no reference made, neither in the Convention nor in the recommendations of the CRC Committee, as to whether the child shall also have the right to change his/her personal name. The choice of the child's names is rather considered, within the ambit of Article 7 CRC, as a natural right belonging to the parents.[87] The Federal Constitutional Court, too, holds the right to naming as being part of the parental rights which is only limited in cases of irresponsible naming.[88]

This view finds its logical equivalent in the German Name Amendment Act (*Namensänderungsgesetz*) according to which no one, neither an adult nor a child, may change his/her names independently but has to initiate a name-changing procedure before the competent authorities,[89] irrespective of whether the individual seeks to change the first name, the surname, or both.[90] If the applicant is a minor, the lawsuit must be filed by the legal representative.[91] In any case, the applicant has to demonstrate a significant reason for changing the name.[92] As a rule, the changing of the child's personal name is permitted only in very special cases and under strict conditions. The family courts may, for instance, change the first name of a child in the course of an adoptionprocedure provided that the adopting parents so request, the child has given his/her consent and the change of the first name is considered as being in the best interests of the child (see Section 1757.4 of the Civil Code). Also the Transsexual Act (*Transsexuellengesetz*) allows a person who does not feel appendant to his/her original sex to officially change his/her first name only after having fulfilled several preconditions. Whereas the minimum age required for this change of name was originally at 25 years, today, after the Federal Constitutional Court, in 1982, has held this age threshold to be contrary to the Basic Law,[93] even children are entitled to change their personal names according to the Transsexual Act; hereby, they do, however, need the consent of their legal representative.[94]

[87] Van Bueren (note 16), at 117; Ziemele in Alen et al. (eds.), *A Commentary on the United Nations Convention on the Rights of the Child*, Volume 7, 2007, Art. 7, p. 11.

[88] See *BVerfGE* 104, 373 (385 et seq.). Under certain circumstances, also the biological father has the right to naming with respect to the child's surname even in cases where the mother does not give consent, see Superior Court of Justice (*Kammergericht*) of Berlin, decision of 23 September 2010, 1 W 70/08, paras. 34–44.

[89] Section 1 of the Name Amendment Act.

[90] See Section 11 of the Name Amendment Act.

[91] Section 2 of the Name Amendment Act.

[92] Section 3 of the Name Amendment Act.

[93] See *BVerfGE* 60, 123 (131 et seq.).

[94] Augstein, *Transsexuellengesetz*, 2012, § 1 MN 5.

3.2.5 Article 9 CRC: Deprivation of Parental Responsibilities and Separation of the Child from His/Her Parents

Article 9 CRC demands from the state parties to ensure that a child shall not be separated from his/her parents against their will, except when competent authorities subject to judicial review determine that such separation is necessary for the best interests of the child. As already mentioned, in Germany, it is the state which supervises parental custody according to the conditions laid down in Articles 6.2 and 6.3 of the Basic Law. Sections 1666 *et seq.* of the Civil Code transform this constitutional mandate into more concrete provisions[95] by stipulating the requirements in which the deprivation of parental responsibilities, partially or completely, is legally admissible. Parents may be deprived of their rights only in cases where the physical, mental, or emotional well-being of the child is gravely endangered because of gross parental failure. As a measure of last resort, i.e., in cases of massive neglect of the child, the state is even competent to take the child out of his/her family in order to (re-)ensure the child's well-being.[96] The separation of the child from his/her parents is, of course, only admissible if other measures have either been unsuccessful or if they will presumably not be sufficient to avert the danger for the child.[97] During the last decades, certain situations have been carved out in case law and in literature as to when state action in order to protect the child must be taken. Especially crimes committed against the child fall into this category, but also the suspicion of the child being sexually abused, the lack of personal hygiene of the child, and strong deficits of the parents in upbringing, e.g., the parents being drug addicts.[98] The competent authority for the partial or complete deprivation of parental responsibilities is the family court. The court has, in principle, discretion as regards the measures to be taken, but the full deprivation of parental responsibilities must be a measure of last resort.[99]

In general, the full deprivation of parental responsibilities goes along with the separation of the child from his/her family. In these cases, Article 6.3 of the Basic Law sets up further (implicit) conditions as regards the possibility to put the child in a public institution for child care or to place the child in a foster family.[100] Finding a new legal family for the child (foster family or adopting parents) is considered to be a more favorable solution with regard to the child's well-being than a placement in a child care institution.[101] Article 20 CRC comes to the same conclusion when

[95] *BVerfGE* 121, 69 (92); further see Brosius-Gersdorf (note 29), Art. 6 MN 190; Olzen in Säcker/Rixecker (eds.), *Münchener Kommentar zum Bürgerlichen Gesetzbuch, Band 7*, 6th ed. 2012, § 1666 MN 1.

[96] von Coelln (note 27), Art. 6 MN 85 et seq.

[97] *BVerfGE* 78, 51 (60).

[98] See *BVerfGE* 107, 104 (118), and the examples given by Veit (note 45), § 1666 MN 14 et seq.; and Olzen (note 95), § 1666 MN 57.

[99] Götz (note 47), § 1666 MN 30.

[100] See Brosius-Gersdorf (note 29), Art. 6 MN 204, with further references.

[101] *BVerfGE* 24, 119 (146–148).

stating that a child temporarily or permanently deprived of his/her family environment shall be entitled to special protection and assistance, and the state shall primarily ensure alternative care such as foster placement or adoption. In addition, it is not excluded that parental responsibilities are retransferred to the parents. The idea of Article 6.2 of the Basic Law is that children should primarily live with their biological parents rather than with compensatory legal parents, if the circumstances permit to do so.[102]

The parent who is deprived of parental responsibilities does keep rights and obligations toward the child even after deprivation. According to Section 1684.1 of the Civil Code, the child has the right to have contact with both parents. Hence, each parent is obliged to have contact with his/her child if the child wants so.[103] Furthermore, one parent may not deliberately hinder the child's contact with the other parent.[104] This is of special importance in cases where only one parent has been deprived of parental responsibilities. However, the obligation to keep contact with the child is not enforceable by law in order to serve the best interests, the well-being, and the development of the child.[105]

3.2.6 Article 14 CRC: The Right of the Child to Freedom of Thought, Conscience and Religion, and Religious Instruction in Public Schools

The right of the child to freedom of thought, conscience, and religion as guaranteed by Article 14 CRC and by Article 4 of the German Basic Law does not hinder the state to install religious education in public schools provided that it is not a mandatory subject for everyone irrespective of religious beliefs. Maintaining the State's obligation of neutrality and the parental educational mandate, respect for freedom of religion or worldview in schools is entrenched in the system.[106] However, Article 7.3 of the Basic Law states that religious instruction shall form part of the regular curriculum in state schools, with the exception of nondenominational schools. Further exceptions, for historical reasons, can be found in Article 141 of the Basic Law. According to this provision, the rules on religious instruction as stipulated in Article 7.3 of the Basic Law shall not apply in any federal state (*land*),

[102] Brosius-Gersdorf (note 29), Art. 6 MN 148. See also ECtHR, *Y.C. v. United Kingdom*, judgment of 13 March 2012, no. 4547/10, § 134 et seq.

[103] Veit (note 45), § 1684 MN 9. See also *BVerfGE* 121, 69 (97).

[104] Götz (note 47), § 1684 MN 5. It is not without problems for the child's well-being that the newly introduced Section 1686a of the Civil Code confers the right to have contact to the biological father even in cases where the child has a legal father and lives with him; see Peschel-Gutzeit, Der doppelte Vater – Kritische Überlegungen zum Gesetz zur Stärkung der Rechte des leiblichen, nicht rechtlichen Vaters, *Neue Juristische Wochenschrift* 2013, 2465 (2466 et seq.). See also the skeptical opinion expressed by ECtHR, *Kautzor v. Germany*, judgment of 22 March 2013, no. 23338/09, § 72.

[105] *BVerfGE* 121, 69 (98 et seq.); Brosius-Gersdorf (note 29), Art 6 MN 191.

[106] Periodic Report of Germany, 20 October 2010 (note 66), para. 113.

such as Bremen, which already had deviating provisions when the Basic Law entered into force.[107]

The mentioning of religious instruction as part of the regular curriculum in Article 7.3 of the Basic Law primarily means that the state is responsible for its curriculum and costs.[108] Parents and guardians, however, have the right to decide whether children shall receive religious instruction or not (see Article 7.2 of the Basic Law). Yet, when the child has reached religious maturity, the decision whether he/she will participate in religious instruction is left up to him/her.[109] Pursuant to Section 5 of the Religious Child Education Act, a child reaches full religious maturity at the age of 14. But already from the age of 12 years onward, the child may not, without his/her will, be educated in a religious confession different from the one he/she belongs to. This provision is considered as being in accordance with the freedom of religion enshrined in Article 4 of the Basic Law.[110]

Religious instruction is given in accordance with the tenets and principles of the religious community concerned, without prejudice to the state's right of supervision. Religious education is, however, not an ecclesiastic event.[111] The state remains responsible for the curriculum which it prepares in conformity with the respective religious principles. Thereby, the state may only employ teachers for religious education which the religious community has approved of through, for instance, either "vocatio" (protestant) or "missio canonica" (catholic).[112] As regards the contents, the dogmata of the respective religious community are taught. Religious education is not just a subject where neutral information is given; religious principles and rites rather form the basis of the courses.[113] However, religious education being primarily a school subject, tolerance and openness vis-à-vis different religions and ideologies are required.[114] Within the federal system in Germany, it is not the Federation (*Bund*) but the federal states (*Länder*) which are competent and responsible for the legislation in educational matters.[115] Therefore, it is up to them to decide the exact curriculum of religious instruction in accordance with Article 7.3 of the Basic Law.

Another problem arises when (female) schoolteachers wear Islamic headscarves in public schools. The CRC Committee was concerned with laws in some of the

---

[107] As to the scope of this provision, see Schmahl in Sodan (ed.), *Grundgesetz*, 2nd ed. 2011, Art. 141 MN 2, with further references.

[108] *BVerfGE* 70, 224 (251); 123, 49 (52 et seq.); Uhle (note 44), Art. 7 MN 48; Robbers in v. Mangoldt/Klein/Starck (eds.), *Grundgesetz, Band 1*, 6th ed. 2010, Art. 7 MN 131 et seq.

[109] Schmitt-Kammler/Thiel in Sachs (ed.), *Grundgesetz*, 6th ed. 2011, Art. 7 MN 52; Uhle (note 44), Art. 7 MN 64.

[110] See Germann in Epping/Hillgruber (eds.), *Beck'scher Online Kommentar zum Grundgesetz*, 2013, Art. 4 MN 27, with further references.

[111] *Cf.* Uhle (note 44), Art. 7 MN 57; Sodan in Sodan (ed.), *Grundgesetz*, 2nd ed. 2011, Art. 7 MN 7.

[112] Uhle (note 44), Art. 7 MN 59. Similarly Kotzur in Stern/Becker (eds.), *Grundrechte-Kommentar*, 2010, Art. 7 MN 37.

[113] *BVerfGE* 74, 244 (252).

[114] Badura in Maunz/Dürig (eds.), *Grundgesetz, Kommentar*, 2012, Art. 7 MN 70 et seq.

[115] Hofmann in Schmidt-Bleibtreu et al. (eds.), *Grundgesetz*, 12th ed., 2011, Art. 7 MN 32.

Länder aiming at banning schoolteachers from wearing headscarves in public schools, as this does not contribute to the child's understanding of the right to freedom of religion and to the development of an attitude of tolerance as promoted in the aims of education under Article 29 CRC.[116] After the decision of the Federal Constitutional Court of 24 September 2003 in the "Ludin" case,[117] however, most of the *Länder* have adopted measures which do not single out a particular religious group when addressing schoolteachers and their religious clothing and outfit.[118]

3.2.7 Article 19 CRC: Prohibition of Physical Punishment of the Child within Family and Beyond

Article 19 CRC states that children have to be protected from all forms of physical or mental violence while in the care of parents, legal guardians, or any other person who has the care of the child. While some German *Länder* originally allowed teachers to physically castigate pupils, physical punishment in schools has been forbidden all over Germany since 1973. Article 86.3 of the Bavarian Education Act (*Bayerisches Gesetz über das Erziehungs- und Unterrichtswesen*), for instance, now expressly prohibits any physical punishment in schools. This rule complies with Article 19 CRC as well as with the ECtHR's case law where the Court has constantly held that corporal punishment in schools violates Article 3 ECHR as it is to be qualified as degrading treatment or punishment.[119]

The question of physical and mental violence against children while in the care of parents or foster families was, however, only regulated in the year 2000, after the CRC Committee had encouraged the German legislator to do so.[120] According to Section 1631.2 of the Civil Code, children now have the explicit right to be raised without any violence whatsoever. Physical punishment, emotional violation, including verbal degradation and other degrading measures, are absolutely prohibited when upbringing a child. None of these measures might be justified as a necessary tool for education. Any kind of violence against a child is regarded as illegal.[121] This does, however, not mean that every form of bodily contact with the child is forbidden.

[116] CRC Committee, Concluding Observations: Germany, UN Doc. CRC/C/15/Add.266, para. 31.

[117] *BVerfGE* 108, 282 (299 et seq.).

[118] This topic is, of course, very complex and still not undisputed; see, e.g., Kokott in Sachs (ed.), *Grundgesetz*, 6th ed. 2011, Art. 4 MN 66–67, with further references as to legislative acts, case law, and legal literature.

[119] ECtHR, *Tyrer v. United Kingdom*, judgment of 25 April 1978, *Europäische Grundrechte Zeitschrift* 1979, 162–168. In *Castello-Roberts v. United Kingdom*, the ECtHR considered further that corporal punishment might also violate the respect for private and family life as established by Article 8 ECHR; see ECtHR, judgment of 25 March 1993, no. 13134/87, § 33 et seq.

[120] See CRC Committee, Concluding Observations: Germany, UN Doc. CRC/C/15/Add.43, para. 30.

[121] Kellner, Die Ächtung der Gewalt in der Erziehung nach neuem Recht, *Neue Juristische Wochenschrift* 2001, 796, at 797. Further see Brosius-Gersdorf (note 29), Art. 6 MN 163.

Grabbing a child by the arm in order to protect him/her from crossing a street is regularly considered as being admissible because it serves the best interests of the child.[122] Also some slighter means of education are held to be permissible such as the lowering of the child's pocket money or banning him/her from watching TV for a limited period of time.[123] Furthermore, it is to be stressed that the prohibition of mental violation does not mean that parents have to fulfill every wish of the child.[124] With Section 1631.2 of the Civil Code, the legislator primarily sought to induce a change in awareness of the public with regard to parenting. The introduction of this provision was therefore accompanied by an awareness campaign entitled "*Dein Kind ist unschlagbar*" ("Your child is unbeatable"),[125] and the proclamation of an annual day of action on 30 April named as "*Tag der gewaltfreien Erziehung*" ("no hitting day"). However, in 2011, a survey conducted by the statistic research institute "*Forsa*" on behalf of the magazine "*Eltern*" showed that four out of ten parents do still occasionally smash or hit their children. Nonetheless, the great majority of parents in Germany today believe it is wrong to do so.[126]

When parents disrespect the prohibition of physical punishment, the family court may take appropriate actions (see Section 1666 of the Civil Code). Furthermore, child welfare offices regularly offer support through counseling in order to ensure a violence-free childhood.[127] They have the specific obligation to protect children from anything and anyone that might endanger their well-being.[128] Finally, children are protected from physical and mental assaults through Section 171 of the Criminal Code. The neglect of one's duty to care for a minor below the age of 16 constitutes a criminal offense provided that this neglect causes the risk of heavily disturbing the child's physical or mental development.[129] Section 171 of the Criminal Code does not only apply to parents but also to guardians, foster families, and persons holding parental responsibilities as well as to any other person officially charged with the care for the child.[130]

---

[122] Kellner (note 121), at 797.

[123] Veit (note 45), § 1631 MN 24.

[124] Kellner (note 121), at 797.

[125] See Periodic of Germany, 20 October 2010 (note 66), para. 164, and Peschel-Gutzeit, Das Recht auf gewaltfreie Erziehung – Was hat sich seit seiner Einführung im Jahre 2000 geändert? – *Familie Partnerschaft Recht 2012*, 195, at 197.

[126] *Cf.* http://www.eltern.de/kleinkind/erziehung/ohrfeigen-klaps.html and http://www.sueddeutsche.de/leben/studie-zu-gewalt-an-kindern-viele-eltern-schlagen-immer-noch-zu-1.1306909. Further see Schmahl (note 4), Art. 19 MN 7, and recently CRC Committee, Concluding Observations: Germany, UN Doc. CRC/C/DEU/CO/3–4, paras. 32–33.

[127] See Section 16 of Book VIII of the Social Code, and Schmahl (note 4), Art. 19 MN 8.

[128] See the tasks and competences stipulated in Section 8a of Book VIII of the Social Code.

[129] Heuchemer in v. Heintschel-Heinegg (ed.), *Beck'scher Online Kommentar zum Strafgesetzbuch*, 2013, § 171 MN 5.

[130] Kühl in Lackner/Kühl, *Strafgesetzbuch*, 27th ed. 2011, § 171 MN 8.

3.2.8 Article 21 CRC: The Rights of the Child in the Adoption System

Article 21 CRC aims at establishing binding conditions for national and intercountry adoption. Unlike Article 3 CRC which gives the best interest of the child only a "primary consideration," Article 21.1 CRC states that within the system of adoption, the best interests of the child shall even be the "paramount consideration." To this aim all persons concerned, including the child, must give their informed consent to the adoption (see Article 21.2 CRC). The German legal order conforms to this condition. According to Section 1741 of the Civil Code, adoption is only permitted in the best interests of the child. This means that the interests of the (future) parents are of no importance.[131] Furthermore, the explicit consent of the child is mandatory for adoption (see Section 1746.1 of the Civil Code); the child's consent cannot be substituted by a representative.[132] However, as minors enjoy only a limited legal capacity, children who are under the age of 14 do additionally need the consent of their legal representative.

Similar prerequisites apply with regard to intercountry adoptions; also, here the informed consent of all parties, including the child, is necessary. Furthermore, Germany is, since 1 March 2002, a member state of the 1993 Convention on the Protection of Children and Co-operation in respect of Intercountry Adoption.[133] The Convention's requirements have been transferred into various federal statutes.[134] According to those regulations, the competent authority, i.e., the Federal Office for Intercountry Adoption (*Bundeszentralstelle für Auslandsadoption*), has to investigate whether the adoption in Germany actually serves the best interests of the foreign child. If this is not the case, the adoption has to be denied. An intercountry adoption shall also be denied if its contents or effects violate the German public order.[135] In any case of intercountry adoptions, an official German adoption agency needs to be engaged in the adoption; private adoptions are not permitted in order to avoid child trafficking.[136] Any unauthorized arrangement of intercountry adoption is a criminal offense which is punishable according to Section 236 of the Criminal Code.

---

[131] Maurer in Säcker/Rixecker (eds.), *Münchener Kommentar zum Bürgerlichen Gesetzbuch, Band 7*, 6th ed. 2012, § 1746 MN 4.

[132] Maurer (note 131), § 1746 MN 15.

[133] *BGBl.* 2001 II, p. 1034.

[134] See, in particular, the Adoption Agency Act (*Adoptionsvermittlungsgesetz, BGBl.* 2002 I, p. 354) and the Effects of Adoption Act (*Adoptionswirkungsgesetz, BGBl.* 2001 I, p. 2950).

[135] Schmahl (note 4), Art. 20/21 MN 33. As to the ambit and scope of the German public order in intercountry adoptions, *cf.* Higher Regional Court (*Oberlandesgericht*) of Cologne, *Neue Juristische Wochenschrift – Rechtsprechungsreport* 2009, 1374.

[136] See Federal Administrative Court (*Bundesverwaltungsgericht*), *Neue Zeitschrift für Verwaltungsrecht* 2011, 1199, at 1200 et seq.; and Schmahl (note 4), Art. 20/21 MN 34.

3.2.9 Article 24 CRC, Read in Conjunction with Article 12 CRC: The Right of the Child to Consent to or to Refuse Medical Treatment

Pursuant to Article 24.1 CRC, state parties recognize the right of the child to the enjoyment of the highest attainable standard of health and to facilities for the treatment of illness and rehabilitation of health. Within this provision, no reference is made to the child's consent to medical treatments. However, there is no doubt that the guiding principle enshrined in Article 12 CRC, according to which the views of the child in all matters affecting him/her shall be given due weight, must also apply to the area of medical treatments.

Under German law, any medical treatment by a medical practitioner is prima facie dogmatically regarded as a physical assault within the meaning of Sections 223, 229 of the Criminal Code.[137] Criminal liability can only be suspended in cases where an informed consent is given prior to the treatment (see Section 228 of the Criminal Code).[138] Yet, if medical treatments are given to minors, the crucial question lies in deciding who is capable of giving the prior consent. In general, it is the patient who has to give the consent personally. In the case of children, however, there is a need to clarify whether the child is sufficiently mature to identify the (short- and long-term) consequences of a given medical treatment. Thereby, the child's maturity to understand the consequences of treatments is independent from obtaining full contractual capability. Whether the child is able to give informed consent has rather to be established for every single medical treatment separately. A 15 year old minor may be able to consent to the taking of a blood sample; however, at the same time he/she will probably not be sufficiently mature to consent to a difficult heart operation.[139]

In cases of immature or very young children, the consent must be substituted by the consent of the parents or the legal representative of the child (see Section 1629.1 of the Civil Code). Under these circumstances, parents do also have the power to consent, within the general rules applicable in a democratic society, to medical treatments of their child without the child's will.[140] However, they have to consider the growing abilities of the child and the child's well-being when exercising their power of representation (see Section 1626.2 of the Civil Code). In some cases, the child may even have a right to veto. For instance, if the medical treatment can be

---

[137] See, e.g., Paeffgen in Kindhäuser/Neumann/Paeffgen (eds.), *Strafgesetzbuch*, 4th ed. 2013, § 228 MN 56; Kühl (note 130), § 223 MN 8.

[138] Paeffgen (note 137), § 228 MN 63.

[139] Rightly Schelling/Gaibler, Aufklärungspflicht und Einwilligungsfähigkeit, *Deutsches Ärzteblatt* 2012, 109, at 110.

[140] Schlehofer in Joecks/Miebach (eds.), *Münchener Kommentar zum Strafgesetzbuch*, 2nd ed. 2011, Vorbem. zu §§ 32 ff. MN 141. See also Schwarz, Verfassungsrechtliche Aspekte der religiösen Beschneidung, *JuristenZeitung* 2008, 1125, at 1128; Weilert, Das Kindeswohl und die Knochenmarkspende Minderjähriger aus verfassungsrechtlicher Perspektive, *Rechtswissenschaft* 2012, 292, at 324, 329.

postponed without any disadvantage for the child, the parents' consent can be overruled by the child's explicit will.[141]

In recent times, the question of male circumcision has been vividly discussed in Germany after the Regional Court (*Landgericht*) of Cologne, on 7 May 2012, had ruled that the circumcision of male babies who are unable to consent to this medical treatment constitutes, in principle, a criminal offense.[142] The opponents of male circumcision, among them the Regional Court of Cologne, put it on the same level with female mutilation.[143] Female mutilation is, in fact, considered a grievous breach of human rights, and it is thus strictly prohibited under German law and can be punished with severe custodial sentences.[144] Some authors therefore also consider male circumcision as being contrary to Article 24.3 CRC according to which state parties shall take all effective and appropriate measures with a view to abolishing traditional practices prejudicial to the health of children.[145] This opinion, though, does not find proof in the practice of the CRC Committee which, until now, restricts its views to the prohibition of female mutilation and only recommends that state parties shall take effective measures to ensure the health of boys and protect them against unsafe medical conditions during the practice of male circumcision.[146] The debate in Germany was finally clarified in December 2012, after a new provision, Section 1631d, had been introduced into the Civil Code.[147] According to this rule, parents of male children are allowed to consent to a circumcision without any medical need, provided that the circumcision is carried out according to the rules of modern medical standards. It is thus rightly presumed that circumcision of boys

[141] Schlehofer (note 140), Vorbem. zu §§ 32 ff. MN 142.

[142] Regional Court (*Landgericht*) of Cologne, judgment of 7 May 2012, JuristenZeitung 2012, 805et seq.

[143] See, besides the Regional Court of Cologne (note 142), e.g., Herzberg, Rechtliche Probleme der rituellen Beschneidung, *JuristenZeitung* 2009, 332, at 334; Putzke, Recht und Ritual – ein großes Urteil einer kleinen Strafkammer, *Medizinrecht* 2012, 621, at 623; Walter, Der Gesetzentwurf zur Beschneidung – Kritik und strafrechtliche Alternative, *JuristenZeitung* 2012, 1110, at 1116 et seq. With convincing arguments dissenting Rox, Annotation to the judgment of the Regional Court of Cologne of 7 May 2012, *JuristenZeitung* 2012, 806, at 807; Wiater, Rechtspluralismus und Grundrechtsschutz: Das Kölner Beschneidungsurteil, *Neue Zeitschrift für Verwaltungsrecht* 2012, 1379, at 1380.

[144] Periodic Report of Germany, 20 October 2010 (note 66), para. 214.

[145] Opinion expressed by, e.g., Rupprecht et al. in Parliamentary Publication (*Bundestagsdrucksache*) 17/11430, p. 8; and Putzke (note 143), at 623.

[146] *Cf.*, e.g., CRC Committee, Concluding Observations: Lesotho, UN Doc. CRC/C/15/Add.147, para. 44; Concluding Observations: South Africa, UN Doc. CRC/C/15/Add.122, para. 33. See also Tobin, *The Right to Health in International Law*, 2011, at 312 et seq.; Schmahl (note 4) Art. 24 MN 20. Furthermore, it is interesting to note that the CRC Committee does neither mention the practice of male circumcision in its recent General Comment No. 15 (2013) on the right of the child to the enjoyment of the highest attainable standard of health (UN Doc. CRC/C/GC/15 of 17 April 2013) nor in its Concluding Observations regarding Germany, of 31 January 2014 (UN Doc. CRC/C/DEU/CO/3–4, paras. 38–39).

[147] *BGBl.* 2012 I, p. 2749.

does usually not endanger the well-being of the child.[148] Only in cases where the contrary is proven, the right of the parents to consent to the circumcision can be denied.[149]

3.2.10 Article 32 CRC: Minimum Age for Admission to Employment

Since more than five decades, the German legal order provides for a minimum age for admission to employment and is thus in accordance with Article 32.2 lit. a CRC. Employment of (young) children is regarded as being illegal. A child in the sense of the Youth Employment Protection Act (*Jugendarbeitsschutzgesetz*) is a person below the age of 15.[150] From the age of 15 years onward until the age of 18, a person is deemed to be an adolescent. Adolescents may be employed for either the purpose of apprenticeship or on-the-job training, or as an employee or home worker, including when rendering similar services.[151] However, there are a number of jobs juveniles over the age of 15 cannot be employed for. According to Section 22 of the Youth Employment Protection Act, it is prohibited to employ an adolescent for jobs that exceed the juvenile's physical or mental abilities; males may not be forced to carry a weight of more than 35 kg, females no more than 15 kg.[152] Furthermore, adolescents may not be exposed to exceeding heat, coldness, or humidity which means that minors may not be employed in slaughterhouses or in cold storage rooms[153]; nor are they allowed to work underground.[154] Against this background, there is also a duty incumbent on the state not to use funeral monuments in cemeteries when there is evidence that the stone originates from quarries of third countries which do not effectively execute the prohibition of child labor.[155] Moreover, juveniles may not be employed on piece-work payment basis as this form of employment is

---

[148] Rixen, Das Gesetz über den Umfang der Personensorge bei einer Beschneidung des männlichen Kindes, *Neue Juristische Wochenschrift 2013*, 257 et seq.; Schmahl (note 4), Art. 3 MN 19, Art. 19 MN 7.

[149] Huber in Säcker/Rixecker (eds.), *Münchener Kommentar zum Bürgerlichen Gesetzbuch, Band 7*, 6th ed. 2012, § 1631d MN 4.

[150] See Section 2.1 of the Youth Employment Protection Act.

[151] More detailed Weyand, *Jugendarbeitsschutzgesetz*, 2012, § 1 MN 3 et seq.

[152] Weyand (note 151), § 22 MN 7.

[153] Weyand (note 151), § 22 MN 15.

[154] Exceptions can be made for employees over the age of 16 years; see Section 24.2 of the Youth Employment Protection Act.

[155] As to this question, see with more details, also with respect to the legal basis necessary for the evidence, Federal Administrative Court (*Bundesverwaltungsgericht*), judgment of 16 October 2013, 8 CN 1.12, paras. 12 et seq.; Bavarian Constitutional Tribunal (*Bayerischer Verfassungsgerichtshof*), *Bayerische Verwaltungsblätter* 2012, 234, at 235, with annotation of Lorenzmeier, *Bayerische Verwaltungsblätter* 2012, 236 (237). Further see Kaltenborn/Reit, Das Verbot der Aufstellung von Grabsteinen aus Kinderarbeit, *Neue Zeitschrift für Verwaltungsrecht* 2012, 925, at 927.

deemed to cause damage to their health and development.[156] Finally, for persons having committed serious crimes, it is strictly prohibited to employ juveniles.[157]

An adolescent is not entitled to decide about his/her employment independently. As minors in Germany are limited in their legal capacity (see Section 106 of the Civil Code), they need consent of the legal representative to conclude contracts, including employment agreements (see Section 107 of the Civil Code). However, according to Section 1631a of the Civil Code, parents have to take into due account the child's abilities, wishes, and affections when exercising their parental right by giving or renouncing consent.[158] Once the legal representative of the child has given consent to taking up the employment, the minor can, from this time on, take all decisions in the context of his/her employment independently (see Section 113 of the Civil Code). Within this field of law, the minor is then no longer limited in his/her legal capacity. A similar situation is given in cases where the minor wants to launch an independent business. Also here, he/she needs the legal representative's consent, but this consent must further be accompanied by an affirmative order from the competent family court (see Section 112 of the Civil Code). After these consents have been given, the minor again enjoys full contractual capability for all matters concerning the business.

3.2.11 Article 32 CRC: Prohibition of Economic Exploitation and Obligations of the Child toward His/Her Parents

Besides establishing a minimum age for admission to employment, Article 32 CRC further stipulates that children shall be protected from economic exploitation and from performing any work that is likely to be hazardous or to interfere with the child's education or to be harmful to the child's health or physical, mental, spiritual, moral, or social development. The German laws are in accordance with these standards. As already mentioned, there are a number of jobs juveniles cannot be employed for because they are considered as being detrimental to the minor's development. To the same aim, the minor's working hours and conditions of employment are strictly regulated by the Youth Employment Protection Act. For instance, juveniles may not work more than 8 h a day and no more than 40 h per week. Their working hours may only be placed between 6 am and 8 pm. They are not allowed to work more than 5 days a week, the 2 days off should, as far as possible, be consecutive.[159] Furthermore, adolescents in employment have to be granted adequate rest periods during their working day which means that they must be admitted a rest

---

[156] See Section 23 of the Youth Employment Protection Act. Further see Weyand (note 151), § 23 MN 1.

[157] See Section 25 of the Youth Employment Protection Act.

[158] Veit (note 45), § 1631a MN 3.

[159] See Sections 8, 14, and 15 of the Youth Employment Protection Act.

period of at least 30 min if they work for 4 h and a half up to 6 h and a rest period of a minimum of 60 min if they have to work for more than 6 h at a stretch.[160] There must be a break of at least 12 h between the end of one working day and the beginning of the next working day.[161] Furthermore, juveniles have the right to an annual paid leave of 30 days. The regulations of the Youth Employment Protection Act, according to which the amount of days for annual paid leave is different for younger adolescents than for older ones,[162] are presumably not applicable anymore after the Federal Labor Court (*Bundesarbeitsgericht*), in 2012, has declared void similar provisions of annual paid leave in public services in view of the prohibition of age discrimination.[163]

A different question arises with regard to the obligations of the child toward his/her parents. According to Section 1618a of the Civil Code, parents and children are obliged to assist each other when in need. This duty applies to any parent-child relationship without any reference to a certain age.[164] It is a lifelong mutual obligation neither side can dispense with[165] and which, in certain situations, also covers mutual financial maintenance and subsistence allowances.[166] Furthermore, Section 1619 of the Civil Code states the obligation of a child toward his/her parents to help with the keeping of the household or a family business, provided that the child lives with the parents and is cared for by them. This obligation is not in conflict with Article 32 CRC, which merely seeks to protect children from economic exploitation and from work that may be harmful to the child's development, because the employer wants to make profit from the children at their expense.[167] On the other hand, marginal or light work, such as child's employments in the family household or business, is rather deemed to be positive and beneficial for the child's development.[168] However, also here, the child's obligations are limited by the well-being of the child; his/her professional and educational ambitions being the absolute limit.[169]

---

[160] See Section 11 of the Youth Employment Protection Act.

[161] See Section 13 of the Youth Employment Protection Act.

[162] Adolescents are admitted an annual paid leave of at least 30 days if they are below the age of 16, of at least 27 days if they are below the age of 17, and of at least 25 days if they are below the age of 18 years; see Sections 19.1 and 19.2 of the Youth Employment Protection Act.

[163] Federal Labor Court (*Bundesarbeitsgericht*), judgment of 20 March 2012, 9 ARZ 529/10, *Neue Juristische Wochenschrift* 2012, 3465.

[164] Enders in Bamberger/Roth, *Beck'scher Online Kommentar zum Bürgerlichen Gesetzbuch*, 2013, § 1618a MN 2.

[165] Peschel-Gutzeit (note 32), at 476.

[166] See, e.g., Section 1649.2 and Section 1601 of the Civil Code.

[167] CRC Committee, UN Doc. CRC/C/20, Annex V, p. 51; Schmahl (note 4), Art. 32–36 MN 7.

[168] Van Bueren (note 16), at 267; Detrick (note 16), at 563.

[169] v. Sachsen Gessaphe in Säcker/Rixecker (eds.), *Münchener Kommentar zum Bürgerlichen Gesetzbuch*, Band 7, 6th ed. 2012, § 1619 MN 3.

4 Conclusion

Although this report confines itself in focusing on selected issues, a first conclusion on the impact of the CRC on the German legal order can be drawn: After the Federal Government has withdrawn its previous reservations to the CRC in 2010, the Convention and its protocols now fully apply in Germany. Since that time at the latest, a remarkable progress in legislation and jurisprudence toward a more child-friendly legal environment can be ascertained. This, of course, does not mean that the German legal order, by now, entirely complies or should even fully comply with all (legally nonbinding) recommendations of the CRC Committee. On the other hand, there is no doubt about the (supplementary) constitutional role which human rights instruments increasingly play in Germany.[170] In some cases they have already led to a shift of views by granting more liberties and more participation rights to children.

[170] Already in 1977, Christian Tomuschat rightly described international instruments for human rights protection as the principal example of supplementary constitution for the Federal Republic of Germany; see Tomuschat, Der Verfassungsstaat im Geflecht der internationalen Beziehungen, *Veröffentlichungen der Vereinigung der deutschen Staatsrechtslehrer* 36 (1978), 51 et seq.

The Implementation of the UN Convention on the Rights of the Child by the State Parties: The Case of Greece

Eleni Micha

1 Introduction

It has been quite some time since Greece had signed and ratified the International Convention on the Rights of the Child.[1] In the 20 years of its application, the Convention has not been implemented to the full extent of the state's plans and commitments. It is true that the Greek state has made significant efforts to comply with its international obligations, with particular reference to the educational and healthcare services. Nevertheless, the state has failed to implement part of its adopted legislation; this has often been due to social pressure and the reluctance of local societies to accept institutional changes, as well as shortage of the necessary financial means, especially due to the latest economic and financial crisis. In consequence, Greece has fallen short of its expectations.

Being aware of these deficiencies, on the occasion of reviewing Greece's Second and Third Periodic Report last year,[2] the Committee on the Rights of the Child has already emphasized the adverse side effects of the current financial crisis on families and public expenditure for social purposes. Accordingly, the Committee invites Greece not to spare any effort and duly consider the social welfare of vulnerable groups

---

This Report which has been finalized in November 2013 and updated in September 2014 has first been published in Vassiliki Koumpli (ed.), Greek National Reports on the 19th International Congress of Comparative Law, Revue Hellénique de Droit International, Vol. 67-I, pp. 687–704, Athens 2014, © Sakkoulas Publications.

[1] Greece signed and ratified the Convention in 1990 and 1993, respectively (Law 2101/1992, Official Gazette A' 192/2-12-1992).

[2] Concluding Observations of the Committee, Document CRC/C/GRC/CO/2-3, 15-6-2012, http://www2.ohchr.org/english/bodies/crc

E. Micha (✉)
School of Law, University of Athens, Sina 14 str., 106 72 Athens, Athens, Greece
e-mail: emicha@law.uoa.gr

O. Cvejić Jančić (ed.), *The Rights of the Child in a Changing World*,
Ius Comparatum - Global Studies in Comparative Law 13,
DOI 10.1007/978-3-319-23189-1_8

of children. In particular, the Committee calls Greece to adopt a nondiscriminatory approach and give priority to the needs of children.[3] Since prohibition of discriminatory treatment, together with the safeguarding of the best interests of the child, constitutes the heart of the protection established by the Convention, all actions undertaken by the member states should aim at the fulfillment of these objectives.

On the same tune, the Greek Ombudsman of the Child calls for appropriate action to be taken for the promotion of children's rights.[4] His efforts culminated in April 2012 with the compilation of an "alternative" report, for the monitoring of the implementation of the Convention by Greece, communicated to the Committee on the Rights of the Child and the state authorities. In particular, the Greek Ombudsman proposed a number of implementation measures including the dissemination of the Convention and coordination of the monitoring efforts by the different actors, state, independent authorities, NGOs, and international bodies.

Following the above, the sources of the available information will be all three Reports of the Greek state submitted to the Committee on the Rights of the Child,[5] the Concluding Observations of the Committee in June 2012 after the review of Greece's Second and Third Periodic Reports, and the Parallel Report submitted by the Ombudsman of the Child in April 2012.[6] In the respective parts of the present report, there will be thorough analysis of the regulatory framework regarding the protection of children's rights in Greece and a respective analysis of the relevant practice of its state organs.

In the first part of the report, the analysis will focus on the notion of "the best interests of the child" and its content, following the recent Greek jurisprudence. Strictly connected to the "best interests of the child" is the nondiscrimination principle as endorsed by the Convention on the Rights of the Child. In consequence, there will be a combined survey of the actions undertaken by Greece for the implementation of the Convention in its domestic legal order in adherence to these principles.

In the second part of the report, there will be a review of the legal provisions, both of the civil and criminal law, referring to the civil status of the child and the treatment of child delinquency. In the third part the analysis will focus on the treatment of the child as a member of the society, namely, as member of its family, school, or working environment. Since some vulnerable groups need special attention, the last part of the report will be devoted to them. To the extent that there is sufficient data on the activities undertaken by the Greek state for their protection,

---

[3] Ibid. p. 2, n. 6.

[4] In 2003, the Greek Ombudsman was assigned with the additional task of defending and promoting children's rights (Law 3094/2003). Consequently, a Deputy Ombudsman for children was appointed, and a new section was established, staffed with an interdisciplinary team comprising jurists, social workers, and psychologists. For additional information on the Ombudsman's mission, see http://www.0-18.gr

[5] The initial state report had been submitted in 2001, whereas the Second and Third Periodic Reports in July 2009 (Document CRC/C/GRC/2-3, http://www2.ohchr.org/english/bodies/crc

[6] Parallel Report to the UN Committee on the Rights of the Child, The Greek Ombudsman, Department of Children's Rights, in http://www.0-18.gr

the analysis will particularly focus on the status of Roma children and children victims of human trafficking or sexual abuse. It is understood that other vulnerable groups, as, for instance, children refugees, children belonging to minority groups as in the Muslim minority of Western Thrace, or children of repatriated Greeks, need special protection by the state, which will comply with its international obligations as envisaged by the Convention on the Rights of the Child. Nevertheless, the respective analysis of the particular legal provisions applicable therein, as well as the practice of the competent state authorities should be the object of a separate report mainly due to the fragmentary character of the respective rules and regulations.

2 The Notion of the "Best Interests" of the Child

Protection of the best interests of the child constitutes a principle of utmost importance. Article 1511 of the Civil Code, in particular, defines the protection of the best interests of the child as the fundamental principle on which to base any decision related to children, either taken by parents or by courts. There is a long established case law of the Greek courts and tribunals based on the notion of the "best interests" of the child.

In a number of recent judgments, the Greek courts referred to the notion of the best interests of the child in its broadest sense and took its beneficial character under consideration. Accordingly, it has been clarified that the notion of the best interests has corporal, material, ethical, spiritual, and psychological aspects which should be used as guiding principles in any decision-making process that concerns the welfare of the child.[7] The judgment 229/2011 is of cardinal importance since the Piraeus Administrative Court of First Instance determined that in cases of administrative expulsion of minors, the best interests of the child have to be the principal criterion for executing the administration's decision.[8] In particular, the Greek Court adjudicated that the detention of a minor with a view to expelling him/her to his/her home country should be a measure of a last resort undertaken by the Greek administration and the conditions of detention should be in accordance with international standards of treating humans. Accordingly, the Piraeus Administrative Court ruled in favor of the minor's immediate release. At the same time, having in mind that the case concerned an unaccompanied minor, the Court communicated the case to the public prosecutor in order to find its place of residence. This order was issued to serve the best interests of the child as interpreted by the Committee for the Rights of the Child. In addition, the notion of the best interests is amply addressed by the

---

[7] In that sense, the exercise of parental custody ought to be awarded according to the level of stability prevalent in the family. Stable relationships of the child with persons other than his/her parents have also to be established. See judgment 13679/2012 of the (one member) Court of First Instance of Thessaloniki in http://www.dsanet.gr

[8] The judgment can be found at http://www.dsanet.gr

Greek courts in awarding the exercise of custody to one parent and visiting rights to the other.[9]

Closely connected to the safeguarding of the best interests is the nondiscrimination principle, another instrument of interpretation implemented for achieving better protection of the rights of children. Access to education for all children, irrespective of their personal or social status, is an example of nondiscrimination. The case of the Roma children would be such an example as enrollment of Roma children to preparatory courses has been provided by the Greek state in order to facilitate their schooling. Another case concerns persons with disabilities and children refugees. In seeking to uphold the principles of best interests and nondiscrimination, in 2007, the state has drafted a National Action Plan with the following objectives: development of the social character of the state and improvement of the health and welfare services provided to Greek citizens and children. In particular, the National Action Plan aimed at the dissemination of the Convention to parents and teachers, establishing cooperation between the network and NGOs and utilizing funds available through the corporate social responsibility. Although a significant part of public expenditure went toward health and social welfare, the conclusion of an accomplished National Plan has not been achieved as initially planned. By his current proposal, the Ombudsman of the Child indicates the need to guarantee access to health and hospital care for all children on a nondiscriminatory basis. There is also a special need to guarantee vaccination and general health care for children without health insurance plans. It is also necessary to ensure the preventive health care of newborns.[10]

Special care is taken for the disabled and mental patients in particular, including children. After the incorporation of the relevant EU directives,[11] Greece introduced a number of statutes relating to children with disabilities. Accordingly, there was a strong support for a wider participation of disabled children or their representatives in the centers of decision-making.

Nevertheless, the implementation of the statutes was poor, and the Committee on the Rights of the Child urges Greece to pay special attention to the needs of children with disabilities along with other vulnerable groups of children (e.g., belonging to minority groups, Roma children, unaccompanied children, etc.). It is of utmost importance to budget for the needs of these vulnerable groups under all circumstances, notwithstanding the fact that a natural disaster or an economic crisis may appear. But above all, the Committee urged Greece to establish a monitoring mechanism to check the proper distribution of funds.[12] In the area of nondiscrimination, public awareness plays a most important role, especially in cases of targeted groups

[9] Judgment 45/2013 issued by the Larissa Court of Appeal (http://www.dsanet.gr). The Court ruled in favor of the children's stay in their father's house during the night and the presence of third persons during those meetings in accordance with the principle of the best interests of the children and not in accordance with the right of the father to enjoy his family rights.

[10] Parallel Report, op.cit., part 9 on health and welfare.

[11] Directives 2000/43/EC and 2000/78/EC.

[12] Concluding Observations, op.cit., n. 18.

such as the mentally ill children. Good practices for combating stigma have been developed within the framework of the Third Community Support Framework (e.g., the activities of the organization "Prometheus" for persons with special needs).[13]

In the framework of the National Action Plan of 2007, an organized and methodical strategy against depression designed by the *Ministry of Health* aimed at changing the negative attitude and prejudice toward children with mental disorders. It is also important to note that both parents of a disabled child are entitled to pension benefits irrespective of age limit. The role of education is crucial at this point, as it constitutes the most efficient way to change the stereotype image for children with disabilities and the discriminatory attitude toward them. To this effect, the drafting of school curricula and textbooks, along with the training of teachers, is a proper means also used by the Greek state in order to change the negative stereotypes.

3 The Child as a Person

3.1 The Civil Law Status of the Child

According to the relevant provisions of the Greek Civil Code, every person under the age of 18 is considered to be a child. After a child is born, its parents or guardians are responsible for submitting its birth certificate to the Registry Office of the town at which it was born. In principle, the birth certificate does not include the child's first name but only its surname and the parents' personal details. Parents are obliged to declare their child's surname in an official statement before their wedding; this statement cannot be revoked.[14] The first name of the child is also ruled by the parents' common statement to the Registry Office. Nevertheless, for practicing Orthodox Christian Greeks, the giving of the first name is connected with the baptism of the child. Accordingly, Greek Orthodox parents are required to submit the christening certificate to the Registry Office, soon after the baptism of their child.

A child born inside wedlock is presumed to have the mother's husband as father. This also holds for a child born within 300 days after the dissolution of a marriage.[15] Nevertheless, the presumption can be rebutted if the mother enters into another marriage or in the case of voluntary act of judicial affiliation by the mother's husband or another man. In case the child bears the mother's surname, that of her husband can be added with the consent of both mother and child.

In case that a child is born after medically assisted reproduction by a surrogate mother, it is presumed that the mother is the one designated by a judgment of the competent court.[16] This can be reversed by legal action contesting the maternity,

[13] The services provided by the organization "Prometheus" are mostly of advisory and therapeutic nature. See http://www.promitheasamke.gr

[14] Articles 1505–1506 of the Greek Civil Code.

[15] Article 1465 of the Greek Civil Code.

[16] Article 1458 of the Greek Civil Code.

within 6 months from the birth of the child. The maternity can be contested by legal action either by the presumed mother or by the surrogate mother, provided that evidence is produced that the child was biologically issued by the latter. Following an irrevocable Court decision, the surrogate mother is considered to be the mother of the child with retroactive effect as from the fact of its birth. In such cases, paternity cannot be contested "if the husband has consented to the medically assisted reproduction of his spouse."[17] In cases of assisted reproduction, sperm banks are obliged to keep records on the identity of the donors. These records are confidential, and only the specially authorized personnel of the Ministry of Health and the judicial authorities have access to them. Consequently, the child being vested with the particular legal interest has the right to access the respective files and obtain information about the identity of its natural father.

3.2 *Nationality and Acquisition of Citizenship*

According to the Code of Greek Citizenship,[18] an individual may acquire Greek citizenship in the following cases:

1. From the time of his/her birth, if the father or mother is already a Greek national, irrespective of him/her having been born in foreign territory.
2. From the time of his/her birth in Greek territory, provided that he/she does not acquire a foreign nationality by right of birth or that he/she is of unknown nationality.
3. An alien born out of wedlock and duly legitimated as the child of a Greek national, becomes Greek national as of the date of legitimization, if at that date he/she has not attained the 18th year of their age.
4. An alien who was adopted by a Greek national before the age of 18, as of the time of his/her adoption.

Acquisition of Greek citizenship by naturalization is possible only if an alien has attained his/her 18th year of age and fulfills the requirements set forth by the Code of Greek Citizenship. The children of a naturalized Greek become Greek citizens if they are under the age of 18 at the time of the naturalization of their parent. In addition, there are some delays in the process of naturalization of minors, for example, in cases of alien children adopted by Greek citizens, due to bureaucratic deficiencies.

[17] Article 1471, par. 2 of the Greek Civil Code as amended by Law 3089/2002 (Official Gazette A' 327/23-12-2002).

[18] The Code of Greek Citizenship was enacted by virtue of Law 3284/2004 (Official Gazette A' 217/10-11-2004). The respective legislation is a combination of jus sanguinis and the jus soli with a view to avoiding such phenomena as children being born without nationality.

The most important development on issues of citizenship was the judgment 460/2013 recently issued by the Greek Council of State.[19] The Supreme Administrative Court ruled against the constitutionality of Law 3838/2010 which treated issues of citizenship for long-term foreign residents in the country. In particular, the Greek Council of State adjudicated that the criterion of long-term residence of parents and children in the domestic territory does not justify their actual admission in the Greek society for the acquisition of Greek citizenship. Even the attendance of the 6-year primary education by the child does not justify a real bond between the parents and the country. Although there was a strong minority of the Court suggesting the opposite, the majority prevailed raising strong disagreement among the doctrine and legal practitioners on the limits of the judicial control.

3.3 *Adoption*

Adoption is considered to be a substitute for a natural family; it is regulated by the Greek Civil Code and the ad hoc legislation introduced by Law 2915/2001.[20] Greece has also incorporated in its domestic legal order, the European Convention of 1967 on adoption and the Hague Convention of 1993 on intercountry adoptions.[21] There are public and private foundling hospitals and care centers which carry out programs of adoption, foster care and day care for infants and young children. The Ministry of Health is supervising the entire process whereas its advisory committees provide consent when a process of adoption is heard before the domestic courts. In this case, a minor at the age of 12 is considered legally capable of giving his/her personal consent before the competent court that decides on their adoption.

As far as interstate adoptions are concerned, originally, these were regulated by specialized services founded by the Presidential Decree 193/1973. Greece has recently ratified the Hague Convention on Protection of Children and Cooperation in Respect of Intercountry Adoptions of 1993.[22] The Ministry of Health & Social Welfare has been assigned to act as the Central Authority. In addition, an Interministerial Committee has been established to deal with pending cases of interstate adoptions. However, there is no proper function of The Hague Convention in the domestic legal order, mainly due to administrative shortcomings. According to the latest report issued by the Ombudsman of the Child, Greek administrative

[19] For the judgment and the respective comments, see the review "Theory & Practice of Administrative Law," issue 1/2013, pp. 20–35 (in Greek).

[20] Articles 1542–1588 of the Greek Civil Code and Law 2915/2001 (Official Gazette A' 109/29-5-2001).

[21] Laws 1049/1980 (Official Gazette A' 114/24-10-1980) and 3765/2009 (Official Gazette A' 101/1-1-2010), respectively.

[22] Law 3765/2009 (Official Gazette A' 101/1-1-2010).

authorities continue to request that Greek courts "legalize" decisions on adoption issued by foreign courts.[23]

In general, the regulation of adoption by the domestic legislation is fragmentary and ineffectual; adoptions organized by private institutions, although permitted by law, are prone to illegal transactions and may even result in trafficking of newborns and infants. The proposal by the Committee on the Rights of the Child to accelerate the relevant procedures with respect to public adoptions, together with stricter state control on private adoptions, may offer solutions to the chronic problems of the adoption system.

3.4 Child Delinquency

In the area of criminal justice, Greece has introduced a number of legislative reforms in order to address various demands and problems regarding the penal treatment of minor offenders. The respective provisions are of a protective and preventive nature in the sense that criminal legislation for minor offenders has a rather educational and reformative, not punitive purpose.

The enactment of Law 3189/2003 on "the reform of juvenile penal legislation" was one of the measures taken to this effect.[24] The main change introduced by the new legislation concerns the limits of criminal liability: the minimum is 8 years of age and the maximum 18 years of age, instead of 7 and 17 years foreseen by the past legislation. Under the influence of the Committee on the Rights of the Child, the distinction between children and adolescents was abolished, and all minors below the age of 18 are considered to be children. There is only one exception to the exclusion of criminal liability for minors: it concerns the cases where the public prosecutor decides that the imposition of a penalty is necessary and applies only to minors who have reached the age of 13. In such circumstances, if a minor has participated in the commission of a crime together with adults, prosecution must be exercised separately; whenever such separation is not possible, the public prosecutor must issue a well-founded decision to justify his refusal.

With regard to the reformatory measures available for minor offenders, Article 122 of the amended Greek Penal Code provides the following measures of reprimand: placement of the minor under the custody of parents or guardians; placement under the responsible supervision of a foster family; placement under the responsible supervision of an institution for minors; placement under probation; initiation of conciliation proceedings between a minor offender and the victim; community service by the minor; participation of the minor in social and psychological programs run by state, municipal, or private institutions; professional or vocational training of the minor; and road traffic education. In imposing the necessary reformatory measures, the competent court has to determine their duration. In any case, only a minor

[23] Parallel Report, op.cit., p. 11.

[24] Official Gazette A' 243/21-10-2003.

of 15 years and older can be confined in a correctional institution.[25] Consequently, there have been changes in the system of correctional confinement for minors. Some of them were successful, others were not. A notable change is the operation of primary and secondary schools in the Avlona juvenile reformatory facility, the largest in the country.[26] Another significant step is the creation of a Central Scientific Council for the prevention and repression of the victimization and criminality of minors, as well as the creation of the "Orestis" network for the protection of minors in 2010. On the other hand, there are serious problems with the treatment of minors, as they are often held in the correctional facilities together with young adults. The practice of the competent authorities not to erase the imposition of previous correctional measures from a minor's penal record is contrary to the spirit of the Convention, since this is also provided by the relevant legislation.

With regard to the special measures applicable to minors in case a particular treatment is required, Article 123 of the amended Greek Penal Code provides the following: placement of the minor under the responsible custody of parents, of a foster family, or of a probation officer; placement of the minor in correctional facilities; the minor's attendance in consultative medical programs; and the minor's referral to a medical or other institution. Such measures are ordered following diagnosis and opinion by a specialized committee of public officials comprising physicians, psychologists, and social workers. Regarding minors who are drug addicts, a psychiatric evaluation and laboratory tests are ordered by the competent courts, as a necessary prerequisite for administering medical treatment. Such measures may be lifted or replaced by a competent court and only at the advice of a group of specialized scientists.

4 The Child and His Social Environment

4.1 Family Care

Caring for a minor child is both a duty and a right of the parents. Parental care includes personal care for the child, management of the child's property, and legal representation of the child in judicial or extrajudicial proceedings. All parental obligations established by the relevant provisions of the Greek Civil Code also include the obligation to take the child's opinion into consideration before making any decision concerning its interests.[27] The present commitment is also included in the legislation on adoption, which expressly foresees that the wishes of the child to be adopted and those of the natural children of the prospective adoptive parent if any,

[25] Law 3860/2010 (Official Gazette A' 111/12-7-2010).

[26] Yet, certain deficiencies, as the lack of trained teachers, constitute an impediment for the proper function of the schools. See the respective remarks and proposals of the Greek Ombudsman of the Child in the Parallel Report, op.cit., p. 21.

[27] Article 1511 of the Greek Civil Code.

are to be heard, depending, of course, on their maturity. The exercise of parental care may be removed from a parent in case he/she is unwilling or unable to exercise these duties.[28] Parental care may be removed from both parents under very strict conditions and following a court's decision.[29] Moreover, parental custody is exercised by both parents even after a divorce or separation. Other solutions may be provided only according to the best interests of the child. However, decisions concerning serious matters of custody, such as name giving, education, and permission to leave the country, must be taken by both parents, even if custody is exercised only by one of them.

In relation to the issue of medically assisted reproduction, special domestic legislation has been enacted in order to cope with its legal, ethical, and economic aspects.[30] Accordingly, the relevant sections of the Family Law as incorporated by the Greek Civil Code have changed in order to keep up with the new scientific developments.

4.2 *Education*

The duration of compulsory education in Greece is 9 years. However, in practice there are no penalties imposed on those responsible for children dropping out of schools. Although there is a decrease in dropout rates, especially from elementary schools, a number of economic and social constraints hinder the realization of the educational goals of the Convention.[31]

Among her numerous efforts, Greece undertook the following steps in order to meet its objectives: a circular issued on 23 June 2010 provides for the compulsory enrollment of all children to public schools, including those of irregular immigrants, even without all the necessary supporting documents.[32]

In order to eliminate social exclusion of minors belonging to minorities (especially of the Muslim minority in the province of Western Thrace) and other vulnerable groups, such as the children of repatriated Greeks, immigrants, ethnic Roma, children with special needs, etc., the Ministry of Education founded a new institution, the "Educational and Vocational Orientation" [and is] seeking the cooperation of parents, employers, and local authorities. With a number of offices operating

[28] Article 1532 of the Greek Civil Code.

[29] The removal of parental care may be ordered only in cases of risk to the physical or moral integrity of the child by its parents or in case of a penalty of over a year's imprisonment imposed on the parents (Articles 1533 and 1535–1537 of the Greek Civil Code).

[30] See the Laws 3089/2002, op.cit., and 3305/2005 (Official Gazette A' 17/27-1-2005), respectively.

[31] The acute financial crisis, the mass influx of immigrants, and social tensions are a few of a large number of problems obstructing the proper implementation of the Convention in the domestic sphere.

[32] Law 3386/2005 (Art. 72) (Official Gazette A' 212/2005) had already provided for the obligatory enrollment of children.

throughout the country, programs on vocational training and appropriate teaching material have helped children with learning difficulties to adjust to their school environment and facilitated their integration. Special institutions for children with speech disorders have been founded, again for the purpose of integration. Nevertheless, and notwithstanding good intentions, this practice has been qualified as discriminatory since it is used for isolating these from other children who are fluent speakers of the Greek language.[33] The institution of intercultural schools also aimed at facilitating the approach between different cultures and creating a multicultural environment. However, the 13 intercultural schools in Greece are not operational in practice, since only a small percentage of foreign pupils attend the respective courses, and Greek pupils are still abstaining.

4.3 Child Labor

With regard to child labor, Greece has made significant progress in enacting new legislation for the protection of minors, either in order to comply with its international obligations or in order to carry out new plans of action in special areas of protection. Nevertheless, the number of children working illegally has increased, especially under the pressure of the economic crisis and the lack of adequate control by the competent social services.[34] The problem of children "working" in the streets is really pressing and demands immediate response. Since 2004, the program "Protection and Social Care of Street Children" instituted by initiative of the state has made considerable effort against the phenomenon of "street children" and illegal child labor. Since a large part of the children working illegally belong to minority groups often comprising foreign nationals, there was an initiative by the Greek state to conclude a bilateral agreement with the state of Albania for close cooperation in the area of child trafficking and their safe repatriation; this initiative has had a positive impact.[35] However, the program did not have the anticipated success. The case of the 500 children who escaped the "Agia Varvara" home between 1998

[33] The judgment of Sampanis and others v. Greece issued by the European Court of Human Rights on 5-6-2008 found a violation of Art. 14 of the European Convention of Human Rights (1950) regarding prohibition of discrimination taken together with Art. 2 of the First Additional Protocol to the Convention regarding the right to education of the Roma children. The Court ruled that the children were denied access to school before being assigned to special classrooms in an annex next to the main school buildings. Therefore, in spite of the authorities' willingness to educate Roma children, the special conditions of school enrollment for them as well as their placement in special classes ultimately resulted in discriminatory treatment, prohibited by the European Convention.

[34] The official data issued from the Ministry of Labor and the National Statistical Service is not always exact. According to the data provided by the Ombudsman of the Child, the number of children aged 15–18 who work is underestimated, since those who drop out of school in order to search for work are more than initially estimated.

[35] A number of intergovernmental meetings with other Balkan countries were launched, e.g., with Bulgaria in 2011, with a view to concluding a cooperation agreement similar to the one concluded with Albania (Parallel Report, op.cit., p. 20).

and 2001 revealed the dearth of a unified approach to the problem. Incompetent record keeping together with limited or inefficient accessibility to the social services required for the comprehensive care of "street children" have been the main causes of the failure to cope with the problem.[36]

In general, a large part of the legislation in force regarding the labor of minors has been enacted in order to implement some significant conventions adopted by the ILO and respective directives of the EU.[37] Accordingly, only minors over 15 years of age can be employed and only under working conditions strictly prescribed by the law. Minors under the age of 15 may engage only in cultural or other similar activities, like theatrical and musical performances, TV/radio recordings, and video shows, but there are strict rules regarding the number of working hours.[38] Following the adoption of ILO Convention No. 182[39] and a number of EU directives, there are certain forms of prohibited child labor. These include night work of adolescents, work in unhealthy environments, work with heavy machinery and dangerous equipment, and work under difficult physical conditions that may jeopardize a minor's life.[40]

Certain exceptions to the above rules and provisions exist with regard to marine professions and minors who are employed in the maritime and fishing industries. Remuneration for minors is provided after 1998 according to the National Labour Agreement concluded after collective negotiations between workers' and employers' unions.

5 Special Cases

5.1 Children Victims of Trafficking and Sexual Abuse

In the combat against human trafficking, there is an enhanced legal framework because the Greek state formulated proper domestic legislation for the purpose of implementing a number of international conventions it had already signed and ratified.

The main focus is on Law No. 3386/2005 on "Entry, residence and social inclusion of third country nationals in the Greek territory," which brought major changes in the Greek Criminal Code.

---

[36] Conclusions on the program "Protection and Social Care of the Street Children," The Greek Ombudsman, Department of Children's Rights (in Greek), March 2004, pp. 16–18 in http://www.synigoros.gr, and Concluding Observations of the Committee, op.cit., paras. 65–66.

[37] Second and Third Periodic Reports of Greece, op.cit., paras. 395ss.

[38] Severe penalties of imprisonment and pecuniary fines are foreseen for those who violate the legislation in question, including parents and persons having custody of minors. Administrative sanctions, including heavy fines, may also be imposed on employers by the labor inspector.

[39] For the text of the Convention and the relevant recommendations, see http://www.ilo.org

[40] Law 3144/2003 (Official Gazette A' 111/8-5-2003).

The present legislation introduced the notion of the "victim of trafficking" regardless of the mode of entry in the country. Therefore, every individual, including minors, who became victim of the offenses described by the law is a victim of human trafficking and requires protection and assistance by the state.[41] In case a minor coming from a third state is characterized as victim of trafficking, he/she is immediately granted a residence permit. For unaccompanied minor victims of trafficking, a special procedure is foreseen in order to locate his/her family or other relatives. Appropriate measures are undertaken for the minor's legal representation before the competent judicial or administrative authorities. A special measure called "period of reflection" was introduced in the present legislation, to enable the victim to cooperate with the police and other competent authorities, if he/she so decides. Although there is no established right to residence in the country, a minor victim of trafficking cannot be deported during this period, and any decision of removal is revoked.[42] Among the significant measures undertaken by the Greek state in the struggle against human trafficking is the national level Operational Action Plan code-named "Ilaeira" that establishes a preventive and suppressive mechanism against the trafficking of women and children.[43]

In addition, Greece has already undertaken certain legislative initiatives in relation to the implementation of its international obligations. In particular, Law 3625/2007 was enacted in order to ratify the additional protocol to the Convention on the Rights of the Child relating to the trafficking of children,[44] and Law 3727/2008 was enacted for the ratification of the Convention of the Council of Europe on the protection of children against sexual exploitation and sexual abuse.[45]

The enactment of Law 3500/2006 for the treatment of family violence is considered to be an important step toward the eradication of phenomena of violence and inhuman treatment against minors.[46] Yet, the ineffective application of this legislation remains a serious impediment to a comprehensive protection of minors who are often victims of violence, sexual abuse, inhuman treatment, and trafficking. The inefficiency of the public services that deal with such complaints and the dearth of trained personnel in schools and other educational facilities are some of the shortcomings already emphasized by the Greek Ombudsman.[47]

---

[41] According to Laws 3064/2002 (Official Gazette A' 248/15-10-2002) and 3386/2005 (op.cit.), the offenses described therein are human trafficking aiming at removing body parts and/or organs of a minor or exploiting a minor's work, procuration, and pandering (Art. 323A of the Penal Code as amended by the legislation in question).

[42] In cases where a residence permit is awarded to the minor, it is valid for 1 year. During that time the minor has access to the labor market and can receive medical treatment and free education.

[43] The initiative plan of "Ilaeira," which was officially presented on 7-8/12/2006, comprises a number of regulations and procedures for cross border and interregional police cooperation among Southeastern European countries.

[44] Official Gazette A' 290/24-12-2007.

[45] The Convention (CETS: 201) entered into force in 1/7/2010, and the domestic law was published in the Official Gazette A' 257/18-12-2008.

[46] Official Gazette A' 232/24-10-2006.

[47] Parallel Report, op.cit., pp. 6–8.

5.2 Vulnerable Groups with Special Focus on Roma Children

Children belonging to minority groups, such as the Muslim minority of Western Thrace, or children belonging to vulnerable groups, such as refugees, deserve special attention and care.[48]

The Roma population in Greece is considered to be a socially vulnerable group due to its particular way of living.[49] Therefore, a series of legislative and administrative measures were undertaken for their protection. Issues of health and family planning, education, and vocational training have been at the core of government initiatives for the integration of the Roma to the Greek society.

In accordance with the respective legislation and the Integrated Action Plan of 2006, a number of sociomedical centers have been established in order to promote primary health care and social protection for the Roma.[50] Among the issues treated at the centers are registration of families and their members, issuance of identification documents, and collective representation of the residents in the centers, housing, and education. Free medical and pharmaceutical care is provided to people who are uninsured, as well as pecuniary benefits for large families. Having established a network of Socio-Medical Centers, the Greek state seeks to raise the awareness of the local people, as well as that of other social institutions, on the problems raised by the phenomenon of the social exclusion of the Roma and their children in particular. With respect to education, the obligatory enrollment of the Roma children to public schools and their attendance on a regular basis is of vital importance for their social integration. So much the Ombudsman of the Child as the Committee on the Rights of the Child has constantly emphasized the need of more enhanced cooperation between the competent authorities, so as to create better living conditions, resolve housing problems, and provide full medical care and health insurance. The Ombudsman of the Child particularly stressed the problem of the Roma omitting to register their newborns as well as adult members in municipal registries, or even their provision of false data. Consequently, due to some recent cases of data falsification, criminal proceedings have been initiated against the responsible public officials in the town registry of Athens who have been discharged from office. The recent case of "Maria," the young child who was found living with a Roma family

---

[48] A case of a group requiring special attention is the Muslim girl minority and the applicability of the Sharia, their religious legislation. The practice of performing marriages among minors, in some cases at a very young age, has already been characterized as a serious problem with respect to the implementation of the Convention on the Rights of the Child. However, due to the limited space available, I shall not proceed to an extensive analysis of the problems concerning vulnerable groups of children requiring special attention. This part of the report will focus only on the Roma children.

[49] Nevertheless, the Roma people are Greek citizens who have the same rights and duties as every other Greek citizen, according to the Constitution and the relevant domestic legislation.

[50] The sociomedical centers have been instituted following a Joint Ministerial Decision of 2006 and were co-funded by the European Community Fund.

since infancy without being its descendant, indicated the need for a more organized and transparent public service regarding the birth registry system.[51] Furthermore, the serialization of the incident by television and radio revealed another aspect of the treatment of the Roma population, namely, its discriminatory character by the media. According to N. Muiznieks, the Commissioner for Human Rights of the Council of Europe, "most news reports, all over the world, have insisted on the ethnicity of the families from which the children have been taken, thus propagating age-old myths portraying Roma as child abductors."[52] Such irresponsible journalism may not only have adverse effects on the lives of Roma, but it may trigger violent reactions and undermine integration efforts.

6 Concluding Remarks

The adoption of a National Action Plan by Greece in 2007 constitutes the focal point of the implementation process regarding the Convention on the Rights of the Child. All the respective measures taken by the Greek member state, i.e., the enactment of appropriate legislation, the adaptation of administrative practice, a number of individual measures, and a series of judgments issued by the domestic courts, all qualify as important positive steps toward the strengthening of the Convention and are accepted as such by both the Committee on the Rights of the Child and the Greek Ombudsman.

However, the absence of specific data and timetable for the application of the Plan, along with the lack of the required infrastructure, constitutes serious impediments as to the evaluation of the progress made.

Certainly, the lack of the necessary financial means constitutes possibly the most significant obstacle for the realization of the Action Plan. The Greek Ombudsman has already proposed the following actions: establishment of a permanent National Coordinating Committee to monitor the realization of the National Action Plan; the decentralization of the health services along with the strengthening of social services in the municipalities throughout the country; the recording and processing of data on the various (public or private sector) structures and services relating to the status of children; the development of support measures for vulnerable groups of minors, for instance, special programs for children with disabilities; and encouragement for better and more cooperation between the competent state services and the various NGOs working in the area. These recommendations seem to be the most feasible solutions for the fulfillment of the obligations deriving by the Convention on the Rights of the Child.

---

[51] Soon after the incident, a number of legislative and administrative modifications have been considered by the competent authorities.

[52] For more information, see http://www.coe.int/t/commissioner/news/2013

Implementation of the United Nations Convention on the Rights of the Child in Indian Legal System

Vishnupriya Yadlapalli

1 Introduction

India has the largest child population in the world. The number of children under the age of 18 years constitutes 41 % of the total population of the country.[1] India's approach to protection and promotion of human rights and child rights derives from the Constitution of India, which provides for affirmative action in favour of children. It also directs the state to ensure that children are not abused and are given opportunities and facilities to develop in a healthy manner in conditions of freedom and dignity. The rights of the child in Indian legal system, particularly with reference to some important issues of the UN Convention on the Rights of the Child, are discussed in detail in this paper.

2 Ratification and Enforcement of the UN Convention on the Rights of the Child in India

The Government of India has ratified the United Nations Convention on the Rights of the Child (CRC) in November, 1992.[2] Article 73 of the Constitution of India states that 'Subject to the provisions of the Constitution, the executive power of the Union shall extend to the matters with respect to which Parliament has power to

[1] Census of India, Government of India, 2013.

[2] www.childlineindia.org.in/UnitedNations-convention-on-the-rights-of-the-child.htm

V. Yadlapalli (✉)
Dean, Faculy of Law, University College of Law, Osmania University,
Hyderabad 500007, Telangana, India
e-mail: vishnu.law14@yahoo.com

O. Cvejić Jančić (ed.), *The Rights of the Child in a Changing World*,
Ius Comparatum - Global Studies in Comparative Law 13,
DOI 10.1007/978-3-319-23189-1_9

make laws; and to the exercise of such rights, authority and jurisdiction as are exercisable by the Government of India by virtue of any treaty or agreement'. Article 253 of the Constitution states that 'Parliament has power to make any law for the whole or any part of the territory of India for implementing any treaty, agreement to Convention with any other country or countries or any decision made at any international conference, association or other body'. Therefore, international conventions like CRC can be enforced in Indian courts without a statute. Any international convention consistent with the fundamental rights and in harmony with its spirit must be read into the provisions of the Constitution. Therefore, the provisions of the CRC in consonance with the fundamental rights can be enforced without a statute. However, the Indian Government made a *reservation* of Article 32 of the CRC regarding the minimum age for admission into employment.

3 The Legal Definition of a Child

All cultures share the view that the younger the children, the more vulnerable they are physically and psychologically and the less they are able to fend for themselves. Age limits are a formal reflection of society's judgment about the evolution of children's capacities and responsibilities. According to Article 1 of the UN Convention on the Rights of the Child 1989, 'a child means every human being below the age of eighteen years unless, under the law applicable to the child, majority is attained earlier'. In India, the census of India defines persons below the age of 14 as children. Most of the government programmes on children are targeted for the age group below 14 years. However, in India, the legal conception of a child has tended to vary depending upon the purpose. Some of the provisions relating to age are discussed hereunder.

The Indian Majority Act, 1875, was enacted in order to bring about uniformity in the applicability of laws to persons of different religions. Unless a particular personal law specifies otherwise, every person domiciled in India is deemed to have attained majority upon completion of 18 years of age. However, in case of a minor for whose person or property, or both, a guardian has been appointed or declared by any court of justice before the age of 18 years, and in case of every minor the superintendence of whose property has been assumed by the Court of Wards before the minor has attained that age, the age of majority will be 21 years and not 18.[3] According to section 11 of the Indian Contract Act, a person below the age of 18 years has no capacity to enter into a contract. The Hindu Minority and Guardianship Act (HMGA), 1956, in Section 4(a) define a 'minor' as a person who has not completed the age of 18 years. The age of majority for the purposes of appointment of guardians of person and property of minors according to the Mohammedan law is also completion of 18 years (the Dissolution of Muslim Marriage Act 1939). Christians (the Indian Divorce Act 1869) and Parsis (the Parsi Marriage and Divorce

[3] The Indian Majority Act, 1875, Section 3.

Act 1936) also reach majority at 18. The age of marriage is 21 years for males and 18 years for females under the Prohibition of Child Marriage Act 2006.

For purposes of criminal responsibility, age limit is 7[4] and 12[5] under the Indian Penal Code, 1860 (IPC). For purposes of protection against kidnapping, abduction and related offences, age is fixed at 16 in the case of boys and 18 in the case of girls.[6] For purposes of special treatment, the age prescribed under the Juvenile Justice (Care and Protection of Children) Act 2000 [Section 2(k)] is 18 for both boys and girls. For the purpose of admission into employment, the term 'child' is defined differently in different labour legislations. For example, the Factories Act, 1948, provides that a person below the age of 14 years is not allowed to work in any factory. The Mines Act, 1952, provides 'no person below the age of 18 years shall be allowed to work in any mine or any part thereof'. Under the Apprentices Act, 1961, a person is qualified to be engaged as an apprentice only if he has completed the age of 14 years. According to the Child Labour (Prohibition and Regulation) Act 1986 [Section 2(ii)], child means a person who has not completed the 14th year of age.

The word 'child' has been used in various legislations as a term denoting relationship, as a term indicating capacity and as a term of special protection. There does not appear to be any criteria or scientific parameters. For instance, in some laws as in the Prohibition of Child Marriage Act 2006, there is a difference between the age of the boy and that of the girl. The minimum age of marriage for girls is 18 but the age of sexual consent under the rape laws is 16 and it is 15 if she is married. The Mines Act defines children as those below 18 years, and the various State Shops and Establishment Acts define the age of a child between 12 and 15 years. In April 2013 the Government of India formulated the National Policy of Children, 2013, which defines the term 'child' as a person who has not completed the age of 18 years. It is necessary that the term 'child' should be defined uniformly in all legislations for all purposes in conformity with the UN Convention on the Rights of the Child, 1989, and the National Policy of Children, 2013.

4 Legal Framework for the Rights of the Child in India

Legislation is one of the main weapons of empowerment of children. India has general framework for the rights of the child, while leaving it to special laws to regulate special rights of the child. The Constitution of India, the fundamental law of the country, came into force on 26 January 1950. It provides a protective umbrella for the rights of children. These rights include right to equality [Article 14]; right to

---

[4] Section 82 of the Indian Penal Code provides, 'nothing is an offence which is done by a child under the age of 7 years'.

[5] Section 83 of the Indian Penal Code provides, 'the age of criminal responsibility is raised to 12 years if the child is found to have not attained the ability to understand the nature and consequences of his/her act'.

[6] IPC Section 361 deals with kidnapping from lawful guardianship.

freedom including the freedom of speech and expression [Article 19(1)(a)]; personal liberty and right to due process of law [Article 21]; right against exploitation [Article 23, 24]; religious, cultural and educational rights [Article 29]; and right to constitutional remedies [Article 32].

In addition to these basic rights, there are certain fundamental rights especially for children. These rights are necessary because of their physical and mental immaturity; the children are especially vulnerable and need special protection. Article 15 of the Constitution prohibits discrimination of citizens on the grounds only of religion, race, caste, sex, place of birth or any combination of them. But subsection 3 states that 'Nothing in this Article shall prevent the state from making any special provision for women and children'. Therefore, laws can be made giving special protection to children. These rights are included in Part III and Part IV of the Constitution. The fundamental rights in Part III are enforceable in courts whereas the directive principles of state policy in Part IV are guidelines and principles that are fundamental to the governance of the country. It is the duty of the state to apply these principles in making laws. If the fundamental rights are violated, a writ petition can be filed in the Supreme Court or the High Court [Article 32 and 226].

Under the Constitution, it is the duty of the state to secure that children of tender age are not abused and forced by economic necessity to enter vocations unsuited to their age and strength [Article 39(e)] and to ensure that children are given opportunities and facilities to develop in a healthy manner and in conditions of freedom and dignity [Article 39(f)]. The directive principles provide for maternity relief [Article 42]. Rights provided under Part IV (directive principles) of the Constitution can be read into the fundamental rights provided in Part III and hence enforceable in courts. Because of judicial interpretation, many of the directive principles have now become enforceable through legal actions before the courts (e.g. the right to education).

It is estimated that there are more than 250 central and state statutes under which the child is covered in India. Some of the important legislations enacted after ratification of the CRC are briefly discussed as follows.

4.1 The Preconception and Prenatal Diagnostic Techniques (Prohibition of Sex Selection) Act 2002

This Act provides for the regulation of the use of prenatal diagnostic techniques for the purpose of detecting genetic or metabolic disorders or chromosomal abnormalities or certain congenital malformations or sex-linked disorders and for the prevention of the misuse of such techniques for the purpose of preconception and prenatal sex determination leading to female foeticide.

4.2 *The Juvenile Justice (Care and Protection of Children) Act 2000 (as Amended in 2006)*

This Act deals with the law relating to juveniles in conflict with law and children in need of care and protection. It provides for proper care, protection and treatment by catering to their development needs, and by adopting a child-friendly approach in the adjudication and disposition of matters in the best interest of children, and for their ultimate rehabilitation through various institutions established under the Act.

4.3 *The Commissions for Protection of Child Rights Act, 2005*

This Act provides for the setting up of independent commissions at the national and state levels to monitor all laws, policies, programmes and administrative mechanisms from a child rights perspective. It also provides for setting up of children's courts for speedy trial of offences against children, including violation of child rights.

4.4 *The Prohibition of Child Marriage Act (PCMA), 2006*

This Act has replaced the Child Marriage Restraint Act, 1929. Some of the important provisions of this Act are child marriage to be made voidable at the option of the contracting party, who was a child at the time of the marriage up to 2 years after obtaining adulthood; provision for maintenance to the female contracting party until her remarriage; and passing of appropriate custody orders by the District Court for children born out of a child marriage. The PCMA, 2006, has enhanced the punishment for male adults marrying a child and for persons performing, abetting, promoting or attending a child marriage, with imprisonment of up to 2 years and a fine of up to Rs. 0.1 million. The offences under the Act are both cognizable and non-bailable.

4.5 *The Right of Children to Free and Compulsory Education Act, 2009*

This Act came into force from April 1, 2010, which provides for that free and compulsory education to all children between 6 and 14 years of age in such manner as the state may, by law, determine. The National Commission for Protection of Child Rights (NCPCR) has been assigned with the responsibility of monitoring the child's right to education.

4.6 The Protection of Children from Sexual Offences Act, 2012

This Act has been passed to strengthen the legal provisions for the protection of children from sexual abuse and exploitation. For the first time a special law is made to address the issue of sexual offences against children. Prior to this Act, sexual offences were covered under different sections of Indian Penal Code (IPC). The IPC does not deal with all types of sexual offences against children and, more importantly, does not distinguish between adult and child victims. This Act defines a child as any person below the age of 18 years and provides protection to all children under the age of 18 years from the offences of sexual assault, sexual harassment and pornography. These offences have been clearly defined for the first time in law. This Act provides stringent punishments which have been graded as per the gravity of the offence.

Besides the above special legislations that deal with children, there are provisions that concern children in various general statutes. Provisions relating to children have also developed in the areas of criminal law, family law, employment law and other aspects of childcare and welfare. There are also specific rules which apply to minors engaged in civil or criminal proceedings or commercial matters. The Code of Criminal Procedure, 1973, lays down various procedures to be followed in a criminal trial and provides for the machinery for the punishment of offenders. The Code of Civil Procedure, 1908, lays down the procedure to be followed in civil trials. The Indian Evidence Act, 1872, deals with the competency of the witness and the value of evidence given by children [Section 112].

Several criminal laws give special protection to children. These statutes include the Indian Penal Code 1860, the Evidence Act 1872, and the Code of Criminal Procedure 1973. The Indian Penal Code, 1860, defines various categories of offences and the punishment for such offences. It has special provisions relating to the causing of miscarriages and injuries caused to the unborn child [IPC Sections 312–318]. In case of child rape, consent cannot be a defence where the child is below 16 years of age. Marital rape is recognized only if the wife is below 15 years [IPC Sections 375 and 376]. There is an enhanced punishment in cases of rape by public servants and custodial rape [IPC sec. 376 (a) (b) (c) (d)], including rape of children in institutions. There are provisions for kidnapping, abduction and buying of minors for the purpose of prostitution, slavery and forced labour [IPC 358–374]. The Immoral Traffic (Prevention) Act, 1956, which was amended in 1987, tries to curb trafficking in young persons, both boys and girls. There are provisions relating to children in the Cable Television Network (Regulation) Act, 1995, and the Prevention of Illicit Traffic in Narcotic Drugs and Psychotropic Substances Act, 1988.

In the area of family law, the personal laws are religion based. The rights of children born to Hindus are governed by the Hindu Marriage Act, 1955, and the Hindu Succession Act, 1956. Christian children are governed by the Indian Divorce Act, 1860, and the Indian Succession Act, 1925. In matters of marriage, maintenance, custody, guardianship, adoption, succession and inheritance, the Muslim children are governed by the Muslim personal law. The Parsi children are governed by the Parsi Marriage and Divorce Act, 1936, and the Indian Succession Act, 1925. An important provision in the Criminal Procedure Code (Cr. PC) 1973 is the order for maintenance of children [Section 125]. Cr. PC Section 125 provides for an order of maintenance of the legitimate or illegitimate child (not a married daughter) who has attained majority, if such a child, by reason of any physical or mental abnormality or injury, is unable to maintain itself.

There are provisions relating to employment of children in the Factories Act, 1948; the Minimum Wages Act, 1948; the Plantations Labour Act, 1951; the Mines Act, 1952; the Merchant Shipping Act, 1958; the Motor Transport Workers Act, 1961; the Payment of bonus Act, 1965; the Beedi and Cigar Workers (Conditions of Employment) Act, 1966; the Bonded Labour System (Abolition) Act, 1976; the Trade Unions Act, 1926; and the various State Shops and Establishment Acts. The Contract Act, 1872; the Indian Partnership Act, 1932; and the Indian Trust Act, 1882, contain provisions relating to civil and commercial rights and liabilities of minors.

A number of policy initiatives, plans and programmes relating to children have been undertaken in India. The policy documents are reference points available for planning and other interventions. Some major policy and plan documents are the following:

- National Policy for Children, 1974
- National Policy on Education, 1986
- National Policy on Child Labour, 1987
- National Plan for SAARC Decade of the Girl Child, 1991–2000
- National Nutrition Policy, 1993
- National Health Policy 2001
- National Plan of Action for Children, 2005
- National Commission for Protection of Child Rights, 2007
- National Policy for Children, 2013

The relationship of the child with the state was rearticulated through the National Policy for Children (NPC), 2013, which replaced the National Policy for Children, 1974, defines the term 'child' as a person who has not completed the age of 18 years. The NPC 2013 indicates the national consensus and clarity on measures to ensure that children grow up healthy and happy – survival, health, nutrition, development, education, protection and participation are the undeniable rights of every child and are key priorities of the policy.

5 Provisions for the Best Interest of the Child

Constitutional provisions, legislations, policies, action plans, schemes and programmes increasingly include the 'best interest of the child' as a guiding principle. Furthermore, constitution of the National Commission for Protection of Child

Rights (NCPCR) has added rigorous focus to ensure consistent application of the principle of the 'best interest of the child'. The 11th Five-Year Plan is committed to creating a protective environment for children through a host of schemes and programmes based on the best interest of the child. The Ministry of Women and Child Development (MWCD) is increasingly focusing on child-friendly approaches, while formulating new policies, legislations, guidelines and programmes. The National Plan of Action for Children (NPAC), 2005, recognizes the best interest of the child in all aspects affecting the child. The principle of best interest of a juvenile or a child in conflict with law was the primary consideration for the amendment of the Juvenile Justice (Care and Protection of Children) Act, 2000 (JJ Act, 2000), in 2006 and is a guiding principle of the Juvenile Justice (Care and Protection of Children) Rules, 2007 (JJ Rules, 2007). The National Human Rights Commission (NHRC) has prepared guidelines for speedy disposal of child rape cases that underline the best interest of the child victims in all procedures followed to prosecute and punish the perpetrators. The Supreme Court and High Courts have kept the best interest of the child as the primary concern while passing judgments. The Integrated Child Protection Scheme (ICPS) concretizes government responsibility for creating a system to protect children in the country from all types of exploitative and vulnerable situations. The National Policy for Children, 2013, which replaced the National Policy for Children, 1974, adopts the best interest of the child as a key principle. However, the interpretation and enforcement of laws in practice is not always in the best interest of the child.

The welfare of the child being the sole and paramount consideration is the principle found at present only in the substantive laws on custody and guardianship of the child. The other substantive and procedural laws are silent on this issue. In fact, the best interest principle should be included in all the substantive and procedural laws including the matrimonial laws, the Civil Procedure Code and the Criminal Procedure Code.

6 The Right of the Child to Know About His/Her Origin

A person's right to know his/her biological or genetic origin raises some of the hardest legal and ethical issues that we have had to face in the last several years. This question arises in case of adopted children, of abandoned or displaced children, of children conceived by artificial insemination or of children born out of wedlock. The principle of the best interest of the child and the child's right to know very often conflicts with other competing rights such as the mother's right to privacy and autonomy and the rights of the adoptive parents.[7]

This right to know is not yet universally accepted or acknowledged as being sufficiently fundamental or vital to give rise to a human right in India. In India the right to life is guaranteed under Article 21 of the constitution, which states that 'no person

[7] Jayna Kothari, 'A difficult road to her roots', the Hindu, 30 March 2013.

shall be deprived of his life or personal liberty except according to procedure established by law'. The right to life has been expanded by the Supreme Court in many important judgments[8] to include the right to privacy and dignity, but questions of personal identity and privacy have not been raised till date. To some extent, concerns of protection of identity and privacy are being raised with respect to the Unique Identification project, but they are not articulated in terms of seeking one's right to identity where such information is not available.

To this end, for the first time, the Karnataka High Court[9] recognized the right to know one's biological origin as a fundamental right under Article 21 of the constitution. The court observed that the right to know one's origin is a dimension of the broader right to ascertain and preserve one's identity. This observation of the court highlights the need to articulate a policy and legal mechanism for openness in adoption and medical records. The legal mechanism needs to recognize such a right to information of one's biological parents and lay down the principles guiding the enforcement of this right in practice which will address the important issue of the right to identity of the child and its protection. The child born out of wedlock has the right to establish the origin regarding nonmarital mother. A child born in wedlock has no right to rebut paternity of the husband of the child's mother.

7 Right to Freedom of Expression and Respect for the Views of the Child

The adoption of National Plan of Action for Children, 2005, was the first step towards strengthening of government's efforts for promoting respect for the views of children and taking them into consideration. Since then actions on promoting participation of children and respect for their views within the family, community, schools and institutions, as well as in judicial and administrative proceedings, in accordance with their age and maturity, have found increased space.

The practice of considering the views of children, especially in cases of contested custody, is increasing, albeit it remains the prerogative of the presiding judge or magistrate. There have been cases where the views of children as young as 10 years have been considered, while in others, the views of 16-year-olds have been overlooked.[10] Greater sensitization of the judges and courts is required that would have better impact, especially as the assessments of the best interests of the child and the influence of the custodian and others can be very subjective.

The JJ Rules, 2007, provides every child the right to express his/her views freely in all matters affecting his/her interest at every stage in the process of juvenile justice. The government continues to enhance freedom of expression among children

[8] Maneka Gandhi v. Union of India, AIR 1978 SC 597.

[9] Ms. Maria Chaya v. State of Karnataka, 2013 (http://clpr.org.in).

[10] Asha Bajpai, Child Rights in India, 2006, p. 126.

through various interventions such as village-level youth clubs, which discuss contemporary social issues, such as gender bias, enrolment drives in primary schools, immunization, drugs and substance abuse, human immunodeficiency virus (HIV)/ acquired immunodeficiency syndrome (AIDS) awareness, etc.

However, facilitating child participation in critical matters and decisions concerning them remains a significant challenge, as children in India are traditionally and conventionally not consulted on matters and decisions affecting their lives in the family and household, the neighbourhood and wider community. Capacity building is required at different levels, especially among caregivers, as they do not have the understanding and skills for involving children's views in matters affecting them. There is a need to move from sporadic efforts at engaging children and listening to their views to institutionalizing participation in programmes for children. There is a need to sensitize the judiciary and court officials for enabling processes and creating an environment, where children's views are heard and considered in judicial proceedings affecting them.

8 Right of Child to Give Consent to Adoption

At present, adoption takes place both formally and informally in the country. Formal adoptions take place under the Hindu Adoption and Maintenance Act, 1956 (applicable to Hindus, Sikhs, Jains and Buddhists, wherein the child gets all the rights of a biological child), and under the JJ Act, 2000, amended in 2006. A child can also be taken as a ward under the GW Act, 1890 (applicable to all other communities, but wherein the child does not have the rights of a biological child). The JJ (Amendment) Act, 2006, has widened the scope of adoption of children by adoptive parents. For the first time, this Act defines 'adoption' in absolute terms as a process through which the adopted child is permanently separated from his biological parents and becomes the legitimate child of the adoptive parents and enjoys the rights, privileges and responsibilities of a biological child. The JJ Act, 2000, makes it mandatory to register all child-care institutions, including orphanages and homes actively taking up adoption, and to ensure that adoptions take place only after proper documentation and scrutiny of prospective parents. The JJ Act 2000 requires that the child's consent be taken into account before the adoption is completed if the child can understand and express his consent, under section 41 (3) of the JJ Act.

9 Intercountry Adoptions

Intercountry adoption is now governed by Guidelines for Adoption from India, 2006, following India's ratification of the Hague Convention in 2003.[11] These guidelines make adoptionprocedures simple and more transparent. These guidelines

[11] Eleventh Five-Year Plan 2007–2012, vol. II, Planning Commission, Government of India.

provide a framework to protect the interests of both biological and adoptive parents along with that of children through the mechanisms of licensing, follow-up reports, documents, etc.; CARA (Central Adoption resource Agency), as nodal authority, promotes domestic adoption and regulates intercountry adoptions in India, as provided under guidelines of the Government of India. It has developed mechanisms to ensure that all orphan, abandoned and surrendered children are expeditiously placed in adoption. Regular inspection is done by CARA to ensure quality childcare and compliance of existing guidelines. CARA ensures that all efforts are made to place a child in his/her own sociocultural milieu in his best interest, before giving him/her in intercountry adoption.[12]

10 Right of the Child to Freedom of Thought, Conscience and Religion

Children's right to freedom of thought, conscience and religion forms an important part of participation rights. The National Plan of Action for Children (NPAC), 2005, states that the government is committed to establishing a civilized, humane and just civil order that does not discriminate on grounds of caste, religion, class, colour, race or sex and which provides information and skills training to children to build their capacities to think and analyse. Religious education is available in schools as an optional subject. Knowledge of the world's great religions is taught in schools as a part of education.

11 Prohibition of Physical Punishment of the Child within or beyond the Family

There is greater awareness in the government on the issue of torture or other cruel, inhuman or degrading treatment, including corporal punishment, which includes abusing, hitting, demeaning a child, etc. by an adult authority figure in the family or outside.

Due to growing sensitization about children's rights at all levels, increasing cases of corporal punishment are being reported. The Study on Child Abuse: India 2007 by the MWCD (Ministry of Women and Child Development) reported that an overwhelming majority of children, that is two out of three children, are victims of corporal punishment. Out of those reporting corporal punishment in schools, 54.28 % are boys and 45.72 % are girls. The study also revealed that more of older children are beaten in schools than younger ones; very high percentage of corporal punish-

[12] Report of Working Group on Development of Children for the 11th Five-Year Plan, Ministry of Women and Child Development, Government of India.

ment is reported in government and municipal schools, and NGO-run schools also reported high percentage of corporal punishment. One of the core objectives of the NPAC, 2005, is to protect all children from neglect, maltreatment, injury, trafficking and sexual and physical abuse. Any person who is in charge of or control over a juvenile or the child; assaults, abandons, exposes or wilfully neglects the juvenile or causes or procures him/her to be assaulted, abandoned, exposed or neglected in a manner likely to cause such juvenile or the child unnecessary mental or physical suffering shall be punishable with imprisonment for a term, which may extend to 6 months, or fine, or both. The JJ Rules, 2007, provide for a suggestion box to be installed in every institution at a place easily accessible to juvenile or child as complaint and redressal mechanism.

With the enactment of the Right of Children to Free and Compulsory Education Act, 2009, which prohibits physical punishment and mental harassment in all educational institutions in the country, the government has strengthened the protection of rights of children.

Under the Indian Penal Code (IPC), 1860, a 'hurt' caused by an 'act' to the 'body' and to the 'mind' constitutes an offence under Section 323. However, in the context of corporal punishment inflicted on children, such a 'hurt' does not constitute an offence. Sections 88 and 89 of the IPC, 1860, provide immunity to a person causing 'hurt' to a child if the act is 'done in good faith, not intending to cause harm, and by consent whether expressed or implied'. Thus, effectively the law does not recognize corporal punishment as an 'offence'.[13]

12 Separation from Family: Deprivation of Parental Responsibilities

Separation from parents in the best interest of the child usually takes place when either parent is not in a position to take care of the child because of poverty, ailment, alcoholism or imprisonment, or when parents are not known, or when children are abandoned, or when children became victims of man-made natural disasters. The NPAC, 2005; the JJ (Amendment) Act, 2006; and the JJ Rules, 2007, recognize the need for care and protection of children, who are separated from parents, including children of prisoners. The JJ (Amendment) Act, 2006, and JJ Rules, 2007, focus on placing children without parental care and support in alternative care within families and use of institutionalization only as a step of last resort. The JJ Rules, 2007, also provide that parents and relatives of a juvenile placed in an institution should be allowed to visit him/her once a month or more frequently in special circumstances. It also provides the juvenile freedom to write and receive letters.

[13] Report of Working Group on Corporal Punishment, National Commission for the Protection of Child Rights, Government of India, 2008.

According to estimates, a large proportion of children in India are destitute, orphan and without parental support. Many of these children get separated, temporarily or permanently, from their family, under vulnerable and exploitative situations or desertion by the family. To safeguard their best interest and their ultimate rehabilitation, legislative provisions have been made and programmes initiated to place these children in community-based alternative care or institutional care. The JJ Act, 2000, and JJ (Amendment) Act, 2006, outline provisions for non-institutional (adoption, foster placement and sponsorship) as well as institutional care. The ICPS (Integrated Child Protection Scheme) provides for sponsorship of education, health, nutrition and other developmental needs of children at risk, to support the family in taking care of the child. Section 43 of the JJ (Amendment) Act, 2006, lays down a provision for developing sponsorship programme for providing supplementary support to families, children's homes and special homes to meet medical, nutritional, educational and other needs of children for improving their quality of life. The state government may make rules for the purpose of carrying out various schemes of sponsorship of children, such as individual-to-individual sponsorship, group sponsorship or community sponsorship. The state has the obligation to prepare the sponsorship programme in consultation with non-governmental organizations (NGOs), Child Welfare Committees (CWCs), relevant government agencies and the corporate sector. The Central Adoption Resource Authority (CARA) promotes domestic adoption for the rehabilitation of orphaned, abandoned and destitute children.

The parent who is deprived of parental responsibilities has the obligation to maintain the separated child and has the right to visit the child periodically if it does not affect the welfare of the child.

13 Right of the Child to Give Medical Consent Independently

A person who has not completed the age of 18 years is said to be a minor and has no capacity to give consent to any contract according to section 11 of the Indian Contract Act, 1872. Hence the child has no right to give medical consent or refuse consent to medical treatment independently until he/she completes 18 years of age. In such condition, the legal guardian of the child can give medical consent.

14 Right of the Child to Change His/Her Personal Name

A person below the age of 18 years has no right to change his/her personal name independently. After attaining the age of 18 years, he/she acquires the right to change the personal name by publishing in the official Gazette.

15 Minimum Age for Admission into Employment

India has the highest number of working children in the world. Children work in all sectors of the economy, i.e. the agrarian, the manufacturing and the service sectors under abusive and exploitative conditions. The estimates on the magnitude of child labour vary due to multiplicity of definitions and different methods of computation. Poverty, parental illiteracy and ignorance and lack of proper educational facilities are the main causes for the employment of children. Employers prefer child labour because of cheap labour and easy to control children.

Legally there is no complete ban on the employment of children in India. No minimum age is prescribed for admission into employment. Children as young as 7 or 8 years are seen working for a living. However, different labour legislations prescribe minimum age of employment differently. The Constitution of India under Article 24 prohibits the employment of children below the age of 14 years in any mine, factory or any hazardous employment. The Child Labour (Prohibition and Regulation) Act 1986 (CLPR Act) came into force by repealing the Employment of Children Act, 1938. The CLPR Act prohibits the employment of a person who has not completed his/her 14th year of age in occupations and processes set forth only in Part A and Part B of the Schedule of the Act (under Section 3). The CLPR Act thus classifies all establishments in two categories, viz., (i) those in which employment of children is prohibited and (ii) those in which the employment of children below 14 years of age is permitted with regulated working conditions. Employment of children is not prohibited in any workshop wherein any process is carried on by the occupier, with the aid of his family, or to any school established by or receiving assistance or recognition from government. Part III of the CLRP Act provides for regulation of conditions of work of children. The period of work of the child on each day shall not exceed 6 hours. The child is not permitted to do work between 6 PM and 8 AM or overtime.

The child has no option to decide about his/her employment. The child is compelled to work under economic necessity and often with the consent of the parents. The CLPR Act violates the right to education of the child guaranteed under Article 21-A of the Constitution of India and also the UN Convention on the Rights of the Child. The government should change the child labour law to ensure the implementation of the right to education law, by banning all forms of child labour entirely.

16 Obligation of the Child Towards Parents

In India, parents, by virtue of being natural guardians of their children, have the right to determine the child's upbringing with regard to religion, education and overall care and development. The child has the obligation to oblige and respect his/her parents.

17 Summary and Conclusion

The above discussed laws and policies tend to work in isolation. The right to education, for instance, is linked to issues of child labour, juvenile justice, child marriages, health and nutrition. The policy perspectives relating to children and childhood are confused. On one hand we have the 93rd Constitutional Amendment stating that it is a fundamental right of children between 6 and 14 years to be in school and also the Right of Children to Free and Compulsory Education Act, 2009, and on the other hand we have the Child Labour (Prohibition and Regulation) Act 1986 laying down that children below 14 years can work in non-hazardous occupations and processes. Further, there is a Prohibition of Child Marriage Act 2006, setting a minimum age of marriage, that declared the marriage voidable at the option of the child contracting party, but not void. The Persons with Disabilities (Equal Opportunities, Protection of Rights and Full Participation) Act 1995 is totally alienated from the education, health and nutrition policies and the children in need of care and protection under the Juvenile Justice (Care and Protection of Children) Act 2000. The JJ Act 2000 has attempted to bring in adoption of children under the Act. But it is not clear about adoption of children whose personal laws do not 'permit' adoption. Laws in India are to be more children-oriented and rights-based in order to be effective. Besides, the rights of children are inalienable and indivisible. They cannot work in isolation. The laws relating to children also have to be interlinked. Perhaps, a single code on children can best protect the interests of the child. The laws and the policies now have to conform to the international standards laid down in the CRC which India has ratified.

A large number of children in India still live much below the standards set by the UN Convention on the Rights of the Child, 1989, and the Constitution of India. They suffer an array of threats to their development, well-being and survival. They suffer from poverty, diseases, famine and war, and they also suffer from acts and omissions of their own caretakers, guardians and parents. Primary education still remains as a paper law and a dream of children for want of allocation of sufficient funds and commitment of the government. Over 100 million children in the age group of 5–14 years in India are deprived of basic education and have no opportunity of going to school (UNESCO Report 2010). India continues to have the highest number of child labourers globally. Millions of children live below poverty with insufficient food and shelter and having no access to health care. Over 300,000 newborns in India die within 24 hours of their birth every year. Out of every three babies in the world dying on the first day of their birth, one is in India (State of World Mothers' Report 2013). There are an estimated one million street children nationwide exposed to violence and exploitation (Achievements, Challenges, Aims and Strategies, UNICEF 2011). According to National Family Health Survey, India accounts for one-third of the world's children who suffer malnutrition. In India, 15 % of children have serious emotional disturbances (World Health Report 2001). Children are discriminated against because of their class, caste or religion. There is no adoption law for children of other religious groups besides Hindus. The continuously declining sex ratio has been a cause of concern among socially conscious demographers and policy makers. Girls are consistently denied equal opportunities to attend and complete primary schooling. Thousands of girls are trafficked and used for prostitution in brothels in cities. The phenomenon of sale of children is universal. Children are also victims of wars, riots, natural calamities, poverty trap and debt burden and globalization.

India's slow and poor implementation of the UN Convention of the Rights of the Child is itself a human rights denial. There are two defaults that affect children, viz., low budgeting of resources and low allocation of attention. These defaults are urgently required correction.

A Study on the Rights of the Child in Iranian Legal System

Habiballah Ahmadi Baloutaki

1 Introduction

Children are the most vulnerable among social groups. Observing their human rights is a great responsibility of governments, societies, and families. The International Convention on the Rights of the Child (CRC) is the first legally binding international instrument for the protection of children's rights. On September 5, 1991, the Islamic Republic of Iran signed the Convention on the Rights of the Child, and the same is ratified on July 13, 1994, with some reservations and conditions. These conditions stated that if any provisions of the Convention contradict Iran's internal and Islamic laws, the latter would override the Convention. This conditional acceptance of the Convention has allowed the violations of children's rights and has prevented the existing legal system from protecting these rights. In this paper, a few examples of how laws in Iran fail to conform to international standards set by the CRC and violate the rights of children are discussed briefly.

2 The Age of Majority

The age of majority may constitute the most important aspect of children's rights in Iranian law. This is the age that a child leaves behind the years of not being responsible for his actions and enters into adulthood, becoming accountable in the eyes of the law. Based on the Article 1210 of the Civil Law as amended in 1962, "the age of majority for boys is 15 lunar years and for girls 9 lunar years." Meanwhile, the first

H.A. Baloutaki, Ph.D. (✉)
University College of Law, Osmania University, Hyderabad, India
e-mail: a.anshan@yahoo.com

O. Cvejić Jančić (ed.), *The Rights of the Child in a Changing World*,
Ius Comparatum - Global Studies in Comparative Law 13,
DOI 10.1007/978-3-319-23189-1_10

article of the Convention on the Rights of the Child states: "For the purposes of the present Convention, a child means every human being below the age of eighteen years unless under the law applicable to the child, majority is attained earlier." As we can see, the first article of the Convention sets up a contrast between an international standard and Article 1210 of Iran's Civil Law, especially with regard to the age of majority for girls. Legal experts and child psychologists acknowledge that the age of majority has an undeniable importance in the life of children and adult responsibility too early in life can result in damaging and irreversible consequences. Legislators bear the responsibility of determining this crucial turning point. Iranian children, especially girls, suffer from oversights in the Islamic Republic's legal system, as some examples below demonstrate.

3 Marriageable Age

In 1931, the first law regarding marriage was passed. It was silent on the legal age for getting married. Article 3 of this law indicated that marrying someone who is not "physically developed" is forbidden and anyone who marries such a person will be condemned to 1–3 years imprisonment in a correctional facility. In 1934, the second chapter of the second volume of the Civil Law described the physical preconditions for marriage. For the first time, in Article 1040, the legislators determined the age for marriage: "Marriage is forbidden for girls under age 15 and for boys under age 18. However, under certain circumstances, with the permission of the public defendant and with the court's approval, exemptions may be allowed, but never to girls under 13 or to boys less than 15 years of age."

In 1974, when the Family Protection Law of 1967 was being revised, the age for marriage was one of the issues that were reviewed. Here, Article 23 of the Family Protection Law was revised to change this age for girls from 15 to 18 and for boys from 18 to 20. This new and special piece of legislation abolished Article 1041 of the Civil Law of 1934. After the Islamic Revolution of 1978, the Family Protection Law lost its legal standing. In 1982, the Islamic Republic's legislators amended the Civil Law, including Article 1041 that addresses the legal age for marriage, and amended this section as follows: "Marriage is forbidden before the age of majority." The notes attached to this Article state that "Marriage is allowed for those under the age of majority with their guardians' permission, if the best interests of the subject are considered."

This article does not codify a legal age for marriage; instead, it refers to the "age of majority." Consequently, the legal age for marriage was reduced to (in solar years) 8 years and 9 months for girls and 14 years and 7 months for boys. In 2001, after 19 years of pleas by human rights defenders, especially those involved with children's rights in Iran, and with the support of international bodies, Article 1041 of the Civil Law was changed by the Expediency Council to the following: "Marriage for girls before attaining age 13 and for boys before attaining age 15 is only allowed by the guardian's permission, with the interests of the subject in mind and by the ruling of a competent court." So after many years, the legal age for Iranian girls for entering into marriage was raised to what is still a young age of 13.

Even though the legal age is defined in this law, it still awards absolute power to the guardians of Iranian children to allow marriage of their minor children, "having their best interest in mind." Based on Article 1180 of the Civil Law and according to Islamic principles, the father and the grandfather are "automatic guardians" of the child. One of the legal rights awarded to these automatic guardians is making decisions about the marriage of their minor child or grandchild. The law provides that such a marriage is legal if the best interests of the child are considered by his or her guardian. However, once this underaged child married off by his or her guardian reaches the legal age, is he or she allowed to nullify the marriage? Most Muslim lawyers and faqihs (expert in Islamic jurisprudence) have responded "no" to this question, arguing that a marriage, entered legally, cannot be nullified later. Even in rare cases where some legal grounds exist to nullify marriages of these underaged victims, a 13-year-old girl or a 15-year-old boy would rarely dare to confront a father and rebel against him because it goes against traditional and cultural norms.[1]

Consequently, Iranian children can not only be subject to forced marriages at the early ages of 13 or 15, but their fathers and grandfathers have full and legal authority to arrange their marriage to whomever they want, as they "have their best interest in mind." In the judiciary system of Iran, there is no legal mechanism to determine what is in the best interest of children and therefore no legal retribution for those who do not act with those interests in mind.

4 Legal Responsibility to Children

Based on Article 49 of the Islamic Penal Law and its notes, children are excused from any punitive responsibility if they commit a crime and, by court decision, can be placed under the supervision of a guardian or in a correctional center for children. Note 1 defines a child as "someone who has not attained the age of majority in religious terms." Note 2 states that if physical punishment is determined to be necessary for guilty children, those punishments must be just and executed with good intentions.

As mentioned earlier, Article 1210 of the Civil Law sets the age of majority for girls at 9 lunar years and for boys at 15 lunar years. Therefore, 9-year-old girls and 15-year-old boys, who are considered adults in the religious sense term by Islamic legislators, can be punished like adults if they commit a crime and can even be subject to physical punishment. The Islamic Penal Law allows severe physical punishments such as whipping, cutting parts of the body, stoning, and execution for those found guilty of a crime. Since 9- and 15-year-old children are considered adults and, as such, held responsible for their acts with possible severe physical punishments if

[1] Lily Pourzand, "Legal Rights of Children in Iran," A Forum on Human Rights and Democracy in Iran, 2007.

they commit crimes, they will be subject to the full force of the law and will not receive reduced punishments. Adolescents are treated as adults in the eye of the law and, if caught committing a crime, face severe punishments.

Iran is only five countries (along with Pakistan, Saudi Arabia, Sudan, and Yemen) that allow the death penalty for individuals under the age of 18. Detained children often do not have the right to due process and are condemned to death, more often. Poor children also do not have sufficient financial means to cover their judicial fees and expenses. The rate of minors sentenced to death in Iran has been rising. Authorities continue to execute children even under pressure from human rights organizations that denounce the practice.[2]

5 Corrective Measures by Parents

The Civil Law of Iran allows parents to punish their children. Article 179 of this law states: "Parents are allowed to punish their child, but this right does not give them authority to go beyond the normal scope." The emphasis of the legislator on not going over the "normal" limits in these punishments does not preclude the parents' cruelty against the child. In the absence of definite and specific criteria, the child's legal protection is compromised and subject to the opinions and interpretations of those involved with such decisions in the courts.

This open-ended right of a parent to punish his child puts children in great danger. Article 220 of the Islamic Penal Law openly states: "A father or a grandfather killing his child will not face the death penalty, but has to pay blood money to the heirs of the deceased and be subjected to a reduced beating sentence." As we can see, the law is tolerant of parents, specifically fathers and grandfathers, punishing children; even the act of killing a child does not render the maximum legal punishment (death penalty). This article fails to comply with international standards of human rights to which the Iranian government is bound and jeopardizes children's lives and safety inside their families.[3]

6 Inheritance of Children

Iranian children, like other Iranian citizens, can inherit from their family members according to laws which define terms of inheritance. The gender of the child plays an important role in this process. According to the laws of the Islamic Republic, a female child's share of an inheritance is half of the share of a male child. As Article

[2] i. Mohammad Mostafaei, "Crime against Children in Iran," Iran Human Rights Documentation Center, 2012.
ii. Raeesi, Denial of Children's Right to Life in Iranian Legal System, 2012.

[3] Rights of the Child, "The voices of Children in Iran," Human Rights NGO, 2012.

907 of the Civil Law states: "If the deceased has no parent but one or more children, the estate is divided as follows: if there is only one child, either male or female, the entire estate goes to him or her. If there is more than one child and all male or all female, the estate is divided evenly among them. If there is more than one child with different genders, the male children inherit twice as much as the female children." Hence, the financial status of Iranian girls can be adversely affected by gender discrimination before they reach adulthood.

7 Citizenship of Children

Some of the most inadequate Iranian laws are those governing citizenship, which has created numerous difficulties for children. In awarding citizenship to a child, only the citizenship of the father matters, not that of the mother. Therefore, if an Iranian woman marries a foreign citizen and gives birth to a child outside Iran, the child cannot acquire Iranian citizenship through the mother.

The lives of many Iranian children have been greatly affected by this law. When they return to Iran with their mothers, they have no legal mechanism through which to acquire Iranian citizenship and no civic rights. They cannot enjoy any social or legal protections and live in a state of constant uncertainty. In order to apply for Iranian citizenship, such children must live in Iran until age 18 and may begin the application process at age 19. As children, they are essentially being punished for not having an Iranian father. They are deprived of educational benefits and other civic rights. If children could become citizens of Iran through their Iranian mothers, this problem would be solved.[4]

8 Children Born Out of Wedlock

Iranian laws fail to protect children born out of wedlock. According to Iranian law, the parents of these "illegitimate" children are defined as "natural" parents as opposed to "legal" parents. Natural parents do not have a legal right to raise their children, according to Iranian law, and can lose custody of them to "legal" guardians. Article 1167 of the Civil Law states: "A child born out of wedlock cannot be attributed to the adulterer or male violator." Therefore, children born out of wedlock cannot inherit wealth or property from their parents, and their parents do not have any financial responsibility towards them. Also, their civic rights such as citizenship or child support can be compromised. These children are deprived from their full civil, legal, and human rights because their parents engaged in an "illegal" relationship.[5]

---

[4] Abghari, Adineh, Introduction to the Iranian Legal System and the Protection of Human Rights in Iran, 2005.

[5] Mahshid Satad Tabaei, "Comparative Study of the Illegitimate Children's Rights under English and Iran Laws," Journal of Basic and Applied Scientific Research, Tehran, 2012.

9 Custody of Children

The custody of children after divorce and the status of those who lose their fathers present still another set of legal setbacks in the context of children's rights. The lack of legal authority for Iranian mothers to manage their children's assets and the absolute rights given to the fathers and grandfathers to control their children's destiny and property is another aspect of the inadequacy of the governing laws.[6]

10 Vulnerability of Children Due to Poverty and Neglect

Although Iran is rich in natural resources, much of the population lives in poverty. According to official reports, 80 % of the Iranian population lives below the poverty line. Children in rural areas are most affected by this problem. Article 24 of the CRC recognizes the "right of the child to the enjoyment of the highest attainable standard of health and to facilities for the treatment of illness and rehabilitation of health." Iran has a very high mortality rate for children under the age of 5 years. Premature birth, pneumonia, pelvic congestion, and diarrhea are the main causes of infant mortality. Although maternal health care has improved in the last few years, malnutrition is still a serious problem among mothers and children, especially in rural areas.[7]

11 Education

Education is free and required up to age of 11 years. In rural areas, however, school attendance is low, particularly among girls. The most far-flung reaches of the country still require numerous improvements in infrastructure. In Iranian society, men enjoy a higher status than women. The Iranian education system propagates the religious belief that women are inferior beings. Among other things, children are taught that women belong to men, who have the right to punish their wives if they disobey them. In spite of this, females have actually outnumbered males in university courses in recent years.[8]

---

[6] Tahir Mahmood, "Family Law Reform in the Muslim world," The Indian Law Institute, New Delhi, 1972.

[7] Audery Ramel, "Children's Rights in the Islamic Republic of Iran," Humanium for Children' Rights, 2012.

[8] Ibid. p. 2.

12 Street Children

Laws governing the lives of children, including homeless children, have created many challenges in Iranian society. Street children have become a serious concern in Iran. Most of these children are not orphans, but usually have drug-addicted parents, which force them to live in the streets. Others are children of refugees or unemployed parents, which force the children to work to help support their families. There are currently an estimated 200,000 children living in the streets. They sleep in abandoned buildings, shipping containers, or vehicles and must find work in order to fulfill their own needs or those of their families. Vulnerable and unsupervised Iranian children are easy prey for adult predators who take any opportunity to abuse them. More than 60 % of these girls have been victims of sexual abuse. An estimated 14 % of Iranian children are forced to work in dangerous and unsanitary conditions. These children usually work in the streets, in automobile or rug factories, or in the sex industry. Their health care and education fall by the wayside without any improvement.[9]

13 Summary and Conclusion

Iran's failure to protect children's rights is not simply a legal problem. It also has social, economic, and cultural dimensions. However, this paper deals with only a few aspects of the discrimination imposed on Iranian children through the legal system. Current law must be changed to conform to international standards of human rights, specifically the rights of children. For years, children's rights activists, along with international supporters, have worked to achieve small changes. Increasing the legal age for marriage is one of them. Yet a human rights crisis exists in Iran today. Children and women need legal protections to achieve freedom and equality. Any attempt to improve the legal status of children and women is a step towards fulfilling the goals of humanity and enhancing human rights. It has become the most important struggle of Iranian society at this time in its history.

---

[9] Supra. Note. 5.

Legal Status of the Child in Japan, Especially in Family Law Matters

Yoshiaki Ohmura

1 Rights of the Child and Legal Framework

On April 22, 1994, Japan ratified the Convention on the Rights of the Child.[1] There had been no comprehensive legal framework concerning the rights of the child in Japan previously, and this Convention remains the only such framework even now.

As for the word "child," the Japanese legal system does not have a unified definition, but some acts have their own definitions of "child" or similar terms as follows:

1. Under 18: Child Welfare Act,[2] Article 4, Paragraph 1; Act on the Prevention, etc., of Child Abuse,[3] Article 2; Act on Punishment of Activities Relating to

This report, which has been finalized in October 2013, has first been published in the International Center for Comparative Law and Politics (ICCLP), Graduate School of Law and Politics, the University of Tokyo (ed.), Japanese Reports for the XIXth International Congress of Comparative Law, Vienna 2014, pp. 222–228, © ICCLP Tokyo 2015.

[1] See the website of Ministry of Foreign Affairs (Japanese). http://www.mofa.go.jp/mofaj/gaiko/jido/. The whole text of the Convention (Japanese and English) is here: http://www.mofa.go.jp/mofaj/gaiko/jido/pdfs/je_pamph.pdf

[2] The whole text of the Act (Japanese and English) is here: http://www.japaneselawtranslation.go.jp/law/detail/?ft=1&re=01&dn=1&co=01&x=31&y=12&ky=%E5%85%90%E7%AB%A5%E7%A6%8F%E7%A5%89%E6%B3%95&page=1

[3] The whole text of the Act (Japanese) is here: http://law.e-gov.go.jp/htmldata/H12/H12HO082.html

Y. Ohmura (✉)
Faculty of Law, Chuo-gakuin University, 451, Kujike, Chiba Prefecture 2701196, Japan
e-mail: yotchan2701196@yahoo.co.jp; yohmura@cc.cgu.ac.jp

O. Cvejić Jančić (ed.), *The Rights of the Child in a Changing World*,
Ius Comparatum - Global Studies in Comparative Law 13,
DOI 10.1007/978-3-319-23189-1_11

Child Prostitution and Child Pornography and the Protection of Children,[4] Article 2, Paragraph 1.

2. Until March 31st following the day when he/she reaches 18: Child Allowance Act,[5] Article 3, Paragraph 1; Child Support Allowance Act,[6] Article 3, Paragraph 1 (depending upon the case, it is possible that a person of 18 or 19 should be treated as a child).
3. Under 20: Act on Welfare of Fatherless Family and Widows,[7] Article 3, Paragraph 1.

Other than the above Acts, Civil Code[8] Article 4 provides that a person under 20 should be treated as a minor. Child and minor are different from each other.

2 Best Interest of the Child

The idea of "best interest of the child (BIC)" is implemented in Japanese Legislation, not as a general provision but as detailed provisions mainly in the field of family law. For example, Article 766 of the Civil Code[9] provides that the interest of the child should be considered with utmost priority, and Articles 834, 834-2, and 835[10] thereof provide that parental rights should be deprived or suspended if the parent violates or is about to violate the interest of their child.

3 The Right to Know His/Her Origin

3.1 The Child Born Out of Wedlock

A child born out of wedlock becomes a "child" of his/her mother in a legal sense when he/she is born from his/her mother. There are some provisions (such as Article 779, Article 780, Paragraph 2 of Article 783, Article 785, Article 787, and Paragraph 2

[4]=The whole text of the Act (Japanese and English) is here: http://www.japaneselawtranslation.go.jp/law/detail/?re=01&dn=1&x=45&y=11&co=1&yo=&gn=&sy=&ht=&no=&bu=&ta=&ky=%E8%99%90%E5%BE%85&page=3

[5]The whole text of the Act (Japanese) is here: http://law.e-gov.go.jp/htmldata/S46/S46HO073.html

[6]The whole text of the Act (Japanese) is here: http://law.e-gov.go.jp/htmldata/S36/S36HO238.html

[7]The whole text of the Act (Japanese) is here: http://law.e-gov.go.jp/htmldata/S39/S39HO129.html

[8]The whole text of the Act (Japanese and English) is here: http://www.japaneselawtranslation.go.jp/law/detail/?re=01&dn=1&x=37&y=17&co=1&yo=%E6%B0%91%E6%B3%95&gn=&sy=&ht=&no=&bu=&ta=&ky=&page=2 and http://www.japaneselawtranslation.go.jp/law/detail/?re=01&dn=1&x=37&y=17&co=1&yo=%E6%B0%91%E6%B3%95&gn=&sy=&ht=&no=&bu=&ta=&ky=&page=3

[9]See note 8 for the text (Japanese and English).

[10]See note 8 for the text (Japanese and English).

of Article 789.[11]) which provide that the mother must formally acknowledge her child born out of wedlock in order to be considered his/her mother, but such provisions have been totally ignored since the judgment of the Supreme Court of April 27, 1962.[12]

On the other hand, as for the father in a legal sense, the situation is quite different. A child born out of wedlock becomes a "child" of his/her father in a legal sense only when the father voluntarily acknowledges his child (Article 779 of Civil Code[13]) or when the child wins in a lawsuit requiring acknowledgment by the father (Article 787 of Civil Code[14]).

In Japan, family relationships are registered in the Family Registration (Koseki) system.[15] In most cases when a child born out of wedlock, the child and his/her mother are shown in the same book of registration, but the father (even if he acknowledges the child) is in another book. In any case, the child is able to request certification of his/her parents' registration (Article 10 of Family Registration Act[16]).

3.2 *The Child Born in Wedlock*

As for the mother, the situation is quite the same as a child born out of wedlock. Those who bear the child is acknowledged to be his/her mother in a legal sense.

On the other hand, as for the father, there are two legal presumptions provided in Article 772 of the Civil Code,[17] namely, that the child born 200 days after the marriage of his/her parents and within 300 days from the day of divorce or annulment or voiding of the marriage. It is possible for the husband to reverse these presumptions by lawsuit towards the child or his/her mother within 1 year from the date when he knew that the child was born, but there is no way to do it for the child or his/her mother.

In the case when a child was born between the marriage of the parents and 200 days after that, there must be no legal presumption that the husband is the father of the child, but it is the practice of Ministry of Justice that in such a case the husband should be treated as the child's father.[18]

---

[11] See note 8 for the text (Japanese and English).

[12] The whole text (Japanese) is here: http://www.courts.go.jp/hanrei/pdf/js_20100319124430129252.pdf

[13] See note 8 for the text (Japanese and English).

[14] See note 8 for the text (Japanese and English).

[15] The whole text of Family Registration Act (Japanese) is here: http://law.e-gov.go.jp/htmldata/S22/S22HO224.html

[16] See note 15 for the text (Japanese).

[17] See note 8 for the text (Japanese and English).

[18] See the following site (Japanese): http://www.sakurai-h.jp/article/10764111.html

3.3 *The Adopted Child*

There are two types of adoption in Japan: ordinal adoption (provided in Articles 792–817 of the Civil Code[19]) and special adoption (provided in Articles 817-2 to 817-11 of the Civil Code[20]). There are differences between these two types of adoption concerning requirements and legal effect thereof, but for both types, the relationship between the adopted child and their biological parents is kept in the Family Registration, and the child may request certification of the registration.

3.4 *The Child Born with Biomedical Assistance*

In Japan, legislation in order to admit biomedical assistance does not exist, and the right of the child to know about his/her biological parents is not secured. A working group under the Ministry of Health, Labor, and Welfare once reported in April 2003 that the child, after they become 15, should have the right to request the information about his/her biological parents, including information that identifies who is his/her parent.[21] However, it has not yet been realized.

4 The Right to Express Views in Family Law Matters

There is no comprehensive provision concerning the right of the child to express his/her views in family law matters. However, in some areas relating to administrative proceedings, there are provisions in which the child may apply for something by himself/herself without involving the parents, i.e., marriage (Article 739[22] of the Civil Code, at 16 or older in case of females and 18 or older in case of males), application of change of surname (Article 791, Paragraph 1[23] of the Civil Code, 15 or older),[24]adoption (Article 797, Paragraph 1[25] of the Civil Code, 15 or older), and admit of dissolution of adoption by consent (Article 811, Paragraph 1[26] of the Civil Code, 15 or older).

---

[19] See note 8 for the text (Japanese and English).

[20] See note 8 for the text (Japanese and English).

[21] See the following site for the report (Japanese): http://www.mhlw.go.jp/shingi/2003/04/s0428-5.html

[22] See note 8 for the text (Japanese and English).

[23] See note 8 for the text (Japanese and English).

[24] No one can change his/her first name without application to and permission from family court based upon justifiable reason. Art. 107-2 of Family Registration Act.

[25] See note 8 for the text (Japanese and English).

[26] See note 8 for the text (Japanese and English).

On the other hand, as for judicial or administrative proceedings, no comprehensive provision clearly states that the child has the right to express his/her views, but according to Article 252 of Family Proceedings Act,[27] or Article 791, 797 etc. of the Civil Code, a child can act without involving his/her parent, etc. in certain kinds of proceedings.

5 Conditions for Intercountry Adoption

According to Article 31 of the Act on General Rules for Application of Laws[28] (the basic act of Japanese conflict of laws), intercountry adoption is governed by the national law of the parties who are willing to be adoptive parents. However, if the national law of the child requires certain conditions (consent of the biological parent(s) or child himself/herself, etc.) concerning adoption, such requirements must also be fulfilled.

6 Freedom of Thought, Conscience, and Religion

Article 20, Paragraph 3 of the Japanese Constitution[29] prohibits the nation or national organs from any religious activity, including religious education. Therefore, it is impossible in any of the national or public schools to carry out religious education. However, the purpose of Article 20, Paragraph 3 of the Constitution is to prevent a certain religious entity from having special privileges, so there is no conflict in the teaching of religion as part of the history or philosophy of the world.

On the other hand, there are many private schools and universities founded by religious entities. Private entities have freedom of religious activity, in this case also including religious education. Therefore, in such schools or universities, there are classes to teach religious matters such as the Bible, etc.[30]

---

[27] The whole text of Family Proceedings Act (Japanese) is here: http://law.e-gov.go.jp/htmldata/H23/H23HO052.html

[28] The whole text of Act on General Rules for Application of Laws (Japanese and English) is here: http://www.japaneselawtranslation.go.jp/law/detail/?re=01&dn=1&x=32&y=17&co=1&yo=%E9%80%9A%E5%89%87%E6%B3%95&gn=&sy=&ht=&no=&bu=&ta=&ky=&page=2

[29] The whole text of Constitution (Japanese and English) is here: http://www.japaneselawtranslation.go.jp/law/detail/?ft=2&re=01&dn=1&yo=%E6%97%A5%E6%9C%AC%E5%9B%BD%E6%86%B2%E6%B3%95&x=59&y=13&ky=&page=1

[30] For example, http://www.sophia.ac.jp/eng/program/undergraduate_c/UG_Theo (Sophia Univ., English), http://www.komazawa-u.ac.jp/cms/undergraduate-e (Komazawa Univ., English) and http://www.kokugakuin.ac.jp/english/shintostudies.html (Kokugakuin Univ., English).

7 Physical Punishment

Article 822 and Article 857 of the Civil Code[31] provide that parents and guardians have authority to reprimand their child and ward, and reprimand is understood to include physical punishment. However, there have been many cases in which parents abused their children under the name of reprimand, creating a severe problem and prompting the enactment of the Act on the Prevention of Child Abuse.[32] Article 14 of the Act provides that the parents must use their authority responsibly, and when they abuse their children, they must not make excuse that such abuse was no more than a reprimand.

As for schools, the provisory clause of Article 11 of the School Education Act[33] clearly prohibits physical punishment under any conditions.

As for child welfare institutions, Article 47, Paragraph 1 of the Child Welfare Act[34] provides that such institutions have the same right as parents concerning the child who has no parent or guardian. Furthermore, Article 47, Paragraph 3[35] provides that such institutions or foster parents have similar rights as the parent concerning reprimand, even if the child has parents or guardians.

8 Deprivation of Parental Responsibilities

The Civil Code has three measures to control parental responsibilities in order to protect the child's interest.

Article 834 of the Civil Code[36] provides that if a parent abuses the child and maliciously abandons the child or it seems impossible or inadequate for the parent to continue his/her responsibility, which may badly harm the child's interest, then the family court may deprive the parents of their parental responsibilities. It is the most severe situation concerning malpractice of parental responsibilities.

Article 834-2[37] provides that if it seems impossible or inadequate for the parent to continue his/her responsibility, which may harm the child's interest, then the family court may suspend the parental responsibilities for a certain period.

Article 835[38] provides that if it seems impossible or inadequate for the parent to continue his/her management of the child's assets, which may harm the child's

[31] See note 8 for the text (Japanese and English).

[32] See note 3 for the text (Japanese).

[33] The whole text of School Education Act (Japanese) is here: http://law.e-gov.go.jp/htmldata/S22/S22HO026.html

[34] See note 2 for the text (Japanese and English).

[35] See note 2 for the text (Japanese and English).

[36] See note 8 for the text (Japanese and English).

[37] See note 8 for the text (Japanese and English).

[38] See note 8 for the text (Japanese and English).

interest, then the family court may deprive the parental right of management (the right of management is understood to be a part of the parental responsibilities, and those parents who are deprived of the management still retain the rest of the parental responsibilities).

If a parent has the whole of his/her parental responsibilities deprived or suspended, the child shall be put under the care of a guardian,[39] just as if the parent had died, but if the parent recovers his/her responsibilities, guardianship ends.

9 Medical Consent

It is said that a child may give or refuse to give medical consent independently, but concerning the age necessary to do so, there is no legal provision and no consensus of opinions among scholars.[40]

10 Employment of Child

Article 56, Paragraph 1 of Labor Standards Act[41] provides that no one may employ a child until the first March 31st after he/she becomes 15 (with exceptions). After that, a child can be employed by contract between the employer and the child himself/herself, provided that the parents of the child give consent to such contract (Article 5, Paragraph 1 of the Civil Code).

Concerning the working hours and conditions of employment of children, Articles 60–63 of the Labor Standards Act[42] provide as follows (just outline):

1. Working hours per week: 40 h, including school hours
2. Working hours per day: 7 h, including school hours
3. Prohibition to use children from 10 pm to 5 am
4. Prohibition to use in dangerous and harmful work
5. Prohibition to use in mine pits

---

[39] Art. 838 Item 1 of the Civil Code.

[40] Concerning this issue, see the following article (Japanese): http://mitizane.ll.chiba-u.jp/metadb/up/irwg10/Jin-H197-06.pdf#search='%E5%8C%BB%E7%99%82%E8%A1%8C%E7%82%BA+%E6%9C%AA%E6%88%90%E5%B9%B4%E8%80%85+%E5%90%8C%E6%84%8F'

[41] The whole text (Japanese and English) is here: http://www.japaneselawtranslation.go.jp/law/detail/?re=01&dn=1&x=46&y=8&co=1&yo=%E5%8A%B4%E5%83%8D%E5%9F%BA%E6%BA%96%E6%B3%95&gn=&sy=&ht=&no=&bu=&ta=&ky=&page=1

[42] See note 41 for the text (Japanese and English).

11 Obligation Towards Parents

The Civil Code[43] provides two kinds of obligations of the child towards his/her parents, as follows. The first is the obligation to recognize the parental rights (Articles 820–824), although there are arguments that it is not the obligation of the child to obey parents but the right of the child to require adequate care from the parents. The second is the obligation to support the parents (Article 877), though such support is mutually required.

12 Discrimination Towards the Child Born Out of Wedlock

There have been various types of discrimination in Japanese society based upon race, sex, sexual orientation, birth, occupation, etc. Among them, one of the most severe and long-lasting discriminations is that against the child born out of wedlock.

Article 900, Item 4[44] of the Civil Code provides that the child born out of wedlock is entitled to only half of the inheritance of the child born in wedlock. That means if a man (A) has two children, one (B) of whom was born from his wife (C) and the other (D) was born from his non-marital partner (E), B will get twice the assets from A in comparison with D, even if D took care of A and B did nothing. It is possible that there was an extramarital affair between A and E, but it is also possible that C and E is in fact the same person.

Even if there are extramarital affairs, it is not justifiable to discriminate against the child for that reason. Moreover, it is not always reasonable to discriminate between two children born from the same parents. Article 2, Paragraph 1 of the Convention on the Rights of the Child is based on the same thinking.

In this matter, the Committee on the Rights of the Child[45] and other related committees of the United Nations recommended to the Japanese Government to revise the law and abolish such discrimination, but the Japanese Government has neglected to do so.[46]

The Grand Bench of the Supreme Court of Japan declared on July 5, 1995 that the above provision (Article 900 of the Civil Code) does not violate the Constitution,[47] but on September 4, 2013, the same Bench reversed the above judgment unanimously and said for the first time that the first half of the provisory clause, Item4,

---

[43] See note 8 for the text (Japanese and English).

[44] See note 8 for the text (Japanese and English).

[45] See: http://www2.ohchr.org/english/bodies/crc/

[46] See Kodomo no kenri jouyaku NGO report renraku kaigi (ed), Kodomo no kenri jouyaku kara mita nihon no kodomo (Gendai jinbunsha, 2011, Japanese).

[47] The whole text (Japanese) is here: http://www.courts.go.jp/hanrei/pdf/js_20100319122945490648.pdf

Article 900 of the Civil Code, violates Article 14 of the Constitution (equality under the law clause).[48] Soon after the above judgment, the Japanese Government began preparations for amendment of Article 900 of the Civil Code in order to abolish discrimination in succession against the child born out of wedlock.[49] At this time (October 15, 2013), it is expected that Article 900 will be amended within a year.

13 Summary

Concerning the rights of the child, there was no comprehensive legal framework in Japan until the National Diet ratified the Convention on the Rights of the Child. Within our domestic legal system, there is an obligation for adults to protect the child. However, in the field of family law, children of 15 years or older are treated like an adult in certain cases. As for fertility assistance, there is not yet sufficient legal basis to manage the parent-child relationships. Concerning the parent-child relationship, we have been using the concept "parental authority" in the Civil Code, but recently the idea of "parental responsibility" is being accepted and the interest of the child is deemed most important. The child born out of wedlock has been discriminated against in the matter of succession, but in September 2013, the Supreme Court made a decision that such discrimination violates the Constitution (equality under the law). The Japanese Government is preparing for amendment of the Civil Code to abolish such discrimination.

[48] The whole text (Japanese) is here: http://www.courts.go.jp/hanrei/pdf/20130904154932.pdf. Furthermore, according to the press, there is one more case in which the Supreme Court decided that the discrimination against the child born out of wedlock violates the Constitution. See http://mainichi.jp/select/news/20130921k0000m040040000c.html (in Japanese).

[49] See http://www.nikkei.com/article/DGXNASDG04041_U3A900C1MM8000/ (Nihon Keizai Shimbun), http://sankei.jp.msn.com/affairs/news/130904/trl13090419130004-n1.htm (Sankei News).

Legal Framework for the Rights of the Child in Portugal

Manuela Baptista Lopes

1 Introduction

The UN Convention on the Rights of the Child (CRC)[1] was signed by Portugal on 26 January 1990 and approved for ratification by Resolution of the Assembly of the Republic No. 20/90 of 12 September 1990, as published in Series I-A of *Diário da República* (the Official Gazette) No. 211/90. The Convention entered into force in the Portuguese legal system on 21 October 1990, less than 9 months after its signature.

2 The Definition of a Child in the Portuguese Legal System

Under the Portuguese legal system, the age limit below which a human being is deemed a child or young person or simply a minor – that is to say, a person who has yet to reach adulthood from a legal perspective – stems from the stipulation in various legislative acts of the age group that is considered to be encompassed by this concept in the specific cases to which those acts apply.

This report follows the *International Academy of Comparative Law*questionnaire designed to solicit a description of the current juridical and normative situation regarding the specific aspects of the rights of children addressed by the questionnaire. It is intended for the *International Congress of Comparative Law*, which will be held in Vienna, Austria, in 2014. As such, the choice of subjects addressed herein focuses specifically on the questions raised in the questionnaire.

[1] Adopted by UN General Assembly resolution 44/25 of 20 November 1989.

M. Baptista Lopes (✉)
Tribunal Constitucional, Lisboa 1249-117, Portugal
e-mail: mbaptistalopes@tribconstitucional.pt

O. Cvejić Jančić (ed.), *The Rights of the Child in a Changing World*,
Ius Comparatum - Global Studies in Comparative Law 13,
DOI 10.1007/978-3-319-23189-1_12

On the subject of the legal capacity of natural persons, the Civil Code stipulates that 'Whoever has not yet turned 18 years of age is a minor'[2]; the Criminal Code says that 'Minors under the age of 16 may not be held' criminally 'liable for the consequences of their acts'[3]; the Law governing the Protection of Children and Young Persons at Risk (Law No. 147/99 of 1 September 1999, hereinafter the LPCJP), which aims to 'foster the rights and the protection of children and young persons at risk, in such a way as to ensure their well-being and full development' (Article 1), establishes that for its purposes, a child or young person is 'a person below the age of 18 years, or a person below the age of 21 years who requests the continuation of an intervention that began before he or she attained 18 years of age' (Article 5[a]); the Law governing Youth Custody, Protection and Re-education (Law No. 166/99 of 14 September 1999, hereinafter the LTC), which is designed to govern state intervention vis-à-vis minors who commit facts which the law defines as criminal offences, particularly in the shape of the possible imposition of a custodial, protective and/or re-educational measure, sets the age of 12 years as the minimum limit for its application – an age below which the only permitted type of intervention is a protective one – and that of 16 years as a maximum, after which one can be held criminally liable.

Given that under the Constitution of the Portuguese Republic (CRP), the CDC itself constitutes internal law,[4] we should also note that its Article 1 defines children as 'every human being below the age of 18 years'.

We may therefore conclude that Portuguese law basically sets two maximum age limits below which a human being may be deemed a child: a civil law limit of 18 years of age and a penal – or more precisely, a para-penal[5] – limit of 16 years.

[2] Article 122, Civil Code.

[3] Article 19, Criminal Code.

[4] 'The norms contained in duly ratified or approved international conventions come into force in Portuguese internal law once they have been officially published, and remain so for as long as they are internationally binding on the Portuguese state' (Article 8[2], CRP).

[5] A para-penal limit is considered to be one that gives rise to an intervention whose goals are not only the protection of the minor but also both his or her education in relation to the need to uphold and abide by the law and his or her reinsertion into community life (resocialisation). When assessing the need for an LTC measure and selecting the right one, due weight must be given to causes that would rule out or mitigate unlawfulness and guilt (Article 2[1], LTC). So while it is clear that from both a theoretical (the legal text and related doctrinal positions) and a practical (the work of law enforcement services) point of view, the LTC does not configure a typically penal intervention, in the light of the same parameters it also unequivocally possesses a para-penal nature derived, apart from anything else, from the fact that the LTC's scope only encompasses cases where minors between the ages of 12 and 16 commit acts which the law qualifies as criminal offences.

3 The Legal Status of the Child

As we can see from the above, in Portugal there is no legal instrument devoted specifically to the rights of the child, in the form of a children's statute, for example. Instead, on the one hand legal texts with a general scope (namely the Constitution, the Civil Code, the Criminal Code, the Labour Code) contain provisions that refer expressly to children; on the other there are texts designed to address matters regarding the rights of children in specific situations (inter alia, the Law governing the Protection of Children and Young Persons at Risk; the Law governing Youth Custody, Protection and Re-education; and the Statute governing Students and School Ethics).[6]

Inasmuch as natural persons acquire their legal capacity when they are born, from the moment of his or her 'complete, live' birth,[7] a child is a subject of rights that he or she possesses the full capacity to enjoy. As such, all the legal texts which govern human and fundamental rights[8] are also intended for children, unless their contents objectively make them inapplicable (e.g. the right to vote).

Given that, as we have already said, norms contained in international conventions form part of national law (the Constitution says that conventional laws are automatically part of Portuguese law, providing that they have been ratified), it is necessary to incorporate them into the corresponding corpus whenever they contain provisions on the subject of children.

A number of constitutional norms – i.e. instructions whose constitutional status means they prevail over ordinary legislation – specifically relate to children. The following especially deserve to be mentioned:

- Norms on family and filiation, especially the establishment of rights and obligations pertaining to fathers' and mothers' rights and duties with regard to the maintenance and upbringing of their children and to parental equality on matters concerning the exercise of rights and the fulfilment of obligations; equal rights for children born in and out of wedlock; the prohibition on separating children from their parents, except when the latter fail to fulfil their fundamental obligations, and even then only by means of a court order; and norms regarding the regulation and protection of adoption (Article 36, CRP)
- Norms on the fundamental social right to healthcare, which specifically refer to the creation of economic, social, cultural and environmental conditions that particularly guarantee the protection of childhood and youth (Article 64, CRP)
- Norms on the protection of maternity and paternity, as eminent social values, which in particular provide for rights during pregnancy and following childbirth from the perspective of the children's interests (Article 68, CRP)

[6] Approved by Law No. 51/2012 of 5 September 2012.

[7] The effective enjoyment of the rights recognised by law to unborn children depends on their birth (Article 66, Civil Code).

[8] Fundamental rights are defined as the human rights expressly enshrined in the Constitution of the Portuguese Republic (CRP).

- An article (69, CRP) that is specifically designated 'Childhood' and establishes the general right of children to protection by society and the state, with express derived secondary rights (enhanced rights for children who are orphaned, abandoned or deprived of a normal family environment and the prohibition of labour by school-age minors)
- An article (70, CRP) specifically entitled 'Youth', which enshrines the right of young persons to a special protection of the effective enjoyment of their economic, social and cultural rights and expressly mentions education, vocational training, culture, work, social security, housing, physical education, sport and leisure time

When it comes to infra-constitutional norms, in practically every area of the law, we can find provisions which, in pursuit of the various constitutional imperatives, concern themselves with the particular vulnerability of young people and the desire to protect them.

4 The Superior Interest of the Child

The concept of the superior or best interest of the child – a truly core concept of the CRC that must be a primary consideration whenever any decision on the subject of children is taken by legislative bodies, courts, administrative authorities and public or private social protection institutions – is widely embodied in Portuguese legislation. However, given that it is an indeterminate or thus far undefined legal concept, at present it is only possible to effectively implement it by means of a case-by-case interpretation or application to a concrete situation.

In Portuguese law, the LPCJP uses the expression 'superior interest' in its definition of the first guiding principle for interventions in relation to children and young persons at risk. Such interventions 'must give priority to the interests of the child or young person', albeit 'without prejudice to due consideration to other legitimate interests within the ambit of the plurality of interests present in the concrete case in question' (Article 4[a]). Also, the Law governing the Organisation of the Custody, Protection and Re-education of Minors (Executive Law No. 314/78 of 27 October 1978, hereinafter the OTM) says that the guiding principles for interventions laid down in the LPCJP are applicable to civil proceedings in the same field. The consideration that must be given to the interests of the child is one of them.

It is clear that the consideration attached to this superior interest applies to interventions in relation to all children, whether or not they are currently at risk and/or the object of civil OTM proceedings. However, even without the explicit designation 'superior' or 'best', the interests of the child appear in all the normative instruments affecting children. This focus derives implicitly from the constitutional precepts described above and explicitly from the Civil Code when it refers to the content of parental responsibilities ('Parents shall, in the interest of their children, be responsible for ensuring the latter's safety and health, providing for their upkeep, directing their education, representing them, even if they are still unborn, and administering their property', Article 1878[1], Civil Code), the LPCJP (particularly, as previously mentioned, the first principle guiding interventions) and the LTE (e.g. on the criterion for deciding which educational measure to choose, Article 6[3] says that this choice must be 'targeted at the interest of the minor'), but this interest is also referred to in more than ten other norms and can also be found in other normative instruments that refer to children. Examples of the latter among many others include the Advertising Code,[9] which says that 'Advertising especially targeted at minors must at all times take their psychological vulnerability into account' (Article 14[1]), and the legislative act on foster care,[10] which requires foster families to 'Pay priority attention to the interests and rights of the child or young person' (Article 21[1][a]).

5 Rights of Children Born In and Out of Wedlock

The Constitution of the Portuguese Republic lays down that 'Children born outside wedlock may not be the object of any discrimination for that reason…'.[11]

One of the many consequences of this principle pertains to the civil law regarding the determination of maternity and of paternity.

Maternity should be declared when the child's birth is registered. If for some reason it is not, the civil registry clerk must send the courts a certified copy of the record, whereupon the Public Prosecutors' Office (MP) is required to attempt to identify the mother and ask her to confirm the child is hers. If the mother does not provide this confirmation, but the evidence that the child is in fact hers is deemed reliable, the MP must then formally investigate the situation.[12]

If maternity is established pursuant to the law, but does not correspond to biological maternity, it may at any time be challenged before a court by any one of a number of persons who possess the legitimacy to do so, including the child himself or herself.[13]

Maternity can also be recognised by means of an action which the child can bring especially for the purpose. Such actions may be lodged while the child who wishes to investigate his or her maternity is a minor or within a legally defined time limit that begins when he or she attains majority or emancipation.[14]

---

[9] Executive Law No. 330/90 of 23 October 1990, with subsequent amendments.

[10] Executive Law No. 11/2008 of 17 January 2008.

[11] Article 36(4).

[12] Articles 1803 and 1808, Civil Code.

[13] The other persons/entities with the legitimacy to challenge maternity are the mother herself, any other person with a moral or material interest in the admissibility of the action to determine maternity and the Public Prosecutors' Office.

[14] Each time it has been called on to pronounce itself on the constitutionality of imposing time limits on actions to investigate maternity or paternity, the Constitutional Court has consistently

As regards paternity, the law establishes a *praesumptio iuris tantum* – a rebuttable presumption – that when the mother is married at the time of the child's birth or conception, the husband is the child's father.[15] However, in such cases, when the mother declares the child's birth, she can say that her husband is not the child's father, whereupon the presumption of his paternity ceases.[16]

The presumption of paternity can also be challenged by the mother's husband, the mother at a later date or the child. In addition, the Public Prosecutors' Office can also make such a challenge at the request of any person who declares himself to be the child's father, if the court first recognises the viability of the request for a declaration of paternity.[17]

Paternity with regard to a child born or conceived out of wedlock can be recognised: by means of an action to acknowledge filiation, which is a personal and voluntary act by which a father recognises that someone is his child, or by means of a court decision in a paternity investigation action.

It should be noted that that the capacity to bring an action to acknowledge paternal filiation pertains to anyone who possesses full capacity to enjoy his legal rights and is over the age of 16 and that minors do not need authorisation from their parents or other legal representatives in order to acknowledge a child as theirs in this way.[18]

Underage mothers representing their child possess the legitimacy to bring an action to investigate the latter's paternity without their own parents' authorisation, but must always be represented in the suit by a special guardian appointed by the court, inasmuch as minors lack procedural legitimacy in general.

Portuguese law also includes a system whereby the Public Prosecutors' Office is required to bring an ex officio action to establish paternity.[19] When a birth is registered with no mention of the father, the registry clerk must send a court a certified copy of the record, which in turn leads to the beginning of this procedure.

The competence to hear ex officio actions to determine both paternity and maternity forms part of the general competence regarding civil OTM proceedings that pertains to the family and juvenile courts.[20]

---

held that such limits must be long enough for the child to be able to exercise his or her rights to personal identity and to the development of his or her personality within the context of the right to know his or her biological roots.

[15] Article 1826, Civil Code.

[16] Article 1832, Civil Code.

[17] Article 1839, Civil Code.

[18] Persons who are legally disqualified due to a psychological anomaly or mental disorder, and those who are clearly of unsound mind when the acknowledgement action is brought, do not possess this capacity.

[19] Articles 1864 et seq., Civil Code.

[20] Cf Article 146(j), OTM.

6 Adoption

The Constitution of the Portuguese Republic is very sparing in its references to adoption. In fact, it is only mentioned in an article entitled 'Family, marriage and filiation', in a paragraph that reads: 'Adoption shall be regulated and protected in accordance with the law, which must lay down swift forms for completion of the respective procedural requirements'.[21] As such, apart from dictating that adoption exist, be protected and be procedurally quick, the Constitution leaves the ordinary legislator a lot of room in which to shape the details of the applicable rules.

When it comes to informing fully adopted children[22] of their biological identity, the Civil Code says that the identity of the prospective adoptive parent cannot be revealed to the adopted child's biological parents, unless the adoptive parent explicitly states that he or she does not object to disclosure. Biological parents, on the other hand, must explicitly object if they do not want their identity to be made known to prospective adoptive parents.[23] The law says nothing about the secrecy of adoption proceedings in relation to the adopted child him or herself.

Pursuant to the Civil Code provisions on the secrecy of the identity of an adopted child's adoptive and biological parents, on the legitimacy to ask for copies of the birth records or certificates of adopted children (a legitimacy that is in principle universal, given that any person is entitled to ask for copies of public records), the Civil Registry Code[24] says that full or photocopies of the records of such persons can only be issued at the request of the persons in question, their descendants or heirs or their forebears, but always without prejudice to the secrecy of the identity of the adopted child's adoptive or biological parents, as provided for in the Civil Code.

Portuguese procedural law also says that both the adoption process and the respective preliminary procedures, including those of an administrative nature, are secret.[25] Breach of this secrecy constitutes a specific legal type of crime, which the applicable norm subjects to imprisonment for up to 1 year or a fine of up to 120 daily units.[26]

---

[21] This is the last paragraph of Article 36 and was not included in the initial text of the CRP (1976), but was added in the first constitutional revision (1982).

[22] This question only arises in cases of full adoption, since it is only then that the adopted child acquires the status of son/daughter of the adoptive parent and the ties between the child and his or her family of origin are dissolved (impediments to marriage do continue to exist). In restricted adoptions, on the other hand, the adopted child retains all the rights and obligations with regard to his or her biological family (cf, respectively, Articles 1986 and 1994, Civil Code).

[23] Article 1985, Civil Code. This means that the secrecy of the identity of adoptive parents is more heavily protected than that of the identity of the child's natural parents.

[24] Executive Law No. 131/95 of 6 June 1995, with subsequent amendments.

[25] Article 173(b), OTM. Cf also Article 164(5).

[26] Article 173-B(3), OTM.

Determining the extent to which the norms laid down in the Civil Code, the OTM and the Civil Registry Code[27] are consistent with the constitutional norm which establishes that the fundamental right to personal identity[28] requires a reconciliation of fundamental rights that may collide or conflict with one another. As is common knowledge, fundamental rights are not absolute but rather relative and subject to the imposition of limits and must give way as far as is necessary in order to safeguard other constitutionally protected rights or interests.[29] The possible unconstitutionality of these norms could only be determined by applying the principle of proportionality in its various facets, but to date the Constitutional Court has not been called on to pronounce itself on this subject.

As we have already said, when it comes to the collision between the right to personal identity on the one hand and the confidentiality and stability of filiation on the other, infra-constitutional law clearly chooses to sacrifice the former. With the exception of the procedures to be observed before marriage, once a court has decreed full adoption, the law does not allow the biological filiation of adopted children to be determined or even for proof of it to be offered.[30]

7 Medically Assisted Procreation

The sole reference to medically assisted procreation (MAP) in the Portuguese Constitution comes in Article 67, under the heading 'Family', which requires the state to regulate assisted procreation in such a way as to safeguard the dignity of the human person. The ordinary legislator is thus given considerable latitude in its ability to shape the details of the applicable regime.

Portuguese law imposes a general duty of confidentiality in relation to the techniques used in medically assisted procreation techniques.[31] Although the exact details of this duty can naturally vary depending on the different stakeholders in each specific case, everyone who is or has been involved in a MAP procedure in any way is under a duty of confidentiality which encompasses the medical act itself, the techniques used and the identity of every participant.

This duty of confidentiality continues to include the nondisclosure of the donor's identity, even to the person born as a result of an assisted procedure. Such persons can,

[27] This list is not exhaustive. For instance, the LPCJP also says that in cases involving implementation of an OTM measure designed to support an autonomous life, the secrecy of the identity of both adoptive and biological parents must be respected in accordance with the provisions of the Civil Code and the OTM.

[28] Article 26(1), CRP.

[29] Article 18(2), CRP.

[30] Article 1987, Civil Code.

[31] Article 15, Law No. 32/2006 of 26 July 2006 (Medically Assisted Procreation Law).

however, obtain relevant genetic information from the competent health service, and they can also obtain information on the existence of any legal obstacle to a proposed marriage from the National Council for Medically Assisted Procreation (CNPMA). In such cases the donor's identity continues to be confidential unless the donor waives that right.

Information on the donor's identity can also be disclosed for important reasons recognised by a court. The legislator has left open the question of whether or not invoking the right to personal identity, within the broader context of the right to know one's origins, is sufficient reason for disclosure, but the norms described above suggest it is not.

This rule of donor anonymity must be seen in connection with Article 10 of the Medically Assisted Procreation Law on the donation of sperm, oocytes and embryos, which determines the cases in which one may resort to such a donation and whose paragraph 2 says that donors cannot be deemed parents of children born by means of a MAP procedure. Given the duty of confidentiality to which both everyone who takes part in these procedures and anyone who in any way learns about the recourse to these techniques or the medically assisted procreation itself is subject, the birth certificate must never mention the fact that the birth followed a MAP procedure.[32]

The Constitutional Court's case law unequivocally considers the right to know the identity of one's biological parents to be part of the protection afforded to the fundamental rights to personal identity and to form a family. However, in the cases in which the court has been called on to pronounce itself on this issue, the question was posed and decided within the context of the establishment of biological paternal/maternal ties and not with reference to medically assisted procreation. If the latter were to come before the court in this respect, it is possible that the conflict between fundamental rights and the ensuing weighing up of the rights at stake might be seen as different.

It is worth noting that the donor anonymity rule was one of the Medically Assisted Procreation Law norms whose material unconstitutionality was raised as part of an abstract ex post facto review of this law requested by a group of Members of the Assembly of the Republic (Parliament). In Ruling No. 101/2009 of 3 March 2009,[33] the court decided not to declare this norm (or indeed any of those before it) unconstitutional.

[32] Article 15(5) of the Medically Assisted Procreation Law expressly provides that 'Under no circumstances shall the birth certificate indicate that the child was born as a result of the use of MAP techniques'.

[33] Published in Series II of *Diário da República* (the Official Gazette) No. 64 of 1 April 2009 and also available at http://www.tribunalconstitucional.pt/tc/acordaos/20090101.html. The Constitutional Court website includes both a summary (http://www.tribunalconstitucional.pt/tc/en/acordaos/20090101s.html) and the full text (http://www.tribunalconstitucional.pt/tc/en/acordaos/20090101.html) of this ruling in English translation.

8 Right of the Child to Be Heard and to Participate in Matters Affecting Him or Her

We have already mentioned the concern about the superior interest of the child in the Civil Code norms on the content of parental responsibilities.[34] The Code also says that children must obey their parents. However, depending on the child's degree of maturity, parents must give weight to the child's opinion about important family issues and recognise his or her autonomy with regard to the organisation of his or her own life.[35,36]

The concepts of degree of maturity, family issues and degree of autonomy when it comes to organising one's own life are indeterminate concepts whose implementation in practice lies with the parents, although they must do so while listening to their children's opinion in accordance with the degree of maturity the parents believe the latter have attained and with the children's own assessment of how important it is for them to be heard on the particular issue at stake. There is thus a certain discretionary margin that gives parents significant latitude to interpret their obligation to listen to their children.

The truth is that the law could have opted for objective (e.g. age) or subjective (e.g. maturity) criteria for establishing the point at which a child's view must begin to be taken into account. Portuguese law has instead favoured the eminently subjective criterion of maturity for fixing this threshold. It therefore falls to the parents and the judge to concretely define this criterion on a case-by-case basis. However, there are situations in which the law does resort to the objective criterion of age. Examples include the 'institute' of adoption, where the adoptee's consent is compulsory whenever he or she is over the age of 12 years, and the adoptive parents' biological children (and/or children who have been adopted prior to the adoption in question) over the age of 12 must be consulted[37,38]; the 'institute' of guardianship, where before appointing a guardian the court must hear the minor if he or she has already

[34] Article 1878 of the Civil Code determines that this extent corresponds to obligations imposed by parentage and that, in the interest of their children, the law obliges parents to ensure the latter's safety and health, to provide for them, to oversee their education, to represent them, even if they are still unborn, and to administer their property.

[35] Article 1878(2), Civil Code.

[36] Here we are only talking about the right to be heard and to play an active role within the family, given that this is the only aspect addressed in the questionnaire that serves as a guideline for this report.

[37] Article 1981(1)(a) and Article 1984(a), Civil Code.

[38] In the case of the biological or previously adopted children of the prospective adoptive parents, this is not consent but merely consultation. However, the court may only disregard a negative opinion on the part of the existing children if there are strong reasons for considering their opposition unjustified.

turned 14[39]; and decisions regarding children's religious education, which only pertain to parents until the young person reaches the age of 16.[40]

Both the capacity to legally recognise a child as one's own and the capacity to manage and dispose of assets that a minor has acquired by working are attained at the age of 16.[41]

The capacity to contract marriage is also acquired at the age of 16,[42] from which point the lack of parental authorisation cannot completely prevent such marriages, but only oppose them in a move that can be overturned by the Civil Registrar.[43]

In all these cases maturity is thus defined by the objective criterion of age.

While the age thresholds of 12, 14 and 16 years are thus important in Portuguese law, one can nevertheless say that broadly speaking the law presumes minors to possess a certain maturity from the age of 7 years, which then progressively increases depending on the particular aspects of life at stake.[44]

Parents may of course disagree with each other as to their children's degree of maturity, how important a certain family issue is and what the children's participation in the organisation of their own lives should be. In such cases, if the parents cannot settle their differences of opinion, and assuming they exercise parental responsibilities jointly,[45] either of them can turn to the courts, which must try to get them to agree. If conciliation continues to be impossible, before giving its decision and unless important circumstances make it unadvisable to do so, the court must hear the child, who is thus given the opportunity to express his or her opinion about the matters in question.

At case law level, the right of children to be heard in cases affecting them is becoming increasingly widely recognised.[46] Whenever it is not actually provided for in the law, this practice is frequently founded on precisely Article 1901 of the Civil Code, as described above. Though its scope is limited to issues of particular importance, this article does offer potential for extended application by analogy.

---

[39] Article 1931(2), Civil Code.

[40] Article 1886, Civil Code.

[41] Articles 1850, 1888(1)(d), Civil Code.

[42] Article 1601(a), Civil Code.

[43] Article 1604(a), Civil Code.

[44] This can be inferred from Article 488 of the Civil Code, with regard to civil liability for unlawful acts: 'Children below the age of 7 years shall be presumed incapable of criminal liability'.

[45] The joint exercise of parental responsibilities is the rule during marriage and also, with respect to issues of significant importance to the life of the child, in cases of divorce, separation from bed and board and declaration of nullity or annulment of marriage (cf Articles 1901 and 1906, Civil Code). As regards cohabiting couples with common children, the law says that when filiation has been established in relation to both parents and the latter live under conditions analogous to those of married couples, the rules governing the exercise of parental responsibility are the same as those applicable during marriage.

[46] Cf unanimous Coimbra Court of Appeal Ruling 450/11.7TBTNV-A.C1 of 20 June 2012, available at http://www.dgsi.pt/jtrc.nsf/c3fb530030ea1c61802568d9005cd5bb/94d01a78963e00ea80257a370048565d.

The scope of Article 147-A of the Law governing the Organisation of the Custody, Protection and Re-education of Minors (OTM) is broader. By making the intervention principles laid down in the Law governing the Protection of Children and Young Persons at Risk (LPCJP) applicable to OTM procedures as well, this article effectively absorbs one of those principles: that children and young persons must be heard (Article 4[i]).[47]

9 Right of the Child to Information

One of the guiding principles for interventions to promote the rights and protection of children and young persons at risk is the obligation to inform (Article 4[h], LPCJP). Pursuant to this principle, both the child or young person and the parents, legal representative or person who has de facto care of him or her have the right to be informed about their rights and about the reasons for the intervention and the ways in which it is to be carried out. As mentioned above, this principle applies to all OTM procedures (Article 147[a], OTM). Indeed, the voluntary jurisdictional nature of procedures applicable to minors would always tend to make this solution possible. In proceedings of this type, the court is not subject to criteria of strict legality, and in each case must adopt the solution it deems most convenient and appropriate.[48] The Law governing Youth Custody, Protection and Re-education (LTC) includes a norm that sets out the rights of the minor, among which is the right to be heard by the judicial authority acting ex officio or at his or her request[49] and to be informed about the rights to which he or she is entitled.[50]

All these institutions and persons – courts, guardians, whether or not they are biological parents or de jure or simply de facto guardians, and social security authorities – must offer the child or young person the information or counselling he or she needs in the situation in question.

10 Intercountry Adoption

As we have already seen, under Portuguese law, potential adoptees over the age of 12 years must consent to the adoption,[51] and if they are over the age of 12, any existing children of the prospective adoptive parents must also be consulted.[52]

---

[47] Cf both unanimous Lisbon Court of Appeal Ruling 3473/05.1TBSXL-D.L1-8 17.11.2011, available at http://www.dgsi.pt/jtrl.nsf/33182fc732316039802565fa00497eec/d7bc9220b76f056080257974004328f8, and the ruling mentioned in the previous footnote.

[48] Article 1410, Code of Civil Procedure.

[49] Article 45(2)(a), LTC.

[50] Article 45(2)(h), LTC.

[51] Full or simple adoption (Articles 1981[1](a) and 1993[1], Civil Code.

[52] Applies to both full and simple adoption.

Intercountry adoption is governed by Executive Law No. 185/93 of 22 May 1993, as amended by Executive Law No. 120/98 of 8 May1998. Portugal is a state party to the Convention on Protection of Children and Cooperation in respect of intercountry adoption (Hague Convention of 29 May 1993).[53]

Portuguese internal law provides for both the placement abroad of minors residing in Portugal for adoption purposes and the adoption of minors residing abroad by persons residing in Portugal.

The placement abroad of minors residing in Portugal with a view to adoption requires a prior court decision, which must include legal measures designed to protect the minor and ensure the suitability of whoever he or she is to be entrusted to with a view to adoption, be it the future adoptive parents themselves or an institution that will then seek to arrange the minor's future adoption.[54]

There is a central authority – the Directorate General of Social Security – which the social security body with responsibility for adoption must always inform of the intention to place Portuguese children residing in Portugal in foreign countries with a view to their future adoption. Foreign adoptions can only take place when timely adoption in Portugal proves impossible.

Portuguese residents who want to adopt minors residing abroad must apply to the social security body covering their area of residence, which will study the application. If it is satisfied that the applicant is suitable for intercountry adoption, this body then transmits the application to the central authority,[55] which in turn sends the relevant information to either the central authority or other competent service in the country where the adoptee lives, or any other entity that is authorised to act as mediator in this field in Portugal or abroad.

11 Right of the Child to Freedom of Thought, Conscience and Religion

As we have noted, the Civil Code says that the decision regarding the religious education of children under the age of 16 rests with their parents. Even so, on this and on any other issue of considerable importance, the parents must nevertheless take both their children's opinion and their degree of maturity into account.

Churches, any other religious communities and organisations representing worshippers who reside in Portuguese territory can all provide religious education at any public basic (primary) and secondary schools they specifically nominate.[56]

---

[53] Approved for ratification by Resolution of the Assembly of the Republic No. 8/2003 of 19 December 2002. Published in Series I-A of *Diário da República* No. 47 of 25.02.2003.

[54] Article 14 of Executive Law No. 185/93 of 22 May 1993, with the wording given to it by Executive Law No. 120/98 of 8 May 1998.

[55] The same central authority is competent with regard to the adoption abroad of minors residing in Portugal.

[56] Article 24, Law governing Religious Freedom (Law No. 16/2001 of 22 June 2001).

To this end they must first register as religious legal persons, which grant them legal personality.

Prior to the current Religious Freedom Law, another legislative act[57] had allowed students to take religious and moral education (EMR) as a full alternative subject to classes in personal and social development. This legislation also allowed all religious faiths with a permanent presence in Portugal to teach EMR classes at public primary and secondary schools.[58]

At present, attendance at EMR classes is still optional, albeit subject to the applicable regime governing absences, but personal and social development classes no longer exist.[59]

The religious authorities of each faith are responsible for curricular programmes and textbooks, but these must be approved in advance by the Minister of Education and must comply with both the constitutional rules and the general principles governing curricular contents. The latter particularly require that academic teaching and training contribute to the internalisation of moral and civic values.

12 Physical Punishment

Portugal is among the countries that prohibit physical punishment within the family.[60] The Criminal Code provisions that typify the crime of domestic violence say that it includes the infliction of 'physical and mental maltreatment, **including corporal punishments**' (emphasis added) on children.[61]

However, while the prohibition on corporal punishment at school or in public or private institutions that care for children is consensual and very widely observed, the case-by-case implementation of the concept within the family still poses difficulties and doubts, in particular, as regards the *quantum* of violence that would justify calling physical punishment 'maltreatment' and the inclusion of the form of conduct within the crime typified by law.

---

[57] Executive Law No. 329/98 of 2 November 1998.

[58] Article 3(1), Executive Law No. 329/98 of 2 November 1998.

[59] If schools feel it appropriate, this subject can nonetheless be offered as an 'additional option'. This format covers subjects that can be created by individual schools as part of their power to manage teaching credits. If the subject does exist, attendance by students is compulsory. Cf *Matrizes do ensino básico e secundário*, available at http://www.dgidc.min-edu.pt/index.php?s=noticias&noticia=353, last accessed on 25 July 2013.

[60] The prohibition on corporal punishment within the family was brought in as part of amendments to the Criminal Code made by Law No. 59/2007, of 4 September 2007.

[61] 'Whosoever, repetitively or otherwise, inflicts physical or psychological maltreatment**, including**, deprivation of liberty and sexual offences … d) **On a person who is particularly defenseless, in particular by reason of age**, disability, illness, pregnancy or economic dependency, **and who lives with the offender**; shall be punished by a term of imprisonment of 1–5 years, if a more severe penalty is not applicable by virtue of another legal provision' (Article 152[1][c] and [d], Criminal Code. Emphases added).

Outside the family environment, persons who inflict physical or psychological maltreatment, including physical punishment, on minors who are in their care, are under their direction or education or are employed by them, are guilty of the crime of maltreatment, which is punishable under the Criminal Code.[62] However, when it comes to defining the concept of physical punishment such that it falls within the scope of the crime of maltreatment, extra-familial situations pose the same degree of difficulty as inter-familial punishment.

Physical punishment at school is one of those subjects that for a long time involved a profound difference between theory and practice. Many child psychologists and pedagogues have always argued that physical punishment is both useless and illegitimate, but their ideas have sometimes also been shared outside the academic domain. In Portugal 120 years ago, an unequivocal legislative stand was taken against physical punishments at school, which were completely forbidden by the 'Ministerial Order establishing several provisions for the standardised regulation of the enrolment and attendance service of primary schools' of 26 September 1893, as published in *Diário do Governo* (the Government Gazette) No. 219 of 28 September 1893.[63] Paragraph 30 laid down that: 'It shall be permitted to stimulate' (students) 'by the use of prizes and punishment; **but corporal punishment shall be expressly prohibited**' (emphasis added).

One can also see that there were some progressive pedagogical trends in Portugal's then non-European territories. The use of punishment per se was clearly encouraged, but teachers were at least advised not to use the spanking paddle,[64] which was the most widely used means of physical punishment at schools at the time. Having said this, these principles remained very theoretical, with little practical application and with actual practices that were at times clearly divergent. In fact, it was only after the Revolution of 25 April 1974[65] that the prohibition on physical punishment at schools and in social institutions was taken seriously.

---

[62] Article 152-A: '1) – Whosoever, having a minor in their care, under their direction or education or as an employee …a) repetitively or otherwise, inflicts on him or her physical or psychological maltreatment, **including** … shall be punished by a term of imprisonment of 1–5 years, if a more severe penalty is not applicable by virtue of another legal provision' (emphasis added). The current text of this particular Civil Code norm was brought in by Law No. 59/2007 of 4 September 2007.

[63] In *Collecção Official de Legislação Portugueza, Anno de 1893*, Lisbon, Imprensa Nacional, 1894.

[64] Ricardo Cabral, The Development of Teacher Education in Portuguese Goa (1841–1961), Concept Publishing Company, New Delhi 2009. Also available at: http://shodhganga.inflibnet.ac.in/; http://shodhganga.inflibnet.ac.in/handle/10603/3280. Accessed on 30 July 2013. "The "Mestres" should not use the "palmatoria" (a wooden cane with a broad end used to hit on the palms as punishment for wrongdoing). They must teach the children with gentleness, patience and good manners. They should teach them with compassion and care as befitting the important post of a Teacher and considering their tender and innocent age" (in Chapter IV). This text is part of instructions addressed to the "mestres" (primary school teachers) by Dom Manuel de Portugal e Castro, viceroy and captain general of India between the years of 1827 and 1835.

[65] The so-called Carnation Revolution (*Revolução dos cravos*), which reinstated a democratic regime in Portugal.

Among other student rights, the student's statute[66] sets out that to the safeguard of the student's safety at school and to respect for his physical and moral integrity, which is clearly equivalent to a prohibition on physical punishment.

13 Termination and Restriction of the Exercise of Parental Responsibility

Portuguese law permits the termination or restriction of the exercise of parental responsibility[67] on various grounds. The law summarises them as all those situations in which one or both parents intentionally contravene or fail in their obligations to their children, with serious detriment to the latter. Situations in which parents are in no condition to fulfil their parental responsibilities by virtue of inexperience, illness, absence or other reasons can also have the same result.[68]

The competence to order this termination or restriction pertains to the courts and can be exercised on application by the Public Prosecutors' Office, any of the minor's relatives or any person who has de facto or de jure care of the minor.

There are also situations in which the law requires that parental responsibility be terminated: e. g. in the case of definitive conviction of a crime which under the law demands it or that of disqualification or incapacity due to mental disorder.

Termination can be total or partial. In the latter case it is restricted to concrete questions regarding representation and management of the child's assets. It may also cover both parents or just one of them and may affect all, one or some of the children.

Parents are never relieved of their maintenance obligations to their children,[69] even if their parental responsibility is terminated.

The exercise of parental responsibilities can be restricted in situations that are not serious enough to justify termination, but in which the safety, health, moral formation or education of a minor are nonetheless at risk. In such cases, parents retain the exercise of those responsibilities regarding everything that is not incompatible with the restrictions imposed by the court.

Termination can entail a variety of different measures, ranging from making a child available for adoption to the various promotion and protection measures included in the Law governing the Protection of Children and Young Persons at Risk: the provision of assistance to the parent(s), or to another family member;

---

[66] Law No. 51/2012 of 5 September 2012, approving the Statute governing Students and School Ethics (establishes the rights and duties of primary and secondary students and the commitment of parents and other members of the educational community to their education and training).

[67] Articles 1913 *et seq.*, Civil Code).

[68] Article 1915(1), Civil Code.

[69] The law defines 'maintenance' as everything that is essential to the recipient's livelihood, housing and clothing, as well as his or her teaching and education if he or she is a minor (Article 2003, Civil Code).

placement with a suitable person; assistance to the young person with a view to his or her ability to live autonomously; foster placement; and placement in a child-caring institution.

14 Consent to the Medical Treatment of Children

Consent by minors to their medical treatment follows the general rule of consent applicable to other acts that are important in life. The capacity to give consent must thus be analysed in the light of the minor's maturity. A lack of capacity in this respect can be overcome by the person(s) with parental responsibility for the minor, acting in accordance with the general terms of the law.

In the case of surgical interventions, however, Portuguese law can be said to be more explicit. Here, it is consent that excludes the unlawfulness of facts that would otherwise constitute actions jeopardising physical integrity.[70] This consent is only effective if given by a person who is over the age of 16 and possesses the judgement needed to assess the meaning and extent of the consent when it is given.[71] The law considers presumptive consent equivalent to effective consent when it is reasonable to assume that the holder of the legally protected interest would have effectively consented to the fact in question if he or she had known the circumstances in which it was carried out.[72]

Whenever a minor's life may be in danger due to a lack of authorisation by his or her parents, a court can give consent instead, under the terms laid down in the LPCJP.

The same applies to refusal of consent. If a minor wishes to refuse consent and his or her parents insist on giving it, a court can intervene and make the minor's position prevail.

15 Right of the Child to a Name

Both the forenames and surnames of Portuguese nationals are essentially immutable, and the (first and/or family) name(s) on a birth certificate can only be altered with the permission of the conservator of the Central Civil Registries under a special name-change procedure.[73]

[70] This even applies to minimally invasive surgical procedures.

[71] Article 38(3), Criminal Code.

[72] Article 39(1) and (2), Criminal Code. An example of presumptive consent is where the time it would take to obtain express consent to a surgical procedure or surgical-medical treatment would represent a danger to life or a serious danger to body or health. In such cases the fact is not punishable despite the absence of express consent.

[73] Article 104, Civil Registry Code.

There are cases where the law itself allows a name to be changed: the establishment of postnatal filiation, adoption[74] and marriage.

Should maternity or paternity be established only after the registration of birth, the surnames of the child may be altered; this change can be requested by both parents or by one parent with the other's consent.

The choice of a child's forenames and surnames rests with the parents; however, if they are unable to reach an agreement, the decision must be taken by a court and must consider the child's interest.[75]

16 Admission to Employment

The minimum age at which a minor can be contracted in order to autonomously engage in a paid activity is 16 years,[76] at which point he or she no longer needs parental consent.

The Labour Code contains a whole subsection on child labour, which particularly regulates the maximum limits on both the normal working period applicable to the minor and night work, as well as the conditions regarding protection of the minor's health and safety.

The law generically prohibits, or at least conditions, work whose nature or the circumstances in which it is carried out are likely to prejudice a minor's physical, psychological or moral development.[77]

[74] In cases of full adoption, the adopted child loses his or her original surname(s) and, with the necessary adaptations, acquires the new one(s) that he or she would have been given in a case of biological filiation. Of the various cases in which the law itself provides for a name change, it is only in that of adoption that the forename(s) can be altered. This alteration is exceptional and can only be ordered by a court at the request of the prospective adoptive parent, if the court considers that this would safeguard the interest of the minor, in particular his or her right to personal identity, and that would help his or her integration into the family (Article 1988, Civil Code). In restricted adoptions the judge can give the child the adoptive parent's(s') surname(s), at the latter's request. The adoptee thus receives a new name in addition to one or more of the surnames of his or her biological family (Article 1995, Civil Code).

[75] Article 1875, Civil Code.

[76] Minors below the age of 16 can only be admitted to employment if they have completed compulsory schooling or are enrolled in and attending secondary education and the work involved is light (Article 68, Labour Code, Law No. 7/2009 of 12 February 2009). If the business is a family one, minors below the age of 16 must work under the supervision and direction of an adult member of their household.

[77] Article 72(2), Labour Code.

17 Children's Obligations Towards Their Parents

The general clause on children's obligations towards their parents says that minors must 'obey their parents or guardian and comply with their precepts'[78] in everything that is not unlawful or immoral.

The Civil Code chapter devoted to the effects of filiation says that parents and their children must afford each other respect, support and assistance and explicitly states that the duty of assistance includes the obligation to provide maintenance and to contribute to family expenses[79] while living under the same roof, depending on each person's own resources. These reciprocal obligations last not just while children are minors, but for as long as a parent-child relationship exists.

The overall framework of maintenance obligations includes the duty of adult descendants to provide parents who need it with maintenance, albeit this is secondary to the primary beneficiary(ies) of that duty – i.e. spouses or former spouses.[80]

[78] Article 128, Civil Code.

[79] Article 1874, Civil Code.

[80] Article 2009(1)(b), Civil Code.

The Rights of the Child: Romanian National Report

Daniela-Anca Deteşeanu

1 Introduction

In Romania, the observance of the rights of the children is ensured through a legal frame consisting in a number of legal instruments, both national and international. In terms of international obligations, Romania is party to the UN Convention on the Rights of the Child since 1990.[1] Starting 2001, Romania became a party to the Optional Protocol of the UN Convention on the Rights of the Child on the involvement of children in armed conflict[2] and to the Optional Protocol of the UNCRC on the sale of children, child prostitution and child pornography.[3] Most of the principles and legal provisions provided by the national legislation are inspired by the provisions of these international instruments.

The main national legal regulations dedicated to the rights of the child are to be found in the Romanian Civil Code, in its recently adopted version[4] and the special law in the field – Law no. 272/2004 – regarding the protection of the child.[5]

[1] Law no. 18/1990, published in the Official Gazette of Romania, Part I, no. 109 from September 28, 1990, republished in the Official Gazette of Romania, Part I, no. 314 from June 13, 2001 (hereinafter "UNCRC").

[2] Law no. 567/2001, published in the Official Gazette of Romania, Part I, no. 692 from October 31, 2001.

[3] Law no. 470/2001, published in the Official Gazette of Romania, Part I, no. 601 from September 25, 2001.

[4] Law no. 287/2009, republished in the Official Gazette of Romania, Part I, no. 505/June 15, 2011, into force from October 1, 2011 (hereinafter "RCC").

[5] Law no. 272/2004, published in the Official Gazette of Romania, Part I, no. 557/June 23, 2004, into force from June 26, 2004 (hereinafter "L272").

D.-A. Deteşeanu (✉)
Faculty of Law, University of Bucharest,
Bd. Mihail Kogalniceanu no. 36-46, Sector 5, Bucharest, Romania
e-mail: daniela-anca.deteseanu@drept.unibuc.ro

O. Cvejić Jančić (ed.), *The Rights of the Child in a Changing World*,
Ius Comparatum - Global Studies in Comparative Law 13,
DOI 10.1007/978-3-319-23189-1_13

RCC regulates the main institutions pertaining to the Civil Law and family law (such as, but not limited to, the right of the child to establish his/her origin, adoption, relations between the child and his/her parents, etc.). L272 has a mixed composition, providing, in the same time, for a general framework of the rights of the child and being the expression of the transposition, into the national law, of the provisions of the UNCRC, but also enumerating the main rights of the child and establishing the national authorities in charge with the observance of application of its provisions.

L272 defines the "child" as being any person who is below the age of 18 and does not possess full civil capacity.[6] RCC provides that a person reaches the age of majority at 18, as a general rule,[7] and that, for the purposes of the legal provisions regarding the protection of the child, a "child" is the person below the age of 18 who did not acquire the full civil capacity, according to the law.[8]

The fundamental rights of the child, as detailed under the UNCRC, are developed in the Romanian legislation in various legal instruments, as follows:

2 General Principles

2.1 Best Interest of the Child

As a true foundation of all other rights of the child, the principle of "best interest of the child" is explicitly provided and detailed in several legal provisions, under both L272 and RCC. L272 provides that all legal regulations, as well as all legal acts concluded in matters related to the rights of the child, shall be subjected to the principle of the best interest of the child. According to the same law, "the best interest of the child" is particularly related to the right of the child to a normal physical and moral development, a balanced social and emotional life and a family life.

The best interest of the child must be observed by the child's parents, legal representatives and guardians and shall prevail in all matters and decisions related to children and taken by the public authorities, authorised private entities and courts of law.

L272 enumerates a number of factors to be taken into consideration when evaluating the best interest of the child: (a) the needs of the child regarding his/her physical, psychological development, education and health, security, stability and relation to a family; (b) the child's opinion, depending on his/her age and degree of maturity; (c) the past of the child, especially considering the cases of abuse, abandonment, exploitation or any other form of violence against the child, as well as the potential

[6] Same definition is provided under Law no. 273/2004 regarding the adoption, published in the Official Gazette of Romania, Part I, no. 557/June 23, 2004, as subsequently modified (hereinafter "L273").

[7] Art. 38 of RCC.

[8] Art. 263 par. 5 of RCC.

situations of risk which may occur in the future; (d) the capacity of the parents or of the persons who are in charge with the child to answer to the child's needs; and (e) the preservation of the personal relations with the persons for whom the child has developed a form of affection.[9]

In RCC, the principle of best interest of the child is explicitly referred to when regulating various civil institutions involving the legal status of the child, such as the case of misunderstandings between parents when exercising their parental rights, adoption, etc. Art. 263 of RCC provides for a legal interpretation regarding the principle of the "best interest of the child", stating that, in order to solve any request/application regarding children, the competent authorities must give all necessary details in order to allow the parties to solve the disputes in an amicable manner. The procedures involving the relations between parents and their children must guarantee that the wishes and interests of the parents are known by the authorities and that the authorities take them into consideration. The procedures involving children must be performed in a reasonable time framework so that the best interest of the child and the family relations shall not be affected.

2.2 *The Right of the Child to Express His/Her Views Freely in All Matters Affecting Him/Her*

The right of the child to express his/her views freely in all matters affecting him/her, as provided under Arts. 12 and 13 of the UNCRC, is detailed under both RCC and L272. As a special law in the field of the child's rights, L272 provides that the child who has discernment has the right to freely express his/her opinion in any matter affecting him/her. The child has the right to be heard in any judicial or administrative procedure in which he/she must participate.

According to L272, "the right to be heard" includes the right of the child to request and receive any pertinent information, to be consulted, to express his/her opinion and to be informed about the consequences of his/her opinion, if it is observed, as well as about the consequences of any decision concerning him/her.[10]

The judicial and administrative authorities must hear the child above 10. A child under the age of 10 can also be heard, if the competent authority considers that his/her hearing is necessary for solving the case. Any child, irrespective of his/her age, may request to be heard. If the requested authority refuses to do so, it must provide reasons for such refuse.

These legal provisions, provided under L272, have been included, in identical terms, in RCC.[11]

---

[9] Art. 2 par. 5 of L272.

[10] Article 24(3) of L272.

[11] Article 264 of RCC.

2.3 The Right of the Child to Freedom of Thought, Conscience and Religion

Art. 32 par. 7 of the Romanian Constitution provides that the State ensures the freedom of the religious education and that, in public schools, the religious education is organised and guaranteed by the law.

L272 provides subsequent details regarding the right of the child to freedom of thought, conscience and religion. The law specifies that the parents shall guide the child, in accordance to their own convictions, in order to choose a religion, taking into consideration the opinion, the age and the degree of maturity of the child. The parents are not allowed to oblige the child to adhere to a certain religion. In case of a child above the age of 14, the religion cannot be changed without the child's consent, while the child over 16 has the right to choose the religion by himself/herself. In case of a child under special protection, the persons who are taking care of the child are prohibited to undertake any actions having as purpose to influence the religious convictions of the child.

According to Law no. 1/2011 regarding the national education,[12] the religious education is compulsory from the elementary school until high school. The same law provides that the pupils who embrace the religions/cults recognised by the State, irrespective of their number, have the right to participate in classes of religion, in accordance to their own religion. Based on the written request of the pupil above 18 or of the parents or legal guardian of the pupil who is a minor, the pupil has the right not to attend the classes of religion.

3 Protection of the Child Through Means of Civil Law

3.1 The Right of the Child to Know About His/Her Origin

While L272 includes the general principle that the child has the right to the determination and the preservation of his/her identity,[13] RCC regulates in detail the legal means in which a child, including the child born out of wedlock, can establish his/her origin.[14]

According to RCC, the child has the right to establish his/her origin regarding the mother, if the child was born out of wedlock or if he/she rebuts the reality of the information mentioned in his/her certificate of birth (the registration of a certain person as being the mother of the child, provided in the certificate of birth). For such purpose, either the child or his/her heirs can lodge an application in the court of law.

[12] Published in the Official Gazette of Romania, Part I, no. 18/January 10, 2011, as subsequently modified.

[13] Art. 8 par. 1 of L272.

[14] Articles 421–440 of RCC.

The right of the child to act in person against the presumptive mother (or of her heirs) is not subject to any statute of limitation, while the child's heirs can act against the presumptive mother (or of her heirs) within 1 year from the date of death of the child.

The child born out of wedlock can establish his/her origin regarding the father only through a judicial procedure. The legal action can be initiated either by the child or by the mother's child (even if the mother herself is under 18) or by the legal representative of the child. The law action has to be lodged against the presumptive father or against the heirs of the presumptive father. The child's right is not subjected to any statute of limitation, but the child's heirs can initiate the legal proceedings within 1 year from the date of the child's death.

In case of the child born or conceived within the marriage, the Romanian civil legislation sets a legal presumption that the husband of the mother is the father of the child born or conceived during marriage. However, this presumption is a relative one and can be rebutted by the mother's husband, by the mother herself, by the biological father or by the child.

The situation of the child conceived under biomedical assistance is a novelty in the Romanian civil legislation, being regulated only starting with 2009, with the adoption of the new RCC (entered into force in 2011).[15] According to the legal provisions, no legal relationship has to be established between the child conceived under biomedical assistance and the biological father. RCC allows the disclosure of certain data regarding the birth of the child only in exceptional circumstances. Article 445 of RCC states that any information regarding the artificial reproduction ("human reproduction medically assisted", as referred to in RCC) is confidential. However, in the cases when the lack of information regarding the human reproduction medically assisted generates a serious risk for the health of the person so conceived or of his/her descendants, the court may authorise the transmission of such information, in a confidential manner, to the physicians or to the competent authorities. RCC provides that the details regarding the artificial reproduction, including the issue related to confidentiality, shall be detailed under a special law. Up to the date of drafting this report, such law has not been adopted.[16]

3.2 *Special Rules Regarding the Rights of the Adopted Children*

RCC and L273 provide for the main rules concerning the adoption of a child. According to the Romanian law, the adoption has as an effect the cease of the family bonds between the adopted child and his/her biological family.

[15] Articles 441–447 of RCC.

[16] The project of the law is currently under the Romanian Parliament's examination.

The information regarding the adoption is confidential, and RCC provides that the modalities in which the adopted child shall be informed about the adoption, his/her biological family and the general legal frame regarding the information on adoption shall be determined by a special law.[17] The special law regarding the adoption, L273, in its recently modified form, provides that the adopted persons have the right to learn about their origins and their past and must be supported when trying to contact their biological parents or biological relatives. The information about the adoption can be given only to major persons. The law provides for the right of the adopted persons to request and obtain general information regarding the institutions that accommodated them before the adoption and their personal past – such as the place and the date of birth – which do not reveal the identity of the biological parents. The identity of the biological parents can be revealed before the moment when the child has acquired the full legal capacity only for medical reasons, based on the request of the adoptive parents, the adopted child, his/her spouse or children, his/her legal representative or a medical institution or hospital. When the adopted person acquires full legal capacity, he/she may request the tribunal to authorise his/her access to the information held by any public authority with regard to the identity of his/her biological parents. In any case, L273 provided for the obligation of the adoptive parents to gradually inform the child about the adoption, as early as possible and with the help of the professionals working in the public institutions specialised in adoptions. In the same time, the information regarding the adoption and the origin of the child, especially the information regarding the identity of the biological parents, as well as the data regarding the medical records of the child and his/her family shall be kept for a minimum of 50 years from the date when the court sentence approving the adoption was issued.

Both L273[18] and RCC provide as a compulsory requirement for the conclusion of the adoption the consent of the child above the age of 10.[19]

The Romanian legislation allows international adoptions. However, the current legal provisions make international adoption a "subsidiary mean", which can be used only if a national adoption is not possible. Even in such case, the international adoption is subject to a number of restrictive conditions. According to Art. 52 of L273, the international adoption of a child having the residence in Romania can be approved by the Romanian authorities only in the following cases: (a) the person who adopts or one of the spouses of the adopting family is relative up to the fourth degree with the adopted child, (b) the person who adopts or one of the spouses of the adopting family is also a Romanian citizen and (c) the person who adopts is the spouse of the biological parent of the adopted child. The children who can be internationally adopted are only the children registered with the Romanian Office for Adoptions – the public authority in charge with the procedures of adoption in Romania. The administrative stage of the procedure is made under the supervision

[17] Art. 474 of RCC.

[18] Art. 14 of L273.

[19] Art. 463 par. 1 letter b of RCC.

of the Romanian Office for Adoptions, while the final stage is a judicial one, the adoption being approved by the court. In any case, the international adoption has to observe the provisions of the Convention on Protection of Children and Co-operation in Respect of Intercountry Adoption, signed in The Hague on May 29, 1993, and ratified by Romania in 1994,[20] to which L273 makes explicit reference.

3.3 *Right to Give Medical Consent*

While L272 provides for a section regarding the protection of health and the well-being of the child, it does not regulate the issues concerning the medical consent of the child. In the same manner, RCC does not provide for any specific rules in this regard. The only provision touching the situation of the child is Art. 68 par. 2 of RCC, which prohibits, in any circumstances whatsoever, the sampling of organs, tissues or cells from minors.

Law no. 95/2006 regarding the reform in the field of health (hereinafter "L95")[21] gives more details regarding the right of the child to give medical consent, establishing three different hypotheses: (1) the consent of the child in case of medical treatment or medical methods of prevention and diagnosis; (2) the consent of the child in case of sampling of organs, tissues and cells; and (3) the consent of the child in case of transplant of organs, tissues and human body cells.

1. In the first situation, Art. 650 of L95 states that the legal age for expressing an informed consent regarding the medical treatment or the medical methods of prevention and diagnosis is 18 years old. The minors (under 18) can give their consent in the absence of their parents or legal representative only in the following situations: (a) emergency situations, when the parents or the legal representative cannot be contacted and the minor has the necessary discernment to understand his/her medical situation and (b) medical situations related to the diagnosis and/or the treatment of reproductive and sexual problems, based on the explicit request of the minor over 16 years.
2. Concerning the sampling of organs, tissues and cells, L95 includes the same prohibition inserted later on in RCC, regarding the prohibition of sampling operations from potential donors who are minors. However, L95 provides for a number of exceptions from this rule. If the donor is a minor and is a relative up to the fourth degree with the receiver of the organ, he/she can donate stem cells. In such cases, if the minor is above 10 years old, he/she can express the consent, but together with the written agreement of the parents or the legal representative. If the minor is under 10, the sampling can be done only with the agreement of the

[20] The Hague Convention on Protection of Children and Co-operation in Respect of Intercountry Adoption was ratified by Romania under Law no. 84/1994, published in the Official Gazette of Romania, Part I, no. 298/October 21, 1994.

[21] Published in the Official Gazette of Romania, Part I, no. 372/April 28, 2006.

legal representative. The law explicitly provides that if the child refuses, either in writing or verbally, any sampling shall be prohibited.
3. Finally, in case of transplant of organs, tissues and human body cells, the consent shall be given by the parents or by any other person who is the legal representative of the minor.

3.4 The Right of the Child to Change the Name

Art. 8 of L272 provides that the child has the right to a personal identity. From the moment of his/her birth, the child has the right to a name. As a general rule, the parents choose freely the name and the surname of the child. The parents can freely choose the surname of the child, subject to the limitations set in Art. 84 par. 2 of RCC, providing that the surname cannot prejudice the public order, the morality or the interest of the child, being prohibited to be registered such surnames as those considered indecent or ridiculous. The name of the child shall be determined based on his/her descent. In the case of an abandoned newborn or a newborn whose descent is unknown, the name of the child shall be determined by decision of the mayor of the municipality where the child has been found.

After the registration of a certain name (and surname) for a person, the change of the name (or surname) can be done only through an administrative procedure, according to Government Ordinance no. 41/2003 regarding the administrative acquire and change of the name of natural persons.[22] In case of minors, the above-mentioned ordinance provides that the application for the change of name shall be done, in the name of the minor, by the parents or, with the approval of the tutorial authority, by the caretaker of the child.

If there is a disagreement between the parents as to the name of the child, the tutorial authority shall decide. In case of the minor who is 14 years old, the minor shall also sign the application. When the parents also change names, the change of the family name of the minor can be requested in the same time with the change of name of the parents. This request can be made separately only for justified reasons.

3.5 The Right of the Child to Work

As a general principle, Art. 42 of RCC provides that the minor can conclude legal acts regarding his/her work, artistic or sport skills or those acts related to his/her work, with the agreement of his/her parents or the legal representative, subject to the provisions of the special laws. In such cases, the child shall exercise the rights and

[22] Published in the Official Gazette of Romania, Part I, no. 68/February 2, 2003.

shall execute the obligations arising out of these acts independently and shall be able to freely use the earnings resulting from his/her work.

More details about the right of the child to work are provided under Law no. 53/2003 – the Labour Code (hereinafter the "Labour Code").[23] According to Art. 16 of the Labour Code, any natural person has the right to work starting from the age of 16. As an exception, a person can conclude a labour contract once he/she is 15 years old, with the agreement of the parents or the legal representatives, if the object of the contract relates to activities suitable for the physical development, aptitudes and knowledge of the child and his/her health, development and professional training are not jeopardised. Children under 15 are prohibited to work. Children under 18 years old are not allowed to work in dangerous environments.

3.6 Obligations of Children Towards Parents

The Romanian legislation provides for a number of general obligations of children towards their parents. Art. 29 par. 3 of L272 sets the general rule that the obligations of the child are determined based on his/her age and degree of maturity, without any interference to his/her rights. However, L272 does not provide for a specific obligation of the child towards his/her parents. Art. 485 of RCC provides for a general obligation of the child – irrespective of his/her age – to respect his/her parents. Articles 513–534 of RCC regulate a general obligation of support between certain persons determined by the law, namely, between spouses, between direct relatives and between brothers and sisters. Therefore, even if the relation between the child and his/her parents is not specifically indicated, this legal provision also covers the obligation of support between the child and his/her parents. This obligation is owed if the parent is in a state of need, not having the necessary means for living, and it consists mainly in providing such means – usually in kind – but if the obligation is not willingly executed in kind, the court of law can determine an allowance (therefore transforming the obligation into a pecuniary one).

4 Protection of Children Through Means of Criminal Law

4.1 Prohibition of Physical Punishment Within and Beyond Family

An important number of national legal instruments ensure the protection of child against any form of maltreatment, exploitation and abuse.

[23] Published in the Official Gazette of Romania, Part I, no. 72/February 5, 2003.

The principle of protection of the child from any form of violence is stated at a constitutional level (Art. 49 of the Romanian Constitution). This principle is developed in the general law governing the legal status of the child – L272. Art. 85 of this law provides that any child has the right to be protected against any form of abuse, neglect, exploitation, trafficking, illegal migration, kidnapping, violence, pornography by internet, as well as against any other forms of violence, irrespective of the environment where these aggressions occur. Any natural or legal person, as well as the child, may inform the competent State authorities – public departments for the protection of the child – about the acts of violence directed against children, so that such authority takes the appropriate measures of protection. The officers working in public institutions where they enter into contacts with children have a legal obligation to urgently inform the public departments for the protection of the child in case of suspicions regarding any form of abuse against children.

If abusive or violent acts have been committed against children by persons who have a duty to care for them, based on a labour relationship, the employer has the legal obligation to inform at once the criminal investigative authorities and not to allow the alleged offender to further perform his/her activities.[24]

Art. 28 of L272 specifically provides that the child has the right to the respect of his/her personality and individuality and cannot be subjected to any form of physical punishments or to other humiliating or degrading treatments. The disciplinary measures against children can be established only by considering the dignity of the child, being explicitly prohibited the physical punishments, or those who jeopardise their physical, psychological or emotional development.

The legal protection of children against any form of violence is ensured through norms of criminal law. The acts of exploitation and violence against children are criminally repressed. The new Romanian Criminal Code,[25] which entered into force in February 2014, incriminates acts such as maltreatment of children (Art. 197), the crimes committed against a family member (Arts. 199 and 200), trafficking of minors (Art. 210), sexual corruption of children (Art. 221) or recruitment of minors for sexual purposes (Art. 222).

In 2003, Law no. 217/2003 regarding the prevention and the fight against family violence has been adopted.[26] Among the most important measures provided under this law are those regarding the creation of emergency centres where protection and assistance (including psychological and legal assistance) are given to the victims of family violence, including children.

The same law provides for the power of the judge to issue an order of restriction, for the purpose of protecting the victims of family violence. Such order may include the prohibition of the offender to contact the children, the removal of the children from the dwelling and their placement in centres of protection or, as the case

---

[24] Art. 96 of L272.

[25] Law no. 286/2009, published in the Official Gazette of Romania, Part I, no. 510/July 24, 2009.

[26] Published in the Official Gazette of Romania, Part I, no. 365/May 30, 2012.

may be, the removal of the offender from the family dwelling and the reintegration of the children.

To such measures may be added the measures of protection provided under L272 (i.e. placement of the child to a family or a person in charge to his/her care or to a specialised institution or specialised supervision of the child) and those provided by Law no. 211/2004 regarding some measures for the protection of the victims of crimes,[27] such as free-of-charge psychological counselling or legal assistance.

4.2 *Deprivation of Parental Rights*

One punitive measure against parents who commit certain criminal offences or maltreat their children is related to the deprivation of parental rights. According to the Romanian Criminal Code,[28] the deprivation of parental rights is provided as a complementary or accessory punishment, in addition to the main punishment (imprisonment or criminal fine). The punishment is applied by the judge if he/she so considers, taking into account the nature and the gravity of the crime, the circumstances of the case and the personality of the offender. While the accessory punishment of deprivation of parental rights is added to the main criminal sanction, the complementary punishment of deprivation of parental rights has to be executed after the execution of the main punishment. The new Romanian Criminal Code provides that the complementary punishment can be determined by the judge for a term between 1 and 5 years.

Following the deprivation of parental rights, as criminal punishment, the judge shall decide the placement of the child, either to a family member, to a specialised caretaker or a specialised institution. The person or the family where such child can be placed must have the domicile in Romania and must be evaluated by the Direction for the Protection of the Child considering criteria such as the moral guarantees and the material means it possesses in order to take care of the child. During the term of placement, the parental rights shall be exercised by the director of the local Direction for the Protection of the Child. As it results from the above mentioned, the parents deprived of parental rights have no rights towards the child. In terms of obligations, L272 provides that the competent local authorities or the judge who decided the placement of the child shall determine the amount of a monthly allowance of the parent(s) for the needs of the child, as provided by the Civil Law. This allowance shall be paid to the local budget. If the parent(s) does not have the means to pay this allowance, the court shall order the parent(s) to provide work for the public interest, instead of providing the above-mentioned allowance.

---

[27] Published in the Official Gazette of Romania, Part I, no. 505/June 4, 2004.

[28] Art. 54, Art. 55, Arts. 65–68 of the new Criminal Code.

5 Summary

Under a general evaluation, the Romanian legislation has implemented the general principles set forth by the UN Convention on the Rights of the Child by various pieces of legislation in both civil and criminal fields. It has to be also emphasised that, with respect to children rights, Romania is also bound by other international obligations arising out from the treaties to which Romania is party to, including those adopted under the framework of the Council of Europe, of outmost importance being the European Convention of Human Rights, as developed by the case law of the European Court of Human Rights.

Legislation (in Chronological Order)

- Law no. 18/1990 for the ratification of the UN Convention on the Rights of the Child, published in the Official Gazette of Romania, Part I, no. 109/September 28, 1990, republished in the Official Gazette of Romania, Part I, no. 314/June 13, 2001.
- Law no. 84/1994 for the ratification of the Hague Convention on Protection of Children and Co-operation in Respect of Intercountry Adoption, published in the Official Gazette of Romania, Part I, no. 298/October 21, 1994.
- Law no. 470/2001 for the ratification of the Optional Protocol of the UNCRC on the Sale of Children, Child Prostitution and Child Pornography, published in the Official Gazette of Romania, Part I, no. 601/September 25, 2001.
- Law no. 567/2001 for the ratification of the Optional Protocol of the UN Convention on the Rights of the Child on the Involvement of Children in armed conflict, published in the Official Gazette of Romania, Part I, no. 692/October 31, 2001.
- Government Ordinance no. 41/2003 regarding the administrative acquire and change of the name of natural persons, published in the Official Gazette of Romania, Part I, no. 68/February 2, 2003.
- Law no. 53/2003 – the Labour Code, published in the Official Gazette of Romania, Part I, no. 72/February 5, 2003.
- The Romanian Constitution, published in the Official Gazette of Romania, Part I, no. 767/October 31, 2003.
- Law no. 217/2003 regarding the prevention and the fight against family violence, republished in the Official Gazette of Romania, Part I, no. 365/May 30, 2012.
- Law no. 211/2004 regarding some measures for the protection of the victims of crimes, published in the Official Gazette of Romania, Part I, no. 505/June 4, 2004.
- Law no. 272/2004 regarding the protection of the child, published in the Official Gazette of Romania, Part I, no. 557/June 23, 2004.
- Law no. 273/2004 regarding the adoption, published in the Official Gazette of Romania, Part I, no. 557/June 23, 2004.
- Law no. 95/2006 regarding the reform in the field of health, published in the Official Gazette of Romania, Part I, no. 372/April 28, 2006.

- Law no. 286/2009 regarding the Criminal Code of Romania, published in the Official Gazette of Romania, Part I, no. 510/July 24, 2009.
- Law no. 287/2009 regarding the Civil Code, republished in the Official Gazette of Romania, Part I, no. 505/June 15, 2011.
- Law no. 1/2011 regarding the national education, published in the Official Gazette of Romania, Part I, no. 18/January 10, 2011.

The Rights of the Child in Scotland

Frankie McCarthy

1 Introduction

Children's rights are an established part of the Scottish legal landscape.[1] The Scottish Government recently affirmed its commitment to making Scotland 'the best place in the world to grow up,'[2] acknowledging the central role played by the United Nations Convention on the Rights of the Child ('the Convention') in pursuit of that goal.[3] With the United Kingdom submitting its fifth report to the Committee on the Rights of the Child ('CRC') in May 2014,[4] this seems an opportune moment to review the current standing of children's rights within Scots family law.

All web addresses cited in this paper were correct as of 18 August 2015.

[1] For a book-length treatment, see A Cleland and E Sutherland, *Children's Rights in Scotland (3rd ed)*, (Edinburgh, W Green, 2009).

[2] Scottish Government, *The 5th UK Government Report to the UN Committee on the Rights of the Child: Scottish Government Submission* (June 2013), p. 2. The Submission is available via the Scottish Government website (scotland.gov.uk) at http://bit.ly/16PNQk1.

[3] *Ibid.*

[4] UK Government, *The Fifth Periodic Report to the UN Committee on the Rights of the Child: United Kingdom* (May 2014), available at http://bit.ly/ZgAt9E

F. McCarthy (✉)
School of Law, University of Glasgow, Glasgow G12 8QQ, Scotland
e-mail: frankie.mccarthy@glasgow.ac.uk

O. Cvejić Jančić (ed.), *The Rights of the Child in a Changing World*,
Ius Comparatum - Global Studies in Comparative Law 13,
DOI 10.1007/978-3-319-23189-1_14

2 The Legal Framework

2.1 Scotland and the United Kingdom

The United Kingdom is made up of three separate legal jurisdictions: England and Wales, Northern Ireland and Scotland.[5] While Anglo-Welsh law is a common law system, Scotland has a mixed legal system combining elements of both civil and common law traditions. Family law in Scotland is not contained within a code, but is set out primarily in legislation emanating from the Scottish Parliament at Holyrood. Some legislation made in the UK Parliament at Westminster and applicable throughout the UK is also of significance. In addition to the legislative material, case law is also relevant. The doctrine of precedent applies, so that Scots judges are bound by decisions of superior Scots courts on the same issues. Neither English legislation nor case law is applicable in Scotland, although the English approach to family law issues can provide a useful comparative perspective and is very influential in certain contexts.[6]

2.2 The UN Convention on the Rights of the Child

The Convention was signed by the United Kingdom on 19 April 1990 and ratified on 16 November 1991. Ratification was originally subject to a number of reservations on issues including employment legislation, juvenile detention and the children's hearings system,[7] but over time, all reservations have been withdrawn. Two declarations remain in place, however. The first states that the Convention is interpreted as applicable only following a live birth. The second states that references to 'parents' will be interpreted to mean only those who, as a matter of national law, are identified as parents. This includes situations where the child has only one legal parent, which may occur as the result of adoption or conception with biomedical assistance.

[5] A referendum on whether Scotland should become an independent country will take place on 18 September 2014. It is not possible here to consider the constitutional implications of a vote in favour of independence, but the domestic Scots law of the child, as outlined in this paper, is unlikely to be altered in its detail.

[6] For an example, see the discussion of the child's right to consent to medical treatment below.

[7] *Reservations and Declaration of the United Kingdom to the UN Convention on the Rights of the Child*, available via the United Nations Treaty Collection website (treaties.un.org) at http://bit.ly/stPC3m

2.3 *Defining 'the Child'*

The age of majority in Scotland is 18, as set out in the Age of Majority (Scotland) Act 1969, s1. For most aspects of legal capacity, however, the age of 16 is actually the more significant milestone. The Age of Legal Capacity (Scotland) Act 1991, s1 provides that a person aged 16 or over has legal capacity to enter into any transaction. A person aged 15 or under therefore has no legal capacity, although various exceptions to this rule are included in the Act, allowing a younger child to enter transactions of a kind commonly entered into by a person of his/her age and circumstances,[8] for example, and giving a child capacity to consent to his/her own adoption at age 12.[9] 'Young persons' aged 16 and 17 also benefit from some additional protections within the law, for example, where a young person enters into a contract that a prudent adult in the same circumstances would not have entered, the contract can be set aside.[10] Fundamentally, however, 16 is the age at which a person becomes fully *capax* in the eyes of the law. Parental responsibilities and rights end when the child turns 16,[11] with the exception of the responsibility to provide direction and guidance, which continues until the child is 18,[12] and the obligation to provide financial support, which continues until the child is 18 (or 25, if in full-time education or training.)[13]

The older Scottish framework of pupils and minors subsists, although only in so far as it does not conflict with the more recent rules of capacity outlined above.[14] The result is that the present-day significance of the older framework is very limited, and the explanation of it given here will accordingly be very brief. Children were divided into pupils (from birth to the age of 12 for girls, and from birth until the age of 14 for boys, the distinction in ages reflecting different ages for attaining puberty) and minors (from 12 or 14 until the age of 18.)[15] A pupil child generally had no active legal capacity, relying on his/her 'tutor' (his/her legal guardian, usually a parent) to carry out transactions on his/her behalf. A minor child had full legal capacity, provided that it was exercised with the concurrence of his/her 'curator' (again, his/her legal guardian.) At 18, full legal capacity was obtained.

[8] Age of Legal Capacity (Scotland) Act 1991, s2(1).

[9] *ibid.*, s2(3). An adoption order in respect of a child aged 12 or over cannot be made without the child's consent: Adoption and Children (Scotland) Act 2007, s32.

[10] Age of Legal Capacity (Scotland) Act 1991, s3.

[11] Children (Scotland) Act 1995, s1(2)(a) and s2(7).

[12] *ibid.*, s1(2)(b).

[13] Family Law (Scotland) Act 1985, s1(1) and (5).

[14] Age of Legal Capacity (Scotland) Act, s1(4).

[15] Erskine, i.7.1.

2.4 Implementation of the Convention in Scotland

The Convention is not directly applicable in Scotland, and there is no individual legal instrument devoted to the rights of the child in this jurisdiction. However, over the past 10 years, the Scottish Government has taken a series of steps to raise awareness of and improve compliance with children's Convention rights.

In 2003, the office of Children's Commissioner for Scotland was created.[16] The Commissioner has a general responsibility to promote and safeguard the rights of children and young people,[17] backed up by various specific obligations including the requirement to consult with children and young people[18] and to produce an annual report highlighting areas of concern in relation to human rights compliance.[19] In 2009, the Scottish Government published an action plan for children's rights entitled *Do The Right Thing*.[20] The action plan identified 21 areas for priority action in response to the CRC's Concluding Observations on the UK report submitted 2 years earlier,[21] ranging from general issues such as the promotion of children's rights within the Government to more particular concerns such as the treatment of 16- and 17-year-olds in the youth justice system. A progress report on the action plan was issued in May 2012.[22]

Perhaps most significantly to date, following a period of consultation in the summer of 2012,[23] the Children and Young People (Scotland) Act 2014 became law in March 2014 and will be brought into force in the next 2–3 years. The Act creates a duty on Scottish Ministers and all public bodies to have due regard to the Convention when exercising any of their functions and includes further responsibilities for the Government to promote and raise awareness of children's rights.[24] Additionally, the powers of the Children's Commissioner will be extended to allow investigations on behalf of individual children and young people.[25]

---

[16] Commissioner for Children and Young People (Scotland) Act 2003.

[17] *ibid.*, s4.

[18] *ibid.*, s6.

[19] *ibid.*, s10. The reports are available on the Commissioner's website (sccyp.org.uk) at http://bit.ly/18VMx2T

[20] *Do the Right Thing: for people who work with children or work on their behalf* (2009) available at http://bit.ly/14GldlR

[21] The UK Report is available via the UNHCR website (unhcr.org) at http://bit.ly/18p2haz. The Scottish contribution to that document was made available by the Scottish Government in its *Report on the Implementation of the UN Convention on the Rights of the Child in Scotland 1999–2007* (2007) available via the Scottish Government website at http://bit.ly/1gZBa94

[22] *Do the Right Thing – a progress report on our response to the 2008 concluding observations from the UN Committee on the Rights of the Child* (2012) available at http://bit.ly/18oPDKF

[23] *Consultation on Rights of Children and Young People Bill* (2011), available at http://bit.ly/1b52WQS

[24] Children and Young People (Scotland) Act 2014, ss1-3.

[25] *ibid.*, s5.

3 Key Convention Rights in National Law

It seems the Scottish Government has no plans at present to place the Convention on a wholly statutory footing, despite support for that option by the respondents to the consultation on the Children and Young People Bill.[26] This does not mean to say that Convention rights are not to be found anywhere within Scots law, however. Specific rights have been incorporated into statute, sometimes on a broad basis, sometimes in relation to particular aspects of family law. The following section will give examples of the Scottish approach by exploring the implementation of key Convention rights under articles 3, 7, 12 and 21.

3.1 Article 3: Best Interests of the Child

The 'best interests of the child' principle is not incorporated in Scotland by way of a broad constitutional norm. However, in the huge majority of legislation regulating the position of children within the law, the welfare of the child is expressly stated to be the paramount consideration. The 'welfare principle' applies to courts determining disputes over parental responsibilities and rights,[27] to state intervention in the lives of children and families,[28] to the adoption process[29] and so on. A more attenuated protection is occasionally found. For example, the UK-wide Child Support Act 1991, which regulates financial support in respect of children who do not reside with one or both parents, requires only that 'regard' be had to the welfare of the child concerned when decisions are taken under this statute.[30]

3.2 Article 7: The Right of the Child to Know His/Her Parents

3.2.1 Traditional Conception

In Scotland, the mother of a child conceived in the traditional way is the woman who gave birth to her. The father is presumed by law to be the man married to the mother between conception and birth,[31] or if she was not married, the man registered as the father on the child's birth certificate.[32]

---

[26] See note 24 above.

[27] Children (Scotland) Act 1995, s11(7)(a).

[28] *ibid.*, s16.

[29] Adoption and Children (Scotland) Act 2007, s14(3).

[30] Child Support Act 1991, s2.

[31] Law Reform (Parent and Child) Scotland Act 1986, s5(1)(a).

[32] *ibid.*, s5(1)(b).

Where there is doubt, it is possible to establish parentage, or to challenge presumed parentage, by way of a civil court action.[33] The court will issue an order declaring a named party to be a parent, or declaring that a presumed parent is not, in fact, a parent, if the position is proved on a balance of probabilities.[34] Proof is normally established by way of DNA profiling. Although the child concerned, a (presumptive) parent or any other person who can demonstrate an interest (e.g. a man who reasonably believes he is the child's father), is entitled to seek a court order, the difficulty in practice is that DNA evidence may be impossible to obtain. The court cannot compel an adult to provide a DNA sample.[35] The court may ask for a sample and 'draw such adverse inference as may be appropriate' from a refusal to provide a sample,[36] but an adverse inference by itself is unlikely to provide proof of parentage on a balance of probabilities. A child of sufficient maturity (presumed at age 12) may consent to giving a DNA sample for herself.[37] For a younger child, consent must be given on her behalf by a person who holds parental responsibilities and rights.[38] Again, such consent cannot be compelled, but an adverse inference can be drawn.

3.2.2 Conception with Biomedical Assistance

A child conceived with biomedical assistance has a right to access information about her conception from the age of 18. Where the donor registered prior to 1 April 2005, the child is entitled to non-identifying information about her biological parents, restricted principally to medical and genetic data. Where the donor registered on or after 1 April 2005, the child is entitled to identifying information.[39]

3.2.3 Adopted Children

The birth certificate of an adopted child in Scotland specifies that the information contained therein is derived from the Adopted Children Register. It is therefore difficult for a parent to conceal the fact of a child's adoption once he/she is of age to read and understand his/her birth certificate. An adopted person has the right of access to his/her birth records, which include the identity of his/her biological parents, from the age of 16.[40] Where a person seeks to exercise that right, the Registrar

[33] *ibid.*, s7.

[34] *ibid.*, s5(4).

[35] *Whitehall v Whitehall* 1958 SC 252; *Torrie v Turner* 1990 SLT 718.

[36] Law Reform (Miscellaneous Provisions) (Scotland) Act 1990, s70.

[37] Age of Legal Capacity (Scotland) Act 1991, s2(4).

[38] Law Reform (Parent and Child) Scotland Act 1986, s6(2).

[39] Human Fertilisation and Embryology Act 1990, s31ZA.

[40] Adoption and Children (Scotland) Act 2007, s55(4)(b).

General must advise his/her that counselling is available,[41] which the local authority is obliged to provide.[42] No other person has an automatic right to information, although they may apply to the court for disclosure of certain information.[43]

3.3 *Article 12: The Right of the Child to Express His/Her Views*

3.3.1 Family Life

Under the Children (Scotland) Act 1995, s6, a person reaching any major decision about a child's life which involves the exercise of parental responsibilities and rights must have regard to any view the child wishes to express on that decision, taking into account the child's age and maturity. A child aged 12 or older is presumed to be sufficiently mature to form a view.

3.3.2 Administrative and Judicial Proceedings

Where a court is asked to make an order in respect of parental responsibilities and rights, or to enable state intervention in a child's life in the form of supervision or taking the child into care, it must have regard to the child's views in respect of the order sought. This includes a specific obligation on the court to ascertain whether the child wishes to express a view at all.[44] The child is again presumed sufficiently mature to form a view at the age of 12.[45] In practice, courts will hear the view of a child of any age, although the view of a younger or less mature child may be given less weight in the decision-making process. Where a child is looked after by a local authority, the child is again entitled to express a view on any decision affecting his/her life.[46]

3.3.3 Advice and Information

The child has no formal right to information and advice in order to form a view, although parents are under a responsibility to provide a child with direction and guidance until the age of 18.[47] A child of sufficient age and maturity (again presumed

[41] *ibid.*, s55(5)(a).

[42] *ibid.*, s55(6) and (7).

[43] *ibid.*, s55(4)(a).

[44] Children (Scotland) Act 1995, s11(7)(b) and s16.

[45] *ibid.*, s11(10).

[46] *ibid.*, s17(3) and (4).

[47] *ibid.*, s1(1)(b) and (2)(b).

at age 12) has capacity to instruct a solicitor in respect of civil matters.[48] Where a child does not have capacity and his/her interests conflict with those of his/her parent, the court may appoint a curator ad litem to represent him/her.[49]

In practice, giving children capacity to sue their parents (or other persons) is of little value unless access to legal aid by children is also ensured. A child aged 12 or over, instructing a solicitor without parental assistance, may apply for civil legal aid or legal advice and assistance, conditional only on the solicitor instructed enclosing a letter confirming that he/she has satisfied himself/herself that the child does indeed have a general understanding of what it means to instruct a solicitor.[50] For a child under 12, the procedure is the same except that the Legal Aid Board reserves the right to query any such letter, for example, if the child appears unreasonably young.[51]

Although the Legal Aid Board appears satisfied that the solicitor's view of the child's capacity is sufficient, the statute actually gives no guidance on who should perform that assessment. In England, where a similar rule exists, the job of assessment of capacity has in some cases been assumed by judges, some of whom have shown hostility to the independent representation of children.[52] In Scotland, there are as yet no reported cases where judges have intervened to declare a child is not of sufficient capacity to instruct a lawyer. However, occasional judicial hostility to the entry of children into the process can be detected. In *Henderson v Henderson*,[53] the concern of the sheriff was the increased drain on the legal aid fund caused by additional parties to an action, particularly where (as in this case) the child's views coincided with those of his/her mother. In *B v B*,[54] Sheriff Principal Bowen refused a 12-year-old child leave to enter the process in respect of an action concerning contact arrangements for himself and his sister on the basis of the markedly more paternalistic concern that it would not be in his best interests to subject him to pressures of the litigation, in addition to which it was not clear that he could give instructions of anything other than a restricted nature.[55] It is arguable whether this decision gave proper weight to the child's right to participate in judicial proceedings affecting his interests.[56]

---

[48] Age of Legal Capacity (Scotland) Act 1991, s2(4A.).

[49] *ibid.*, s1(3)(f).

[50] This is the test set out in the Age of Legal Capacity (Scotland) Act, s2(4A).

[51] The legal foundation of the right to apply for legal aid under the age of 16 is found in the Legal Aid (Scotland) Act 1986, ss.28B-S. Legal aid must be 'in the *best* interests of the child' under s28D(3).

[52] *Re H* [1994] All ER 762.

[53] 1997 Fam LR 120.

[54] 2011 SLT (Sh Ct) 225.

[55] The case was complicated by the fact the child had previously been represented by a curator, in whom he had lost confidence part way through the proof after 5 days of evidence had been heard. The sheriff principal was understandably influenced by the fact that, had the child been permitted to enter the process in his own right, the witnesses would likely have had to be recalled for fresh cross-examination and the proof further delayed.

[56] But see *Fourman v Fourman*, 1998 Fam. L.R. 98, where the sheriff commented positively on the appropriateness of a 14-year-old child's decision to join the action as party minuter, with independent legal representation.

3.4 *Article 21: Adoption*

3.4.1 Child's Consent to Adoption

A child has capacity to consent to his/her own adoption at age 12.[57] An adoption order in respect of a child aged 12 or over cannot be made without the child's consent.[58]

3.4.2 Intercountry Adoption

The UK is a signatory state to the Hague Convention on Protection of Children and Co-operation in Respect of Intercountry Adoption of 1993[59] ('the Hague Convention), which was implemented in Scotland by way of the Adoption (Intercountry Aspects) Act 1999. It is highly unusual for children habitually resident in Scotland to be placed for adoption in a country which is not also a signatory to the Hague Convention, and that process will not be considered here.

Prospective adopters habitually resident in another Hague Convention country are subject to the same eligibility criteria as domestic adopters. Applications can be made by couples (defined as persons who are married, in civil partnership, or who live together as if married or in civil partnership)[60] or by single persons. A single applicant must prove that he/she is not a member of a couple,[61] unless he/she is a step-parent applying to adopt the child of his/her spouse or partner.[62] Applicants must be at least 21 years old.[63]

In order to be considered for adoption, the child must be under 18 years of age, and intercountry adoption must have been assessed as in the best interests of the child.[64] The assessment is carried out by the local authority, with consideration of recommendations made by the adoption panel and of the views of the child where appropriate.[65] Where prospective adopters are identified, the adoption panel makes recommendations on their suitability, and the local authority again determines whether the proposed placement is in the child's best interests having regard to the panel's recommendations and the child's views.[66] The adoption cannot proceed

[57] Age of Legal Capacity (Scotland) Act 1991, s2(3).

[58] Adoption and Children (Scotland) Act 2007, s32.

[59] 32 ILM 1134.

[60] Adoption and Children (Scotland) Act 2007, s29(3).

[61] *ibid.*, ss30(1)(b) and (2).

[62] *ibid.*, ss30(1)(3).

[63] *ibid.*, ss29(1) and 30(1).

[64] Intercountry Adoption (Scotland) Regulations 1999, reg 30.

[65] *ibid.*, regs 22–24.

[66] *ibid.*, regs 25 and 26.

unless the local authority has met the prospective adopters, they have visited the child and the local authority is content for the adoption to proceed.[67]

4 Current Issues in Children's Rights

The implementation of specific Convention rights by way of legislation does not tell the whole story of the Convention's influence on Scots family law. Consideration of some currently topical issues in respect of the law on children's rights will help to illustrate the broad impact the Convention has had on lawmakers and the judiciary, whilst also highlighting areas in which work remains to be done. A key theme in this section is balance: where should the balance be struck between the right of a child to protection and the right to autonomy or self-determination? Relatedly, what is the correct balance between the rights of parents and the rights of children? Although arguments can be made as to whether the balance has been correctly struck in each of the following examples, it is nevertheless encouraging to find that the rights and needs of children at the heart of the decisions which have been made.

4.1 Religious Education and the Right to Freedom of Thought, Conscience and Religion

In Scotland, regional education authorities have an obligation to make available both religious observance and non-confessional religious instruction in all state-funded schools,[68] unless a resolution to discontinue this has been passed by the education authority and approved by electors in that local authority area.[69] Although not prescribed by statute, governmental policy guidance to education authorities indicates that the content of these activities should reflect the full range of faiths, or absence of faith, of pupils and teachers within the school community.[70]

Parents have the right to withdraw their children from both observance and instruction,[71] failing which attendance will be required as it would be for any other lesson. An interesting question is whether the child has an independent right to withdraw from religious activities once of sufficient age and maturity. The child's right to education is incorporated into domestic statute in Scotland,[72] along with a

[67] *ibid.* reg 27(6).

[68] Education (Scotland)Act 1980, s8(1).

[69] *ibid.*, s8(2).

[70] Scottish Government, *Curriculum for Excellence – provision of religious observance in schools* (2011), available at http://bit.ly/WHT3pf

[71] Education (Scotland) Act 1980, s9.

[72] Standards in Scotland's Schools Act 2000, s1.

right to express his/her views on educational decisions which affect his/her life.[73] As discussed below, a 'mature minor' has the right to consent to medical treatment,[74] with some authority suggesting that he/she is also entitled to refuse such treatment, even where this conflicts with his/her parents' wishes or may not be in his/her best interests.[75] By analogy, it could be argued that a mature minor should be entitled to withdraw from religious observance or non-confessional education even if this conflicts with the wishes of his/her parents. There is no reported instance of such a situation being brought to the attention of the courts, however, so the question remains unresolved at present.

4.2 Physical Punishment and the Right to Protection from Abuse

Physical punishment of children is not permitted in schools or other institutions that take care of children.[76] Child minders and foster carers are prohibited from using corporal punishment on children in their care.[77] Physical punishment by persons holding parental responsibilities and rights will normally be categorised as criminal assault. However, a defence of 'justifiable assault' may be invoked. The court will determine whether an assault is justifiable having regard to the nature of the punishment, the reason for it and the circumstances in which it took place; its duration and frequency; any physical or mental effect on the child; the child's age; the child's personal characteristics including sex and state of health at the time of the punishment; and any other relevant circumstances.[78] An assault will not be considered justifiable where it includes a blow to the head, shaking or use of an implement.[79]

In 2008, the CRC emphasised that the current law on physical punishment of children does not comply with the terms of the Convention and reiterated the recommendation made in previous reports that all forms of corporal punishment within the family be prohibited as a matter of priority.[80] The Scottish Government, in its contribution to the UK report submitted in 2014, appeared unmoved, with no plans

[73] *ibid.*, s2.

[74] Age of Legal Capacity (Scotland) Act 1991, s2(4).

[75] *Houston, Applicant*, 1996 SCLR 943.

[76] Standards in Scotland's Schools Act 2000, s16.

[77] *ibid.*, ss16 and 19.

[78] Criminal Justice (Scotland) Act 2003, ss51(1) and (2).

[79] *ibid.*, s51(3).

[80] UN Committee on the Rights of the Child (CRC), *Consideration of reports submitted by States parties under article 44 of the Convention: Convention on the Rights of the Child: United Kingdom of Great Britain and Northern Ireland*, 20 October 2008, CRC/C/GBR/CO/4, paras 40–42. Available at: http://www.refworld.org/docid/4906d1d72.html

to change the law.[81] This is an area in which the rights of parents could be said to have been prioritised at the expense of the rights of children. Full implementation of the Convention might be needed to effect change.

4.3 Deprivation of Parental Responsibilities and the Right to Family Life

The court is empowered to deprive a person of some or all of his/her parental responsibilities and rights.[82] In deciding whether to make such an order, the welfare of the child is the paramount consideration, and no order should be made unless it would be better for the child to do so than not.[83] The court must also take into account any views expressed by the child concerned, subject to his/her age and maturity.[84]

The court is also empowered to make a permanence order[85] or an adoption order[86] in respect of the child where such an order is sought by the local authority responsible for the child. The welfare of the child is again the paramount consideration guiding both the local authority and the court.[87] A permanence order has the effect of vesting primary responsibility for the child's residence in the local authority[88] and may also deprive the child's parents of some or all of their responsibilities and rights.[89] A child subject to a permanence order is likely to be placed with a foster family or in local authority care, including residential care. He/she may or may not continue to have contact with his/her parents. Depending on the circumstances, the child may eventually return to living with his/her parents, whose rights will be restored. Alternatively, he/she may remain with a foster family or in local authority care until he/she reaches full legal capacity at the age of 16. As a final alternative, a child subject to a permanence order may later be adopted,[90] although a permanence order is not a necessary prerequisite to adoption.

An adoption order removes rights from the birth parents[91] and vests them in the adoptive parents.[92] This cannot normally be done without the consent of the

---

[81] Scottish Government, *The 5th UK Government Report to the UN Committee on the Rights of the Child: Scottish Government Submission* (June 2013), p. 18.

[82] Children (Scotland) Act 1995, s11(2)(a).

[83] *ibid.*, s11(7)(a).

[84] *ibid.*, s11(7)(b).

[85] Adoption and Children (Scotland) Act 2007, s80.

[86] *ibid.*, s28.

[87] Children (Scotland) Act 1995, s16; Adoption and Children (Scotland) Act 2007, s14(3).

[88] Adoption and Children (Scotland) Act 2007, ss80 and 81.

[89] *ibid.*, s82.

[90] *ibid.*, s28(5).

[91] *ibid.*, s35.

[92] *ibid.*, s28(1).

birth parents.[93] Parental consent can be dispensed with if the parent is deceased, cannot be found or is incapable of giving consent.[94] More controversially, parental consent can be dispensed with by the court where required for the child's welfare.[95] This provision was challenged on the grounds that it did not comply with the rights of birth parents under article 8 of the ECHR, but the UK Supreme Court found the interference with parents' rights to be justified by the need to protect the rights of the child, bringing the legislation within the ambit of article 8(2) ECHR.[96]

It is possible for conditions to be attached to an adoption order, including the condition that the child should continue to have contact with his/her birth parents.[97] Accordingly, a form of 'open adoption' is available in Scotland, although 'simple adoption' on the French model, whereby the child retains his/her birth name and inheritance rights, cannot be done here.

4.4 'Mature Minors' and Consent to Medical Treatment

A child under the age of 16 may consent to surgical, medical or dental treatment where, in the opinion of the practitioner treating him/her, he/she is capable of understanding the nature and possible consequences of that treatment.[98]

Whether the power to consent to treatment carries with it the power to refuse treatment is not clear. The legislation enabling a 'mature minor' to give consent to medical treatment in Scotland is a statutory recapitulation of the decision in the English case of *Gillick v West Norfolk and Wisbech Area Health Authority*.[99] In that case, Lord Scarman indicated that:

> [...] parental right yields to the child's right to make his own decisions where he reaches a sufficient understanding and intelligence to be capable of making up his own mind on the matter requiring decision.[100]

The implication seems to be that parental rights come to an end once the child reaches sufficient maturity. This is a logical extension of the common law principle that one adult cannot override the consent of another. In the sole Scottish authority commenting on the issue, *Houston, Applicant*,[101] the sheriff was satisfied that a mother could not give consent to medical treatment of her 15-year-old son, who had

---

[93] *ibid.*, ss31(1) and (2).

[94] *ibid.*, ss31(1), (2)(b) and (3)(a)-(c).

[95] *ibid.*, ss31(1), (2)(b) and (3)(d).

[96] *S v L (also known as ML v ANS)* [2012] UKSC 30.

[97] *ibid.*, s28(3).

[98] Age of Legal Capacity (Scotland) Act 1991, s2(4).

[99] [1985] 3 All ER 402.

[100] *ibid.*, at 422a.

[101] 1996 SCLR 943.

been assessed as capable of understanding the decision and had clearly refused treatment. The decision in the case did not turn on this issue, however, meaning the views of the court have less force than they might have had. Scottish academic commentators tend to the view that the right to consent carries with it the right to refuse[102] and current National Health Service guidance to medical professionals in Scotland recommends that where a competent person under 16 refuses treatment, the refusal must be respected.[103]

English case law subsequent to *Gillick* suggests a different interpretation, however. In *Re R* (A Minor),[104] Lord Donaldson suggested that a mature minor and his/her parent were both 'keyholders' to consent, and either might use his/her key regardless of the position of the other. This view was reiterated in *Re W*.[105]

The weight of evidence favours an interpretation that a mature minor is able to refuse treatment in Scotland. Until a Scots court is able to give a view on the English authorities, however, it is difficult to claim that this interpretation is a definitive statement of the law.

4.5 Right to Change of Name

A child has no independent right to change his/her personal name in Scotland. A person holding parental responsibilities and rights is empowered to register the child's name on birth[106] and also to make a change to the name registered by way of substitution, addition or omission on one occasion prior to the child's 16th birthday.[107] A child could not make a change without concurrence of his/her parent(s). Were a conflict to arise between parent and child, in principle, the child could ask the court to resolve the dispute,[108] which it should by reference to the welfare test.[109] The practicality of such a solution is doubtful, however.

[102] L Edwards, "The right to consent and the right to refuse" 1993 *Juridical Review* 52; S Elliston, *The Best Interests of the Child in Healthcare* (2007, Routledge Cavendish), p. 112.

[103] *A Good Practice Guide on Consent for Health Professionals in NHS Scotland* (2006, Scottish Executive Health Dept), ch 2.

[104] [1991] 4 All ER 177.

[105] [1992] 4 All ER 62.

[106] *M v C* 2002 SLT (Sh Ct) 82.

[107] Registration of Births, Deaths and Marriages (Scotland) Act 1965, s43. Where two or more people hold parental rights, a joint application must be made.

[108] Children (Scotland) Act 1995, ss11(2)(d), (3)(a) and (5).

[109] *ibid.*, s11(7).

4.6 Employment

Regulation of employment is not contained within one statute, but rather is dealt with on a piecemeal basis primarily in local authority bye-laws. As a general rule, children are not allowed to work in factories or industrial sites, in licenced premises such as betting shops or pubs, and more generally, may not undertake work that may be harmful to their health, well-being or education. Normally, it is not possible for a child younger than 13 to be employed in any capacity, other than as a performer (e.g. acting or modelling). A producer seeking to employ a child as a performer must acquire a performance licence from the local authority in respect of that child. The local authority will not grant the licence unless satisfied that the child's education will not suffer as a result.

At 13, a child can be employed by his/her parents to do occasional light gardening or farmwork, or by other parties to do occasional light work of a kind specified in local bye-laws. At 14, a child can be employed to do light work for 5 h on a Saturday and 2 h on school days and Sundays, but not before 7am or after 7pm, and not for more than a total of 12 h per week. During school holidays, a weekly limit of 25 h applies, and a child must be allowed at least two work-free weeks. The same limitations apply at age 15, except that the daily cap is raised to 8 h per day on a Saturday and the weekly cap to 35 h during school holidays. Parental consent is not usually required.

Once a person turns 16 and reaches school-leaving age, he/she is dealt with under adult employment law. She can obtain a full-time job (40 h per week) and is liable to pay National Insurance. However, the national minimum wage is set at a much lower rate for 16- and 17-year-olds (£3.72 per hour), and a slightly lower rate for 18–20-year-olds (£5.03 per hour), than for those aged 21 and over (£6.31 per hour.)

4.7 Children's Responsibilities

Scots law does not lay down any obligation of the child towards his/her parents.

5 Conclusion

It is encouraging to see the Scottish Government's expressed commitment to children's rights backed up by concrete developments in the law. Many of the key rights encompassed by the Convention have found their way into legislation, with the welfare principle in particular long established as a key stone of child law in Scotland. The wider influence of the Convention can also be felt in the legal responses to currently topical issues, where increasing recognition of the capacity of children to make autonomous decisions in areas such as medical treatment and education is to be welcomed. The passing into law of the Children and Young People (Scotland) Act 2014 is the most significant step yet towards implementation of the Convention in domestic law.

However, Scotland must not rest on its laurels. The continuing availability of the 'justifiable assault' defence remains difficult to reconcile with the welfare principle, and the practical difficulties attending the child's right to express a view in judicial and administrative proceedings need to be addressed. At the most fundamental level, regardless of the extent to which the Convention has influenced Scottish national law, it still does not form part of Scottish national law. Perhaps this omission is one the Government might be persuaded to rectify before the Convention reaches its 25th anniversary.

The Rights of the Child in Serbia

Nevena Vučković Šahović and Ivana Savić

1 Introduction

The Republic of Serbia is one of the "new" states on the world map. In 2006, after almost 90 years of being incorporated in broader state unions, Serbia has become an independent state.

The implementation of the Convention on the Rights of the Child (hereinafter: *the CRC* or *the Convention*) in Serbia has been impacted by the long-term consequences of the wars in the region during the 1990s and transition from socialist to market economy. The current political situation in Serbia is characterised by a struggling coalition government, still inadequate rule of law, high degree of corruption, mismanaged economy and slow decentralisation process. Needless to say, all this has an impact on the realisation of the rights of child in the country. A large number of children in Serbia still live in poverty.[1] Persistent political problems shift focus from economic issues and stall reforms. Two major economic problems are unemployment and low level of productivity.[2]

[1] See Government of the Republic of Serbia. 2011. *First National Report on Social Inclusion and Poverty reduction in the Republic of Serbia: The Status of Social Exclusion and Poverty Trends in the period 2008–2010 and future priorities.*

[2] See World Bank Europe and Central Asia region Poverty Reduction and Economic Management Department (ECA PREM). 2012. *South East Europe: Regular Economic Report No.3. From Double-Dip Recession to Accelerated Reforms.*

N.V. Šahović (✉)
Svetozara Markovica 24, Beograd 11000, Serbia
e-mail: vnevena17@gmail.com

I. Savić, L.L.M.
Bulevar vojvode Putnika 12a, Beograd 11000, Serbia
e-mail: ivana.savich@gmail.com

O. Cvejić Jančić (ed.), *The Rights of the Child in a Changing World*,
Ius Comparatum - Global Studies in Comparative Law 13,
DOI 10.1007/978-3-319-23189-1_15

Serbia still struggles with negative attitudes towards the rights of the child, which can be witnessed in any stratum of the society. That includes teachers, social workers, judiciary, health professionals, members of Parliament, government officials and many others.[3] Often, efforts to implement the CRC or to claim rights of the child involve not only legal but also social and moral actions to overcome obstacles imposed by the dominant social discourse. Due to still conservative approaches to the rights of the child, some pertaining areas are difficult to deal with in Serbia. For example, violence against children is a big problem in Serbia – the attitude towards violence against children, particularly in schools and families, is still very conservative. Furthermore, corporal punishment is still an acceptable disciplinary measure in the upbringing of children, and though forbidden by law, it is still often used in educational, state care and penitentiary institutions. An increase and change in the nature of violence, especially peer violence, is of particular concern.[4]

This paper offers insight into the implementation of selected rights of the child in Serbia and suggests some general and law reform-specific recommendations for improvements.

2 The State of the Rights of the Child

The ratification of the Convention on the Rights of the Child by the Republic of Serbia has enabled direct implementation of the Convention in the national legislation. The Convention was ratified in 1990 (by the Socialist Federative Republic of Yugoslavia) when the Law on Ratification of the Convention on the Rights of the Child[5] was adopted. Serbia, as one of the former Yugoslav republics and an independent State since 2006, has undertaken the commitments made upon ratification.

Since the initial ratification of the CRC, Serbia has significantly improved its legal framework for the rights of the child; however it is still not enough. Over the years the Republic of Serbia has made significant efforts to harmonise national legislation with the Convention and adopt numerous laws that significantly advance the rights of the child in the country. Some of the laws of particular importance are Family Law (2005),[6] Law for Prevention of Discrimination against Persons with

[3] See The Children's Coalition for Reporting on Child Rights in Serbia. 2008. *Alternative Report-Child Rights in Serbia: the Children's Perspective*. The Children's Coalition for Reporting on Child Rights in Serbia. available at: http://www.crin.org/resources/infoDetail.asp?ID=16483&flag=legal

[4] Petrović, Marija… et al. 2013. Izveštaj o ostvarivanju opštih mera primene Konvencije o pravima deteta U Republici Srbiji. Beograd: Centar za prava deteta, p. 17

[5] Official Gazette of SFRJ – International contracts N° 15/90 and Official Gazette of SRJ – International Contracts N° 4/96 and 2/97

[6] Family Law (Official Gazette of Republic of Serbia, N° 18/2005 and 72/2011)

Disabilities (2006),[7] Law on Juvenile Criminal Offenders and Criminal Protection of Juveniles (2006),[8] Law on the Foundations of the Education System (2009),[9] Law on the Prohibition of Discrimination (2009),[10]Law on Registry Books (2009),[11]Public Information Law (2009),[12]Law on Associations (2009),[13] Law on Social Protection (2011),[14] etc.

Serbia does not have a special legal instrument which is devoted to the rights of the child. Of particular importance is that the 2006 Constitution of Serbia (hereinafter: *the Constitution*) for the first time guaranteed the rights of the child, more specifically the right to a personal name, the right to birth registration, the right to learn about his/her origins, the right to preserve his/her own identity, and the right to protection from psychological, corporal, economic or any other form of exploitation or abuse, and guarantees equal treatment of children born out of wedlock.[15] Additionally, the Constitution guarantees child rights[16] and their protection by law. Such a constitutional provision is a guarantee of the codification of the rights of the child, namely, through the adoption of *lex specialis* for the rights of the child, Child Rights Law.[17] However, in spite of the efforts made, particularly by the Protector of Citizens,[18] to initiate the adoption of such law, it is still missing. Hence, within the Serbian legal system, there are over 80 laws relevant to the realisation of rights in the Convention of the Rights of the Child and its optional protocols. Such regulation of the rights of the child represents an obstacle for a proper realisation of those rights, especially as it complicates access to justice for children and effective protection of rights. Such a legal framework for the rights of the child would indicate also that in each and every area relevant thereof, there should be specialised professionals for working with and for children, which is currently not the case. The lack of effective mechanisms for monitoring of the implementation of the rights of the child represents another obstacle.

---

[7] Law for Prevention of Discrimination against Persons with Disabilities (Official Gazette of Republic of Serbia, N° 33/2006)

[8] Law on Juvenile Criminal Offenders and Criminal Protection of Juveniles (Official Gazette of Republic of Serbia, N° 85/2005)

[9] Law on the Foundations of the Education System (Official Gazette of Republic of Serbia, N° 72/2009 and 52/2011)

[10] Law on the Prohibition of Discrimination (Official Gazette of Republic of Serbia, N° 22/2009)

[11] Law on Registry Books (Official Gazette of Republic of Serbia, N° 20/2009)

[12] Public Information Law (Official Gazette of Republic of Serbia, N° 43/2003, 61/2005, 71/2009, 89/2010- Constitutional Court Decision and 41/2011- Constitutional Court Decision)

[13] Law on Associations (Official Gazette of Republic of Serbia, N° 51/2009 and 99/2011- other laws)

[14] Law on Social Protection (Official Gazette of Republic of Serbia, N° 24/2011)

[15] Constitution, Art. 64

[16] *Ibid.*

[17] Similarly to that see UN Doc. CRC/C/SRB/CO/1

[18] The institution is also known as Ombudsperson.

2.1 Definition of the Child

The Serbian legal system does not have universally accepted definition of the child. However, the general age below which a human being is deemed a child is derived from the concept of age of majority, which is reached at the age of 18.[19] Furthermore, different laws use different terms to define the child and age limit, as well as terms related to children.

The Constitution of the Republic of Serbia[20] considers that a child is a person who has not reached the age of majority,[21] except in Article 32 on the right to a fair trial in which it refers to children as *minors*. It is interesting to note that not only the Constitution but also other laws use the term *minor*, a term that describes a person who is under the age of legal competence. The use of the term *minor* reflects a paternalistic approach to children, which influences the legal position of children in Serbia as objects rather than subjects of rights. Furthermore, the laws differentiate between children within the different age groups by defining them as *younger* and *senior minors*. Even though it is necessary to acknowledge different levels of development and competencies within the age group 0–18, we consider the term *minor* as an inappropriate term, and we believe that the terminology relating to the definition of the child should be changed so as to properly reflect the essence of the rights of the child: the child.

The Family Law does not explicitly define the child. The Law considers a child as a person who has not reached the *age of majority*. In addition, when it comes to legal capacity of children, the Law makes a distinction between persons under the age of 14 that are regarded as *younger minors* and persons below the age of 14 and under the age of 18 that are regarded as *senior/mature minors*. When it comes to social protection of children, the Law on Social Protection defines the child as a *minor* and *child* without making any distinction within the age group 0–18,[22] which indicated that within the social protection system all children are regarded equally.

In criminal matters, the concept of the child significantly differs from the concept of the child in family and social welfare matters. The Criminal Code[23] defines the child as a person under 14 and *minor* as a person between the age of 14 and 18.[24] However, the Criminal Code in its Article 163[25] introduces the term *young people* without defining it, which brings additional legal uncertainty, especially taking into account that there is a definition of youth in the Serbian legal system. Similarly to that, the Law on Juvenile Criminal Offenders and Criminal Protection of Juveniles defines children as persons under the age of 14, and persons aged 14–18 are regarded

---

[19] Constitution, Art. 37 and Family Law, Art. 11

[20] Right to a fair trial

[21] Age of 18

[22] Art. 41

[23] Criminal Code (Official Gazette of Republic of Serbia, N° 85/2005, 88/2005 – corrected, 107/2005 – corrected, 72/2009, 111/2009 and 121/2012)

[24] Art. 112, paras. 9–10

[25] Violation of Labour Rights and Social Security Rights

as *juveniles*,[26] among which there is a distinction between younger, aged between 14 and 16, and older, aged between 16 and 18.

As noted above, there is a definition of *youth* in the Law on Youth[27] that represents the codification and recognition of the rights of the youth within Serbian legal system. According to the Law, a youth is defined as person above the age 15 and under the age of 30.[28] Such definition of the youth leads to the conclusion that in accordance with that Law, a child is a person under the age of 15, and hence that different legal regime would apply to children below and above the age of 15 which might be in conflict with regime imposed by other laws.

In general, in the Republic of Serbia, it could be considered that the age limit below which a human being is deemed a child is 18 years, but not in all circumstances, which amounts to an unequal treatment of the child in domestic legislation. Such inconsistencies in definition of the child additionally complicate the realisation, protection and advancement of the rights of the child and could be eliminated by introduction of a supreme norm in a comprehensive and organic child rights act.

2.2 *Specific Rights of the Child*

2.2.1 Best Interest of the Child

The best interest of the child is not only one of the rights in the CRC[29] but also one of the basic principles of that treaty. The best interest of the child is referred to in the Constitution only in the context of revoking all or specific rights of one or both parents by a court ruling, only if such action is in the best interest of the child, but not in other matters.[30] However, such a constitutional limitation is somewhat overcome by Article 6, paragraph 1 of the Family Law: "everyone is under the obligation to act in the best interest of the child in all activities related to the child". Furthermore, the Family Law refers to the best interest of the child in other provisions – life with parents, personal relationship, exercise of parental rights, adoption, foster care and divorce.

2.2.2 The Right to Participation

The second basic principle of the Convention on the Rights of the child is enshrined in its Article 12, which obliges states parties to enable respect or the views of the child. The popular term used for that right is the *right to participation*.[31] Serbian

---

[26] Additional problem is of a semantic nature: in Serbian language there is one word for both *minor* and *juvenile*.

[27] Law on Youth (Official Gazette of Republic of Serbia, N° 50/2011)

[28] Art. Art. 3, para. 1

[29] CRC, Art. 3

[30] Art. 65

[31] CRC, Art. 12

Family Law does not proclaim as a principle the right of the child to express his/her views within his/her family. However, the Law foresees the right of the child to freely express his/her opinion in particular legal proceedings.[32] A child who has reached the age of 10 may freely and directly express his/her opinion within every court or administrative proceeding where his/her rights are decided upon. In addition, a child who has reached 10 years of age may address the court or an administrative body, by himself/herself or through another person or institution, and request assistance in realisation of his/her right to free expression of opinion.[33] The child does not need to grow up to a certain age before he/she can enjoy the right to express his/her views, except in cases of court and administrative proceedings for which it is required that the child is at the age of 10 or above.[34] Furthermore, according to Article 65 of the Family Law, a child has the right to duly receive all information necessary to form his/her own opinion. Depending on the given circumstances, a certain type of professional will be relevant and tasked with providing the child information that is necessary to form his/her opinion – i.e. health professional is in charge for providing the necessary information on the medical treatment. The Family Law foresees that the child who has reached 10 years of age and who is capable of reasoning has to give his/her consent to adoption.[35]

2.2.3 Right to Identity

The Convention on the Rights of the Child recognises rights of the child to acquire and preserve identity,[36] which encompasses several rights such as the right of the child to birth registration, right to name, right to know his/her origins, right to acquire a nationality and a right not to be a subject of illicit transfer and non-return.

The Constitution of the Republic of Serbia in the Article 64 recognises a right of every child to know about his/her origin, which is in compliance with the Convention. Similarly, Article 59 of the Family Law recognises the right of the child to know about his/her origin and at the same time imposes limitations to this right. The limitations introduced by the Family Law are related to the biological identity or genetic and medical information important for the child, that includes, but it is not limited to the establishment of the biological maternity and paternity.

The mother of the child is considered to be the woman who gave birth to the child and who is registered as such in the register of births. The maternity of the woman entered in the register of births as the child's mother can be contested, and hence the child and the woman claiming to be the child's mother have the right to establishment of maternity.[37] If the woman who gave birth to the child is not entered

---

[32] Art. 65

[33] Ibid.

[34] Ibid.

[35] Art. 98

[36] CRC, Arts. 7, 8 and 11

[37] Family Law, Art. 43

in the register of births as the child's mother, her maternity may be established by a final court judgment.

The situation with the establishment of paternity slightly differs than that relating to the establishment of maternity. If paternity is not established by acknowledgement, it may be established by a final court judgment. The establishment of paternity in such cases can be initiated by the child, the mother and the man claiming to be the child's father.[38] Paternity can also be contested. The paternity of a man entered in the register of births as the child's father can be contested by the child, the mother, the mother's husband and the man claiming to be the father, if he, by the same action, requests the establishing of his paternity.[39] In Serbian law, an adopted child has a right to know who his/her biological parents are. A child who has reached the age of 15 and who is able to reason has the right to inspect the register of births and other documentation related to his/her origin.[40]

When it comes to a child conceived with biomedical assistance, he/she has a right to know who his/her parents are. Family Law defines the mother of the child conceived through biomedical assistance as the woman who gave birth to the child. If the child is conceived through biomedical assistance by a donated ovum, the maternity of the woman who donated the ovum may not be established.[41] Similarly to that, the mother's husband or mother's cohabitee is to be considered the father of the child conceived through biomedical assistance if he gave prior written consent to the procedure of biomedically assisted fertilisation, and paternity in such cases cannot be contested. If the child is conceived through biomedical assistance by donated semen cells, the paternity of the man who donated the semen cells may not be established.[42] The Law on Infertility Treatment and on Biomedically Assisted Procreation[43] goes even further and prohibits establishment of maternity and paternity of donors of biological material.[44] According to the Law on Infertility Treatment and on Biomedically Assisted Procreation, the child conceived with biomedical assistance has a right to know the donor's medical data only if legitimate medical reasons exist,[45] but it does not regulate in which situations legitimate medical reason exists.

Every child has the right to a name. However, according to the Family Law, the child who has reached the age of 10 and who is capable of reasoning has the right to give consent to the change of his/her personal name, while the child who has reached 15 years of age and who is able to reason has the right to change his/her

[38] Family Law, Art. 55

[39] Family Law, Art. 56

[40] Family Law, Art. 59

[41] Family Law, Art. 57

[42] Family Law, Art. 58

[43] Law on Infertility Treatment and on Biomedically Assisted Procreation (Official Gazette of Republic of Serbia, N° 72/2009)

[44] Arts 65 and 66

[45] Art. 64

personal name.[46] The child's surname may be changed upon establishment of maternity or paternity or upon contesting of maternity or paternity.[47] An adopted child's surname may be changed according to the surname of one or both adopters.[48] The child who has changed his/her surname by adoption may take back his/her surname after the termination of adoption by annulment.[49]

2.2.4 Freedom of Religion

Serbia is a secular state. However, in 2000 the religious education was introduced into the Serbian educational system. Article 22 of the Law on Primary Education[50] and Article 27 of the Law on Secondary Education[51] introduce religious education along with the civic education as an optional subject. In accordance with Article 20 of the Law on Primary Education and Article 24 of the Law on Secondary Education, religious education should teach about traditional churches and religious communities. The curriculum for religion studies is adopted in agreement between the Minister of Education and the Minister of Religion, at the agreed proposal of the traditional churches and religious communities that are Serbian Orthodox Church, Islamic Community, Catholic Church, Slovakian Evangelical Church, Jewish Community, Christian Reformed Church and Evangelical Christian Church.

2.2.5 Intercountry Adoption

Serbia has not ratified the Hague Convention on Protection of Children and Co-operation in Respect of Intercountry Adoption,[52] even though the Law on ratification is in procedure of adoption.[53] The Family Law and the Law on Nationality of the Republic of Serbia regulate intercountry adoption.[54] When it comes to the intercountry adoption, there are three situations:

---

[46] Art. 346

[47] Art. 349

[48] *Ibid.*

[49] Art. 349

[50] Law on Primary Education (Official Gazette of Republic of Serbia, N° 50/92, 53/93, 67/93, 48/94, 66/94 – Constitutional Court Decision, 22/2002, 62/2003 – other law, 64/2003 – correction of other law, 101/2005 – other laws and 72/2009 – other law)

[51] Law on Secondary Education (Official Gazette of Republic of Serbia, N° 50/92, 53/93, 67/93, 48/94, 24/96, 23/2002, 25/2002 - correction, 62/2003 – other law, 64/2003 – correction of other law, 101/2005 – other law, 72/2009 – other law and 55/2013 – other law)

[52] Hague Conference on Private International Law, *Hague Convention on the Protection of Children and Co-operation in Respect of Intercountry*, 29 May 1993, 33

[53] http://www.paragraf.rs/dnevne-vesti/140213/140213-vest2.html

[54] Law on Nationality of the Republic of Serbia (Official Gazette of Republic of Serbia, N° 135/2004 and 90/2007)

1. When a foreign citizen or a stateless person wants to adopt a child with foreign citizenship before Serbian authorities, the right to adoption is recognised as a general right.
2. When an adopter who holds Serbian citizenship wants to adopt a child who holds foreign citizenship or a child without citizenship before the Serbian authorities, such a child has a general right to be an adoptee if Serbian authorities have grounds to accept jurisdiction over that adoption case.
3. When foreign citizen wants to adopt a child of Serbian citizenship, the following conditions foreseen by Article 103 of the Family Law must be met:
   - That adopters cannot be found among domestic citizens. It is to be considered that adopters cannot be found among domestic citizens if more than 1 year has passed from the day of entry of data on the future adoptee in the Unified Personal Register of Adoptions.
   - That the minister responsible for family protection gave his consent to adoption. Exceptionally, the minister responsible for family protection can grant adoption to a foreign citizen before the time limit of 1 year, if that is in the best interest of the child.

2.2.6 Obligations of the Child Towards Parents

When it comes to obligation of the child towards his or her parent(s), Article 66 of the Family Law states that the child has the duty to help his/her parents in accordance with his/her age and maturity. Furthermore, the child who earns wages or has income from property has the duty to partially provide for his/her own support, the support of his/her parent and minor brother or sister, under the conditions of the Family Law.[55]

2.2.7 The Right to Medical Consent

In accordance with the Law on Protection and Promotion of Patients' Rights,[56] the child who has reached the age of 15 and who is capable of reasoning and who has received a prior notice about the medical treatment has a right to give medical consent independently.[57] If the child who has reached the age of 15 and who is mentally competent refuses proposed medical treatment, the authorised healthcare professional is obliged to require the consent of the child's legal guardian.[58]

---

[55] Art. 66

[56] Law on Protection and Promotion of Patients' Rights (Official Gazette of Republic of Serbia, N° 45/2013)

[57] Art. 19, para. 4

[58] Art. 19, para. 5

2.2.8 Prohibition of Corporal Punishment

In Serbia there is no general prohibition of corporal punishment. According to Article 45 of the Law on the Foundations of the Education System, corporal punishment is prohibited in preschool, primary and secondary educational institutions. Similarly, corporal punishment is also forbidden in social welfare institutions as well as in correctional institutions. Family Law prohibits violence against children and foresees corporal violence against a child by his/her parent as a reason for full deprivation of the parental responsibilities.[59] However, the Law does not define corporal violence. Furthermore, the Law is silent on corporal punishment, which leads to the conclusion that corporal punishment could be considered as corporal violence, but it has to be judged on a case-by-case basis. In the Serbian legal system, such punishment of the child by parents is neither allowed nor prohibited. The system only envisages a sanction in the event of abuse, neglect or violence against the child by his/her parents. Hence, in cases when corporal punishment of the child by his/her parents has elements of corporal violence, the parents can be sanctioned by the full deprivation of parental responsibilities along with sanctions foreseen by the Criminal Code.

2.2.9 Deprivation of Parental Responsibilities

Full and partial deprivation of parental responsibilities is foreseen by the Family Law.[60] Full deprivation of parental responsibilities is foreseen in situations when a parent abuses rights that comprise a part of parental rights (corporal, sexual or emotional abuse of the child; exploitation of the child by forcing him/her to excessive labour, or to labour that endangers the moral, health or education of the child, or to labour that is prohibited by law; instigation of the child to commit criminal acts; accustoming the child to indulge in bad habits; and any other way of rights abuses) and when a parent grossly neglects duties that comprise a part of parental rights (child abandonment; lack of care for the child he/she lives with; avoidance of child support or maintenance of personal relations with the child he/she does not live with or impediment of the maintaining of personal relations of the child with the parent the child does not live with; intentional and undue avoidance of creation of conditions for cohabitation with the child who is living in a social service institution for user accommodation; and any other way of gross neglect of duties that comprise a part of parental rights).[61]

A parent who exercises the rights or duties that comprise a part of his/her parental rights unconscionably may be partially deprived of parental rights. A parent who exercises parental rights may be deprived of the rights and duties of protecting,

---

[59] Art. 81

[60] Arts. 81–2

[61] Family Law, Art. 81

raising, upbringing, educating and representing the child, as well as of managing and disposing of the child's property. A parent who does not exercise parental rights may be deprived of the right to maintain personal relations with the child and of the right to decide on issues that significantly influence the child's life.[62] Only the court is competent for deprivation of parental responsibilities, both full and partial deprivation.[63] If the child's parents are fully deprived of parental responsibilities, the child can be adopted,[64] placed in foster care[65] and placed under guardianship.[66] A court decision on full deprivation of parental rights deprives the parent of all rights and duties that comprise parental rights, except the duty of supporting the child.

2.2.10 Right to Employment

According to Article 24 of the Labour Law, the minimum age for admission to employment is 15. Similarly, according to Article 25 of the Labour Law, if a child at the age of 15 or above wants to engage in work, he/she can only do with written consent of parents, adoptive parents or foster parent and upon certification from the competent healthcare body substantiating that he/she is capable of performing such tasks that are stipulated in the labour contract and that these tasks are not harmful for his/her health. The Labour Law in Articles 84–88 regulates special protection of children[67] on the labour market. Full-time working hours for persons below the age of 18 shall not exceed 35 hours per week or 8 hours per day.[68] Additionally, in the Article 88, the Law prohibits overtime and redistribution of working hours for employees below the age of 18, and it only allows work at night in cases of work in the area of culture, sports, art and advertising and when it is necessary to continue work discontinued due to the action of force majeure, under the condition that such work lasts for a definite period of time, that it has to be urgently completed and that the employer has no other older employees available. In such cases, the employer must provide supervision of work of employees below the age of 18 by a person of full age. In Article 84, the Labour Law specifies the list of jobs on which the child cannot be employed – jobs involving strenuous corporal work; work underground, under water and at excessive heights; noxious radiation or substances that are toxic, carcinogenic or causing inherited diseases; and health risks related to cold, heat, noise or vibrations and jobs that may, pursuant to advice of the competent health authority, increase health and life risks and be harmful in light of overall adolescents' health.

[62] Family Law, Art. 82

[63] Family Law, Arts 81–82

[64] Art. 91

[65] Art. 113

[66] Art. 124

[67] The Law uses term *adolescents*.

[68] Labour Law, Art. 87

3 Conclusion

There are many challenges and tasks for Serbia in order to better implement the CRC. Some of those include, but are not limited to, improvement of the legal reform, such as adoption of the child Rights Law; poverty eradication among children; increased and specified budget allocation for children; a higher level of political interest, knowledge and attention to children; fundamental reform of the education system, in accordance with international standards; improvement of healthcare for children, including adolescent health; better quality education and information dissemination on child rights, in as broad as possible spectrum of beneficiaries, in particular, children, their parents, teachers and health workers; facilitation of an efficient child protection system (emergency interventions) from all forms of abuse and exploitation, including ones in the context of trafficking, occurring through media and availability of harmful information on the internet; and improvement of legal and practical conditions that would enable the child's access to justice.[69]

Needles to say, further law reform in Serbia in the areas relevant for the rights of the child is necessary. However, even the best law is but a piece of paper if it does not enable actual exercise of rights of the child. Therefore, further law reform, followed by efficient and effective mechanisms for implementation remains the biggest challenge for children in Serbia.

---

[69] See UN Doc. CRC/C/SRB/CO/1.

The Rights of the Child in Solomon Islands' Plural Legal System

Jennifer Corrin

1 Introduction

Solomon Islands is made up of 26 islands and hundreds of islets, lying about 1600 km north-east of Australia. It has a land area of 30,000 km^2, about the same size as Belgium, and is spread out in a 1360 km long, double chain. The country has a population of about 516,000, with over 80 vernacular languages spoken. About 80 % of people live in rural areas.[1] Solomon Islands was a British protectorate from 1893 until 1978, when it became an independent member of the Commonwealth.[2] It has a Westminster style of State government,[3] coexisting with a traditional chiefly system.[4]

From 1999 to 2002, Solomon Islands endured civil strife. This worsened the countries' economic problems. Levels of poverty are still rising and a large number of children are affected by this.[5] Added to the logistical and language barriers, this has made it very difficult for Solomon Islands to make any progress in living up to its international law commitments.

---

[1] Solomon Islands National Statistics Office, *Key Social Indicators* (2012) Census 2009, http://www.spc.int/prism/solomons/index.php/social

[2] *Solomon Islands Independence Order 1978* (UK).

[3] *Constitution of the Solomon Islands 1978* (SI) ('*Constitution*'), s 9. The *Constitution* is scheduled to *Independence Order 1978* (UK).

[4] *Constitution*, art 114(2)(b) acknowledges the chiefly system and provides that the Parliament must legislate for the role of chiefs in the government. The *Provincial Government Act* Cap 118 (SI) provides for the administration of local government by provincial assemblies.

[5] UN Committee on the Rights of the Child (CRC), *UN Committee on the Rights of the Child: Comments on State Party Report: Solomon Islands*, 6 June 2003, CRC/C/15/ADD.208, available at: http://www.refworld.org/docid/3df59ecb2.html [accessed 5 November 2013], [44].

J. Corrin (✉)
Centre for Public, International and Comparative Law, TC Beirne School of Law,
The University of Queensland St Lucia Campus, Brisbane, Queensland 4072, Australia
e-mail: j.corrin@law.uq.edu.au

O. Cvejić Jančić (ed.), *The Rights of the Child in a Changing World*,
Ius Comparatum - Global Studies in Comparative Law 13,
DOI 10.1007/978-3-319-23189-1_16

2 Solomon Islands Legal System

In order to understand the complexities of the law relating to children in Solomon Islands, it is necessary to have some background on the pluralistic legal system. The supreme law, at least from the State's perspective, is the *Constitution of Solomon Islands 1978*. This *Constitution* has been under review for about 10 years and a draft federal constitution is being considered.[6] Legislation is ranked next in order of priority. Where there is no Act of Solomon Islands' Parliament covering a situation, UK Acts of general application may apply.[7] In theory, UK Acts and customary laws are on par, but in practice, the legislation usually prevails. Since its independence, Solomon Islands' courts are not bound by the decisions of foreign courts and are free to develop their own jurisprudence.[8] However, English common law up to that date is retained in force.[9] The *Constitution* states that customary law is to prevail over English common law and equity,[10] although this provision is rarely complied with.[11]

It must also be kept in mind that for many people the *Constitution* and legislation are foreign concepts and customary laws are far more relevant.[12] This is particularly the case in the rural sector and especially in relation to personal laws, including laws governing children.[13]

Customary laws are largely unwritten and do not form a homogenous body of rules for the whole country, but differ from place to place. This often makes it difficult to say what those laws are in any particular case. However, some generalisations are possible. Customary laws place emphasis on group norms and obligations, rather than individual rights. Members of a community group (generally based on kinship) have reciprocal obligations to care for each other by providing food, shelter and other necessities. These obligations apply particularly to young, sick and elderly

---

[6] Draft Federal Constitution of Solomon Islands, available at: http://www.sicr.gov.sb/2011%20Draft%20Fed%20Const%20of%20SI.pdf [accessed 11 November 2013].

[7] *Constitution*, sch 3, para 1.

[8] *Constitution*, sch 3, para 4(1).

[9] *Constitution*, Sch 3, para 2(1)(c).

[10] *Constitution*, Sch 3, para 2(1)(c): 'the principles and rules of the common law and equity shall have effect as part of the law of Solomon Islands, save in so far as … in their application to any particular matter, they are inconsistent with customary law applying in respect to the matter'. See also, *Kasa v Biku* (Unreported, High Court, Solomon Islands, Muria CJ, 14 January 2000), available via www.paclii.org at [2000] SBHC 62.

[11] Jennifer Corrin and Don Paterson, Introduction to South Pacific Law (Palgrave MacMillan, 3rd ed, 2011) 47–48.

[12] See Jennifer Corrin Care, 'Wisdom and Worthy Customs: The Role and Operation of Customary Law in the South Pacific' (2002) 80 *Reform* 31, 34. Compare *K v T* [1985–1986] SILR 49.

[13] See, for example, in relation to Solomon Islands and Vanuatu, Kenneth Brown, *Reconciling Customary Law and Received Law in Melanesia* (Charles Darwin University Press: Darwin, 2005) 38–40.

members of the group. Accordingly, customary norms provide an informal safety net to vulnerable Solomon Islander children.[14]

Solomon Islands, like other common law States in the Pacific, has a dualist system[15] in which international treaty law does not become part of domestic law unless specifically incorporated by legislation.[16] To date, there is no legislation in Solomon Islands which specifically introduces the *UN Convention on the Rights of the Child* (the 'Convention')[17] or any other international texts into the internal order.[18]

As discussed below, a *Child Rights Bill* was drafted in 1997 by Solomon Islands' National Advisory Committee on Children and sought to give binding effect to the Convention, but the bill has not yet been adopted by Parliament nor circulated for comments.[19] In the interim, the High Court of Solomon has stated, in the context of prosecution of a child for murder, that the Government of Solomon Islands has 'the responsibility indeed the obligation to enact legislation that will give effect to these conventions [including the CRC]'.[20] In the absence of such legislation, the court would 'do all within its powers to protect juveniles within the safeguards provided by the Constitution … and the *Juvenile [Offenders] Act*'.[21] On the other hand in *K v R*, which was a bail application in relation to the same defendant and same case, a differently constituted High Court held the requirements of conventions including the CRC were 'already well reflected' in domestic legislation, making further legislation unnecessary.[22] This case is discussed further below in this report.

[14] Solomon Islands Government, *Reports Submitted by State Parties under Article 44 of the* Convention: *Solomon Islands*, UN Doc CRC/C/51/Add.6 (12 July 2002) 8.

[15] As opposed to a monist system. In the US, for example, a treaty becomes part of the domestic law of the country once it has been ratified according to the constitution.

[16] Solomon Islands, as a common law country, follows the UK's dualist approach: *R v Bow Street Metropolitan Stipendiary Magistrate*; *Ex parte Pinochet Ugarte (No 1)* [2000] 1 AC 61 at 81 (Lord Slynn of Hadley), cited in Gillian Triggs, *International Law: Contemporary Principles and Practices* (Chatswood: LexisNexis, 2006) 107. See also Corrin Care (2006, 51, 59). See also Sue Farran, *Human Rights in the South Pacific: Challenges and Changes* (Abingdon, Routledge-Cavendish, 2009) 62.

[17] *Convention on the Rights of the Child*, 1577 UNTS 3 (ratified 10 April 1995) ('Convention')

[18] The only small island of the South Pacific to have done this is Vanuatu: see, for example, *Convention on the Elimination of all Forms of Discrimination against Women (Ratification) Act* Cap 235.

[19] Dennie Iniakwala, 'Solomon Islands' (statement by Dr. Dennie Iniakwala, Head of Delegate and Co-Chair of the National Advisory Committee on Children during the Presentation of the National Initial CRC Implementation Report to the Committee on the Rights of the Child, Geneva, 26 May 2003) 4

[20] *R v K* (Unreported, High Court, Solomon Islands, Naqiolevu J, 12 July 2005) available via www.paclii.org at [2005] SBHC 80.

[21] Cap 14.

[22] *K v R* (Unreported, High Court, Solomon Islands, Palmer CJ, 16 September 2005) available via www.paclii.org at [2005] SBHC 150. His Honour specifically mentioned s 7 of the Constitution (giving effect to art 37 of the Convention) and the *Juvenile Offenders Act*, the *Penal Code* and the *Criminal Procedure Code* (giving effect to art 37(b) of the Convention).

Notwithstanding the lack of domestic legislation incorporating the Convention, in general international law does have a persuasive effect.[23]

2.1 Conventions and Protocols

From 1892 to 1978, Solomon Islands was a British protectorate.[24] During that time, the UK government acceded to a number of international human rights instruments on its behalf. However, the Convention is a post-independence document, to which Solomon Islands acceded independently on 10 April 1995.[25] Solomon Islands is also a signatory to the First Optional Protocol to the Convention on the Rights of the Child on the Involvement of Children in Armed Conflict[26] and the Second Optional Protocol to the Convention on the Rights of the Child on the Sale of Children, Child Prostitution and Child Pornography.[27] It is not party to the Third Optional Protocol to the Convention on the Rights of the Child on a Communications Procedure, nor to the Protocol to Prevent, Suppress and Punish Trafficking in Persons Especially Women and Children supplementing the United Nations Convention against Transnational Organized Crime.[28]

Solomon Islands initial report to the Committee on the Rights of the Child ('CRC') was due in 1997, but was not submitted until 2002.[29] The Report was considered by the CRC in 2003.[30] The Committee's observations on the report highlighted the lack of specific legislation governing children's rights and emphasised the need to bring domestic legislation and customary laws in line with the principles of the Convention.[31] The Committee also criticised the lack of definition of 'best interests of the child' and noted that the importance of the principle was not reflected

[23] See, e.g. *Soeasi V R* (Unreported, High Court, Solomon Islands, Naqiolevu, J), 7 December 2007, available via www.paclii.org at [2007] sbhc 159.

[24] See *Pacific Order in Council 1893* (UK); John Nonggorr, 'Solomon Islands' in Ntumy (ed) *South Pacific Island Legal Systems* (Honolulu: University of Hawaii, 1993) 268.

[25] *Convention on the Rights of the Child*, 1577 UNTS 3 (ratified 10 April 1995).

[26] Optional Protocol Relating to the Convention on the Rights of the Child on the Involvement of Children in Armed Conflict (2002) 2173 UNTS 222; signatory 24 September 2009.

[27] Optional Protocol to the Convention on the Rights of the Child on the Sale of Children, Child Prostitution and Child Pornography (2002) 2171 UNTS 227; signatory 24 September 2009.

[28] Protocol to Prevent, Suppress and Punish Trafficking in Persons, Especially Women and Children, supplementing the United Nations Convention against Transnational Organized Crime (2003) 2237 UNTS 319.

[29] UN Committee on the Rights of the Child (Crc), UN Committee on the Rights of the Child: State Party Report: Solomon Islands, 12 July 2002, Crc/C/51/Add.6, available at: Http://www.Refworld.Org/Docid/3df59ecb2.Html [Accessed 5 November 2013].

[30] UN Committee on the Rights of the Child (Crc), UN Committee on the Rights of the Child: Comments On State Party Report: Solomon Islands, 6 June 2003, Crc/C/15/Add.208, available at: Http://www.Refworld.Org/Docid/3df59ecb2.Html [Accessed 5 November 2013].

[31] Committee on the Rights of the Child, Concluding Observations: Solomon Islands, 33rd sess, UN Doc CRC/C/15/Add.208 (2 July 2003) 2.

in the practices of decision-makers. The Committee recommended that further training be given on the meaning and implementation of the best interest of the child. The Committee also noted the risk that informal (customary) adoption would lead to female children being used as de facto domestic workers and recommended that Solomon Islands 'take all necessary measures to end the practice of informal adoption'.[32]

No report has been submitted since and there is no adequate data collection mechanism in place. The CRC noted that this was a hurdle to monitoring and evaluating the progress of implementation of the Convention.[33]

3 The Definition of Child

The Convention requires that parties define childhood as the period prior to attaining the age of 18 years, for all legislation. As mentioned above, in 1997 a *Child's Rights Bill* was drafted, which would have introduced this change in line with the Convention. To date the bill, which is discussed further below, has not been enacted.[34]

3.1 Personhood and Age of Majority

In Solomon Islands a child is deemed to be a person when the child has completely proceeded in a living state from the body of his/her mother.[35] A child becomes a person capable of being killed when he/she is born alive, whether or not he/she is breathing, or has independent circulation and the navel string is severed.[36]

The age of majority is still governed by the common law in Solomon Islands and is therefore 21. Persons under that age were referred to as 'infants', but 'minor' is now the preferred term. Apart from the common law age of majority, specific statutes

[32] Committee on the Rights of the Child, Concluding Observations: Solomon Islands, 33rd sess, UN Doc CRC/C/15/Add.208 (2 July 2003) 8.

[33] UN Committee on the Rights of the Child (Crc), UN Committee on the Rights of the Child: State Party Report: Solomon Islands, 12 July 2002, Crc/C/51/Add.6, available at: Http://www.Refworld.Org/Docid/3df59ecb2.Html [Accessed 5 November 2013], [15].

[34] Dennie Iniakwala, 'Solomon Islands' (statement by Dr. Dennie Iniakwala, Head of Delegate and Co-Chair of the National Advisory Committee on Children during the Presentation of the National Initial CRC Implementation Report to the Committee on the Rights of the Child, Geneva, 26 May 2003) 4; UNICEF, *Solomon Islands "Plus 5" Review of the 2002 Special Session on Children and World Fit for Children Plan of Action Country Report* (UNICEF 2007) 2.

[35] *Penal Code* Cap 5, s 201.

[36] *Penal Code* Cap 5, s 208. Section 206 of the Penal Code provides that a woman commits infanticide where she causes the death of her child and 'the balance of her mind was disturbed by reason of her not having fully recovered from the effect of giving birth to the child or by reason of the effect of lactation consequent upon the birth of the child'.

impose a variety of ages at which responsibility or protections will apply. The age specified depends to a large extent on the purpose of the legislation. The main statutes regulating the age at which a person is deemed to be a child are in the field of crime, criminal responsibility, criminal procedure and correctional services, civil procedure, voting, employment and adoption. The relevant legislation includes:

AdoptionAct 2004
Affiliation, Separation and Maintenance Act Cap 1
Constitution
Correctional Services Act 2007
Juvenile Offenders Act 1972
Labour Act Cap 73, part VII
Penal Code Cap 26
Solomon Islands Courts (Civil Procedure) Rules 2007

The principal provisions are discussed below.

3.2 Adoption

The *Adoption Act 2004* defines a child, referred to somewhat archaically as an 'infant', as a person under the age of 18.[37]

3.3 Maintenance

Under the *Affiliation, Separation and Maintenance Act*, an affiliation order expires when the child reaches 16, or at 13 if the child is earning a sufficient amount to maintain him or herself.[38] However, an order may be made or extended beyond 16 if the child is studying or training for a trade, profession or vocation or there are special circumstances.[39]

3.4 Criminal Responsibility

The *Penal Code*[40] introduces an irrebuttable presumption of law that a person under the age of 8 years cannot be criminally responsible for any act or omission. Accordingly, a child under 8 cannot be guilty of an offence. The Penal Code also

[37] *Adoption Act 2004*, s 2(1).

[38] *Affiliation, Separation and Maintenance Act* Cap 1, s 7.

[39] Section 8.

[40] Cap 26, s 14.

introduces a rebuttable presumption of law that a child under the age of 12 is not criminally responsible for an act or omission, unless the child knew that what he/she was doing was wrong.[41]

In *R v Rakaimua*[42] Muria CJ put the evidential burden of raising immaturity on the defence:

> [A] person under eight years of age will be excused of any criminal responsibility for his act or omission. A person who is eight years but still under 12 years will also be excused from criminal responsibility unless it is proved that the person had the capacity to know that he ought not to have done what he did or made the omission at the time the act was done or omission was made. The defence says that the accused in this case is a person who was less than 12 years of age at the time of the commission of the offence and who then did not have the capacity to know that what he did would cause death. ... It is for the prosecution to show by evidence that the defence of immature age raised by the accused must be excluded. But I think I can also say without shifting the burden of proof to the defence that the accused must point to some evidence supporting the suggestion that he was of immature age at the time and which may help to raise doubt in the Court's mind.

This approach is more problematic than it may first seem. In Solomon Islands many people do not hold a birth certificate.[43] And even oral evidence may be problematic, as some people do not know their date of birth. It is not unusual for people to assess their approximate age, and that of family members, by reference to an important event, for example, the date of Independence.

The CRC has recommended that the minimum age for criminal responsibility in Solomon Islands should be raised to 12, which it considers to be the internationally acceptable minimum age of criminal responsibility.[44] The CRC also stated that the use of two minimum ages, that is 8 for the rebuttable presumption and 12 for the rebuttable presumption, was confusing. The Committee considered that it might lead to discriminatory practices and to the lower age being used for very serious crimes such as murder.[45] A review of the *Penal Code* and the *Criminal Procedure Code* was referred to Solomon Islands Law Reform Commission ('SILRC') on 1 May 1995. However, this was not acted upon until 2008, when an Issues Paper ('Criminal Issues Paper') was published.[46] The Criminal Issues Paper raised the

---

[41] Cap 26, s 14.

[42] (Unreported, High Court, Solomon Islands, Muria CJ,15 March 1996]) 4–5 available via www.paclii.org at [1996] SBHC 13.

[43] The CRC expressed concern that society at large is not aware of the importance of birth registration: UN Committee on the Rights of the Child (CRC), UN Committee on the Rights of the Child: Comments on State Party Report: Solomon Islands, 6 June 2003, CRC/C/15/ADD.208, available at: http://www.refworld.org/docid/3df59ecb2.html [accessed 5 November 2013], [28].

[44] UN Committee on the Rights of the Child (CRC), *UN Committee on the Rights of the Child: State Party Report: Solomon Islands*, 12 July 2002, CRC/C/51/Add.6, [417–418], [431–434] available at: http://www.refworld.org/docid/3df59ecb2.html [accessed 7 November 2013.

[45] Committee on the Rights of the Child, General Comment No 10 (2007) Children's rights in Juvenile Justice CRC/C/GC/10.

[46] Solomon Islands Law Reform Commission *Review of Penal Code and Criminal Procedure Issues Paper 1*, November 2008.

question of raising the age of criminal responsibility and whether there should be only one age prescribed.[47] A final report has not yet been published by the SILRC.

For the purposes of criminal responsibility, a male under the age of 12 is presumed to be incapable of having sexual intercourse.[48]

3.5 Juvenile Offenders

The *Juvenile Offenders Act* defines a child as being under the age of 14 years.[49] A young person is someone 14 or over and under the age of 18.[50] A child cannot be imprisoned unless he/she is a serious repeat offender.[51] As there are currently no juvenile detention facilities in Solomon Islands, children and young persons are not imprisoned unless they are apprehended together with adults, tried as a group and convicted of committing a 'grave crime'.[52]

When a child is being prosecuted, the Act states that only members and officers of the Court, parties to the case, their advocates or authorised representatives and other persons directly concerned with the case are allowed to attend.[53] Publication of the child's name, address, school, photograph or anything likely to lead to the identification of the child or young person before the court is also prohibited.[54]

3.6 Correctional Services

The *Correctional Services Act* 2007 defines a 'young prisoner' to mean any prisoner under the age of 18 years and to include any prisoner under the age of 21, who, in the opinion of the commissioner, commandant or court, may be at risk of harm in a correctional centre.[55] The Act contains special provisions for dealing with children (that term is not defined) and young persons (which is not defined, but presumably bears the same meaning as 'young prisoner'), including keeping young male prison-

[47] Solomon Islands Law Reform Commission *Review of Penal Code and Criminal Procedure Issues Paper 1*, November 2008, [4.10–4.13].

[48] *Penal Code* Cap 5, s 14.

[49] Cap 14, s 2.

[50] *Juvenile Offenders Act* Cap 14, s 2.

[51] *Juvenile Offenders Act* Cap 14, s 4(4).

[52] UN Committee on the Rights of the Child (CRC), *UN Committee on the Rights of the Child: State Party Report: Solomon Islands*, 12 July 2002, CRC/C/51/Add.6, [417–418], [431–434] available at: http://www.refworld.org/docid/3df59ecb2.html [accessed 7 November 2013]; *Juvenile Offenders Act* Cap 14, s2. The schedule defines 'grave crimes' as murder, attempted murder, manslaughter, unlawful wounding, unlawful poisoning and causing grievous harm.

[53] *Juvenile Offenders Act* Cap 14, s 4.

[54] *Juvenile Offenders Act* Cap 14 s 4(a), (b).

[55] *Correctional Services Act 2007* s 2.

ers separate from adults[56] and making arrangements for separation or contact with their family or other persons in the best interests of a child or young person.[57] In addition to the normal rights, a young prisoner has the right:

(a) *To be provided with suitable education consistent with community standards*
(b) *As far as practicable, to have access to parents, siblings and family members*
(c) *To have access to advice and support*[58]

The Act also provides for the minister to make regulations for female prisoners and their children consistent with the rights and obligations of international conventions and recognised standards, including the rights of women to feed and care for their infant children whilst in a correctional centre.[59] The *Correctional Services Regulations 2008* do not appear to have made any provision in this regard. As required by the Juvenile Justice Act,[60] a juvenile detention centre has been set up in the capital and is inspected annually by the ICRC (Fiji).[61]

3.7 *Child Victims*

The *Penal Code* sets a limit of 15 years of age for crimes to be classified as crimes against children. These include indecent assault,[62] abduction,[63] sexual defilement,[64] unlawful sexual intercourse[65] and disposing of minors for immoral purposes.[66] For the purpose of the offence of child stealing, a child is a person under 14.[67] For the purposes of procurement, the age of a child is a person under 18 or 21 depending on the nature of the offence.[68]

It is also an offence to neglect a child. The duty is placed on the head of the family and tenants of a house in which a child is living to provide for the necessaries of life for any child under 15 under their care.[69] In addition it is an offence for employers not to provide food, clothing or lodging for servants or apprentices under 15.[70]

[56] *Correctional Services Act 2007* s 34(2).
[57] *Correctional Services Act 2007* s 34(3).
[58] *Correctional Services Act 2007* s 40(2).
[59] *Correctional Services Act 2007* s 75(2).
[60] Cap 14 s 17(1).
[61] CRIN, *Solomon Islands: Child Rights References in the Universal Periodic Review*, available at: http://www.crin.org/resources/infodetail.asp?id=25544 [accessed 10 November 2013], [77].
[62] *Penal Code* Cap 5, s 141.
[63] *Penal Code* Cap 5, s 254.
[64] *Penal Code* Cap 5, s 143. If the child is under 13, the crime is classified as a felony: s 142.
[65] *Penal Code* Cap 5, s 143.
[66] *Penal Code* Cap 5, s 150.
[67] *Penal Code* Cap 5, s 253.
[68] *Penal Code* Cap 5, s 144.
[69] *Penal Code* Cap 5, s 204.
[70] *Penal Code* Cap 5, s 212.

The SILRC Criminal Issues Paper raises questions about amending criminal law and procedure, including the law relating to children, for discussion.[71] The SILRC completed its report on reform of sexual offences in the *Penal Code* in June 2013.[72] The underlying principles for reform used to formulate the recommendations included the need to provide protection for children from all forms of sexual abuse and exploitation and the provision of effective systems for prosecuting cases in a child-sensitive manner. The recommendations include the introduction of new offences to protect children from sexual abuse.[73]

The other statute which deals with children as victims is the recently passed *Immigration Act 2012*, which makes provisions for trafficking in person offences. The Act provides that a person commits an offence of trafficking in children if the trafficked person is under 18.[74] The penalty for this offence is either a fine of up to 90,000 penalty units or imprisonment up to 10 years or both.[75] The Act has not yet come into force.

3.8 Civil Procedure

For the purposes of civil procedure, a 'child' is defined as meaning a person under the age of 18 years.[76] A child is regarded as being under a disability and, as discussed below, special rules are in force, designed to protect their interests.

3.9 Voting

The Constitution prescribes the qualification age for electors as 18.[77] This accords with the definition of the child in article 1 of the CRC.[78]

---

[71] Solomon Islands Law Reform Commission, *Review of Penal Code and Criminal Procedure Issues Paper 1*, November 2008.

[72] Solomon Islands Law Reform Commission *Review of the Penal Code and Criminal Procedure Code: Second Interim Report – Sexual Offences* June 2013 available at http://www.lawreform.gov.sb/files/reports/Final-sexual_offences_report_2013_v4_12_June.pdf

[73] Solomon Islands Law Reform Commission *Review of the Penal Code and Criminal Procedure Code: Second Interim Report – Sexual Offences* June 2013 recommendations 12, 14–27, p. 25–32.

[74] Section 77.

[75] *Immigration Act 2012*, s 77.

[76] Solomon Islands Courts (Civil Procedure) Rules 2007, Sch 4.

[77] *Constitution*, s 55(1)(b).

[78] Article 1.

3.10 Marriage

The minimum age of consent for minors who qualify as Solomon Islanders[79] to enter into a marriage under State law is 18 or 15 with the consent of the father.[80] In the absence of the father, consent may be given by the child's mother or, in her absence, the child's guardian.[81] The SILRC has recommended that the minimum age for customary marriage, which is currently regulated by the customary law pertaining to the parties to the marriage, should be regulated to fall in line with the minimum age for marriage under State law, subject to a lower age applying in exceptional circumstances, including pregnancy where marriage is in the best interests of the unborn child.[82]

For minors who are not Solomon Islanders, the minimum age of consent is unclear. If the *Marriage Act 1949* (UK) applies in Solomon Islands as an Act of general application, the age is 16.[83] However, the High Court has held that this Act does not apply as its 'complicated statutory framework' prevents it from being an Act of general application.[84] If the 1949 Act is not part of the law of Solomon Islands, the common law imports a minimum age of consent of 14 for a male and 12 for a girl.[85]

Raising the age of consent to 18 for all children in Solomon Islands would give some protection against arranged or forced marriages.[86]

3.11 Employment

In April 2012, Solomon Islands ratified ILO Convention 182.[87] However, appropriate domestic legislation has not been passed. The *Labour Act*[88] sets 12 as the minimum age for employment.[89] It also sets 15, 16 and 18 years as ages that govern

[79] See further Jennifer Corrin, 'A Question of Identity: Complexities of State Law Pluralism in the South Pacific' (2011) 61 (1) Journal of Legal Pluralism and Unofficial Law 143–169.

[80] *Islanders Marriage Act* Cap 171 (SI), s 10.

[81] *Islanders Marriage Act* Cap 171 (SI), s 10.

[82] LRC, *Review of the Penal Code and Criminal Procedure Code: Second Interim Report Sexual Offences*, 2013, recommendation 13a.

[83] *Marriage Act 1929* (UK), s 2.

[84] *Mahlon v Mahlon* [1984] SILR 86, 87–88.

[85] *Arnold v Earle* (1758) 2 Lee 529.

[86] Kenneth Brown, Jennifer Corrin Care 'Putting Asunder: Divorce and financial relief in Solomon Islands 2005 *Oxford University Commonwealth Law Journal*, 96.

[87] ILO Normlex. *Ratifications for Solomon Islands*; accessed November 5, 2013; http://www.ilo.org/dyn/normlex/en/f?p=1000:11200:0::NO:11200:P11200_COUNTRY_ID:103193

[88] Cap 73, Part VII.

[89] *Labour Act* Cap 73, s 46.

different protective provisions in the Act. The Act is discussed further below. The *Constitution* guarantees protection from slavery and forced labour for everyone, including children.[90]

4 Domestic Law

4.1 Human Rights Protection

There is no specific written law devoted to the rights of the child, although the Bill of Rights within the Constitution extends to children as well as adults.[91] Protected rights include:

- Right to life[92]
- Right to personal liberty[93]
- Freedom from inhumane treatment, including inhuman or degrading punishment[94]
- Protection of the law[95]
- Right to freedom of thought, religion or belief[96]
- Right to freedom of expression[97]
- Right to freedom of movement within Solomon Islands[98]
- Protection from discrimination on the ground of colour, race, place of origin, creed or sex or political opinion[99]

These rights and freedoms are subject to exceptions, including public interest.[100]

A *Child Rights Bill* was drafted in 1997 by the National Advisory Committee on Children (NACC).[101] This body was established by Solomon Islands' Cabinet in

[90] *Constitution*, s 6.

[91] *Constitution*, ch II.

[92] *Constitution*, s 4.

[93] *Constitution*, s 5.

[94] *Constitution*, s 7.

[95] *Constitution*, s 10.

[96] *Constitution*, s 11.

[97] *Constitution*, s 12.

[98] *Constitution*, s 14.

[99] *Constitution*, s 15.

[100] See *Constitution*, s 3: the rights and freedoms are 'subject to such limitations of that protection as are contained in those provisions, being limitations designed to ensure that the enjoyment of the said rights and freedoms by an individual does not prejudice the rights and freedoms of others or the public interest'.

[101] Dennie Iniakwala, 'Solomon Islands' (statement by Dr. Dennie Iniakwala, Head of Delegate and Co-Chair of the National Advisory Committee on Children during the Presentation of the National

August 1993 and consists of representatives of government, non-governmental organisations (NGOs) and church organisations. The NACC has an advisory role to the government and has formulated a National Policy on Children 2010–2015. There is also a National Youth Policy 2007, which was formulated by the Ministry for Women, Youth and Children's Affairs in 2007. To date neither policy has been endorsed by the Cabinet.[102] Since the formulation of the National Policy on Children, the NACC does not appear to have been active, although it is referred to in Solomon Islands' 2013 budget as having 'the mandate to advise Cabinet on all issues affecting children, coordinate implementation of CRC, and develop and disseminate advocacy materials that promote the interests and rights of the child'.[103]

The *Child Rights Bill* 1997 sought to give the CRC (especially arts 6, 13, 14, 15, 16, 31, 32, 36, 37 and 40) the force of law. The draft bill has not been put before Parliament. According to Solomon Islands' 2002 Report to the Committee, Solomon Islands Law Reform Commission ('SILRC')[104] was, at that time, in the process of reviewing existing laws in this area. NACC was intending to make a submission to the LRC on point[105] but to date this does not appear to have been done.[106] The CRC has stated that it is encouraged by the establishment of this body, but concerned about its effectiveness.[107]

4.2 *The Best Interests of the Child*

Article 3 of the Convention provides that in all actions involving children, the best interests of the child shall be a primary consideration (the 'welfare principle'). The *Constitution* does not enshrine the welfare principle; however, it is referred to in at least two statutes in force in Solomon Islands.

Initial CRC Implementation Report to the Committee on the Rights of the Child, Geneva, 26 May 2003) 4.

[102] UN Committee on the Rights of the Child (CRC), UN Committee on the Rights of the Child: State Party Report: Solomon Islands, 12 July 2002, CRC/C/51/ADD.6, Available at: http://www.refworld.org/docid/3df59ecb2.html [accessed 5 November 2013], [20].

[103] The Honourable Rick Houenipwela MP, *Solomon Islands Budget 2013: Budget Strategy and Outlook* (Solomon Islands Ministry of Finance and Treasury, 2013).

[104] Law Reform Commission Act Cap 15.

[105] UN Committee on the Rights of the Child (CRC), UN Committee on the Rights of the Child: State Party Report: Solomon Islands, 12 July 2002, CRC/C/51/Add.6, available at: http://www.refworld.org/docid/3df59ecb2.html [accessed 5 November 2013], [20].

[106] The NACC is not amongst the list of those who made submissions to the LRC on the Review of the Penal Code and Criminal Procedure Code, although it is listed as having been consulted: LRC, Review of the Penal Code and Criminal Procedure Code: Second Interim Report Sexual Offences, 2013, App 1.

[107] UN Committee on the Rights of the Child (CRC), UN Committee on the Rights of the Child: Comments on State Party Report: Solomon Islands, 6 June 2003, CRC/C/15/Add.208, available at: http://www.refworld.org/docid/3df59ecb2.html [accessed 5 November 2013, [7].

Like its British predecessor,[108] which was in force in Solomon Islands as an Act of general application, the *Adoption Act 2004* incorporates the welfare principle[109] but falls short of spelling out that the best interests of the child are the paramount consideration in adoption proceedings.[110] The Act does not elaborate on the factors to be taken into account in determining 'welfare' in this context. Relevant considerations include, but are not limited to, the health of the applicants.[111]

The High Court has considered the welfare principle in four of the seven cases applying the Act since its commencement in 2008.[112] Although the Court has not in any case used the language of the Act (the 'welfare of the infant'), it has referred to the 'best interests' of the child,[113] the 'interests' of the child[114] and the 'wellbeing' of the child.[115] In assessing welfare, the High Court has considered the health and finances of the prospective adoptive parents,[116] their education level and employment,[117] and their ability to provide a secure home and good future for the child.[118]

The welfare principle is enshrined more emphatically in the context of guardianship proceedings. The *Guardianship of Minors Act* is a statute of general application which was in force in England on 1 January 1961 and consequently applies in Solomon Islands by virtue of the *Constitution*. The Act requires the court to regard the welfare of the child as the first and paramount consideration.[119] The paramountcy

---

[108] *AdoptionAct 1958* (UK).

[109] *AdoptionAct 2004*, s 9(1)(b): 'The court before making an adoption order shall be satisfied... that the order if made will be for the welfare of the infant'.

[110] The welfare principle is stated in even stronger terms by the Convention in relation to adoption: art 21 provides that the system of adoption within a country must ensure that the best interests of the child are not just 'a' but 'the' paramount consideration.

[111] *Adoption Act 2004*, s 9(2).

[112] *Re Rabaua* (Unreported, High Court, Solomon Islands, Mwanesalua J, 27 July 2012) available via www.paclii.org at [2012] SBHC 77.

[113] *Re Armstrong* (Unreported, High Court, Solomon Islands, Mwanesalua J, 2 April 2012) available via www.paclii.org at [2012] SBHC 26; *Re Rabaua* (Unreported, High Court, Solomon Islands, Mwanesalua J, 27 July 2012) available via www.paclii.org at [2012] SBHC 77.

[114] *Re Duinkerke* (Unreported, High Court, Solomon Islands, Mwanesalua J, 2 September 2011) available via www.paclii.org at [2011] SBHC 82.

[115] *Re Matautia* (Unreported, High Court, Solomon Islands, Mwanesalua J, 21 March 2013) available via www.paclii.org at [2013] SBHC 22.

[116] *Marumaru v Wetara* (Unreported, High Court, Solomon Islands, Mwanesalua J, 28 July 2009) available via www.paclii.org at [2009] SBHC 28; see also *Re Rietveld* (Unreported, High Court, Solomon Islands, Mwanesalua J, 3 February 2012) available via www.paclii.org at [2012] SBHC 9.

[117] *Re Lizza Rabaua* (Unreported, High Court, Solomon Islands, Mwanesalua J, 27 July 2012) available via www.paclii.org at [2012] SBHC 77.

[118] *Re Wetara* (Unreported, High Court, Solomon Islands, Mwanesalua J, 21 November 2012) available via www.paclii.org at [2012] SBHC 130.

[119] *Guardianship of Infants Act 1925* (UK) s 1: *Principle on which questions relating tocustody, upbringing, etc. of infants are to be decided*: *Where in any proceeding before any court (whether or not a court within the meaning of the Guardianship of Infants Act 1866) the custody or upbringing of an infant, or the administration of any property belonging to or held on trust for an infant,*

of the welfare principle has come into conflict with the patriarchal values underpinning customary laws. In at least four reported cases, it has been held that customary rights of custody were subordinate to the welfare of the children. In *Sukutaona v Houanihou*,[120] *Re B*,[121] *K v T*[122] and *Sasango v Beliga*,[123] the welfare of the children was held to be the paramount consideration, and customary custody arrangements were rejected as they were not regarded as being in the child's best interests.[124]

Although the desire of the courts to protect the welfare of children in this area can be readily understood, at least by European observers, the legal basis for this is rather dubious. Whilst para 3(1) of the *Constitution* states that 'Acts of Parliament' shall prevail over customary law, this has been held to refer to Acts of the Parliament of Solomon Islands only, and not to Acts of the Parliament of Great Britain. This means that the *Guardianship of Minors Act 1925* is, at best, on a par with customary laws.

4.3 The Right to Information About Parents

There is no specific legislation allowing a child to know about his/her origin as required by Art 7 of the CRC. Nor does a child have any right to challenge the paternity of his or her mother's husband, whether the child was born during the marriage or not. Nor does either parent or any other person have a specific right to challenge paternity. However, in many areas of Solomon Islands, people still live in small communities and there is no room for secrecy on questions of parenthood. Further, if affiliation proceedings are commenced, the court may hear any evidence produced in support or defence of the claim, which could include evidence from the child.[125] Affiliation proceedings may only be commenced by the mother, who must be single at the time of the birth of the child.[126] 'Single' is defined to include a married woman who is living apart from her husband.[127] Proceedings must normally be

or the application of the income thereof, is in question, the court, in deciding that question, shall regard the welfare of the infant as the first and paramount consideration, and shall not take into consideration whether, from any other point of view, the claim of the father, or any right at common law possessed by the father, in respect of such custody, upbringing, administration or application, is superior to that of the mother, or the claim of the mother is superior to that of the father.

120 [1982] SILR 12.

121 [1983] SILR 223.

122 [1985–86] SILR 49.

123 [1987] SILR 91.

124 It should be noted, however, that the Court in each of the four cases made it clear that it regards custom as relevant to a determination of where the child's best interest lies.

125 *Affiliation, Separation and Maintenance Act* Cap 1, s 5(1).

126 Section 3.

127 Section 2.

commenced before the birth of the child[128] or within 3 years after the birth of the child.[129] However, proceedings may also be commenced if the putative father has made provision for the child's maintenance before or within 3 years after the birth or, if he left Solomon Islands within that 3 year period, within 12 months after his return.[130]

An adopted child does not have the right to know who his or her biological parents without a court order. The *Adoption Act* 2004 requires an Adopted Children Register to be kept by the Registrar General.[131] The index of the register is open to inspection by the public.[132] However, details of the biological parents are not kept on that register. Rather they are kept in another register complied under the Act, which links entries in the Adopted Children Register with 'Adopted' entries in the Registers of Births.[133] That register is not open for inspection except under a High Court order.[134] This means that in order to discover the names of birth parents, a child must obtain an order from the High Court of Solomon Islands. Given the geographic and economic obstacles which may limit a child's ability to access the High Court, the provisions may amount to a violation of the Convention.[135]

Neither does an adopted child have the right to know other non-identifying data about his/her biological parents, such as medical data, social status, religion and political convictions. There is no law in force which relates to children conceived with biomedical assistance and such procedures are not offered in Solomon Islands. In fact, there is breakdown of health services and many regional hospitals and clinics do not have adequate supplies.[136]

4.4 Consideration of the Child's Background

In situations where children are removed from their family environment, the Convention provides that due consideration should be given to the 'desirability of continuity in a child's upbringing and to the child's ethnic, religious, cultural and linguistic background'.[137]

---

128 Section 3(a).

129 Section 3(b).

130 Section 3(c) and (d).

131 *Adoption Act* 2004, s 18(1).

132 *Adoption Act* 2004, s 18(3).

133 *Adoption Act* 2004, s 18(4).

134 *Adoption Act* 2004, s 18(5).

135 Article 7.

136 UN Committee on the Rights of the Child (CRC), UN Committee on the Rights of the Child: Comments on State Party Report: Solomon Islands, 6 June 2003, CRC/C/15/ADD.208, available at: http://www.refworld.org/docid/3df59ecb2.html [accessed 5 November 2013], [40].

137 *Convention*, art 20(2).

Consideration of a child's background is particularly relevant in the context of intercountry adoption proceedings, where the child may be permanently removed from Solomon Islands. Under State law, only a person domiciled in Solomon Islands may make an application for adoption.[138] An order may only be made where the child has been in the care of the applicant for at least three consecutive months immediately preceding the date of the order. This condition is strictly enforced. Applicants are normally expected to be resident in Solomon Islands,[139] but the High Court may allow non-residents to apply.[140] Section 12 of the *Adoption Act 2004*, in particular, seems formulated to facilitate adoptions by non-residents. This provides that a person who is not domiciled in Solomon Islands and wishes to adopt a child under the law of another jurisdiction may apply for a provisional adoption order allowing them to remove the child for up to 2 years.[141]

It is unclear whether intercountry adoptions are allowed under customary laws. This will depend on the rules applying in the community to which the child belongs. However, if, for example, the adoptive parents wanted to apply for a passport in order for the child to leave the country, the customary adoption would have to be endorsed by the High Court, and this would bring the factors listed in the *Adoption Act 2004*, including whether the making of an adoption order will be for the welfare of the infant into play.

There is no express provision for the above matters to be taken into account when an order depriving a parent of custody is made under the *Affiliation, Separation and Maintenance Act*, although similar issues arise in such cases as in adoption cases.

4.5 The Right to Be Heard

As mentioned above, the Constitution guarantees the right to freedom of expression for everyone, including a child.[142] This is subject to exceptions, but none of these are specific to children. However, this constitutional provision is at odds with customary laws, according to which children must respect their elders and may not have a right to speak in village proceedings. The CRC has recommended that Solomon Islands 'promote and facilitate, within the family, the school, the courts and administrative bodies, respect for the views of children and their participation in all matters affecting them'.[143]

[138] *Adoption Act* 2004, s 3(1).

[139] *Adoption Act* 2004, s 3(5).

[140] *Adoption Act* 2004, s 12.

[141] *Adoption Act* 2004, s 26(1).

[142] *Constitution*, s 12(1).

[143] UN Committee on the Rights of the Child (CRC), UN Committee on the Rights of the Child: Comments on State Party Report: Solomon Islands, 6 June 2003, CRC/C/15/Add.208, available at: http://www.refworld.org/docid/3df59ecb2.html [accessed 5 November 2013],[27(b)].

Where a child is involved in State court proceedings relating to his or her family, there is no absolute right to be heard, but the court may take account of a child's views. Where a child is old enough to express a view, they will invariably be allowed to express this where the court is deciding on custodial and access arrangements where there is a dispute between the parents.[144] In practice, the courts write to the Social Welfare Office to request a social welfare enquiry background report on the applicants and children concerned.[145] Most courts consider children of 12 years and above to be competent to give evidence.[146] In the juvenile court, a child or young person[147] is entitled to give an opinion or evidence.[148]

As mentioned above, in civil proceedings, a child under 18[149] is regarded as being under a disability[150] and may only commence, defend or conduct proceedings through a litigation guardian,[151] who may be appointed for them by the court.[152] If the court does not make an appointment, this may be done by the child's legal representative filing a sworn statement that a person has agreed to take on the role and that they are a proper person to take on the role and have no adverse interest.[153]

There is no specific legislative provision for the child to be given information or advice about the proceedings. However, if a litigation guardian is appointed on application[154] or by the court of its own motion,[155] that person will have an ethical duty to ensure the child has information and advice appropriate for his or her level of understanding.[156] Additionally, the Constitution provides for the Office of

---

[144] See, e.g. *Sima v Thomas* (Unreported, High Court, Solomon Islands, Muria CJ, 27 October 1995), available via www.paclii.org at [1995] SBHC 60.

[145] UN Committee on the Rights of the Child (CRC), *UN Committee on the Rights of the Child: State Party Report: Solomon Islands*, 12 July 2002, CRC/C/51/Add.6, [417–418], [431–434], available at: http://www.refworld.org/docid/3df59ecb2.html [accessed 7 November 2013], [224]. See, e.g. *K v T* [1985–86] SILR 49.

[146] See further, Catherine Crosby-Currie, 'Children's Involvement In Contested Custody Cases: Practices and Experiences of Legal and Mental Health Professionals 20:3 *Law and Human Behavior* (June 1996), 289–311.

[147] See *Juvenile Offenders Act* Cap 14 s 2: 'child' is defined as a person under the age of 14 years; 'young person' is defined as a person between the ages of 14 and 18 years.

[148] *Juvenile Offenders Act* Cap 14 s 9(1).

[149] Solomon Islands Courts (Civil Procedure) *Rules 2007*, Sch 4.

[150] Solomon Islands Courts (Civil Procedure) *Rules 2007*, Rule 3.17.

[151] Solomon Islands Courts (Civil Procedure) *Rules 2007*, Rule 3.19.

[152] Solomon Islands Courts (Civil Procedure) *Rules 2007*, Rules 3.18 and 3.20.

[153] Solomon Islands Courts (Civil Procedure) *Rules 2007*, Rule 3.24.

[154] *Solomon Islands Courts (Civil Procedure) Rules 2007*, Rule 3.24.

[155] *Solomon Islands Courts (Civil Procedure) Rules 2007*, Rules 3.18 and 3.20.

[156] See, e.g. *The Legal Practitioners (Professional Conduct) Rules 1995*, para 9(2): 'A legal practitioner shall always be frank and open with his client and with all others so far as his client's interest may permit and shall at all times give his client a candid opinion on any professional matter in which he represents that client'.

Public Solicitor[157] to provide legal aid, advice and assistance to persons in need and in particular:

(a) *To provide legal aid, advice and assistance to any person in need who has been charged with a criminal offence*
(b) *To provide legal aid, advice and assistance to any person when directed to do so by the High Court*[158]

Notwithstanding, the CRC has expressed concern that adolescents do not have appropriate access to information.[159]

The *Adoption Act* 2004, which came into force in 2008,[160] does not make a child's consent a prerequisite to an adoption order being made. The *Adoption Act 2004* provides that the Court shall give 'due consideration' to the wishes of the infant. However, it does not give a child a right to object to adoption, regardless of their age or level of understanding. In fact, the consent of the infant seems to be expressly excluded by s 6(2) which states 'the consent of any person to the making of an adoption order in pursuance of an application (not being the consent of the infant) may be given ... without knowing the identity of the applicant for the order'. Only the consent of both parents and any guardian of the child is required.[161] The requirement for consents of the parents and guardian may be dispensed with in limited circumstances, namely, where the person whose consent is required has (a) abandoned, neglected or persistently ill-treated the infant, (b) cannot be found or is incapable of giving consent or is withholding his consent unreasonably or (c) is certified to be insane by a qualified medical practitioner.[162]

The procedure laid down in the *Adoption Act* requires a court hearing before an order will be granted.[163] Whilst there is no specific requirement for the child's consent, the court must consider whether an adoption order is in the best interests of the child.[164] The Court is empowered to appoint a guardian ad litem for the child.[165] Except where at least one of the applicants is a parent, an adoption order cannot be made in respect of a child under the compulsory school age unless the applicant has given at least 3 months' notice to the local authority. Where the child is old enough to express an opinion, the court may, but is not required to, give the child an opportunity to be heard and take the child's wishes into account. For example, in *Re Okini Manu*, Palmer J did not expressly refer to the child's welfare, but he did consider the

[157] *Constitution*, s 92(1).

[158] *Constitution*, s 92(4).

[159] UN Committee on the Rights of the Child (CRC), UN Committee on the Rights of the Child: Comments on State Party Report: Solomon Islands, 6 June 2003, CRC/C/15/ADD.208, available at: http://www.refworld.org/docid/3df59ecb2.html [accessed 5 November 2013], [42(a)].

[160] LN 145/2008.

[161] *Adoption Act* 2004, s 6(1)(a).

[162] *Adoption Act* 2004, s 7.

[163] *Adoption Act* 2004, s 3.

[164] *Adoption Act* 2004, s 9.

[165] *Adoption Regulations 2008*, reg 6.

child's preference that the adoption order be granted.[166] However, most cases have focused on the ability of the adoptive parents to care for the child and the consent of the child's current guardians.[167]

The *Adoption Act* does not apply to customary adoptions,[168] which are common. The rules governing such adoptions differ from place to place.[169] Given the status-based norms which often underlie customary laws, it is unlikely that the child's consent would be required.

4.6 Freedom from Discrimination

The Constitution protects all citizens, including children, against being treated in a discriminatory manner by a public officer or person exercising legal or public authority.[170] Accordingly, children cannot be excluded from enrolling at a State school because of their religious belief. In addition to the State-run schools, which provide free education for years 1–9,[171] a large number of primary and secondary schools are operated by the five main Christian denominations. These schools conduct obligatory religious education in accordance with that denomination's beliefs.[172] 90 % of the population in Solomon Islands professes to be affiliated to one of the five main Christian denominations (Church of Melanesia, Roman Catholic, South Seas Evangelical Church, United Church and Seventh Day Adventist). There is a strong interdenominational Christian influence in the country and most public gatherings start and finish with a prayer. Whilst church schools give preference to students who are members of their particular faith, some offer places to students from other faiths.[173]

---

[166] (Unreported, High Court, Solomon Islands, Palmer J, 30 July 1999) available via www.paclii.org at [1999] SBHC 74.

[167] *In re Armstrong (Infant) [2012] SBHC 26; HCSI-CC 8 of 2012 (2 April 2012)* http://www.paclii.org/cgi-bin/sinodisp/sb/cases/SBHC/2012/26.html?stem=&synonyms=&query=adoption%20and%20act%20and%202004; *Marumaru v Wetara [2009] SBHC 28; HCSI-CC 238 of 2009 (28 July 2009)* http://www.paclii.org/cgibin/sinodisp/sb/cases/SBHC/2009/28.html?stem=&synonyms=&query=adoption%20and%20act%20and%202004; *Re Lizza Rabaua (A Minor) [2012] SBHC 77; HCSI-CC 48 of 2012 (27 July 2012).*

[168] Adoption Act 2004, s 28.

[169] UN Committee on the Rights of the Child (CRC), *UN Committee on the Rights of the Child: State Party Report: Solomon Islands*, 12 July 2002, CRC/C/51/Add.6, [417–418], [431–434], available at: http://www.refworld.org/docid/3df59ecb2.html [accessed 7 November 2013], [225].

[170] *Constitution*, s 15.

[171] The Free Fee Education Policy has been in operation since 2009, but this only covers operational costs.

[172] UN Committee on the Rights of the Child (CRC), UN Committee on the Rights of the Child: State Party Report: Solomon Islands, 12 July 2002, CRC/C/51/ADD.6, Available at: http://www.refworld.org/docid/3df59ecb2.html [accessed 5 November 2013], [173].

[173] UN Committee on the Rights of the Child (CRC), UN Committee on the Rights of the Child: State Party Report: Solomon Islands, 12 July 2002, CRC/C/51/Add.6, available at: http://www.refworld.org/docid/3df59ecb2.html [accessed 5 November 2013], [172].

Further, under the Constitution, all citizens, including children, are accorded freedom of thought, conscience and religion, unless this individual right interferes with the rights of others or with the public interest.[174] Accordingly, in theory, no person attending a school is compulsorily required to receive religious instruction in a particular faith. Further, the Solomon Islands Country Report states that 'Anyone who is under 18 years of age is required to have the consent of his/her guardian before he/she can receive religious instruction'.[175] However, in some areas of the country, the only secondary school is provided by a particular Church. In such cases, a child may have little choice other than to attend that school and receive instruction in the school's faith. In State secondary schools, Bible Studies is a compulsory subject in the first 3 years. Students then choose whether or not to pursue Bible Studies as an elective in their fourth and fifth years.[176]

4.7 *Corporal Punishment and Ill-Treatment*

It is a criminal offence for anyone over 15 to 'wilfully assault, ill-treat, neglect, abandon or expose' a child under 15 who is in their care.[177] It is also an offence to cause or procure a child to be 'wilfully assaulted, ill-treated, neglected, abandoned or exposed' by another.[178] However, a proviso to this section preserves the right of 'any parent, teacher, or other person, having the lawful control of a child or young person to administer reasonable punishment' to a child under 15.[179] However, if corporal punishment is severe, it may amount to inhumane treatment which is prohibited by the Constitution.[180]

In *R v Rose*[181] a teacher was prosecuted under the *Penal Code* for caning two 10-year-old pupils in the sight of their classmates. The defendant raised the defence of 'reasonable punishment'. Ward CJ held that in deciding on reasonableness, the Court must consider whether the punishment is reasonable on the facts and that the question of whether it offends section 7 of the Constitution should be borne in mind as part of that assessment. Any infliction of corporal punishment on a child that was inhuman or degrading must, in the light of that provision, be unreasonable punishment.[182]

[174] *Constitution*, s 12.

[175] UN Committee on the Rights of the Child (CRC), UN Committee on the Rights of the Child: State Party Report: Solomon Islands, 12 July 2002, CRC/C/51/Add.6, available at: http://www.refworld.org/docid/3df59ecb2.html [accessed 5 November 2013], [169].

[176] UN Committee on the Rights of the Child (CRC), UN Committee on the Rights of the Child: State Party Report: Solomon Islands, 12 July 2002, CRC/C/51/Add.6, available at: http://www.refworld.org/docid/3df59ecb2.html [accessed 5 November 2013], [173].

[177] *Penal Code* Cap 26, s 233(1).

[178] *Penal Code* Cap 26, s 233(1).

[179] *Penal Code* Cap 26, s 233(4).

[180] Section 7.

[181] [1987] SILR 45.

[182] [1987] SILR 45, 50–51.

In determining whether the conduct was degrading, His Lordship held that s 7 should be interpreted in the light of present-day conditions and the commonly accepted standards in Solomon Islands at the time. He considered that, whilst the very old cases established the defence of reasonable correction, the generally accepted standard of what is reasonable has changed radically since then. If the manner of inflicting corporal punishment was 'outside the standards normally accepted and expected today, the possibility that the victim will feel humiliated [was] increased'.[183] However, in view of the fact that the extent of the punishment inflicted was slight and did not breach the Code of Discipline in the school's Teachers Handbook and that the victims agreed that their actions disrupted the assembly, no conviction was entered. This reasoning would appear to apply equally to a parent or other family member who physically chastises a child.

It is also an offence to ill-treat, neglect or abandon a child under 15 or cause the child to be treated in that way or to be exposed to unnecessary suffering or injury to health.[184] A parent or person who is legally liable to maintain a child under 15 is deemed to have neglected the child in a manner likely to cause injury to health if the parent or other person has failed to provide adequate food, clothing, medical aid or lodging for the child.[185] A further deeming provision provides that if it is proved that the death of a child under 3 was caused by suffocation while the infant was in bed with a person over 15 who went to bed drunk, that person will be deemed to have neglected the child in a manner likely to cause injury to its health.[186] Conviction for any of these offences under the Penal Code carries a penalty of up to 5 years imprisonment.[187]

However, the police do not tend to pursue allegations of ill-treatment of children and prosecutions under the Penal Code and human rights cases under s 7 are rare. Churches and the Red Cross Handicapped Centre are the only organisations that investigate such cases.[188] There are no mandatory reporting procedures in place and no State services for child victims of abuse. The local community, extended family or the church may in some cases provide protection and support.[189]

The comments made by the CRC in response to Solomon Islands first report suggested that Solomon Islands should place a prohibition of all forms of physical and

[183] [1987] SILR 45, 50–51.

[184] *Penal Code* Cap 26, s 233(1).

[185] *Penal Code* Cap 26, s 233(2)(a).

[186] *Penal Code* Cap 26, s 233(2)(b). The exception to this is where the child suffocates due to disease or choking.

[187] *Penal Code* Cap 26, s 233(1).

[188] UN Committee on the Rights of the Child (CRC), UN Committee on the Rights of the Child: State Party Report: Solomon Islands, 12 July 2002, CRC/c/51/add.6, available at: http://www.refworld.org/docid/3df59ecb2.html [accessed 5 November 2013], [193].

[189] UN Committee on the Rights of the Child (CRC), UN Committee on the Rights of the Child: State Party Report: Solomon Islands, 12 July 2002, CRC/c/51/add.6, available at: http://www.refworld.org/docid/3df59ecb2.html [accessed 5 November 2013] [193]–[194].

mental violence, including corporal punishment, against children.[190] No action has yet been taken on this and corporal punishment is still widely practiced within the family, schools and other institutions.[191]

4.8 Deprivation of Parental Rights

Under State law, both parents may be deprived of parental rights if the child is made a ward of court. A father may be deprived of rights of custody and access under the *Affiliation, Separation and Maintenance Act*[192] on grounds which include adultery, desertion, cruelty and neglecting to maintain his children. This will result in a decree of judicial separation being issued by the magistrates' court.[193]*The Affiliation, Separation and Maintenance (Amendment) Act 1992* introduced a procedure for obtaining wide-ranging protection orders for spouses where domestic violence is established.[194] This procedure might also be used to deprive a parent of custody and access. The orders that can be made include an order prohibiting the respondent from using or threatening to use violence against a child.[195] Such orders may be made ex parte on an interim basis for a maximum of 28 days.[196] Orders may also be made requiring the respondent to leave the matrimonial home[197] and/or prohibiting the respondent from entering the matrimonial home.[198] A power of arrest may be attached to the order if the magistrates' court is satisfied that the respondent has physically injured the child and considers that this is likely to happen again.[199] A police officer may arrest without warrant a person who breaches such an order.[200]

On an application for an affiliation order, the *Affiliation Separation Maintenance Act* also empowers the magistrates' court or a local court to give custody of the child to someone other than the mother if the mother is not a fit and proper person to have custody of the child, or she has died, become of unsound mind or is in prison.[201]

---

[190] UN Committee on the Rights of the Child (CRC), UN Committee on the Rights of the Child: Comments on State Party Report: Solomon Islands, 6 June 2003, CRC/C/15/Add.208, available at: http://www.refworld.org/docid/3df59ecb2.html [accessed 5 November 2013], [30]–[30(a)].

[191] UN Committee on the Rights of the Child (CRC), UN Committee on the Rights of the Child: Comments on State Party Report: Solomon Islands, 6 June 2003, CRC/C/15/Add.208, available at: http://www.refworld.org/docid/3df59ecb2.html [accessed 5 November 2013], [30].

[192] Cap 1.

[193] Section 11.

[194] *Affiliation Separation Maintenance Act* Cap 1, ss 22–24.

[195] *Affiliation Separation Maintenance Act* Cap 1, s 22(2)(b).

[196] *Affiliation Separation Maintenance Act* Cap 1, ss 22(5) and (6).

[197] *Affiliation Separation Maintenance Act* Cap 1, ss 22(3(c)(i).

[198] *Affiliation Separation Maintenance Act* Cap 1, ss 22(3)(c)(ii).

[199] *Affiliation Separation Maintenance Act* Cap 1, ss 24)(1).

[200] *Affiliation Separation Maintenance Act* Cap 1, ss 24(2).

[201] *Affiliation Separation Maintenance Act* Cap 1, s 9(1).

Application for such an order may be made by a social welfare officer, the Provincial Secretary or any other public officer appointed by him, the putative father or the mother.[202]

Under the *Penal Code*, where a child under 16 is found guilty of a crime, the parents or guardians of the child may be ordered to pay fine, costs or compensation.[203] However, parents may only be deprived of custody under the *Penal Code* if they have caused, encouraged or favoured seduction, prostitution or unlawful detention of a female child under 18.[204]

Under indigenous customary laws, the position is more complex. As mentioned above, customary laws are not homogenous and, in the event of misbehaviour on the part of a parent, the position will depend on the customary laws of the group to which the parents belong. This may be further complicated where the parents come from different parts of the country and are governed by different customary regimes. As a general rule it can be said that the patriarchal norms of customary laws make it very unlikely that a father would be deprived of parental rights or responsibilities. This is particularly the case where bride price has been paid.[205]

There is no official State system offering alternative care for children whose parents are unable or unsuitable to look after them. However, the social system in force means that the community as a whole takes on responsibility for children within it.[206] This system, known in Melanesia as the 'wantok' system means that relatives or adults in the broader social network will take over the parenting role if this becomes necessary. This may take the form of customary adoption, which is a common occurrence, but is perhaps closer to a fostering arrangement, as it does not usually cut the ties with natural parents.[207]

4.9 Medical Treatment

In Solomon Islands, the child's consent to medical treatment is not required. Nor does he/she have a right to refuse consent to medical treatment. If there is opposition to a parent's decisions regarding medical treatment of a child, a child

---

[202] *Affiliation Separation Maintenance Act* Cap 1, s 9(2).

[203] *Penal Code* Cap 5, s 38.

[204] *Penal Code* Cap 5, s 152.

[205] Jennifer Corrin and Kenneth Brown, 'Marit Long Kastom: Marriage in the Solomon Islands', *International Journal of Law, Policy and the Family* 18 (2004) 52, 75.

[206] Kenneth Brown, *Reconciling Customary Law and Received Law in Melanesia: The Post-independence Experience in Solomon Islands and Vanuatu*, Charles Darwin University Press, NT Australia, 2005.

[207] Kenneth Brown, *Reconciling Customary Law and Received Law in Melanesia: The Post-independence Experience in Solomon Islands and Vanuatu*, Charles Darwin University Press, NT Australia, 2005.

(through a litigation guardian) or a third party with sufficient interest could make an application to the High Court to have the child made a ward of court. This procedure results in the court taking control of decisions relating to the child.[208]

4.10 Change of Name

At common law a person's name is the name that they are known by, so from this perspective, there is nothing to prevent a child from changing his or her name. However, a child does not have the right to change his or her name as it exists on official State records until he/she reaches 21. A change of name can be effected by deed poll, which is legal document, binding only on the person executing it. Such a document can be executed by the child's parents on the child's behalf.

4.11 Employment

The *Labour Act*[209] sets 12, 15, 16 and 18 years as the ages that govern different protective provisions in the Act. The Act sets 12 as the minimum age for employment,[210] 15 for working in an industrial undertaking or on a ship (other than a school ship or training ship or under an approved school or college),[211] 16 for working underground in a mine[212] and 18 for working underground in a mine[213] or on a ship without a certificate of fitness,[214] on a steam ship as a trimmer or stoker[215] or on night shifts in an industrial undertaking.[216] Employers in an industrial undertaking and every master of a ship must keep a register of all employees under 18.[217]

The penalty for breaching any of these provisions is a fine of $500.[218] However, reasonable belief that the person was old enough to be employed is a defence.[219]

---

208 See, e.g. *Macleod v Macleod*, High Court, Solomon Islands, Ward C.J, 8 August 1991, available via www.paclii.org at [1991] SBHC 47; HC-CC 131 of 1989 (8 August 1991).

209 Cap 73, Part VII.

210 *Labour Act* Cap 73, s 46.

211 *Labour Act* Cap 73, s 47.

212 *Labour Act* Cap 73, s 48.

213 *Labour Act* Cap 73, s 49(a).

214 *Labour Act* Cap 73, s 49(c).

215 *Labour Act* Cap 73, s 49(b).

216 *Labour Act* Cap 73, s 49(d).

217 *Labour Act* Cap 73, s 50.

218 *Labour Act* Cap 73, s 52.

219 *Labour Act* Cap 73, s 51(2).

The magistrate dealing with the charge may determine the age of the child, where this is disputed acting on such evidence as he/she thinks fit.[220]

Hiring children under 15 and girls under 18 for prostitution is prohibited by the *Penal Code*.[221] Other than this, there is no prohibition on the jobs that a child may do. Nor is there any regulation of a child's working hours or other conditions of employment.

Generally, children are entitled to choose their own employment, but given the prevailing cultural norms, a child is unlikely to go against his or her parents' wishes when choosing employment. The exception is apprenticeship of a child aged 14–16, where the deed is required to be signed by a parent or guardian.[222] The child's consent is also required.[223] Children over 16 may apprentice themselves.[224] The term of apprenticeships must not exceed 5 years.[225]

In 2002, the Committee on Economic, Social and Cultural Rights (CESCR) recommended that Solomon Islands consider ratifying the main International Labour Organization Conventions relating to economic, social and cultural rights. These include Convention No. 182 concerning the Prohibition and Immediate Action for the Elimination of the Worst Forms of Child Labour,[226] which was ratified in 2012.[227] The government collaborated with the ILO to implement a Decent Work Programme for 2009–2012, designed to promote decent employment for youth; no specific activities appear to have been launched under this programme.[228]

4.12 Rights on Arrest and Conviction

Article 37 of the Convention includes rights to freedom from torture and cruel, inhuman or degrading treatment or punishment; freedom from capital punishment and life imprisonment without possibility of release; freedom from unlawful or arbitrary deprivation of liberty; and, on imprisonment, the right to be treated with

---

[220] *Labour Act* Cap 73, s 51(1).

[221] Cap 26, ss 144(1)(a),149(1).

[222] *Labour Act* Cap 73, s 54.

[223] *Labour Act* Cap 73, s 54.

[224] *Labour Act* Cap 73, s 56.

[225] *Labour Act* Cap 73, ss 54 and 56.

[226] ILO. Fact Sheet: Solomon Islands. Status Report. Bangkok: 2009, available at: http://www.ilo.org/wcmsp5/groups/public/-asia/-ro-bangkok/-ilo-suva/documents/publication/wcms_155871.pdf [accessed 5 November 2013].

[227] ILO Normlex. *Ratification for Solomon Islands*, accessed November 5, 2013; http://www.ilo.org/dyn/normlex/en/f?p=1000:11200:0:NO:11200:P11200_COUNTRY_ID:103193.

[228] UN Committee on the Rights of the Child (CRC), UN Committee on the Rights of the Child: Comments on State Party Report: Solomon Islands, 6 June 2003, CRC/C/15/ADD.208, available at: http://www.refworld.org/docid/3df59ecb2.html [accessed 5 November 2013], [6].

humanity and respect and in a manner appropriate to his or her age. More particularly, on incarceration, children are normally to be separated from adults and allowed to maintain contact with their family and provided with prompt access to legal and other appropriate assistance.

The adequacy of Solomon Islands legislation to protect the rights of a child set out in Article 37 was considered in *K v* R, which has been referred to earlier in this report.[229] This was a bail application on behalf of a boy aged 17 who was charged with murder and with being a member of an unlawful society, the 'Guadalcanal Liberation Front'. Since his arrest in October 2003, he had been held in an adult prison for nearly 2 years. In seeking bail, defence counsel referred to Solomon Islands obligations under international texts. The Court noted that in murder cases (which carry a life sentence),[230] bail was only granted in exceptional circumstances.[231] In refusing bail, Palmer CJ held that the relevant conventions (the Universal Declaration of Human Rights, the International Covenant on Economic, Social and Cultural Rights, the International Convention on the Elimination of All Forms of Racial Discrimination and Convention on the Rights of the Child) had to be read subject to the domestic legislation and the *Constitution*. His Lordship stated that 'Much of what is contained in those Conventions and international instruments are already well reflected in our domestic legislation'. More particularly, he held that Article 37(a) of the Convention was reflected in s 7 of the Constitution, which guarantees protection from slavery and forced labour for everyone, including children.[232] His Lordship also dismissed the argument that a mandatory life sentence of imprisonment for murder contravened Article 37, as, if convicted, an accused might apply to the Committee on the Prerogative of Mercy for a pardon under s 45 of the Constitution. His Lordship was also of the view that Article 37 (b), which protects a child from unlawful or arbitrary deprivation of liberty, was 'more than adequately catered for in the Juvenile Offenders Act, the Constitution, the Penal Code and the Criminal Procedure Code'.

5 Reciprocal Obligations

Generally, customary laws are founded upon respect for elders and for the family. Accordingly, in many areas of the country, children are obliged to look after their parents and to support them to the best of their ability. The penalty for not doing so is likely to be community condemnation or, in extreme cases, ostracism. However,

---

[229] (Unreported, High Court, Solomon Islands, Palmer CJ, 16 September 2005), available via www.paclii.org at [2005] SBHC 150, affirming *R v K* (Unreported, High Court, Solomon Islands, Naqiolevu J, 12 July 2005), available via www.paclii.org at [2005] SBHC 80.

[230] *Penal Code* Cap 5, s 200.

[231] *R v Kong Ming Khoo* (Unreported, High Court, Solomon islands, Ward CJ, 1991) 2, available via www.paclii.org at [1991] SBHC 24.

[232] *Constitution*, s 6.

as discussed above, customary laws can also benefit vulnerable children by creating obligations on members of the same social group to provide them with food and shelter.[233]

6 Conclusion

There is an urgent need for comprehensive child rights legislation to be passed by Parliament in order to implement the terms of the Convention. Rather than adopting a bill modelled on foreign legislation, this should be drafted to take into account the circumstances of Solomon Islands. As recommended by the CRC, Solomon Islands needs to 'strengthen the mechanisms required to harmonise its constitutional provisions and its domestic and customary legislation written provisions and principles of the Convention as soon as possible'.[234]

Solomon Islands is a country where traditional means of awareness raising and training do not always succeed. The CRC has recommended wide dissemination of the initial report and written replies submitted by Solomon Islands, but logistical difficulties, language diversity and cultural differences all pose problems for such initiatives. Creative solutions are required such as those suggested by the CRC, which include 'audiovisual aids such as picture books and posters, in particular at the local level and through the mass media'.[235] However, even these suggestions underestimate the difficulties in combating ingrained status-based norms.

The second, third and fourth reports are now overdue and this is obviously a burden which the country finds difficult to shoulder.

Bibliography

Books

Brown, Kenneth. 2005. *Reconciling customary law and received law in Melanesia: The post-independence experience in Solomon Islands and Vanuatu*. Darwin: Charles Darwin University Press.

Corrin, Jennifer, and Done Paterson. 2011. *Introduction to South Pacific law*, 3rd ed. Melbourne: Palgrave Macmillan.

---

[233] Solomon Islands Government, *Reports Submitted by State Parties under Article 44 of the* Convention: *Solomon Islands*, UN Doc CRC/C/51/Add.6 (12 July 2002) 8.

[234] UN Committee on the Rights of the Child (CRC), UN Committee on the Rights of the Child: Comments on State Party Report: Solomon Islands, 6 June 2003, CRC/C/15/ADD.208, available at: http://www.refworld.org/docid/3df59ecb2.html [accessed 5 November 2013].

[235] UN Committee on the Rights of the Child (CRC), UN Committee on the Rights of the Child: Comments on State Party Report: Solomon Islands, 6 June 2003, CRC/C/15/ADD.208, available at: http://www.refworld.org/docid/3df59ecb2.html [accessed 5 November 2013], [18(b)].

Farran, Sue. 2009. *Human rights in the South Pacific: Challenges and changes*. Abingdon: Routledge-Cavendish.
Fraenkel, Jon. 2004. *The manipulation of custom: From uprising to intervention in the Solomon Islands*. Sydney: Pandanus Books.
Steiner, Henry J., and Phillip Alston. 1996. *International human rights in context: Law politics, morals*. Oxford: Clarendon Press.
Triggs, Gillian. 2006. *International law: Contemporary principles and practices*. Chatswood: LexisNexis.

Articles

Baird, Natalie. 2011. To ratify or not to ratify?: An assessment of the case for ratification of international human rights treaties in the Pacific. *Melbourne Journal of International Law* 12: 1.
Butler, Petra. 2008. Margin of appreciation – A note towards a solution for the Pacific? *Victoria University of Wellington Law Review* 39: 687.
Corrin Care, Jennifer. 1999. Customary law and human rights in Solomon Islands. *Journal of Legal Pluralism and Unofficial Law* 43: 135.
Corrin Care, Jennifer. 2006. Negotiating the constitutional conundrum: Balancing cultural identity with principles of gender equality in post-colonial South Pacific societies. *Indigenous Law Journal* 5: 51.
Corrin, Jennifer, and Kenneth Brown. 1999. Conflict in Melanesia – Customary law and the rights of Melanesian women. *Commonwealth Law Bulletin* 24: 1334.
LAWASIA. 1992. Report on a proposed Pacific Charter of Human Rights. *Victoria University of Wellington Law Review* 22: 99.
Renshaw, Catherine, Andrew Byrnes, and Andrea Durbach. 2010. Human rights protection in the Pacific. *New Zealand Journal of Public and International Law* 8: 117.
Tamata, Laitia. 2000. Application of the human rights conventions in the Pacific Islands courts. *Journal of South Pacific Law* 4.

Chapters in Edited Books

Thaman, K. 1999. A Pacific Island perspective of collective human rights. In *Collective human rights of Pacific peoples*, ed. Nin Thomas. Auckland: University of Auckland.

Conference and Occasional Papers

Corrin, Jennifer. 2008. *Only skin deep? Law reform and the reality of human rights in the South Pacific*. Paper presented at the Australasian Law Reform Agencies Conference, Port Vila, Vanuatu, 10–12 Sept 2008.
Zorn, Jean. 2000. *Women, custom and international law in the Pacific*. Occasional Paper No 5. Port Vila: University of South Pacific.

Reports and Other Documents

Committee on the Rights of the Child. 2002. *List of issues: Solomon Islands*. UN Doc CRC/C/Q/SOL/1.

Committee on the Rights of the Child. 2003. *Concluding observations: Solomon Islands*. 33rd sess, UN Doc CRC/C/15/Add.208 (2 July 2003).

International Council on Human Rights Policy (ICHRP). 2009. *When legal worlds overlap human rights, state and non-state law*. Geneva: ICHRP. Available at SSRN: http://ssrn.com/abstract=1551229

New Zealand Law Commission. 2006. *Converging currents: Custom and human rights in the Pacific'*. Study Paper No 17. Wellington.

Solomon Islands Government. 2002. *Reports submitted by state parties under Article 44 of the convention: Solomon Islands*. UN Doc CRC/C/51/Add.6, 12 Jul 2002.

Solomon Islands National Constitutional Congress and The Eminent Persons Advisory Council. *1st 2009 Draft Federal Constitution of Solomon Islands*, 26 Jun 2009.

UNICEF. 2007. *Solomon Islands "Plus 5" review of the 2002 special session on children and world fit for children plan of action*. Country Report.

Les droits de l'enfant mineur d'âge en droit espagnol après la Constitution de 1978

Gabriel García Cantero

1 Introduction

Si bien le code civil espagnol promulgué en 1889 s'inspire en général dans le code Napoléon, cependant il avait adopté à l'époque les règles du Droit canon sur le mariage et la famille; d'autre part il se fait écho de la conception patriarcale de celle-ci dominante dans la société européenne du XIX siècle, et basée sur la supériorité hiérarchique du mari et du père, avec la conséquence de la soumission de la femme, et aussi de l'enfant au pouvoir de son mari, et de leur parents (d'abord le père et après sa mort, la mère) ou du tuteur. En général dans le Cc de 1889, on ne parlait absolument pas des droits de l'enfant mineur d'âge.

La Constitution de 1978 a changé radicalement la perspective de la situation juridique de l'enfant mineur en Espagne. Le titre I de celle-ci règle les droits et les devoirs des citoyens, et pour la première fois on peut parler d'un *Droit civil constitutionnel*. L'art. 10 ouvre le titre avec cette règle impérative :

1. La dignité de la personne, les droits inviolables qui lui sont inhérents, le libre développement de la personnalité, le respect de la loi et aux droits d'autrui sont le fondement de l'ordre politique et de la paix sociale.
2. Les normes relatives aux droits fondamentaux et aux libertés que la Constitution reconnait seront interprétées d'accord avec la Déclaration Universelle des Droits Humains et les Traités internationaux sur les mêmes matières ratifiés par l'Espagne.

En conséquence, cet article déclare ouvertement que notre Constitution s'inspire directement dans le texte de l'ONU de 1948 et, en plus, elle invoque aussi les futurs

G. García Cantero, (✉)
Professeur émérite de Droit civil, Faculté de Droit, Université de Zaragoza,
C/ Pedro Cerbuna 12, Zaragoza 50009, Espagne
e-mail: ggarcia@unizar.es

O. Cvejić Jančić (ed.), *The Rights of the Child in a Changing World*,
Ius Comparatum - Global Studies in Comparative Law 13,
DOI 10.1007/978-3-319-23189-1_17

traités internationaux, signés par l'Espagne sur la matière comme un moyen d'interpréter celle-là, ainsi qu'on a crée la procédure adéquate pour la ratification de les dits traités. Les droits fondamentaux ne sont pas créés par l'État mais seulement ils sont reconnus par la Constitution. Pour l'avenir aussi la voie légale y est bien dessinée. Donc, on peut conclure que notre Constitution de 1978, avait bien préparé d'avance la réception en Espagne de la Convention de 1989.

Il y a d'autres préceptes constitutionnels dont la cite est obligée :

Art. 12: Les espagnols son majeurs d'âge aux 18 ans.

Art. 16: 1. Sont-elles garanties la liberté idéologique, religieuse et de culte des individus et des communautés sans d'autres limites pour se manifester que le nécessaire pour maintenir l'ordre public protégé par la loi. 2. Personne ne pourra pas être obligé a déclarer sur son idéologie, religion ou croyance. 3. Aucune confession religieuse aura caractère officiel. Les pouvoirs publiques tiendront compte des croyances religieuses de la société espagnole et maintiendront des rapports de coopération avec l'Église catholique et les autres confessions.

L'art. 20.4 dispose expressément que *la protection de la jeunesse et de l'enfance* sont des limites à la liberté de penser, de presse et d'information.

L'art. 27 règle minutieusement la liberté d'enseignement et d'éducation :

1. Tous ont droit à l'éducation. On reconnait la liberté d'enseignement. 2. L'éducation a pour objet le plein développement de la personnalité humaine dans le respect aux principes démocratiques de la vie en société et aux droits et libertés fondamentaux. 3. Les pouvoirs publics garantissent le droit qui assiste aux parents pour que leurs enfants reçoivent la formation religieuse et morale qui sont d'accord avec leurs convictions personnelles. 4. L'enseignement basique est obligatoire et gratuite. (...) 7. Les professeurs, les parents et, dans leur cas, les élèves interviendront dans le control et la gestion de tous les centres d'enseignement soutenus par l'Administration avec des fonds publiques ...

Le chapitre 3ème du Titre I traite « *Des principes recteurs de la politique social et économique* ». La doctrine l'interprète dans le sens qu'il ne contient pas de droits fondamentaux, mais des *principes* qui dans l'avenir vont inspirer la politique de l'état espagnol. Ils ne peuvent pas être invoqués devant les tribunaux qu'après une loi ordinaire qui les développe en soit promulguée (art. 53.3); mais son importance pratique a été remarquable comme l'inspiration de la politique législative et comme critère d'interprétation du droit positif dans les années successives.

En voici les principes constitutionnels les plus importants par rapport à notre sujet:

Art. 39. 1. Les pouvoirs publiques assurent la protection social, économique et juridique de la famille. 2. Les pouvoirs publiques assurent aussi ***la protection intégrale des enfants****, égaux devant la loi et indépendamment de sa filiation, et [la protection] de leurs mères indépendamment aussi de leur état civil. La loi va faciliter la recherche de la paternité . 3 . Les parents ont le devoir de prêter assistance de toute classe aux enfants nés à l'intérieur ou en dehors du mariage, pendant sa minorité et aussi dans les autres cas détermines par la loi. 4. Les mineurs jouiront de la protection établie dans les traités ou les accords internationaux qui veillent pour leurs droits.*

Art. 48. Les pouvoirs publiques vont promouvoir les conditions pour la participation libre et efficace de la jeunesse au développement politique, social, économique et culturel.

Art. 49. Les pouvoirs publiques vont réaliser une politique de prévision, traitement, réhabilitation et intégration des handicapés physiques, sensoriels et psychiques, auxquels ils vont prêter l'attention spécialisée due à son état, et aussi ils vont les protéger spécialement afin de qu'ils puissent jouir de tous les droits que ce Titre octroie à tous les citoyens.

Art. 54. Une loi organique va régler l'institution du « Defensor del Pueblo » (Ombudsman), en tant que haut Commissionné du Parlement (« Cortes Generales »), élu par celui-ci pour la défense des droits établis dans ce Titre avec le pouvoir de surveiller l'activité de l'Administration et à la charge d'en rendre compte au Parlement.

Je me permet de souligner l'expression que l'art. 39.2 CE utilise à propos de la *protection intégrale des enfants*, en tant que principe inspirateur de la politique social et économique. Le mot *intégral* veut dire, en espagnol, que la protection est totale, c.a. d. dans tous les cas, de manière absolue et sans exception, toujours en priorité à l'égard des autres intérêts aussi protégés par la loi. Peut être c'est la première fois que notre législateur constitutionnel a utilisé cet adjectif dans ce sens si fort.

2 Le nouveau droit civil espagnol de la personne et de la famille après la Constitution de 1978

La position juridique de l'enfant mineur en Espagne a dû changer radicalement après la promulgation de la Constitution en vigueur. Tout d'abord il y a des règles constitutionnelles que sont directement applicables (par ex. la majorité d'âge à 18 ans, au lieu de 21 ans du Cc), et il y a d'autres dispositions que les tribunaux considèrent qui révoquent tacitement le Cc. Mais la réforme produite par le texte constitutionnel a été si profonde qu'a partir de l'année 1981, le législateur ordinaire est obligé de promulguer différentes lois sur une *nouvelle régulation civil* du mariage et des régimes matrimoniaux, de la filiation matrimoniale et non matrimoniale, de la tutelle, de l'adoption, ainsi que leurs conséquences dans le Droit de successions et d'autres matières connexes (par ex. la nationalité), qui affectent aussi directement ou indirectement aux droits des mineurs.

De sorte qu'au fur et à mesure que le législateur ordinaire a développé le chapitre 3ème, titre I, de la Constitution, il apparaît ce que la doctrine espagnole appelle le *Système publique de la protection des mineurs* dont les *notes caractéristiques* sont les suivantes :

- (1ª) L'assistance publique aux mineurs en situation d'abandon est de la compétence de certains organes administratifs, lesquels doivent qualifier celle-ci sans l'intervention du Juge. On considère l'abandon (*desamparo)* comme la privation de l'assistance morale et matérielle due à l'enfant.
- (2ª) En principe l'intervention administrative a pour but la réinsertion du mineur abandonné dans sa famille d'origine et subsidiairement l'intégration dans une nouvelle famille après la rupture des liens juridiques avec celle-là.

- (3ª) À la mesure du possible on cherche l'intégration de l'enfant abandonné dans la famille ample ou étendue d'origine avant que dans une autre famille.
- (4ª) Pour l'assistance publique de l'enfant abandonné on préfère d'abord l'accueil familiale au lieu de l'accueil chez des institutions.
- (5ª) En présence de plusieurs frères ou sœurs abandonnés on cherche, dans la mesure de possible, une solution unifiée pour tous (donc, l'accueil dans la même famille ou centre).
- (6ª) La compétence attribuée à l'Administration possède un caractère dynamique, parce qu'elle comprend aussi tous les *situations du risque* pour les mineurs, ainsi que tous les autres cas d'accueil légal des mineurs ainsi que tous les placements en vue d'adoption. Dans ces hypothèses la compétence de l'Administration est exclusive sauf un recours finale aux tribunaux civils. En fait, la nouvelle législation a privilégié les compétences de l'Administration sans pour autant éliminer la compétence de ceux-là. Mais surtout, il faut remarquer que,
- *(7ª) On établie comme principe informateur de tout le système de protection publique des mineurs la primatie de l'intérêt de ceux-ci.*

3 La Convention de 20 novembre 1989, approuvée par l'Assemblée Générale de l'ONU, et la Loi espagnole Organique 1/1996, du 15 janvier, de la protection juridique du mineur (LOPJM)

La Convention de 1989 de l'ONU a été ratifiée par l'Espagne le 30 novembre 1990, et elle a donné lieu a la Loi de 1996 de la Protection Juridique du Mineur (LOPJM) et quelques années plus tard à la Loi d'Adoption International de 2007 (LAI). Mais le législateur espagnol a tenu compte aussi de la « Carte Européenne des Droits de l'Enfant » de 1992.

En synthèse on peut bien établir que la Convention de 1989 a trouvé une législation nationale dûment disposée pour mieux recevoir le Droit international, parce que la Constitution de 1978 en avait anticipé le principe fondamental.

Dans son Exposée de Motifs (numéro 2) on dit que la LOPJM suppose une réforme en profondeur des institutions traditionnelles de protection de mineurs réglés dans le Cc, en instituant un cadre juridique très ample qui oblige à tous les pouvoirs publiques, ainsi qu'à toutes les institutions dédiées aux mineurs, à leurs parents et familiaux et à tous les citoyens en général. Les profondes transformations sociales intervenues dans la société ont produit un changement dans le *statut* social du mineur qui va permettre d'élaborer un *système des droits humaines de l'enfance*, dont émane la reconnaissance de la pleine capacité juridique pour devenir titulaire de droits le mineur d'âge ainsi qu'une capacité progressive pour pouvoir les exercer. En conséquence, cette loi va établir un concept des personnes mineurs d'âge comme des sujets actifs, participatifs et créatifs capables de modifier sa propre sphère d'action personnelle et sociale, ainsi que de promouvoir la recherche de satisfaire personnellement leurs propres besoins et celles des autres. L'état actuel de la science permet d'affirmer que la meilleure forme de garantir socialement et juridiquement la protection de l'enfance est celle de promouvoir l'autonomie des enfants en tant que sujets des droits.

Selon l'art. 1° la Loi s'applique aux mineurs de 18 ans qui se trouvent dans le territoire espagnol, sauf que la loi personnelle applicable détermine une âge mineure.

L'art. 2° établi le principe général suivant : Dans l'application de cette Loi *l'intérêt supérieure des mineurs sera préférable à tout autre principe légitime concurrent.* Les mesures à adopter en faveur des mineurs auront toujours un caractère éducatif. Les limites à la capacité d'agir des mineurs seront l'objet d'interprétation restrictive.

Les matières réglées dans la LOPJM sont les suivantes :

- Art. 3°: Sources de Droit international.
- Art. 4°: Droit à l'honneur, à l'intimité et à sa propre image.
- Art. 5°: Droit à l'information.
- Art. 6°: Droit à la liberté idéologique.
- Art. 7°: Droit de participation, d'association et de réunion.
- Art. 8°: Droit à la liberté d'expression.
- Art. 9°: Droit a être entendu.
- Art. 10°: Les mesures administratives pour faciliter l'exercice des droits des mineurs.
- Art. 11°: Principes de l'action administrative.
- Arts. 12°–22°: Actuation administrative face aux situations de manque de protection sociale des mineurs.

Dans les Dispositions Additionnelles on établie de règle la compétence de la jurisdiction gracieuse dans le cas des protection des mineurs en suivant les normes suivantes :

(a) Le Juge et le Ministère Public doivent agir *ex officio* dans l'intérêt du mineur, en suppléant la passivité des parties particulières et en lui donnant conseil sur leurs droits et la façon de corriger les défauts de leurs demandes;
(b) Les mineurs n'ont pas besoin d'un Avocat ou d'un Avoué pour agir devant les tribunaux;
(c) La tierce opposition sera résolue dans la même procédure sans obliger au mineur à utiliser la procédure contentieuse.

4 La Loi 54/2007, de 28 décembre, de l'adoptioninternationale (LAI)

Cette Loi est promulguée en application de la Convention de l'ONU de 1989, mais aussi de la Convention de La Haye de 1993, ratifiée par l'Espagne le 30 juin 1995. Elle remplace les règles en vigueur du Droit international privé ainsi que complète celles du droit civil espagnol sur l'adoption.

La raison d'être de la LAI s'explique dans son l'Exposé des Motifs (numéro 1) :

« Le nombre croissant des adoptions constituées à l'étrangère supposent à la fois un défi juridique pour le législateur national qui doit fournir les instruments juridiques précises pour que l'adoption se réalise avec toutes les garanties légales et aussi protéger l'intérêt supérieur des mineurs à adopter, en facilitant le développement harmonique de l'enfant dans un foyer familiale adéquat. Mais tout cela à l'intérieur d'un scrupuleux cadre de sécurité juridique au profit de tous les participants à l'adoption international, et principalement de l'enfant adopté. L'expérience nous a permis d'apprécier l'opportunité d'une loi qui va empêcher la dispersion normative en vigueur et en unifiant toute la législation applicable spécialement le Droit international privé ».

La Loi a pour object une régulation systématique, cohérente et actualisée de la matière, divisée en trois Titres :

- I. Dispositions générales
- II. Normes de Droit International Privé relatives à l'adoptioninternationale
- III. D'autres mesures de protection de mineurs.

On tiendra compte des solutions juridiques contenues dans cette importante Loi dans les réponses aux questionnaire.

5 Les réponses au questionnaire

5.1 Ratification de la Convention sur les droits de l'enfant

Espagne a ratifié la Convention de 1989 le 30 novembre 1990.

5.2 Définition de l'enfant

J'aimerai clarifier une simple *question terminologique* qui parfois en langue espagnole peux faire tomber en erreur les traductions de l'anglais ou du français. En général dans la langue courante on parle de : « niño », « adolescente », et « joven », sans y établir une claire délimitation d'âge; on est appelé « niño » avant d'arriver à l'usage de la raison (jusqu'à 7 ans environ); l' « adolescente » a déjà la capacité naturelle de raisonner et de vouloir (entre 7 ans et 12-14 ans environ); le « joven » se trouve en train d'arriver à la majorité d'âge ou bien il l'a franchie récemment (on le considère après 14 ans environ). Donc, en espagnol c'est pas tout à fait exacte de dire « Convención de los Derechos del Niño », traduction qu'on prend littéralement du texte français (« Convention du Droit des *Enfants* ») ou anglais (« Convention on the Rights of the *Child* »). Il semble plus correcte d'utiliser le nom « menor » (donc j'utilise habituellement la phrase : « **Convención de los Derechos del menor** » = Convention des droits du mineur ou des mineurs).

En droit espagnol la majorité d'âge est fixée à 18 ans, selon l'art. 11 de la Constitution et l'art. 315 Cc qui dit : « La majorité d'âge commence aux 18 ans accomplis. – Pour calculer cette âge il faut compter le jour de la naissance comme un jour complet ».

5.3 Instrument légal dévoué aux droits des mineurs

En droit espagnol il y a un réel et complet instrument légal dévoué aux droits des mineurs; il y a d'abord un état civil du mineur, et aussi une catégorie spéciale des droits sociaux des mineurs et tout cela c'est la conséquence des plusieurs facteurs concurrentes.

Tout d'abord après la promulgation de la Constitution de 1978 on prend le départ de la Déclaration des Droits de l'Homme de l'ONU de 1948, laquelle devra y être utilisée pour interpréter le Titre I de la Constitution en matière des droits fondamentaux et des libertés, et aussi on s'engage implicitement à ratifier les successives traités ou Conventions sur cette matière. En conséquence, ce Droit civil constitutionnel a donné lieu en Espagne à une réforme en profondeur du Cc en matière des personnes et de la famille. Finalement la Convention de 1989 a été développée par une Loi spécial de 1996 la LOPJM qui, en partie, réitère et en partie complète ce cadre de protection du mineur en droit espagnol. Il y a donc, une régulation civile de la position juridique du mineur (le *status* de la minorité d'âge) complétée par un système publique de protection sociale du mineur, créé progressivement à partir 1978 et presque fini dans nos jours.

5.4 Le principe de l'intérêt supérieur de l'enfant

Le questionnaire énumère une liste des **matières sélectionnées** que le droit espagnol, de sa part, a dû intégrer d'accord à la Convention de 1989. Il s'agit de douze points bien choisis, parfois d'une grande portée, et d'autres plutôt sur des aspectes plus concrètes, qui à l'heure actuelle sont discutés encore dans certains pays et sur lesquels il n'y a pas toujours l'accord unanime dans la doctrine espagnole. À la fin je me permets d'ajouter quelques autres qu'à mon avis on pourrait les traiter aussi dans ce Congrès.

Le principe de l'intérêt supérieur de l'enfant (art. 3 du Convention) existait déjà en Droit espagnol dès 1978 et il vient d'être ratifié ou confirmé – donc, renforcé – en Espagne. Cet intérêt se manifeste dans toutes les formes indiquées au questionnaire (Constitution, Code civil et Loi spéciale d'intégration [LOPJM du 1996], et aussi inclus dans des principes généraux, ou bien en forme très détaillé dans des normes plus concrètes et déterminées).

5.5 L'origine d'un enfant

Le Code civil permet à l'enfant né en dehors du mariage et aussi à leurs parents biologiques soit de réclamer leur filiation, ou leur lien de paternité et de maternité, soit d'attaquer une filiation ne correspondant pas à la filiation biologique et attribuée erronément à une autre personne.

À la différence du régime primitif du Cc de 1889, la Loi de 1981 et d'accord à l'art. 39.2 Constitution a facilité l'introduction du principe de *liberté de larecherche de la filiation* non matrimoniale moyennant toute sorte des preuves y inclues les preuves biologiques. D'accord au régime ancien de filiation, dans la société espagnole et par rapport à la filiation illégitime les statistiques montraient, au moment de la Transition politique (1975), que la moitié environ des mères non mariées reconnaissaient volontairement leur enfant, que dans le 20 % de cas ils le reconnaissaient tous les deux parents, et seulement dans un 5 % environ de cas le père tout seul l'avait reconnu; et en conséquence qu'il y avait le 25 % environ de cas où l'enfant en était abandonné de fait à la naissance pour les deux parents de sorte qu'il était inscrit au Registre civil comme *fils de parents inconnus.* Après la Loi de 1981 le panorama sociale en Espagne commence à changer : la mère célibataire améliore son prestige social (parfois elle refuse ou s'oppose à la reconnaissance du père biologique, et fait tout de son mieux pour l'empêcher), le nombre des enfants abandonnés a diminué graduellement après cette date, et surtout la plupart des actions exercées par la mère contre le père biologique a réussi devant les tribunaux. Il faut ajouter encore que les parents biologiques de l'enfant non matrimonial peut-être en été mariés à un tiers au moment de la conception ou de la naissance de celui-ci, et que la loi auparavant mettait beaucoup d'obstacles à détruire la présomption de paternité légitime. Mais la preuve biologique généralisée après la Loi détruisait la présomption de légitimité, de sorte que les actions de la réclamation de paternité ou de maternité vont prévaloir habituellement contre le père ou la mère déjà mariés.

En bref, le régime actuel du Cc est le suivant :

5.5.1 Origine biologique de l'enfant

L'enfant non matrimoniale pourra réclamer sa filiation biologique, s'il y a possession d'état, pendant toute sa vie : art. 131 Cc. (il serait le cas ou les parents non mariés parmi eux vivent ensemble avec leur fils sans l'avoir reconnu, ainsi ils maintiennent des rapports de fait avec lui, mais ils non pas assumé volontairement son rôle légal).

Aussi l'enfant pourra réclamer sa filiation quand il n'y a pas possession d'état; dans ce cas l'enfant ignorait en fait sa filiation biologique dont les preuves il découvre plus tard : il pourra la réclamer aussi pendant toute sa vie (art. 133 Cc.). Il serait le cas si après sa naissance il a été abandonné et successivement interné dans une institution d'accueil dans laquelle il vit jusqu'à sa majorité. Dans certains cas même ses héritiers pourront exercer l'action de réclamation de filiation pendant un délai de 4 ans après son décès si les preuves de la filiation sont découvertes dans ce période de temps.

L'action de réclamation de paternité ou maternité correspond aussi aux parents s'il n'y a pas possession d'état, et cette action est imprescriptible (art. 132); les cas sont plutôt rares dans la pratique (par exemple, les parents ont abandonnés leur enfant et après ça ils changent d'opinion, ou bien la mère cache la naissance au père qui connait le fait de la naissance seulement quelques années plus tard).

Si les parents biologiques ou l'un d'eux sont mariés à un tiers il y en a plusieurs solutions légales :

(a') le père ou la mère biologiques pourront à tout temps reconnaître volontairement leur enfant, soit au moment de l'inscription au Registre de l'État civil ou à un moment postérieure;

(b') par contre, les parents biologiques se taisent toujours et, en conséquence l'enfant est attribuée faussement au mari; c'est le cas le plus complexe parce que la possession d'état favorise la filiation matrimoniale de l'enfant; le père biologique une fois informé des faits pourra attaquer d'abord la filiation matrimonial attribuée au mari, et simultanément réclamer sa paternité non matrimoniale pendant tout sa vie; cette action pourra en être exercé par le père dans son propre nom et aussi au nom de son fils mineur; et une fois que celui-ci arrive à la majorité l'action d'attaque et de réclamation lui correspondent aussi à l'enfant pendant toute sa vie.

À remarquer qu'on se posse ici un cas limite : C'est quand l'enfant procréé par un homme divers du mari a été bien accepté au sein de la famille matrimoniale dans laquelle il s'élevé, ou bien le mari dupe a pu pardonner l'adultère de sa femme, tout en restant ignorant de la réalité l'enfant lui-même. Est-ce que le vrai père biologique aura le droit de troubler la paix de ce foyer? Il y a des auteurs et même de systèmes juridiques qu'y mettent d'obstacles (un délai de prescription de l'action, par exemple). Dans le droit espagnol le Tribunal Constitutionnel en 2005 et 2006 a annulé partialement l'art. 133 Cc en éliminant quelque limitation temporelle (auparavant, un an à partir de la connaissance des faits ou de l'inscription au Registre) à l'action exercée par le père biologique. En conséquence et d'accord à la jurisprudence de la Cour Suprême, en tout temps, soit l'enfant non matrimoniale que son père biologique ou tous les deux pourront réclamer la filiation pendant toute leur vie en attaquant d'abord la filiation matrimoniale erronément attribuée.

5.5.2 L'enfant adopté

Quant aux *enfants adoptés* l'art. 180.5 Cc dispose que ceux-ci, une fois atteint l'âge de la majorité ou pendant sa minorité représentés par leurs parents adoptives, ont le droit de *connaître tous les données relatives à leur origine biologique*. Il faut savoir que la législation espagnole déclare secrète la procédure de l'adoption, de sorte que dans la pratique la famille d'origine n'arrive pas à connaître *de visu* la famille d'adoption (à différence, par exemple, de la législation allemande). Il n'y a qu'une seule classe d'adoption, qui produit un lien de filiation que l'art. 108 al. 2 Cc égalise quant à ses effets au filiation matrimoniale; en Espagne, l'adoption une fois approuvé par le Juge rompt les liens existants avec la famille d'origine, sauf quant aux empêchements du mariage. Dans le Registre civil, après la constitution de l'adoption on ouvre une nouvelle inscription au marge de la naissance à l'enfant adopté, en même temps qu'on conserve l'inscription primitive de celui-ci dont la consulte cependant doit être approuvée par le Juge. Si on adopte un enfant de filiation inconnue et après de constituer l'adoption il vient d'être reconnue ou le juge en déclaré sa filiation, ces faits ne changent pas celle-là, laquelle reste irrévocable, sauf dans de cas exceptionnels (art. 180 Cc). Mais on respecte l'art. 7.1 de la Convention (L'enfant … aura le droit dés sa naissance à un nom, à en acquérir une nationalité et, *à la mesure du possible, à connaître leur parents* …). C'est à dire, l'enfant adopté dispose de moyens juridiques pour connaître son origine, mais sans modifier son état civil. L'expérience nous montre que chez beaucoup des adoptés il existe un profond sentiment pour connaître personnellement et en vue d'entretenir des rapports humains avec leur parents. Dans ce but ils s'engagent souvent à des recherches coûteuses que la loi civile, à mon avis, doit favoriser.

5.5.3 L'enfant né par l'usage de techniques médicalement assistées

Quant aux *enfants nés par l'usage de techniques médicalement assistées* il faut dire qu'en 1988 l'Espagne a été l'un des pays pionniers pour les accepter très amplement dans le système de la filiation, et que cette Loi a été modifiée en 2003 avec le même esprit d'ouverture. Le Tribunal Constitutionnel en 1999 en avait accepté la première loi, même si, en apparence, celle-ci serait contraire à l'art. 39.2 de la Constitution (parce qu'on interdit la libre recherche de la filiation). Ici nous intéresse souligner que la loi permet que la technique soit-il applicable à une femme mariée, hétérosexuelle ou homosexuelle, ou à une femme qui vit en union de fait, et même à une femme qui vit toute seule. La doctrine civiliste critique souvent cette législation, parfois contradictoire et parfois donnant lieu à des problèmes plutôt artificiels (fécondation post mortem) ou à des graves conflits de conscience. Les principes qu'inspirent cette législation sont les suivants :

(a') La filiation des enfants nés avec les techniques de procréation médicalement assistée est soumise au régime établi dans les lois civils, sauf les exceptions établis dans la Loi spéciale;

(b') Dans aucun cas l'inscription dans le Registre civil pourra indiquer que l'enfant est né de ces techniques;

(c') Ni la mère ni son mari, une fois qu'ils l'ont accepté formellement, en donnant son consentement préalable et expresse à une fécondation déterminée réalisée avec l'intervention de donateur, ils ne pourront pas s'opposer, dans aucun cas, à la qualification comme filiation matrimoniale de l'enfant né moyennant ces techniques.

Cela signifie que l'enfant né est considéré matrimonial malgré qu'on a utilisé pour la procréation le sperme d'un tiers anonyme, parce qu'il y a prohibition légale et absolue d'attaquer la filiation de celui-là. La recherche de la filiation reste impossible malgré la disposition de l'art. 39.2 de la Constitution. Et s'il s'agit d'un mariage célébré par deux femmes après 2005, la compagne de celle-ci qui l'a enfanté pourra l'inscrire comme fils propre. Serait-il un cas d'un nouveau-né qui aura légalement deux mères et aucun père. Mais la prohibition d'attaquer cette filiation matrimoniale n'oblige pas à l'enfant et quelques auteurs pensent à la possibilité de réclamer la paternité du vrai père (malgré que son identité est presque impossible de connaître en fait), ou au moins que sa filiation ne serait pas matrimoniale mais non matrimoniale dont le père reste inconnu. Jusqu'a présent des cas pareils ne se sont présentés à ma connaissance devant les tribunaux espagnols.

(d') Si la femme vit en union de fait, son compagne doit donner aussi son consentement formel à l'usage des techniques lequel constitue un titre pour lui attribuer la filiation non matrimoniale du nouveau-né. La solution c'est la même si l'homme qui a donné son consentement non cohabite pas avec la femme malgré qu'il a donné son consentement. La loi laisse aussi en vigueur la réclamation judiciaire de filiation par le nouveau-né (il serait peu probable que sa mère pendant la minorité de l'enfant représente à celui-ci devant les tribunaux, mais après la majorité l'enfant pourra exercer personnellement l'action de réclamation de sa filiation biologique).

(e') Le mari ou l'homme qui vit avec la femme pourront établir par écrit que leur sperme crioconservé puisse être utilisé pour féconder la femme dans un délai de 12 mois après sa morte, et la naissance d'un enfant comme résultat de cette fécondation produira les mêmes effets que dans le cas (a') décrit. Donc, on a autorisée la fécondation *post mortem*, pourtant très combattue par la doctrine en raison des éventuels conflits héréditaires.

(f') Il est interdit la gestation par substitution ou par de mères porteuses.

(g') Malgré le principe de l'anonymat de la donation du sperme, la loi permet que l'enfant né de ces techniques en puisse obtenir une *information générale du donateur* de sperme sans y inclure son identité, laquelle seulement pourra être communiquée à l'enfant quand il y aura des circonstances extraordinaires qui mettent en danger la vie ou la santé de celui-ci, ou bien s'il existe une procédure criminelle, mais sans qu'un aucun cas la révélation de l'identité du donateur puisse en être utilisée pour déterminer la filiation de l'enfant.

5.6 Le droit d'exprimer librement son opinion et d'être entendu

Les droits reconnus au mineur aux arts. 12 et 13 de la Convention sont-ils reconnus dans le droit espagnol : Il y a des règles très détaillées dans la LOPJM.

L'art. 5 de LOPJM déclare à ce propos :

> « Droit à l'information : 1. Les mineurs ont le droit de rechercher, recevoir et utiliser toute l'information adéquate à son développement.
>
> 2. Les parents ou tuteurs et les pouvoirs publiques doivent veiller afin que l'information qui reçoivent les mineurs soit-elle véritable, plurielle et respectant les principes constitutionnelles.
>
> 3. Les Administrations publiques doivent promouvoir la production et diffusion des matériaux informatifs et d'autres adressés spécialement aux mineurs et qui respectent les principes indiqués, en même temps qu'elles doivent faciliter l'accès des mineurs aux

services d'information, documentation, bibliothèques et d'autres services culturels. Elles doivent veiller aussi pour que les messages adressés aux mineurs puissent promouvoir les valeurs de l'égalité, de la solidarité et du respect aux autres, en écartant les images de violence, exploitation des rapports parmi les personnes ou qui reflètent un traitement dégradant ou sexiste.

4. Des normes spéciaux vont garantir que la publicité ou les messages adressés au mineurs ou émis dans la programmation adressée à ceux-ci ne leur produise des dommages moraux ou physiques.

5. En tout cas, le Ministère Publique et les Administrations publiques ont la compétence en matière de protection des mineurs et en conséquence ont le devoir d'exercer les actions pour la cessation et la rectification de la publicité illicite ».

L'art. 9 de LOPJM dispose littéralement :

« Droit à en être entendu. 1. Le mineur a le droit d'être entendu, soit-t-il dans l'intérieur de la famille que dans toute procédure administrative ou judiciaire dans lequel il soit directement concerné et puisse aboutir à une résolution qui affecte à son sphère personnelle, familiale ou social.- Dans la procédure judiciaire la présence du mineur devant le juge sera faite de forme adéquate à sa situation personnelle et au développement de celle-ci en préservant toujours son intimité.

2. L'exercice de ce droit pourra se faire de façon personnelle par le mineur lui-même ou à travers de son représentant désigne quand il ait capacité naturelle pour le faire. Si tout cela ne serait-il pas possible ou convenable pour le mineur, on pourra connaître l'opinion de l'enfant à travers de son représentant légal sauf s'il a d'intérêts contraires au mineur, ou bien moyennant d'autres personnes qui par sa profession ou par un rapport de confiance avec lui puissent la transmettre objectivement.

3. Si le mineur demande d'être entendu directement ou par son représentant, pour le refuser le Juge devra motiver la résolution négative et la communiquer au Ministère Public et au sollicitant ».

Quant au droit du mineur à y être entendue on peut conclure :

- L'art. 9 établie le droit de l'enfant mineur d'âge d'être entendu à l'intérieur de la famille et l'accomplissement de ce droit est confié aux parents et au tuteur. Les arts. 154 et 268 Cc établissent le contenu de l'autorité parentale et celui du tuteur, avec les mêmes limites : « si les enfants ont capacité naturelle ils doivent toujours être entendus par leurs parents avant d'en prendre des décisions qui les affectent »; « les tuteurs devront exercer sa charge d'accord avec la personnalité des mineurs, en respectant son intégrité physique et psychologique ». Mais la Sociologie nous montre plutôt à l'heure actuelle des certains cas ou les mineurs se révoltent contre leurs parents et parfois ils les maltraitent, de sorte que sont ceux-ci qui, quelques fois agissent, devant le juge pour réclamer; sans pour autant dire que les parents despotiques ou violents face à leur enfants aient disparus du tout dans la pratique judiciaire.
- L'art. 9 établie aussi le droit du mineur d'être entendu devant les tribunaux ou les organes administratives; la loi ne fixe pas l'âge à partir de laquelle il pourra l'exercer. Dans des cas concrètes la loi attribue au Juge la faculté de déterminer qu'en raison des circonstances concurrentes le mineur a la capacité naturelle de s'exprimer; en matière d'adoption l'âge de 12 ans c'est le minimum pour consentir à sa propre adoption (art. 177.1 Cc), et par dessous cette âge le Juge est obligé seulement à l'entendre « si tuviere suficiente juicio » (art. 177.3.3 Cc)

c.à.d. si le mineur en dispose de capacité naturelle de penser et de vouloir. Cette règle civile pourra être généralisée pour tous les cas d'intervention du mineur devant le juge ou l'autorité administrative. D'autre part, la Loi de la Procédure civil de 2000 permet au juge de célébrer la séance sans publicité quand les mineurs y sont intéressés (arts. 138.2 et 754) afin de protéger son intimité. En tout cas l'art. 9 de la LOPJM obligera soit au juge soit à l'autorité administrative à admettre les différentes formes d'intervention du mineur y prévues.

- Quant aux moyens juridiques :

À mon avis, l'avancement technique de la société de l'information tout récemment produit obligera peut être le législateur à *moderniser* le texte de ces articles quelque peu obsolètes étant donné les facilités octroyés à tous - et pas seulement aux mineurs – pour obtenir l'information en général ainsi que l'objectif légal de réussir à avoir un certain *control de l'information adressée aux mineurs*, d'accord à l'art. 8 de la LOPJM.

5.7 Les droits de l'enfant dans le domaine de l'adoption

À partir de l'âge de 12 ans l'adopté devra consentir librement devant le Juge sa propre adoption, et l'adoptant devra avoir au moins une différence de 14 ans avec celui-là (*adoptio imitatur naturam*). Si tel consentement manque, l'adoption sera nulle absolument. En dessous de cet âge le Juge devra seulement l'entendre s'il a la capacité naturelle; autrement leurs parents ou le tuteur devront y consentir.

La Loi 54/2007, de 28 décembre (LAI) établie les conditions de l'adoptioninternationale :

- le but de la LAI c'est de garantir que les adoptions internationales se réalisent justement en faveur de l'intérêt supérieur du mineur, mais aussi des intérêts des adoptants et aussi de tous ceux qui interviennent dans cette procédure (art. 2);
- à cet objet l'adoption international des mineurs devra respecter les principes de l'art. 21 de la Convention de 1989, et aussi de la Convention de La Haye de 29 Mai 1993; en particulier, l'Espagne devra inclure les standards et sauvegardes de celle-ci quand elle signe des Accords dans la matière avec des États qui n'ont pas souscrit ce dernier Accord (art. 3);
- seulement pourront développer des fonctions d'intermédiation dans cette adoption les organes administratifs désignes dans la LAI (c.-à-d. les « Entidades Públicas de Protección de Menores » et les « Entidades de Colaboración ») autorisés soit dans les pays d'origine que dans les pays du destin des mineurs (art. 4);
- il est absolument interdit de formaliser des adoptions de mineurs quand le pays d'origine de ceux-ci se trouve en situation de guerre ou au milieu d'une catastrophe naturelle (art. 4);
- le séjour d'un mineur étrangère en Espagne à l'occasion d'un programme de vacances, ou d'études ou pour en recevoir traitement médical ne pourra pas en être utilisé pour l'adopter sans que finisse celui-là et le mineur ait commencé un programme d'adoption (art. 4);

- l'adoption international ne pourra pas produire des bénéfices financières à l'exception des frais strictement nécessaires pour en satisfaire le coût (art. 4);
- la Loi règle en détail l'activité en Espagne des « Entidades Públicas competentes en materia de protección de menores » (pour la plupart elles sont des organes de la Communauté Autonome du domicile des adoptants), ainsi que des « Entidades Colaboradoras de Adopción International » (qui possèdent compétence exclusive dans la matière et qui ont besoin d'une autorisation spéciale) (arts. 5 à 9, LAI);
- l'Administration espagnole doit déclarer l'aptitude (« idoneidad ») des adoptants, laquelle est valable pendant trois ans (art. 10); une fois approuvée l'adoptioninternationale les adoptantes sont obligés d'informer successivement l'Administration du pays d'accueil sur l'évolution du rapport avec le mineur adopté et au but de remplir les conditions établies par l'État d'origine (art. 11);
- la LAI contient aussi des règles du Droit international privé á propos de l'adoption (arts. 14 à 31) qui remplacent les règles contenues jusqu'à présent dans le Cc.

5.8 Le droit à la liberté de penser, de conscience et de religion

Le mineur a le droit à la liberté de penser, de conscience et de religion. Ceci est établi à l'art. 6ª LOPJM, qui ajoute que l'exercice des droits qui découlent de cette liberté aura seulement des limitations établies par la loi exigés par le respect des droits et libertés fondamentaux des autres, et aussi que les parents ou les tuteurs ont le droit et le devoir de collaborer pour que le mineur exerce cette liberté de façon qu'elle puisse contribuer à son développement intégral.

Les Écoles publiques et subventionnées ont l'obligation d'offrir l'enseignement religieuse des différentes confessions reconnues en Espagne, et les parents et les tuteurs ou les mineurs eux-mêmes à partir d'un certaine âge, ont la liberté de choisir l'enseignement d'accord à leurs convictions, ou bien de ne pas suivre aucune; l'enseignement religieuse est donnée par les ministres de chaque confession ou par des personnes autorisés par celle-ci et comprend l'instruction doctrinale et morale de la Religion.

5.9 Châtiment corporel de l'enfant

Les châtiments physiques sont interdits, soit à l'intérieur de la famille, à l'École ou dans les institutions concernant les mineurs.

Dans la rédaction primitive du Cc on disait à l'art. 155-2°, que les parents avaient à l'égard de leurs enfants la faculté de les corriger et même de les châtier d'une manière modérée. Mais en raison de l'application de l'art. 19 de la Convention on a éliminé cette faculté, et au lieu de cette règle on a établi que les parents, dans l'exercice de l'autorité parentale pourront solliciter l'aide de l'autorité. Et d'accord à l'art. 268, les tuteurs devront exercer sa charge d'accord à la personnalité de leurs pupilles, en respectant son intégrité physique et psychologique. Le Code pénal punie aussi tous les actes adressés contre l'intégrité physique ou psychique des mineurs commis soit à l'intérieur comme en dehors de la famille, et en général d'une manière plus aggravée étant donné la condition vulnérable de la victime.

5.10 Privation des droits parentaux

La loi prévoit la possibilité de priver aux parents de l'autorité parentale. Les motifs sont très amples (par des actes intentionnels ou simplement fautifs, ou bien par des raisons objectives), ainsi que les différents tribunaux compétents (en voie criminelle, civile ou même administrative) et aussi par la durée de la privation (définitive, transitoire, temporelle). La norme s'inspire toujours dans le bien-être du mineur, de sorte qu'on accorde à l'autorité compétente des facultés discrétionnaires (pas tellement arbitraires).

L'art. 170 Cc dispose : « Le père ou la mère pourront être privés de l'autorité parentale, totalement ou partiellement, par un arrêt fondé dans l'inaccomplissement des leurs devoirs inhérents à celle-ci ou bien prononcée dans une procédure criminelle ou matrimoniale. – Les Tribunaux pourront, en vue du bénéfice et intérêt de l'enfant, accorder la récupération de l'autorité parentale quand a-t-il cessé la cause qui avait déterminé la privation ».

La privation pourra en être accordée dans une procédure civile spéciale; ils sont légitimés pour la demander le mineur lui-même et son représentant volontaire, l'autre parent et le Ministère Publique. La privation pourra-t-il constituer une peine accessoire imposée en raison de la condamnation pour un délit contre le mineur. Aussi dans une procédure de divorce le juge pourra aussi déclarer la privation de l'autorité parentale en raison des faits prouvés à l'égard de chaque parent. Si l'enfant est déclaré administrativement abandonné, on produit automatiquement la suspension de l'autorité parentale à la suite de la tutelle légale attribuée à l'organe administratif chargé de la protection des mineurs dans le territoire; ce procédure pourra aboutir à constituer l'adoption de l'enfant.

Quant aux motifs de la privation, il faut dire que dans l'inaccomplissement des devoirs peuvent rentrer tous les motifs énumérés à l'art. 19.1 de la Convention.

Qui va s'occuper de l'enfant après la suspension ou la cessation de l'autorité parentale? Il n'y a pas des règles générales en droit espagnol et il faut en tenir compte de chaque cas. En principe l'autorité parentale sera exercée par l'autre parent qui est-t-il déclare innocent; si tous les deux sont coupables, on ouvre la tutelle. Dans le cas d'abandon l'Administration pourra choisir une institution spécialisée s'il est convenable pour l'enfant. Le placement dans une famille est fréquemment utilisé par l'Administration dans le cas d'enfants abandonnés; il y a plusieurs modalités de ce placement (en vue d'adoption, à caractère permanente ou temporaire, etc.).

Si la privation de l'autorité parentale a été temporaire la loi prévoit normalement le retour au foyer d'origine une fois que la cause de la privation a disparue. En tout cas le bien-être de l'enfant devra inspirer à l'autorité compétente la décision la plus adéquate.

Même si la privation de l'autorité parentale reste définitive le rapport juridique parent - enfant n'est pas absolument disparu. Le parent reste obligé aux devoirs légaux par rapport à son fils, même s'il est devenu majeure d'âge (par exemple, le devoir d'aliments en cas de besoin). D'autre part le parent privé de l'autorité a le droit de succéder *ab intestat* à son fils, à moins que celui-ci l'ait déshérité expressément.

L'art. 155-1° Cc dispose aussi que les enfants ont le devoir de respecter toujours à leurs parents. Finalement, quant au droit de visite, si au moment de la mort le père en prison demande au juge la permission de voir son fils desheredité par lui-même, ou bien par qui il a été déshéritée, on pourra nier cette demande qui cherche peut-être la réconciliation parmi eux? (bien sur, l'enfant majeur d'âge pourra dénier la visite accordée par le Juge…).

5.11 Consentement médical

Pour répondre à cette question il faut en tenir compte des règles suivantes : L'art. 162 Cc détermine le contenu de l'autorité à l'égard de la représentation légale des enfants :

> « Les parents qui exercent l'autorité parentale disposent de la représentation légale de leurs enfants mineurs non émancipés. Mais il y a des exceptions : 1° Les actes relatifs aux droits de la personnalité ou d'autres cas, lesquels l'enfant d'accord aux lois et selon sa propre maturité peut réaliser par soi-même […]».

La loi tient compte, en général, de l'évolution physique et psychique de la personnalité du mineur pour lui accorder progressivement la capacité d'agir tout seul. Il y a une rémission à d'autres lois. D'accord à l'art. 9.3 de la Loi de 14 novembre 2002 de l'Autonomie du Patient, le mineur devra donner son consentement pour le traitement médicale s'il en dispose de la capacité de comprendre et de vouloir sans l'intervention des parents; autrement le consentement serait-il octroyé par les représentants légaux ayant écouté préalablement l'enfant s'il a rempli les 12 ans. Si le mineur a accomplie 16 ans, les parents ne peuvent pas représenter l'enfant en cas de traitement médical. Mais en cas d'un grave risque pour la vie du mineur, les parents donnent toujours son avis qui sera tenue en compte pour le facultatif. Ce régime est applicable soit pour accepter que pour refuser un traitement médicale du mineur.

5.12 Changement du nom par le mineur

Tout d'abord une explication sur une singularité du droit espagnol. Depuis toujours la femme espagnole a conservé son nom propre après son mariage et elle le transmet à son enfant (également qu'il le transmet son mari). Il y avait, pourtant, une question discutée de la hiérarchie des noms. Avant les dernières réformes la loi avait établie que l'enfant matrimoniale portait d'abord le nom de son père et après le nom de sa mère. Mais une loi de 1999 a réformé l'art. 109 Cc permettant aux parents de se mettre d'accord avant de l'inscription de la naissance de son fils sur l'ordre des noms à imposer au nouveau-né; autrement l'ordre sera le traditionnel. L'ordre accordé par les parents pour le premier enfant sera le même pour les enfants successifs, et cette faculté ne pourra pas s'exercer par le parents qu'une seule fois. Mais il y a maintenant une règle nouvelle : « Chaque enfant, au moment d'arriver à la majorité d'âge a la faculté de changer l'ordre de ses noms »; mais ce changement n'aura d'effet que pour lui-même et pas pour ses frères ou soeurs.

Tout changement de filiation produit pendant la minorité sera suivi du changement du nom de l'enfant (par exemple, si une adoption a été formalisée, ou une filiation non matrimoniale a été déclarée par le Juge). D'autre part, les parents pendant la minorité de l'enfant peuvent changer leurs noms pour des différents motifs, et cela affecte toujours leurs enfants mineurs. Mais ceux-ci ne peuvent pas, avant d'arriver à la majorité, prendre l'initiative de changer son nom.

S'il s'agît des enfants nés hors mariage il faut en tenir compte de la reconnaissance du nouveau-né. Si l'enfant est reconnu par le père et la mère, le nom de l'enfant sera le même que l'enfant matrimonial. Mais s'il est reconnu seulement par sa mère, celle-ci donnera à son fils ses deux noms et dans le même ordre; mais la loi l'autorise pour qu'au moment de l'inscription la mère change l'ordre de ses propres noms imposées au nouveau-né au but de ne pas publier son origine.

Quand j'emploi le mot *nom* je traite conjointement le prénom et le nom de famille (*first name and surname).*La Loi du Registre civil permet à chaque personne pour des diverses motifs, de changer l'un ou l'autre, ou tous les deux.

5.13 Le contrat de travail du mineur

La capacité d'agir ou d'exercice dans le Droit du travail ne coïncide pas avec le Cc. La doctrine spécialisée en établi le cas suivants :

(a) Les majeurs d'âge, les mineurs émancipées selon le Cc (par mariage, par la concession des parents ou par le juge), mais aussi ceux qui ont été émancipés de fait, jouissent de pleine capacité pour contracter son travail.

L'émancipation de fait se produit quand les parents ont consenti que son enfant vit indépendamment, c.-à-d. à son coût et normalement, mais pas nécessairement, en domicile séparé. Les parents pourront retirer son consentement à la vie indépendante, et on accepte aussi le consentement tacite (art. 7, b, de le

Statut de Travailleurs). Le salaire appartienne au mineur et il l'administre librement.

(b) Disposent-ils d'une capacité d'agir limitée les majeurs de 16 ans non émancipes. Ceux-ci peuvent contracter son travail avec l'autorisation de leurs parents, même tacite, laquelle est révocable. L'autorisation tombe sur le travail et non sur la vie indépendante et il faut la donner cas pour cas.

(c) Selon l'art. 6,1, b) de le Statut de Travailleurs il est prohibé l'accès au travail des mineurs en dessous de 16 ans. Les Traités internationaux signés par l'Espagne acceptent dans certains cas le travail des mineurs à partir de 14 ans. D'autre parte, ce mineur a la possibilité de se marier avec la licence du juge (art. 48, 2 Cc), et le mariage produit l'émancipation et de ce fait le travailleur serait inclus sub a).

L'ancien « contrat d'apprentissage » est remplacé par le « contrat pour la formation » (art. 11,2 du Statut). L'art. 40, 2 de la Constitution établie que le droit à la formation des travailleurs est un principe de la politique sociale et économique. L'entreprise pourra offrir un contrat pour la formation aux mineurs entre les 16 et les 21 ans, d'une durée entre 6 mois et 2 ans (4 ans pour les handicapés).

5.14 Les devoirs de l'enfant à l'égard de ses parents

Chaque être humain du fait de sa naissance dans un foyer normal, c.a. d. quand leurs parents son mariés, maintien-t-il des rapports juridiques, pas seulement avec ses père et mère, mais il rentre aussi dans les liens de la famille ample auxquelles appartiennent ceux-ci. Le fait d'en avoir arrivé à la majorité d'âge suppose la fin de l'autorité parentale exercée sur lui jusqu'à 18 ans, mais il ne rompe pas les liens juridiques avec sa famille - étroite ou ample – qui l'accompagnent toujours jusqu'a sa mort. Dans les dernières temps la doctrine en Europe à approfondi le thème de la *solidarité parmi les générations* (sujet du Congrès Internationale de Lyon du juillet 2011, dont les Actes viennent d'être publiées). Dans plusieurs pays européens on voit souvent à l'heure actuelle la génération de grands parents aider économiquement à leurs fils est petit-fils dans la crise mondiale qui nous angoisse. Cette situation sociale est liée à beaucoup de facteurs changeants d'une époque à une autre, d'un pays à un autre. Mais il y a un minimum qu'on a conservé, plus ou moins, dans tous les codes civils européens.

- Pendant la minorité et sous certains conditions les parents peuvent utiliser les fruits des biens appartenant aux mineurs pour contribuer équitablement aux charges de la famille si l'enfant vit avec eux (art. 165.2 Cc);
- Si les ascendants de l'enfant – déjà majeur normalement en ce moment et ayant formé sa propre famille – se trouvent en besoin, le devoir de solidarité parmi les générations se concrétise dans le devoir légal d'aliments (art. 143, numéro 2°, Cc), qui en Espagne oblige seulement les personnes liés par la sang (en France inclut aussi aux alliés);

- Les ascendants à défaut de descendants ont droit à une réserve héréditaire (art. 807-2° Cc); dans le même cas, les ascendants succèdent ab intestat à leurs petits-enfants (art. 935);
- Les enfants pendant toute sa vie ont le *devoir de respecter* leur parents (art. 154.3. n° 2 Cc); et par analogie aussi à leurs aïeuls qui par la Loi de 21 novembre 2003 ont le droit de maintenir des rapports personnels avec leurs petits-enfants;

  Tout ce qui est dit à l'égard des enfants matrimoniaux on les applique aussi aux enfants nés hors mariage quand leur filiation est reconnue par leurs parents.

  À mon avis tout cela est déjà prévu à l'art. 8.1 de la Convention (le mineur a le droit à conserver les rapports familiaux sans intrusion illicite).

5.15 D'autres droits des mineurs dans la Convention de 1989

Évidemment le répertoire des droits des mineurs est plus étendu que celui qui est prévu dans le questionnaire. En tout cas il faut féliciter Mme la Rapporteur pour en avoir choisi des points très chauds dans la doctrine et la praxis de plusieurs pays du monde. Bien sûr que d'autres questions telles comme les enfants-soldiers, ou le travail forcé des mineurs, ou bien le régime d'esclavage ou quasi-maintenu dans certaines régions de l'Afrique, ou le tourisme international combiné avec la prostitution des mineurs organisée dans certains régions d'Asie, souleve encore l'émotion et la proteste indignée des juristes un peu partout dans le monde.

Pour ma parte je me permets d'ajouter le thème de *lagarde partagée des enfantsen cas de crise de la couple*. Depuis longtemps la recherché sociologique et psychologique (et aussi le cinéma) nous montre que les enfants mineurs sont les victimes immédiates de la rupture du foyer, même si les lois s'efforcent de déclarer que « la séparation, la nullité et le divorce n'exemptent pas leurs parents de l'accomplissement de ses obligations par rapport à leurs enfants » (art. 92.1 Cc). Dans la pratique des pays occidentaux normalement la loi ne prévoit pas que les enfants puissent participer à la procédure du divorce, par exemple, pour s'opposer à celui-ci (en fait on a constaté que certains enfants du divorce pensent toujours obsédées à leur propre responsabilité pour la rupture de leur foyer); en fait, selon le droit en vigueur, seulement les enfants sont entendus dans le procès matrimonial pour que le juge puisse mieux attribuer sa garde à l'un ou l'autre des parents. Habituellement les tribunaux espagnols en avaient attribuée la garde des enfants à la mère dans le 90 % environ des litiges. Maintenant la loi a été réformée en 2005 admettant la *garde partagée* sous certaines conditions. Les tribunaux on réagi timidement face à la réforme, et le pourcentage de cas de celle-ci a augmenté jusqu'à le 12 ou 13 %. La solution c'est pas simple et beaucoup des conditions y sont nécessaires pour que la garde partagée soit-elle efficace. Est-ce que ce thème on pourrait l'examiner et discuter comparativement? Si l'intérêt de l'enfant devrait en avoir la primauté sur tous les intervenants dans la rupture de la vie en commun, pourquoi pas on ne le tient compte plus amplement dans la procédure en cas de la crise du foyer à l'intérieur duquel il est naît et où il s'élève?

Bibliographie

Sur le droit en vigueur la bibliographie espagnole est très abondante. J'ai utilisé deux ouvrages fondamentaux parfois inspirés avec de différences d'orientation et du style mais qui jouissent tous les deux d'une complète information et qui sont très appréciés par la doctrine civiliste actuelle:

LACRUZ *et altri:* "Elementos de Derecho civil", IV, "Familia" (2éme édition revue par Joaquín RAMS ALBESA) ed. Dykinson (Madrid 2005).

MARTÍNEZ DE AGUIRRE *et altri*: "Curso de Derecho Civil (IV) Derecho de Familia", 4éme édition, ed. Colex (Madrid 2013).

Pour suivre l'histoire du thème après le Cc de 1889, avec abondante information de droit comparé, il faut citer:

CASTÁN TOBEÑAS, "Derecho civil español, común y foral", IV "Derecho de familia", tome V volume I (12ème édition à la charge de GARCÍA CANTERO et CASTÁN VÁZQUEZ) ed. Reus, Madrid 1995; et tome V volume 2, (10ème éd. à la charge de GARCÍA CANTERO et CASTÁN VÁZQUEZ), Madrid 1995.

POST SCRIPTUM: En Espagne la Loi du 28 juillet 2015 vient de compléter la LOPJM, ainsi qu'en comblant quelques lacunes que le rapport ci-après en avait dénoncé (5,6); mais surtout les aspects administratifs et le principe du meilleure intérêt de l'enfant. Cette loi a perfectionné aussi la LAI pour mieux répondre aux exigences internationales.

The Rights of the Child in the Netherlands: A Family Law Perspective

Ton Liefaard and Machteld Vonk

1 Introduction: The Netherlands Embracing the UN Convention on the Rights of the Child

The Netherlands do not belong to the first countries that have ratified the UN Convention on the Rights of the Child (CRC). On the contrary, it took until the 8th of March 1995 before the CRC entered into force for the Kingdom of the Netherlands,[1] after ratification by the Dutch Parliament on the 24th of November 1994.[2] 166 countries preceded the Netherlands.[3] The Dutch government assumed that the Netherlands were meeting many of the obligations laid down in the CRC and that ratification would not require significant adjustment of national law and policies.[4] Despite this assumption, a number of new Acts and policies have been developed since 1995, including the adoption of the prohibition to use violence against children in the domestic setting in 2007, supported by a number of national plans of action to address child abuse and neglect the development of the 2005

The research for this chapter was concluded on the 1st of January 2014.

[1] The Kingdom of the Netherlands currently consists of four States (the Netherlands, Aruba, Curacao and St. Maarten), which are all bound by the CRC. The three Caribbean islands, Bonaire, Saba and St. Eustatius are part of the Netherlands as special municipalities.

[2] Kingdom Act of 24 November 1994, *Bulletin of Acts and Decrees* 1994, 862; *Treaty Series* 1995, 92 (Act sanctioning the CRC).

[3] M. Blaak e.a (eds.), *Handboek Internationaal Jeugdrecht*, Leiden: Defence for Children 2012, p. 49.

[4] J. Doek, 'De ratificatie van het Verdrag voor de Rechten van het Kind. Enige beschouwingen over de mogelijke gevolgen voor de Nederlandse rechtspraktijk', *NJCM-Bulletin* 1995, pp. 10–21.

T. Liefaard (✉) • M. Vonk
Department of Child Law, Leiden Law School,
Steenschuur 25, 2311 ES Leiden, The Netherlands
e-mail: t.liefaard@law.leidenuniv.nl; m.j.vonk@law.leidenuniv.nl

O. Cvejić Jančić (ed.), *The Rights of the Child in a Changing World*,
Ius Comparatum - Global Studies in Comparative Law 13,
DOI 10.1007/978-3-319-23189-1_18

Youth Care Act, regulating the administration of youth care and child protection, which included a *right* to youth care and a special Act for juveniles deprived of their liberty in custodial institutions in 2001 (i.e. Youth Custodial Institutions Act), and the establishment of a Children's Ombudsperson in 2011. In addition, research indicates that there is an increase in the number of court cases in which the CRC plays a role, which has contributed to the development of a certain children's rights jurisprudence.[5]

It is fair to say that the CRC did not have the 'game changing' impact on the Netherlands as it did have on other countries. This probably is one of the reasons why the ratification of the CRC has not resulted in major adjustments of statutory law, including the Dutch Constitution. Unlike other countries such as South Africa or, nearer by, Belgium, the Netherlands have not included special children's rights provisions in their,[6] nor have they drawn up special children's acts regulating child protection or juvenile justice. In addition, the CRC has not led to a critical and holistic assessment of the Dutch legal system as far as the position of children is concerned. This seems particularly true for the area of family law, in which notions such as the best interests of the child were already common good, significantly influenced by the increasing amount of case law of the European Court of Human Rights.

This chapter analyses a number of issues related to family law and some related areas, such as labour law, in light of the UN Convention on the Rights of the Child.[7] It will start by addressing some relevant general principles, such as the definition of the child, the best interests of the child principle and the right to be heard. Subsequently, a number of family law issues will be analysed, including (inter country) adoption, parental responsibilities and medical decision making.

Before starting, it is important to underscore that the Dutch legal system can be characterized as monistic. This means that international law is considered to be part of the domestic legal order. Based on article 93 of the Dutch Constitution, provisions of international treaties are legally binding after ratification and can be directly applicable. In addition, provisions of international law are superior to provisions of national law (s. 94 of the Constitution). In light of this, it is also important take into account that the Dutch legal system has been under significant influence of the European Convention on Human Rights and the case law of the European Court of Human Rights. This has also affected the position of children in family law during the past 30 years.

---

[5] J.H. de Graaf et al. De Toepassing van het Internationaal Verdrag inzake de Rechten van het Kind in de Nederlandse Rechtspraak. Deel II, Amsterdam: Centre for Children's Rights Amsterdam 2015. M.M.C. Limbeek & M.R. Bruning, 'The Netherlands', in: T. Liefaard & J.E. Doek (eds.), *Litigating the Rights of the Child. The UN Convention on the Rights of the Child in Domestic and International Jurisprudence*, Dordrecht: Springer Science+Business Media 2015, pp. 89–104.

[6] T. Liefaard & J.E. Doek (eds.), *Litigating the Rights of the Child. The UN Convention on the Rights of the Child in Domestic and International Jurisprudence*, Dordrecht: Springer Science+Business Media 2015.

[7] The main focus in this contribution lies at the CRC. In addition, some reference will be made to other relevant international legal instruments, such as the European Convention on Human Rights.

2 General Principles

2.1 Definition of the Child: Minority

The CRC defines a child as 'every human being below the age of 18 years unless under the law applicable to the child, majority is attained earlier' (Art. 1 CRC). The Dutch definition of minority corresponds with this definition of the child and can be found exclusively in the Dutch Civil Code (hereinafter: DCC), that is, a minor under Dutch law is someone who has not yet reached the age of 18 and does not fall under the two possible ways of attaining majority before the 18th birthday (s. 1:233 DCC).[8] The first way to attain majority is to marry or to register as civil partners (s. 1:31 DCC). This can only be done in case of pregnancy and when both partners are 16 or older, or when the Ministry of Security and Justice gives permission due to compelling reasons.[9] The second way to attain majority is that a female minor can be declared adult by the juvenile court based on section 1:253ha DCC. This rule is meant to enable a 16- or 17-year-old mother to exercise parental responsibility over her child; parental responsibility can only be exercised by those who have the legal status of majority.

2.2 Best Interests of the Child Principle

One of the general principles of the CRC, as defined by the UN Committee on the Rights of the Child, concerns the best interests of the child principle. According to Art. 3(1) CRC, '[i]n all actions concerning children, whether undertaken by public or private social welfare institutions, courts of law, administrative authorities or legislative bodies, the best interests of the child shall be a primary consideration'.[10] Even though the Dutch Constitution does not enshrine this fundamental principle of international children's rights, it can be regarded as one of the cornerstones of Dutch Family Law, regulating the position of minors, parents and legal guardians, and of the child protection and youth care system.[11] The best interests of the child principle serves as the foundation of Dutch law regulating the position of the child with the aim to secure the child's right to development (see Art. 6 CRC). In addition, it can

---

[8] For a translation of the Dutch Civil Code in English, see H.C.S. Warendorf, R. Thomas and I. Curry Sumner, *The Civil Code of The Netherlands*, Kluwer Law International, May 2013.

[9] There is currently a bill in the Dutch parliament that would abolish the possibility for a pregnant 16–17-year-old minor to marry and thus acquire majority. The reason for this amendment is to protect children from forced marriage. *Parliamentary Documents II* 2012/13, 33 488, nr. 2 (Wet tegengaan huwelijksdwang).

[10] See also General Comment No. 14 (2013) on the right of the child to have his or her best interests taken as a primary consideration (art. 3, para. 1), UN Doc. CRC/C/GC/14.

[11] In the Dutch juvenile justice system the best interests of the child principle can be considered part of the pedagogical approach towards children in conflict with the law.

be argued that the principle also contributes to the protection of the child and his or her family against interference by the State.[12] In this regard, it is important to note that the jurisprudence of the European Court of Human Rights under Article 8 ECHR, in which the best interests of the child have been recognized as a key principle, has had significant influence on the position of children and parents in Dutch Family Law and child protection.[13]

The principle has been embedded in law and/or jurisprudence, either explicitly or implicitly. An example of the latter concerns Article 1:247 DCC which stipulates that parents' responsibility for the care and upbringing of the child includes that they are responsible for the mental and physical well-being of the child as well as his or her safety and that they have to foster the development of their child's personality. This responsibility corresponds with Art. 18(1) CRC which stipulates that parents have the primary responsibility for the upbringing and development of their child and that his or her best interests are their basic concern. In light of this, s. 1:254 DCC, in which the ground for a family supervision order can be found, implicitly refers to the best interests of the child as well by providing that the court can issue a family supervision order if required by the need to protect a child against a serious threat of his or her physical or mental interests or health.

In terms of explicit references to the best interests of the child, there are many family law provisions in which the principles serve as a protective minimum, which enables the court to reject a certain request if granting it were contrary to the best interests of the children involved.[14] An example concerns a joint request of one parent with parental responsibility, and a third person, with no custody over the child, but with family life, to exercise joint parental responsibility (s. 1:253t DCC). Such a request can only be rejected if the court has reasons to assume that granting it would neglect the child's best interests. Other family law provisions give courts the competence to order a certain decision to protect the best interests of children; either the court order would serve the child's best interests or the best interests of the child demand a specific court order.[15] An example is the appointment of a guardian *ad litem* in cases concerning the care and upbringing of the child (s. 1:250 DCC). The court can appoint a guardian *ad litem* if the court considers this required by the best interests of the child. Another example concerns the denial of access to the child or information about the child on the basis of the protection of his or her best interests (s. 1:377a(3)(d), 1:377b(2) and 1:377c(1) and (2) DCC).

The above-mentioned decisions require that the court is informed on the basis of best interests of the child assessment; one could argue that the best interests of the child principle serves as a procedural safeguard (i.e. it must be taken into account). Given the inherent vagueness of the principle (i.e. it implies a case by case analysis), it may be assumed that courts clarify how best interests of the child assessment have influenced their decision. However, sometimes, it is up to the court to decide which

[12] Asser/De Boer 1* 2010/813 & 814.

[13] See, e.g. Asser/De Boer 1* 2010/842.

[14] Asser/De Boer 1* 2010/814a with reference to many examples.

[15] Asser/De Boer 1* 2010/814a with reference to many examples.

of the possible outcomes of a certain case is considered in the best interest of the child, i.e. a substantive assessment by the court itself[16]; this is, for example, true if the court ought to decide on parental responsibility and has to choose between two parents (s. 1:253d(3) DCC) or in case of a dispute between parents with parental responsibility concerning the upbringing of the child (s. 1:253a DCC).

It is important to note that the best interests of the child principle does not imply that it has to be paramount. As ruled by the Dutch Supreme Court with reference to Art. 3(1) CRC, the best interests of the child have to be taken into account as a primary consideration.[17] This does, however, not mean that other interests are not relevant or cannot have priority over the interests of the child.[18]

2.3 *Right to Be Heard*

The right of the child to be heard, as laid down in Art. 12 CRC, is considered another general principle of the CRC. Dutch law makes no explicit reference to this principle, but one comes across different provisions concerning the right of children to be heard. These are generally related to formal proceedings, such as judicial proceedings in matters of family law or child protection. As far as the exercise of parental responsibility is concerned, the Dutch Civil Code does not acknowledge the right to be heard (see s. 1:247 DCC). This touches upon the question to what extent parents are, based on Art. 12 CRC, compelled to guarantee the right to be heard within the family environment. It goes beyond the scope of this contribution to elaborate on this. However, it is interesting in this context to note that Section 1:249 DCC requires children to heed the rights and responsibilities given to their parents in the context of their parental responsibilities and the interests of the other family members.

Under Dutch civil law, a child is legally incompetent to take legal action or to access the court. It is assumed that the child's parents represent him or her in legal matters (s. 1:245(4) DCC).[19] In case of a (potential) conflict of interest between parent(s) and child, the court can appoint a guardian *ad litem* to represent the child (see arts. 1:250 and 1:212 DCC). In addition, the law provides for an informal way to access the family court in matters concerning access (s. 1:377g DCC) or parental custody (s. 1:251a(4) and 1:253a(4) DCC), which is available for children of 12 or older, or for children younger than 12 but who can be considered competent enough.

---

[16] Asser/De Boer 1* 2010/814a.

[17] It should be noted that the Dutch translation refers to '*the*primary consideration' (translated and emphasized by authors).

[18] The Netherlands Supreme Court, 25 April 2008, *NJ* 2008, 414.

[19] M. Limbeek, De bijzondere curator: een volwaardig sluitstuk van rechtsbescherming?, in: J.H. de Graaf e.a. (eds.), *Rechten van het Kind en Waardigheid*, Nijmegen: Ars Aequi Libri 2013, p. 199.

Furthermore, there are some exceptions with regard to the legal incompetence of children. Some concern matters of child protection. A child of 12 or older may request, *inter alia*, to end the family supervision order (s. 1:256(4) DCC), to replace the youth care agency responsible for the enforcement of the family supervision order (s. 1:254(5) DCC) or to end or shorten a placement in alternative care (s. 1:263(2) DCC). In addition, a child of 12 or older who is placed in an institution of closed youth care is considered fully competent to take legal action. The same is true for children in closed youth care under the age of 12 who can be considered competent (s. 29a(2) Youth Care Act). Children in closed youth care are also entitled to a court-appointed lawyer (s. 29f(2) Youth Care Act).

A key provision is Article 809 of the Code of Civil Procedure, which stipulates that every child of 12 years or older has the right to express his or her views in family court proceedings.[20] The court can decide not to hear the child if it considers the case of minor importance. The court can rule similarly if it assumes that the child is not capable of forming his or her views due to a serious physical or mental disorder (s. 809 jo. 802 Code of Civil Proceedings) or if is assumes that either the child is not willing to be heard or hearing the child might jeopardize his or her health.[21] Recently, the Netherlands Supreme Court underscored the significance of the right to be heard, with explicit reference to Art. 12 CRC, and ruled that if a child has not been properly invited to be heard by the court, the court cannot rule not to hear the child (i.e. give a final decision without providing the child with the opportunity to be heard) without a sufficient reasoning why one of the above-mentioned exceptions applies.[22]

The court can also decide to hear a child younger than 12. In case of child maintenance, the law provides that the child must be 16 or older. The court can however decide to hear a child under 16. In child protection cases, the court can order a temporary family supervision order without hearing the child, if immediate action is required. This hearing should be held within 2 weeks after the order (s. 809(3) Code of Civil Proceedings).[23] A similar regulation applies in case of placement in closed youth care (see s. 29f and 29d Youth Care Act). However, in such cases, a child has to be heard by the court, unless the court observes that child is not willing to be heard.

In practice, the courts tend to hear children separately from other interested parties, such as the parents. The regulation of proceedings on child law cases[24] provides some rules in this regard. Only if a child is younger than 12, the child will in principle be heard with the other interested parties present. If the child is heard separately

---

[20] This age limit corresponds with the minimum age of criminal responsibility, which is a deliberate decision of the legislator; J.H. de Graaf, 'De paradox van de toegenomen kinderrechten', in: J.H. de Graaf e.a. (eds.), *Rechten van het Kind en Waardigheid*, Nijmegen: Ars Aequi Libri 2013, p. 19.

[21] The Netherlands Supreme Court, 1 November 2013, ECLI:NL:GHSGR;2012:5085, para. 3.3.5.

[22] The Netherlands Supreme Court, 1 November 2013, ECLI:NL:GHSGR;2012:5085, para. 3.3.6.

[23] J.E. Doek & P. Vlaardingerbroek, *Jeugdrecht en jeugdzorg*, Amsterdam: Elsevier 2009, p. 110–111.

[24] Procesreglement civiel jeugdrecht, 12[e] druk, April 2013, para 7.

(i.e. the general rule) the court must give a summary to other interested parties (cf. Art. 6 ECHR's principle of 'equality of arms').[25]

In conclusion, Dutch law has build in an age limit at 12 years with regard to the question whether or not a child must be heard and whether or not a child can be assumed to have legal competence to take legal action in certain specific cases. This age limit corresponds with other age limits, one of which concerns medical decisions that will be addressed below. However, it does not correspond with the recommendation of the UN Committee on the Rights of the Child not to set these kinds of age limits, based on the assumption that every child should in principle be considered capable of expressing his or her views.[26] Even though setting an age limit like this one can be defended from the perspective of legal certainty and equality or for practical reasons, it is interesting to note that the existence of the age limit of 12 years has not been questioned when the Dutch government ratified the CRC, while its practical implications maybe far reaching, particularly for children underneath that age.[27]

3 Parent-Child Relationships: Parentage, Knowledge of Genetic Origins and Adoption

3.1 Birth Registration and Name

One of the first aspects to look into when considering the rights of children in family law is the rights enshrined in Article 7 of the CRC: *The child shall be registered immediately after birth and shall have the right from birth to a name, the right to acquire a nationality and. as far as possible, the right to know and be cared for by his or her parents.*[28] Birth registration in the Netherlands needs to take place within 3 days of the birth of the child (s. 1:19e(6) DCC). The child's mother has the capacity to declare the birth with the birth registrar, but the child's father has the duty to make such a declaration; if he fails to do so, he may be fined (s. 1:19e(6) DCC). If the child has no father, this duty falls on other persons specifically named in s. 1:19e(3) DCC. In case no declaration is made, this duty falls on the Burgomaster (s. 1:19e(5) DCC). Clearly the aim of the legislation is that no child remains unregistered. At the registration of the birth, the child's first name(s) and surname must be registered (s. 1:4 and 1:5 DCC). Parents are free to choose a first name for their child as long as it is not unsuitable or is not also used as a surname, unless this surname

---

[25] M.R. Bruning, 'Equality of arms bij jeugdbescherming', *FJR* 2007, 1. Zie ook J.H. de Graaf, 'De paradox van de toegenomen kinderrechten', in: J.H. de Graaf e.a. (red.), *Rechten van het Kind en Waardigheid*, Nijmegen: Ars Aequi Libri 2013, p. 21–23.

[26] General Comment No. 12, The right of the child to be heard, UN Doc. CRC/C/GC/12, para. 21.

[27] T. Liefaard, *The Rights of the Child to Be Taken Seriously*, Inaugural lecture, 19 November 2013 (unpublished).

[28] The right to nationality under Dutch law falls outside the scope of this paper.

is commonly used as a first name (s. 1. 4(2) DCC). The child's surname depends on the mother's relationship status and/or the choice made by the parents between the name of the birth mother or the name of the other legal parent or the name of the birth mother and the other person with parental responsibility (s. 1:5 DCC).[29] Where the child's parents are unknown, the child will be given a temporary first name and surname by the birth registrar, awaiting a decision on the child's name by Royal Decree (s. 1:5(10) DCC). It is very difficult to change a name once it is registered on the birth certificate under Dutch law. There are different procedures and different grounds for changing first names and for changing surnames. More importantly, minors have not been given the capacity to instigate civil proceedings by themselves; therefore, an application for change of a first name or surname needs to be filed by the child's statutory representative (this will usually a parent with parental responsibility).[30] The request for a change of a first name will have to be submitted with the District Court, and the applicant will have to prove that he has a substantial personal interest in changing his first name(s), which is not always easy to prove in practice.[31] A change of surname will only be granted in a limited number of cases and requires a Royal Decree (s.1:7(3) DCC and *Besluit Geslachtsnaamswijziging* hereafter *BG*). There are a number of general grounds for surname change (s. 1 BG), and there are a number of grounds relating to the acquisition and later change of a surname pursuant to parental separation and new family formation. Once the child has reached the age of 18, he may file an application to have his surname changed into the surname of the partner of his parent, provided this partner has taken care of him for some time during his minority, into the surname of his other parent or into his original surname, if it has been changed during his minority (s. 4–6 BG). Such possibilities also exist when the child is under 18, but then again the child's statutory representatives will have to file the application, and a number of extra requirements are applicable (s. 3 BG).

3.2 *Biological Parents, Legal Parents and Knowledge of Origins*

What rights does a child have with regard to a biological parent who is not a legal parent? In order to answer this question, we need to distinguish between the right to know who this biological parent is on the one hand and the right to establish a legal parent-child relationship with this parent on the other hand.[32] The last issue will be

[29] Under Dutch law a child can have a legal mother or a legal mother and a legal father at birth or (as of 1 April 2014) two legal mothers (s. 1:198 and 1:199 DCC).

[30] Section 1:234(1) and 1:245(4) DCC).

[31] Section 1:4(4) DCC. Examples of successful applications for name changes are for instance names that have a religious connotation that no longer complies with the applicants life choices.

[32] M.J. Vonk, Weten, kennen en erkennen: kinderen van ouders die niet samen zijn, *NTM-NJCM Bulletin* 2013 jaargang 38, nr. 4. http://machteldvonk.files.wordpress.com/2013/08/02-art-njcm-2013-nr-4_vonk.pdf

discussed first. Biology is no longer the only basis on which parenthood can be based. In the past few decades, the intention to become a parent (consent to conception) has also become an important basis. The most recent example of this is the upcoming change in Dutch law that will become effective on 1 April 2014 and will allow two women to both become legal mothers to the same child as of the moment of birth. Whether this will happen automatically depends on their relationship status and the use of unknown or known donor sperm.[33]

The paternity of a child born to an unmarried mother may be established against the biological father's will by the District Court on the application of the mother (within 1 year of the child's birth and until the child reaches the age of 16) or the child (no time limit) (s. 1:207 DCC). If a child is born within a marriage, the mother's husband will automatically be the child's legal father, even if he is not the child's biological father (s. 1:199 DCC). Both the legal father, the legal mother and the child can file an application to deny the legal father's paternity if he is not the biological father. The father and mother can only do this within a very limited time frame after birth (mother) or after starting to suspect that the legal father is not the biological father (legal father). There are some circumstances that make denial impossible for the legal mother and the legal father, even where the father is not a biological parent, for instance, where they both consented to the use of donor sperm or where the legal father knew the mother was pregnant with another man's child at the time he entered into a marriage. These exceptions do not apply to the child. The child has the right to challenge the legal parenthood of a non-biological parent, regardless of the manner in which the child was conceived, until 3 years after she started to suspect that the legal father is not her biological father, and if this suspension started growing during her minority, he has until 3 years after he has reached majority (s. 1:200(6) DCC).[34]

The right to know one's biological parents has become increasingly important in the Netherlands over the past 30 years and lead to the introduction of legislation in 2004 concerning the right to donor data of children conceived through artificial reproduction techniques with donor sperm and/or eggs.[35] Clinics and professionals involved in artificial reproduction with donor material have a duty to pass on information about the donor (including person identifying information) to the Donor Data Registry (s. 2 DDARA). In this Registry, the donor's medical information is stored, as well as background information and person identifying information.

[33] M. J. Vonk, Same-sex parents in the Netherlands, *Homoparentalite? Approche Comparative*, Société de legislation comparée Français, Paris 2012, p. 13–39.

[34] For extensive information on Dutch legal parenthood see M.J. Vonk, *Children and their parents: A comparative study of the legal position of children with regard to their intentional and biological parents in English and Dutch law*, Intersentia – Antwerp, 2007. http://igitur-archive.library.uu.nl/dissertations/2007-1219-220809/index.htm

[35] Wet donorgegevens kunstmatige bevruchting Stb. (Donor Data Artificial Reproduction Act hereafter referred to as DDARA). For information in English on this Act, see: P.M. Janssens, A.H. Simons, R.J. van Kooij, E. Blokzijl and G.A. Dunselman, A new Dutch Law regulating provision of identifying information of donors to offspring: background, content and impact, *Human Reproduction*, 2006, Apr. 21 (4): 852–6.

The information in the donor's medical records may only be provided to the doctor of the child conceived with biomedical assistance (s. 3(1)(a) DDARA). The child, once he has reached the age of 12, can request other data about his biological parent, such as physical features, education, profession, characteristics, etc. (s. 3(1)(b) DDARA). The child's legal parent(s) may also request non-identifying information until the child reaches the age of 12 (s. 2(1)(c) DDARA). These data may not lead to the identification of the donor. Once the child has reached the age of 16, he may apply for the person identified as his biological parent to be revealed to him (s. 3(2) DDARA). In principle, this information will be provided to the applicant unless the donor can prove that he has a substantial personal interest in the information being kept secret. In this decision, the consequences for the child of non-disclosure need to be born in mind. Children conceived outside a clinical setting or children conceived before the entry into force of the earlier mentioned Act have to rely on case law by the Dutch Supreme Court and the European Court of Human Rights for their claim to access information about their biological parent(s). In the late 1980s and early 1990s, two cases established the boundaries of this right in the Netherlands.[36] In the latter of these cases, the Dutch Supreme Court established on the basis of Article 8 ECHR and Article 7 CRC (which the Dutch government at that time had not yet ratified) that access to information about a person's origins is an essential part of a person's right to identity.[37] In principle, the child's right to information about his or her origins outweighs the interests of the biological parent, unless the biological parent can prove that he has a substantial interest in the information not being revealed. However, the first problem with the right to know origins is the fact that children will have to know that one or both parents are not the biological parents. In the context of adoption, there is an implied duty in the Netherlands on adoptive parents to inform their adopted child that they are not his original parents (status information); an adoption order will not be granted if the prospective adopters are unwilling to tell the child about his adoptive status.[38] Subsequently, the adopted child has a right to obtain information about his original/biological parents (information about origins). In practice, it will of course depend on the availability of the information, whether the child will come to know who his biological parents are. Section 30 of the Hague Convention on Intercountry Adoption imposes on states a duty to ensure that information about the child's origins held by them is preserved. Moreover, States must ensure that the child (or the child's representative) may have access to this information. In Dutch intercountry adoption law (s. 17d Wobka),[39] the adopted child, the (prospective) adopters or the child's statutory representative has been given the right of access to the adoption file that the licence holder has in his possession.

---

[36] For more information on the issue, see R. Blauwhof, *Foundational Facts, Relative Truths: A Comparative Law Study on Children's Right to Know Their Genetic Origins*, Antwerp: Intersentia 2009.

[37] Dutch Supreme Court, 15 April 1994, NJ 1994, 608.

[38] For instance, District Court Leeuwarden 10 May 2000, ECLI: RBLEE:2000: AA5749.

[39] This Act will be discussed in more detail later on.

In the context of artificial procreation with donor eggs/sperm, there has been discussion on the issue of status information: are parent obliged to tell their children they were donor conceived? In response to a recent extensive evaluation of the Donor Data Act,[40] the *staatssecretaris* stated that he is not willing to take measures to force parents to provide this information to their children. He favours measures that support openness about donor conception but confirms that it is the choice of parents when and how they inform their child about its conception.[41] The issue of information about a child's origins is very topical in the Netherlands at present; it also played a very prominent role in the parliamentary debates on the new law on lesbian motherhood that will enter into force on 1 April 2014.

In a recent case concerning an intercountry adoption from India, the Arnhem Court of Appeal stated that the fact that children have a (clausulated) right to know who their biological parents are does not mean that possible biological parents have a corresponding right to know who their children are.[42] In this case, an Indian couple claimed that their son (born in 1997) had been abducted in 1999 and was subsequently adopted by a Dutch couple (who followed all the applicable rules). They asked the court to establish on the basis of DNA testing that they were indeed the boy's biological parents. The boy was unwilling to cooperate with the DNA testing, and both the court and the court of appeal dismissed the Indian couple's request. This judgment reflects the Dutch idea in parentage law that a biological father outside the child's family unit cannot rebut the paternity of the child's legal father; only the child, the mother and the legal father have been given this right.

3.3 *Intercountry Adoption*

Family formation can also take place by means of adoption. Since there are very few children residing in the Netherlands available for adoption, intercountry adoption is the most common form of adoption. In 2011, 563 children were adopted through intercountry adoption in the Netherlands, 28 children were adopted domestically by new parents and 435 children were adopted by the life partner of their parent. Of this last group, the overall majority (351) of children were adopted by the mother's female life partner.[43] Dutch law requires the child over 11 years of age to be (given the opportunity to be) heard during the adoption proceedings. A judge will not make

---

[40] H.B. Winter et al. *Evaluatie embryowet en wet donorgegevens kunstmatige bevruchting*, Den Haag, ZonMw, 2012, Reeks evaluatie regelgeving http://www.zonmw.nl/uploads/tx_vipublicaties/embryowet-wdkb_webversie.pdf

[41] Letter of the staatssecretaris of 11 July 2013 concerning his reaction the evaluation of the aforementioned Act *Standpunt op evaluatie Embryowet en Wet donorgegevens kunstmatige bevruchting* kenmerk 124775-105375-PG

[42] Court of Appeal Arnhem, 13 September 2012, ECLI:NL:GHARN:2012:BX7942

[43] These data were obtained from *Centraal Bureau voor de Statistiek* (Dutch Statistical Agency) on 6 January 2014 http://statline.cbs.nl/StatWeb/publication/?VW=T&DM=SLNL&PA=80496NED&D1=a&D2=a&D3=a&HD=110809-1444&HDR=G1,T&STB=G2

adoption orders if the child who is 12 years or older objects to the adoption (s. 1:228(1)(a) DCC). Where a younger child object to adoption and this child is considered able to reasonable asses his own interests in the matter, the adoption order will not be granted either. Other requirements for adoption under Dutch law can be found in Sections 1:277–1:232.

In the context of intercountry adoption, three legal instruments are relevant: the Hague adoption Convention, the Dutch Placement of Foreign Foster Children Act (*Wobka*)[44] and the sections in the Dutch Civil Code mentioned before. In the case of national adoptions, the rules in the Dutch Civil Code will apply; in the case of international adoptions, the *Wobka* applies; and if the child is adopted from a country that is party to the Hague Adoption Convention, this convention applies as well. Since the requirements of the Hague Adoption Convention apply for all signatory states and are easily accessible to interested parties, the focus in this section will be on the requirements that prospective adopters residing in the Netherlands are faced with if they want to adopt a child from abroad. The regulations that cover this process are laid down in the *Wobka*. First of all, prospective adopters will have to apply for consent to adopt *(beginseltoestemming)*.[45] The process from the submission of the application for consent to adopt and actually bringing the adopted child to the Netherlands will take 3–5 years. Both single persons and married couples are eligible to apply for intercountry adoption. Couples who are living together or have entered into a registered partnership cannot apply jointly for intercountry adoption. One of the couple will have to apply, and the other partner can later adopt the child through partner adoption in the Netherlands. The maximum age difference between the adopter and the child is 40 years.[46] If a couple or one partner in a couple submits an application for consent to adopt, the age of the eldest partner of the couple will be taken into account, even where this is not the partner who applies for the consent to adopt. Moreover, the child to be adopted may not be 6 years or older upon entry into the Netherlands, unless it concerns a sibling of a child already adopted by the same person(s) or a group of siblings given up for adoption that cannot be separated without causing them serious harm.[47] A home study will take place before the consent to adopt can be granted.[48] If the prospective adopter is part of a couple, the other partner will also be involved in the home study. In all adoption procedures, domestic or intercountry, the child's best interests are a paramount consideration.[49]

[44] Wet van 8 December 1988, houdende regelen inzake de opneming in Nederland van buitenlandse pleegkinderen met het oog op adoptie.

[45] Section 2 Wobka.

[46] Section 3(1) and section 5(7) Wobka.

[47] Section 8(a) Wobka.

[48] Section 5 Wobka.

[49] Section 1:227(3) DCC.

4 Being a Child in a Family: Participation and Development and Limits to Parental Autonomy

The preamble of the CRC recognizes that 'the child, for the full and harmonious development of his or her personality, should grow up in a family environment, in an atmosphere of happiness, love and understanding' and 'the child should be fully prepared to live an individual life in society, and brought up in the spirit of the ideals proclaimed in the Charter of the United Nations, and in particular in the spirit of peace, dignity, tolerance, freedom, equality and solidarity'. In these extracts from the CRC, the tension between two important elements in the parent-child relationship stand out, on the one hand the safe and harmonious childhood in a family environment and on the other hand the duty of parents and others to nurture the growing independence and autonomy of the children concerned and prepare them for life as an adult. This means on the one hand that the safety of children in their family home must be safeguarded (they should, for instance, be protected from physical violence) and on the other hand that children should be able to become increasingly independent in their decision-making, for instance, concerning their own health or employment. Both issues concern the scope accorded to the exercise of parental responsibility on the one hand and the rights and interests of the child on the other hand. How has the Dutch legislator solved these issues where the position of a child in his family is concerned?

4.1 *Physical Punishment*

Parental responsibility in the Netherlands includes the right and duty of its holder to care for and raise the child.[50] This includes the care and responsibility for the mental and physical well-being of the child and promoting the development of the child's personality (s. 1:247(2) DCC). Since 2007, the Dutch Civil Code states that holders of parental responsibility will not submit the child to physical or mental punishment/abuse or any other form of humiliating treatment (s. 1:247(2) DCC). The inclusion of this ban on physical punishment in the Civil Code is mainly a moral appeal on parents and does not contain any punitive measures. Moreover, there has been discussion about the meaning of physical punishment/abuse, for instance, does slapping a child once on the hand when it tries to take a cookie from the cookie jar

[50] Parental responsibility can be invested in legal parents, but also the legal parents' partner who is not a legal parent upon their joint request. However, there is a maximum of two persons who can hold parental responsibility with regard to a child (s. 1:245(3). For more information on Dutch parental responsibility, see C.G. Jeppesen de Boer, *Joint parental authority: a comparative legal study on the continuation of joint parental authority after divorce and the breakup of a relationship in Dutch and Danish Law and the CEFL principles*, Antwerp: Intersentia, 2008.

after it has been told several times not to do so physical abuse?[51] The Dutch Criminal Code does include punitive measure for parents and others, such as schoolteachers or child care professionals, who subject a child to physical punishment.[52] The Dutch Criminal Code (s. 300 and onwards) distinguishes between different categories of *infliction of bodily harm on a person*, from simple to grievous and ultimately bodily harm resulting in death (either negligent, on purpose or premeditated); each category has its own range of penalties. Important in the context of physical punishment within the family is Section 304 of the Dutch Criminal Code which gives judges the possibility to increase the possible punishment with one third, if the bodily harm is inflicted on a family member, such as a child. In 2011, the government launched an extensive scheme to prevent and sanction child abuse *Kinderen veilig* (Children safe) that proposes a multidimensional approach to child abuse. Recent Acts such as the *Wet tijdelijk huisverbod* (Act temporary ban from the family home) under which a perpetrator of domestic violence can be banned from his home for a period of time and the *Wet voorwaardelijke sancties* (Act suspended sanctions) which among others broadens the possibilities to force perpetrators of child abuse/domestic violence to undergo treatment or counselling support this approach.[53]

4.2 Discharge of Parental Responsibility

If child abuse occurs within the family, a judge can impose child protection measures, such as a care and supervision order, and ultimately parents can be discharged of their parental responsibility. Voluntary discharge of parental responsibility will only take place if the parent concerned is unfit or unable to fulfil the duty of caring for or raising the child (s. 1:266 DCC). If the holder of parental responsibility does not agree with the voluntary discharge of parental responsibility, he may be discharged nonetheless in a number of circumstances listed in Section 1:268 DCC. These circumstances include the situation where a lighter child protection measure has been in place for some time (either a care and supervision order pursuant to s. 1:254 DCC for 6 months or a care and protection order pursuant to s. 1:261 DCC for 18 months), but this has not led to and is not expected to lead to the removal of the threat to the child's moral or mental interests or his health on which the order was based in the first place (s. 1:268(2)(a)). Another ground for involuntary discharge pertains to the situation where one of the parents has been discharged, but the children remain under the influence of this discharged parent unless the other parent is discharged as well (s. 1:268(2)(b) DCC). The third ground for involuntary discharge concerns the situation where the parent with parental

[51] http://www.rijksoverheid.nl/onderwerpen/kindermishandeling/documenten-en-publicaties/richtlijnen/2011/11/28/actieplan-aanpak-kindermishandeling-2012-2016-kinderen-veilig.html

[52] See in this context paragraph 41 of General Comment 13, which requires States to combat physical or humiliating forms of discipline at schools.

[53] http://www.nji.nl/Beleid-WetDOUBLEHYPHENen-regelgeving.

responsibility is unable to determine his will due to disturbed mental faculties (1:268(2)(c) DCC).

At present there are two child protection measures that terminate a parent's parental responsibility: (in)voluntary discharge (*ontheffing)* as described in Sections 1:266–1:268 DCC and disqualification (*ontzetting*) as described in s. 1:269 DCC. Discharge (whether voluntary or not) is motivated by the holder's inability to meet the needs of the child, whereas disqualification is motivated by the holder's (culpable) behaviour with regard to the child concerned. Grounds for disqualification include abuse, gross neglect, irresponsible behaviour, serious disregard of instructions given by the institution for family guardianship under a care order or a criminal conviction for the wilful participation in a criminal offence with a minor under the parent's responsibility or the commissions of a criminal offence involving the child, such as sexual abuse. At the request of the Child Care and Protection Board (*Raad voor de Kinderbescherming*) or the public prosecutor, the District Court may discharge a parent of parental responsibility. A request for disqualification may be filed with the district court by the other parent, a relative by blood or marriage of the child up to and including the fourth degree, the Child Protection Board or the public prosecutor (s. 1:270(1) DCC)). If the child has been raised by others for some period of time and there is a well-founded fear that the parent with parental responsibility will reclaim or take back the child even where this is not in the child's best interest, these others may also apply for disqualification of the parent (s. 1:269(1)(e) and s. 1:270(2). It is important to note that disqualification is requested and ordered very infrequently. Discharge/disqualification is not necessarily permanent. Parents can request to be reinvested with parental responsibility if this is in the interest of the child concerned, and the parent is capable of a sustained exercise of his responsibilities for the mental and physical well-being of the child (s. 277(1) new DCC).

In the near future, these two types of discharge will become one (s. 1:266 new DCC). The ground for terminating a parent's parental responsibility will be that the circumstances in which the child is raised constitute a serious threat to the child's moral or mental interests or his health and that the parent is not able to exercise (or resume the exercise of) his responsibilities for the mental and physical well-being of the child within a period of time that is acceptable in view of the child's personality and development. Whether or not the parents' consent to this child protection measure is no longer of consequence. Moreover, under this new provision, parents can be discharged of their parental responsibility at or shortly after the moment of the child's birth. The grounds mentioned earlier for disqualification will be summarized under the heading abuse of parental responsibility (s. 1:266(1)(b) new DCC). The new measure can be requested by the Child Protection Board, the public prosecutor and the person who is not a parent, but has been taking care of the child as part of his family for more than a year (s. 267(1) new DCC). The institute for family guardianship (*Bureau Jeugdzorg)* can request it indirectly through the Child Protection Board.

If a parent is deprived of his parental responsibility, the other parent with parental responsibility will hold it alone (s. 274(1) DCC).[54] If there is no other parent with parental responsibility after deprivation, the judge will appoint a guardian; this guardian will exercise guardianship over the child.[55] In the context of child protection, this will generally be an institution for family guardianship. The institution for family guardianship will place the child in foster care with a family or in an institution, depending on the needs of the child and the availability of foster families. The child will have a right to contact with his parents and parents have a right and duty to maintain contact with the child, unless it is not in the child's interests that contact be maintained.[56] Parents have a right to information about the child and will still be liable to pay child maintenance (s. 1:392 DCC).

4.3 Medical Treatment

Parental responsibility includes the care for the child's physical and mental health. What happens if parent and child have different ideas about the child's mental health and measure that may be taken to improve the child's health? Under Dutch law, parental responsibility ends when a child turns 18, but that does not mean that children have right to make important decisions about their own life by themselves. For instance, in the field of medical treatment, child participation starts at a reasonably early age. In the case of medical treatment provided to a child less than 12 years of age, the consent of both holders of parental responsibility will have to consent to the treatment. Where the child has reached the age of 12 but has not yet turned 16, both the child and the holders of parental responsibility need to agree to the treatment (s. 7:450(2) DCC). Treatment cannot take place if the child does not agree, unless the child is legally incapable (*wilsonbekwaam*). There are two circumstances that allow for treatment to be given to the child, without the parent's consent. First of all, treatment can take place without parental consent if refraining from treatment would lead to substantial harm for the child. An example would be the treatment of a sexually transmitted disease. The parents need not be informed of the medical treatment that will or has taken place. Secondly, if the agreement of the holder(s) of parental responsibility cannot be obtained, treatment can take place if the minor has considered the consequences of the treatment and decides to have it nonetheless. In this case, parents will in principle need to be consulted. If, for example, a 13-year-old child needs a blood transfusion but the parents refuse to consent because their

---

[54] If the parent who is deprived of parental responsibility held it with a person who is not a legal parent, for instance, a new partner, the other parent may ask the court to invest him with sole parental responsibility to the detriment of the partner s. 1:253v (6) DCC. In this text, the term parent with parental responsibility includes the partner who is not a legal parent unless explicitly excluded.

[55] Section 1:275 DCC.

[56] Sections 1:377a, 377c DCC and section 42(2) Uitvoeringsbesluit Wet op de Jeugdzorg (*Additional regulations pertaining to the Youth Care Act*).

religion does not allow for blood transfusions, treatment can take place if the child desires it. However, if the parents want the blood transfusion to take place, but the 13-year-old child refuses to consent, it cannot take place. If the child is legally incapable and objects to the treatment, it may take place without the minor's consent if it concerns treatment of a serious nature and it is necessary to prevent substantial harm to the minor under certain circumstances (WGBO 7:465(6) DCC). Once the minor has reached the age of 16, it is only his consent that is required for medical treatment, unless the child is legally incapable (s. 7:447(1) and s. 7:450(3) DCC).

4.4 Employment

In principle, the minimum age for admission to employment in the Netherlands is set at 16 years.[57] However, under certain circumstances, children can be allowed to work from the age of 12 years. This concerns only 'lighter' forms of employment (e.g. newspaper delivery, an alternative sanction or a social internship). The child has the right to decide independently about his/her employment once it reaches the age of 16 years;[58] before that age, he needs the consent of his statutory representative.[59] However, in case the minor below the age of 16 does work and the legal representative does not object within 4 weeks, consent is presumed to have been obtained.[60] Minors are protected by labour laws. Apart from certain provisions in the more general Working Hours Act, for children aged from 12 to 16 years, there are specific regulations relating to child labour[61] that are concerned with working hours and conditions for different types of labour. Conditions for employment of children of 16 or 17 years old can be found in the Arbeidsomstandighedenbesluit *(Working Conditions Resolution)*. Children aged from 12 to 16 may only perform certain types of work. Children aged 16 or 17 are allowed to perform almost every job, but for 'risky activities', supervision is required. Furthermore, they are not allowed to work with dangerous substances.

5 Conclusion

In conclusion, it is safe to say that on the whole, the rights and interests of children play a role of substance in Dutch Family Law, despite the absence of a special Children's Act or explicit references to the general principles of international children's rights. The assumption that Dutch law was already largely in conformity with

---

[57] Section 1:2 jo. 3:2 Working Hours Act (*Arbeidstijdenwet*).

[58] Section 7:162(1) DCC.

[59] Section 1:234 DCC.

[60] Section 7:162(1) DCC.

[61] Nadere regeling kinderarbeid *(Additional Regulation Child Labour)*.

the CRC at the time of its ratification has prevented critical reflections on prominent existing legal standards, such as the age limit of 12 years as the dividing line between competence and incompetence to be heard in judicial family law proceedings, to have an independent legal status or to take medical decisions. In this contribution, it has been indicated that such a critical reflection would have been appropriate. Nevertheless, some interesting developments in the area of Dutch Family Law have been identified, showing that the CRC, in conjunction with the ECHR, have increasingly been used as frames of reference to sharpen the protection of the rights of children in family matters.

The Rights of the Child: United Kingdom National Report

Jenny Driscoll

1 Introduction

The United Kingdom (UK) comprises Great Britain (England, Scotland and Wales) and Northern Ireland. There are three legal jurisdictions, with England and Wales sharing jurisdiction, although the Welsh Government has recently consulted on the possibility of creating a separate Welsh legal jurisdiction. A number of 'overseas territories' also come under the jurisdiction of the UK. In its most recent Concluding Observations, the United Nations Committee on the Rights of the Child (2008) expressed significant concerns about the implementation of the principles of the Convention in the overseas territories, but space does not permit further consideration of those regions here.

At the time of writing, the Welsh Assembly has legislative competence only in those areas expressly 'conferred' on it by the Government of Wales Act 2006 and listed in Schedule 7 thereto. The Scottish Parliament, by contrast, is empowered to legislate on all matters which have not been expressly 'reserved' in the Scotland Act 1998, Schedule 5. In Northern Ireland, the Assembly has full legislative competence over any matters which are not explicitly 'excepted' or 'reserved'. 'Excepted' issues remain within the domain of the UK Parliament at Westminster, but the

The author gratefully acknowledges the assistance of Dr Julie Doughty, Cardiff University; Professor Kathryn Hollingsworth, Newcastle University; Professor Laura Lundy, Queen's University Belfast; Dr Claire McDiarmid, University of Strathclyde; and Paola Uccellari, Director of the Children's Rights Alliance for England (CRAE) through feedback on earlier drafts. Any mistakes are entirely the author's own.

J. Driscoll (✉)
Department of Education and Professional Studies, School of Social Science and Public Policy, King's College London, Franklin-Wilkins Building, Rm 2/15 Waterloo Bridge Wing, Waterloo Road, London SE1 9NH, UK
e-mail: Jenny.driscoll@kcl.ac.uk

O. Cvejić Jančić (ed.), *The Rights of the Child in a Changing World*,
Ius Comparatum - Global Studies in Comparative Law 13,
DOI 10.1007/978-3-319-23189-1_19

Assembly may legislate in respect of 'reserved' issues subject to certain conditions (Northern Ireland Act 1998 Schedules 2 and 3). All the devolved institutions must act in accordance with the European Convention on Human Rights, which has been incorporated into domestic legislation through the Human Rights Act 1998, and with European Union law. This report covers all four nations, indicating where there are significant differences between countries.

The Convention was ratified by the UK on 16th December 1991 and the reporting process of the United Nations Committee on the Rights of the Child is undertaken in relation to the UK as a whole, but national governments and non-governmental organisations may prepare separate reports. The most recent Concluding Observations were made in response to the Third and Fourth Periodic Report of the United Kingdom (2007). The United Kingdom submitted its Fifth Periodic Report in May 2014, with concluding observations expected in 2016. The Scottish Government published a separate submission for the Fifth UK Government Report in June 2013.

In this article, after an explanation of the definition of a 'child' in UK law and of the way in which the 'best interests' of the child relate to the 'welfare principle' underpinning UK family law, the key issues raised by the United Nations Committee on the Rights of the Child in its Concluding Observations in 2008 are set out, followed by commentary on significant developments since that date, including the UK Government's Fifth Periodic Report (2014), and then the specific issues additionally raised by the general reporter regarding family law relations.

2 The 'Child' and Children's Rights in UK Law

A child is defined in different ways in relation to different aspects of law in the UK, but for most purposes a child is a person under the age of 18. The Children Act 1989 section (s) 105 defines a child as 'a person under the age of eighteen' and the Family Law Reform Act 1969 s1(1) states that 'a person shall attain full age on attaining the age of eighteen' (England and Wales). Similar provisions apply in Northern Ireland, under the Children (Northern Ireland) Order 1995 s2(2) and the Age of Majority Act (Northern Ireland) 1969 s1(1). In Scotland, the situation is a little more complex. The parental responsibilities and rights listed under s1 of the Children (Scotland) Act 1995 only apply to children under 16, save for the duty to provide appropriate guidance, which subsists to the age of 18 (s93(2)). Scotland's Children's Hearing System applies to children to the age of 16, extending to 16 and 17 year olds in some circumstances.

UK law does not recognise the unborn child as a legal person, and therefore the foetus has no rights of his/her own until birth[1] and his/her father has no rights in relation to him/her, although the unborn child capable of being born alive may be regarded as having some 'conditional' rights in relation to injury or assault prior to

[1] *Paton v British Pregnancy Advisory Service Trustees* [1979] QB 276.

birth (see MacDonald 2011). The AbortionAct 1967 prohibits abortion in England, Scotland and Wales except (i) prior to 24 weeks' gestation where there is risk of injury to the mother's physical or mental health or that of her existing children; or (ii) where termination is regarded as 'necessary to prevent grave permanent injury to the physical or mental health of the pregnant woman'; or (iii) where continuance of the pregnancy would involve 'greater risk to the life of the pregnant woman than termination'; or (iv) where there is a substantial risk that if the child were born he or she would 'suffer from such physical or mental abnormalities as to be seriously handicapped' (Abortion Act 1976 s1(1)). The Abortion Act does not apply to Northern Ireland, where recent guidance (Department of Health, Social Services and Public Safety, April 2013) states that the 'circumstances where a termination of pregnancy is lawful in Northern Ireland are highly exceptional' (1.3) and that it is 'illegal to perform a termination of pregnancy unless it is necessary to preserve the life of the pregnant woman, or there is a risk of real and serious adverse effect on her physical or mental health, which is either long term or permanent' (1.4).

There is no specific legal instrument in England or Northern Ireland devoted to the rights of the child. In Wales, a general framework, the Rights of Children and Young Persons (Wales) Measure 2011, requires Welsh ministers, when making decisions concerning legislation and/or policy, to have regard to (a) part 1 of the United Nations Convention on the Rights of the Child (UNCRC); (b) articles 1–7 of the Optional Protocol to the Convention on the Rights of the Child on the involvement of children in armed conflict, except article 6(2); and (c) articles 1–10 of the Optional Protocol to the Convention on the Rights of the Child on the sale of children, child prostitution and child pornography. From 1st May 2014, this duty applies to Welsh ministers when exercising any of their functions. Section 4 makes provision for a reporting system on compliance with the duty and s6 for the amendment of legislation in accordance with recommendations made in such reports. The Children and Young People (Scotland) Act 2014 requires ministers to review what steps might be taken to further implementation of the UNCRC and to take appropriate actions in response to such review and to promote awareness and understanding of the UNCRC. It also imposes reporting duties on certain public authorities to enhance scrutiny of the public sector's approach to implementation.

3 The Best Interests of the Child

In all three jurisdictions, family law is underpinned by the 'welfare principle'. Under the Children Act 1989 s1(1) and the Children (Northern Ireland) Order 1995 article 3, the *court* is required to give '*paramount* consideration' to the welfare of the child in making decisions in relation to a child's upbringing. In Scotland, the court or children's hearing is required to give '*paramount* consideration' to the welfare of the child throughout the child's childhood in determining any matter concerning that child (Children (Scotland) Act 1995 s16 and Children's Hearings (Scotland) Act 2011 s25). The welfare principle also applies to adoption agencies under the Adoption and Children Act 2002 and equivalent legislation. Under the Children's Hearings (Scotland) Act 2011, which covers youth justice as well as safeguarding law, a children's hearing or court may make a decision that is inconsistent with the requirement imposed by s25(2) to regard the need to safeguard and promote the welfare of the child throughout the child's childhood as the paramount consideration if it considers that it is necessary for the purpose of protecting members of the public from serious harm (whether physical or not), and in coming to the decision, the hearing/court is to regard the need to safeguard and promote the welfare of the child throughout the child's childhood as a *primary* consideration. There is additional provision in the Children and Young Persons Act 1933 s44(1) (England and Wales) that '[e]very court in dealing with a child or young person who is brought before it, either as an offender or otherwise, shall have regard to the welfare of the child or young person…'.

The welfare principle does not apply to other administrative or legislative institutions, including social care, nor to parents, and is more paternalistic – and arguably therefore less conducive to children's rights (MacDonald 2011) – than article 3. In 2008, the UN Committee on the Rights of the Child criticised the UK for failing to ensure that article 3 is implemented 'in all legislative and policy matters affecting children, especially in the area of juvenile justice, immigration and freedom of movement and peaceful assembly' (2008, para 26). Some progress has been made since then. A number of statutory provisions include a requirement that public authorities exercise their functions having regard 'to the need to safeguard and promote the welfare of children' (e.g. Children Act 2004 s11 (applies to children's social care authorities, health authorities, police, youth offending bodies); Education Act 2002 s175; Borders, Citizenship and Immigration Act 2009 s55). This duty has been interpreted with reference to article 3 in some secondary legislation, for example, statutory guidance issued under the Borders, Citizenship and Immigration Act 2009 s55 requires that '… the best interests of the child will be a primary consideration (although not necessarily the only consideration) when making decisions affecting children' (paragraph 2.7). The Supreme Court has sought to interpret domestic legislation in a way compatible with the UNCRC, for example, ruling that the best interests of a child must be a primary consideration when considering whether a decision to remove an illegal immigrant is a necessary and proportionate response with regard to the European Convention on Human Rights 1950 article 8.[2] In the High Court, recent decisions in planning law[3] and in relation to the eligibility of prisoners who are mothers for childcare resettlement leave[4] have applied this approach more widely. However, in the absence of direct statutory implementation, administrative bodies may be slow to incorporate the best interests principle in routine practice.

---

[2] *ZH (Tanzania) v Secretary of State for the Home Department* [2011] UKSC 4.

[3] *AZ v Secretary of State for Communities and Local Government* [2012] EWHC 3660 (Admin) and *Stevens v Secretary of State for Communities and Local Government* [2013] EWHC 792 (Admin).

[4] *R (MP) v Secretary of State for Justice* [2012] EWHC 214 (Admin).

The last decade has seen some wider policy initiatives to promote a more child-focused and holistic approach to children's services. In England, this took the form of the *Every Child Matters* (DfES 2003) agenda, but although the five core principles of this strategy remain embedded in the Children Act 2004, the Government has not promoted the initiative further. In Scotland, *Getting It Right for Every Child* (GIRFEC) (Scottish Government 2008, updated 2012) applies to all agencies working with children and families and aims to support targeted intervention to enhance child well-being across agencies. The eight well-being indicators are for children to be safe, achieving, healthy, active, responsible, nurtured, respected and included. In 2013, the Scottish Government commissioned a report on how GIRFEC relates to and endorses the principles of the UNCRC (Aldgate 2013). Similarly, Wales has adopted seven core aims for work with children and young people, based on the principles of the UNCRC (Welsh Assembly Government 2004). Northern Ireland has developed six key outcomes, focusing on the extent to which children are healthy; enjoying, learning and achieving; living in safety and stability; experiencing economic and environmental well-being; contributing positively to community and society; and living in a society that respects their rights (OFMDPM 2006).

4 Key Issues Raised in the 2008 Concluding Observations

The Committee welcomed the UK's then imminent withdrawal of reservations to articles 22 and 37(c) of the Convention; the adoption of some legislation in relation to children's rights, such as the Children Act 2004 and the Childcare Act 2006; the creation of the Equality and Human Rights Commission; and references to the Convention in domestic case law. Although the Children's Plan for England 2007 and the creation of the Department for Children, Schools and Families were also praised, these have since been abolished. The Committee expressed concern that the UK had not ensured that all legislation is compliant with the Convention and recommended incorporation of the Convention into domestic law through the introduction of a Bill of Rights as well as the development of an overarching policy for implementation and evaluation at the state party level. However, Government proposals for a British Bill of Rights under consideration in the run-up to the 2015 General Election involved repeal of the Human Rights Act 1998 rather than the incorporation of additional international treaties.

The Committee found a 'general climate of intolerance and negative public attitudes towards children, especially adolescents' (p. 6), evidenced in the media; in restrictions in children's freedom of assembly and movement; in the continued sanctioning of physical punishment of children in the home; in a punitive approach to children in the youth justice system, including an unacceptably low age of criminal responsibility (viz. 10, save in Scotland where it is 8, although the age of prosecution was raised to 12 by the Criminal Justice and Licensing (Scotland) Act 2010); failure to restrict custody to a sentence of last resort; and continued use of physical restraint in custody. The Committee was concerned at high rates of child substance misuse and bullying and poor play infrastructures, particularly for disabled children. Although the Committee praised greater statutory provision with regard to the views of the child, it highlighted continuing inadequacies in relation to the implementation of article 12 in education law and policy and in relation to disabled children. It also drew attention to the consequences of poverty and inequality in the UK, particularly in relation to access to health and education services; high rates of teenage pregnancy in lower socio-economic groups; and the increasing gap in infant mortality rates between the rich and poor. The Committee expressed alarm at the prevalence of child maltreatment and pointed to deficiencies at the national strategic level in monitoring; provision of alternative care; and support for child victims. It called for greater state support for parents in their child-rearing responsibilities, as well as improved access to services for children suffering mental ill health and disabled children.

5 Significant Developments Since the Consolidated Third and Fourth Periodic Report

There have been some positive developments since 2007. In the Fifth Periodic Report (HM Government 2014), the Government cites significant improvements in some outcome indicators, including a fall in child deaths and in the infant mortality rate; lower rates of child drug and alcohol use and of teenage pregnancy; and reductions in first-time entrants to the criminal justice system and in children in custody. Reforms to strengthen the independence and power of the Children's Commissioner for England and improve provision for children with special educational needs have been introduced through the Children and Families Act 2014. In its most recent report on the *State of Children's Rights in England*, CRAE (2013) applauded expression of a 'strong commitment' to improving outcomes for looked-after children and proposed reforms to adoption and family justice, although CRAE raised concerns as to whether the proposals would 'prioritise the rights of parents over the best interests of the child' (CRAE 2013, p. 3).

In their midterm report, the UK Children's Commissioners (2011) welcomed the commitment to end child detention for immigration purposes (although it does not appear that this has been entirely achieved) as well as the proposed measures in Wales and Scotland outlined above, but drew attention to ongoing concerns in five areas in particular: participation, disabled children, child poverty, asylum-seeking children and youth justice. The Commissioners observed that child participation has yet to become mainstream practice and that children still have limited advocacy rights or none in Northern Ireland. They considered progress to removing barriers for disabled children's access to services to have been inadequate since 2008. They were concerned that children in the immigration system whose age was disputed are still not given the 'benefit of the doubt' and that identification and protection of child trafficking victims was poor.

In relation to youth justice, whilst finding that the Scottish Children's Hearing System was more efficient in diverting children from the youth justice system, in general, the Commissioners considered that youth justice systems required reorientation towards prevention and diversion. CRAE (2013) has also criticised the government's refusal to raise the age of criminal responsibility and to ensure that children aged 17 are treated as such in the criminal justice system. Some progress has been made in relation to the last criticism: under the Legal Aid, Sentencing and Punishment of Offenders Act 2012, 17 year olds are now treated as children for the purposes of remands, and all children remanded to custody will be treated as looked-after children (children in state care). Furthermore, in April 2013, the High Court ruled that treating 17 year olds in police custody as adults is unlawful;[5] as a result of which, The Police and Criminal Evidence Act 1984 Code C has been amended to give additional rights to 17-year-olds, including safeguarding through access to an 'appropriate adult', and s42 of the Criminal Justice and Courts Act 2015 (not yet in force as at August 2015) will amend the definition of 'arrested juvenile' under the Police and Criminal Evidence Act 1984 to include 17-year-olds.

CRAE (2013) has also expressed concern that in some respects compliance with the UNCRC has regressed since 2008, primarily as a result of resource issues arising from the global recession. Areas of particular concern were worsening child poverty; cuts in legal aid making it more difficult for children to access justice; and the government's failure to assess the impact of fiscal measures on children's rights. A report from the Office of the Children's Commissioner (2014) is highly critical of the Government's draft Child Poverty Strategy 2014–2017, which is unlikely to meet the aim of abolishing child poverty by 2020.

Provisions in the Anti-social Behaviour, Crime and Policing Act 2014 are expected to restrict further children's freedom of assembly and movement. Recently enacted age discrimination legislation (Equality Act 2010) does not apply to children. Revelations of widespread sexual exploitation of adolescents have highlighted concerns as to the care of older vulnerable children, but reductions in statutory guidance in child protection may weaken children's access to protective services, whilst deregulation in education is likely to impact negatively on children's access to appropriate education in sex and relationships, drugs and alcohol, and citizenship.

In Scotland, there appears to be a more optimistic assessment of the Scottish parliament's commitment to children's rights. In response to the *Concluding Observations*, the Scottish Government published an action plan (Scottish Government 2009) and more recently a progress report on the action plan (Scottish Government 2012). In its report of September 2012, Together (formerly Scottish Alliance for Children's Rights) recognised a 'clear commitment from the Scottish Government to enable children to realise their rights under the UNCRC and to improve its implementation across Scotland' (p. 1), but also highlighted a gap between policy and practice, although the Children and Young People (Scotland) Bill did not escape criticism in the media for lacking a preventative focus and

[5] *R (on the application of HC) v Secretary of State for the Home Department* ([2013] EWHC 982 (Admin)), initiated by Just 4 Kids Law.

support for families and for excessive surveillance of family life. Furthermore, the Scottish Government (ruled by the Scottish National Party since 2011) acknowledged in its *Submission to the United Nations Committee* (Scottish Government 2013b) that its proposed programme of reforms will be limited by UK Government policy and expressed outright criticism of the UK Government's welfare reforms.

The Welsh Government also published an action plan in response to the 2008 Concluding Observations, entitled *Getting it Right* (2009), and reported on its progress against the plan (Welsh Government 2013). In March 2012, the Welsh Government also introduced the Children's Rights Scheme, which sets out the arrangements to monitor compliance with the duty to have regard to children's rights laid down in the Rights of Children and Young Persons (Wales) Measure (the Measure). The *Getting it Right update* (Welsh Government 2013) highlighted a focus on participation rights through the Measure and a commitment to opportunities for play, especially for disabled children, but acknowledged that educational attainment in Wales needs to be addressed to enable competition at international level. An interim report by Save the Children (2013) concluded that the Measure presents an unprecedented opportunity to promote children's rights in Wales (although its claim that the Measure amounts to incorporation of the UNCRC in Welsh law is inaccurate) and lauded the awarding of the first Right to Play award by the International Play Association in 2011 to Wales in recognition of progress made in this area. However, as in Scotland, fiscal restraints and a gap between policy and current practice were regarded as threats to further progress, and the report pointed to a dearth of robust data about children's lives, including in relation to mental health; maltreatment and bullying; sexual exploitation and trafficking; and the experiences of minority groups of children. The report also expressed concern that the Social Services and Well-being Bill in its (then) current draft gave insufficient attention to children's rights and outcomes.

6 Specific Issues in Relation to Family Law

6.1 The Right of the Child to Know About His/Her Origin

Case law recognises the child's right to know of his or her natural parents unless his/her welfare demands otherwise.[6] However, in England and Wales, provisions under the Welfare Reform Act 2009 schedule 6 to amend the Births and Deaths Registration Act 1953 to require registration of the name of the father where the parents are not married (ss2A and 2B) (subject to some exceptions set out in s2B(4)) are not currently in force. In Scotland, the Registration of Births, Deaths and Marriages (Scotland) Act 1965 s18 precludes unmarried fathers from being named on the birth certificate unless there is agreement, a court order or statutory declarations by both parents. Similar provisions apply in Northern Ireland under the Births and Deaths Registration (Northern Ireland) Order 1976 Art. 14(3).

[6] *A* v *L* (*Contact*) [1988] 1 FLR 361.

Under the Family Law Act 1986, any person may apply to the court for a declaration that a person named in the application is/was the parent of another person named (s55A) or for a declaration that the applicant is the legitimate child of his or her parents (s56). The court may order testing under the Family Law Reform Act 1969 s20(1) and will usually do so in recognition of the child's right to know his or her parents. However, save in relation to applications under the Children Act 1989, children are not able to make their own applications to court and will therefore need to be represented by a litigation friend (usually the Official Solicitor).

Adoption orders in the UK are usually 'closed', that is, there is no face-to-face contact between the child and his or her birth parents after adoption, and the general duty on local authorities to promote such contact to children in their care under the Children Act 1989 s34 is removed by the Adoption Agencies Regulations 2005 reg 45.2. In England, Wales and Northern Ireland, adopted children have a right on adulthood (i.e. at 18) to ascertain the identity of their birth parents (see the Adoption and Children Act 2002 ss56–65 and the Disclosure of Adoption Information (Post-Commencement Adoptions) Regulations 2005 (AIR) for the legal framework in relation to disclosure of information relating to adoption orders made since December 2005). During the adopted child's childhood, *Statutory Guidance on Adoption* (Department for Education (DfE) 2013) and the Adoption Agencies Regulations 2005 reg 35 require the preparation of a 'life story book' and 'memory box' to be prepared within ten working days of the adoption ceremony (Guidance para 5.50) and for a 'later life letter' to be prepared for the child when older, to explain his or her family background and the circumstances leading to his or her adoption (para 5.51). In Scotland, the National Care Standards (Adoption Agencies) 2005 assure that at 'an appropriate age', children will be provided ('as far as possible') with their 'full birth history and genetic history' to ensure that they have the information they need for 'a healthy adult life and possible future parenthood'. Standards 10–12 allow children over 16 to access their records, find out about their birth family and make contact with them.

Children born by donor conception will be able to obtain data, including identifying data, on donors on adulthood where it was supplied after 1st April 2005 (Human Fertilisation and Embryology Authority (Disclosure of Donor Information) Regulations 2004 reg 2(3)). An applicant under 18 may only be given non-identifying information (including as to ethnicity, religion, medical screening, occupation, interests and skills (reg 2(3A)). However, legal commentators have drawn attention to the need to ensure that the method of conception is indicated on birth certificates to enable children to exercise this right.

6.2 The Child's Right to Express His/Her Views Freely in All Matters Affecting Him/Her

The child has no specific right to express his or her views in matters affecting him or her in her home environment in England, Wales and Northern Ireland; however, the European Convention on Human Rights has been incorporated into UK law through the Human Rights Act 1998, and the right to freedom of expression under article 10 of that Convention applies to children as to adults. In Scotland, the Children (Scotland) Act 1995 section 6(1) requires a person reaching any major decision which involves exercise of parental rights or responsibilities to have regard so far as practicable to the views (if she or he wishes to express them) of the child concerned, taking account of the child's age and maturity. A child 12 years of age or more is expressly presumed to be of sufficient age and maturity to form a view.

In relation to administrative or judicial proceedings, in England and Wales and Northern Ireland, where a court is considering whether to make, vary or discharge private or public family law orders, the court shall have regard to the ascertainable wishes and feelings of the child concerned, to be considered in the light of his or her age and understanding (Children Act 1989 s1(3): Children (Northern Ireland) Order 1995 Art. 3(4)). In private law proceedings (i.e. those between family members or carers and not involving the state), the court is only required to have regard to the child's ascertainable wishes and feelings where the proposed order is opposed by one of the (adult) parties (CA 1989 s1(4)(a), C(NI)O 1995 s3(4)(a)). Local authorities are also required to ascertain and take into account children's views in relation to the provision of services (CA 1989 s17(4A)) or accommodation (CA 1989 s20(6)), decisions in respect of children in state care (s22(4) and s22(5)), as well as in relation to adoption (Adoption and Children Act 2002 s1(4)). In Scotland, the Children's Hearings (Scotland) Act 2011 strengthens measures to ensure that children's views are heard, including through s121 (which requires the chair to ensure that documentation adequately reflects the child's views unless it is not appropriate to do so, taking into account the age and maturity of the child). Additionally, s122 (not yet in force) will impose a requirement on the chair of the hearing to inform the child of the availability of advocacy services, unless it is not appropriate to do so, taking into account the age and maturity of the child. Children in England and Wales have no express right to information and advice, but in public family law proceedings the child is represented by both a lawyer and a guardian (the latter through the Children and Family Court Advisory and Support Service (Cafcass)). The guardian is responsible for advising the court as to the child's wishes and feelings and providing information, advice and support to the child and family (Criminal Justice and Court Services Act 2000 s12(1)). In private family law proceedings, a court *may* ask Cafcass or a local authority to report to the court on the welfare of the child (CA 1989 s7), which will include communicating the child's wishes and feelings to the court. In Northern Ireland, the Children (Northern Ireland) Order 1995 s60 makes provision for reports to the court on matters relating to the child's welfare.

6.3 Right to Give Consent to Adoption

The Adoption and Children Act 2002 s1(4) requires the adoption agency to have regard to the child's wishes and feelings, considered in the light of their age and understanding, but does not give the child the right to consent. In Scotland, unless the court is satisfied that the child is incapable of consenting, an adoption order may not be made in respect of a child who is aged 12 or over unless the child consents (Adoption and Children (Scotland) Act 2007 s32).

6.4 Conditions for Intercountry Adoption

Intercountry adoption in the UK is permitted where the child cannot be cared for in any suitable manner in his or her own country; adoption would be in the best interests of the child and with respect for his or her fundamental rights as recognised in international law; the adopter has been assessed by an adoption agency as eligible and suitable to adopt from overseas; and no profit is made from the process. It is governed by the Adoption and Children Act 2002 in England and Wales, the Adoption and Children (Scotland) Act 2007 in Scotland and the Adoption (Intercountry Aspects) Act (Northern Ireland) 2001 in Northern Ireland. Three types of intercountry adoption are distinguished: Hague Convention (the adoption is recognised in the UK and the child acquires British citizenship); 'designated list' (the adoption is recognised in the UK but the child does not acquire British citizenship); and 'other' (the adoption is not recognised in UK law and the prospective adopters must apply for an order on return to the UK).

6.5 The Right of the Child to Freedom of Thought, Conscience and Religion

In England and Wales, maintained schools (excluding special schools) must provide religious education for all registered pupils in accordance with schedule 19 of the School Standards and Framework Act 1998 (Education Act 2002 s80 (England) or s101 (Wales) and SSFA 1998 s69(1)) and a daily act of collective worship (SSFA 1998 s70). Teaching must 'reflect the fact that religious traditions in Great Britain are in the main Christian whilst taking account of the teaching and practices of the other principal religions represented in Great Britain' (Education Act 1996 s375(3)), but parents (and pupils from the academic year after that in which they attained 16) may request withdrawal from religious education under SSFA 1998 s71, and arrangements may be made for alternative religious provision elsewhere. Schools with a 'religious character' may make provision for instruction in accordance with the religious tenets espoused by the school and well-being and community cohesion'.

In Scotland, the Education (Scotland) Act 1980 s8 provides that public and grant-aided schools shall be open to pupils of all denominations, but that parents may withdraw their children from religious instruction and observance at school. In June 2013, a petition was lodged at the Scottish Parliament calling for *parental* opt in to religious observance (but not education) to replace *parental* opt out.

In Northern Ireland, the provision of Religious Education must be included in the curriculum for all children up to the age of 16 in all publicly funded schools under the Education (Northern Ireland) Order 2006 Art. 5, as must be a daily act of collective worship (Education and Libraries Order (Northern Ireland) 1986 Art. 21(1)). Parents have the right to withdraw their child from part or all of religious education or collective worship (ibid. Art. 21(5). There is no opt out provision for children of any age.

6.6 *Physical Punishment of the Child Within and Beyond the Family*

6.6.1 Institutions

The Education Act 1986 s47 made physical punishment illegal in maintained schools and was followed by the School Standards and Framework Act 1998 s131 in relation to independent schools and establishments for preschool age children (amending s548(1) of the Education Act 1996). Scotland outlawed physical punishment in educational establishments in 2000 (Standards in Scotland's Schools etc. Act 2000, s16) and Northern Ireland in 2003. Physical punishment is also barred in children's homes (Residential Establishments – Child Care (Scotland) Regulations 1996, reg 10(2); Children's Homes Regulations 2001 reg 17(2); Children's Homes Regulations (Northern Ireland) 2005 reg 16 and Children's Homes (Wales) Regulations 2002 reg 17(5)), foster homes (Fostering Services (England) Regulations 2011 Schedule 5 para 2(c) and Fostering Services (Wales) Regulations 2003 schedule 5 para 8) and by child day-care providers in England, Scotland and Wales (e.g. Child Minding and Day Care (Wales) Regulations 2010 reg 23(5)). In Northern Ireland, there is no legislative provision in relation to childcare, but standard 6 of the Child Minding and Day Care for children aged under 12 Minimum Standards (2012) requires that physical punishment is neither used nor threatened. A review commissioned by a previous government recommended that physical punishment be rendered unlawful in all settings outside the child's family or household (Singleton 2012), but the current Government has not acted upon the recommendations.

Within custodial institutions, physical punishment is not authorised, but neither is there an explicit prohibition. Furthermore, there has been considerable concern over the use of restraint techniques to control young offenders in secure settings (see e.g. Smallridge and Williamson 2008). Youth justice has not been devolved to Wales, but the Howard League for Penal Reform regards the All Wales Youth Offending Strategy 2004 as indicative of a more encouraging approach in its emphasis on young offenders as children first and offenders second.

6.6.2 Within the Family

There remains an anomalous common law defence of 'reasonable punishment' to a charge of common assault against a person over 16 having care of a child. In response to European Court of Human Rights case law,[7] the government limited but did not abolish the defence in England and Wales through the introduction of the Children Act 2004 s58. The current extent of the defence is uncertain, as 'reasonable punishment' is not defined and the defence is not available for more serious offences such as assault occasioning actual bodily harm, but whether actual bodily harm or common assault is charged is a matter of prosecutorial discretion. The UN Committee on the Rights of the Child expressed its concern that the UK has failed to prohibit corporal punishment in the family in its Concluding Observations in 2008, but the Fifth Periodic Report states that while the Government does not 'condone any violence towards children', it takes the view that 'a mild smack does not constitute violence and that parents should not be criminalised for giving a mild smack' (p. 21). A recent attempt to remove the reasonable punishment defence in Wales was unsuccessful. In Northern Ireland, there is a similar defence pursuant to the Law Reform (Miscellaneous Provisions) (Northern Ireland) Order 2006 Art. 2. In Scotland, the law is somewhat clearer, but no more compatible with children's UNCRC rights and is set out in the Criminal Justice (Scotland) Act 2003 s51, which allows the defence of 'physical punishment carried out in exercise of a parental right or of a right derived from having charge or care of the child where such assault is 'justifiable'. In determining that issue, the court must have regard to (a) the nature of what was done, the reason for it and the circumstances in which it took place; (b) its duration and frequency; (c) any effect (whether physical or mental) which it has been shown to have had on the child; (d) the child's age; and (e) the child's personal characteristics (including, without prejudice to the generality of this paragraph, sex and state of health) at the time the assault was inflicted. Excluded from the definition of a justifiable assault are (a) a blow to the head, (b) shaking or (c) the use of an implement. The *UK country report of the Global Initiative to End All Corporal Punishment of Children* (June 2015) calls for explicit prohibition of all corporal punishment in all institutions accommodating children in conflict with the law and alternative care settings, including public and private day care, in the UK.

7 Deprivation of Parental Responsibilities

In England and Wales and Northern Ireland, parents lose parental responsibility upon adoption of their child (which requires a court order), whereupon the child becomes the legal child of the adopter(s) (Adoption and Children Act 2002 s67;

[7] *A v United Kingdom* (1998) 27 EHRR 611.

Adoption (Northern Ireland) Order 1987 Art. 40). Birth parents do not lose parental responsibility when a child is in care to the local authority pursuant to a court order, but share parental responsibility with the local authority, which is able to determine the extent to which others exercise parental responsibility in so far as it is necessary to safeguard or promote the child's welfare (Children Act 1989 s 33(3) and (4)). An unmarried father who acquired parental responsibility through agreement with the mother, court order or registration may lose parental responsibility by court order, and a child may make an application for such an order with leave of the court (Children Act 1989 s4(2A)), which will only be given if the court is satisfied that the child has sufficient understanding to make the application (s10(8)). Case law suggests parental responsibility will only be revoked in extreme circumstances, such as the infliction of severe injuries on the child[8] or where the father sexually abused the mother's elder daughters.[9] In Scotland, the Children (Scotland) Act 1995 utilises the concept of parental responsibilities and rights and under s11(2); the court may deprive a person of some or all of those responsibilities and rights, but s11(11) states that an order made by the court shall have the effect of depriving a person of a parental responsibility or parental right only in so far as the order expressly so provides and only to the extent necessary to give effect to the order. In all countries, a range of interested parties may be granted parental responsibility, including step-parents and persons having a residence order in relation to the child. Unmarried fathers who lose parental responsibility pursuant to s4(2A) nonetheless are responsible for their child's financial upkeep and may be permitted contact. All parents are also entitled to notice of proceedings, for example, for care or supervision orders or for adoption.

8 Independent Right to Give/Refuse Medical Consent

In England and Wales, the Family Law Reform Act 1969 s8 allows children over 16 to consent independently to their own medical and dental treatment. In relation to consent, children under 16 are accorded similar rights over decisions to those over 16 if they are assessed to be 'competent' within the meaning laid down by the House of Lords in *Gillick* v *West Norfolk and Wisbech Area Health Authority*.[10] However, case law on refusal of treatment has ruled that parental consent to treatment may override that of the competent minor aged over or under 16. The High Court retains unlimited jurisdiction over children under 18 and may also authorise treatment against a child's wishes. The child's welfare will be the court's paramount consideration, and medical treatment will only be recommended by doctors if regarded as being in the patient's best interests. To date, there has been no reported case of a court allowing a child to refuse life-threatening treatment. Although there

---

[8] *Re P (Terminating Parental Responsibility)* [1995] 1 FLR 1048.

[9] *CW v SG* [2013] EWHC 854 (Fam).

[10] [1986] AC 112.

is statutory provision for competent children to refuse court-ordered medical or psychiatric assessments or examinations (Children Act 1989 s38(6) and s43(8); Children (Scotland) Act 1995 and Children (Northern Ireland) Order 1995), case law[11] confirms that the High Court may overrule these children also. The situation in Northern Ireland is the same as that in England and Wales, as the inherent jurisdiction of the High Court applies. In Scotland, a person aged 16 or over has legal capacity to enter into a 'transaction', a term which includes 'the giving by a person of any consent having legal effect' (Age of Legal Capacity (Scotland) Act 1991, s 1(1)(b) and s9). The right of young people under 16 who are considered to be competent to consent to medical treatment is confirmed in statute (Age of Legal Capacity (Scotland) Act 1991, s 2(4)). Whether the refusal of a competent child to medical treatment can be overridden in Scotland is unclear.

9 Right to Change His/Her Personal Name Independently

In England and Wales, it is lawful to use or be known by any name, provided that there is no intention to deceive or defraud. However, evidence of a change in name may be required for many purposes. Application for the formally recognised change of a child's name may be made by deed poll executed by a person with parental responsibility and requires the consent of all persons with parental responsibility and a declaration that the application is for the benefit of the child. Where a child is over the age of 16, the child's consent is also required (Enrolment of Deeds (Change of Name) Regulations 1994, reg 8). Where all persons with parental responsibility do not consent, application may be made to the court for a specific issue order under s8 of the Children Act 1989. A child may only apply for a specific issue order with leave of the court, which will only be given if the court is satisfied that the child has sufficient understanding to make the application (s10(8)). If leave is granted, the court will determine the issue on the basis that the child's welfare is the paramount consideration (s1(1)). In Scotland, a child can change his/her name independently once they reach the age of 16 (Registration of Births, Deaths and Marriages (Scotland) Act 1965 s43(5)). For children under 16, the application must be made by a 'qualified applicant' (s43(4)), defined as (a) where only one parent has parental responsibilities in relation to the child, that parent; (b) where both parents have such responsibilities in relation to the child, both parents; and (c) where neither parent has such responsibilities, any other person who has such responsibilities (s43(9A)). There is no 'benefit' provision, but limitations on the number of times that names may be changed. In Northern Ireland, application for one change of name and one change of surname may be made in relation to children under 18 by the qualified applicant (which may comprise more than one person with parental responsibility) (Births and Deaths (Northern Ireland) Order 1976 Art. 37).

---

[11] See, for example, *South Glamorgan County Council v W & B* [1993] 1 FLR 574.

10 The Minimum Age for Admission to Employment

In England and Wales, the Children and Young Persons Act 1933 s18 as amended regulates the part-time work of children aged 14–15, but is subject to variation through local bye-laws, which may make provision for the employment of children aged 13. Fortin concludes that the resulting arrangements are 'not only extremely confusing, but fail to protect [children] adequately' (2009, p. 109). Broadly, children under 13 may not be employed, save in relation to performance work which cannot be undertaken by an older person. Children aged 13–15 may only be employed in 'light' work. Children aged 14 and 15 may be employed for no more than 2 h on school days (including 1 h before school), to a maximum of 12 h in a school week and only between 7 am and 7 pm. A child under 18 may not be employed in street trading; industrial undertakings; work beyond the child's physical or psychological capacity or involving harmful exposure to toxic or carcinogenic substances or radiation; work in which there is a risk to health from extreme cold or heat, noise or vibration; work in which there may be risk to the young person's safety; gambling; or on ships. Requirement for parental consent to the child's employment is governed by local authority bye-laws (DCSF 2009). Scottish law has similar provisions, including for regulation of this issue by local authorities, under the Children and Young Persons Act 1937 ss28 and 30. The Education (Scotland) Act 1962 s136 prohibits the employment of children under 16 in factories, quarries and mines. Northern Ireland imposes a minimum age of employment of 13, governed by The Children (Northern Ireland) Order 1995 Art. 135, which also specifies that no child shall be employed before the close of school hours on any day on which he is required to attend school; or before seven o'clock in the morning or after seven o'clock in the evening on any day; or for more than 2 h on any day on which he is required to attend school (subject to exceptions laid down by regulations, including in relation to child performers). Provision is also made to exclude children from street trading and the employment of children in any occupation 'likely to be injurious to his life, limb, health or education, regard being had to his physical condition'.

11 Conclusion

The current status of children's rights in the UK reflects the remnants of a paternalistic culture and an ambivalent commitment to the concept of children as rights holders. Children have no legal obligations towards their parents and no right to vote before the age of majority. The central Government at Westminster is predominantly concerned with fiscal considerations (see p. 10 of the Fifth Periodic Report) and has indicated it may repeal the Human Rights Act 1998, through which the European Convention on Human Rights is incorporated in UK law, in response to high-profile immigration cases. It has not signed the *Optional Protocol to the*

Convention on the Rights of the Child on a Communications Procedure, which provides an international complaint mechanism for children who consider their rights to have been violated and which opened for ratification in February 2012, but the Fifth Periodic Report states that it will keep this under review. In contrast to the Westminster parliament, there appears to be a strong will to prioritise children at policy level within the devolved administrations, although it might be considered that such policies are more often concerned with children's welfare than their autonomy rights. Furthermore, a number of commentators have drawn attention to the failure of practice to match rhetoric. Whilst resources are scarce in the current economic climate, article 4 requires state parties to undertake appropriate measures for the realisation of children's economic, cultural and social rights 'to the maximum extent of their available resources'. To date, the UK Government has not demonstrated a commitment to children's rights commensurate with its economic standing.

Bibliography

Aldgate, J. 2013. *UNCRC: The foundation of getting it right for every child*. Scottish Government. http://www.togetherscotland.org.uk/resources-and-networks/resources-library/detail/?resource=347. Last accessed 18 August 2015.

Department for Children, Schools and Families (DCSF). 2009. Guidance on the employment of children London DCSF. https://www.gov.uk/government/publications/guidance-on-the-employment-of-children, last accessed 18th August 2015.

Department for Children, Schools and Families (DCSF). 2010. *Religious education in English schools: Non-statutory guidance*.https://www.gov.uk/government/publications/religious-education-guidance-in-english-schools-non-statutory-guidance-2010. Last accessed 18 August 2015.

Department of Health, Social Services and Public Safety (DHSSPS). 2013. *The limited circumstances for a lawful termination of pregnancy in Northern Ireland: A guidance document for health and social care professionals on law and clinical practice*. Belfast: DHSSPS.

Fortin. 2009. *Children's rights and the developing law*. Cambridge: Cambridge University Press.

Global Initiative to End All Corporal Punishment of Children. 2013. *UK country report*. http://www.endcorporalpunishment.org/progress/country-reports/uk.html, last accessed 18 August 2015.

HM Government. 2003. *Every child matters: Change for children*. London: Department for Education and Skills.

HM Government. 2014. *The fifth periodic report to the UN committee on the rights of the child: United Kingdom*.http://tbinternet.ohchr.org/_layouts/treatybodyexternal/Download.aspx?symbolno=CRC%2fC%2fGBR%2f5&Lang=en. Last accessed 18 August 2015.

MacDonald, A. 2011. *The rights of the child: Law and practice*. Bristol: Family Law.

Office of the Children's Commissioner. 2014. *Response of the Office of the Children's Commissioner to the government's child poverty strategy 2014–17*. London: Office of the Children's Commissioner. https://www.childrenscommissioner.gov.uk/publications/response-governments-hild-poverty-strategy-2014-17, last accessed 18 August 2015.

Office of the First Minister and Deputy First Minister (OFMDFM). 2006. *Our children and young people – our pledge – A ten year strategy for children and young people in northern Ireland 2006–2016*. Belfast: OFMDFM.

Save the Children. 2013. *Rights here, right now: Are children's rights a reality in Wales?* http://resourcecentre.savethechildren.se/library/rights-here-right-now-are-childrens-rights-reality-wales-wales-ngo-interim-report, last accessed 18 August 2015.

Scottish Government. 2009. *Do the right thing.* http://www.scotland.gov.uk/Publications/2009/08/27111754/0. Last accessed 18 August 2015.

Scottish Government. 2012. *Do the right thing progress report.* http://www.scotland.gov.uk/Publications/2012/05/3593. Last accessed 18 August 2015.

Scottish Government. 2013a. *A guide to getting it right for every child.* http://www.scotland.gov.uk/Topics/People/Young-People/gettingitright/introduction. Last accessed 18 August 2015.

Scottish Government. 2013b. *The 5th UK government report to the UN committee on the rights of the child: Scottish Government Submission.*

Singleton, Sir R. 2010. *Physical punishment: Improving consistency and protection.* DCSF- 00282-2010.

Smallridge, P., and A. Williamson. 2008. *Independent review of restraint in juvenile secure settings.* London: Ministry of Justice. http://webarchive.nationalarchives.gov.uk/20130401151715/https://www.education.gov.uk/publications/standard/youthcrime/page1/restraint-review, last accessed 18 August 2015.

Together (Scottish Alliance for Children's Rights). 2012. *State of children's rights in Scotland 2012.*http://www.togetherscotland.org.uk/resources-and-networks/state-of-childrens-rights-reports/. Last accessed 18 August 2015.

UK Children's Commissioners. 2011. *UK Children's Commissioners' midterm report to the UK state party on the UN convention on the rights of the child.* http://www.childrenscommissioner.gov.uk/publications/uk-childrens-commissioners-midterm-report-state-party-un-convention-rights-child-report, last accessed 18 August 2015.

UK Government. 2007. *The consolidated 3rd and 4th periodic report to the UN committee on the rights of the child.* http://tbinternet.ohchr.org/_layouts/treatybodyexternal/Download.aspx?symbolno=CRC%2fC%2fGBR%2f4&Lang=en, last accessed 18 August 2015.

United Nations Committee on the Rights of the Child. 2008. Forty-ninth session: Consideration of reports submitted by states parties under article 44 of the convention – *concluding observations: United Kingdom of Great Britain and Northern Ireland* CRC/C/GBR/CO/4.

Welsh Assembly Government. 2004. *Children and young people: Rights to action.* Cardiff: Welsh Assembly Government.

Welsh Government. 2009. *Getting it right 2009.* http://dera.ioe.ac.uk/10867/, last accessed 18 August 2015.

Welsh Government. 2013. *The getting it right update 2013 – Action plan addressing the concluding observations of the UNCRC committee (2008).* dera.ioe.ac.uk/17378/2/130131updateen.doc, last acessed 18 August 2015.

Youth Justice Board. 2012. *Code of practice for managing the behaviour of children and young people in the secure estate.*http://www.justice.gov.uk/youth-justice/custody/behaviour-management/restraint-minimisation-strategies. Last accessed 11 Sept 2013.

The State, Parents, Schools, "Culture Wars," and Modern Technologies: Challenges Under the UN Convention on the Rights of the Child

Nora V. Demleitner

1 Introduction

The United States has signed but not ratified the UN Convention on the Rights of the Child (CRC), which makes it one of the only three countries that do not fully participate in this almost universally ratified human rights treaty.[1] With its signature, the US government has indicated not only its general support for the principles of the CRC and the protection of the human rights of children, but also signaled US compliance with these norms.[2] In recent decades, the US Senate has generally been

This report was first published in 62 Am. J. Comp. L. 491–514 (Summer 2014), available at http://www.ingentaconnect.com/content/ascl/ajcl/2014/00000062/a00101s1;jsessionid=90f712cict74j.alice. That issue contains the US National Reports compiled for The XIXth International Congress of Comparative Law, held in Vienna in July 2014.

I am grateful to Max Hyman, W&L '14L for his research assistance.

[1] http://treaties.un.org/Pages/ViewDetails.aspx?src=TREATY&mtdsg_no=IV-11&chapter=4&lang=en (listing signatories and ratifiers of CRC as of Oct.14, 2013). The other two countries are Somalia, which only in 2012 reestablished a national government after decades of civil war, and South Sudan, which became a member of the United Nations in July 2011. The United States has ratified two of the three additional protocols to the CR. *See* http://treaties.un.org/pages/ViewDetails.aspx?src=IND&mtdsg_no=IV-11-c&chapter=4&lang=en (listing signatories and ratifiers of the Optional Protocol to the Convention on the Rights of the Child on the Sale of Children, Child Prostitution and Child Pornography as of Oct. 14, 2013) *and* http://treaties.un.org/pages/viewdetails.aspx?src=treaty&mtdsg_no=iv-11-b&chapter=4&lang=en (listing signatories and ratifiers of the Optional Protocol to the Convention on the Rights of the Child on the Involvement of Children in Armed Conflict as of Oct. 14, 2013).

[2] UNICEF, *Introduction to the Convention on the Rights of Child: Definition of key terms, available at* http://www.unicef.org/crc/files/Definitions.pdf.

N.V. Demleitner (✉)
Washington and Lee University School of Law, Lexington, VA 24450, USA
e-mail: demleitnern@wlu.edu

O. Cvejić Jančić (ed.), *The Rights of the Child in a Changing World*,
Ius Comparatum - Global Studies in Comparative Law 13,
DOI 10.1007/978-3-319-23189-1_20

reluctant to ratify international treaties in the human rights area for domestic reasons, including preservation of states' rights, sovereignty concerns, questions of constitutionality, rejection of international accountability, and fears of foreign interference in the US legal system.[3] Parental rights organizations have objected to ratification of the CRC, fearing it would empower children.[4]

This paper focuses on some of the core principles of the CRC and their application under US law. As the laws of individual states rather than federal law govern many of these central issues, this can lead to distinct approaches, especially as new technologies impact family relations, including conception. Many of the most intractable cultural issues in the United States involve children or arise in the context of primary and secondary education, often pitting children against parents or against the state.

The curious role of children in the United States may be displayed nowhere better than in the criminal justice context. For the sake of children, US sentencing has become ever harsher over the last 35 years. Enhancements have been applied to drug sellers who are offering illegal narcotics near schools;[5] child sexual offenders and those watching child pornography on the Internet have witnessed a dramatic lengthening of their sentences and at the same time have been exposed to lifelong registration and community notification statutes. They have been barred from living near schools and daycare centers and even from frequenting playgrounds.[6]

On the other hand, children have also experienced the harshness of the criminal justice process. In the late 1980s, the fear of crime became amplified because of the image of the "superpredator," the adolescent, ruthless, violent offender.[7] In response, states allowed for or even mandated the transfer of juveniles into the adult criminal justice system.[8] Some states sentenced offenders as young as 13 to life-without-parole. This trend has been reversed only in recent years through Supreme Court cases that barred the death penalty and mandatory life-without-parole for those who committed homicide while under age 18.[9] It also prohibited life-without-parole

---

[3] See, e.g., Natalie Hevener Kaufman & David Whiteman, *Opposition to Human Rights Treaties in the United States Senate: The Legacy of the Bricker Amendment*, 10 Hum. Rts. Q. 309 (1988).

[4] See, e.g., parentalrights.org. For a full discussion of the arguments for and against ratification, see Congressional Research Service, Luisa Blanchfield, *The United Nations Convention on the Rights of the Child*, April 1, 2013.

[5] For criticism of these sentence enhancements, see, e.g., Aleks Kajstura, Peter Wagner & William Goldberg, *The Geography of Punishment: How Huge Sentencing Enhancement Zones Harm Communities, Fail to Protect Children* (July 2008), *available at* www.prisonpolicy.org/zones/.

[6] For a critique of these developments, see Kelly K. Bonnar-Kidd, *Sexual Offender Laws and Prevention of Sexual Violence or Recidivism*, 100(3) Am. J. Pub. Health 412 (2010).

[7] Shay Bilchik, Office of Juvenile Justice and Delinquency Prevention, *Challenging the Myths*, Juvenile Just. Bull. (Feb. 2000), *available at* www.ncjrs.gov/pdffiles1/ojjdp/178993.pdf.

[8] For an example, see Human Rights Watch, *No Minor Matter: Children in Maryland's Jails* (1999), *available at* www.hrw.org/reports/1999/maryland/.

[9] Roper v. Simmons, 543 U.S. 551 (2005) (juvenile death penalty unconstitutional); Miller v. Alabama, 567 U.S. ___, 132 S. Ct. 2455 (2012) (mandatory life-without-parole sentence unconstitutional when applied to a juvenile convicted of a homicide offense).

for juvenile non-homicide offenders, in recognition of the mental and emotional differences between adults and children.[10] The criminal justice system is indicative of the tension in which US society and the US legal system often find themselves with respect to the treatment and protection of children.

As the political culture in the United States values limited government and protections of the individual against the state, even the juvenile justice system extends extensive procedural protections to children. They have, however, been employed to justify harsher penalties. In general, US law emphasizes rights rather than duties, an approach in which it varies, for example, dramatically from the African Charter on the Rights and Welfare of the Child.[11] Despite that political and legal belief structure, the common law has established duties based on special relationships, including those between husband and wife and a parental duty to reasonably protect a child. Explicit duties of children to parents appear limited to special situations. A child may owe a parent a duty of care, for example, when the child voluntarily takes custody of an ailing parent in a way that prevents others from providing care to that parent.[12]

This paper will begin with definitions of "child" and "parent" and then turn to the core concept of "best interests of the child" and its application in select contexts. Next, it looks at three areas in which the rights of parents, children, and the state have come to clash—the right to speech, to information, and to freedom of religion—especially in the public school setting. All of these issues reflect ongoing changes in technology, society, and law, situating children at the center of crucial societal conflicts in the United States.

2 Who Is a "Child"?

The authority to determine who is a child and what rights that person carries is divided between the federal and state governments. At common law, the age of majority was generally 21 years. Today the age of majority is regulated legislatively. While most people deem 18 the age of majority, the law appears more fluid.[13] With the exception of the right to vote—which the US Constitution grants at 18 years due to a constitutional change in 1971[14]—most of the rights of children are age dependent and may extend beyond 18 or end before that age. State legislatures regulate the specific numerical age at which individual rights arise.[15] Such regulation may accord with the CRC's approach that increasing rights (and responsibilities) be

---

[10] Graham v. Florida, 560 U.S. 48 (2010).

[11] Art. 31.

[12] See Restatement (Second) of Torts § 314A (1965).

[13] See Stanley v. Stanley, 112 Ariz. 282 (1975) ("majority or minority is a status rather than a fixed or vested right and [ ] the legislature has full power to fix and change the age of majority").

[14] U.S. Const. amend. XXVI, § 1.

[15] See 43 C.J.S. *Infants* § 2 (Westlaw 2013).

given to children as their age and maturity increase (up to the age of 18 unless otherwise determined under a country's law),[16] though US law extends this concept of maturation beyond 18 in select areas. It appears that the CRC prefers individual assessment of a child's maturity, though in some contexts, it may accept at least a presumption of maturity or allow for a global age-based determination on efficiency grounds.

The specific age at which a child is legally considered an adult varies depending on the context. For example, the Alaska legislature sets the default age of majority at 18 years. For select purposes, however, Alaska lowered that age. These include ownership of long guns (allowed at age 16, without parental consent) and consent to sexual contact (16 years, but elevated to 18 years if the child's sexual partner "has legal authority over the child").

On the other hand, Alaska has raised the age of majority above and beyond the general statutory age of majority for select purposes, such as possession of tobacco (19 years) and possession of alcoholic beverages (21 years). While many of these increases and decreases are specific to individual states and may be explained either by cultural differences between states or by specific incidents that have driven legislative change, others are based on federal mandates.

In all states, purchase and public possession of alcoholic beverages are allowed only at age 21, though many states permit exceptions to these general rules.[17] When the federal government tied federal highway funds to the purchase or public possession of alcohol by those under 21, over time every state changed its law so as to guarantee its receipt of federal monies.[18] Even though Congress would have been barred from legislating a national drinking age, it achieved the same goal through its power of the purse.

In addition to the constitutionally based provision on voting age, other federal (and state) constitutional provisions may regulate certain aspects of the age of majority. The federal constitution's equal protection mandate, for example, bars state legislatures from declaring different ages of majority applicable to females and males, even in situations where biological and emotional maturity may differ.[19]

The Supreme Court has indicated increasing interest in child development concepts, especially in the sentencing area. It declared the execution of those who committed a capital offense while under the age of 18 unconstitutional, relying on child development literature, which finds children fundamentally different from adults as

[16] CRC art. 1.

[17] National Institute on Alcohol Abuse and Alcoholism, Alcohol Policy Information System, *Underage Drinking: Possession/Consumption/Internal Possession of Alcohol*, *available at* http://alcoholpolicy.niaaa.nih.gov/underage_possession_consumption_internal_possession_of_alcohol.html?tab=maps (listing exceptions to rule).

[18] National Minimum Drinking Age Act of 1984, 23 U.S.C. § 158.

[19] See, e.g., Craig v. Boren, 429 U.S. 190, 204 (1976) (a state law allowing females who are 18 years old to purchase nonintoxicating beer, while barring purchase of such beer by males under the age of 21, constituted unconstitutional discrimination in violation of the equal protection clause); Stanton v. Stanton, 421 U.S. 7, 17 (1975) (in the context of child custody, no valid distinction regarding the age of majority can be made on the basis of gender).

their judgment and emotional maturity are not yet fully developed.[20] The Court has recently applied this line of jurisprudence also to life-without-parole sentences.[21] Whether this approach will carry over into other areas of the law remains an open question. At this point, it presents a welcome reprieve for some young offenders, at least at the high end of sentencing.

As the CRC defines "child," a definition generally accepted in the United States, even though with respect to some rights and obligations the specific age cutoff may vary, it fails to provide a definition of "parent." In light of modern technological changes, that definition and the implicit rights and duties have become increasingly complicated. Recently, the US Department of State ruled that US citizenship will transmit to a child born to a US citizen mother but conceived with the egg of a non-US citizen. The definition of "parent" will likely cause further questions in the years ahead and present challenges in different areas of the law. For purposes of this paper, the term will be used in its commonly understood meaning.

3 Parental Rights

Generally, the state grants parents broad leeway in educational and parenting choices for their children, including ways to punish children. Only in exceptional circumstances will parents be deprived of their rights because of abuse or neglect. Schools, however, are frequently held to a different and higher standard than parents. Societal norms, for example, have evolved with respect to corporal punishment in schools and continue to undergo changes, though they have not yet impacted parental freedom in that area.

3.1 Corporal Punishment

The Supreme Court decided in 1977 that corporal punishment in schools does not violate the 8th Amendment prohibition on cruel and unusual punishments.[22] Currently, half of the states regulate corporal punishment statutorily, with some banning it, while others allow it expressly.[23] Within the family, physical punishment of

---

[20] Roper v. Simmons, 543 U.S. 551 (2005).

[21] Miller v. Alabama, 567 U.S. ___, 132 S. Ct. 2455 (2012) (mandatory life-without-parole sentence unconstitutional when applied to a juvenile convicted of a homicide offense); Graham v. Florida, 560 U.S. 48 (2010) (life-without-parole unconstitutional for those who committed non-homicide offense before turning 18).

[22] See Ingraham v. Wrights, 430 U.S. 651, 671 (1977).

[23] See Corporal Punishment in Public Schools, 0040 SURVEYS 7 (2007) (Westlaw).

children remains permitted,[24] apparently under a general belief that "some" corporal punishment benefits (or at least does not harm) a child. There is no debate in the United States about the international community's moving increasingly to a total prohibition on the physical punishment of children, including in families, under CRC Article 19.[25]

3.2 *Loss of Parental Rights*

Even in the United States, physical punishment is limited by considerations of the child's best interest. Should parents violate such restrictions, they may lose their parental rights. Physical harm is not the sole ground for such a decision. Under federal law, child abuse and neglect is defined as including sexual, emotional, and physical abuse, exploitation, and abandonment.[26] Many state statutes provide for the deprivation of parental responsibility upon a finding that a parent is guilty of a federal or state crime against children.[27] The state may also terminate a parent's right to have a relationship with her child pursuant to a finding of abuse or other event that shows that the parent is "unfit"—but the finding of unfitness must be made by at least clear and convincing evidence.[28] In addition, incarceration longer than 15 months may cause termination of a parent's legal responsibility for their child. Because of the negative impact of such a forced separation on parent and child, in recent years some criminal justice policies, such as drug courts, have been developed in part to keep the family unit together.[29]

---

[24] See 6 Am. Jur. 2d *Assault and Battery* § 28 n.1 ("A parent, or one acting in loco parentis, does not commit an assault and battery by inflicting corporal punishment on a person subject to the person's authority, if the parent remains within the legal limits of the exercise of that authority.").

[25] See, e.g., Elizabeth T. Gershoff, *More Harm Than Good: A Summary of Scientific Research on the Intended and Unintended Effects of Corporal Punishment on Children*, 73 Law & Contemp. Probs. 31, 54–56 (2010) (discussing social science research detailing negative effects of corporal punishment and adoption of bans on such punishment in dozens of countries around the globe).

[26] Federal Child Victims' and Child Witnesses' Rights Act of 2009, 18 U.S.C. § 3509 (West, Westlaw through 2013) ("[T]he term 'child abuse' means the physical or mental injury, sexual abuse or exploitation, or negligent treatment of a child."). *See also* 42 Am. Jur. 2d *Infants* § 18 (West, Westlaw through 2013).

[27] *See* 59 Am. Jur. 2d *Parent and Child* § 34 (West, Westlaw through 2013). For examples of how states define child abuse and neglect, *see generally* U.S. Department of Health and Human Services, Administration for Children & Families, *Child Welfare Information Gateway, What Is Child Abuse and Neglect?* (2008) *available at* https://www.childwelfare.gov/pubs/factsheets/whatiscan.cfm.

[28] *See* 53 A.L.R.3d 605 (West, Westlaw through 2013); 59 Am. Jur. 2d *Parent and Child* § 34 (West, Westlaw through 2013).

[29] *See*, e.g., Myrna S. Raeder, *Special Issue: Making a Better World for Children of Incarcerated Parents*, 50 Family Ct. Rev. 23, 27 (2012); *A Jailhouse Lawyer's Manual*, Chapter 33: Rights of Incarcerated Parents, Columbia Hum. Rts. Rev. 896 (9th ed. 2011).

Courts and state administrative agencies, such as child protective services, may deprive a parent of parental responsibility.[30] A state's choice in these tools is a matter of preference, and the federal constitution only requires that the parent's procedural due process rights be honored, which means notice and an opportunity to be heard. States vary in their provision of trial by jury for proceedings involving termination of parental rights.[31] Any of these procedural protections only apply to the permanent termination of parental rights but not to temporary removal of children from the home.

In most states, both the parent and the child have the right to an attorney, paid by the state if they cannot afford one, because of the gravity of the rights at stake in termination proceedings. In about a dozen states, however, children continue to remain unrepresented.[32]

When a child has been abused or neglected, she becomes a ward of the state, which means dependent on the court. It is the task of the court to preserve the child's relationship with her parents if at all possible. This mandate aligns with CRC Article 9, which asks that states keep parents and children together unless such a separation is necessary because the parents, for example, have dissolved their relationship and live separately or because of abuse or neglect of the child. Under US law, if preserving this relationship would lead to the continuance of abuse, neglect, or instability in the child's life, a court may provide a new permanent and stable home for the child.

As the court explores the feasibility of preserving the child-parent relationship, the two parties will initially be separated only temporarily. The state can house children for a short period of time, upon the government's further evaluation of the fitness of the parents or the home for the children, with the assumption that the child will be returned home. If the parent is abusive, she/he can be removed from the home, and through a protective order be ordered to cease contact with the child. Children may also be put in the care of another family member, a situation that can be temporary but also evolve into long-term placement. Should no suitable family member be available, children can be placed in foster care. Within a year in foster care, it should be determined whether children will eventually be put up for adoption. This process has been accelerated to avoid the long-term placement of children in foster care. As domestic adoptions can be fraught with difficulties and many individuals prefer to adopt young children, many children remain in foster care until

[30] *See* Child Abuse, 0080 SURVEYS 18 (2007) ("The agency to whom suspected abuse is reported is often a state child protection office that is not hindered by the same constitutional restrictions to which traditional law enforcement agencies are subject. These agencies are sometimes allowed to take custody of children prior to actually proving that abuse has occurred.").

[31] See 102 A.L.R.5th 227 (2002).

[32] Erin Shea McCann & Casey Trupin, Kenny A. *Does Not Live Here: Efforts in Washington State to Improve Legal Representation of Children in Foster Care*, 36 Nova L. Rev. 363 (2012).

they age out of the system at 18. This happens currently to 11 % of all children in foster care.[33]

Even though the state can completely and irrevocably terminate the rights of a parent to a relationship with their child, it must prove the need for such a deprivation by clear and convincing evidence. This is a very high standard because natural parents have a "fundamental liberty interest . . . in the care, custody, and management of their child [that] does not evaporate simply because they have not been model parents or have lost temporary custody of their child to the State."[34] On the other hand, parents whose parental rights have been terminated do not appear to owe their former (legal) child any duties, though this may differ from state to state.

When a child's interest is at stake, including the termination of parental rights, the CRC, under Article 3, requires that state and private welfare agencies, the legislature, administrative agencies, and the judiciary make the "best interests of the child" standard their primary consideration. The next section will define the standard under US law and apply it in a number of different settings. It will conclude with a critique of the application of the standard to individual situations in which the child is involved directly but a refusal to apply it when a child's welfare is at stake indirectly or when application of the standard would require societal changes.

4 The Best Interests of the Child Standard

Many of the distinctions between those below and those above the age of majority seem to be driven by considerations of the best interests of the child, a standard that originated in the United States.[35] As a matter of both common and statutory law, best interests of the child have been the guiding principle in many US jurisdictions for more than 125 years.[36]

[33] Children's Rights, *Facts About Aging Out*, *available at* http://www.childrensrights.org/issues-resources/foster-care/facts-about-aging-out/.

[34] Santosky v. Kramer, 455 U.S. 745, 753 (1982).

[35] Lynne Marie Kohm, *Tracing the Foundations of the Best Interests of the Child Standard in American Jurisprudence*, 10 J. L. & Family Studies 337 (2008).

[36] See Howard Davidson, *A Model Child Protection Legal Reform Instrument: The Convention on the Rights of the Child and Its Consistency with United States Law*, 5 Geo. J. on Fighting Poverty 185, 191 (1998). Not all child-related legislation necessarily serves a child's best interest. The United States, for example, still permits recruitment of 17-year-olds (with parental consent) into its military. *See Join the Military: Eligibility Rules*, *at* www.military.com/join-armed-forces/eligibility-requirements. Human rights law on this issue continues to evolve. See Jonathan Todres, Mark E. Wojcik & Cris R. Revas, The U.N. Convention on the Rights of the Child: An Analysis of Treaty Implications and of U.S. Ratification 123 (2006) [hereinafter Todres, Wojcik & Revas].

4.1 Best Interests Defined

States may adopt the best interest standard either through legislation or through judicial decision-making. Today, all 50 states have laws that require use of this standard in many areas of law, including child labor, education, adoption, custody, and placement of children.[37] Federal law also uses the concept when addressing child welfare issues under its jurisdiction. Legislative proposals to change the focus of the standard, in some cases to increase parental rights, have generally failed.[38]

All states of the union, the District of Columbia, and several US territories have statutes that direct courts to consider the best interest of the child when making important life decisions.[39] With respect to custody decision, many state statutes specify a number of nonexclusive factors to consider. Common among these factors are (a) the health, safety, and welfare of the child, including the petitioning parents' capacity to provide medical care, clothing, sustenance, and emotional support; (b) the existence of domestic violence in the home, and whether the party seeking custody is the perpetrator; (c) the child's relationship to the parties seeking custody; (d) the mental and physical health of the parents seeking or defending custody; (e) and the present or probable future stability of the child's social environment. The last factor compares the child's greater support system in the current environment, including relationships with friends and family, with the probable state of a future support system after a given custody ruling. The test, therefore, allows for great flexibility and adaptability, which also makes it subject to criticism especially on grounds of unequal application.

Since the best interest standard is prevalent in US law, commentators on the CRC have generally argued that its implementation in the United States "would require little or no adjustment in [its] long-standing history of attempting to keep the 'best interests of the child' at the forefront of judicial and legislative activity."[40] This may, however, not be true for all individual requirements under the CRC, especially as many pose novel issues. This includes the right of children to preserve their identity under CRC Article 8, which includes "nationality, name and family relations …."

[37] For a discussion of the movement toward a different standard in custody cases, see Richard A. Warshak, *Parenting By The Clock: The Best-Interest-of-the-Child Standard, Judicial Discretion, and the American Law Institute's "Approximation Rule,"* 41 Baltimore L. Rev. 83 (2011).

[38] High-profile adoption cases have questioned the rights of parents in contrast to the "best interests" of the child. *See* Annette R. Appell & Bruce A. Boyer, *Parental Rights* vs. *Best Interests of the Child: A False Dichotomy in the Context of Adoption*, 2 Duke J. Gender L. & Pol'y 63 (1995).

[39] See U.S. Department of Health and Human Services, Administration for Children & Families, *Child Welfare Information Gateway, Determining the Best Interests of the Child* 1 (2012), *available at* https://www.childwelfare.gov/systemwide/laws_policies/statutes/best_interest.pdf.

[40] Todres, Wojcik & Revas, *supra* note 36, at 126.

4.2 The Right to Identity

In light of modern reproductive technology, DNA testing, and changing family relations, the definition of "family relations" has come under pressure. Under common law, the mother's husband was assumed to be the child's biological father. Today, a child may file a paternity suit to rebut the paternity of that person and any other person claiming to be a father or bestowed with the title of a parent by a court. In such situations, the court is free to compel a putative parent, or a person whose parental status is challenged, to submit to DNA testing.[41]

Children born out of wedlock are permitted to sue to establish paternity. Whether they are able to establish their relationship with a putative parent through blood and/or genetic tests depends on the nature of the procedure,[42] as blood tests may generally be used only to exclude paternity, but not to confirm paternity status over the objection of a parent.[43]

Legal parenthood and questions of identity may, in some situations, also pose challenges for same-sex couples. The Department of State appears to have recognized just recently the child of a lesbian couple as "born in wedlock" if the child is conceived from the egg of one woman and carried by the other. For a woman, therefore, "mother" becomes defined as being the genetic or the gestational and legal mother of the child, at least under one set of legal rules. How this will impact other legal concepts of parenthood and issues of identity remain open questions.

The right to know one's identity looks different for adopted children. In most US jurisdictions, adopted children do not have a right to find out who their biological parents are as most adoptions are "closed."[44] Some jurisdictions allow an adopted child to learn identifying data about his/her biological parents upon a showing of good cause, and federal courts of appeal have upheld such legislation as constitutional. In many states, an adopted child does not have the right to discover even non-identifying data about their biological parents, including medical information or religion. Only a few states now require the inclusion of non-identifying information (medical and social histories) that can be released on request of the adopted child.[45] There is no indication of a substantial trend away from closed or near-closed adoptions.

The courts of two states, Tennessee and Oregon, notably diverge from the majority approach.[46] In those states, a child may obtain access to identifying data relating to their biological parents if disclosure is in the best interest of the child. Courts in

---

[41] See 41 Am. Jur. 2d *Illegitimate Children* § 31 (Westlaw 2013).

[42] See 14 C.J.S. *Children Out-of-Wedlock* § 97, § 76 (Westlaw 2013).

[43] See 41 Am. Jur. 2d *Illegitimate Children* § 31 (Westlaw 2013).

[44] See U.S. Department of Health and Human Services, Administration for Children & Families, *Child Welfare Information Gateway*, *Access to Adoption Records* (June 2012), *available at* https://www.childwelfare.gov/systemwide/laws_policies/statutes/infoaccessap.pdf.

[45] See 1 Leg. Rts. Child. Rev. 2D § 6:12 (2d ed.) (Westlaw 2012).

[46] Janet Leach Richards, *Medical Confidentiality and Disclosure of Paternity*, 48 S.D. L. Rev. 409, 427–28 (2002–03).

both states have subordinated the parents' constitutional claims to a privacy interest in personally identifying data to the state's interests in the disclosure of parental identity inherent in administering adoptions.[47]

Modern technological advances increase the relevance and the stakes of decisions surrounding the discoverability of one's biological parents. Perhaps not surprisingly, in cases of artificial insemination by donor (AID) disclosure of the donor's medical data as well as non-identifying data is held to a standard similar to the disclosure of the identity of the natural parent of an adopted child.[48] In most states, children conceived through AID are unable to gain access to information relating to their natural biological donor, though at least 18 states have passed laws that allow such children to gain access upon a showing of cause. The California Court of Appeals, for example, held that the constitutional interest in maintaining anonymity was limited and outweighed by the state's interest in preserving children's right to discover their identity.[49] Only a small number of state courts have held that biological donors have a lower constitutional privacy interest in non-identifying than in identifying data, causing the states' interest in disclosure to override the lowered privacy interest.

While modern family relations with their frequent distinctions between biological, social, and legal parent(s) may constitute the most challenging frontier of the law, wide variety exists between countries with respect to rules on children's names and name changes.[50]

4.3 Changing One's Name

When a child requests change of his first or determination or change of his last name, courts apply the best interest standard.[51] When changes of the last name are considered, courts turn to the factors employed in custody cases: the effect of the change on the preservation and development of the child's relationship with each parent; the identification of the child as part of the family unit; the length of time that the child has used the surname; the preference of the child if the child is of sufficient maturity to express a preference; whether the child's surname is different from the surname of the child's residential parent; the embarrassment, discomfort, or

[47] See Does 1, 2, 3, 4, 5, 6, & 7 v. State, 164 Or. App. 543, 565 (1999) ("Because a birth mother has no fundamental right to have her child adopted, she also can have no correlative fundamental right to have her child adopted under circumstances that guarantee that her identity will not be revealed to the child."); Doe v. Sundquist, 2 S.W.3d 919, 926 (Tenn. 1999) (denying birth mothers' claims that Tennessee statute allowing children put up for adoption to obtain identifying data about their birth parents after attaining the age of 21 violated mothers' constitutional rights).

[48] See Lucy R. Dollens, *Artificial Insemination: Right of Privacy and the Difficulty in Maintaining Donor Anonymity*, 35 Ind. L. Rev. 213, 217 (2001).

[49] See Johnson v. Superior Ct., 95 Cal. Rptr. 2d 864, 864 (Ct. App. 2000).

[50] See, e.g., *Thanks, mum: Governments find reason to regulate the names of children*, The Economist, January 14, 2012.

[51] See 65 C.J.S. *Names* § 24 (Westlaw 2013).

inconvenience that may result when a child bears a surname different from the residential parent; the important ties to family heritage, ethnic identity, and cultural values; and the parental misconduct or failure to maintain contact with and support of the child.[52]

At the birth of a child, parents generally choose a child's first name without state interference. Should a child petition for change of name, the court considers the following issues in light of the best interests of the child: the child's preference; the effect of the change of the child's name on the preservation and development of the child's relationship with each parent; the length of time the child has borne a given name; the degree of community respect associated with the present and proposed names; the difficulties, harassment, or embarrassment that the child may experience from bearing the present or proposed name; and the existence of any parental misconduct or neglect.[53]

Even though parents are left largely free in their choice of a given name for their child, a child's name change will be subject to a searching test, presumably to ascertain the child's rationale and seriousness of purpose and to avoid negative repercussions from a name change. The court's goal is clearly to protect the child's interest in these rare cases.

4.4 Critique

Historically, the best interest test may have hidden gender bias and continues to be applied disparately to different socioeconomic, racial, ethnic, and religious groups. In addition, use of the test in some areas of the law conceals the poor treatment to which other areas of the law, such as the criminal justice system, subject children. Only recently has the US Supreme Court acknowledged that children's intellectual and emotional development differs dramatically from that of adults, leading to restrictions on the most arduous and punitive sanctions imposed, including the death penalty and life-without-parole.

When children are the object of the decision-making, as in the cases outlined above or in custody situations, the best interest standard will be applied, even though perhaps not always equally. It has not been expanded, however, to the situations in which the state's decision will have a dramatic impact on the child even though the law does not exert its force upon the child directly. Two such situations involve the criminal sentencing of a parent (in criminal prosecutions unrelated to the child) and the decision to deport the noncitizen parent. In both of these cases, the existence of a child or the importance of the relationship between the parent and the child are rarely considered, barring extraordinary situations, despite an increasing array of literature indicating the negative consequences of parental, and especially maternal, incarceration or deportation.

Over the last two decades, the number of prisoners who have at least one minor child has increased substantially, so that in 2010 2.3 % of all minor children living

---

[52] See *id.*

[53] See *id.*

in the United States had at least one incarcerated parent. Almost half of all prisoners have a minor child. Black children were 7.5 times and Hispanic children 2.5 times more likely to have a parent in prison than white children.[54] A recent study has found a substantial impact of parental imprisonment on a child's educational attainment, later unemployment, and involvement with the criminal justice system, especially following maternal incarceration. Perhaps most surprisingly, the same study found that the impact of maternal incarceration extends beyond the child to the entire community by depressing college graduation rates of young people educated in schools where between 10 % and 20 % of other children had an incarcerated parent.[55] The US criminal justice system, as the legal system as a whole, is individually oriented and therefore only rarely allows for consideration of third-party interests at sentencing. The US Sentencing Guidelines, for example, indicate that "family ties and responsibilities are not ordinarily relevant in determining whether a departure [from the otherwise applicable guidelines sentence, which is primarily based on the offense of conviction and the offender's criminal history] may be warranted."[56]

A similar situation involves the deportation of noncitizen parents. As the United States subscribes to the *ius soli* (and *ius sanguinis*) principle of citizenship, even the children of undocumented migrants born in the United States automatically obtain citizenship. With the parents remaining without a legal status, however, if a removal order issues, they (and their children) face the choice between returning to the parents' country of citizenship or separating the family, often with serious long-term emotional and financial consequences. Parental arrest and detention, in addition to ultimate removal and long-term bans on return, inflict serious psychological harm on children.[57] Only recently has the US Immigration and Customs Enforcement issued a policy outlining enforcement priorities and prosecutorial discretion, with the goal of "not unnecessarily disrupt[ing] the parental rights of both alien parents or legal guardians of minor children."[58] How successfully that policy has been implemented and whether it has served children well may be too early to assess.

---

[54] Bureau of Justice Statistics, Lauren E. Glaze & Laura M. Maruschak, *Parents in Prison and Their Minor Children* (Aug. 8, 2008; rev. Mar. 30, 2010), NCJ 222984.

[55] John Hagan & Holly Foster, *Children of the American Prison Generation: Student and School Spillover Effect of Incarcerating Mothers*, 46 Law & Soc'y Rev. 37 (2012).

[56] U.S. Sentencing Commission Guidelines Manual, §5H1.6. *Family Ties and Responsibilities (Policy Statement)* (2013).

[57] See, e.g., Dorsey & Whitney LLP, Report to the Urban Institute, *Severing a Lifeline: The Neglect of Citizen Children in America's Immigration Enforcement Policy* (2009).

[58] U.S. Immigration and Customs Enforcement, *11064.1: Facilitating Parental Interest in the Course of Civil Immigration Enforcement Activities* (Aug. 23, 2013). For a critique of the memorandum as failing to allow for individual consideration, see Mills Legal Clinic at Stanford Law School & Center for Justice and International Law, *Supplemental Report on Prosecutorial Discretion and Family Unity Addressing U.S. Government Policies Issued After Submission of Petitioners' Report in support of the Public Thematic Hearing on Human Rights of Migrants and Legislative Reform in the United States before the Inter-American Commission on Human Rights (149th Period of Sessions) pursuant to Article 66 of the Rules of Procedure of the Inter-American Commission on Human Rights, available at* www.law.stanford.edu/sites/default/files/project/443312/doc/slspublic/13-10-22%20FINAL%20Supplemental%20Report.pdf.

Failure to consider children's interests and well-being when a state decision will impact them dramatically has negative effects societally and systemically. Even though the best interest standard permeates many areas of judicial and agency decision-making, it remains inapplicable when the child's fate is not directly at issue despite it being indirectly affected.

Application of the best interest standard or direct imposition of state measures on children implies their right to provide input, though not necessarily the right to make a decision.

5 Abortion, Custody, Adoption: Children's Rights to Express Their Views

CRC Articles 12 and 13 guarantee that a child has meaningful opportunities to express her views freely in all matters affecting her, though this does not necessarily imply decision-making authority. The First Amendment's protection of freedom of speech extends to children though children seem to possess lesser rights to expression than adults under the same circumstances, especially if the state can show a compelling state interest in restricting a child's right to express an opinion.[59]

In criminal proceedings, juveniles accused of crimes are guaranteed due process during both the pretrial and trial stages under the 5th, 6th, and 14th amendments, which includes the right to be heard.[60] As victims of criminal offenses, children also have a right to participate in the criminal justice process, though the process may have to be accommodated, especially for younger children.

The weight of the child's opinion in family matters and health issues, the most frequent situations in which such right will be exercised, increases with the age and maturity of the child.[61] Three areas—abortion, custody, and adoption—may be of particular importance to children and especially older children.

5.1 Abortion

With respect to one highly charged issue, abortion, it has been hotly debated where the power to make a final decision resides and how to weigh a child's opinion. States may not impose a blanket provision requiring the consent of a parent or person standing in the position of a parent to the abortion of an unmarried minor.

---

[59] Congressional Research Service, Henry Cohen, *Freedom of Speech and Press: Restrictions to the First Amendment* (2009); 1 Children & the Law: Rights and Obligations § 1:7 (Westlaw 2012).

[60] See Kent v. United States, 383 U.S. 541, 554 (1966); *see also* In re Gault, 387 U.S. 1, 12–18 (1967).

[61] See Virginia Mixon Swindell, *Children's Participation in Custodial and Parental Right Determinations*, 31 Hous. L. Rev. 659, 674–76 (1994).

The Supreme Court invalidated a state statute that required minors to secure written parental consent before having an abortion.[62] Instead, the Court suggested alternative procedures if the state wishes to still restrict minors' abortions.

Pregnant minors are entitled to show that they are sufficiently mature and well informed to make the abortion decision themselves upon consultation of a doctor but without any parental consent. Should the minor be insufficiently mature to make such a decision, the court can determine independently that an abortion is (not) in the best interests of the child. The so-called judicial bypass has been established to protect minors and shield them from having to share their plans with their parents.

The decisions on a minor's right to consent to an abortion have influenced judicial guidance on other medical procedures. The Supreme Court suggested, for example, that a state requiring a minor's written consent for other procedures besides abortion may be equally constitutional, as long as the surgery is sufficiently serious.[63] How the courts will react, for example, to the desire of a minor to have a sex change surgery that lacks parental support remains an open question.

The state or a third party may have less power to override a child's refusal to undergo surgery than it has regarding a child's wish to have surgery.[64] The weight given to a child's refusal is a function of the court's determination of the child's maturity and competence to make reasoned decisions. These two factors also play a determinative role in a court's assessment of a minor's views in custody situations.

5.2 *Custody*

The most common situation in which children are heard is custody cases. Many states allow a child to express a preference in custody hearings, and in most states, the District of Columbia, and Puerto Rico, the child's preferences are considered in custody rulings. In the great majority of American states, children do not need to attain a specific numerical age before being allowed to participate in custody proceedings affecting them or before the child's stated preferences be given weight in

---

[62] See Planned Parenthood of Cent. Missouri v. Danforth, 428 U.S. 52, 72 (1976); Swindell, *supra* note 61, at 672–73.

[63] See *Planned Parenthood*, 428 U.S. at 67 ("As a consequence, we see no constitutional defect in requiring it only for some types of surgery as, for example, an intracardiac procedure, or where the surgical risk is elevated above a specified mortality level, or, for that matter, for abortions.").

[64] Ross Povenmire, *Do Parents Have the Legal Authority to Consent to the Surgical Amputation of Normal, Healthy Tissue from Their Infant Children?: The Practice of Circumcision in the United States*, 7 Am. U. J. Gender Soc. Pol'y & L. 87, 102 (1999). The United States, under federal law, prohibits female genital mutilation, sometime referred to also as female circumcision, unless health considerations counsel in favor of it. 18 U.S.C. §116 (2012). Male circumcision is permitted and remains widespread in the United States, though the national rate of newborn circumcision has been dropping over the last few years. The latter, of course, precludes participation of the child in the decision-making.

the court's best interest analysis.[65] Instead, most courts look to the "maturity" of a child—specifically whether the child has, to the court, sufficiently developed emotional and intellectual capacity necessary to make an informed decision regarding her preferences. The weight courts assign to the preferences of a child scales with the level of maturity the judge observes.[66] Some states, however, take a hybrid approach, specifying age minimums for some purposes in child custody hearings but directing the judge to determine maturity holistically for other purposes in the same hearing.

In California, for example, children age 14 and older are permitted to address the court regarding custody and visitation, unless, pursuant to a finding on the record, the judge determines that "doing so is not in the child's best interests."[67] Children under the age of 14 may participate in custody hearings affecting them, but do not, like children over 14 years, benefit from a presumption in favor of their participation.

Notably, state courts give varying degrees of weight to the preferences of a mature child in best interest custody determinations. The first states that gave *controlling and mandatory* weight to child preference in custody determinations were four southern states: Georgia, Mississippi, Tennessee, and Texas.[68] There is some speculation that the American South's traditional allocation of more responsibility to children motivated this approach. In more recent years, however, most states have moved away from a mandatory scheme to a best interest approach that preserves judicial discretion.

Some of the states require children be "informed" before they are allowed to state a preference or before the judge can determine the weight of this preference. In child custody proceedings, a guardian ad litem or special attorney has the power to move discovery and get information from either of the two parents to enable the child to make an informed decision about which of the parents she/he prefers to have primary custody.[69]

---

[65] See Child Custody Prac. & Proc. § 4:11 (Westlaw through Mar. 2012).

[66] See Barbara A. Atwood, *The Child's Voice in Custody Litigation: An Empirical Survey and Suggestions for Reform*, 45 Ariz. L. Rev. 629, 634 (2003) (noting that 80 % of Arizona judges surveyed considered the preferences of older teenagers to be "very significant" in their decision-making, while only 40 % of judges interviewed would give similar weight to the preferences of children aged 11–13 years, and 70 % of judges interviewed agreed that the preferences of very young children are given "no significance at all" in their best interest custody determinations).

[67] Cal. Fam. Code § 3042(c), (d) (West, Westlaw through 2013).

[68] See Kathleen Nemechek, *Child Preference in Custody Decisions: Where We Have Been, Where We Are Now, Where We Should Go*, 83 Iowa L. Rev. 437, 445 (1998).

[69] Child Custody Prac. & Proc. § 12:13 at n. 5 (Westlaw 2012) (providing a diverse list of jurisdictions that require the appointment of an attorney who is granted the same powers of discovery as the other parties). *See* Andrea Khoury, *The True Voice of the Child: The Model Act Governing the Representation of Children in Abuse, Neglect, and Dependency Proceedings*, 36 Nova L. Rev. 313, 317 (Spring 2012) ("There is also the same lack of uniformity within the states, regardless of statutory guidance. In one county there may be a 'lawyers for children' program, and lawyers are regularly appointed, and in another county in the same state, there is no such similar program, and courts will appoint nonlawyers or Court Appointed Special Advocates (CASAs).").

Child custody decisions may come at any point in a child's life, and the same holds true for adoptions, though the participation and decision-making role of children in the adoption process is more substantial.

5.3 Adoption

Adoptions generally require greater child involvement in the decision-making than custodial arrangements.

> In many states, if the child being adopted is over a certain age, he or she must consent to the adoption. The age of children who must give their consent to adoption generally ranges from 10 to 14. Absence of such consent is apparently an absolute bar to adoption. The preferences of younger children may also be considered by the court, but are not binding.[70]

While many adoptions occur within the United States, the United States is also involved in intercountry adoptions, as a net "importer" of children.[71] Congress ratified the 1993 Hague Convention on Protection of Children and Co-operation in Respect of Intercountry Adoption and made national legislation applicable to all adoptions "involving US residents"—apparently as parents or children.[72] This legislation (and the Convention) requires that all groups that offer cross-border adoption services in connection with a US person must satisfy certain accreditation requirements and be approved by US accreditation entities.

Accreditation standards mandate that the agency provide the putative parents a copy of the medical records of the child in English. To protect the child, the agency must conduct a thorough background report, including a home study, of the prospective parents. The adoption service must bill on a fee-for-service basis, not a contingency fee basis. In addition, the adoption service must disclose fully its policies and practices, the disruption rates of its placements for intercountry adoption, and all fees charged for such adoptions. These rules have been developed to protect potential parents from exploitation and children from illicit transfer and trafficking. This is particularly important as children in intercountry adoptions tend to be younger and are often unable to participate in the adoption process. Despite the heightened protections for both sides implicit in these requirements, intercountry adoptions have created diplomatic tensions between the United States and some sender countries.[73]

---

[70] 1 Leg. Rts. Child. Rev. 2D § 6:5 (2d ed.) (Westlaw 2012).

[71] U.S. Department of State, Bureau of Consular Affairs, Office of Children's Issues, *FY2012 Annual Report on Intercountry Adoptions* (Jan. 2013), *available at* adoption.state.gov/content/pdf/fy2012_annual_report.pdf. Despite a high total number of foreign adoptees, per capita the United States ranks only in the middle of highly developed Western democracies with respect to the total number of children adopted from abroad. *See* Australian InterCountry Adoption Network, *International Adoption Statistics*, *available at*www.aican.org/statistics.php.

[72] See 42 U.S.C. § 14901–54 (2000); 2 Am. Jur. 2d Adoption § 46 (Westlaw 2013).

[73] See Council of Europe Parliamentary Assembly, Written declaration 536: *Intercountry adoption: Children as hostages of international relations*, Doc. 13113 rev. (January 29, 2013).

Above section has focused on the relationship between children, their parents, and the state, largely in its judicial or legislative role. Many other legal areas involving children's rights heavily implicate (public) schools.

6 School and Work

Depending on state laws, schooling from an age range between 5 and 8 up to 16 and 18 is compulsory in the United States. That requirement can be fulfilled through school attendance or homeschooling. Approximately 3 % of American children are being homeschooled. Ten percent attend private rather than public schools.

Children may take on paid work outside the home while still in school, as envisioned in CRC Article 32 para. 2 point a. Federal and state laws regulate child labor. Regulations include restrictions on the number of hours children can work, what times of day a child may work, what general occupations are fit for children, what specific tasks children can perform, and under what conditions they may perform those jobs.

Federal law mandates the minimum age for employment, without parental consent, at 16 years, except for agricultural work.[74] The federal minimum age for non-agricultural employment is 14 years, which means that even with parental consent, a child under 14 years may not work.[75] Under federal law, the hours a child can work during the week also depend on the age of the minor—14-year-olds are permitted to work significantly fewer hours than 16-year-olds. Under US Department of Labor regulations, workers between the ages of 16 and 18 years are prevented from engaging in employment the department finds to be particularly hazardous or detrimental to their health or well-being.

Agricultural employment does not require a minimum age. While child labor laws do not apply to a child working on her parent's farm, they apply generally to a child working on a farm owned by someone other than her parents. With parental consent, children as young as 12 may work on such a farm, in some states for up to 12 h and without being paid minimum wage. Children's farm work—and work in the entertainment industry—remains poorly regulated. For many American children in rural areas, therefore, agricultural work may be a regular part of their lives, leaving less time for school-related work. Rural schools and educational attainment during primary and secondary school do not seem to be measurably below those in more urban or suburban settings; college attendance rate, however, is lower.

Schools themselves have frequently been the flash point of children's rights, especially the right to expression and the concomitant right to information, to allow for the formation of an opinion, which can then be expressed. Both aspects are encapsulated in CRC Article 13 subject to limited exceptions outlined there.

---

[74] See 29 U.S.C. § 203(e)(4)(l) (2006).

[75] See 29 C.F.R. § 570.2 (West, Westlaw through May 2013).

7 Access to Information: Tensions Between Parents, Schools, and Children

The Convention explicitly guarantees the right to information, while the First Amendment only implicitly protects the right of access to information as such access is a necessary condition for the meaningful exercise of the right to free expression. Even in the case of adults, the right to information remains insufficiently developed.[76]

In a case indirectly involving children, the Supreme Court struck down a federal law that had prevented the mailing of unsolicited advertisements relating to the availability of contraceptives, in part because the law denied parents information necessary to make informed decisions about birth control and discuss it with their children.[77] The law remains unsettled when the child's desire for information conflicts with her parents' wishes, however. In this case, the courts must (or should) determine the extent and nature of the child's autonomous liberty interest—as distinct from her freedom of speech—as it is closely connected to the right to information.

A child's autonomy interests inevitably conflict with constitutional principles protecting the parents' rights to control and raise their children free from (most) governmental interference.[78] Parents have a recognized liberty interest in raising their children by the methods they desire and are given great latitude in making choices for their children—including, a parent's decision to remove her child from otherwise mandatory lower education for religious and social reasons—seemingly without consideration of the child's wishes.[79] Minor children do not have any constitutional rights in the home that can be enforced against their parents, including the right to speech or information unless their parents give them such rights.[80]

Outside the home, parents and governments may influence children's access to information. Both government regulations and parental preferences will be less certainly enforced outside the home against a child who is considered "mature," since the child's First Amendment rights and constitutional interest in autonomy increase with age and maturity. Courts do not employ numerical age to decide dispositively a child's (lack of) maturity. A "mature" child's right to information is said to be strongest when access to that information is necessary for meaningful exercise of another fundamental right, such as that of protecting a would-be mother's decision to obtain an abortion—even if the would-be mother is legally a minor. Healthcare

[76] See Stanley v. Georgia, 394 U.S. 557, 564 (1969) ("It is now well established that the Constitution protects the right to receive information and ideas. 'This freedom (of speech and press) . . . necessarily protects the right to receive . . . .'"); Catherine J. Ross, *An Emerging Right for Mature Minors to Receive Information*, 2 U. Pa. J. Const. L. 223, 227, 230–31 (1999).

[77] See Bolger v. Young Drugs Prods. Corp., 463 U.S. 60, 74 (1983).

[78] See Prince v. Massachusetts, 321 U.S. 158, 166 (1944).

[79] See Wisconsin v. Yoder, 406 U.S. 205, 224–35 (1972).

[80] Both 42 U.S.C. § 1983 and U.S. Const. Amend. XIV only prevent deprivation of civil liberties by state actors.

providers, therefore, may provide information necessary for informed consent to a medical procedure, including abortion and contraception, to minors.[81]

Most states allow parents to have significant control over the public school education of their children.[82] However, they cannot prevent public schools from teaching topics that they find morally offensive.[83] Many of these disputes have centered on sexual education as well as the teaching of evolution in public schools. In those situations, the state must allow for parents to seek alternatives to public schooling and cannot limit what parents teach their children.[84] On the other hand, school boards—with or without the consent of parents—have the authority, for example, to ban certain books from the curriculum and from school libraries, as long as they do not do so because they merely disagree with the content but rather because of the educational suitability of the content.[85]

In public school settings, the right to freedom of expression, including the reception of information, has frequently collided with the right to religious freedom.[86]

8 Religion in School: The "Culture Wars"

Among the core CRC articles is 14, which guarantees children the right to freedom of thought, conscience, and religion. Under the US Constitution, freedom of religion is guaranteed though the United States perceives itself as having a religious (largely Judeo-Christian) citizenry. For that reason, the US Supreme Court has developed extensive jurisprudence on how to assure the separation of church and state without unduly burdening the exercise of religious practice.

Education about religion, though not religious instruction, is available in public schools, as both an obligatory and an optional subject. Instruction about world religions, for example, is perfectly acceptable though attempts to teach religion in public schools would likely lead to Establishment Clause[87] challenges because public schools are state actors. Those challenges can be overcome if the teaching activity satisfies a three-part test.[88] First, the law under scrutiny must "reflect a clearly secu-

[81] Belloti v. Baird, 443 U.S. 622 (1979).

[82] See Ross, *supra* note 76, at 247 n. 120 (providing a list of state statutes that allow parents to opt out or provide substitute education that they choose on controversial topics, and statutes that require the school to give notice to the parents of students if the school curriculum contains education on controversial topics).

[83] See Brown v. Hot, Sexy, and Safer Prods., Inc., 68 F.3d 525, 533–34 (1995).

[84] See Ross, *supra* note 76, at 247.

[85] Bd. of Educ., Island Trees Union Free Sch. Dist. No. 26 v. Pico, 457 U.S. 853 (1982).

[86] Approximately 10 % of children in the United States in prekindergarten through 12th grade are enrolled in private schools, with about 80 % of all private schools being religiously affiliated. Council for American Private Education, *Facts and Figures*, at www.capenet.org/facts.html.

[87] U.S. Const. Amend. I ("Congress shall make no law respecting an establishment of religion ….").

[88] See Comm. for Pub. Educ. & Religious Liberty v. Nyquist, 413 U.S. 756, 772 (1973).

lar legislative purpose," which has been interpreted to mean that the law's explicit *purpose* cannot be designed to advance or inhibit religion.[89] Second, the law must "have a primary *effect* that neither advances nor inhibits religion" (emphasis added). Third, the law must be religiously neutral to "avoid excessive entanglement with religion."[90] Public schools can therefore mandate that students study subject matters relating to religion, so long as the school curriculum, including religious studies, reflects a secular legislative purpose—such as to teach social studies or literature—and so long as the primary effect of the curriculum is not to inhibit or advance certain religious ideals.[91] Beyond these restrictions, states are given substantial leeway—substantively and procedurally—in creating public school curricula.[92]

On numerous occasions, religiously motivated school boards have attempted to weave religious ideals into mandatory school courses, for example, by requiring the study of "intelligent design" or "creation science" along with evolution theory, restricting the teaching of evolution theory, or requiring abstinence-only sexual education. Courts are accustomed to applying the judicially created Establishment Clause test in such situations. The Supreme Court struck down a Louisiana law requiring that god-creation viewpoints be presented whenever evolution science was discussed in the classroom because the law served no secular purpose.[93]

The courts also held policies in Dover, Pennsylvania, unconstitutional when a largely religiously conservative school had adopted a classroom disclaimer that specifically referenced "intelligent design" (a relabeling of "creation science") as an alternative theory to evolution science and later voted to change the ninth-grade biology curriculum to "make ninth grade biology students 'aware of gaps/problems in Darwin's theory and of other theories of evolution, including, but not limited to, intelligent design.'"[94] Such efforts by local school boards continue in religiously conservative communities throughout the United States.

Ironically, religious activists have occasionally seized onto the requirement to avoid "religious entanglement" to justify their introduction of religious views into school curricula. Some have argued that evolution science promotes atheism or the absence of god, which is "a religion," and therefore sole presentation of this science

[89] See Wallace v. Jaffree, 472 U.S. 38, 56 (1985).

[90] See, e.g., Walz v. Tax Comm'n of City of New York, 397 U.S. 664 (involving property tax exemptions to religious institutions).

[91] See Hall v. Bd. of Sch. Comm'rs of Conecuh Cnty., 656 F.2d 999, 1001–03 (5th Cir. 1981).

[92] See Sch. Dist. of Abington Twp. v. Schempp, 374 U.S. 203, 300 (1963) ("To what extent, and at what points in the curriculum, religious materials should be cited are matters which the courts ought to entrust very largely to the experienced officials who superintend our Nation's public schools.").

[93] See Edwards v. Aguillard, 482 U.S. 578, 581 (1987). *See generally* Edward J. Larson, *Teaching Creation, Evolution, and the New Atheism in 21st Century America: Window on an Evolving Establishment Clause*, 82 Miss. L.J. 997, 1020 (2013).

[94] Kitzmiller v. Dover Area Sch. Dist., 400 F. Supp.2d 707 (M.D. Penn. 2005).

"theory" itself violates the Establishment Clause.[95] Courts, however, have rarely permitted the presentation of religious views to balance "antireligion."

With the Supreme Court having closed most other doors to the promotion of religious beliefs regarding the origins of humankind, religious activists have instead attempted to find a secular purpose for "Darwin disclaimers," which are notices provided to students that evolution science is "only a theory" to be considered among other explanations for the origins of humankind, including creation science, intelligent design, or other explanations involving a divine source. Religious activists in state legislatures have also sponsored laws that instruct local school districts to "promote critical thinking skills" by listing scientific theories that are deemed by statute to be "rightly subject to critical analysis," including "evolution, the origin of life, global warming, and human cloning."[96] These disputes, as curious as they may appear to non-Americans, are an integral part of the American legal system where the tension between religious freedom and the avoidance of state-sponsored religions inherent in the First Amendment often plays out in the school setting.

9 Conclusion

The CRC covers broad territory. Whether US law always conforms to its requirements remains questionable, especially in light of the diversity of approaches within the United States. The most difficult questions under both the CRC and the US Constitution and its laws pertain undeniably to the clash of rights between parents, the state, and children, many of which occur in the public school setting.

The United States would benefit from participating in a global dialogue on these challenging issues. This is particularly true as modern technology may expand the concept and undermine the traditional notion of parent. US scholars and practitioners may also gain perspective and insight from the different understanding or application of legal concepts, such as the best interest standard.

[95] See Blog: Religion & American Law, *Evolution and Atheism: Is There a Connection?* (Oct, 6, 2013), *available at* http://religionandamericanlaw.blogspot.com/2013/10/evolution-and-atheism-is-there.html.

[96] See Larson, *supra* note 93, at 1008–32.

The Rights of Children: An Uzbek Perspective

Iroda Djuraeva

1 Introduction

Since its independence in 1991, Uzbekistan has ratified six major United Nations human rights instruments and more than 70 international conventions and treaties on human rights.[1]

9 December 1992 served as the date of ratification of the UN Convention on the Rights of the Child (hereafter Convention) in Uzbekistan that led to undertaking the national legislation review from the point of its conformity with the Convention.

The Constitution of Uzbekistan[2] provides state protection of families, particularly for mothers and children.[3] The primary statutes in the field of children's rights are Family Code[4] of the Republic of Uzbekistan (hereafter FC RUz) and the Law on Guarantees of the Rights of the Child. For the first time, the law sets the international legal definition of a child as a person below 18 years and also enshrines the following notions: orphaned children, socially vulnerable children, disabled children, etc. (Article 3).[5] FC RUz devotes a special section to the rights

[1] Available at http://www.parliament.gov.uz/en/events/international/2814 (accessed December 25, 2014).

[2] *The Constitution of the Republic of Uzbekistan* adopted on 8 December 1992 at the 11th session of the Supreme Council of the 12th convocation. As amended by the Law of the RUz dated 16 April 2014, No. 366.

[3] *Ibid.*, art 45, 64–66.

[4] *Semejnyj Kodeks Respubliki Uzbekistan* [Family Code of the Republic of Uzbekistan] adopted on 30 April 1998, No. 607-I. As amended by the Law of RUz dated 20 January 2014, No. 365.

[5] *Zakon o garantijach prav rebenka* [Law on Guarantees of the Rights of the Child] dated 7 January 2008, No. 139. As amended by the Law dated 24 December 2009, No. 239.

I. Djuraeva (✉)
Attorney at Law firm "Mukhiddinova I Partnyory", Bodomzor way str., 1A,
Tashkent city, Uzbekistan
e-mail: iroda.d@gmail.com

O. Cvejić Jančić (ed.), *The Rights of the Child in a Changing World*,
Ius Comparatum - Global Studies in Comparative Law 13,
DOI 10.1007/978-3-319-23189-1_21

of minors under which the children are considered as persons with both personal and property rights.[6]

There are also other legal acts that in one way or another cover matters related to children's participative and protective rights such as Civil Code, Labor Code, Criminal Code, Criminal Procedural Code, Civil Procedural Code, the Law on Protection of Citizen's Health, the Law on Education, the Law on Freedom of Conscience and Religious Assemblies, Resolution of Cabinet of Ministers "On approval of the required legislative acts on the implementation of the Family Code of the Republic of Uzbekistan," and Resolutions of Supreme Court Plenum of the Republic of Uzbekistan.

At first sight these adopted legal acts sufficiently extended the rights of the child; however, let us review the implementation of these provisions in practice.[7]

2 The Best Interests Principle

The best interests of the child[8] principle first appeared at the international level in provisions 2 and 7 of the Declaration on the Rights of the Child, 1959.[9] For many years this principle has been implemented in various forms[10] in different countries and over a range of international legal instruments particularly in relation to children's custody disputes. In Uzbekistan this principle has been also integrated into domestic legislation and practice. However, Family Code does not provide a clear

[6] *Family Code*, s 11, 13.

[7] The experience of lawyers in practice has been applied in this report. Respondents' group includes judges, prosecutors, legal practitioners, and guardianship body and has been interviewed on specific issues of the application of family legislation in practice.

[8] Convention Article 3's use of the phrase "best interests of the child" borrows its language directly from US law. The best interests of the child have been a guiding principle in US law for more than 125 years. Prior to the existence of the states of North and South Dakota, the Code for their predecessor territory invoked the best interests of the child in 1877 as a factor for a court to consider when deciding whether and to whom to award custody or guardianship of a child. See further Codes of Territory of Dakota §127 (1877) cited in LeAnn Larson LeFave, "Origins and Evolution of the 'Best Interests of the Child'" Standard 34 S.D. L. Rev. 159. 470 (1989).

[9] *Declaration of the Rights of the Child,* available at http://www.unicef.org/lac/spbarbados/Legal/global/General/declaration_child1959.pdf (accessed September 23, 2014).

[10] Principle 2 of the 1959 Declaration provides the stronger legal threshold that the best interests of the child shall be the paramount consideration in contrast to the primary consideration in the CRC. (See Trevor Buck, *International Child Law*. 2nd ed. (London: Routledge, 2011), p. 127.) There is difference between "primary" and "paramount." The word "paramount" emphasizes that the child's best interests are determinative. If a child's interests are paramount, it is difficult to see any other consideration being seriously taken into account. "Primary," by contrast, means first. That a child's best interests should be "first consideration" is an exhortation to consider specifically the best interests of the child and to give the child's best interests greater weight than other considerations. Michael Freeman, *Article 3. The Best Interests of the Child* in: A. Allen, J. Vande Lanotte, E. Verhellen ... A Commentary on the United Nations Convention on the Rights of the Child. (Boston: Martinus Nijhoff Publishers, 2007), p. 60.

formulation of a general requirement, namely, that the best interests of the child shall be primary consideration as Article 3 of the Convention stipulates. At the same time, there are many references in Uzbek family legislation to the interests of the child. For example, Article 75 FC RUz states that parental rights cannot be exercised in contradiction with children's interests; in accordance with part 2 of Article 70 FC RUz, if the parents reside apart and the parent with whom the child lives is wishing to give the child his or her own surname, the guardianship and trusteeship body shall resolve this issue depending on the interests of the child and taking into account the other parent's opinion; and adoption is allowed only in the interests of the child (Article 151 FC RUz). Yet Uzbek court practice has not developed a unified approach for a definition of the child's interests; however, the paragraph 3 of the Resolution of the Supreme Court Plenum[11] emphasizes that courts must take a decision that would correspond to the interests and wishes of minors. The child's interests are defined by Uzbek court practitioners upon two criteria: subjective (the opinion of the child, of parents) and objective (upbringing, standard of living). For instance, in determining with which of the parents the child is to live after dissolution of the marriage, the court considers the following: the child's affection to each of the parents and to brothers and sisters, parental care and attention for the children, the age of the child and the moral and personal characteristics of the parents, the parents' relationship to each other and the parent-child relationships, and the ability to create an environment for the child's upbringing and development (the parent's occupation, working hours, financial stability, and marital status); however the benefit of parent's financial stability is not considered as a decisive factor for child's custody to this or that parent. The court may take into account the wish of the child who has reached the age of 10, to live with one of the parents.[12]

3 The Right of the Child to Know About His or Her Origin

3.1 The Right to Know About the Father v. the Interests of the Child's Mother

Both Article 65 of FC RUz and Article 13 of Law on Guarantees of the Rights of the Child provide a child with the right to know about his or her parents. However, realization of this right may cause certain issues. For instance, whether a child born out of wedlock or conceived with artificial insemination has the right to claim any information about his or her father from the mother. Uzbek family legislation does not stipulate any provision that would oblige the mother to provide such

[11] *Postanovlenie Plenuma Verchovnogo Suda Respubliki Uzbekistan "O praktike primenenija sudami zakonodatel'stva pri razrešenii sporov, svjazannich s vospitaniem detej"* [Resolution of the Supreme Court Plenum of the Republic of Uzbekistan "The practice of application of the legislation by the courts when considering disputes on the children's upbringing"] dated 11 September 1998, No. 23. As amended by Resolution of Supreme Court Plenum dated 11 December 2013, No. 21.

[12] *Ibid.*

information. On the one hand, the record about the father may be a secret of mother's personal life and its disclosure may lead to violation of her right to privacy that is enshrined in the Constitution of Uzbekistan (Article 27). On the other hand, information about the father will create an opportunity to establish paternity and consequently will affect the child's maintenance and inheritance rights.[13] But such conflict of interests is not encountered in practice[14] as most often the mother is the initiator of the establishment of fatherhood.

Upon reaching the age of 18, the child is also enabled to claim establishment of paternity, with exception of the following cases: when the information about the father in the child's birth certificate is made on the basis of the marriage certificate or upon a joint application of the child's father and the mother on establishing paternity.[15] The record about the father in the child's birth certificate proves the child's descent from this person (paragraph 5).[16] Hence, in these cases, the child is not able to get the recognition of paternity of his or her biological father, until the information about the father in the child's birth certificate is judicially annulled. But according to Article 63 of the FC RUz, only a person who has been recorded as the father or mother of the child is entitled to dispute in court the record within 1 year from the time when he or she knew or should have known of the record. Thus, the child has no right to dispute paternity in such a case, and as a consequence, there is no possibility to establish paternity by judicial decision.

It should be also noted that in the event of the death of a person who claimed himself a father of the child but was not married to the child's mother, the court is entitled to verify his fatherhood. In the event of the death of a person who was not married to the child's mother, the court is entitled to verify this fatherhood, i.e., the fact that the child was descendent of this person.[17]

---

[13] Under Article 64 of FC RUz in case where paternity is established in registry office or in the court, the child born out of wedlock has the same rights and duties with respect to the father and to his relatives as the children born within marriage.

[14] According to the comments of respondents group: Attorney at law firm "Mukhiddinova i Partnyory" with work experience of 32 years and Judge of inter-district civil court of Mirzo Ulugbek district of Tashkent city with work experience of 6 years.

[15] *Postanovlenie Kabineta Ministrov "Ob udtverždenii neobchodimych normativnych aktov po realizacii Semejnogo kodeksa" Priloženie No. 1 Pravila registracii aktov graždanskogo sostojanija.* [Resolution of the Cabinet of Ministers "On approval of the required legislative acts on implementation of the Family Code of the Republic of Uzbekistan" Appendix No. 1 Rules of registry of civil status] dated 12 April 1999, No. 171. As amended by the Resolution of Cabinet of Ministers dated 22 September 2014, No. 269.

[16] *Postanovlenie Plenuma Verchovnogo Suda "O primenenii sudami zakonodatel'stva pri rassmotrenii del ob ustanovlenii otcovstva* [Resolution of Supreme Court Plenum "On application of legislation by courts when reviewing cases on establishment of paternity"] dated 25 November 2011, No. 8.

[17] *Ibid.*, Paragraph 17, 18.

As to the children conceived with artificial insemination, Uzbek law states that married persons who have given their written consent to the artificial fertilization or embryo implantation (in cases by foreign donor) and had a child through these methods will be recorded in the register of birth as the child's parents.[18]

Disputes on the right of the child conceived with biomedical assistance to claim information about the father have not been considered in court practice. In addition the record about parents made in registry office proves the child's origin from them as it is mentioned above.

3.2 *The Right to Know About the Biological Parents v. the Interests of Adopters*

There is inconsistency of norms within Uzbek family legislation: on the one hand, the right of the child to know his or her parents that is enshrined in Article 65 FC RUz but, on the other hand, the confidentiality of adoption (Article 153 FC RUz), which prohibits the disclosure of the information about the child's origin, including identity of birth parents as well as medical history. Apparently that adopted child will not be able to exercise this right as the law provides for safeguarding of secrecy of adoption by changing the child's name, surname, patronymic, the date and the place of birth within Uzbekistan if the child is below the age 10. Besides, disclosure of secrecy of adoption entails criminal responsibility (Article 125 of Criminal Code).[19] The only way to obtain information about the biological parents seems to be with the adopter's consent. However, in the event when it is required to get the child's consent to adoption who has reached the age of 10 (Article 155 FC RUz), in my opinion, confidentiality of adoption is not needed, since it will not be a secret to this child. Therefore, it is possible to assume that in such cases the child might have the right to claim the data about his or her natural parents, but it is not yet enshrined in the law.

Thus, the right of the child to know about his or her origin is more likely declarative provision since there are no corresponding procedural norms that would provide realization of this right.

---

[18] *Family Code*, art 207 (5).

[19] *Ugolovnyj Kodeks Respubliki Uzbekistan* [Criminal Code of the Republic of Uzbekistan] approved by the Law of RUz dated 22 September 1994, No. 2012-XII and entered into force on 1 April 1995 in accordance with Resolution of Supreme Counsel of RUz dated 22 September 1994, No. 2014-XII. As amended by the Law of RUz dated 20 August 2015, No. 391.

4 Transnational Adoption

Before, in Uzbekistan adoption had been effected by the decision of the khokim[20] of region and khokim of city upon the application of persons wishing to adopt the child. Since 2013 the court is authorized to review domestic and intercountry adoption.[21] This novelty indicates that Uzbek government pays a crucial attention primarily to the best interests of children in adoption matters. However, international adoption of children, who are citizens of Republic of Uzbekistan, is not quite widespread. For instance, according to the statistics,[22] from 1999 to 2013 total adoption of Uzbek children by US citizens amounted to 57. Uzbekistan is not a party to *Hague Convention on Protection of Children and Co-operation in Respect of Intercountry Adoption, 1993*. The process of adopting a child by the citizens of CIS countries is exercised in accordance with the terms of *Minsk Convention, 1993*[23] and bilateral agreements. In other cases Uzbek law governing adoption procedure is to be applied, namely, Articles 151–167, 237 of FC RUz.

4.1 Requirements for Adoption

One of the essential requirements for transnational adoption in Uzbekistan is the respect for the "subsidiarity" principle.[24] This principle is set in Article 154 FC RUz under which is a list of persons who have a pre-emptive right to adopt the child: relatives of adoptee regardless of their residence; a person with whom the adoptee lives; persons who adopt siblings, so as not to break up the family ties between them; stepmother and stepfather; citizens of the Republic of Uzbekistan; and persons who have lost children due to illness or accident. Besides, in accordance with paragraph 28 of Regulation on adoption of minor children and giving the child for upbringing into family (foster care), only those foreign nations, whose countries

[20] The institution of the khokim (regional chief administrator) is the traditional form of authority in Uzbekistan which has been sanctioned by historical experience.

[21] *Zakon Respubliki Uzbekistan o vnesenii izmenenij i dopolnenij v nekotorie normativnye akty* [Law of the Republic of Uzbekistan on Making Amendments and Additions in Some Legal Acts] dated 30 April 2013, No. 352. This Law adopted by Legislative Chamber of Oliy Majlis on 20 March, 2013 and approved by the Senate on 28 March, 2013. As amended by the Law of the RUz dated 26 August 2015, No. 393.

[22] *Statistics*, available at http://adoption.state.gov/about_us/statistics.php (accessed September 23, 2014).

[23] *Convention of CIS Countries on Legal Assistance and Legal Relations in Civil, Family and Criminal Matters (Minsk Convention)* dated 22 January 1993 was ratified by the resolution of the Supreme Council of the RUz on 6 May 1993, No. 825-XII and became effective for the Republic of Uzbekistan on 19 May 1994.

[24] State of origin must determine that an intercountry adoption is "in the child's best interests" after due consideration has been given to possibilities of placement within its own state, in other words, a "subsidiarity" principle. See further Trevor Buck, *International Child Law* (London: Cavendish publishing limited, 2005), p. 158.

have their diplomatic missions in Uzbekistan, are eligible to adopt the child who is the citizen of Republic of Uzbekistan.[25]

The next noteworthy prerequisite for adoption is the consent given by particular persons established by law. They are as follows: birth parents, adopter's spouse, and the child. In case where parental consent is not required, the child's guardian or the administration of state institution for children left without parental care give their consent to adoption. It should be noted that consent of the child is necessary if he or she has reached the age of 10 years. The child's consent to adoption is established by guardianship and trusteeship bodies or by court when considering adoption cases. There is one exception of this rule, that if the child has been already living with adopter and recognizes him or her as a parent, then the child's consent is not required.[26] The third condition is that prospective parents must personally participate at all stages of adoption process. Adopters are obliged personally to meet with the child and to make a contact with him or her. Also under Uzbek law, adopters may be adult persons of both sexes.[27] The age difference between the prospective adoptive parent and the child must be at least 15 years, except in the case where the child is being adopted by a stepparent.

According to the comments of respondent's group, the child is eligible for adoption in the following cases: in the event of parents' death; when the parents give their notarized consent to adoption; if the parents are deprived by court of parental rights, are recognized by court as legally incapable and missing, or are declared deceased; and if his or her parents have not visited him or her in children's home or medical institution for more than 1 year without valid reasons.[28]

5 The Right of the Child to Express His or Her Views

5.1 The Age When the Child Is Capable of Forming His or Her Views

Article 68 of FC RUz contains information about the child's right to express his or her views in resolving any issue in the family affecting his or her interests, as well as to be heard in any judicial or administrative hearings. However, this provision does not stipulate a minimum age for when the child is capable of forming his or her

---

[25] *Položenie ob usynovlenii nesoveršennoletnich detej, prinjatii detej v sem'ju i na vospitanie (patronat)* [Regulation on adoption of minor children and giving the child for upbringing into family (foster care)] of the Resolution of Cabinet of Ministers of RUz dated 12 April 1999, No. 171.

[26] *Family Code*, art 155,156.

[27] *Ibid.*, art 152.

[28] Respondents' group: Specialist of guardianship and trusteeship body responsible for protection of minors of Mirabad district with work experience of 5 years.

own views[29] on the issue of place of residence. Since family law provides obligatory consent of the child who has reached the age of 10, in resolving certain cases where the child's vital interests are the subject matter, it is reasonable to assume that starting from this age the child is capable of making up his or her own mind on the matter requiring decisions.

5.2 *Involvement of the Child in the Process of Making Decision*

5.2.1 In Custody and Contact Disputes

Article 68 of FC RUz is applied particularly often in the disputes on child custody. In practice exploring the views of the child has its specifics and it is up to the age criterion. Uzbek court first empowers guardianship and trusteeship body to carry out the inspection of the conditions of the child's life as well as person(s) applying for custody. In its turn, the guardianship and trusteeship body must provide the court with the certificate of inspection as well as with the conclusion on the merits of the dispute (paragraph 13).[30]

Then the court orders a psychological examination to find out the child's opinion (age category up to 10 years). In accordance with paragraph 28 of Resolution of the Supreme Court Plenum[31] exploring the children's views, their attachment to the parties shall be conducted by the department of public education during the inspection. If either of the parents disagrees with examination findings and the court will find it necessary to interview the child, then this interview should be carried out regarding the child's age and maturity, in the presence of a teacher and without any influence

[29]The Committee interprets the term "views" as going beyond developed views, to include feelings, insights, interpretations, concerns, and ideas. Implementation of Article 12 requires recognition of and respect for nonverbal forms of communications such as play, body language, facial expression, or drawing and painting, through which very young children make choices, express preferences, and demonstrate understanding of their environment. The Committee on the Rights of the Child therefore discourages the introduction of age limits, either in law or in practice, that restrict the child's right to participation in decision-making. See Gerison Lansdown, *Every Child's Right to be Heard: A Resource Guide on the UN Committee on the Rights of the Child General Comment No. 12*, (UK: Save the Children, 2011), p. 21. Available at http://www.unicef.org/adolescence/files/Every_Childs_Right_to_be_Heard.pdf (accessed September 19, 2014).

[30]*Položenie ob opeke i popečitel'stve, Priloženie No. 1 k Postanovleniju Kabineta Ministrov "Ob udtverždenii normativno-pravovych aktov po realizacii Zakona "Ob opeke i popečitel'stve"* [Regulation on guardianship and trusteeship bodies. Appendix No. 1 Resolution of Cabinet of Ministers "On approval of the legislative acts on implementation of the Law of the Republic of Uzbekistan "On guardianship and trusteeship body"] dated 22 September 2014, No. 269.

[31]Resolution of the Supreme Court Plenum of Republic of Uzbekistan "The practice of application of legislation by courts when considering disputes on the children's upbringing" dated 11 September 1998, No. 23.

on the child. However, courts very rarely authorize such an interview in the courtroom due to the negative impact on the child's mental health.

According to the survey of court practitioners,[32] the opinion of the child who has reached the age of 10 is usually heard in the courtroom in the presence of a teacher. Under paragraph 3 of Resolution of the Supreme Court Plenum, the court may take into account the wishes of the child, who has reached the age of 10, to live with one of the parents. Hence, the child's view is heard and is taken seriously by the court in conjunction with other evidences of the case.

As to visitation rights, in legal practice, the right of the child to contact is not perceived as an autonomous right, and the realization of this right fully depends on the application of one of the parents residing apart from the child or other relatives to establish the order of meetings with the child. However, the court when reviewing such cases takes into consideration the child's interests and wishes.

5.2.2 In Criminal and Administrative Proceedings

A special status of the child in criminal cases is derived from Uzbek Criminal Code. As a rule criminal responsibility starts upon reaching the age 16. But for some crimes that pointed out in Article 17 of Criminal Code, criminal responsibility starts from the age of 13, 14, or 18. Thus, the minimum age for criminal responsibility is established at the age of 13.[33]

The Right to Have a Legal Representative
According to Articles 54, 60, and 121 of Criminal Procedural Code (hereafter CPC),[34] minors, under the age of 16 years, accused of criminal offenses as well as victim or witness of the crime, are interviewed with the presence of their legal representative. The representative may be the child's parent, adopters, guardians, or other type of advocate.

The Right to Have a Legal Attorney
Uzbek law stresses that participation of legal attorney is mandatory in cases where minor is charged with crime, both at the stage of investigation and in court.[35] This rule is to be applied even when the minor refuses of legal assistance. Evidences

---

[32] Respondents' group: Judge of the inter-district civil court of Mirzo Ulugbek district of Tashkent city with work experience of 11 years in the judicial system, including 5 years in the prosecutor's office; Chairman of Uchtepa inter-district civil court of Tashkent city with work experience of 20 years.

[33] M.Kh. Rustambaev, *Commentary to Criminal Code of the Republic of Uzbekistan.* (Tashkent: O'qituvchi, 2004), pp. 149, 643.

[34] *Ugolovnyj processual'nyj Kodeks* [Criminal Procedural Code] approved by the Law of RUz dated 22 September 1994 No. 2013-XII and entered into force on 1 April 1995 in accordance with Resolution of Supreme Counsel of RUz dated 22 September 1994, No. 2014-XII. As amended by the Law of RUz dated 20 August 2015, No. 391.

[35] *Ibid.*, art 51. See also: *Postanovlenie Plenuma Verchovnogo Suda "O sudebnoj praktike po delam o prestuplenijach nesoveršennoletnich"* [Paragraph 3 of Resolution of the Supreme Court Plenum

collected without participation of a lawyer, in cases where his or her involvement is obligatory, are considered as void.

The Right Not to Be Compelled to Give Testimony
Under Article 121 of CPC, witness and victim of crime under the age of 16 years are not warned about the criminal responsibility for refusing to give testimony or for giving false testimony in advance.

The Right to Have a Free of Charge Assistance of an Interpreter
According to CPC, individuals including children involved in criminal proceedings may ask for an interpreter. In practice most often schoolteachers are invited as interpreters at public expense, i.e., free of charge.[36]

In practice, at the stage of investigation, some cases where minors were being interrogated with violation of the abovementioned provisions of the law such as an interview of minors without legal assistance and legal representative are encountered.[37] But in the event of such violation of minors' rights which is also considered as breach of procedural law, the case is to be sent to extra investigation or the judgment is to be annulled.[38]

5.2.3 In Decisions Regarding Medical Treatment

With regard to the issue of child's right to medical treatment, the first question to be asked is whether the child is sufficiently autonomous or has the requisite capacity to provide the consent to the treatment. Under Uzbek domestic legislation, the minor over the age of 14 years is entitled to give voluntary informed[39] consent to medical

"Court practice on cases in regard to minors charged with crime"] dated 15 September 2000, No. 21. As amended by Resolution of the Supreme Court Plenum dated 13 December 2012, No. 19.

[36] Respondents' group: Attorney at law firm "Mukhiddinova i Partnyory" with work experience of 20 years.

[37] Information received from reference group: Assistant of the Prosecutor of Tashkent city with work experience of 9 years in the prosecutor' office; Attorney at law firm "Mukhiddinova i Partnyory" with work experience of 20 years.

[38] Respondents' group: Assistant of Prosecutor of Tashkent city with work experience of 9 years in the prosecutor' office; Attorney at law firm "Mukhiddinova i Partnyory" with work experience of 20 years.

[39] To be informed, a child should be able to understand the nature of the medical treatment, the risks and seriousness of the procedure, the potential benefits, the alternatives, the possibility of refusing consent, and medical consequences which such a refusal could entail. (See Geraldine Van Bueren, *The International Law on the Rights of the Child*. (The Netherlands: Martinus Nijhoff Publishers, 1998), p. 310.) In New Zealand, under the Code of Health and Disability Service Consumers' Rights 1996, health practitioner must judge whether a particular child is competent to give informed consent. This judgment will be based upon the child's understanding and maturity and the gravity of medical procedure in question. Children as consumers under Code must be consulted in a manner relevant to their age. See in greater detail: Claire Breen, *Age Discrimination and Children's Rights. Ensuring Equality and Acknowledging Difference*. (Boston: Martin Nijhoff Publishers, 2006), p. 53.

treatment or to refuse treatment.[40] According to Article 26 of Law on Protection of Citizen's Health, consent to medical treatment in regard to children below the age of 14 is given by parents or by another legal representative. In the absence of the parents or another legal representative, the decision on medical treatment is made by physicians' concilium, and – if it is impossible to summon the concilium – by physician in charge of the case with further confirmation of hospital administrator and legal representative. This provision is more likely declarative. In practice cases, when the child's view regarding treatment differed from that of his or her parents were not encountered. As a rule, decisions concerning medical treatment of minors rest with their parents.

6 The Right of the Child to Preserve His or Her Identity

The right of children to a name is fundamental, as a name is the first point of reference both for the child and society as a means of identifying the child and the child's family. It is for this reason that this right is particularly important for nonmarital children.[41] Furthermore, where a child remains unregistered, it is easier to abduct, sell, or induce that child into prostitution, and a child may become stateless as a result of non-registration.[42] Uzbekistan undertook effective legal measures to prevent such cases. In particular, under paragraph 14 of the Rules of registry of civil status, the child shall be compulsory registered after the birth in registry office at the birth place or at the place of residence of his or her parents.

The child's right to a name, surname, and patronymic is enshrined in Article 9 of the Law on Guarantees of the Rights of the Child and Article 69 of FC RUz. The name shall be given to the child upon an agreement of parents. It should be noted that law does not stipulate any restrictions with respect to the parents' right to name their child; parents may choose any name they wish.[43] The registry office cannot refuse to satisfy the parents' requests; they can only give a recommendation if the selected name is discordant or does not harmonize with patronymic. Although in

---

[40] *Law on Guarantees of the Rights of the Child*, art 22; See also: *Zakon ob ochrane zdorov'ja graždan* [Law on Protection of Citizen's Health], art 19, dated 29 August 1996, No. 265-I. As amended by Law of RUz dated 19 May 2010, No. 246.

[41] Geraldine Van Bueren, Op.cit. p. 117.

[42] Trevor Buck, Op.cit, p. 131.

[43] Similar rule is enshrined in Japanese law. Under Koseki (registration system under which every family, husband, wife, and unmarried children is registered with government. Birth, marriage, divorce, and death are recorded as is the relationship between each person) there are no restrictions on the parents' right to name their child; however, in one case the registry office refused to register the name on the grounds that it was an abuse of that parental right (Judgment of the Tokyo Family Court, Hachioji Branch on 31 January 1994, Hanrei Jiho (1486), pp. 56–61. See further: Yukiko Matsushima, "Controversies and Dilemmas: Japan Confronts Convention" in Michael Freeman, *Children's Rights: A Comparative Perspective*. (England, USA: Dartmouth, 1996), p. 133.

most cases, parents choose traditional names for their children.[44] Besides, under paragraph 166 of the Rules of registry of civil status, the child is entitled to personally apply to the registry office for changing his or her name, surname, or patronymic upon reaching the age of 16. The registry office is entitled to change the child's name upon joint request of the parents before the child reaches the age of 16. But, the name or surname of the child who has reached the age of 10 can be changed only with his or her consent.[45]

The surname of the child is determined by the parents' surname. If the parents have different surnames, the child is given the father's or mother's surname upon an agreement between the parents. Upon request of the parents, a child may be given a surname derived from the first names of his or her grandfather from both the father and mother lines according to national custom.[46]

When a divorce or separation is granted and the parent with whom the child lives wishes to give the child his own surname, the guardianship and trusteeship body shall resolve this issue depending on the child's interests (e.g., the child is accustomed to the previous surname or on the contrary he or she wishes to have the same surname as all family members) and taking into consideration the opinion of the other parent.[47] However, the opinion of the other parent residing apart from the child is not considered as obligatory.

If the child is born to an unmarried mother, in the absence of a joint application of the parents and court's decision on establishment of paternity, the surname of the child's father will be written down in the Register of birth as the mother's surname; first name, patronymic, and nationality of the child – according to the mother's statement.[48] If the child is born to an unmarried parents and paternity has not been legally established, a guardianship and trusteeship body depending on the interests of the child has the right to change the child's surname to the mother's surname that she has on the date of her application with such request (part 3 Article 70 FC RUz).

7 The Right of the Child to Labor

In accordance with the Law on Guarantees of the Rights of the Child, the minimum age of employment is set as 16, although in special cases, at the age of 15 with the parent's written consent, a minor may start part-time light work which is not harmful to his or her health and moral development and does not disrupt his or her

[44] Respondents' group: Deputy Head of the municipal justice department on the registry office.

[45] *Family Code*, art 70.

[46] *Ibid.*, art 69.

[47] Consideration of other parent's opinion means that he or she should be notified about the submission of request to guardianship and trusteeship body on the changing the child's surname and his opinion should be heard.

[48] *Family Code*, art 207 (3).

education in his or her free time.[49] Employees under age 18 are hired only after a medical examination, and thereafter until the age 18, they are subject to compulsory annual medical examination (part 3 Article 239 of Labor Code[50] RUz (hereafter – LC RUz)). Uzbek labor law envisages special protection to minors in its regulation of working hours and conditions. For example, for minors aged between 16 and 18, working hours are set no more than 36 h a week and for those aged between 15 and 16 years, no more than 24 h a week (Article 242 LC RUz). A minor's vacation cannot be less than 30 calendar days (Article 244 LC RUz). Article 241 LC RUz contains the list of work prohibited for minors because of negative impact on their health and moral development. This list includes work with hazardous materials, underground work, and job which requires moving heavy weights over the limits established for them. Besides, Uzbek government approved the list of occupations with unfavorable working conditions to which it is forbidden to employ persons under the age 18.[51] Minors cannot work overtime, at night, or during weekends and holidays.

After ratification of International Labor Organization's Worst Forms of Child Labor Convention № 182 on 24 June 2008 and Minimum Age Convention №138 on 6 March 2009, provisions prohibiting forced labor were added to the Labor Code (Article 7), the Code of Administrative Responsibility was amended with provisions prohibiting the use of minors' labor (Article 49–1), and the Criminal Code was amended with provisions prohibiting trafficking of minors ((a) part 3 Article 135) and involvement of minors in antisocial behavior (Article 127).

8 Deprivation of Parental Rights

Under family legislation,[52] the parents (one of them) are deprived of parental rights if they: avoid to perform their parental responsibilities, including avoiding the payment of the alimony; refuse without valid reasons to take their child from maternity department or from other medical center, educational establishment, or institution for the social protection of the population, or other similar institutions; abuse their parental rights, including child maltreatment, physical or mental violence against child; suffer from chronic alcoholism or drug addiction; and have committed premeditated crime against the life or health of their children or against the life or health of the spouse. This list of grounds is exhaustive. According to Article 80, FC RUz cases on deprivation of parental responsibilities are considered by court. One of the parents, prosecutor, and guardianship and trusteeship bodies responsible for

[49] *Law on Guarantees of the Rights of the Child*, art 20.

[50] *Trudovoj kodeks* [Labor Code of the Republic of Uzbekistan] adopted on 21 December, 1995 and came into effect on 1 April, 1996. As amended by the Law of RUz dated 20 August 2015, No. 391.

[51] This list is approved by the Resolution of Ministry of Labor and Social Protection of Population and Ministry of Health, registered by Ministry of Justice of RUz, dated 29 July 2009, No. 1990.

[52] *Family Code*, art 79.

protection of the rights of children may submit the application on termination of parental rights to the court.[53] Besides, Uzbek family law provides the child with the entitlement to personally appeal to the court or to guardianship and trusteeship body upon reaching the age of 14 with the claim to protect his or her rights, particularly in cases when parents (one of them) fail to fulfill or improperly fulfill their rights involved in the child's upbringing and education or when they abuse the parental rights.[54] But in legal practice, this right is more likely declarative, since it is not supported by specific procedural means.

The guardianship and trusteeship body keeps the records on the dysfunctional families. According to the comments of the respondents' group, in the event of immediate threat to the child's life and health, a guardianship and trusteeship body has the authority to take the child from his or her parents, to notify immediately the prosecutor, and to apply to the court within 7 days with a claim on deprivation of parental rights. When the court issues a termination of parental rights decree, a guardianship and trusteeship body has to find a place for the child. In the first place, they search for the child's relatives. In the absence of relatives, the child is transferred for upbringing into foster family or can be adopted, or a legal guardian is appointed. If these forms of placement of the child fail to implement, then the child will be placed in the institution for orphans and children without parental care.[55]

The parents deprived of parental rights lose all the rights based on the fact of kinship with the child, including the right to receive maintenance from the child and the right to privileges and allowances established for citizens with children. Nevertheless, the termination of parental rights does not relieve the parents of the responsibility to support the child. The child whose parents (one of them) are deprived of parental rights retains the ownership of the dwelling premises or the right to use this dwelling. Guardianship and trusteeship body of region (city) at the place of residence of orphans and children without parental care shall exercise a control over preservation of residential premises for orphans and children without parental care. In the event of detection of unlawful sale of these living premises, guardianship and trusteeship body has to apply to the court within 5 days of the date of detection with a claim on the recognition of such transaction void (paragraph 10).[56] Besides, if this child is not adopted, then he or she maintains property rights

---

[53] See also: paragraph 18 of Resolution of the Supreme Court Plenum of RUz "The practice of application of legislation by courts when considering disputes on the children's upbringing" dated 11 September 1998, No. 23.

[54] *Family Code*, art 67 (5).

[55] Respondents' group: Specialist of guardianship and trusteeship body responsible for protection of minors of Mirabad district with work experience of 5 years.

[56] *Položenie "O porjadke obespečenija žilymi pomeščenijami detej-sirot i detej ostavšichsja bez popečenija roditelej" Priloženie No. 1 k Postanovleniju Kabineta Ministrov "O merach po obespečeniju žilymi pomeščenijami detej-sirot i detej ostavšichsja bez popečenija roditelej"* [Regulation on the procedure of providing residential premises for orphans and children without parental care. Appendix no. 1 to the Resolution of Cabinet of Ministers "On the measures of providing dwellings for orphans and children without parental care] dated 2 August 2010, No. 164. As amended by the Resolution of Cabinet of Ministers dated 9 December 2014, No. 338.

based on fact of kinship with his or her parents and other relatives, including the right of inheritance.[57]

The court has the authority taking into account the child's opinion to dismiss the restoration of parental rights claim, if it contradicts the child's interests. Besides, the restoration of parental rights in respect of a child who is 10 years of age or older is possible only if this child consents to restoration. Restoration of parental rights is not allowed in cases where the child is adopted and adoption is not canceled.[58]

Furthermore Uzbek law also provides criminal responsibility in case of physical punishment of children.[59]

9 The Right of the Child to Freedom of Thought, Conscience, and Religion

Article 17 of Law on Guarantees of the Rights of the Child provides the right of the child to freedom of thought, conscience, and belief; however, the law states that freedom of the child's opinion and its expression can be restricted in the procedure established by law. Since Uzbekistan declares separation of education system from religion, it is not allowed to include religious subject into curriculum (Article 7).[60] Under Uzbek law, the private religious education is also forbidden.[61]

Schoolchildren and students who attend state schools and universities cannot wear religious clothing and any religious symbols. According to Article 14 of Law on Freedom of Conscience and Religious Assemblies, citizens of the Republic of Uzbekistan (with exception of members of religious organizations) are not allowed to appear in public institutions wearing religious clothing. It should be noted that this is both a political and legal controversial issue worldwide.[62] From Uzbek per-

---

[57] *Family Code*, art 81 (4).

[58] Paragraph 21 of Resolution of the Supreme Court Plenum of RUz "The practice of application of legislation by courts when considering disputes on the children's upbringing" dated 11 September 1998, No. 23.

[59] *Criminal Code*, art 110 (2) a. See also: *Postanovlenie Plenuma Verchovnogo Suda "O sudebnoj praktike po delam o pričinenii umyšlennogo telesnogo povreždenija* [Resolution of the Supreme Court Plenum "Court practice on cases about infliction of intentional corporal punishment"] dated 27 June 2007, No. 6. As amended by Resolution of Plenum of Supreme Court dated 13 December 2012, No. 19.

[60] *Zakon o svobode sovesti i religioznych organizacijach* [Law on Freedom of Conscience and Religious Assemblies]. New edition approved by the Law dated 1 May 1998, No. 618-I. As amended by Law dated 31 December 2008, No. 197.

[61] *Ibid.*, art 9.

[62] Controversies surrounding the wearing of religious clothing, particularly in public institutions such as schools, universities, and public service offices, found their way to the European Court of Human Rights in two important decisions. The first, Dahlab v Switzerland, involved a school teacher who was banned from teaching in a primary school because she dressed in traditional, modest clothing including a headscarf. The second case, Şahin v Turkey, involved a university

spective, it can be explained as that Uzbekistan is a secular country where the separation of state and religion is enshrined in law.[63] In addition, the said provisions do not contradict to the Constitution of Uzbekistan (Article 31) and the terms of Convention that in greater detail and at the same time gently said about correlation of state laws, which are secular and the right of the child to freedom of religion (§3 Article 14 of Convention).

Under Uzbek law, all matters concerning the child's upbringing and education are resolved by the parents' mutual agreement, depending on the interests of the child and taking into consideration the child's opinion (Article 75 FC RUz). The kind of issues in which religion children are to be brought up in, when those responsible for children cannot agree on the choice of religion, is not raised in practice. In Uzbekistan predominantly children follow their parent's religion. But it is not a compulsory condition. There are a number of states in which children already possess the right to have and adopt a religion of choice under their national law.[64] Uzbek law does not provide any special norm which would allow the child to choose or to change the religion, and at what age the child can enjoy this right. However, the law does not prohibit doing this either. Furthermore, the Constitution of Uzbekistan provides for general provision under which everyone including children has the right to profess or not to profess any religion (Article 31).

10 The Child's Duty to Support His or Her Parents

Unlike some other countries in which children are legally obliged to assist their parents in the household,[65] Uzbek family law does not enshrine such an obligation of the child since personal non-property duties cannot be settled by law. They are more likely regulated by moral and ethical principles as a facet of child's upbringing. As to property responsibilities of the child, under civil law, minors aged between 14 and 18 can be personally financially responsible for property damage. If a minor does not have any property or other source of income enough to reimburse the

student who was prohibited from study because she wished to wear a headscarf in her lectures and examinations. Carolyn Evans, *The "Islamic scarf" in the European Court of Human Rights,* available at http://www.law.unimelb.edu.au/files/dmfile/download89441.pdf (accessed September 19, 2014). See also: Jon Henley, "France to Ban Pupils' Religious Dress," Jane Kramer, "Taking the Veil: How France's Public Schools Became the Battleground in a Culture War," The New Yorker (New York, US), 22 November 2004, 58., Clare MacCarthy, "Danish Muslim Dismissed for Wearing Headscarf Loses Court Case," Financial Times (London, UK), 19 December 2003, 10.

[63] *Law on Freedom of Conscience and Religious Assemblies,* art 5.

[64] In Switzerland children above the age of 16 are allowed to choose for themselves the religion to which they wish to adhere and the same applies in Finland for those above the age of 15. See Geraldine Van Bueren, Op.cit. p. 158.

[65] See § 1619 of German Civil Code (BGB) in series "German and European Laws" 2nd ed. (Moscow: Wolters Kluwer, 2006), p. 417.

damage, then this property damage must be reimbursed by his or her parents, adopters, or guardian, unless they prove that damage is not their fault (Article 994).[66]

Nevertheless, the law provides that able-bodied adult "children" are obliged to maintain their disabled[67] in need of assistance[68] parents (Article 109 FC RUz). A specific feature of such cases is that the court when calculating alimony takes into consideration all able-bodied adult children of parent-plaintiff since all of them are obliged to support their parents, and it does not matter whether the parent-plaintiff brings a lawsuit against only one child or all of them. In each case this issue is solved by the court based on the particular circumstances of the case. For instance, the court takes into account which of the children, in what forms and in what amount has provided support for the parent and which of them has not; financial and marital status of both parties (taking into consideration all sources that form the income of the parties). It's also essential for the court to explore the reasons that led a disabled parent to apply for judicial procedure for recovery of maintenance. Adult children are also obliged to bear extra expenses made by his or her parent due to serious illness and other valid reasons (Article 111 FC RUz). Able-bodied adult children are not relieved of obligation to take care and to provide financial support even if their parents are maintained by state or non-state institutions.

Children may be relieved of this duty, if the court finds that his or her parents in the past fail to fulfill their parental responsibilities (Article 113 FC RUz). Children are also relieved of paying alimony to his or her parents who deprived of parental rights and their rights have not been restored by the court decision.

11 Concluding Remarks

To sum up, it should be noted that prior to ratification of the Convention, the rights of children in Uzbekistan were not enshrined in the law as autonomous rights and were considered as the object of parental care.[69] The ratification has brought about the transformation of Uzbek family law. Overall, the compliance of Uzbek legislation with Convention is quite good. This paper was to highlight positive develop-

---

[66] *Graždanskij Kodeks Respubliki Uzbekistan* [Civil Code of the Republic of Uzbekistan] Approved by the Laws dated 21 December 1995 No. 163-I and 29 August 1996 No. 256-I. As amended by the Law dated 20 August 2015, No. 391.

[67] Disabled persons are men who attain the age of 60 and women 55 (Article 7), as well as those who are handicapped (groups I and II) (Article 15). *Zakon o gosudarstvennom pensionnom obespečenii graždan* [Law on State Pensions for Citizens] dated 3 September 1993, No. 938-XII. As amended by the Law dated 4 December 2014, No. 379.

[68] The parents who are in need of assistance means that these parents are not able to provide a decent life for themselves due to small proportion of allowance or pensions or not receiving them, as well as due to the lack of other source of income. See L.M. Pčelinceva, Family Law of Russia. 6th ed. (Moscow: Norma Infra-M, 2012), p. 405.

[69] See *Kodeks o brake i sem'e Uzbekskoj SSR* [The Code on Marriage and Family of Uzbek SSR] dated 1 October 1969. As amended on 1 January 1983.

ments as well as to illuminate obstacles that are currently impeding to broader realization of children's rights in our country. For instance, for the first time, the child's right to express his or her views is enshrined in law, and legal practice has developed the mechanism that provides the child with opportunity to be heard in judicial proceedings either directly or through psychological test depending on the age criteria. Furthermore, the Family Code sets certain cases when obligatory consent of the child who has reached the age of 10 years is needed. The court when trying the cases on custody and contact disputes primarily takes into consideration the child's interests. In addition, a guardianship and trusteeship body makes efforts to place the child without parental care into a family in the first place. However, yet children are not deemed sufficiently autonomous right holders as it is defined in Convention. Some rights of children (e.g., the right to contact) are considered from the perspective of parental rights and responsibilities. Other provisions of law, such as the right to know about his or her origin and the right to protection (in part that enables the child to personally apply to the court upon attaining the particular age), remain rather declarative than real due to the lack of respective mechanism of their implementation in procedural law.

Despite Uzbek criminal legislation provides for special status of minors in criminal proceedings, juvenile justice does not exist as an independent branch of judiciary. Presently criminal cases in regard to minors are not considered by a competent, independent, and impartial authority, as required by Article 40 of the Convention, but they are decided by the judge of general jurisdiction.

La transposition de la Convention de l'ONU sur les droits de l'enfant en droit Venezuelien

Alberto Blanco-Uribe

1 Introduction

1.1 Antécédents

La préoccupation de l'humanité par le bien être de l'enfant au niveau planétaire et non seulement de chaque Société ou Etat isolément est décimononique. Elle s'est manifesté de manière explicite, il y a presqu'un siècle, à l'occasion du travail de la vieille Société des Nations, étant approuvée, le 26 novembre 1924, la Déclaration des droits de l'enfant, dite Déclaration de Genève,[1] texte très bref où les « hommes et femmes du monde », reconnaissent en termes d'égalité et de non discrimination, ces simples principes :

« *Premier : L'enfant doit être mis en conditions de se développer normalement depuis le point de vue matériel et spirituel.*

Deuxième : L'enfant affamé doit être alimenté, l'enfant malade doit être attendu, l'enfant déficient doit être aidé, l'enfant inadapté doit être établi, l'orphelin et l'abandonné doivent être recueillis et aidés.

Troisième l'enfant doit être le premier à recevoir des secours en cas de calamité.

Quatrième : l'enfant doit être mis en conditions de pouvoir gagner sa vie et doit être protégé de toute exploitation.

Cinquième : L'enfant doit être éduqué en lui inculquant le sens du devoir qu'il a de mettre ses meilleures qualités au service du prochain ».

Ultérieurement, plus de trois décades après, l'Assemblée Générale des Nations Unis, ayant auparavant approvée la Déclaration universelle des droits de l'homme,

[1] https://sites.google.com/site/associationaidhs/test/les-droits-de-l-enfant

A. Blanco-Uribe (✉)
Universidad Central de Venezuela, Edificio Avila, Piso 2, Oficina 2B,
Avenida Principal de Las Mercedes, Caracas, Venezuela
e-mail: albertoblancouribe@gmail.com

O. Cvejić Jančić (ed.), *The Rights of the Child in a Changing World*,
Ius Comparatum - Global Studies in Comparative Law 13,
DOI 10.1007/978-3-319-23189-1_22

le 10 décembre 1948, où il a été consideré que l'enfant, « *par son manque de maturité physique et mental, a besoin de protection et d'attentions spéciales* », a corrigé et dicté le 20 novembre 1959 une nouvelle Déclaration des droits de l'enfant,[2] qui contient dix principes, dont les deux premiers disposent que:

> « *L'enfant doit jouir de tous les droits énoncés dans la présente Déclaration. Ces droits doivent être reconnus à tous les enfants sans exception aucune, et sans distinction ou discrimination fondées sur la race, la couleur, le sexe, la langue, la religion, les opinions politiques ou autres, l'origine nationale ou sociale, la fortune, la naissance, ou sur toute autre situation, que celle-ci s'applique à l'enfant lui-même ou à sa famille* ».
>
> « *L'enfant doit bénéficier d'une protection spéciale et se voir accorder des possibilités et des facilités par l'effet de la loi et par d'autres moyens, afin d'être en mesure de se développer d'une façon saine et normale sur le plan physique, intellectuel, moral, spirituel et social, dans des conditions de liberté et de dignité. Dans l'adoptionde lois à cette fin, l'intérêt supérieur de l'enfant doit être la considération déterminante* ».

Cependant, ce qui compte souligner, c'est que l'humanité ne s'est pas conforme avec des simples principes établis dans desdocuments internationaux d'une immense notoriété, c'est vraie, mais dont leurvaleur n'allait pas plus loin que d'être du «soft law», demandant des efforts d'interprétation dans le domaine du «ius cogens» et la suprématie des droits de l'homme, sinon, qu'au bénéfice de la sécurité juridique et de la garantie de réponse protectrice l'ordonnancement juridique, au sein de la même Assemblée Générale, à peine, encore une fois, trente ans après, a été approuvée et a commencé le processus de signatures et ratifications de la Convention relative aux droits de l'enfant,[3] le 20 novembre 1989, où les Etats assument de véritables obligations juridiques internationales ("hard law"), fondées sur les postulats centraux de ses articles 2.1, 2.2, 3.1 et 4 :

> «*Les Etats parties s'engagent à respecter les droits qui sont énoncés dans la présente Convention et à les garantir à tout enfant relevant de leur juridiction, sans distinction aucune, indépendamment de toute considération de race, de couleur, de sexe, de langue, de religion, d'opinion politique ou autre de l'enfant ou de ses parents ou représentants légaux, de leur origine nationale, ethnique ou sociale, de leur situation de fortune, de leur incapacité, de leur naissance ou de toute autre situation*».
>
> «*Les Etats parties prennent toutes les mesures appropriées pour que l'enfant soit effectivement protégé contre toutes formes de discrimination ou de sanction motivées par la situation juridique, les activités, les opinions déclarées ou les convictions de ses parents, de ses représentants légaux ou des membres de sa famille*».
>
> «*Dans toutes les décisions qui concernent les enfants, qu'elles soient le fait des institutions publiques ou privées de protection sociale, des tribunaux, des autorités administratives ou des organes législatifs, l'intérêt supérieur de l'enfant doit être une considération primordiale*».
>
> «*Les Etats parties s'engagent à prendre toutes les mesures législatives, administratives et autres qui sont nécessaires pour mettre en oéuvre les droits reconnus dans la présente Convention*».

---

[2] A.G. Res. 1386 (XIV), 14 U.N. GAOR Supp. (No. 16) p. 19, ONU Doc. A/4354 (1959). http://www.udaf36.fr/Documents%20de%20base/Textes%20fondamentaux/droitsdesenfants.pdf

[3] A.G. Res. 44/25 http://www2.ohchr.org/french/law/crc.htm

Une si grande acceptation eu ce traité international, qu'il est entré en vigueur rapidement le 2 septembre 1990, ayant été ratifié pour les débuts 2012 par 193 Etats. Le Venezuela l'a signé le 26 janvier 1990 et l'a ratifié presque d'immédiat et sans réserves par loi du 20 juillet 1990.[4]

1.2 Problème

L'abime, typique dans des pays avec peu de culture juridique quotidienne, entre l'entrée en vigueur conforme à la loi, des normes juridiques, indépendamment de la hiérarchie qu'elles étalent dans l'ordonnancement juridique, dans un coté, et de l'autre coté, leur efficacité réelle, est visible aussi dans ce thème. C'est-à-dire, que la seule ratification de la Convention ne conduit pas, tout simplement, vers une amélioration effective, significative et automatique de la situation vitale des enfants. Et ceci, plus grave encore nonobstant la dictée des lois internes de transposition de la Convention, qui ne sont pas complètement appliquées par les opérateurs juridiques y compris, notamment, les juges et les autorités administratives de protection des enfants.

1.3 Objectif

Le présent rapport, avec support documentaire dans les textes normatifs qui prétendent développer le mandat conventionnel international de garantir les droits de l'enfant au Venezuela, s'efforce de démontrer qu'au moins sur un plan simplement formaliste et normatif, la Convention se trouve dûment transposée dans le droit interne.

2 Développement

2.1 Cadre constitutionnel

La Constitution en vigueur a été adoptée par référendum populaire en décembre 1999,[5] après son approbation par l'Assemblée Nationale Constituante, étant le plus important de celle-ci, le traitement sublime en vigueur qui est donné aux droits humains comme modèle de constitution garante du dénommé nouveau constitutionalisme latino-américain.

[4] Publiée au journal officiel N° 34.541 du 29 août 1990.

[5] Publiée au journal officiel N° 36.860 du 30 décembre 1999. http://pdba.georgetown.edu/Constitutions/Venezuela/ven1999.html

Dans ce sens, en partant de l'idée iusnaturaliste, marquée dans son exposition de motifs, de la liberté et égalité de la personne, comme attribut ontologique limitant de l'actuation étatique, commence dans ses articles 2 et 3, en déclarant le pays comme un Etat démocratique et social de droit et de justice, qui défend comme valeur supérieure de son ordonnancement juridique et de son actuation la prééminence des droits de l'homme, étant une finalité essentielle de l'Etat, la défense et le développement de la personne et le respect à sa dignité et la garantie de l'accomplissement des principes et droits consacrés en elle.

A continuation suivie, son article 19 souligne le respect et garantie des Droits de l'homme, comme obligation des organes du pouvoir public, devant les assurer en accord au principe de progressivité et sans discrimination, non seulement en vue de la Constitution, sinon aussi des traités internationaux sur les droits de l'homme ratifiés, sur lesquels, l'article 23 prévoit que possèdent hiérarchie constitutionnelle et prévalaient dans l'ordre interne, dans la mesure, qu'ils contiennent des normes sur son profit et exercice plus favorables à celles établies par la Constitution et la Loi, étant d'application immédiate et directe par les Tribunaux et autres organes du pouvoir public.

Plus en avant, son article 203, signale la classique réserve légale garante, mais le fait de manière plus rigide, en exigeant que la loi développant les droits de l'homme, soit une loi organique, ce qui demande à satisfaire des exigences formelles qu'assurent la participation des minorités présentes au sein du parlement, au moment de son adoption.

Finalement, en concret, quant aux droits de l'enfant, ses articles 75 et 78, en reprenant les idées centrales de la Convention, disposent que :

«Les garçons, filles et Adolescents ont le droit de vivre, d'être élevés ou élevées et de se développer au sein de leur famille d'origine. Exceptionnellement, lorsque ceci ne soit pas possible ou contraire à leur intérêt supérieur, auront le droit à une famille de substitution en conformité à la Loi. L'adoptionpossède des effets similaires à lafiliationet s'établie toujours en bénéfice de l'adopté ou de l'adoptée, en conformité à la Loi. L'adoption internationaleest subsidiaire de la nationale».

«Les garçons et les filles et adolescents sont sujets pleins en droit et ils seront protégés par la législation, organes et tribunaux spécialisés, lesquels respecteront, garantiront et développeront les contenus de cetteConstitution, de la Convention sur les Droits de l'Enfant et autres traités internationaux touchant cette matière et ayant été souscrits et ratifiés par la République. L'Etat, la famille et la société assureront avec priorité absolue, protection intégraleà l'enfant. Pour ceci, il sera pris en compte son intérêt supérieur dans les décisions et actions qui les concernent. L'Etat promouvra son incorporation progressive à la qualité de citoyen actif et de citoyenne active et une entité rectrice nationale dirigera les politiques pour la protection intégrale des garçons, filles et adolescents».

Ce qui précède, sans préjudice de dispositifs qu'interdissent l'esclavage et la traite des enfants, (article 54), assurent le droit à l'information des enfants (article 58), ou consacrent des droits qui sont applicables aux enfants comme personnes.

2.2 *Cadre legal*

Comme instrument juridique spécial, dédié à la tutelle des droits de l'enfant, se trouve la Loi cadre, qui développe le thème: la Loi Organique pour la Protection des Garçons, Filles et Adolescents dictée en 2007[6] avec quelques reformes et dérogatoires partielles. Dans son article 1 est défini son objet comme celui de garantir à tous les garçons, filles et adolescents, des conditions d'égalité et de non discrimination (article 3), et de priorité absolue (article 7), l'exercice plein et effectif de leur droits et garanties, sous la clause du «*numerus apertus*» et spécialement ceux qui sont énumérés par la Convention relative aux droits de l'enfant (articles 10 et 11), étant l'Etat ténu de prendre toutes les mesures administratives, législatives, judiciaires et d'autres que soient nécessaires (article 4).

Avant tout, nous avons qu'à son article 2 on entend pour enfant toute personne ayant moins de douze ans et par adolescent ceux qu'ayant eu douze ans, n'arrivent pas encore aux dix-huit ans, et en cas de doute la personne sera considerée comme enfant ou adolescent selon le cas, pour sa meilleure protection. Partant de la même idée, qui n'a pas encore eu les dix-huit ans, sans sous –classifications selon l'article 1 de la Convention, est assumé comme de l'enfance :

> «*Au sens de la présente Convention, un enfant s'entend de tout être humain âgé de moins de dix-huit ans, sauf si la majorité est atteinte plus tôt en vertu de la législation qui lui est applicable*».

Dans un autre ordre d'idées, il est à remarquer que ce corps normatif est omni compréhensif de la matière liée à la jouissance et exercice des droits de l'enfant, laissant en marge textes spéciaux, soumis à celui-ci dans sa qualité de loi cadre, comme c'est le cas entre autres, de la Loi sur les procédures spéciales en matière de protection familiale de garçons, filles et adolescents.[7] En conséquence, il s'agit d'une loi cadre générale, que dans quelques cas régle directement le développement de certains droits de l'enfant, sans exclure l'autre technique législative de confier celui d'autres de ces droits à des lois spéciales. En plus, étant une loi clairement destinée à la protection des droits de l'enfant, simultanément elle fomente et encourage la participation active de l'enfant dans la résolution de ses affaires, assistant alors à un texte légal très complet, car il instaure aussi l'appareil institutionnel indispensable pour atteindre ses propos, établi les procédés et typifie les délits et leur sanctions.

En tout cas, n'importe l'interprète ou l'applicateur de toute législation de sauvegarde de ces droits, c'est qui est vrai, c'est que son travail doit être accompli en suivant le chemin de l'intérêt supérieur de l'enfant (article 8), ce qui se trouve ordonné comme nous l'avons vu dans l'article 78 de la Constitution, en accord avec l'article 3.1 de la Convention. Pour ceci, il est aussi présente dans les lois spéciales, comme à l'article 5.9 de la Loi sur les procédures spéciales en matière de protection familiale de garçons, filles et adolescents.

---

[6] Publiée au journal officiel extraordinnaire N° 5.859 du 10 décembre 2007.

[7] Publiée au journal officiel N° 39.570 du 9 décembre 2010.

La définition de la portée de l'intérêt supérieur de l'enfant se trouve au dit article 8, comme suit :

«L'intérêt supérieur du garçon, fille et adolescent est un principe d'interprétation et d'application de cette Loi, lequel est d'obligatoire accomplissement dans la prise de toutes les décisions qui concernent les garçons, filles et adolescents. Ce principe est dirigé à assurer le développement intégral des garçons, filles et adolescents ainsi que la jouissance pleine et effective de leurs droits et garanties.

Premier Paragraphe: Pour déterminer l'intérêt supérieur des garçons, filles et adolescents dans une situation concrète il doit s'apprécier :

a) L'opinion des garçons, filles et adolescents.

b) Le besoin d'équilibre entre les droits et garanties des garçons, filles et adolescents et leurs devoirs.

c) Le besoin d'équilibre entre les exigences du bien commun et les droits et garanties des garçons, filles et adolescents.

d) Le besoin d'équilibre entre les droits des personnes et les droits et garanties des garçons, filles et adolescents.

e) La condition spécifique des garçons, filles et adolescents comme personnes en plein développement.

Deuxième Paragraphe. En application de l'intérêt supérieur des garçons, filles et adolescents, au cas où il y aurait des conflits entre les droits et intérêts des garçons, filles et adolescents, face à d'autres droits et intérêts également légitimes, prévaudront les premiers».

Ainsi, en ce qu'il s'agit du contenu dogmatique de la loi en analyse, avant tout, est soulignée la longue énumération, simplement énonciative et complémentaire des droits prévus dans la Convention, contenue entre ses articles 15 et 116, où est apprécié, par exemple, les droits à la vie, au nom et à l'identification, à la nationalité, à connaître l'identité de père et mère et à obtenir ses attentions, à une famille, à un niveau de vie adéquat, à l'environnement, à l'intégrité personnelle, à la liberté de pensée, conscience et culte, à la liberté, à la santé, à l'éducation, à la recréation, à l'honneur, à l'information, à la liberté d'expression, à opiner et être entendu et tants d'autres, sur lesquels se feront des commentaires.

Entrons ensuite à l'analyse de quelques droits de l'enfant, en partant du questionnaire établi par la rapporteuse générale du topique.

2.2.1 Le droit à connaître son origine

En premier lieu, le droit à connaître son origine, prévu dans l'article 7.1[8] de la Convention, trouve sa transposition dans l'article 25:

«Tous les garçons, filles et adolescents, indépendamment de safiliation, ont le droit de connaître leur pères et leur mères, ainsi que d'avoir leur attention, sauf quand ceci soit contraire à l'intérêt supérieur».

[8] «L'enfant est enregistré aussitôt sa naissance et a tout-de-suite le droit à un nom, le droit d'acquérir une nationalité et, dans la mesure du possible, le droit de connaître ses parents et d'être élevé par eux».

Cette prévision est totalement ample, dans le sens que l'enfant né hors mariage, aura le droit de faire établir son origine sur le père non marital, à travers de l'action d'inquisition de la paternité et également peut le faire le père biologique.

Et, dans les mêmes termes, l'enfant né dans le mariage a le droit à protester la présomption de paternité du mari de sa mère, et peut le faire aussi le père biologique.

D'un autre côté, l'enfant adopté ou conçu avec assistance biomédicale, n'a pas le droit de savoir qui sont ses parents biologiques, mais dans son intérêt supérieur il a le droit de connaître d'autres informations non d'identification tels que les données médicales.

2.2.2 Le droit d'exprimer son opinion librement dans toutes les affaires qui l'affectent

En second lieu, **ledroit d'exprimer son opinion librementdans toutes les affaires qui l'affectent**, prévu dans les articles 12.1, 12.2 et 13.1[9] de la Convention, trouve sa transposition dans les articles 67 et 80 :

«Tous les garçons, filles et adolescents ont le droit d'exprimer librement leur opinion,...»
«Tous les garçons, filles et adolescents ont le droit
a) à exprimer librement leur opinions sur les affaires où ils aient de l'intérêt.
b) à que leurs opinions soient prises en compte en fonction de leur développement.
Ce droit s'étend à tous les milieux où se développent les garçons, filles et adolescents, parmi ceux-ci: le milieu étatique, familial, communautaire, social, scolaire, scientifique, culturel, sportif et de recréation.

Premier Paragraphe: Il est garanti à tous les garçons, filles et adolescents l'exercice personnel et direct de ce droit, spécialement dans toute procédure administrative ou judiciaire, qui conduise vers une décision qu'affecte leurs droits, garanties et intérêts, sans autres limites que celles qui dérivent de leur intérêt supérieur.

Deuxième Paragraphe: Dans les procédures administratives ou judiciaires, la comparution du garçon, fille ou adolescent, se réalisera de la forme la plus adéquate à sa situation personnelle et développement. Dans les cas de garçons, filles et adolescents avec des nécessités spéciales ou d'incapacité, on doit garantir l'assistance de personnes qui pour leur profession ou relation spéciale de confiance, puissent transmettre objectivement leur opinion.

Troisième Paragraphe: Lorsque l'exercice personnel de ce droit ne résulte pas convenable à l'intérêt supérieur du garçon, fille ou adolescent, celui-ci s'exercera par intermédiaire de son père, mère ou représentants ou responsables pourvu que ceux-ci ne soient pas de partie intéressée ni aient des intérêts contraires à ceux du garçon, fille et adolescent, ou à travers d'autres personnes qui, par leur profession ou relation spéciale de confiance puissent transmettre objectivement leur opinion.

---

[9] «1. Les Etats parties garantissent à l'enfant qui est capable de discernement le droit d'exprimer librement son opinion sur toute question l'intéressant, les opinions de l'enfant étant dûment prises en considération eu égard à son âge et à son degré de maturité.
2. A cette fin, on donnera notamment à l'enfant la possibilité d'être entendu dans toute procédure judiciaire ou administrative l'intéressant, soit directement, soit par l'intermédiaire d'un représentant ou d'une organisation approprié, de façon compatible avec les règles de procédure de la législation nationale». «1. L'enfant a droit à la liberté d'expression».

Quatrième Paragraphe: L'opinion du garçon, fille ou adolescent uniquement sera contraignant, lorsque la loi ainsi l'établisse. Personne peut forcer aux garçons, filles ou adolescents à exprimer leur opinion, spécialement dans des procédures administratives ou judiciaires».

Il faut faire mention à propos de que l'article 8 exige qu'il soit appréciée l'opinion de l'enfant, dans le processus de détermination de son intérêt supérieur, et l'article 86 lui reconnaît le droit de défendre ses droits par lui-même.

Donc, il est évident que l'enfant a le droit d'exprimer son point de vue en matière du droit de famille, dans sa famille et dans des procédures administratives o judiciaires, et à recevoir information et assessorat afin de former son point de vue, du côté des tribunaux de justice, les autorités du bien être, ses avocats et représentants légaux, sans nécessité d'avoir atteint un certain âge.

Cependant, cette opinion ne sera toujours contraignant pour les autorités, sauf qu'une loi l'établisse, mais seront toujours obligés de les considérer, en vue du suprême intérêt de l'enfant.

2.2.3 Le droit de donner son consentement pour son adoption

En troisième lieu, il est apprécié que l'enfant de douze ans ou plus a **le droit de donner son consentement pour sonadoption**, en conformité à l'article 414.a:

«*Pour l'adoptionil faut les consentements suivants :*
a) De la personne à être adoptée si elle a douze ans ou plus».

2.2.4 Les conditions pour l'adoptioninternationale

En quatrième lieu, à propos des **conditions pour l'adoptioninternationale**, la loi dispose (article 407) que les garçons, filles et adolescents ayant leur résidence habituelle au Venezuela:

«*Uniquement peuvent se considérer aptes pour uneadoptioninternationale, lorsque les organismes compétents examinent toutes les possibilités de son adoption au... Venezuela et constatent que l'adoption internationale répond à l'intérêt supérieur du garçon, fille ou adolescent à être adopté*».

2.2.5 Le droit à la liberté de pensée, de conscience et de religion

En cinquième lieu, **le droit à la liberté de pensée, de conscience et de religion** prévu à l'article 14.1[10] de la Convention, est transposé dans l'article 35:

[10] «Les Etats parties respectent le droit de l'enfant à la liberté de pensée, de conscience et de religión».

«Tous les garçons, filles et adolescents ont le droit à la liberté de pensée, conscience et religion.

Le père, la mère, représentants ou responsables ont le droit et le devoir d'orienter les garçons, les filles et les adolescents dans l'exercice de ce droit, de façon qu'il contribue à leur développement intégral».

Dans cette perspective, au Venezuela elle est optative l'éducation religieuse, dans les écoles privées qui l'offrent et se limite à l'enseignement de quelques religions en particulier, telles que la catholique, la juive ou la musulmane, sans qu'elle soit impartie la connaissance générale sur les grandes religions du monde. Aux écoles publiques l'éducation religiose este absente.

2.2.6 L'interdiction de la punition physique des enfants

En sixième lieu, quant à **l'interdiction de la punition physique des enfants**, dans et hors la famille, selon l'article 19.1[11] de la Convention, nous avons les articles 32 et 32-A qu'établissent:

«Tous les garçons, filles et adolescents ont le droit à leur intégrité personnelle. Ce droit comprend l'intégrité physique, psychique et morale.

Premier Paragraphe. Les garçons, filles et adolescents ne peuvent pas être soumis à tortures ni à d'autres peines, traitements cruels, inhumains ou dégradants.

Deuxième Paragraphe. L'Etat, les familles et la société doivent protéger tous les garçons, filles et adolescents contre toute forme d'exploitation, mauvais traitement, tortures, abus ou négligences capables de nuire à leur intégrité personnelle. L'Etat doit garantir des programmes gratuits d'assistance et attention intégrale aux garçons, filles et adolescents qu'aient souffert des lésions à leur intégrité personnelle».

«Tous les garçons, filles et adolescents ont le droit au bon traitement. Ce droit comprend une éducation non violente, fondée sur l'amour, l'affection, la compréhension mutuelle et le respect réciproque et la solidarité.

Le père, la mère, représentants, responsables, tuteurs, tutrices, familiers, éducateurs et éducatrices devront employer des méthodes non violentes dans l'éducation, la formation, et correction des garçons, filles et adolescents.

En conséquence, il est interdit tout type de châtiment physique ou humiliant. L'Etat, avec l'active participation de la société doit garantir des politiques, programmes et mesures de protection adressés à l'abolition de toute forme de punition physique ou humiliante des garçons, filles et adolescents. On entend par punition physique, l'usage de la force, en exercice des autorités parentales d'élevage et d'éducation, avec l'intention de causer quelque degré de douleur ou d'incommodité corporelle, afin de corriger, contrôler ou changer le comportement des garçons, filles et adolescents, pourvu qu'il ne constitue pas un fait punissable.

On entend par punition humiliante, tout traitement offensif, dénigrant, dévalorisant, stigmatisant ou ridiculisant, réalisé dans l'exercice des autorités parentales d'élevage et d'éducation afin de corriger, contrôler ou changer le comportement des garçons, filles et adolescents, pourvu qu'il ne constitue pas un fait punissable».

---

[11] «Les Etats parties prennent toutes les mesures législatives, administratives, sociales et éducatives appropriées pour protéger l'enfant contre toute forme de violence, d'atteinte ou de brutalités physiques ou mentales, d'abandon ou de négligence, de mauvais traitements ou d'exploitation, y compris la violence sexuelle, pendant qu'il est sous la garde de ses parents ou de l'un d'eux, de son ou ses représentants légaux ou de toute autre personne à qui il est confié».

Ainsi la punition physique de l'enfant est interdite dans et hors la famille et se trouve sanctionnée dans les articles 254 et 352, avec prison d'un à trois ans et privation de l'autorité parentale.

2.2.7 La privation de la responsabilité parentale ou autorité parentale

En septième lieu il se trouve, conjointement avec l'antérieur, l'article 352, qui prévoit la possibilité de **la privation de la responsabilité parentale ouautorité parentale:**

«Le père ou la mère ou les deux peuvent être privés de l'autorité parentalequant à ses fils ou filles, quand :

a) Ceux-ci soient maltraités physique, mental ou moralement.

b) Ceux-ci soient exposés à toute situation de risque ou menace aux droits fondamentaux du fils ou de la fille.

c) Ils manquent aux devoirs inhérents à l'autorité parentale.

d) Ils essaient de les corrompre ou de les prostituer ou ils soient complices de leur corruption ou prostitution.

e) Ils abusent d'eux ou d'elles sexuellement ou les exposent à l'exploitation sexuelle.

f) Ils soient dépendants de substances alcooliques, stupéfiants ou psychotropiques ou autres formes graves de pharmacodépendance qui puissent compromettre la santé, la sécurité ou la moralité des fils ou filles, même quand ces faits n'occasionnent des sanctions pénales pour son auteur.

g) Ils soient condamnés ou condamnées pour des faits punissables commis contre les fils ou les filles.

h) Ils soient déclarés mis en question ou mise en question.

i) Ils refusent de leur prêter l'obligation de manutention.

j) Ils incitent, facilitent o permettent que le fils ou la fille exécute des actes qu'attentent contre son intégrité physique, mentale ou morale.

Le Juge ou la Juge s'occupera de la gravité, réitération, procédé arbitraire et l'accoutumance des faits».

Cette décision uniquement peut être prise par un tribunal de protection et le juge, que même inexplicablement n'a pas l'habitude de le faire, se trouve faculté pour prendre, entre autres, les mesures de l'article 466:

«a) Mesure de cautionnement ou d'interdiction de sortie du pays au garçon, fille ou adolescent, père, mère représentants ou responsables ou tierces personnes qu'exercent la responsabilité de l'éducation.

b) Restitution de la garde au père, mère ou tierces personnes qu'exercent la responsabilité de l'éducation en cas de rétention indue du garçon, fille ou adolescent.

c) Garde provisoire au père, à la mère ou à un familier du garçon, fille ou adolescent.

d) Régime de cohabitation familière provisoire.

e) Placement familial ou dans entité d'attention provisoire pendant les diligences pour la procédure de placement familial.

f) Séparation de la personne qui maltraite un garçon, fille ou adolescent, de son entourage.

g) Rétention du passeport du garçon, fille ou adolescent.

h) Restitution de biens ou mobiliers du foyer, propriété du garçon, fille ou adolescent, de sa mère ou père, pour garantir le droit à un niveau de vie adéquat.

i) Autorisation pour voyager en cas d'extrême nécessité dûment prouvée, pour garantir le droit à la vie ou santé du garçon, fille ou adolescent».

D'un autre côté, le père privé de l'autorité parentale maintient avec l'enfant son obligation de manutention (article 366).

2.2.8 Le droit de donner son consentement médical

En huitième lieu, la loi ne prévoit pas de manière explicite un **droit de donner son consentement médical de façon indépendante, ni un droit de nier son consentement pour quelque traitement médical de forme indépendante**, ceci faisant partie du droit à opiner dans les affaires qui puissent l'affecter avec ou sans de caractère contraignant et en vue de l'intérêt supérieur de l'enfant.

2.2.9 Le droit de changer son nom personnel

En neuvième lieu, la loi ne contemple pas **le droit de changer son nom personnel (prénom et nom) sous une forme indépendante.**

2.2.10 Les droits au travail

En dixième lieu, en ce qui concerne les **droits au travail** à qui fait référence l'article 32[12] de la Convention, nous avons l'article 96 qui fixe l'âge minimum pour l'emploi, quatorze ans, pouvant être autorisés ceux qui aient eu les douze ans, pourvu qu'il ne soit pas affecté son droit à l'éducation et l'activité ne soit pas dangereuse, ni nocive pour leur santé et développement.

D'un autre côté, implicitement on observe le droit de l'enfant à décider sur son travail de forme indépendante, quand l'article 100 dispose que:

> *«Il est reconnu aux adolescents à partir des quatorze ans, le droit de célébrer validement des actes, contrats et conventions collective en relation avec son activité de travail et économique; ainsi que, pour exercer les respectives actions pour la défense de ses droits et intérêts y compris le droit de grève, devant les autorités administratives et judiciaires compétentes».*

[12] «1. Les Etats parties reconnaissent le droit de l'enfant d'être protégé contre l'exploitation économique et de n'être astreint à aucun travail comportant des risques ou susceptible de compromettre son éducation ou de nuire à sa santé ou à son développement physique, mental, spirituel, moral ou social.
2. Les Etats parties prennent des mesures législatives, administratives, sociales et éducatives pour assurer l'application du présent article. A cette fin, et compte tenu des dispositions pertinentes des autres instruments internationaux, les Etats parties, en particulier :
a) Fixent un âge minimum ou des âges minimums d'admission à l'emploi;
b) Prévoient une réglementation appropriée des horaires de travail et des conditions d'emploi;
c) Prévoient des peines ou autres sanctions appropriées pour assurer l'application effective du présent article».

Quant aux conditions de travail, en plus des dispositifs dédiés à régler la syndicalisation, le droit de grève, le droit aux vacances, l'examen médical annuel, la sécurité sociale et bien d'autres thèmes, l'article 102 en particulier fait référence à la journée de travail :

«La journée de travail des adolescents ne pourra pas excéder les six heures par jour et devra être divisée en deux périodes, et aucune ne sera pas plus grande de quatre heures. Entre ces deux périodes, les adolescents et adolescentes pourront profiter d'un repos d'une heure. Le travail hebdomadaire ne pourra pas excéder les trente heures.

Il est interdit le travail d'adolescents en heures extraordinaires».

Et, quant aux travaux pour lesquels un mineur ne peut pas être employé, l'article 94 mentionne uniquement la généralité de ceux qui puissent troubler son éducation ou soient dangereux ou nocifs pour sa santé et son développement intégral.

2.2.11 Les obligations de l'enfant envers ses parents

En onzième et dernier lieu, en ce qui concerne si existent des devoirs ou des obligations de l'enfant envers ses parents l'article 93.h prévoit:

«Honorer, respecter et obéir ses parents, représentants ou responsables, pourvu que ces ordres ne violent pas ses droits et garanties ou contreviennent l'ordonnancementjuridique».

3 Résumé

Entreprenant l'analyse de l'acte juridique interne le plus important, à travers lequel on prétend au Venezuela, transposer les principes et mandats contenus dans la Convention relative aux droits de l'enfant, dans ce qu'a été appelé «*l'intérêt supérieur de l'enfant*», on prétend déterminer si ceci a été bien fait, au moins dans la perspective purement formelle.

Alberto Blanco-Uribe Avocat et spécialiste en Droit administratif de l'Universidad Central de Venezuela (UCV). DESS en Droit de l'Environnement et DEA en Droit Public de l'Université Robert Schumann, France. Spécialiste en Justice Constitutionnelle et spécialiste en Droits de l'Homme et Garanties Constitutionnelles de l'Universidad de Castilla-La Mancha, Espagne, Maître en Droit UCV et Universidad de Castilla-La Mancha, Professeur Agréé en Droit Constitutionnel et en Droits de l'Homme UCV. Coordinateur Général de la Chaire Libre des Droits de l'Homme UCV.

Questionnaire for the Section IV A: Public International Law

The UN Convention on the Rights of the Child and Its Implementation in National Law: 25 Years After

The UN General Assembly adopted the UN Convention on the Rights of the Child on 20 November 1989, which entered into force on 2 September 1990. Hence, it is of paramount importance to explore, 25 years after entry into force of the convention, which of the rights have been implemented and which are the most salient problems and difficulties in its implementation.

The questionnaire does not encompass all the rights of the child provided for by the convention but mainly those related to family law relations:

1. Has your country ratified the UN Convention on the Rights of the Child?
2. If so, when was the convention ratified?
3. Does your legal system regulate the age below which a human being is deemed a child?
   - If so, which statute regulates it (family law statute, special statute on the rights of the child, constitution)?
   - What is the age limit below which a human being is deemed a child?
4. Is there a special legal instrument in your legal system which is devoted to the rights of the child?
   - If your answer is yes, what does this instrument encompass?
     (a) General framework for the rights of the child, while leaving it to special laws to regulate special rights of the child
     (b) Protective law aimed at protecting the rights of the child without regulating the participative rights of the child
     (c) Complete law that includes all rights of the child (participative and protective, as well as providing for the authority in charge of law enforcement)

O. Cvejić Jančić (ed.), *The Rights of the Child in a Changing World*,
Ius Comparatum - Global Studies in Comparative Law 13,
DOI 10.1007/978-3-319-23189-1

5. Implementation of the provisions of the convention in national legislation:

   (A) Is the best interest of the child (BIC – Article 3) implemented in the legislation of your country and how:

   - By constitutional norms, by family law or by other statutes?
   - By a general provision about BIC or by more detailed provisions?
   - If the BIC is regulated in greater detail, what does it encompass?

   (B) The right of the child to know about his/her origin (Article 7):

   - Does a child born out of wedlock have a right to establish his/her origin regarding nonmarital mother and nonmarital father? Who else has that right (mother, biological father, someone else)?
   - Does a child born in wedlock have a right to rebut paternity of husband of his/her mother (the presumed father)? Who else has that right (mother, her husband, biological father, someone else)?
   - Does an adopted child have a right to know who his/her biological parents are (identifying data about his/her biological parents)?
   - If not, does an adopted child have a right to know other non-identifying data about his/her biological parents, such as medical data, social status, religion, political convictions and so on?
   - Does a child conceived with biomedical assistance have a right to know who his/her biological parents are (identifying data about his/her biological parents)?
   - If not, does a child conceived with biomedical assistance have a right to know other non-identifying data about his/her biological parents, such as medical data, social status, religion, political convictions and so on?

   (C) The right of the child to express his/her views freely in all matters affecting him/her (Articles 12 and 13) – manner of implementation:

   - Does the child have a right to express his/her view in family law matters within his/her family?
   - Does the child have a right to express his/her view in administrative or judicial proceedings?
   - Does the child need to attain a certain age before he/she can enjoy the right to express his/her view?
   - Does the child have a right to information and advice in order to form his/her view?
   - Who is in charge of providing the child with the said information and advice (court, guardianship or welfare authority, special lawyer or special representative of the child)?

   (D) Does the child have a right to give his/her consent to adoption?
   If a child possesses such a right, what age is required for the consent?

   (E) What are the conditions for intercountry adoption?

(F) The right of the child to freedom of thought, conscience and religion (Article 14):

- Is religious education available in schools as an obligatory or optional subject?
- If so, what is taught as part of such religious education: religious instruction or knowledge of the world's great religions (religious culture or the like)?

(G) Is physical punishment of the child within and beyond family forbidden (Article 19)?

- Physical punishment of the child is forbidden in schools and other institutions that take care about children (social welfare institutions and similar ones).
- Physical punishment of the child is forbidden within family for the parents, guardians, foster family and any other person who holds parental responsibilities.
- Does your legal system envisage a sanction in the event that parents physically punish a child?
- If so, what sanctions are envisaged?

(H) Does your law provide for the possibility of deprivation of parental responsibilities?

- If so, which grounds for deprivation are foreseen (abuse of parental rights, gross neglect of children, physical or mental violence, injury or abuse, maltreatment or exploitation, including sexual abuse, something else – Article 19 para. 1)?
- Which body is competent for deprivation of parental responsibilities (court, administrative authority, another body)?
- What type of protective measure or alternative care is envisaged in the event of deprivation of parental responsibilities (placement in a suitable institution for child care, foster placement, kafalah of Islamic law, adoption, something else)?
- Does the parent who is deprived of parental responsibilities keep any rights and/or obligations towards the child after deprivation?

(I) Does the child have a right to give medical consent independently? Which age is required for this right?
Does the child also have a right to refuse consent to medical treatment independently?
Which age is required for this right?

(J) Does the child have a right to change his/her personal name (first name and surname) independently? What age is required for such right?

(K) What is the minimum age for admission to employment in your country (Article 32 para. 2 point a)?

- Does the child have a right to decide about his/her employment independently or does he/she need parental consent?
- Is there any legal regulation of the child's working hours and conditions of employment?
- Does the law specify the jobs for which a minor child cannot be employed?

(L) Does your national law lay down any obligation of the child towards his/her parents?

Index

O. Cvejić Jančić (ed.), *The Rights of the Child in a Changing World*, Ius Comparatum - Global Studies in Comparative Law 13,
DOI 10.1007/978-3-319-23189-1

CPSIA information can be obtained at www.ICGtesting.com
Printed in the USA
BVOW06*0822271115

428607BV00004BA/16/P

9 783319 231884